Environmental Governance

In memory of Gabriella

Environmental Governance

INSTITUTIONS, POLICIES AND ACTIONS

Arild Vatn

Professor of Environmental Sciences, Department of International Environment and Development Studies, Norwegian University of Life Sciences, Ås, Norway

EE Edward **Elgar**
PUBLISHING

Cheltenham, UK • Northampton, MA, USA

Published by
Edward Elgar Publishing Limited
The Lypiatts
15 Lansdown Road
Cheltenham
Glos GL50 2JA
UK

Edward Elgar Publishing, Inc.
William Pratt House
9 Dewey Court
Northampton
Massachusetts 01060
USA

Paperback edition 2016

A catalogue record for this book
is available from the British Library

Library of Congress Control Number: 2015943193

ISBN 978 1 78100 724 2 (cased)
ISBN 978 1 78100 725 9 (eBook)
ISBN 978 1 78536 362 7 (paperback)

Typeset by Servis Filmsetting Ltd, Stockport, Cheshire
Printed and bound in Great Britain by TJ International Ltd, Padstow, Cornwall

Contents in brief

Full contents

Acknowledgments

Writing a book is a process that includes colleagues, students, friends and family. The number of people to thank is numerous. Many of the ideas presented here have been discussed at conferences, in seminars, in classrooms, in restaurants, around various kitchen tables. While I certainly do not recollect all the discussions that made a difference, I would first like to thank the following people from outside my department for inputs that have been helpful in clarifying my ideas and pointing me towards material I have been unaware of: David Barton, Erik Gómez-Baggethun, Lars Bakken, Lars Berger, Frank Biermann, Dan Bromley, Kate Farrell, John Gowdy, Konrad Hagedorn, Juha Hiedanpää, Tim Jackson, Sharachchandra Lélé, Petter Jensen, George Kajembe, Christian Kerschner, Valborg Kvakkestad, Joan Martinez-Alier, Roldan Muradian, Richard Norgaard, John O'Neill, Jouni Paavola, Felix Rauschmayer, Karen Refsgaard, Jan Åge Riseth, Inge Røpke, Per Kr. Rørstad, Katrine Soma, Clive Spash, Tone Smith Spash, Sigrid Stagl, Sian Sullivan, Oran Young and numerous PhD students participating in the Thor Heyerdahl summer schools in environmental governance since 2011.

If possible, I am even more indebted to colleagues at the Department of Environment and Development Studies. There are numerous seminars, discussions in projects and when teaching together that have influenced my thinking tremendously. I am especially grateful to Pål Vedeld for his encouragement and discussions over many years about issues related to environmental governance. Moreover, in preparing the text, I have had help from several colleagues. First of all, I would like to thank Marianne Aasen. She has read all chapters in draft form and offered insightful comments not least to help ensure consistency across the various chapters. Added to that, several have commented on specific chapters: Tor A. Benjaminsen, Ian Bryceson, Bill Derman, Marit Heller, Darley Kjosavik, John A. McNeish, Synne Movik, Nadarajah Shanmugaratnam, Ellen Stenslie and Pål Vedeld, as well as Ståle Navrud at the NMBU School of Economics and Business. The comments have been very helpful while also challenging. I am impressed by and very grateful for the engagement in my project.

I would also like to thank Raymond A. Samndong for helping out with literature reviews for the sections of Chapter 12 covering pastures, irrigation and fresh water fisheries, and Victorija Viciunaite for help with drawing figures and checking the reference list. I will also thank the Thor Heyerdahl Institute for financing part of the time spent to prepare the text and the department for granting me a sabbatical to be able to finish the writing.

Finally, I would like to thank you Gabriella. You passed away in the process of writing the book. Your encouragement and support was always very important to me – in life, but also in the form of strong memories.

Arild Vatn
NMBU, Ås, Norway
20 April 2015

Abbreviations

CBA	cost–benefit analysis
CBD	Convention on Biodiversity (UN)
CBFM	community-based forest management
CDM	clean development mechanism
CER	certified emission reduction
CFCs	chlorofluorocarbons
CH_4	methane
CITES	Convention on International Trade in Endangered Species (UN)
CO_2	carbon dioxide
COP	Conference of the Parties
CPR	common-pool resource
DDT	dichlorodiphenyltrichloroethane
EEZ	exclusive economic zone
EGS	environmental governance system
ENGO	environmental non-governmental organization
EROI	energy return on investment
EU	European Union
EU ETS	EU Emissions Trading System
FAO	Food and Agriculture Organization (UN)
GATT	General Agreement on Tariffs and Trade
GDP	gross domestic product
GM(O)	genetically modified (organism)
IAD	institutional analysis and development (framework)
IBRD	International Bank of Reconstruction and Development
ICA	International Co-operative Alliance
ICSID	International Centre for Settlement of Investment Disputes
IENGO	international environmental non-governmental organization
IGO	intergovernmental organization
IMF	International Monetary Fund
INGO	international non-governmental organization
IPCC	Intergovernmental Panel on Climate Change
IQ	individual quota
ITQ	individual tradable quota
IUCN	International Union for Conservation of Nature

JFM	joint forest management
MAC	marginal abatement costs
MAUT	multi-attribute utility theory
MCA	multicriteria analysis
MEA	Millennium ecosystem assessment
MEC	marginal environmental costs
$MtCO_2$	metric tons of carbon dioxide
Mtoe	million tons of oil equivalent
N	nitrogen
N_2	nitrogen – molecular form
N_2O	nitrous oxide
NGO	non-governmental organization
NO_x	(mono-)nitrogen oxides (NO and NO_2)
NPV	net present value
O_2	oxygen – molecular form
OECD	Organisation for Economic Co-operation and Development
OPEC	Organization of the Petroleum Exporting Countries
P	phosphorus
PCB	polychlorinated biphenyl
PES	payments for ecosystem services
PFM	participatory forest management
PGP	provider gets principle
pH	measure of acidity (from Latin *potentia Hydrogenii*)
POPs	persistent organic pollutants
ppm	parts per million
PPP	polluter pays principle
REDD+	reducing emissions from deforestation and forest degradation
SO_2	sulfur dioxide
SPS	sanitary and phytosanitary (measures) (part of the WTO agreement)
TAC	total allowable catch
TRIPS	Trade-Related Aspects of Intellectual Property Rights
TTIP	The Transatlantic Trade and Investment Partnership
UN	United Nations
UNCLOS	United Nations Convention on the Law of the Sea
UNEP	United Nations Environment Programme
UNFCCC	UN Framework Convention on Climate Change
UPF	utility possibility frontier
VOC	volatile organic compound
WHO	World Health Organization
WMO	World Meteorological Organization

WTA	willingness to accept
WTO	World Trade Organization
WTP	willingness to pay
WUA	water user association
WWF	World Wide Fund for Nature

1

Introduction

The quality of our environment – for example, water, air, soils and biological resources – is changing. While these resources are fundamental to human survival and well-being, the way they are utilized makes us worry about future living conditions for both humans and other species. This concerns pollution, and the health of ecosystems and of humans. It involves loss of biological diversity, reducing the resilience and adaptive capacity of natural systems. It also concerns climate change and the changes this implies for life across the globe. Finally, the greatest challenges may follow from the combined effects of these changes.

Environmental resources are, in a fundamental sense, *common resources*. You breathe the same air as your neighbor. If you pollute the air, others will also have to endure the consequences. Water passes through landscapes linking various uses, making discharges a common problem. If you are situated 'upstream' in space or time, you may not worry. All consequences or costs are shifted to others – including future generations.

Some may invoke that land is not a common resource. Land can be divided by legal and physical means – for example, fences. Nevertheless, land is the host of species, of biological resources that obey neither institutional nor physical barriers. Water moves through land and soils interact with the air, so environmental resources typically exist as parts of interlinked systems, as interactive processes. Therefore, it is now standard to talk about biogeochemical processes involving the interlinked processes of biota, land, water and air. The evolution of biological life has itself invoked tremendous changes in the composition of the atmosphere, the dynamics of soils and so on (Graves and Reavy, 1996). Seen from a geological time perspective – that is, billions of years – life has, so to speak, created its own conditions.

These physical and biological interdependencies imply that human lives are also interdependent. The relationship between humans and their physical environments is not only a relationship between humans and nature, it is also as much a relationship between other humans – to others that have to endure the consequences of one's own actions.

1.1 The environment – conflict and coordination

The interdependencies described above imply that environmental issues are characterized both by *conflicts* as well as by great needs to *coordinate* action.

1.1.1 Environmental conflicts

Conflicts of interest to us are of two main kinds. First, there are conflicts related to *access to environmental resources* as livelihoods, as the basis for economic activity. Basic needs like food and shelter all depend on access to natural resources. Land is the fundamental asset – as the basis for agriculture and forestry. Land also offers resources like metals, oil and hydroelectric power, and is space for the construction of homes, roads, cities and so forth.

As long as there are enough resources for everybody and all resources are of equal quality, the conflict potential is low. This is rarely the case, however, since land is a finite resource with variable quality. This creates interdependency because of rivalry in use. If a resource is used or consumed by one person, it cannot at the same time be used or consumed by others. Therefore, human history is full of conflicts over access to resources. It is a basis for wars between groups or nations as well as conflicts within these entities. We observe conflicts between various economic strata or classes, where some do not even own their own labor – slaves; where some 'own' nothing *but* their own labor – for example, landless people; while others own resources even at the global scale.

Second, there are conflicts related to what may be termed *side-effects* of economic activity. Use of environmental resources results in effects beyond the intended production – for example, loss of biodiversity and pollution. Land is cleared for agriculture, for construction, for mining and so on. This changes the opportunities for others through changes in the landscape and the dynamics of ecosystems, among other things. Also important is the flow of matter following economic activity. Production and consumption result in waste. Over time, the volume of waste equals the amount of resources extracted from the environment and included in the economic process. Some waste is harmless, but much of it changes the conditions for ecosystem functioning and human activities. This is even the case with many naturally produced compounds if their concentrations become too high. Moreover, we have to think in much wider terms regarding waste than what turns up in our waste bins. The economic process has much wider waste-creating implications.

As an example, the use of fossil fuels has resulted in vast emissions of carbon dioxide (CO_2), influencing the composition of the atmosphere and hence the climate. Industrial production of nitrogen (N) for agriculture has doubled the amount of biologically accessible nitrogen. This has been important for increasing food production, but it also influences biological life by losses to water and air from both production and consumption. Lost to water, especially coastal areas, it increases the basis for algae growth and reduces water quality. Lost to air it may be deposited over forests and change biological dynamics. Nitrogen losses may also cause climate change. Similarly, emissions of sulfur and toxic compounds – from heavy metals, dichlorodiphenyl-trichloroethane (DDT), dioxin and pesticides – all influence health directly and our living conditions more generally through influencing species loss and the working of ecosystems. One example is a growing concern about the effect of this on nature's pollination capacity, not least through reduced stocks of functioning bee communities (Kluser and Peduzzi, 2007).

The second type of conflict is about who may impose costs on whom. Is the polluter free to pollute and let others carry the costs, or do the potential victims of pollution have the right to be protected? These are fundamental questions of our time. While some of the involved conflicts are symmetrical, others are asymmetrical. Symmetry implies that those polluting are also enduring the consequences. Asymmetric conflicts exist when side-effects are unequally distributed, sometimes influencing only others. Upstream factories or households may pollute the water of a river without experiencing any negative effects themselves. Present generations may shift costs of various kinds onto future generations. The capacity to protect oneself from environmental degradation may also vary. While reduced water quality may affect all people in an area, the rich may have the capacity to install cleaning facilities that are far beyond the reach of the poor. While climate change affects the whole globe, the poor have less capacity to defend themselves (Martinez-Alier, 2002).

1.1.2 Coordination

The aspect of coordination can also be divided into two, following the above division of conflicts. First is the *coordination of access to and use of resources*. If it is not clarified who can use a resource, conflicts may escalate as everybody lives under the continual uncertainty of 'losing what they physically possess'. Creating rules about who may hold which resources may be favorable to all as it settles the conflicts about access. Certainly, the more uneven the distribution is, the greater the chance that conflicts may develop. Favored groups may use elaborate measures to disguise the fact that certain interests are privileged – for example, arguing about 'faith', what is 'natural', and referring to 'the rule of law'. Being able to make advantages accepted or invisible is important in creating strong power bases in any society.

There are also coordination problems related to the form of use of environmental resources. People may find it desirable to produce jointly, as in firms. This demands coordination. Similarly, people may want to specialize in a specific production – say grain – implying that they depend on others to supply their other needs. Hence, markets, public production plans or community cooperation are necessary for ensuring that the wider set of needs is covered.

Second, we have the *coordination issues following from side-effects* of production and consumption. From the individual's point of view, it may seem best to continue to, for example, ignore pollution from an agricultural practice to a water body, as he or she has to carry all costs of changing this action, while everyone using the water shares the gains. The individual gains from free-riding. To ensure that the quality of the resource is retained, it is necessary for the group to establish some rules that ensure that the sum of emissions is within some limit that maintains water quality. Even though there is a potential gain for everybody, it may still be challenging to ensure cooperation.

While the efforts to coordinate resource use within a group may be challenging, the problems are substantially increased if conflicts are asymmetric. Under symmetry there is a gain of coordination for all, while noting the temptation to free-ride on others' efforts. In the case of asymmetric side-effects, not all will gain from coordinated action. The issues are equally challenging in both space and time. In the case of upstream polluters of rivers, they gain from polluting. This is a cost free way to handle waste. All costs appear downstream. One might argue that it is more than fair that upstream people stop imposing costs upon those downstream. Nevertheless, they may choose to ignore such arguments and continue their practice. Similarly, present generations may shift costs to later generations from, for example, high own consumption levels. To find a coordinated solution to this type of problem is even more challenging when we consider people who do not have a direct say at all.

Choosing to coordinate is a normative issue. First, it is a normative issue if one seeks a solution to resource distribution conflicts and side-effects at all. Next, the choice of coordinated solution – including whose interests to protect – is also a normative consideration. This shows that to study environmental governance is to engage in issues that are fundamentally ethical.

1.2 The main argument of the book

This book is about how people and societies handle the issues of coordination and conflict regarding use and protection of their physical environments. It is about clarifying what characterizes the challenges and how people have gone about solving them. It concerns how we should study these issues to facilitate a better understanding of how and why we have created present challenges. It is, however, also about facilitating thinking about better solutions to growing problems.

Studies in the field of environmental governance need to be *interdisciplinary* – crossing over the social–natural science divide as well as integrating insights from various social sciences. Building on such a perspective, the book offers a set of distinct messages:

1. *The human spheres of action – specifically the economy – are subsystems of the physical environment.* All human action is in one way or another linked to the physical environments we live in. In this sense, it has to 'obey the laws of nature'. All production depends on inputs of environmental resources and influences environmental processes. Figure 1.1 illustrates these relationships.

    Sun energy is the basis for all life, while the economy also depends on the material inputs from the environment – be it the biosphere, the lithosphere and so on. A fundamental issue of environmental governance is concerned with how we 'manage' the flows of inputs and waste, including how we maintain the functional capacities of environmental processes. As emphasized above, this is an issue involving both conflict and need for coordination.

Note: The numbered arrows are flows of 1: inputs; 2: waste.

Figure 1.1 The economy–environment interaction

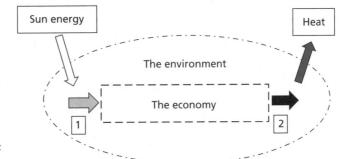

2. *Environmental conflicts are of different kinds and create specific challenges for coordinated solutions.* Environmental challenges vary a lot according to their physical and biological characteristics. Problems related to forests, fish, water and air are quite different. While fish move, trees do not. While water issues are typically local or regional, problems related to air pollution are sometimes global. Some problems are physically rather simple like dividing land between different owners, while others are complex in that it is difficult to foresee consequences of various actions. Examples are loss of biodiversity and climate change.

    For the topic of this book, it is, moreover, important to recognize the different kinds of conflicts involved. The characteristics of the environmental resources and their various uses will interact and establish a certain pattern of interdependencies between people. We have already emphasized the difference between symmetric and asymmetric problems. The size of groups involved – a result of both the dynamics of the resources involved and patterns of habitation – is also important to the challenges involved. Finally, we have the differences in economic development, social and political cultures that influence the form of conflict and the opportunities for coordinated solutions.

    Given interdependencies, coordination demands collective action. The role of the state – the necessity for state action in this field – will be analyzed from different angles, emphasizing both strengths and weaknesses. The role of civil society also manifests as very important.

3. *Environmental problems are fundamentally about human action and analyzing them demands a good understanding of human motivation.* Studying environmental problems is as much about studying human action as about understanding environmental makes. In relation to this, the issue of human motivation is core. What makes us do what we do? On this core issue, the social sciences seem to be broadly split in two – between individualist and social constructivist positions. The former states that humans are autonomous actors searching for actions that maximize their individual utility. Autonomy – in the individualist sense – implies that social processes do not influence the preferences a person holds. Moreover, the individual only considers actions that increase his or her own utility. Neoclassical or mainstream economics is the main theoretical position supporting such a view of human motivation and action.

    On the other hand, the social constructivist position departs from both the above premises. First, preferences are seen to be influenced by the society in which a person is raised or lives. Second, people may act according to the norms of that society, which may imply that they act in ways that are not necessarily the best for themselves, but realize the values or goals behind the norm. Anthropology, sociology and classical institutional economics have developed based on this understanding.

4. *Institutions matter – institutions are the 'means' that humans use to coordinate activities and to handle conflicts.* This book is based on a distinct understanding of what institutions are and do. I understand institutions as humanly created 'rules' that not only protect certain interests or values, but also facilitate coordination. They may take the form of conventions, norms or various types of rights – for example, property rights. We will look more deeply into this later. For now, it suffices to think about institutions as 'rules'.

Institutions define the 'borderlines' between the economy and its environment – see Figure 1.1 – as well as the internal structures of the economy and its surrounding society. It is through institutions that we define who has access to various environmental resources – for example, use or property rights. Moreover, institutions define who has the right to shift costs upon whom. Do the rules protect the polluter or the victims? Or, maybe there are no rules, giving actors an implicit 'right' to emit polluting substances?

This book is based on the observation that institutions form people. Institutions are not just rules that limit certain actions – for example, norms or laws saying that you are not permitted to pollute, cut certain trees, or throw trash. Institutions may also form the meaning of various situations and the ideas of what it is right to do. Hence, the institutions of a society influence the preferences of the members of that society. Furthermore, institutions influence the kinds of motivations that form the basis for action. Some institutional structures like markets facilitate individualistically oriented actions, while institutional structures like communities and families support actions based more on norms about what is better for the group or even for others outside the group.

This book is about governance. For now, we may define governance as about shaping social priorities – the formulation of goals – and how these should be realized. Implicit in this is how conflicts are acknowledged and possibly resolved and how human coordination is facilitated. Institutions are very important elements in any governance system. They define which actors are involved in the formulation of goals, which roles they are permitted to play, and how they may interact. More specifically, institutions are important because they influence:

(a) which rights and responsibilities the actors involved have – that is, how power is distributed;

(b) how demanding/costly it is to interact/coordinate actions between different actors and which knowledge and expertise are considered 'relevant' and 'sound';

(c) what kinds of motivations are dominating this interaction.

So, while the characteristics of the environmental problem are important, so are the attributes of the institutions involved as they define the space for possible outcomes of an environmental conflict. These are complex issues, and a core aim of the book is to help develop our understanding of various aspects of this nexus.

5. *Knowledge is very important for action, but often contested.* Natural and social systems are both complex. This implies that they can be described and understood in multiple and often incompatible ways. Moreover, changing use of environmental resources or institutions has uncertain outcomes. Prior to action we cannot know for sure what will happen. We all have to be conscious about this when studying environmental conflicts and discussing alternative solutions. It is hard to deliver 'safe proofs' of what causes a problem and how it can best be remedied. Inaction may easily be the result as this offers opportunities for various interests to confuse processes of necessary change.

    The climate change debate illustrates this. The fight between most climate researchers and climate 'skeptics' is about whether climate change is happening and the role played by emissions of climate gases like CO_2. The complexities involved offer space for, for example, questioning the forecasts made by climate models. At the same time, the assumptions of these models can be tested against observation, and combining data from experiments and global trends in the climate makes it possible for us to become more certain about what causes the trends we observe. Arguments like CO_2 being a natural compound and therefore cannot cause problems, that CO_2 emissions cannot result in increased temperatures and so on, still survive the debate. This does not mean, however, that these views are not overwhelmingly disproved by natural science research.

    This book takes a critical realist position in relation to the above. This position states that the physical world exists independently of our consciousness about it. There are aspects that our senses and instruments can observe and hence describe well, but there are also properties that cannot be observed or well described. What we experience will, moreover, be influenced by the concepts we use, the way we classify objects and so on. While this implies that a search for objective truth is not possible in a fundamental sense, it is possible to discriminate between descriptions and define which is the better given the present status of knowledge.

6. *The present institutions seem unable to solve the kind of environmental problems we are facing; therefore, we need to look for new solutions.* The argument behind this message is complex and can only be described in a very rudimentary form here: the institutions we have established over the last

centuries have been based on strengthening independent choices – for example, firms/corporations as operating in markets. This development has facilitated economic growth, which has – despite vast and even deepened inequalities – taken many out of poverty. Economic growth has, however, also created heavy pressures on the environment and threatens the long-run basis for future well-being. Environmental policies have been established to reduce negative impacts when they appear. We nevertheless observe a conflict between an economic system with institutions demanding growth to work well and an environment that cannot manage the intensifying pressures thereof. The argument is that this conflict cannot be handled with the present environmental policy programs. It seems to demand a fundamental restructuring of the economy, making it much less dependent on growth. It demands firms that are socially and ecologically responsible. Hence, future environmental governance should be much more oriented at restructuring the institutions of the economy and not limit itself to developing regulations given these structures.

As consumption reaches affluent levels, welfare gains from economic growth are small – maybe non-existent. Environmental costs thereof are, on the other hand, increasing at an escalating rate. Hence, it should be easy to accept that we should direct our economy differently. This is, however, not happening. I hope that the book will make it easier to understand why this is so. Moreover, I would also like to help the reader to begin to think constructively about what the alternatives could look like.

While most publications in the field of environmental governance focus on environmental policy, taking the basic institutions of the economy largely as given, this book is based on a different focus and understanding. It proceeds from the view that apprehending the challenges we face and the dominating formats of environmental governance put in place demands a thorough analysis of the economic processes and the institutions that govern these. Hence, the institutions of the economy and economic policy at large are as important for the study environmental issues as the specific environmental programs.

As is clear from the above, the book has both a descriptive and normative orientation. It aims at helping readers to develop their understanding of what causes environmental degradation and how it could be reduced. It is interdisciplinary, while framed within the tradition of classical institutional economics – see, for example, Vatn (2005). I draw on a series of insights from political economy, ecological economics, sociology, political science, anthropology, political ecology and natural sciences. While the economic processes are a very important topic for the book, I develop a position that is different from standard rational choice theory and the individualist understanding of human action found in neoclassical/mainstream economics.

As already noted, there is a dividing line in social science – between those supporting rational choice/individualist models and those supporting more social constructivist positions. While the former dominates mainstream economics, the latter dominates sociology, anthropology and classical institutional economics. Political science is divided more or less into two equally large 'camps'. While this book is oriented to analyzing environmental governance from the perspective of classical institutional economics, it also intends to inform the reader about alternative positions. To acquire a deeper insight into these positions, the reader must go to disciplinary sources. The intention here is to offer further understanding of the institutionalist way of thinking by contrasting it to other positions.

1.3   The structure of the book

The book is divided into five parts. Part One is called 'Human Action and the Environment' and comprises two chapters. In Chapter 2, I describe some of the dominant environmental problems of today. I analyze the causes behind the present status, including both economic and political factors. I classify environmental resources and show how their varying characteristics influence the potential conflicts that may arise.

In Chapter 3, we go deeper into characterizing the kinds of conflicts and coordination problems that may arise in the realm of the environment. I also discuss what kind of options there are for resolving environmental conflicts. In some cases, this may involve gains for all parties, but, typically, it will not, and society has to decide which interest to support. Chapter 3 outlines key arguments of the book in a simple and non-technical way.

In Part Two – 'The Theory of Institutions and Human Action' – I develop the theoretical tools for the analyses that follow. In Chapter 4, I ask 'What are institutions?' The focus is first of all on the meaning of the concept. The chapter includes sections on how institutions form actors – individual and collective – and their relationships to each other. The concept of power will be emphasized as I look at institutions as power structures. The book is based on a distinct understanding of what institutions are and do, and it will be contrasted with other core positions. The chapter closes with an analysis of the role institutions play in the economic process.

Chapter 5 is focused on theories of motivation and human action. Understanding what characterizes human action is core to studying environmental governance. The chapter covers models from standard rational choice through non-rational behavior to those of plural rationality. The main argument of the present book is that human action is motivated in different ways – sometimes by own interests only, sometimes by the interest of the group one belongs to and sometimes even by the interests of others. A key role of institutions is to define what kind of rationality is expected in specific contexts of choice. In some settings, institutions facilitate individual choice and individual interests, while in other contexts cooperation is more pronounced. As environmental problems are collective problems, understanding what facilitates cooperation is very important.

In Part Three, the focus is on 'The Theory of Environmental Governance'. In Chapter 6, I present a framework for environmental governance analyses based on the understanding of institutions and human action as discussed in Part Two. The concept of environmental governance and its various definitions is first discussed. Thereafter I develop the framework step by step, starting with the concept of resource regime – the economic institutions. Next, I include actors and institutions governing the political process and processes of civil society. Together with the resource regime, these elements comprise the elements of governance structures. Including environmental resources and technology completes the framework for studying environmental governance systems.

In Chapter 7, I turn to the issue of how to evaluate governance structures. I first develop a set of criteria with reference to the concept of legitimacy – emphasizing both the legitimacy of the process of decision-making ('input') and the results obtained ('output'). I take this further into an analysis about how governance structures influence environmental action – a key aspect of its legitimacy. Here I emphasize how different governance structures influence people's rights, the cost of interaction (transaction costs), the perception of environmental problems and finally the motivation for action. All of these aspects influence both the processes and outcomes of environmental governance – hence its legitimacy. I close the chapter with a brief discussion of what may motivate changes in governance structures – the theory of institutional change.

Part Four is about 'Markets and Governance'. The market is presently the most important governance structure regarding resource use. Moreover, while environmental governance used to be very much about correcting markets, there is a trend directed at establishing markets to create better governance. Hence, understanding what markets are and do is crucial for the study of environmental governance.

In Chapter 8, I briefly present the standard theory of markets, including how supply and demand is understood. While this theory sees markets as 'natural phenomena', I describe, in parallel, markets as a socially created governance structure. The chapter also includes a critical review of the claim that markets are efficient governance structures. In Chapter 9, I follow up on the perspective of markets as socially created by offering a brief history of the institutions around trade and the actual creation of the actors of markets – the producers and the consumers.

The fifth and last part of the book is about 'Environmental Governance in Practice'. It is by far the largest section, including five chapters. In Chapter 10, I look at the process of policy formulation, covering first the stages of an 'idealized' decision-making process. The chapter also includes sections on the main discourses and strategies in present environmental governance – emphasizing government-, market- and community-oriented strategies. I reflect on the aspect of multilevel governance – noting that environmental effects go beyond key decision-making units from the local level to become the global issues. The chapter closes with a section focusing on a set of international environmental agreements, illustrating the complexities and conflicts characterizing environmental decision-making.

Environmental governance may be described as (1) a process of goal-making – of setting priorities – and (2) of changing governance structures to try to create what is desired. Certainly, it is a messy process, and the distinction is mainly of analytical value. In Chapter 11, I focus on different ways to create inputs to the process of formulating goals. I look at some key characteristics of evaluating 'what it is better to do' – both at the level of the individual and the social. Next, I introduce the concept of value-articulating institutions – explaining how the process of evaluation and its outcomes are influenced by its institutional framing. Thereafter I present three types of evaluation procedures – cost–benefit analysis, multicriteria analysis and deliberative methods – emphasizing especially what kind of assumptions they are based on and what type of values they are able to include.

In Chapter 12, I turn to the issue of changing governance structures to promote more environmentally friendly action. I discuss first the potentials of making changes in the basic resource regime. Thereafter I look at experiences with various regimes and policy instruments in a set of environmental policy areas. First, I review research regarding institutions governing use and protection of environmental resources like forests, fish and biodiversity. Next, I look at policy instruments used in the area of pollution – for example, emissions to water and air, of greenhouse gases and issues related to waste treatment. The chapter closes with a theoretical assessment of the various policy instruments visited like the legal, the economic and the informational.

I already mentioned the turn in environmental governance towards a greater use of markets. Chapter 13 is devoted to a deeper analysis of this trend. I present first the theory of markets in environmental governance. Next, I discuss to what extent observed developments really are a 'turn to the market', concluding that state command plays a profound role. I evaluate the legitimacy of the changes observed based on experiences with, for example, payments for ecosystem services, carbon markets and biodiversity offsets. Last, I discuss alternative governance structures for REDD+ – the emerging policy area regarding reduced deforestation and forest degradation.

There are some serious problems with the dominating models of environmental governance. The book therefore concludes with a chapter called 'Environmental Governance – the Need for New Institutions'. Here I sum up the weaknesses of present models and discuss various alternative directions to take – including modifications of present structures and sketches of more radical changes. I think the situation demands a new direction and some fundamental restructuring of the institutions that form our economies. Ideas may come from the study desk; workable solutions have, however, to be crafted in practical contexts – among millions of motivated individuals and groups. Hopefully, the tools and ideas presented in this book are helpful in supporting such processes.

Part One

Human action and the environment

In this book, the environment refers to the natural environment – to the physical space in which human activities take place and from which we acquire the resources necessary for sustaining our lives. This refers to land, air and water and the biological and physical resources and processes included.

In this first part, I look at various ways of conceptualizing the environment – different ways of understanding what the environment is and how it functions. While nature is complex, it can be described and understood in different ways. By choice of perspective, we orient our analysis and possible recommendations in certain directions. Hence, being aware of alternative descriptions and what the strengths and weaknesses are of each is very important.

I will also focus on the relationships between humans and the environment. While this implies a distinction between 'humans' and 'nature', I note that this is a necessity for analysis, while not representing an ontological position. Certainly, humankind is part of nature, evolves with and within it. At the same time, humans operate as if nature is distinct from us – something 'out there', important for sustaining our lives.

As emphasized, environmental problems are foremost conflicts between humans. Human–nature interactions represent human-to-human relations forced upon us by a common environment. The aim of this part of the book is therefore also to categorize such relations and conflicts. In doing so, I aim to show how our understanding and descriptions of the environment influence how we perceive conflicts and what resolutions are relevant, if even possible.

2

The environment

The aim of this chapter is to offer a basis for later analyses of environmental governance and policy. I start with showing two different ways that the natural environment is presented in the scholarly literature – the environment as 'materials' and the environment as 'interlinked processes'. These are complementary as well as competing perspectives. Thereafter I look at changes observed in key parts of the natural environment as influenced by human action – for example, biodiversity loss, climate change, water and land use changes and various forms of pollution. In this second part of the chapter, I mainly make use of the 'process perspective'. The chapter closes with a short discussion of the causes of environmental degradation.

2.1   Characterizing the environment

2.1.1   The environment as stocks and flows of materials and energy

From an anthropocentric perspective, one way to perceive the environment is as stocks and flows of materials and energy. The environment offers materials and energy that are necessary to sustain a host of life forms. Regarding the human species, it now 'consumes' a tremendous amount of natural resources. Some are renewable and some are non-renewable. Measuring the stock of non-renewables and the stock and reproduction rates of renewables is a useful way to describe the environment. This regards how much land is available for agriculture, the stocks and flow of forest products, the stocks and flows of fish, the stocks of fossil fuels and the stocks of metal ore and so on.

A key issue following the perspective of the environment as materials and energy regards whether there will be enough resources to sustain the present or even increased consumption levels in the future as well as allowing the world's poor to catch up. There is no simple answer to this issue. There are reasons to worry that we might run out of (some) resources – see, for example, Meadows et al. (1992) and Kerschner et al. (2013). Others are not so worried. According to Robert Solow – a typical representative of a dominant view among economists – there will always be a substitute (Solow, 1974, 1993). While this could be so in many cases, the reasoning neglects that for some resources there are no substitutes – for example, phosphorus as a necessary element of photosynthesis/food production. Nevertheless, the fundamental issue regarding 'enough physical resources' is one of energy availability and knowledge. When resources are used, they typically disperse. They are not lost from the earth, but are turned into waste and become (much) more costly to access. Resources typically end up in the oceans. This is also so for phosphorus. The energy cost of retrieving phosphorus from ocean water is, however, very high.[1]

There is another important issue involved when looking at use and dispersal of materials – interrupted dynamics. Changing the surface of the earth by creating agricultural fields, establishing cities, building infrastructures and so forth changes the conditions for natural ecosystem dynamics. Emissions of various types of waste – from production and consumption – have their own implications for these dynamics. Here I include a wide understanding of what waste is – that is, all 'losses' including emissions from combustion engines, factories, mining sites and so on. Actually, all resources we introduce into the economy, all new compounds that we create from these, become waste at some point. This follows from the laws of thermodynamics. The importance of land use changes and emissions may be tremendous. The next section offers a way in which we can understand these effects, focusing on the environment as a set of interlinked processes.

2.1.2 The environment as a set of interlinked processes

Flows of matter and energy and interactions between species at different levels form the basis for ecosystems. The development within modern ecology (e.g., Odum and Barrett, 2005; Levin, 2009) and the various earth sciences, including studies of the atmosphere, hydrosphere, oceans and biosphere (e.g., Steffen et al., 2005), emphasize the interdependencies between different parts and processes of entire systems, all the way from individual organisms, through populations, ecosystems, and up to global-level processes. Hence, the concept of the earth system is introduced (e.g., Schellnhuber, 1999).

The interdependencies between abiotic and biotic processes can be illustrated by the development of the composition of the atmosphere. We believe that the original atmosphere was similar to the gases in volcano eruptions, consisting mainly of water vapor (80 percent), carbon dioxide

(12 percent) and sulfur dioxide (7 percent). There was no oxygen and almost no nitrogen (1 percent) (Graves and Reavy, 1996). As a result, not least from biological processes, this composition has changed tremendously, also altering the conditions for life. By the evolution of the cyanobacteria some 3.5 billion years ago, the production of atmospheric oxygen began. Through photosynthesis, carbon dioxide (CO_2) and water was transformed into organic matter (e.g., sugar) with oxygen (O_2) as 'waste'. Over time, plant production changed the balance between O_2 and CO_2 in the atmosphere, making the appearance of aerobic life forms possible. While the level of O_2 in the atmosphere has now reached 21 percent, the level of CO_2 was reduced to approximately 280 ppm before the start of the industrial era around 1750 (Steffen et al., 2005).[2] Nevertheless, due to biological, but also other processes like suspension of CO_2 in seawater, vast amounts of carbon have over time been moved into different parts of the environment like soils, seawater, sea beds and in geological formations (e.g., fossil carbon). Through the burning of fossil fuels, the level of CO_2 in the atmosphere has been increasing and the yearly average is now approaching 400 ppm (IPCC, 2014a).

Similarly, ecosystems recycle matter and energy in more or less closed loops where what is waste from one species – for example, litter from trees – is a resource for other species like fungi and bacteria, turning litter into compounds that the trees can later access. Recycling is also involved in predator–prey interactions. While ecology traditionally tended to emphasize balance or equilibrium states, modern ecology emphasizes much more variability and change. There are both equilibrium and non-equilibrium processes.

Stability, variability and change

Plants and animals are highly ordered systems. Genetic, hormonal and neural controls maintain steady states within limits. This is necessary for an organism to exist. Life depends on a certain level and type of order. Ecosystems, however, have no such tight controls. They are characterized by "pulsing states within limits" (Odum and Barrett, 2005, p. 6).

Over longer time frames, species, even ecosystems, appear and disappear. Changes may follow shifts in weather patterns, in species competition, volcanic activities and so on. The 'browning' of the Sahara some 6000 years ago was caused by changes in the climate that seem to have been triggered by a small change in the distribution of solar radiation on the surface of the earth, with amplified effects due to biophysical feedbacks (Claussen et al., 1999). Species invasions may change landscapes quite substantially even over rather short time periods. The invasion of the Siberian spruce in Scandinavia, peaking about 2000 years ago and taking over a landscape dominated by deciduous trees, is one among many examples (Ohlson et al., 2011).

Variability is different from change, while depending on the time frame referred to. Given a chosen time frame, something may appear as change, which given a longer time frame is better described as a variation around a quite stable average. We observe this in seasonal variations in temperatures, precipitation and plant growth. We also observe it in longer time frames as in the case of glacial cycles. The famous Vostok ice core data show a rather regular pattern of CO_2 concentrations and inferred temperatures over the last 400 000 years through four glacial–interglacial periods of about 100 000 years each (Petit et al., 1999) where glacial periods with lower temperatures/CO_2 levels dominate shorter periods with higher temperatures/CO_2 levels. The explanation of this cyclical variability seems to relate both to variation in the earth's orbit around the sun and in changes regarding the angle of the earth's axial tilt (the so-called Milankovitch cycles). However, earth surface temperature is also influenced by the capacity of the atmosphere to absorb sun energy (e.g., CO_2 levels), the albedo (the fraction of light reaching the surface that is reflected back into space) and the intensity of the sun. Volcanic activities also play a role (Keller and Botkin, 2008). While volcanic activity is a separate mechanism, the other mechanisms are interlinked through the effect of sun energy and temperatures on, for example, ice formation and plant growth, influencing next both the albedo and CO_2 levels in the atmosphere.

Cycling and connectivity

A second issue concerns cycling of matter and energy, and the various connectivities within the system. Through various biogeochemical processes we observe cycles even at the global scale of various compounds important for life like calcium, carbon, nitrogen, phosphorus and sulfur (e.g., Schlesinger, 1991).

Hydrological cycles, ocean and atmospheric movements are key elements of cycling movements of both matter and energy. The hydrological cycles – through rainfall, erosion, percolation through soils and movements to lakes and oceans – is a core motor in cycling of matter. Depositions on land have been important for many agricultural systems – for example, the large river dynasties of the Middle East and Asia. Rivers tie land to the sea with nutrient inputs important for biological life, not least in coastal areas.

Ocean currents are as important, transporting nutrients far away from where they originated and greatly influencing the opportunities for life, also beyond coastal areas. Similarly, these currents transport energy from equatorial zones to higher latitudes, making temperature variations across the globe much lower than they would otherwise have been. Also, atmospheric movements transport energy and have a similar effect on temperature variations. Winds are also important for transport of matter, causing depositions both on land and on sea surfaces (Steffen et al., 2005).

While I have emphasized abiotic processes, biological dynamics are very important for the process of cycling matter and even for weather patterns. Nitrifying bacteria play a key role in the nitrogen cycle, making nitrogen available for plant growth both in terrestrial and aquatic ecosystems. Plants play a key role in the carbon cycle. Figure 2.1 depicts the main elements of the 'natural' terrestrial carbon cycle.

Note: The numbers are global sums in billions of tons of carbon for the pre-industrial world. In the case of fluxes, measurements are per year. Soils are the largest pool for carbon globally. The carbon sequestration through photosynthesis (Pn) equals net primary production (NPP) plus losses through respiration (Ra) and losses of volatile organic carbon (VOC). Carbon in NPP has the capacity to increase the soil pool, but in equilibrium losses through respiration (Rh) equals inputs to soils and losses through fires. The yearly capture of carbon through photosynthesis is about 6% of the plant and soil pools altogether.

Source: Based on Steffen et al. (2005, Figure 2.34).

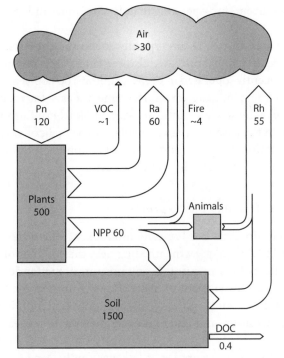

Figure 2.1 Main elements of the terrestrial carbon cycle, billions of tons of carbon in pools and fluxes

Processes operate at different scales

As already indicated, the processes we are looking at here operate at different scales both in time and space. At the local level, issues like pests, fires, precipitation and loss of key species are of specific interest. A fire may totally change a landscape (for a while), but have a rather small impact on wider geographical scales. A pest might hit locally, but not spread. Different ecosystems are characterized by different compositions of species and diverse hydrological conditions, therefore operating very differently concerning nutrient use and storage. Plant growth and carbon sequestration vary greatly across a landscape.

Other processes operate at higher scales both in time and space. The changing composition of the atmosphere is a very good illustration of how lengthy a process may be – actually operating at scales over billions of years. At the same time it is linked to local processes as every biologically active part of the surface of the globe has delivered 'inputs' to the process by, for example, sequestering CO_2 and releasing O_2. Glacial processes are regional, but with global consequences – for example, the level of the sea. Wind systems and ocean currents are operating mainly at regional and global scales.

While local processes are typically performing at faster time scales than the regional and global ones, we also see large variations here. Glacial processes have 'recently' operated in cycles of about 100 000 years. Other climatic phenomena may operate on shorter time scales – for example, a few hundred years like the so-called little 'Ice Age' in Northern Europe between 1550 and 1850. In the case of ocean currents, we may talk of years or even months as relevant time frames, while weather phenomena like low pressure may cross an ocean or continent in just a few days.

Linkages across scales and across processes

Natural processes are typically interlinked. The water cycle influences terrestrial biological growth, affecting next the volumes of sequestered carbon. The effect of ocean currents on transport of matter depends – among other things – on the amount of matter flowing from rivers. Vegetation influences the effects of wind and water on erosion. Vegetation is also very dependent on precipitation, as it also influences precipitation itself.

While the list of examples of linkages can be long – actually infinite – our interest here is more about how we can understand and classify these linkages. We observe that local and faster processes typically deliver inputs to slower regional and global ones. This is typical for all major matter cycles. An example is algae that absorb calcium and phosphorus from seawater that themselves may have originated from eroded rocks. Algae have an average life expectancy ranging from a few days to a year or two. The absorbed calcium and phosphorus may end up on the sea bed and then be included in geological processes that over very long time scales produce rocks rich in these compounds. Another is the emission of gases – for example, CO_2 – from plants, animals and soils, influencing the long-run composition of the atmosphere.

At the same time, global processes frame local ones. The composition of the atmosphere affects how much solar radiation will be captured by the atmosphere, then influencing local climates. The ocean currents have a tremendous effect on both local climates and availability of nutrients for species like fish.

So, how is it that these linkages do not produce complete chaos? First of all, sun energy that flows to the earth is high-quality energy that has the capacity to support the formation of ordered systems from single species to the global level. Certainly, we know yet of no other planet where life exists, so it may seem that the conditions have to be rather extraordinary for life to develop and sustain itself. Second, the living bodies as well as the earth system are characterized by feedbacks that are very important for the way the system operates.

There are two types of feedbacks – positive and negative – or *amplifying* and *stabilizing* feedbacks, as defined by Chapin et al. (2009). Amplifying feedbacks augment changes in a process and tend therefore to destabilize a system. One example could be increased temperatures that may result in melting of glaciers and sea ice, next resulting in reduced reflection of sun rays as the surface gets darker (reduced albedo). The effect of this will be higher temperatures, more melting of ice, even higher temperatures and so on.

Stabilizing feedbacks have the opposite property. They occur when two processes or components interact and growth in one causes a decline in the other. One example is temperature increase resulting in more precipitation, with cloud formation that may lower temperatures. Another is predator–prey relationships where increase in prey facilitates growth in the predator population, which tends to keep both populations fluctuating around intermediate levels. A third is the balance between plants and animals where plant growth reduces CO_2 and increases O_2 levels in the atmosphere, while animals living off these plants produce the reverse. The difference between the more stable cell/organism and the more fluctuating ecosystem as referred to above, relates to differences in these feedback mechanisms.

Resilience and thresholds

Systems characterized by amplifying feedbacks destabilize themselves. For a system to be sustained over (some) time, the existence of stabilizing feedbacks is necessary. In relation to this, we need yet another concept to be able to characterize systems. This is the concept of *resilience* (Holling, 1973; Chapin et al., 2009; Gunderson et al., 2010). Chapin et al. (2009, p. 9) define resilience as "the capacity of the system to absorb a spectrum of shocks and perturbations and still retain and further develop the same fundamental structure, functioning, and feedbacks". Hence, resilience has some commonality with the concept of *robustness*. However, where robustness means maintenance of system performance, the concept of resilience includes the capacity of a system to change and adapt, while still remaining within critical thresholds. Figure 2.2 illustrates key aspects.

As Chapin et al. (2009, p. 11) state, the "resilience of the system. . .is the likelihood that it will remain in the same state despite perturbations". In (a) a basin of attraction of a (eco-)system is described by the curved line. The location of the ball represents the state of the system. The attractor basin defines possible states. If we think of a forest, an external shock – for example, a fire – will kill many plants and trees and hence the state of the system changes – illustrated by the position of the ball moved up the side of the attractor basin from its equilibrium as defined by the basin. If the forest has the capacity to re-establish after this change – that is, it is resilient – this could be illustrated with the ball moving back to the bottom of the basin.

Moving to (b) through (e), a series of different types of systems and system resiliences is described. In (b) an unpredictable system is illustrated. The change in the state of the system depends entirely on the shock or perturbation. This is a system without any (strong) feedbacks. In (c) we

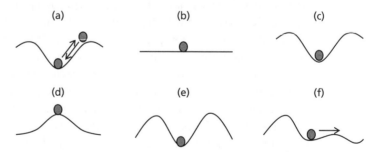

Source: Based on Chapin et al. (2009).

Figure 2.2 System stability and resilience

have a system with stabilizing feedbacks as in (a). In (d) we encounter a situation where feedbacks amplify the external shock. In (e) we see changes in the internal feedback structure as compared to (a). In (f) changes appear that may make the system easily 'flip' – that is, leave the basin of attraction and enter another. An example of the latter is an oligotrophic lake (low on nutrients) that over time is exposed to high inflows of nutrients, shifting its dynamics – including species composition – as it becomes eutrophic.

The concept of a *threshold* or *tipping point* is important in relation to the above. A threshold is a level of a state variable of a system – for example, the level of nutrients in a lake – that if passed makes the system 'flip' – the lake becomes eutrophic. In panel (a) of Figure 2.2, the threshold is the limit of the basin. A development up until the threshold will typically not result in changes in the sense that the system can still return to its original state after the external shock. When the threshold is passed, abrupt alterations may happen. A rubber band may illustrate the idea of a threshold. You may stretch it far without anything happening to its structure. Stop stretching it and it returns to its original length. If you stretch it beyond a certain point – the threshold – it breaks and the original shape cannot be retained.

2.2 A degrading environment

The relevance of the above for environmental governance regards whether human activities are pushing environmental systems beyond important thresholds or if they are resilient enough to sustain human production and consumption. In the following we shall look at five key areas – that of biodiversity and biodiversity loss, climate change, freshwater and land, nitrogen and phosphorus, and, finally, chemical pollution and aerosols. It will only be possible to give a brief summary of a few key aspects for each kind of problem and the type of challenges we are facing. As issues and challenges are different, the structure of each section will vary somewhat.

2.2.1 Biodiversity and biodiversity loss

Defining biodiversity is difficult. It is about variation in biological potential. In relation to that, definitions typically cover three levels – diversity within species, between species and between ecosystems. Wilson (2001, p. 377), hence, defines biodiversity as follows:

> The variety of organisms considered at all levels, from genetic variants belonging to the same species through arrays of species, to arrays of genera, families, and still

higher taxonomic levels; includes the variety of ecosystems, which comprise both the communities of organisms with particular habitats and the physical conditions under which they live.

The number of known/named species is in the order of 1.5 million (Dolman, 2000; Keller and Botkin, 2008). This is, however, only a proportion of all species on earth. Keller and Botkin (2008) indicate that the total number could be in the order of 3–10 million. Stork (1997) and Mace et al. (2005) offer even higher estimates, that is, 5–15 million and 5–30 million respectively. Biodiversity richness is typically highest in the tropics. Many tropical forest areas are characterized as biodiversity 'hotspots' (e.g., Myers et al., 2000; Lamoreux et al., 2006).

Changes in the composition of species are a natural process. Over time species become extinct as new ones appear. To be able to develop the kind of resilience that characterizes biological systems, they have to produce some randomness. This serves to constantly develop and 'test' better ways of adaptation. It creates 'searches' within the available state space through processes like genetic mutations. Variation increases and the system becomes better able to handle shifts in environmental conditions – see, for example, Nicolis and Prigogine (1989).

While change is a natural and a necessary element of living systems, the speed of species loss may cause concern. Present extinction rates are estimated to be about 100–1000 times higher than the 'natural' level (Pimm et al., 1995; Mace et al., 2005). Without action, the speed is actually expected to increase. Rockström et al. (2009, p. 15) conclude that "currently about 25 percent of the species in well-studied taxonomic groups are threatened by extinction". This does not imply that mass extinction did not happen before the human species colonized the world. The first of the five periods of extinction we know of happened 450 million years ago (Keller and Botkin, 2008). The fourth is maybe the most famous, appearing about 65 million years ago and causing the extinction of dinosaurs. It is thought to have been caused by a large asteroid hitting the earth. A key observation from these prior mass extinction periods is that it takes a long time for ecosystems to recover. While uncertain, the literature indicates millions of years (e.g., Novacek and Cleland, 2001).

The present high level of losses is, to a large extent, a result of human activities. This is a new dimension. Important factors are land conversion, land fragmentation and pollution – see also the sections below. Due to climate change, pressures are increasing.

Why are biodiversity and its loss important? As we have seen, biological processes play a key role in maintaining the dynamics of various other natural processes. Different species fill different niches – that is, they maintain different processes of importance for the larger system they are part of. Some bacteria are specialists at converting nitrogen gas in the atmosphere to biologically accessible nitrogen important to all other species. Different types of plants are specialized to capture sun energy through photosynthesis under specific conditions. Various species typically feed on different types of plants. Bacteria and fungi of different forms decompose organic material so that nutrients again become available for plants to grow. Many species – plants, bacteria and fungi – also remove pollutants from water, soil and air. From a functional perspective, diversity is therefore important for ensuring that various processes are maintained.

Moreover, variation is a kind of security. Diversity within a species increases the chance for it to survive if external conditions change. Similarly, an abundance of species maintaining a certain function in an ecosystem increases the chance of that system surviving despite species becoming extinct. Variation and redundancy are important for the resilience of ecosystems. Ehrlich and Ehrlich (1992) use the 'rivet-popper' problem as an analogy to this. Airplanes are constructed with considerable redundancy; thus, the removal of a single rivet from a wing would not cause a crash. However, "the continuous removal of numerous rivets will sooner or later lead to disaster" (Ehrlich and Ehrlich, 1992, p. 226).

While a certain stability of ecosystems is also very important for the human species, biodiversity is important for more direct economic reasons. Certainly, food production is highly dependent on a variety of species. While only about 110 plant species provide the basis of almost all food in the world (Dolman, 2000), variation in genetic material is crucial for the long-run functioning of the food system. This is not least important for the ability to develop new crops in the face of environmental change, capacity to combat diseases and so on. Also important is the role various plants play in both 'traditional' and 'modern' medicine. The whole industry of biotechnology depends on natural variation.

Finally, maintenance of biodiversity is important for recreational, cultural and aesthetic reasons. Variety is a source of both cultural identity and experience. Ethical arguments based on the position that various life forms have an equal right to exist are covered in the UN General Assembly World Charter for Nature from 1982.

2.2.2 Climate change

Climate change is also a natural phenomenon, but, as in the case of biodiversity, human activities play a key role in the changes we are now observing. Climate change includes alterations in the patterns of temperature, precipitation and wind and how these vary across seasons. Many factors influence the climate. The amount of sun energy hitting the earth's atmosphere is key. The composition of the atmosphere, the reflective capacity of the earth's surface and the capacity of oceans to store and transport heat are also of great importance.

As already emphasized, this complex interplay has resulted in quite substantial climatic variations over geological time horizons. Over the last 400 000 years there have been four rather similar glacial–interglacial periods, where phases of low temperatures/low levels of CO_2 and methane (CH_4) in the atmosphere dominate those with higher levels – Figure 2.3. The ultimate cause behind the changes is believed to relate to solar radiation reaching the atmosphere and various feedback responses of 'the earth system'.

Note that in the last 10 000 years – the Holocene – the pattern is somewhat unusual. The temperature has stabilized at a high level, including less variability over shorter time frames. It has been argued that the observed stability was a necessary condition for agriculture to appear about 10 000 years ago. It has also been argued that we might soon be heading for a new Ice Age. Recent research – for example, Berger and Loutre (2002) – points in a quite

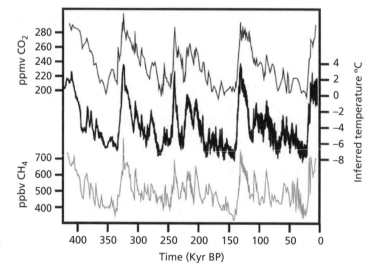

Note: kyr = 1000 years; ppmv = parts per million by volume; ppbv = parts per billion by volume.

Source: Steffen et al. (2005, Figure 1.3).

Figure 2.3 Estimated levels of carbon dioxide (CO2; upper graph), methane (CH4, lower graph) and temperature (middle graph)

different direction, with any new Ice Age being at least 50 000 years ahead –
that is, not accounting for effects of anthropogenic emissions.

Since the start of the Industrial Revolution, we observe a gradual
change in levels of CO_2, CH_4 and N_2O (nitrous oxide) – Figure 2.4. The
Intergovernmental Panel on Climate Change (IPCC, 2007a) has estimated
that since 1750, two-thirds of the CO_2 emissions have come from fossil fuels
and one-third from land use changes. This relation has changed over time,
with fossil fuels and the production of cement playing a relatively more
important role more recently. About half of the emitted carbon is retained
in oceans and on land (plants and soils). The rest is building up the concentration in the atmosphere. CH_4 emissions originate in wetlands, ruminant
animals, rice agriculture, burning of biomass and waste dumps. As opposed
to CO_2, we observe a slowdown of CH_4 emission growth in recent years. N_2O
emissions are largely linked to agriculture – the use of nitrogen fertilizers and
land use changes. Other gases like chlorofluorocarbons (CFCs) also play a
role. Nevertheless, CO_2 dominates with regard to radiative forcing.[3]

Global climate models are used to predict future developments in, for
example, temperatures and precipitation. Important inputs are projections of
future emissions of greenhouse gases. Figure 2.5 shows a selected set of such
scenarios for temperature developments until the year 2100. These estimates
typically predict temperature increases for 'business-as-usual scenarios'

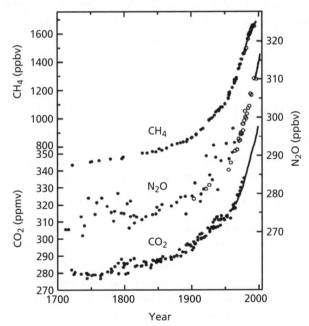

Note: ppmv = parts
per million by volume;
ppbv = parts per billion by
volume.

Source: Steffen et al. (2005,
Figure 2.3).

Figure 2.4
Greenhouse gases
in the atmosphere
since 1700

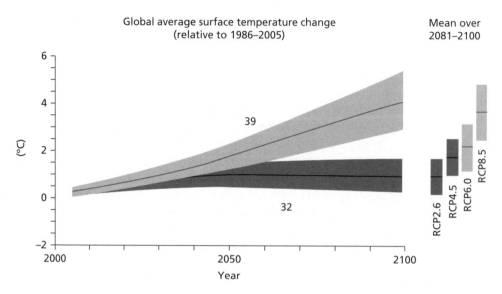

Note: RCP = representative concentration pathways.

Source: IPCC (2014a, Figure 2.1 (b)). Climate Change 2014: Synthesis Report. Contribution of Working Groups I, II and III to the Fifth Assessment Report of the Intergovernmental Panel on Climate Change, Figure 2.1 (b). [Core Writing Team, Pachauri, R.K. and Meyer, L. (eds.)]. IPCC, Geneva, Switzerland.

Figure 2.5 Temperature predictions

in the range of 2–5.5°C compared to a reference level of the mean of the period 1986–2005. IPCC (2014a, p. 8; original emphasis) writes: "Scenarios *without additional efforts to constrain emissions*... lead to [representative concentration] pathways ranging between RCP6.0 and RCP8.5. RCP2.6 is representative of a scenario that aims to keep global warming *likely* below 2°C above pre-industrial temperature". This demands substantial mitigation efforts. Temperatures will continue to increase in business-as-usual scenarios, indicating a temperature rise in the order of 3–12°C by the year 2300.

Per capita emissions of greenhouse gases/CO_2 volumes are typically much higher in developed as compared to developing countries, although China is now the country with the largest total emissions. Table 2.1 shows data of CO_2 emissions per capita (exclusive of land use change) from a selected set of countries.

The variation across countries is tremendous. While the level of economic development as measured by the gross domestic product (GDP) influences emissions per capita, other factors also count like the composition of fossil fuels,[4] access to energy sources other than fossil fuels, the efficiency of energy and transport sectors, whether the country is a large oil producer and so forth. It is hence notable that Qatar has the highest per capita emissions, while

Table 2.1 Emissions of CO_2 per capita and in total for a selected set of countries, 2010[a]

Country	$MtCO_2$ per capita	Million $MtCO_2$ total per country
Qatar	40.5	70.4
United States of America	17.6	5428.6
Australia	16.9	372.8
Kazakhstan	15.2	248.5
Germany	9.1	744.8
United Kingdom	7.9	493.1
China	6.2	8280.1
Sweden	5.6	52.5
Brazil	2.2	419.4
India	1.7	2007.2
Tanzania	0.2	6.8

Note: [a] Land use changes excluded.

Sources: World Bank (2015); CDIAC (2015).

China has recently surpassed Sweden in per capita levels of CO_2 emissions. It is estimated that 73 percent of the total global greenhouse gas emissions come from CO_2.[5] This percentage is typically somewhat higher for developed countries and lower for developing ones (World Resources Institute, 2012).

There are a lot of uncertainties concerning climate change and its future development. First, the development in emissions is uncertain and depends not least on political decisions. Second, the role of various stabilizing and amplifying feedbacks is uncertain. We have already emphasized that land and sea retain about half of the CO_2 emissions. This is a huge stabilizing factor, while there is uncertainty for the future due to complex interactions between temperature, CO_2 concentrations and nutrient cycles. It is likely that these natural stabilizing feedbacks will weaken during the present century. This tendency seems most certain for oceans (Steffen et al., 2005).

Also important are the amplifying feedbacks following from melting ice and the thawing of permafrost soils. The former will reduce albedo, which next reduces reflection of sun energy back into the universe. Hence, more of the energy will be trapped as heat. The latter involves potential release of large amounts of CH_4, which is now stored in frozen soils. If the latter happens, there is the risk that 'a natural process' – instigated by human activities – may speed up global warming tremendously. This could force an attractor shift despite reduced human emissions.

Consequences of global warming for the biota – humans and other species – are many. They are also uncertain – not only because of uncertainties regarding expected emission levels and various feedbacks. There is also a lack of knowledge related to how a defined increase in temperature influences the dynamics of ecosystems. There will be direct effects like precipitation, frequency of floods and droughts, erosion, severe storm events, sea level rise, ocean currents and their dynamics. Biota will also be indirectly affected through changes in production of organic matter, availability of freshwater, distribution of diseases, species adaptation, ocean acidification and so on.

There is no space in this chapter for in-depth coverage of these issues, but I will briefly mention some issues with regard to three areas: food production, health and ocean acidification. Regarding food availability, analyses are typically based on emission scenarios resulting in a global temperature increase by the end of this century in the order of 2–3°C (e.g., Fisher et al., 2001; Cline, 2007; Nelson et al., 2009; Thornton, 2011). Most analyses point towards increased food production in mid- to high latitudes, while there will be a decrease in lower latitudes – tropical areas – that is, where food shortage is already a problem. While Nelson et al. (2009) indicate the greatest effects for South Asia, Cline (2007) suggests that Africa south of the Sahara will be hardest hit.

Concerning health effects, problems will again mainly appear in developing countries. IPCC (2007b, p. 48) summarizes this in the following way:

> The health status of millions of people is projected to be affected through, for example, increases in malnutrition; increased deaths, diseases and injury due to extreme weather events; increased burden of diarrhoeal diseases; increased frequency of cardio-respiratory diseases due to higher concentrations of ground-level ozone in urban areas related to climate change; and the altered spatial distribution of some infectious diseases.

Looking finally at ocean acidification, we have already emphasized oceans as sinks for CO_2. While this is positive in the sense that it reduces atmospheric concentrations, it results in lower pH (measure of acidity) in ocean waters. IPCC (2014a) indicates an increase in ocean acidity in the order of 50–100 percent. As Rockström et al. (2009) emphasize, many marine organisms – especially those protecting themselves with calcium carbonate shells – are very sensitive to changes in pH. They also note problems for coral reef formation. Generally, acidification will lower the survival and growth of many marine organisms, influencing both sea ecosystems and the capacity of the sea to capture CO_2.

We have already emphasized the uncertainties in model projections. I will close this section by making two observations. First, almost all projections of impacts of climate change are based on 'middle range' temperature changes. Researchers are reluctant to make analyses of 'high' temperature scenarios as this implies 'stretching' the models beyond temperature levels where they offer a reasonable level of certainty. This results in risks being systematically under-communicated.

Second, many amplifying and stabilizing processes are not included in the models. Rockström et al. (2009) note that climate models only include 'fast feedbacks' like changes in water vapor, clouds and sea ice. Hence, they yield temperature increases in business-as-usual scenarios that are in the range of 2–4.5°C. Referring to Hansen et al. (2008), they note that including 'slow feedbacks' such as decreased ice sheet volume, changed vegetation distribution and inundation of continental shelves gives projections in the order of 4–8°C. The potential cascade of amplifying feedbacks this could release raises serious questions about the level of risks we are facing.

2.2.3 Freshwater and land

Freshwater

The hydrological cycle is fundamental to life. Water is necessary for all forms of biological life. Water, moreover, transports nutrients and other materials not only important for life in the sea, but also for wetlands and sedimentation on land. Water is both a stock and a flow resource. Concerning stocks, most of the water is stored in the oceans (96.5 percent). About 1 percent is saline groundwater. Hence, freshwater amounts to only 2.5 percent of the total. Of this again, 70 percent is stored in glaciers (Shiklomanov, 1993). Nevertheless, the 0.8 percent of the total volume that appears as freshwater in lakes, soils, subsoil aquifers and rivers is vast – about 10 million km³.

Concerning flows, the total amount of precipitation per year is globally about 500 000 km³. Of this, 22 percent (110 000 km³) falls over land (Postel et al., 1996). While humans also appropriate water from storage like groundwater and lakes, we are most dependent on rainwater in our activities. This is even more so as groundwater basins and lakes are dependent on rainwater for their replenishment.

Regarding human use of freshwater resources, Molden (2007) presents global estimates indicating that human withdrawals of renewable water resources in the year 2000 were globally close to 9 percent. Postel et al. (1996) conclude that humanity uses about 36 percent of precipitation. The main difference between the two sources is that Postel et al. include water use in all ecosystems influenced by human appropriation as defined by Vitousek et al. (1986). Molden (2007) uses data from the Food and Agriculture Organization (FAO), focusing only on agriculture, industry and domestic uses.

It is estimated that over 25 percent of the global population lives under severe conditions of water stress (Vörösmarty et al., 2000). Similarly, Palaniappan and Gleick (2011, p. 1) indicate that "about one-third of the world's population lives in countries with moderate-to-high water stress". According to the United Nations (UN, 2009a) the situation all the way from Northern Africa, through the Middle East/Arabian peninsula, through Turkey, Iran and so on, to India and Northern China, is characterized by so-called 'physical water scarcity' or is approaching scarcity. The same situation is found in the southwest of the USA and Mexico. Most of Africa south of the Sahara is characterized by 'economic water scarcity'. This means that there is enough rain compared to the size of the population, but people face difficulties due to lack of means to access the available water.

The use of groundwater is rising rapidly on a global scale. The United Nations (UN, 2009a) estimates that at present about 20 percent of water used for human purposes – especially for irrigation in agriculture – comes from this source. The figure is most probably underestimated as there are many uses not accounted for. Groundwater use has tended to lower water tables in many parts of the world, indicating unsustainable water use – see, for example, Konikow and Kendy (2005); Rodell et al. (2009). It is also noteworthy that only 2 percent of precipitation over land is infiltrated into groundwater. It should further be mentioned that Molden (2007) estimates that 25 percent of the world's rivers now run dry before they reach the ocean.

Looking at the situation for the world's groundwater resources, the UN (2009a, p. 131) notes:

> [that a] more sobering conclusion drawn from detailed local aquifer studies is that where groundwater services are in heavy demand, much of the good quality groundwater has already been used. Contemporary recharge to shallow aquifers has become seriously (perhaps irrevocably) polluted, and relaxing water abstraction and pollution pressure on aquifers will take considerable time.

Regarding water quality, problems span issues all the way from lowered drinking water quality due to bad sanitation; eutrophication of lakes, rivers and coastal waters due to emissions of nutrients; to the spread of various toxic substances that influence all types of water bodies. The situation is again different across the globe. Concerning quality, the situation has actually been improved in many respects in the developed regions of the world. This is due not least to better sanitation facilities and some regulations related to use of toxic substances. While there still are many issues in these parts of the world, the situation is much more difficult in the developing countries. Diarrhea is a big problem especially in Sub-Saharan Africa and South Asia – causing almost 2 million deaths in these regions in 2004 according to the World Health Organization (WHO, 2008). Use of pesticides affects water quality and human health. Regulations of toxic substances are weak.

Human use also influences the dynamics of ecosystems and conditions for other species. Human appropriation simply implies less available water for natural ecosystems. Hence, it becomes an issue of not only how much water is available, but also how much should be left for the reproduction of natural systems. Most worrying perhaps is the estimate that biodiversity in freshwater species was halved between 1970 and 2005 (UN, 2009a). This is most probably the effect of eutrophication, emissions of toxic substances and regulations of water flows.

Land

Total land area of the globe is 149 million km². This is less than 30 percent of the surface of the earth. More than 40 percent is not well suited for habitation. Deserts and glaciers cover – as an example – about 30 percent of total land surface. Table 2.2 gives an overview of various land uses in 2009 based on FAO data.

Table 2.2 Different categories of land and land uses – 2009

Land category	Area in 1000 km²	Area in %
Total land area	148 940	100
Arable land	13 812	9.3
Pastures, meadows etc.	35 078	23.6
Forests	40 387	27.1
Other	40 880	27.4
Inland water	4 557	3.0
Antarctica	14 226	9.6

Source: FAO (2012a).

According to the FAO, about 9 percent of the land surface of the earth is arable (crop) land. Including pastures/meadows, agricultural use is about 34 percent. Ramankutty et al. (2002) argue that arable land is actually larger than documented by the FAO. Using remote sensing, they estimate arable land to be almost 18 million km^2 in 1990 (about 12 percent of total land mass). While there are uncertainties with this method, they argue that official statistics may under-report cropland – especially in China. As forests may also represent opportunities for grazing lands, the distinction between pastures and forests is likely very uncertain. Meyer and Turner (1992) indicate an area almost the double of the FAO in the category 'grassland/pasture'. Certainly, much of the areas included in this estimate are extensively grazed.

Ramankutty and Foley (1999) assess that the amount of arable land has more than quadrupled from the year 1700. According to them, the amount of cropland was at that time 4 million km^2 globally. In 1900 it was about 11.5 million km^2, increasing another 50 percent to reach 18 million km^2 by the end of the last century. From 1700 to 2000, the population increased tenfold. As a result of this, cropland per person has diminished substantially. Using the data from Ramankutty and Foley (1999), we see a reduction from approximately 0.7 ha per capita in 1900 to about 0.3 ha per capita in 1990. Most of this reduction has actually come about since 1950 and reductions have continued to date. Despite this, the number of malnourished people has been rather constant since 1970 – in the order of 800 and 900 million people (MEA, 2005). This implies that the percentage of malnourished people – while still far too high – has been reduced from 24 to 13 percent globally. Nevertheless, about 10 million people are estimated to die from malnourishment every year (Steffen et al., 2005).

Substantial increases in yields following expanded use of inputs like fertilizers (see Section 2.2.4), pesticide use, irrigation and development of new crop varieties explain why reduced agricultural area per capita has not resulted in increased malnutrition. The total world grain harvest almost tripled from 877 million tons in 1961 to 2433 million tons in 2010. To be able to combat malnutrition, to feed a growing population and meet changes in diet, it has been estimated that food production may need to be increased globally by 70 percent – even 100 percent in developing countries – by 2050 (FAO, 2009). In relation to this, it is notable that the growth in world total grain harvests per year is reduced from 2 percent in the period 1961–85 to about 1.2 percent thereafter.

Generally, we seem to be heading towards a period of increased competition over land resources. For the moment, there are at least three important issues to note. First, more land seems needed for feeding a growing and partly undernourished population. Second, there are increased demands for land to produce biofuel as a substitute for fossil fuels to combat climate change. Third, there are strong arguments in favor of halting deforestation – both to protect biodiversity and to combat climate change as it is estimated that deforestation/land use change is the cause of emissions of CO_2 in the order of 10–12 percent (IPCC, 2014b).[6]

According to the FAO (2010), deforestation was on average about 16 million ha (0.16 million km^2) per year between 1990 and 2000. This trend has slowed down since 2000 so that average levels are estimated to be about 13 million ha. Due to afforestation and natural expansion, net losses were about half of this level. Hence, forest cover expanded in Europe and Asia, while decreasing in Latin America, Africa and Oceania. Given twentieth-century trends, we should expect a cumulated loss of forests in the order of 10 percent for the twenty-first century (Ramankutty and Foley, 1999). The situation for wetlands is even worse. According to Katz (2006), about half of the world's wetlands have disappeared since 1900.

The total size of various land use categories is important for maintaining biodiversity and habitats of different kinds. The structure of the 'produced' landscapes, is, however, also essential. Habitat fragmentation – the splitting up of species habitats into smaller units – causes disintegration of populations. This will next increase the risk of extinction. While reducing fragmentation is demanding given the various conflicts over different uses, constructing corridors to create contacts between habitats is a favored strategy.

Added to the issue of competition over land, food production may face a series of further future challenges. One is land degradation. The picture is, however, quite complex, uncertain and heavily debated – see, for example, Robbins (2012). Bai et al. (2008) have undertaken a global assessment of land degradation in the period 1981–2003. Their conclusion is that there has been an overall increase in net primary productivity of land.[7] At the same time about a quarter of the land area suffered from a decline in productivity – identifying these areas to be mainly found in Africa south of the equator, but also Southeast Asia and the Pampas. They note that areas typically emphasized as degraded – like the Middle East, South and Central Asia are "represented by only relatively small areas of degradation" in this period. Hence, they conclude, "most areas of historical land degradation have become stable landscapes with stubbornly low levels of productivity" (Bai et al., 2008, p. 231).

Steffen et al. (2005) emphasize a second issue, the effect of aerosol particle loadings and ozone concentrations on crop production. A case study from East Asia has observed up to 30 percent reduced solar irradiation, implying similar losses in yields. Comparable effects are documented in Pakistan.

A third set of issues concerns use of pesticides and fertilizers. While pesticides play a very important role in maintaining the production capacity of many agricultural systems – not least high-yield monoculture based – issues are raised concerning the long-term sustainability of their use (MEA, 2005). Similar challenges are faced in the field of fertilizer use. The latter is the topic of the next section.

2.2.4 Nitrogen and phosphorus

Increased use of fertilizers has played a key role in the growth in global agricultural production. Increased availability of nitrogen and phosphorus has been especially important. Nitrogen is often a limiting factor for the productivity of ecosystems/growth of crops. While there are huge amounts of nitrogen gas (N_2) in the atmosphere, it is not accessible to plants if not converted to nitrate or ammonia. If we go back to about 1900, most biologically accessible nitrogen came from natural processes. Looking at terrestrial systems, biological fixation (by microorganisms – free living or in symbiosis with leguminous plants) was in the order of 100 million tons per year. The production in oceans was of a similar magnitude (blue-green algae). Added to that was a volume of about 5 million tons fixed by lightening. There was also crop residues and manure. This was, however, recycled nitrogen fixed by nature. The extra input from human activity came mainly from legume and rice production, estimated to be about 15 million tons in 1890 (Galloway, 2005).[8]

With the invention of industrial methods of producing ammonia and nitrates in the early twentieth century, the availability of biologically accessible nitrogen has vastly increased. However, the use of industrially produced fertilizers grew rather slowly until 1960 where the volume reached about 13 million tons of nitrogen.[9] By 2002, the figure had reached 87 million tons per year (FAO, 2012a). If we add nitrogen fixed through leguminous crops (40 million tons), nitrogen that is oxidized through fossil fuel combustion (about 20 million tons) and human-induced burning beyond the natural level (about 10 million tons), we get a yearly total of about 160 million tons, which is larger than natural fixation by terrestrial systems (MEA, 2005; Steffen et al., 2005). A prognosis by MEA (2005) points towards a further increase from 2000 to 2050 in the order of 100 million tons per year.

If we look at phosphorus, we observe a similar trend. Actually, human activity is relatively more important in this case. According to Jahnke (2000), phosphorus used in fertilizers and detergents amounts to 12.5 million tons. This should be compared to a natural rate of release at about 2.2 million tons per year due to weathering of phosphate-rich rocks and soil processes (Reeburgh, 1997).

There are two key issues concerning sustainability of present practices. First, the level of losses of nutrients to various ecosystems is important. Second, future availability of phosphorus is a growing concern. Looking at losses, these may change the dynamics of ecosystems. Nitrogen and phosphorus are lost from fields to water in large quantities. Added to this is nitrogen from combustion, resulting in abrupt shifts in both freshwater and marine ecosystems (e.g., Carpenter, 2005; Zillén et al., 2008). Eutrophication and algae blooms as a related phenomenon are a typical result across the globe. As Rockström et al. (2009) emphasize, nutrient losses to the environment erode the resilience of these systems. Also worrying is the loss in the form of nitrous oxide (N_2O), which is one of the most important greenhouse gases. While IPCC estimates that 1 percent of all nitrogen in fertilizers ends up as N_2O in the atmosphere, Crutzen et al. (2007) argue that the overall level could be in the range of 3–5 percent.

Both nitrogen and phosphorus are fundamental elements of plant production, but it is only in the case of phosphorus that there are any issues concerning future availability. Estimates regarding accessible phosphate rock reserves vary substantially. Van Kauwenbergh (2010, p. vii) concludes that "phosphate rock concentrate reserves to produce fertilizer will be available for the next 300–400 years". Cordell et al. (2009) indicate a time frame that is much shorter: 50–100 years. Whatever is the better estimate, research in this field raises issues concerning present practices and the need to develop an agricultural system with much higher levels of phosphorus recycling.

2.2.5 Chemical pollution and aerosols

Chemical pollution

Chemical pollution includes heavy metals, organic compounds of industrial origin and radioactive compounds. Such pollution both influences human health and the survival of a wide range of species. The release of chemicals follows from production and use of a series of new compounds developed for commercial reasons – for example, pesticides, industrial coolants, lubricants, plastic additives, flame retardants and so on – and as a side-effect of economic activity – for example, the release of heavy metals from coal burning and mining.

It is estimated that there are about 100 000 'industrial' chemicals on the world market. Toxicity data exist for just a few thousand of these and we literally know nothing about their combined effects (Rockström et al., 2009). Problems observed concern various disorders and also death. Some chemicals act as endocrine disruptors – that is, they affect the hormone system – which may cause birth defects, cancer and learning disabilities. Sexual development problems are also observed. Some compounds may travel across the whole globe – like mercury – and become concentrated through the food chain. They are particularly causing problems for species at the top of the chain.

A specific issue concerns the time it takes from a chemical being released into the environment to proving its effects. With reference to persistent organic pollutants (POPs) like polychlorinated biphenyl (PCB), dioxin and dichlorodiphenyltrichloroethane (DDT), Steffen et al. (2005, p. 226) note:

> The persistence of organic pollutants in continental aquatic systems is almost always high, and their degradation products can sometimes be more toxic than the parent compound. Dealing with such water quality issues can be slow, as it often takes a decade or longer for the effects of a newly introduced compound to be thoroughly analysed and several more decades or longer for deleterious effects to work their way through food webs from primary producers to predators.

This kind of delay creates challenges for policy formulation.

Aerosols

Aerosols are suspensions of small solid particles or liquid droplets in another gas, and can be natural or human-made. Examples are clouds, dust, smog and smoke. Cloud formation is a natural phenomenon, but the concentration of aerosols has been greatly amplified not least through burning of fossil fuels. Tsigaridis et al. (2006) have estimated that the concentration of most aerosols influenced by human activities has doubled since pre-industrial times.

Aerosols result in a series of respiratory problems, causing both death and reduced life quality. It is estimated that reduced outdoor urban air quality results in about 800 000 premature deaths per year. Exposure to indoor smoke is even more dangerous – causing about 1.6 million deaths. These problems are most extensive in developing countries, especially in Asia (Rockström et al., 2009).

I have already mentioned consequences of aerosols on food production in certain regions where coal plays a cornerstone in energy delivery. They also result in loss of freshwater fish through acidification. Aerosols have a cooling effect on the climate, and it is estimated that it currently reduces the effect of greenhouse gases by about 10 percent (Myhre, 2009). It may also affect for example, monsoon circulations (Lau and Kim, 2006).

2.2.6   Are we approaching limits?

Referring back to the issue of resilience, there are two aspects of special interest. First, we might ask if the changes we cause to ecosystems and their interactions are pushing them beyond important thresholds. Second, we might wonder if the speed of change is higher than the systems' inherent capacity to adapt.

Problems appear on different scales. We have already mentioned examples of local and regional systems having 'flipped'. Rockström et al. (2009) ask whether there are any boundaries at the planetary scale, and if so, if any of these have already been transgressed. They identify ten such boundaries – climate change, ocean acidification, stratospheric ozone depletion, global phosphorus cycles, global nitrogen cycles, biodiversity loss, global freshwater use, land system change, atmospheric aerosol loading and chemical pollution.

Defining limits on the scale of the planet is very difficult and the authors – top experts in their various fields – note that their assessment is both preliminary and very uncertain. It is still important to try to establish insights in this form as far too much of the research is focused on single issues mainly at local level, for one compound only or only for one type of change. Hence, the overall picture is lost in 'details'.

Rockström et al. are able to define a planetary boundary for all but atmospheric aerosol loading and chemical pollution. They conclude that the planetary limit is transgressed with regard to biodiversity loss, climate change and nitrogen loading. In the case of biodiversity, they indicate a planetary boundary of extinction at a rate ten times that of 'normal'. As the present extinction rates are in the order of 100–1000 that of normal, they conclude that we are way over the boundary.

Regarding climate change, the authors define a boundary for CO_2 concentrations at 350 parts per million (ppm). Based on paleoclimatic data, they define a 'danger zone' somewhere within the range of 350–550 ppm. As the present level is about 400 ppm, they conclude that this boundary is also transgressed. Due to increased levels of other greenhouse gases – for example, CH_4 and N_2O – Rockström et al. note that looking just at the radiative forcing of CO_2 is only part of the story. They conclude, however, that the present cooling effect of aerosols just about nullifies the effect of other greenhouse gases. The negative effect of aerosols, however, on human health and acidification is a strong argument for reducing their emissions, influencing the climate change boundary.

Looking then at nitrogen, the authors define a limit of 25 percent of the current volume of human-produced biologically accessible nitrogen compounds – specified as 35 million tons per year. They emphasize that this is "a first guess" (Rockström et al., 2009, p. 13). If they are in any way close to what is a reasonable limit, we see again what great challenges humanity faces. While there are possibilities to increase efficiency in the use of nitrogen in agriculture, feeding a growing population with reduced levels of nitrogen fertilizers is very demanding.

Rockström et al. also emphasize that we are close to the limits concerning phosphorus and ocean acidification. The situation is – according to them – a bit better for land system change, global freshwater use and stratospheric ozone depletion. In the case of land use, the authors define the limit of cropland as 15 percent of ice-free land surface. According to the estimates they use, we are currently at 10–13 percent. Hence, the authors indicate that we have some space left at the global level, while one may wonder about effects on biodiversity.

I think it is wise to look at these evaluations as indications of serious challenges facing humanity. I also think they are helpful attempts to orient our focus in the right direction. Trying to define boundaries is, moreover, important, while there will be a lot of uncertainty and disagreement about what issues to emphasize, if or when global limits are the best way to define thresholds and where the thresholds seem to lie.

2.3 What causes environmental degradation?

As we have seen, human use of resources and influence on ecosystem dynamics has increased tremendously since the Industrial Revolution. The pace has been especially high since 1950. How do we explain this? We can start by examining the formula $I = P \times A \times T$. It measures human impact (I) on the environment as a product of P = population, A = affluence and T = technology – see

Ehrlich and Holdren (1971). The formula is correct 'by definition', but it is necessary to look behind it to better understand the issues involved.

Offering a quick recap of the human impact, it is estimated that 10 000 years ago there were roughly 5 million people living on earth, mainly hunters and gatherers. Around this time the 'invention' of agriculture occurred, with new technologies forming the basis for a gradual shift in human survival strategies and resource use. By selecting and sowing seeds, by clearing land and tilling the soil, domesticating animals and so on, the capacity to produce food for human consumption increased substantially. Hence, 2000 years ago, the estimated population had grown to about 200–300 million (Cohen, 1995). Various types of metal were discovered, expanding the capacity to produce tools.

Despite the extension of the resource base, the growth of the human population was still slow. By the year 1500 it was in the order of 500 million (ibid.). The expansion was mainly related to increasing the amount of land for agriculture and some expansion in the use of metals. We observe, however, no fundamental changes in the type of resources used and crop yields do not seem to have increased (Evans, 1980). Population growth seems therefore to have been rather slow up until the start of the Industrial Revolution. By 1800 we reached the first billion, and the speed now increased substantially, with the population reaching 2.5 billion in 1950 (Goldewijk, 2005) and passing 7 billion late in 2011. So while it took 1500 years to double the population based on 'pure' expansion of land used for agriculture, we see almost a tripling over the last 60 years. Note also that in the same period, living conditions improved substantially for a large fraction of humanity and the average life expectancy increased by almost 45 percent from the period 1950–55 to 2005–10: from 46.6 to 67.6 years respectively (UN, 2009c). Despite the tremendous challenges regarding the life situation for the over 2 billion living in extreme or moderate poverty[10] in 2011 (World Bank, 2014a), this is informative of the great advances in nutrition and health care (see also Viner et al., 2011).

This very rapid development has, however, been dependent on a tremendous growth in resource use. The most important is access to fossil fuels and the various technological developments expanding use of such fuels, resulting in substantial increase in crop yields, in use of metals and minerals and the production of many new chemical compounds and products. Table 2.3 gives an overview of human energy use since 1850.

Until 1850, biomass dominated as energy source. By 1900 biomass and coal were equally important. Thereafter fossil fuels took over as main source.

Table 2.3 Global energy use in Mtoe[a] – 1850–2005

	Coal	Oil	Dry gas	Nuclear	Hydro	Geothermal/ Sun	Wind	Biomass	Total
1850	49.6							284.4	332.1
1900	460.0	20.7	5.3		1.8			423.6	888.9
1950	986.3	535.9	153.6		41.2	1.2		488.8	2145.6
1980	1805.5	3173.6	1242.9	186.4	147.7	12.4	0.07	781.3	7258.2
2005	2922.7	3995.7	2366.2	721.8	251.3	45.9	13.2	1195.8	11 484.0

Note: [a] Million tons of oil equivalents.

Sources: Laherrere (2006) and personal information from Laherrere (2012).

From about 1950, we observe a strong growth in energy use where most of the expansion comes from fossil fuels. Biomass use has also increased, while its relative importance is reduced from 22 to about 10 percent. The data on biomass are very uncertain not least because much of what is used is not sold. The use of hydropower and later also nuclear power complete a picture of rapid growth. Total energy use in 1950 is estimated to be about 2150 Mtoe (million tons of oil equivalents). In 2005 total use had grown more than five times to 11 484 Mtoe. This development has certainly created vast opportunities for expanding human activity. As an illustration, one barrel of oil (159 liters) is equivalent to 12 man-years in energy terms (Hicks and Nelder, 2008). With a population of 7 billion, the average energy offered by fossil fuels is equivalent to 100 man-years per person. Certainly, the distribution of that power is very skewed – both between and within countries.

Behind this trend lies technological development and expanded knowledge. As important is the development in economic institutions like property rights, business organization and market expansion (Bernstein, 2005). Actually, these changes began several hundred years ago and preceded the Industrial Revolution. In the post-World War II period we see a stronger integration between different economies, not least based on changes in the trade regimes fostering substantial increases in international trade. The focus on economic growth as the core aim of almost all economies across the globe has been very strong.

Taken together, we note that from 1950 to 2005 world GDP increased almost nine-fold from about 5.3 to 47.1 trillion dollars (based on IMF, 2012 and OECD, 2003 – measured in 1990 US dollars). As the population grew from

2.56 billion in 1950 and 6.46 billion in 2005 (UN, 2012a), average GDP per capita increased about 3.5 times in this 55-year period.

The above figures are stunning – not least if we compare developments before the Industrial Revolution. Steffen et al. (2005) show time series over the last 100–250 years covering energy consumption, GDP, population, water use, fertilizer use, number of transport vehicles, fully exploited fisheries, damming of rivers, species extinction, atmospheric concentrations of CO_2, N_2O and CH_4 and so on. They all match exponential developments quite well.

The role of technology in this process is two sided. The $I = P \times A \times T$ formula indicates that the better the technology, the lower the impact – for example, if a better engine can produce the same amount of work with half the use of fuel, impact is also halved. At same time, we note that new technology makes it possible to expand economic activity beyond what was earlier possible. Land can be more easily cleared; minerals and energy sources previously unavailable become accessible. Moreover, as technological change makes production cheaper, resources are freed that can be used to expand consumption. The so-called 'Jevons paradox' therefore implies that while more efficient production could spare the environment, the room that is created for increased consumption of resources counteracts this potentially positive effect.

The picture drawn above provides the overall global picture. It masks a lot of variation between and within countries. For example, while average consumption levels have increased about 3.5 times from 1950 to 2005, the income for the average Norwegian has increased almost 6.5 times. Nevertheless, as already mentioned, there are more than 900 million malnourished in the world and there are 2.2 million people – almost 40 percent of the population on earth – living on 2 US dollars or less per day. Notable also is that the share of total pre-tax income of the 1 percent richest in the USA in the 1970s was below 10 percent, but rose above 20 percent in 2006–08 (Piketty and Saez, 2003).

2.4 Main messages

In this chapter, I have aimed at characterizing important aspects of the natural environment and I have looked at how human appropriation and use have influenced its status. I have described the natural environment partly as a stock of materials and energy and partly as a system of interlinked processes. These are complementary, but also to some extent competing descriptions. The resource perspective emphasizes availability over space and time. The question is whether we will run out of resources and if so, what will be the consequences. The process perspective emphasizes the dynamics of environmental systems, noting that there are a tremendous number of interlinkages creating both stability and variation. A key issue concerns how human appropriation and use of environmental resources may not only reduce availability of these, but also force changes in the dynamics of environmental systems, thus changing their functioning. This may next influence their resilience, stability and capacity to sustain living systems – including human societies.

I have offered an overview of the status of the natural environment regarding a set of key environmental resources and processes – that is, biodiversity and biodiversity loss, climate change and the effects of freshwater and land use, of use of fertilizers and chemical pollution and aerosols on the functioning of natural systems. The conclusion was that humans have had substantial impact on the quality and dynamics of all these areas and that in all fields there is degradation of environmental capacities. It is very difficult to say which changes are the most serious. The literature seems to emphasize biodiversity loss and climate change as most problematic.

The changes observed have grown in magnitude over the last 200–300 years, with an escalation after 1950. They follow from expanded economic activity where increased use and transformation of natural habitats, emissions of industrially produced 'non-natural' compounds and tremendous increases in waste production (in its broadest sense) are key elements. Hence, the challenges faced are a result of changed human–nature interactions. Behind this lie policies for economic growth, technological and institutional change. I will return to these aspects in later chapters.

NOTES

1 In the very long run, geological processes naturally 'recycle' resources. See Schlesinger (1991) for estimated average circulation periods for key chemical compounds.
2 The level of CO_2 has varied between 200 and 280 ppm during the last 400 000 years.
3 Radiative forcing is the measurement of the capacity of a gas or other forcing agents to affect the energy balance.
4 The amount of CO_2 per unit of energy is higher in coal than in oil, which is again higher than gas. Coal plays a very important part in energy production in countries like China.
5 Such a calculation demands defining the relative forcing of different gases. Estimates vary according to the time horizon set for such an analysis.
6 The absolute level of emissions from deforestation and land use changes has not changed that much over the last century. It seems to have doubled in the first ten years after World War II though, compared to the level in the first half of the century. It fell again after 2000. Due to large increases in CO_2 emissions, the

percentage has fallen from more than 50 percent of total carbon emissions in 1900 to about 17 percent in 1970 and 11 percent in 2010 (IPCC, 2014a).

7 While correcting estimates for changes in rainfall, they have not been able to correct for, for example, changes in land use.

8 Some very minor volumes from guano should also be mentioned.

9 The figure is for 1961 – the earliest year the FAO offers data on fertilizer production.

10 The World Bank defines extreme poverty as living on less than 1.25 US dollars per day. The similar figure for moderate poverty is 2 US dollars.

3

The environment – an arena for conflict and coordination

In this chapter, I present various perspectives on how to understand human interaction in the realm of the environment. First, I will look at a set of classifications of environmental processes and resources from a social science/ economics perspective, expanding on the natural science-dominated perceptions presented in Chapter 2. All of them have been important for analyses of human–nature relationships with quite distinct implications for policy-making. Thereafter, we shall look into a stylized case to illustrate the kind of challenges humans face when interacting in a common environment and discuss ways in which potential conflicts could be handled. Based on this, I discuss ways to classify human conflicts concerning the environment. I close the chapter with a brief discussion regarding how we can approach the issue of 'truth' in a situation characterized by complexity and the fact that there are limits to observation.

3.1 Classifying environmental processes and resources

To analyze environmental issues, we need to define what the core aspects or dimensions are. In this section, I will emphasize four characterizations often used in economic and social science analyses.

3.1.1 Nature as capital

Viewing the natural environment as capital means to think about it as inputs to the process of producing goods or services for human consumption. By using this concept, the environment is in principle made equal to other types of capital in production like manufactured capital (machines, buildings etc.) and human capital (skills, knowledge etc.).

There are two quite distinct issues arising from looking at nature as capital. First, capital typically has a price. It is acknowledged that defining the monetary value of nature is difficult, but it is argued that this is, in principle, not that different from, for example, valuing the manufactured assets of a firm. Second, various types of manufactured capital can be substitutes for each other – for example, insulating a building is a substitute for (alternative to) investing in heating equipment. From a capital perspective, there is emphasis on how different natural capitals can be substituted for each other or with manufactured or human capital. An example could be increased use of irrigation equipment as an alternative to using more land in food production. While I will return to the issue of pricing the environment in Chapter 11, here I will look more into the issue of substitution.

Why is this issue important? If natural and human-made capitals are substitutes, there are no specific environmental resources that need to be protected for the future. Manufactured capital can simply replace natural capital. There has been some conflict over this view, leading to the distinction between the concepts of *weak* as opposed to *strong sustainability* (Toman et al., 1995). Weak sustainability is based on the assumption that natural capital and human-made capital are substitutes. Future living conditions can be sustained or even made better through expanding the volume of human-made capital as a substitute for natural capital. Strong sustainability implies that there is no opportunity for substitution between the two groups of capital. Conserving nature is necessary to ensure as good living conditions for the future as for the present.

None of these extremes offer a reasonable understanding of the actual capacities of the two groups of resources. It is more reasonable to distinguish between natural capital that has, respectively do not have a substitute. The concept of *critical natural capital* (Nöel and O'Connor, 1998) emphasizes that there are some natural resources that cannot be substituted or where substitution is limited. Examples of non-substitutable resources are those that are necessary for biological growth, like oxygen, nitrogen, carbon dioxide, phosphorus and water. Whether the issue of non-substitutability is something to bother about depends on whether or not sources are abundant. As we have seen, issues have already arisen concerning phosphorus and fresh water. Fertilizers are a substitute for land in agriculture – the same total yield can be produced on less land using fertilizers. We cannot, however, use just fertilizers. These resources are therefore substitutes only to a certain degree.

The distinction between no and limited substitution can also be illustrated by looking at water. A plant needs a certain amount of water to grow. At the same time, different types of, for example, irrigation systems, can sustain that need by different amounts of water. Drip irrigation uses more manufactured capital and less water compared to irrigation by flooding the land. Moreover, the most fundamental types of critical natural capital are not necessarily the various compounds themselves, but the dynamics or functioning of the biosphere and its various life support systems, as emphasized in Chapter 2. What becomes critical is to avoid pushing the system beyond essential thresholds. Perrings (1997) offers a framework for how to analyze the issue of substitution between capitals in such a situation.

3.1.2 Nature as services

The concept of ecosystem services – see, for example, Daily (1997); Costanza et al. (1997) – also strongly emphasizes nature's value for humans. The Millennium Ecosystem Assessment team (MEA, 2005) worked extensively on the concept. They divided ecosystem services into four types: (1) provisioning services (e.g., food, water, fiber and fuel); (2) regulating services (e.g., regulation of climate, water and disease); (3) cultural services (e.g., spiritual, aesthetic, recreation and education); and (4) supporting services (e.g., primary production, nutrient cycling and soil formation).

This way of conceptualizing nature 'equalizes' it to human-produced services. The provisioning services influence human well-being directly. The cultural services offer direct satisfaction or experiences. Regulating and supporting services are seen as important in ways that are more indirect. They ensure that the dynamics of the natural environment are reproduced, sustaining human health and the capacities of the provisioning and cultural services.

Biodiversity plays a role in 'producing' all the above services. It has, however, been argued that it is not reasonable to look at nature only in terms of human welfare. O'Neill et al. (2008) emphasize that we do not only live *off* and *in*, but also *with* nature, implying that nature is valuable in its own right. This can be seen as the dominant 'ethics' especially of animal rights activists/theorists. In this discourse one focuses at nature's rights and animal rights (e.g., Regan, 1988; Nash, 1989).

One should note that the shift in the 1990s towards emphasizing 'services' was driven by many biologists and ecologists themselves. It seems to be motivated by the idea that people and politicians will value nature more highly – that is, be willing to take protection more seriously – if they understand how important nature is for humans. The perspective of nature as a service is often taken further by claiming that as such it should have a price, otherwise there will be insufficient provision. Different actors advance this way of thinking. An important representative is 'The Economics of Ecosystems and

Biodiversity' project (TEEB, 2010). While this may seem quite innocuous at first glance, it is a reflection of the fact that economic language and market ideas are gradually gaining a stronger position in areas where this did not use to be the case.

3.1.3 Nature as common and nature as rival

Environmental resources are under stress. One might understand that to be due to the lack of a price. Another way to approach the issue is to look at what characterizes environmental resources and ask what makes them specifically vulnerable to overuse. As emphasized in Chapter 2, the environment is characterized by interlinkages. In some cases, effects are quite direct and typically local – for example, appropriating water such that less becomes accessible for neighbors. In other cases – for example, cutting down a forest – indirect effects are also important, like the influence on global carbon cycles.

In relation to this, two aspects are important: (1) whether the act of one person reduces what is available for others, and (2) how easy it is to limit effects of acting just to those that undertake the act. While (1) is about rivalry in use or in consumption, (2) regards how easy it is to exclude some people from using the resource – see Table 3.1.

If a resource is rival, it will be unavailable to others if used or consumed; a standard example is a piece of bread. In the case of water in a lake with few people living around it, water may, however, be seen as so abundant that the drinking of it by one person does not influence water availability to others. Rivalry is low and unimportant for practical purposes. Similarly, information and knowledge is non-rival. TV signals are non-rival.

If we move to exclusion, there are actually two issues involved. First, we have the question of who gets access to a resource. Second, there is the issue of how to handle side-effects – effects of one person's use on other people's opportunities. In the case of water in a river, the first question concerns who is permitted to use the water. The second issue concerns how the use of some having access influences the availability or quality of the water for other users.

Table 3.1 shows four stylized situations given that rivalry is either high or low and exclusion is either easy or difficult. Goods with high rivalry and easy exclusion of others are typically called 'private goods'. Examples of such goods are all kinds of commodities like bread, bottled water, clothes, cars, and so on. The case of a low level of rivalry and easy exclusion is called 'club' or 'toll' goods. A classic example is television signals that can be turned into

Table 3.1 A general classification of goods and resources

		Exclusion	
		Easy	Difficult
Rivalry in use and/or consumption	**High**	'Private goods'	'Common-pool resources'
	Low	'Club goods'	'Public goods'

Sources: Based on Randall (1987); Ostrom et al. (1994).

cable TV systems – that is, exclusion is made possible. The challenge in such cases is not about overuse of a good or resource. It is rather about how those producing the good or service – the TV programs – can ensure that they are paid for their activities.

If rivalry is low, but exclusion is difficult, we approach so-called 'public goods'. The standard example is military defense and police – systems that offer protection to everybody living in a country or municipality. Hence, the individual may ask why he or she should pay for this security. If everybody else pays, the individual gets the service for free. If nobody else pays, it does not help if the single individual pays. This creates the challenge of *free-riding*, typically demanding some forced payment like taxation to ensure delivery. The characteristics of the resource create this challenge.

If an environmental resource is characterized by low rivalry – being a public good – there is really no problem as these resources are produced and maintained naturally. There is no problem of provision. Issues appear, though, when the resources are used to an extent where use becomes rival and they become what in Table 3.1 are called 'common-pool resources' (CPRs). It is often difficult to exclude people from using environmental resources – recall the characteristics of our physical environments as extensively discussed in Chapter 2. We may therefore face severe problems regarding overuse. Almost all environmental resources were originally 'public goods'. As human use became more extensive, various resources went from being non-rival to becoming rival. Currently, most land and much available water are in this category. Even in the case of air, rivalry is now apparent – we have already talked about the effects of CO_2 emissions and air pollution.

The various types of CPR problems operate at different scales across time and space. While appropriation of water mainly produces local and immediate effects – for example, use of water from a small river or lake – CO_2 emissions have global effects and influence living conditions for coming generations. How demanding it is to handle a CPR problem depends on how many people are involved. In the case of the small river, the number may be low. If they as a group have the right to exclude others – making the resource exclusive to themselves – they may be able to develop systems to handle side-effects from use within the group. In the case of climate change, 7 billion people are presently involved in creating the problem. Exclusion in the sense that not everybody should get access to the air is certainly not an option. Hence, there is a need to define how much each can emit. Making 7 billion people agree on that is a daunting task.

The difficulty or cost of exclusion may vary with what dimension of a resource we look at. Land is fairly easy to divide into pieces owned by individual actors, firms, communities or public bodies. In this way exclusion is established for the land itself. However, this does not ensure exclusion concerning all processes in which the land is included – like the water cycle. Depending on the status of the forest, water may cause erosion, moving soil/soil particles from land to rivers or onto other pieces of land. Water may also carry nutrients from land to aquatic systems. The magnitude of this will depend on how the land is used. Similarly, land is always interacting with the air, again depending on how the land is used. As we have seen, some land uses have substantial impact on emissions of greenhouse gases.

Another issue is that of classifying goods and defining property rights. Property rights are a way to exclude. They influence who gets access to a certain resource (point 1 above). It may also influence how easy it will be to handle side-effects (point 2). There is a tendency in the literature to link private goods to private property, public goods to public property and so on. This is a mistake. Characterizing resources and defining property rights are two different things. While certain characteristics of a resource may make it difficult or even impossible to attach a certain type of property right to it – for example, making air into private property – societies have a host of opportunities for how they arrange exclusion; what kinds of property rights they define. As an example, health services would most probably qualify as 'private goods'. Many countries have, nevertheless, made it a public responsibility, considering good health a human right. Education may be organized both under private and public arrangements, while use is non-rival. These choices are based on value assessments and not on technical properties of the services involved.

3.1.4   Nature as complex

In Chapter 2, I introduced the issue of complexity. Here I expand into a discussion on implications for human–nature relationships. No common definition of complexity exists. Definitions refer, however, typically to the idea of systems. More specifically, complexity is understood as interaction between parts that can be identified to form some sort of a whole. A standard phrase in this field is the observation that 'the whole is more than the sum of its parts'. There are emergent properties (Odum and Barrett, 2005).

The opposite view – the reductionist vision – implies that, for example, ecological features can be reduced to biological, which in turn can be reduced to chemical and, finally, physical characteristics. The idea is that understanding the parts makes it possible for us to understand the whole. While this vision has advanced human understanding of the world around us, it has not enabled us to fully understand the dynamics of systems as consisting of interacting parts. It has, however, facilitated the division of the natural sciences, resulting in a lot of instrumental knowledge, which has proven useful for 'engineering' natural systems. At the same time, the problems that have appeared because of such engineering show the limits of the reductionist vision.

Fertilizer and pesticide use in agriculture can illustrate this. Problems created by, for example, establishing monocultures have been 'corrected' by adding nutrients and killing weeds chemically. This is 'functional' at the chemical level. It creates, however, problems at the level of species and ecosystems. Another example is geoengineering – for example, climate engineering in the form of reflecting more of the sunlight back into space. While reducing the temperature effect of CO_2, it does not solve the problem of ocean acidification. Its effect on changed distribution of sunlight across the globe is another aspect not captured with a focus only at temperature.

Uncertainty and ignorance characterize complex systems. Stirling (1998) differentiates between four types of uncertainty. First, there is *risk*. This is a situation with known outcomes and probabilities and expected values can be computed. An example would be a 50–50 chance of getting ten apples or nothing. The expected value would in this case be five apples. In a situation where outcomes are known, but probabilities cannot be assigned, we have *uncertainty*. Risk and uncertainty are the traditional categories found in the literature, but complexity theory has resulted in further additions. There is *ambiguity*. This is a situation where outcomes are poorly defined, but probabilities may still be definable. Finally, there is *ignorance*, where there is no basis for defining (a complete list of) outcomes. This implies that probabilities cannot be defined, either.

The challenge lies not least with ignorance. The emergent properties of complex systems implies by necessity some level of ignorance – even irreducible ignorance (Faber et al., 1996; Giampietro, 2003; Mayumi and Giampietro, 2006). Therefore, the complexity vision of the environment has some strong policy implications. One is the form of proof demanded for action as well as non-action. Let us say that we might fear that chemical X has a long-term negative impact on species Y. We could think of two 'rules of proof' here. The first would be to show that there would be harm. The other is to prove safety. Given ignorance, neither harm nor safety can be determined with (reasonable) certainty. Consequently, if the rule is to prove harm, evidence that harm will happen often cannot be produced 'up front'. Similarly, it is equally difficult to prove safety. Hence, if proof of harm is demanded, a basis for the regulation of the chemical will rarely be produced. If safety must be documented, there will be few chemicals 'released'.

The historically dominant 'rule of proof' has been proving harm, making it very difficult to ensure environmental protection. This has resulted in the formulation of the 'precautionary principle'. The Rio Declaration formulates it this way:

> In order to protect the environment, the precautionary approach shall be widely applied by States according to their capabilities. Where there are threats of serious or irreversible damage, lack of full scientific certainty shall not be used as a reason for postponing cost-effective measures to prevent environmental degradation. (UNEP, 1992, Principle 15)

More 'radical' versions of the concept also exist – for example, the 'strong precautionary principle'. Sachs (2011, p. 1288) states:

> The Strong Precautionary Principle shifts the burden of proof on the safety of a product or activity from government regulators to private firms. I define it as the view that: (1) regulation should presumptively be applied when an activity or product poses serious threats to human health or the environment, even if scientific uncertainty precludes a full understanding of the nature or extent of the threats; and (2) the burden of overcoming the presumption in favor of regulation lies with the proponent of the risk-creating activity or product.

3.2 Interests, conflict and coordination

As human action in the realm of the environment is interdependent, situations where uses are rival or uncertain can cause conflicts between different interests. Societies then need to define whose interests should be protected. An aspect of this concerns coordination of competing uses. I will look into this by presenting a constructed case covering various types of conflicts and forms of possible coordination mechanisms. This section is core to the whole book, as the rest of the text is largely about going more deeply into various aspects of the issues raised below.

Looking at conflict and coordination raises both technical and normative issues. Withdrawing water from a river, a lake or an aquifer demands different technical solutions and involves different types of uncertainties. Biological resources vary in their dynamics. There are, for example, some unique issues characterizing the management of a fish stock as compared to a forest.

Normative issues regard values and interests. Which principles should guide access to resources and the treatment of side-effects and of ignorance? Who should have the right to catch the fish or use the water? Who should carry the costs of side-effects? How should uncertainties regarding future possibilities and problems be handled? Related to this is also the issue of what motivates human action. To what extent do people emphasize their own interests only? How willing are they to think about consequences of their actions for the wider group of people involved? In the following example, I will make different assumptions to illustrate the issues involved. A more thorough and systematic treatment will follow in later chapters.

The case we shall look at – use of water resources in a river – should be thought of as 'idealized' as well as 'typical'. It is simplified, while offering opportunity to look at several common/regular challenges when a natural resource/environmental system is used by a group of people. The setting is as follows. Some people have moved into an area through which a river flows. No one lived there before. They live in families, but see themselves as members of the wider group or community. The number of households was rather small at the start – about 30. The group decided where each household could settle and what land could be cleared for growing crops. They also depended on using the water in the river. This use developed over time. We shall focus mainly on that part of the story.

3.2.1 Coordination problems with little or no conflict

From the beginning, water was used for drinking, cleaning clothes and for people washing themselves. The first issue that came up concerned where and when to bathe. They wanted to make this into a 'ceremony' where they took baths together. This demanded an agreement on which day to clean themselves. They had already set up a system they called 'mooning', based on the cycle of the moon with each cycle counting 28 nights. They therefore decided to meet and bathe every seventh evening – that is, four times per 'mooning'. Some argued that the group should meet every four nights. They liked to wash more often and argued that this would fit equally well to the cycle of a 'mooning'. As all wanted to bathe together, this was not a big issue. Some argued that if they did it every seventh day, it could be placed both at full moon and new moon. This was seen as an intriguing argument and the dwellers finally settled for this. Every bathing at new moon was termed 'mooning rebirth' and the ones at full moon were called 'mature mooning'. At these events, extra food and drinks were provided.

The above parable shows the construction of a convention. They could have chosen any system given that they all came at the same evening. When to meet was a secondary issue and the group was able to settle the issue easily. To get there, however, we observe that multiple other conventions or rules had to exist. The group needed a common language to express their views and proposals. They needed structure in how to reach a common decision. It demanded a system of counting. Deciding a fixed cycle of days also seems to have been important. Maybe they thought that it would be easier to know when to meet with a fixed system. Perhaps using the moon phases as the point of reference was chosen as it was easy to know when to meet. The latter illustrates the need for simplification – choosing conventions that simplify interaction.

3.2.2 Coordination problems with conflicting interests, but with possibilities for an informal solution

Over time the group grew and a decision was made that new households should settle upstream and create a sub-village. The people continued to have regular contact and land remained held in common. The people in the new sub-village maintained the bathing convention, but over time they established their own bathing place for practical reasons.

Livelihoods gradually changed. People started to keep animals. These were watered in the river, and as numbers increased, water quality started to degrade. There was rivalry as one could not water animals in the upstream

Table 3.2 Consequences of different watering strategies for upstream and downstream farmers

		Downstream farmers	
		Use water where they live	Move further down-stream when using water
Upstream farmers	**Water animals where they live**	I 50 100	II 70 100
	Move animals further downstream for watering	III 100 80	IV 30 80

Note: In each cell, the upper right figures are payoffs for downstream farmers and the lower left for the upstream ones.

sub-village and at the same time retain clean water for those living downstream. The water in the river had moved from being a public good to a common-pool resource. People downstream argued that those living upstream should stop watering their animals upstream and instead move them down the river beyond the downstream sub-village for watering. Hence, they proposed to exclude part of the river for watering animals. People upstream argued that this was not their problem. Pointing to the capacity of the river to clean itself, they argued that if people downstream wanted better quality, they could move further down to cleaner parts of the river to drink, wash and bathe and so on. For illustrative purposes, let us define the following relative gains of the various strategies as in Table 3.2.

The figures in Table 3.2 are so-called payoffs and can be viewed as measures of utility. Figures in the upper right corners refer to downstream farmers, while those at the bottom left refer to the upstream ones. Payoffs are asymmetric – that is, different for the two groups involved. (For an example of a symmetrical case, see Box 3.1.) The downstream farmers depend on the strategy of the upstream ones, while upstream farmers are not influenced by what downstream farmers do. This is captured in the utility for the two groups. If the upstream farmers continue to water animals where they live, they get the same relative payoffs as before, independent of what the downstream farmers do (cells I and II). The value is set to 100. If they decide to follow the demands of the downstream farmers, payoffs go down as they have to use resources to move the animals every day. The reduced payoffs (80) in cells III and IV illustrate this.

BOX 3.1

A SYMMETRICAL 'GAME' – THE PRISONER'S DILEMMA

In the literature, many environmental problems are depicted in the form of a symmetrical game. It is called the 'prisoner's dilemma' game as it was first described for a situation where two people were caught and accused of committing a crime together, but where the police had no firm evidence. By offering a lower level of imprisonment if each exposed the other criminal, the police could structure the situation such that both – if thinking only about themselves – would tell the truth.

The prisoner's dilemma catches key characteristics of symmetrical environmental issues. Table 3.3 below shows a situation close to that in the text just assuming that animals are watered in a small lake instead of a river. Using the language of game theory, building a small pond by the lake for watering animals is called 'cooperate', while watering directly in the lake is called 'defect'. We simplify by assuming that only two households/farmers live by the lake and both hold animals.

When reading the figures, note that payoffs in the right upper corner of each cell relate to farmer A and the payoffs at the left bottom relate to farmer B. While cooperation offers the best solution for the two together, each farmer would gain from defecting if the other cooperates. Actually, as the situation is

depicted, whatever farmer A does, it is best for farmer B to defect. If farmer A cooperates, farmer B will gain 100 if defecting and only 85 if cooperating. Similarly, if farmer A is defecting, farmer B should again defect as 70 (defecting) is better than 60 (cooperating). As the situation is symmetrical, both will choose to defect given that they only think about their own interests. This is the case despite the fact that if both cooperated, they would be better off. Playing the strategy that is individually best is called a Nash equilibrium.

Environmental problems typically involve many agents. Moreover, it is rather unusual that the payoffs are exactly symmetrical. Typically, costs of doing nothing hits harder on some, while much of the costs of taking action falls on others. Those driving less by car cause fewer environmental problems, but face the same consequences concerning air quality as those driving a lot. In the case of climate change, costs will mainly fall on later generations.

The above assumes that people decide (only) on the basis of individual payoffs. As will be discussed later, this cannot be taken as a given. Rather, people can communicate and define common notions of what is 'right'/collectively favorable as opposed to 'individually best'.

Table 3.3 Farmers watering animals presented as a prisoner's dilemma

		Farmer A			
		Cooperate		Defect	
Farmer B	Cooperate	I	85	II	100
		85		60	
	Defect	III	60	IV	70
		100		70	

The only way downstream farmers can retain original payoffs is if upstream farmers stop watering animals upstream and move them downstream (cell III). If they do not stop, downstream farmers could choose to move further downstream. Balancing the costs of moving against the gain in the form of gradually better water quality, the best result they can get is 70 (cell II). This is a helpful strategy, because if they do as before, the payoff is even lower (50 – cell I). For downstream farmers to move downstream if upstream farmers move down (cell IV) is a 'non-option', as they just increase problems for themselves (take on costs to move to a place with worse water quality).

If no common agreement is reached – if everybody chooses on the basis of the above payoffs – solution II will be the logical result. Upstream farmers will not stop watering/move and downstream farmers will have to make the best out of the situation by moving further down when in need of water. They will recognize, however, that total payoffs measured as the sum of payoffs to upstream and downstream farmers are greatest if they choose solution III. On the other hand, there is no way to achieve this without action that goes beyond each group doing separately what is best for themselves.

Changed preferences due to taking wider issues into account

One way the conclusion could be altered is if preferences change. Upstream farmers may realize that if they change their behavior, it could be possible to recreate the previous good relationship with the downstream villagers. Considering this wider issue, they may realize that not only are there costs related to moving animals downstream for watering, there are also gains.

Table 3.4 Consequences of different watering strategies for upstream and downstream farmers – changed preferences by upstream farmers

		Downstream farmers	
		Water animals where they live	Move animals further downstream for watering
Upstream farmers	Water animals where they live	I 50 90	II 70 90
	Move animals further downstream for watering	III 100 95	IV 30 95

Moreover, they may realize that if they move animals together, they can reduce costs. Finally, there is grass along the paths down the river, which is valuable as extra feed. They may simply change their preferences as depicted in Table 3.4.

If the payoffs are changed this way, the best for both parties is that the upstream farmers move downstream. There is no conflict anymore.

Norms and self-restraint

The above 'dream-like' scenario is perhaps not very reasonable. In conflicts of the above type, 'dreams' or 'win-wins' are rare. What then, are the options for downstream farmers? They may argue that total gains are highest if upstream farmers water their animals downstream. The total payoff in cell III of Table 3.2 is 180, while the present adaptation in cell I only offers 150 in total. This argument may produce ridicule from upstream farmers, whose interests are protected by the status quo solution. However, downstream farmers could go further and argue that the action of the upstream farmers is bad behavior. It is against the norm of respecting other people's interests. The downstream farmers could also refer to when the group moved to this river, showing how important it was for them to cooperate. At that time, they practiced the norm of 'all for one and one for all'. This kind of argument might change the situation: (1) Upstream farmers may feel socially bound by such a norm and while they have to take on extra costs, they realize that it is wrong of them to spoil the water for those downstream. (2) Upstream farmers may become concerned about their position in the wider village community. People in favor of the cooperative solution may make complaints or upstream farmers may just sense that downstreamers feel bad about their practice. They expect the negative reactions to be such that it does not pay to stick to the original position.

While both arguments result in self-restraint among upstream farmers – that is, they do their watering downstream – the type of reasons invoked in 1 and 2 are very different. Case 1 refers to a common norm of what is acceptable behavior. The payoffs/gains for upstream farmers are not changed compared to Table 3.2. They simply accept that it is right to respect the interests of downstream dwellers. Another decision rule is invoked. In case 2, the payoff has changed. The fear of becoming a 'bad neighbor' with lower social standing reduces the individual utility of watering upstream. If this feeling reduces the payoff of present practice to less than 80, it becomes individually rational for the upstream farmers to water animals downstream. Note that there is an important distinction here. While the fear of being picked on refers directly to own utility, the issue of social standing may go beyond the perspective of individual utility. It may also refer to issues like self-respect or the norm of duty, which goes beyond a simple utility calculation of pleasure and pain. It takes us back to some of the reasoning around case 1 above and cannot be captured by changing the payoffs in Table 3.4.

Threats

If moral persuasion does not work, downstream farmers might use another strategy. They might threaten upstream farmers that they will start taking their own animals even further upstream to pollute the water for upstream farmers. It is costly for them, but they may still do it to demonstrate their disagreement, hoping that the upstream farmers then realize that they really have no alternative but to change their practice.

The problem with retaliation is that a 'war' may break out between the two sub-villages. The downstream villagers may be uncertain about the outcome of such a development. It may destroy whatever is left of good neighborhood and social cohesion within the wider community of farmers.

Side payments

If they do not dare threaten, there are further options to pursue. Since the downstream farmers seem to gain more from upstream farmers taking their animals downstream to water them than it costs for upstream farmers to do so, a side payment from the downstreamers to the upstreamers could result in a situation that is better for both.

We now encounter the problem of comparing individual utilities. So far, we have implicitly assumed that a utility of 100 is the same for all farmers. Such an assumption is not innocuous, as comparing utility across individuals is a complex issue (see Chapter 11). Nevertheless, let us assume that it is possible to construct a numeraire into which both groups can translate their utilities. Money is one such numeraire. Let us therefore shift assumptions and presume that the payoffs in Table 3.2 are monetary estimates.

If so, downstream farmers should be willing to pay those upstream up to 30 monetary units to make them water downstream – that is, to get from situation II in Table 3.2 where their payoff is 70 to situation III where their original payoff is 100. They would still be as well off (see also Table 3.5). If downstream farmers pay the upstream farmers 20 units to water down-

Table 3.5 Potential for side payments

		Downstream farmers	
		Water animals where they live	Move animals further downstream for watering
Upstream farmers	Water animals where they live	I 50 100	II 70 100
	Move animals further downstream for watering	III **100 (70+)** ↙ 20–30 ↙ **80 (100+)**	IV 30 80

Note: Original values (cf. Table 3.2) in bold. Figures in parentheses in cell III show the result of a side payment.

stream, upstream farmers would be as well off as if they continued the present practice. By doing this, there are still ten monetary units left that they could divide and both groups would be better off than in the present situation (cell II; cf. 70+ and 100+ in cell III).

Added to the problem of monetization, there are two more issues attached to this solution – one concerning the rights distribution, the other the costs of negotiating agreement about compensation. Regarding the first, downstream farmers may not want to pay, despite the potential gain, since that would be to give upstream farmers a 'right' to pollute the river. They may ask why the present situation should be turned into the reference point for negotiations. Downstream farmers may claim that they have the same right to clean water as those upstream. They also may argue that responsibility should be with upstream farmers. These should either change their practice or pay down-stream farmers a compensation for the nuisance. The downstreamers may also wonder if making side payments would spoil the community spirit. If every-body is free to claim payments for refraining from doing something that is con-sidered a nuisance by others, it will pay to create nuisance to demand payments to stop creating that nuisance, and the solidarity of the community may erode.

When it comes to the negotiation costs, downstream farmers realize that if the process of negotiating the conditions for a payment demands more resources than the net gain of ten monetary units, the strategy of paying will be a waste. If there are many actors involved, negotiation costs could be quite substantial. The same is the case if the disagreement is strong. Hence, the (expected, but uncertain) high costs of negotiating could block the option of side payments.

3.2.3 Conflicting interests handled by a third party

Because of the above issues, downstream farmers may not be interested in pursuing the side payment avenue. They start thinking that what the community needs is a system that can handle conflicts. There have also been some conflicts over clearing of forests for agricultural land as even land is gradually becoming rival. While this conflict is not as tense as the one regarding watering animals, they see that it could easily develop in that direction as the number of households in the area is growing and the need for land increases.

After thinking about what could be done, those living downstream propose to select a group of people from both sub-villages to decide in matters like the above. This way, a third party in the form of a village council can formulate rules and define whose interests should be protected during conflicts. While persuasion, threats and side payments operate directly at the level of the parties, establishing a council implies creating a power of decision-making above the parties themselves. They believe that such a system would make decisions easier and make it possible to reconcile conflicts like the water issue.

At a gathering between the sub-villages, downstream farmers propose that they set up such a council. They argue that it is important to have a system to settle disputes and to make rules that everybody should follow. They also emphasize that this will simplify processes. The discussion in the sub-villages goes on for a while. Upstream farmers are afraid that such a council could rule against their interests in the water case. More generally, people are worried that council members will become too powerful and favor their own interests. At the same time, they acknowledge that the land use conflicts will increase and that some resolution must be sought. After a rather long process, the villagers decide to establish a council of seven members with one elected as head. Rules for how the election is to be undertaken, duration of serving, and so on, are defined. Emphasis is put on what the role of a village council member implies; that is, what it means to act on behalf of the community and as a third party in disputes.

Regarding the water conflict, the council considers several options, including closing parts of the river for watering animals, defining certain times of the day for watering upstream and downstream, or leaving the situation as it is. Some of the members in the council are upstream farmers and find themselves a bit squeezed between the interests of (fellow) upstream farmers and the issue of finding a solution that is considered fair. Cutting a long story short, the council finally concludes that parts of the river should be closed for watering animals, but allowing establishment of ponds along that part of the river where animals could drink, given that outlets from these ponds were not directed back into the river. This solution created some costs for upstream farmers and, after a hard fight in the village council, downstream farmers had to accept to pay parts of the costs. In the end, upstream farmers realized that their situation had actually improved. It reduced their costs compared to having to move animals every day. They could even use the 'dirty' water to flood their fields and realized that this way they could increase yields.

Pond building and the subsequent use of water for flooding fields over time led to the idea of an irrigation scheme. While the river was rather small, this created no real problems in the beginning. There were ample amounts of water. A shock went through the village one day, however, when it was clear that the secretary of the village board had taken part of the money paid by the downstreamers to finance pond building and used it for personal advantage. The secretary was fired and had to pay back what was taken. The villagers established a control committee to follow the activities of the board, including delivering a report at a yearly village assembly.

As time went by many households settled further from the river. The village council therefore started to discuss how they could organize the system so that everybody got the water they needed. They established an irrigation committee with the authority to make rules about the development of systems for channels, a rotation system for when various households could use the water and how and when maintenance on channels and so forth should be done. The system worked well, and farmers in the downstream sub-village adopted this practice. Ever larger volumes of water were appropriated, and in the dry season this had substantial impact on the water level downstream of our two sub-villages. However, there were also settlements further down. One day, members from one of these communities came visiting. They simply asked: 'Where has our water gone?'

3.3 Classifying environmental conflicts

3.3.1 The basic categories: 'we' vs 'they'

The above parable and the example in Box 3.1 can be helpful as a starting point for classifying environmental conflicts. We can divide between the following basic types:[1] first, within a group – 'we' conflicts; and second, between one group of people and another group – 'they' conflicts. A 'we' conflict is described in Box 3.1. There are more than one farmer/household living close to the lake who all water their animals there. Assuming that everybody contributes to the pollution problem and everybody is affected, we have a 'we' conflict. The same people that created it face the consequences. As shown in Box 3.1, cooperation will offer the best result for the group in total, but assuming individually rational actors, they will continue to deteriorate the water. Agreed-upon norms or actions by a third party could break this logic. One could expect that since 'all are in the same boat', internal norms of the community could work successfully.

There may, however, be different communities living along the lake, and they may not cooperate. People talk about 'us' as opposed to 'them'. We have a 'they' conflict. The above case of upstream–downstream farmers is also a 'they' conflict, where the characteristics of the resource makes the interdependence asymmetrical. Here, the practice of unregulated watering is purely a good for one group and bad for another. Here not all are in the same boat, and *ceteris paribus* it is less plausible to expect that the conflict can be settled directly between the groups – see the discussions in Section 3.2.

The wider context of social relationships may be as important as the specificity of the environmental issue for the severity of the conflict. At the end of the parable presented above, people from a neighboring village appeared. While the physical problem between the two villages is similar to that between the two sub-villages – our community – it is not certain that these villages can find a common solution the same way our community did.

Table 3.6 Symmetrical vs asymmetrical conflicts

		Causes	
		Symmetrical	Asymmetrical
Effects	Symmetrical	I	II
	Asymmetrical	III	IV

3.3.2   Symmetrical vs asymmetrical conflicts

Thinking further about the issue of interdependencies, one can differentiate between symmetry and asymmetry both in what causes problems and how the effects are distributed – see Table 3.6.

The pure 'we' and 'they' conflicts as described above are found in cells I and IV. The situations described by cells II and III are hybrids including elements of both 'we' and 'they'. To expand the picture, present problems that fit cell I could be local water pollution from wastewater, local air pollution from widely used heating facilities and cars, queuing, fishing in a common lake, cutting trees in a common forest and so on. Certainly, in almost any case of this kind, some are creating more nuisances/appropriating more resources than others and some are more adversely affected than others. Hence, almost no environmental conflict is strictly symmetrical.

Examples of IV are abundant. Climate change is a core example. Emissions vary tremendously between people in different countries, as well as within. While people in the South are emitting generally much less than people in the North, they will, on the other hand, be the hardest hit by climatic impacts. Acid rain is another case belonging to IV, where the wind carries emissions that deposit over large distances.

Moving to II, we would include various local polluting activities, where just some of the people living in the area produce the emissions, while all have to endure them. Pollution from factories is a typical example. Emissions from heating facilities only supplying parts of the population would be of this kind. Concerning III, we encounter situations where 'what everybody does' has consequences that are unequally shared. Wastewater pollution could illustrate this. All households create wastewater, while emissions may be concentrated in certain points in the landscape – for example, rivers or lakes. Situations with different sensitivities to a common practice – for example, pollution and noise from car driving – may serve as another example.

One systematic cause of asymmetry is variation in economic and political positions. Poor people use fewer resources – hence emit less – and are less able to defend themselves against negative effects both individually and collectively (politically). Examples abound across the globe of how the poor suffer most from environmental degradation. Mining, oil drilling, extraction of oil from tar sands, logging, shrimp farming and dam construction are all examples of activities that demand land/space that constitute livelihoods for people. Moreover, the methods involved in resource extraction often result in polluted soils, groundwater, rivers and lakes. Conflicts of this kind are numerous – see, for example, Martinez-Alier (2002).

While the above type of examples are quite easy to observe and understand, there are also more subtle processes involved. Export of toxic waste from the North to the South is one example. Robbins (2012) describes poor residents of Accra (Ghana) who make a 'living' from buying, sorting and processing hazardous waste in the open and without any protection. As opposed to the above examples, they do so 'voluntarily'. It is, however, voluntary only in relation to their life situation. Another case is the movement of economic activities – not least industrial production – in the same direction, bringing with them various emissions that are often less regulated as environmental legislation is typically weaker in the South than in the North – see also Chapter 12.

Poverty may also cause environmental destruction as in the case of deforestation following from the need for firewood and land for agriculture. Alternative energy sources like electricity and fertilizers are simply unavailable due to low income. At the same time, changes of this kind – while reducing some problems – may create others like loss of livelihoods/ecosystems through damming and nutrient losses that could potentially result in eutrophication.

3.3.3 The aspect of spatial scale

Asymmetries are often linked to spatial scales. The further away from the source a consequence appears, the greater the chance for the conflict to be asymmetric. A good illustration is offered in Martinez-Alier (2002, p. 67) where he talks about the so-called 'chimney war' in Germany:

> Complaints about pollution from sulphur dioxide pollution led to the building of taller and taller chimneys of up to 140 metres even before 1890. The authorities ordered the tall chimneys to be built in order to pacify protests in the immediate surroundings. The factory owners complied willingly in order to disperse the pollution over a large territory where, it was hoped, it would be mixed up with the pollution from other factories, thus evading responsibility in judicial cases which required cause-and-effect proof of the source of the damage.

While this example not only applies to Germany, it illustrates quite well the relationships between space, physical interaction and socio-political relations. Building smoke stacks moves the pollutant to another area – making it a clear-cut 'they' conflict. If these 'others' are not part of a wider socio-political 'we', the problem will most typically endure over time. In the above case, much of the pollutants were deposited in Germany, which resulted in pressures on the federal government to institute regulations. Pollutants were, however, also transported by wind across national borders. It took a longer time before any relevant international regulations were in place – that is, the Convention on Long-range Transboundary Air Pollution from 1979 (Chasek et al., 2014) – again see Chapter 12.

While physical, social and political spaces are all important for characterizing an environmental conflict, and each has their distinct importance, the relationships are often quite complex. Political power is necessary to institute regulations. States play an important role in combating environmental problems, while international coalitions may be necessary to support national regulations. Environmental groups may be stronger in the international arena than nationally where industrial lobbies dominate. Likewise, Ministries of Environment may push for international agreements to strengthen their national case.

3.3.4 The time dimension

A conflict of the 'we' type may have a 'they' conflict added to it. People living around a lake may, as mentioned, cause nuisances to each other. These problems may be enduring and affect people not yet born. Typically, problems build up over time – the issue of pushing the system beyond essential thresholds – see Section 3.1.1. Hence, gains of polluting the lake – that is, avoidance of cleaning costs, and so on – benefit the present generation, while (most of) the costs are carried by the next.

Following our analyses in Chapter 2, there is no doubt that the present generation – and unevenly so – shifts high levels of costs upon coming generations. Nevertheless, it takes time for consequences to accumulate. The problem is that future people are not able to voice their interests and demand changes. Martinez-Alier (2002) emphasizes that problem resolution often demands conflict exacerbation. He makes the point that it is only when the conflict becomes strong, that enough political pressure can be released to ensure the necessary shifts in rights structures – to turn the present tide of cost shifting.

3.4 Complexity, uncertainty and knowledge

What is a problem and how it should be understood is not a straightforward issue. Our understanding is based on the concepts we have developed and on the theories we use to interpret what we observe. At the base of this is the language. According to the philosopher Ludwig Wittgenstein ([1922] 1974, p. 68, paragraph 5.6; original emphasis): "*The limits of my language* mean the limits of my world". Moreover, due to the complexities involved, the objects or processes we are looking at can be described in different ways. As we have seen, complexity also implies various forms of uncertainty.

We hinted at this when starting this chapter by emphasizing different ways of perceiving nature – as capital, as services, as common and rival, and as complex. Complexity implies that it may be quite difficult to agree on what is the best characterization of the topic or system one is studying. While new concepts sometimes appear to describe a phenomenon, science also expands through translating concepts from one area to another – through metaphorical transfers. Mirowski (1989) documents how the model of mechanics with its concepts of equilibrating forces was incorporated into mainstream economics' understanding of markets. There are other perceptions of the economic system that emphasize imbalance and change and use metaphors from biology instead of physics – see Hodgson (1996) on evolutionary economics. Embarking on one metaphor may put conceptualization on a specific track. Looking at nature as capital may make you next talk about nature as a bank – see the TEEB (2012) homepage. Certainly, the conceptualizations – which metaphors are used – matter for how one thinks about and approaches what is observed.

The issues we cover here are quite demanding. I will only be able to scratch the surface. Let us start with a brief comment to the distinction between (naive) empiricism and (radical) relativism in science. An empiricist position – as understood here – implies two main things. First, the world – the reality – exists independent of our conceptualizations of it. Next, it is possible for science to clarify what characterizes this reality – to establish an objective truth through observation. Truth is independent of human constructs like our concepts. Relativism emphasizes, however, that truth is entirely subjective. In its most radical form, relativism means that the external world depends on our conceptualization of it.

Taken literally, both positions are problematic. A (naive) empiricist position eschews the fact that the real world goes beyond what can be observed, and that what we observe depends on our concepts. Moving to the relativist position, its view that observations depend on concepts is valid, while it is problematic to assume that our conceptualization generally influences the objects themselves. Sayer (1992, p. 61; original emphasis) comments on the latter: "Non-realists reject objectivity;[2] from the correct point that the objective properties of something can't be known independently from our ("subjective")[3] thoughts about them, they wrongly conclude from this that they can only *exist* if they are thought about".

Critical realism – see, for example, Bhaskar ([1975] 2008, 1989); Sayer (1992); Maxwell (2012) – offers a valuable alternative way to understand these difficult issues. This position perceives the world as divided into three distinct ontological layers: the 'real', the 'actual' and the 'empirical'. The 'real' refers to potentials or tendencies of various objects. The 'actual' refers to the events, behaviors, and so on that take place. The 'empirical' refers to the observations or perceptions of such objects and events. Hence, the leaf hanging on a branch has the potential to fall, due to gravity. It also has the potential to continue hanging due to the powers of the twig. In the autumn, the latter potential is weakened. A wind may rip the leaf off or it may fall gently, while in neither cases following a straight line due to aerodynamic forces. So the real is the various potentials, the actual is the event of a falling leaf with all its twists and turns, the empirical is the observations we make of this process. Due to the relative importance of the forces involved, we can predict that the leaf will fall, but not when and how. This does not mean that patterns do not appear – leaves tend to fall close to the stem of the tree – but we must talk of tendencies rather than laws. Moreover, this understanding of potentials implies that systems of parts will be characterized by emergent properties, properties that depend on the tendencies or potentials of the parts involved and the way these potentials interact.

The implication for science is that it becomes an ongoing process in which concepts and theories are improved to understand the mechanisms and relationships studied – for example, Newton's idea of gravity was fundamental to better understanding the fact observed over and over again that 'free objects' fall to the ground. It, also implies, however, that empirical observation alone cannot fully explain what is happening. Theories regarding the potentials involved are needed to make observations intelligible. This is not least important when observing human action. We may observe somebody helping someone that has fallen when crossing the street. We observe the action, while we do not observe the motivation that causes the action. It has to be inferred from theorizing about what could make somebody 'offer a helping hand'. Our theorization may prove to be wrong. Knowledge or truth claims are fallible.

There are differences between the social and natural sciences that need to be commented on in relation to the above. First, while conceptualization in the natural sciences does not influence the potentials of various objects – for example, calling something gravity does not influence the falling leaf – creating concepts like a 'class', a 'norm' and so on, may actually influence the identity and potentials of actors. Even more fundamentally, the language itself defines, even creates, potential for action in the social sphere.

Second, the social structures and relations we create – the values they are based on – are not given or neutral. Hence, we cannot strive for objectivity when studying the social world in the same sense as when looking at the physical. This does, however, not imply that social relations can or should be treated in completely relativistic terms. On the contrary, exactly because they are human-made, they are open to reasoned critique about what is the better conceptualization, and the better thing to do. Such critique is crucial – see Bhaskar (1989, 1991). The argument made is that values and institutions, since they are collectively created, can be both discussed and evaluated across individuals. In this specific sense, they are 'objective'. Moreover, the social world – the institutional structures we make – are both common to us and exist independently of us as specific individuals. This world is thus also 'objective' in the sense that it can be observed and studied as social 'facts'. It is, however, not 'natural' or neutral.

One may ask if knowledge is dependent on our theorizing and conceptualization, might it be vulnerable to 'manipulation'? According to Baert (2005, p. 89) the post-structuralist[4] "conceives of knowledge as forever entangled in (and unable to transcend) intricate power relations" while "critical realism reaffirms the emancipatory status of the social sciences".

This does not imply that knowledge may not be manipulated in political power games. The observation that truth is fallible does not imply, however, that 'anything goes'. A recent example in the field of climate policy is enlightening. A few years ago, a series of publications was released that document the deliberate production of disinformation regarding climate change science – see, for example, Union of Concerned Scientists (2007); Hoggan and Littlemoore (2009); Oreskes and Conway (2010) – with the main activities found in the USA. The process includes the establishment of the Global Climate Coalition (1989–2002) – covering a group of businesses and formed as a response to establishment of the Intergovernmental Panel on Climate Change (IPCC) and actively opposing policies to reduce greenhouse gas emissions. It also includes a well-noted campaign by ExxonMobil copying the strategies of the tobacco industry used to fight research that documented health consequences of smoking. The Union of Concerned Scientists (2007, p. 3) emphasizes that ExxonMobil has "Manufactured uncertainty by raising doubts about even the most indisputable scientific evidence". Critical realists would note that by exposing such use of data through reasoned critique one is able to distinguish between real uncertainty and the manufactured ones.

3.5   Main messages

In this chapter, we first looked at different ways to classify and describe nature/the environment – that is, nature as capital, nature as services, nature as common and rival, and finally nature as complex. These descriptions are all constructed as a basis for studying human–nature relationships. It is notable that they have relevance for different types of analyses – for example, the complexity perspective is more relevant when analyzing issues where there are clear elements of ignorance. As important is the way the different characterizations will frame the analyses we make. Thinking in terms of 'capital' or 'services' directs the analysis differently from, for example, looking at the issues from the perspective of nature as 'common'. While I might find the perspectives of nature as common and rival, and the complexity vision as most promising and relevant, my main message is not to say that these are the only ones to use. My aim, rather, is to raise awareness regarding the importance of being conscious about the effects of different framings – both when framing own analyses and when observing how the environment is perceived in e.g., policy-making processes. There is much power in being able to ensure what perspective becomes the basis for policies.

The fact that our environment is important for sustaining our lives, that it is, moreover, common and often characterized by limits/rivalry, makes use and protection of these resources and processes both conflictual and demanding coordination. In relation to that, I have tried to systematize the types of conflicts involved and how they could possibly be resolved. I have looked at the level of conflict and how that may influence the form of solutions that could appear. I argued that some problems are pure coordination problems, and as such most probably solved by developing certain conventions regarding preferred actions – like deciding on days to meet in our story on the river villages. Conflicts may be more intense, demanding the development of, for example, norms, threats, side payments or changed preferences to ensure some resolution. It was, however, noted that some conflicts could be so deep that these institutions would not be durable. The solutions that could be made 'horizontally' would not be found effective/legitimate. Then creating and using the power of a third party could be necessary – that is, 'vertical' or hierarchical power. While a simple story, it captures some of the more fundamental dynamics that I will elaborate on throughout the book. This regards how institutions define access to resources – for example, property rights – how they influence perceptions – like what is possible to do – how they influence the costs of coordinating action – that is, transaction costs – and finally how they influence preferences about what is best to do/the kind of motivation that characterizes choice.

An alternative – and equally important issue regarding classification of conflicts – concerns who is involved and how consequences of environmental problems are distributed. One aspect here regards whether the conflict is at the level of the individual, the group that the individual defines himself or herself as belonging to, or if it is about 'us' vs 'them'. Similarly, the conflict is expected to be different if it is symmetrical or asymmetrical. Environmental problems are typically asymmetrical, which makes them extra demanding to resolve. Asymmetries may, moreover, operate across both space and time.

This book is influenced by the perspectives of critical realism. With its distinctive way of thinking about complexity, it helps us to understand the importance and limitations of observations. It also offers a way to critically engage in evaluating different descriptions and discourses regarding both their factual and normative basis. For students and practitioners in the field of environmental governance, this is a crucial issue.

NOTES

1 One may also envision 'I' conflicts – that is, conflicts between different interests of the same person. I do not include such conflicts here as there is no social dilemma – no interdependencies between actions of different people.
2 Sayer defines three forms of objectivity – see Sayer (1992). Objectivity regards "the nature of things regardless of what we or others may think about them" (p. 58).
3 Sayer also defines three forms of subjectivity – see Sayer (1992). Subjectivity concerns "what we think, experience, believe or feel about something" (p. 58).
4 Referring to the work, of, for example, Derrida, Foucault and so on.

Part Two

The theory of institutions and human action

As emphasized in Part One, environmental problems are to a large extent about human relationships. They concern how we intrude into each other's lives by using, changing and protecting certain environmental resources and processes. Such interdependencies are governed by institutions as social constructs that form and inform action.

In this part of the book, I will first define and explain the concept of an institution. I see institutions as rules and regularized practices. They define what values and interests should have priority in a society. They also support coordination of action. Institutions influence action by defining what is expected, what is seen as 'normal behavior' in various settings. They define who has access to certain resources and what such access implies regarding acceptable uses.

As we saw in Chapter 2, humanity is facing some daunting challenges both at local, national and international levels regarding maintenance of environmental resources and processes. Environmental governance is about agreeing on what priorities should be made and then deciding on how to ensure that these priorities materialize. That implies changing action, which can be facilitated by changing institutions. Ultimately, Part Two is about presenting and discussing existing knowledge regarding the relationships between institutions and actions.

4

What are institutions?

I have already mentioned institutions several times, but have not defined the concept. In this chapter, I will both define it and develop its meaning and importance. I start by presenting some examples of institutions in everyday life. Next, I will define the concept as used in this book. In Section 4.3, we will look at the relationships between individuals and institutions. To study institutions, we need an understanding of the concept of power both as a key aspect of institutions themselves as well as of the process of forming them. This will be the topic for the fourth section of this chapter. I will finally introduce the readers to competing positions within institutional theory to further clarify the perspective on institutions used in this book.

4.1 Institutions in everyday life

Institutions are human constructs. They form relations between people and structure human interaction. When we grow up, we learn about the institutions of the specific society. We may not do so consciously, as institutions are often just 'the ways things are done'. They may seem natural to us, and we may not recognize that institutions are made by people – are socially constructed.

The way we greet is a typical example. As a child, we learn how to greet other people. We may just copy what adults do, or adults may tell the child that it should greet and how this should be done. The child learns what kinds of clothes to wear on various occasions; it may learn on which side of the street to walk; it learns about the convention of time, what to eat, when to go to bed and so on. He or she also may learn that it is wrong to lie and take what belongs to others.

The list could have been made extensively long. The main point is that there are many 'rules' about how to behave especially in relation to other people. These 'rules' – or institutions – are what we and others are expected to abide by in certain situations. While greeting could be done in many different ways, rules may simplify life in the sense that they provide expectations concerning what we and others know should be done, for example, by shaking hands. This way institutions create a certain level of stability. The institution of time likewise makes it easier to organize activities. Institutions may also be significant beyond such practical functions. Learning ways of behaving may be important in forming our personality. We in a sense become what we are used to doing.

You may say that in your culture you do not greet by hand, but rather offer a hug. Yes, people have different customs depending on what community they live in. So institutions are specific to communities, cultures and so on. People greet in different ways across the globe. Some drive on the right, others on the left. Customs of clothing vary, as do food traditions. Societies do, however, typically have common rules about these kinds of issues.

Institutions may also be constructed to support one interest against another. Some may own land; some may not. Some are 'upper class' while others are 'ordinary people'. Some may be permitted to pollute while others have to endure the effects thereof. Societies often produce 'stories' about why things are as they are, referring to, for example, inequality as 'natural'. Institutions are, however, not created by nature. People create them. Stories about 'the natural order of things' may rather be viewed as a way to protect interests favored by institutions.

4.2   Defining institutions

Institutions take a variety of forms; therefore, agreeing on a common definition is difficult. Such a definition will, moreover, have to depend on how one understands human action. Before exploring these issues, I start by presenting the definition we will use in this book:

Institutions are the conventions, norms and formally sanctioned rules of a society. They provide expectations, stability and meaning essential to human existence and coordination. Institutions support certain values, and produce and protect specific interests.

The definition describes institutions according to both their *form* and *what they do*. Regarding the former, we often distinguish between informal and formal institutions, with conventions and norms characterized as informal. Concerning what institutions do, I note that they create order – facilitate coordination – as well as take sides in conflicts. They may be developed to support certain values as opposed to others. They may also be set up to protect specific interests. As emphasized earlier, in a world of scarce and interlinked environmental resources, the action of one influences the opportunities for others. Thus, a key issue regards which individual or position gets access to what resource and how this access is protected. The above definition tries to capture the duality of interaction – of coordination and conflict. Conventions are oriented at ensuring coordination. Norms, and even more clearly, the formally sanctioned rules, are important where there is conflict, defining which interests should be protected.

One may ask why institutions are also essential to human existence. Can humans not exist without institutions? Robinson Crusoe lived alone for many years and was able to carry on with his life. What Daniel Defoe showed, however, was not a self-contained individual, but rather an individual who continued to live his life by the institutions he had learned in England before being shipwrecked.

The point is that a person could certainly live physically without institutions. What we consider specifically human about Crusoe, however, is the institutions of which he was a carrier. These social constructs gave meaning to his life as they also formed his character and personality. Institutions are – according to this understanding – not only external rules. They also form the individual as he or she learns what is expected or meaningful to do in various situations (see also Bourdieu, 1989; Scott, 2014).

4.2.1 Conventions

Conventions may take a variety of forms. They have, however, one common feature: they simplify by *combining certain situations with a certain act, solution or understanding*. Conventions help structuring behavior and this way both create ordered interactions and simplify choice situations. They solve *coordination problems* and operate typically where there are no conflicts or conflict levels are low – see the parable in Chapter 3 and the choice of days for bathing in the river.

The language is a set of conventions, as well as the 'institution of all institutions'. It is a 'meta' ordering, as it provides a structure within which one can formulate other specific institutions. It is these 'other' institutions that will interest us the most. The number of conventions and the form they may take are prodigious. Some areas are specifically evident:

- *the conventions of the language:* syntax and semantics;
- *measurement scales:* time, temperature, length, weight, volume, value (money) and so on;

- *directions:* north, south, latitude, longitude and so on;
- *acts in certain situations:* types of greeting, dress codes, food standards, conventions concerning how to do specific construction work, how to behave in the traffic and so on;
- *codified perceptions:* models of interpretation of physical and social 'facts'.

While conventions generally simplify life and make coordination in a complex world possible, we observe a slight difference between coordination instruments such as the metric system and dress codes. While being able to measure the length of a piece of cloth is a requirement for selling and buying cloth, it is unimportant whether it is measured in centimeters or inches, as long as we are accustomed to the metric. Dressing as a merchant, a farmer or a judge is a different matter. Certainly, clothing has a common practical function in that it protects us from the cold and functions well given the tasks to perform. However, it also communicates meaning as it expresses the identity of the person wearing it.

As implicit in the above, conventions may take the form of practices as ways of acting that may not necessarily be communicated by oral/written language but are learned through observing how 'things are done'. A key element of this is what we call habits. Some habits are purely individual – not institutions. Most are, however, typical for groups of people, for communities, even whole cultures. Hence, they are institutionalized practices.

The aspect of codified perceptions concerns cognition and common perspectives regarding how we understand the world around us. These perceptions are already 'conventionalized' through the concepts we use when categorizing objects, relations and processes. Codified perceptions also include standardized interpretations – for example, conventional ways of understanding phenomena like 'gravitation', 'inflation', 'money', 'gender' and so forth.

Institutions must be interpreted. We may make errors or misunderstand the situation. Everybody has observed this and experienced the confusion that it creates. Sometimes it is a rather innocent issue – for example, when a person comes wearing a tie to a gathering where others observe the 'casual' code. In the traffic, a misunderstanding may create great danger. Hence, traffic conventions have over time often been legally codified and punishments are often attached to breaking these rules.

4.2.2 Norms

Norms also take a variety of forms. They are distinguished from a convention since they combine a certain situation with a *required* act or solution that supports an underlying *value*. A norm is a prescription intended to support a certain definition of how we should treat others, how to behave and so on. Typical examples are rules like 'you should greet people'; 'you should not lie'.

Norms are about developing and sustaining certain types of relations between people. They are the archetype of institutions in *civil society*. People live in societies and the number of interrelated acts is vast. It is here that the aspect of value comes in. The distinction between a norm and a convention can be illustrated by the norm to greet others when we meet. This norm may be based on the value of showing respect for and acceptance of the other. The way we greet is, however, a convention.

In the case of norms, what is at stake is foremost the creation of human character, human values and what is considered proper human relations. While coordination aspects are also involved, norms go further. They define the right way to act. We may have the problem of contaminated water because people discharge pollutants. A norm saying that you should not discharge such matter may be enough to change the behavior, even though it is individually tempting to continue the practice.

Norms take sides as they protect values and support certain interests. The example of pollution indicates a conflict at least in the sense that the immediate interest of the individual would be to pollute. The norm establishes that pollution is not acceptable. If somebody breaks a norm, fellow citizens may criticize him or her. When a norm is fully internalized, however, a person will tend to follow it independently of any external sanctions. The understanding of what this means varies across the literature. Some emphasize that breaking a norm creates a *feeling of guilt*, and that the level of guilt feeling determines whether the norm is adhered to or not – see, for example, Ostrom (1998). Others like March and Olsen (1995) emphasize that people follow the norm by principle – because it is the *right* thing to do.

There is nothing intrinsically good to norms. They may sometimes be quite discriminating. They may define somebody as more worthy than others, of higher social ranks and so on. The Indian caste system is a rather subtle example, legitimized by normative structures referring to natural orders. Some people are Brahmins; others are Shudras. Certainly, it is very effective for an interest to be protected by a rule that appears 'natural'.

4.2.3 Formally sanctioned rules: legal relations

As already indicated, conflicts are sometimes too strong to be handled only by establishing norms or conventions. Formally sanctioned rules, for simplicity just 'formal rules', are different from the above categories in two ways. They combine a certain situation with an act that is *required or forbidden* and that is governed by *third party sanctioning*. Such a sanctioning system may be based in formal law with the state as third party. Less formalized structures may also have third party mechanisms – for example, the village council in our Chapter 3 parable. Violating what is prescribed implies formalized punishment like being fined or imprisoned. Note that we referred above to reactions by fellow citizens. This is control among 'likes'. The difference to third party punishment is therefore that this authority stands above the conflicting parties.

As emphasized by Bromley (1989), legal relations are fundamental to creating order in modern societies, not least in the form of economic relations. They exist where interests are or may be explicitly *conflicting* and the collective finds it necessary to empower the regulation of this conflict by formalized control through the authority of the police and the court system.

Wesley Hohfeld, a legal scholar of the early twentieth century, developed a structure of fundamental legal relations (Hohfeld, 1913, 1917). He distinguished between static and dynamic relations or correlates – Table 4.1.

Static refers to a given relation between, for example, individuals Alpha and Beta, while dynamic relates to the power to change a legal relation. The first of the static correlates is right vs duty. If Alpha has the right to a certain good – let us say timber from a piece of land – then Beta is not allowed to cut down the trees. Beta is bound by a duty to let Alpha decide what to do with the resource. If Beta does not follow what is prescribed, the formal power of the collective – the third party – is used to punish Beta.

Table 4.1 The four basic legal relations

		Alpha	Beta
Static correlates		Right	Duty
		Privilege	No right
Dynamic correlates		Power	Liability
		Immunity	No power

Source: Hohfeld (1913, 1917).

The second static correlate – privilege vs no right – is different in that Alpha is free to behave in a certain way towards Beta, and Beta has no right to oppose this act. A privilege may imply that Alpha is free to cross some land despite the fact that it is owned by Beta. In Scandinavia, as an example, it is 'every man's right' to walk in any forest to pick berries and so on. In Hohfeld's terminology, this is a privilege.

The dynamic correlates are divided into power vs liability and immunity vs no power. Concerning the former, Alpha has the power to voluntarily create a new legal relation, which affects Beta. Alpha may be the parliament of a state and Beta its citizen. Alpha may define a new law concerning the regulation of polluting substances. When this is set up, Beta must follow the regulation or accept punishment. At the fellow citizen level, we may have a situation where Beta wants to cross Alpha's land because Beta wants to cut down some trees on his or her land and it is impossible to sell the timber without crossing Alpha's land. In this case, a contract may be established defining what Beta must do in order to be allowed to cross the land. As the property owner Alpha has the power to define these demands, Beta is obliged to comply. Otherwise, there will be no contract. We observe how it is the right, the static term, to a specific piece of land that gives Alpha the power to set the conditions – that is, the dynamic aspect.

Immunity means that Alpha is not subject to Beta's attempt to create a new legal relation, which binds Alpha. Alpha may have a right to cross Beta's land protected by an immunity rule. Beta may want to sell the land, but he or she is not free to change Alpha's right. The land may be sold, but Alpha's right stays the same. Alpha has immunity and Beta has no power to change the relation.

As we have seen, to make a legal relation binding – to ensure that Alpha's right is observed by Beta – a third party must be instituted that has the power to force Beta. Legal relations are in general triadic. They dictate what Alpha may or may not do towards Beta, and, in the event of non-compliance, some kind of reaction from this third party will follow.

4.3   Institutions as social constructs

People create institutions. It is obvious that it will take two or more people, normally large groups, to construct an institution. Let us use another parable – the creation of the meal. In this simple story there are only two people at the beginning – A and B. At some point, they decide to make a table and to sit at that table while eating. Later they have children and as they observe this routine, they start to copy it. While the parents recognize that they created the routine, the children do not see it as socially created. For them it is just how these things are done and reproduced as they themselves stick to the habit.

Certainly, there never was such a situation with the first couple. Things developed gradually. Nevertheless, the simple parable is helpful. It mirrors the fact that *people both shape institutions and are shaped by them*. The story also shows that there are actually three phases in the process of making institutions – of institutionalization – see Berger and Luckmann (1967):

1. *Externalization*. This is the process whereby subjectively constructed routines take form and are expressed. It is the stage of establishing, for example, the meal routine. The routines are visible, but they still belong only to those creating them.
2. *Objectivation*. This is the situation when others observe the routines as existing 'facts'. They have retained an existence independent of those creating them and stand out as 'things'. What the parents subjectively choose has become objectively real for the children.
3. *Internalization*. This is the stage where the children reproduce the institutions. When they play in the garden, they also have 'meals'. The process of internalization is often called 'socialization'.

A and B, who constructed the routines, can change them rather easily. Berger and Luckmann (ibid., 76–7) emphasize the following:

> What is more, since they themselves have shaped this world in the course of a shared bibliography which they can remember, the world thus shaped appears fully transparent to them. . . . All this changes in the process of transmission to the new generation. The objectivity of the institutional world 'thickens' and 'hardens', not only for the children, but (by a mirror effect) for the parents as well.

As the parents' choice becomes 'the way these things are done', it also 'captures' the parents of the parable. The very existence of the institution creates expectations that even the creators must respond to. This is the 'mirror effect'.

While the three phases generally appear in sequence for the individual, they are continuously ongoing if we look at society as a whole. In the perspective presented here, the society is a subjective product of human beings – of groups of people. People may choose to, for example, greet with the right hand, while they could have gone for 'the rule' of hugging. Nevertheless, this way of greeting becomes objectively real for those observing that it is always done this way. It takes on an objective form since it comes to exist independently of the creators. Finally, it reproduces itself constantly via the social creation of each individual being born into this society and learning its institutions. Subjective forms become 'social facts'.

Internalization may not happen as smoothly as described above. Children may not always do what is expected. Parents may have to punish the child by telling her or him that what was done was wrong or bad. The child may not yet have fully internalized the norm. Over time, internalization happens or the norm will 'die'. Institutions are dependent on being continuously reproduced.

The above story of the parents and their children captures the time dimension only partially. History is not that of two generations. The process of human development and the creation of societies have been going on for hundreds of thousands of years, first in small bands, later in tribes and settlements such as villages and towns. Finally, nation states and even today's international organizations and treaties are all examples of institutionalization processes. The complexity of social organization is vastly increased. It is not only about creating the everyday practical institutions of meals and greetings. It is also about individual and collective rights and the complex sets of roles that appear in modern societies. Parallel to this, the actors have also changed. In the beginning individuals and small groups played core roles. Later organizations of different kinds – for example, guilds, firms, civic organizations, political parties, governments and so on – have become much more important as actors in the institutionalization processes.

The fact that humans have always organized themselves into groups is undeniable. There is strong evidence that we could not have survived in early times without the ability to organize and cooperate (Ostrom, 2000). People fought against various predators and other groups of people, but humans are not especially strong or fast. Organizational talent – the talent of social construction – was an important element in our capacity to survive and expand. For long periods, humans operated in rather small groups. This implies that the development of institutions occurred under conditions of great social cohesion. People depended on each other, and external pressures from both natural forces and other human groups most probably had the effect of strengthening internal solidarity. The individual was social from the very beginning. The creation of rules occurred in a situation where trust, obligation and reciprocity were important (Barkow et al., 1992). Whether the situation was such that bands of individuals with a greater propensity to cooperate had a natural selection advantage is a hypothesis that can never be directly tested. Evolutionary psychology documents, however, that people have inherited the propensity to learn norms, which is similar to the inherited ability to learn grammatical rules (Pinker, 1994).

4.4 The role of power

As already emphasized, institutions facilitate cooperation as well as taking sides. Both aspects relate to power.

4.4.1 What is power?

Like the concept of institutions, the concept of power is difficult to define, and the understanding varies substantially across the literature. In the social sciences, definitions typically refer to the capacity to act, and as a relationship between actors. One may emphasize power as an actor's ability to realize his or her interests or goals. It may also be defined as the ability to control one's environment, including the behavior of other agents.

Robert Dahl (1957, pp. 202–3) defined power in the following way: "A has power over B to the extent that he can get B to do something B would not otherwise do". Dahl studied behavior especially in organizations and political bodies. Studying visible conflicts is important, but his definition was criticized for omitting conflicts that do not become visible (e.g., Bachrach and Baratz, 1963). Even in what we would term democratic societies, processes may not be open and conflicts may be suppressed.

Steven Lukes took this perspective even further. He noted that "A may exercise power over B by getting him to do what he does not want to do, but he also exercises power over B by influencing, shaping or determining his very wants" (Lukes, 2005, p. 27). He therefore talked about three views on or 'faces' of power:

- the one-dimensional view focusing on observable behavior and decision-making (e.g., Dahl);
- the two-dimensional view also including non-decision-making; issues that are suppressed (e.g., Bachrach and Baratz);
- the three-dimensional view, adding the power to form people's interests and wants – Lukes's own position.

There are several challenges when analyzing the last two power dimensions, as the focus is on what did not happen and is not directly observable. The specific point included in the three-dimensional view implies that people want something that is not their 'real' interest. Here

Lukes comes close to the concepts of 'alienation' and 'false consciousness' as emphasized in the Marxian-oriented literature. The problem is not that this could not happen. There is much of what is important that is unobservable. The challenge is, nevertheless, how to study such processes, as they 'show up' not only in lack of action, but also in lack of awareness by the self – by the people whose interests have been perverted. This seems to introduce a normative element about what a good life is or should look like. The observation is that some people are not offered the opportunity to live such a life. At the same time, invisible power that molds people's desires and expectations is very 'effective'. Systems for social stratification – by class, caste and so on – could be seen as examples of such forms of power.

In relation to this, Gaventa's (1980) study of latent conflicts is interesting. He asked why situations of discrimination and oppression could be sustained without resistance or revolt. He concluded that social elites use their power to prevent people participating in decision-making and to accept that this is how things should be – see the two- and three-dimensional views above. Elites form the will of the suppressed. Various kinds of social myths may play a significant role.

Gaventa also recognized that for the suppressed to be able to enter the decision-making arena, they need to overcome the mechanisms of the two- and three-dimensional views. They need first to develop and articulate what they see as their real interests and next ensure that these are accepted as legitimate issues for political decision-making. An obvious example of this is the establishment of representative democracy and the right to vote as an alternative to the previously existing autocratic power systems/dictatorships. The first step was the establishment of the idea of an alternative system and the creation of an identity of the ruled as political subjects – that is, as thinking of themselves as somebody who ought to have the right to engage in the decision-making process. A part of this was to challenge the legitimacy of autocratic power.

Using eighteenth- and nineteenth-century Europe as an example, the institution of voting was created first for a sub-group of men – that is, those owning land/property. Next, the idea that owning property was constitutive of political rights was challenged and the right was expanded to all men. The superiority of men was finally challenged and voting rights were also given to women. Then we are into the twentieth century. What now seems an obvious right was created not least through changing the self-understanding of those previously not thus empowered.

Power is not only about domination; it is also what makes action possible – note the distinction between 'power over' and 'power to'. To support the powerless does not imply avoiding power, but to empower. Learning to read is empowering. The same concerns other practical and theoretical skills as well as increased access to decision-making processes. At a systems level, we note that institutional structures influence how easy it is to cooperate/coordinate action. Hence, facilitating cooperation also has an important power dimension to it. While one often envisions that the power of one may reduce the power of somebody else, this is not always the case.

4.4.2 The sources of power

Defining the forms of power is one thing; specifying its sources is another. Power depends on access to resources, but the meaning of this is not straightforward. Etzioni (1975) divides power into three: what he calls *coercive, remunerative* and *normative* power. Coercive power may be based on brute force, but in modern societies, structural or rule-based forms of coercive power are much more important. This concerns the power of the state – for example, the power to issue laws and the subsequent power of the police and court systems. Leadership of organizations and firms is coercive power – the power to command – based on the rules defined for these entities. Remunerative power concerns the capacity to make people act in desired ways through payments/incentives. Economic power rests on ownership to resources and materializes typically in markets. Nevertheless, states may also use remunerative power in the form of subsidies and taxes. Finally, normative power concerns symbolic rewards, esteem and prestige, moral persuasion and so forth.

Etzioni's understanding of power overlaps Lukes'. His categories are relevant for all faces of the three-dimensional view. Coercive and remunerative power play a relatively more important role at the level of decision-making and controlling agendas, while normative power is more important in forming people's wants or perceived interests.

While Etzioni's way of defining sources of power is quite abstract, power can also be defined more concretely. Below I list a few of the most important:

- *Brute force*. This is a non-institutionalized form of power, operating both at the level of individuals, groups and conflicts between countries in the form of war.
- *Rights*. These are institutionalized forms of power extending the rightholder's capacities and limiting other people's power upon her or him. Property rights are a special source of power generating access to

economic resources to cover own needs, but also directing other people through remunerative action. It rests on the power of a third party.

- *Knowledge.* Controlling the development and distribution of knowledge and conceptual frames implies specifying what the issues are, how they should be understood and what demands action. Being ignorant about an issue implies that you cannot act upon it. Creating ignorance is a way to disempower.
- *Capacity to produce.* Creating economically valuable resources is important both for ensuring (some level of) independence and establishing remunerative power.
- *Capacity to organize.* Through 'pooling' one's capacities, organizing strengthens the capabilities and position of individuals to become members of a group. More generally, high *costs of interaction* disempower people.
- *Capacity to motivate.* Influencing people's motivational structures is a way to direct action. Moral persuasion is part of this.

Analyses of power are found within different disciplines with varying emphasis and understanding of what generates power. Some have developed theories that are best suited to studying political processes and decision-making in organizations. Others have looked at the dynamics of families, communities and civil society at large. Some have looked at firms and at markets. While there are certain common aspects across all these fields – for example, Lukes's model – the source and forms of power are typically described as quite contextual. What could become a source of power greatly depends on the specific conditions.

4.4.3   Power and sustainability

While there are many different definitions of sustainability, the emphasis on the intergenerational aspect is key. Hence, sustainable development has been defined as "development that meets the needs of the present without compromising the ability of future generations to meet their own needs" (WCED, 1987, Chapter 2, Section IV, paragraph 1).

Theories of power typically reflect that actors are self-interested and use their power to establish conditions that are better for themselves. From this perspective, sustainability creates a vast challenge. As future generations do not currently exist, they have no say in decision-making. They are powerless in the most fundamental sense as the present generation can impose whatever condition on future generations. The latter have no say in decision-making; they are fundamentally unable to form agendas; and the present generation defines their interests as a function of how we develop institutions and organizations into which the next generation will be included and formed.

Understanding power as the capacity to get what one wants, does, however, not preclude acts on behalf of others. It is not only 'power over' or 'power to', but also power 'with'. This regards what interest power is made to serve. There is hence nothing in the concept of power that precludes the powerful from taking other people's interests into account – be it within the present or future generations.

To clarify this it may be helpful to return to the distinction between 'we' and 'they' types of conflict. The 'prisoner's dilemma game' – see Box 3.1 – illustrated a 'we' conflict with powerless actors. The structure of the game forced them to choose a strategy with results far from the best obtainable. Creating ways to cooperate could make it possible to break the logic of the game, as allowing communication could produce better results.

In the case of a 'they' conflict, the situation is different. There is typically no potential gain for all – as with the upstream/downstream dwellers of Chapter 3. Turning to the intergenerational issue – which is also upstream/downstream, now in the time dimension – the power rests in the hands of the present generation. The future ('downstream') generations depend on the mercy of the present generation for defining which living conditions they will have to operate under. Handling such issues demands focus on the normative underpinning of action. It becomes necessary to think about what obligations we have towards coming generations. While much of the present literature on power relations looks at obligations as constructed by powerful actors to suppress the interests of others, sustainability demands changed focus. The actor must ask what obligations it has towards others, while these others are unable to exercise any power to define that obligation and ensure that it is respected. This is the fundamental challenge of sustainability.

4.4.4 Power and institutions

Institutions are important in forming power relations and as sources of power. Cognitive and normative structures form the perceptions and the self-understanding of various individuals and groups. How we interpret physical and social 'facts' depends on our knowledge and the type of models we have learned regarding interpretation. Normative and cognitive structures define our position in society as we see it. They also include 'visions' about why things ought to be in certain ways. This is core in Lukes's understanding.

Bourdieu (1989) places a similar emphasis on this by using the concept of symbolic power. Socially created conventions and norms of a society imply and reflect domination. Hence, there is both an epistemic and normative power element underlying the institutions of a society.

At a more tangible level, we have rights to resources and positions in decision-making. Access to resources is fundamental to what kind of lives we can live. Power in decision-making regards both how we can ensure such access and what relations we have to others – whether in political as well as economic and social processes. Institutions may be formulated to ensure participation as well as exclusion. These issues may be quite subtle. The right to vote may be universal, while some feel this right does not empower them – the situation for many minorities.

Regarding power and institutions, I will finally emphasize the capacity of a society to coordinate action when wanted. Typically, coordination is a demanding challenge for any society, meaning that the power to coordinate is weak. Summarized, institutions influence power relations in the following ways:

- *Epistemic and normative power.* This concerns the capacity to influence people's knowledge/perceptions, self-understanding, preferences, subjective interests and values as embedded in the conventions and norms of a society.[1]
- *Positional power.* This concerns access to resources and positions in decision-making processes in a wide sense. Core here is the defined rights structure.
- *Coordination power.* This regards the capacity to coordinate human action towards common goals. Such power depends both on institutional and organizational structures of society and how demanding/costly it is to coordinate activities given the form of such structures.

These powers are linked in various ways. Positional power may be important for having epistemic and ideological power. Similarly, rights structures and cognitive/normative aspects influence how easy it is to coordinate since common perceptions and norms simplify communication and create trust.

From the start of the section on power, the focus was on the actions of certain actors – for example, how A could get B to do what he or she wanted. Throughout our analysis, the role of institutional structures has become more and more prevalent. People act and exercise power. At the same time, their power is very much embedded in their positions within the institutional structures as defined by their positions and rights/access to resources. This duality of agency and structure is a core aspect of social science and in understanding power. Some authors put more emphasis on agency as the basis for power relations and others on institutional structures.

A basic understanding underlying this book is that one cannot focus *either* on agency *or* on structure. Both are important, as actors form institutions and are then formed by them. So those having the power to change institutions will themselves be influenced by these institutions. They operate as constraints not only for the powerless. Private property offers advantages to those being able to accumulate resources. They do, however, also have to follow the rules and practices for such accumulation.

Anthony Giddens (1984) has been central in developing our understanding of the interdependencies between actors and structures. He sees power as integrated into the institutions of a society. Human actors create and change the institutions – they define the laws, norms and conventions of a society. At the same time, the institutions structure the activities humans undertake. They even form the actors, as we have seen.

4.5 Different understandings of institutions

The concept of an institution is differently defined and understood across the social sciences. To provide anything close to a complete overview would demand a book of its own. Hence, in putting together the following few pages, I have had to make some serious simplifications – see Figure 4.1.

The main distinction is between those defining institutions as organizations and those defining them in some way as 'rules, symbols and practices'. Concerning the latter group, we may distinguish between rational choice-based and constructivist-based understandings of institutions.

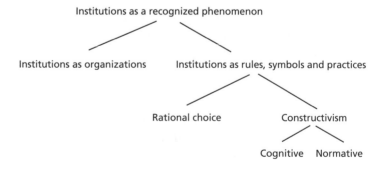

Figure 4.1 Different ways of understanding institutions

Defining institutions as organizations is quite typical within political science. There is a problem in the sense that the distinction between actors and institutions becomes blurred. Organizations are actors. Certainly, institutions form them – for example, rules defining who can be members, how decisions can be made, who can represent and so on. Nevertheless, they are actors and since institutions also shape individuals, there is no fundamental difference at that level. Hence, I will leave this position aside, while noting that when reading the literature about environmental governance many define organizations as institutions – see, for example, Miles et al. (2002); Chasek et al. (2014).

What interests us here is the distinction between the rational choice position and constructivist theories. It concerns the understanding of human action including the relationship between institutions and human action. Following from that, there is also a distinction concerning how to understand institutional change. While we have already commented on aspects of such change above, I will cover this latter issue more systematically in Chapter 7.

4.5.1 Rational choice institutionalism

Rational choice institutionalism – or the individualist position as it may also be termed – dominates economics and substantial parts of political science. We should note that most economists are not much engaged in institutional analyses. There is, however, a sub-tradition called 'new institutional economics' that has been very instrumental in developing rational choice institutionalism.

The neoclassical economic model

Explaining rational choice institutionalism demands a brief presentation of the model of neoclassical economics. This has been the dominating model within economics and includes the most developed exposition of rational choice.[2] Following Lakatos (1974), Becker (1976) and Eggertsson (1990) we may define the following *core* of the neoclassical model:

- rational choice as maximizing individual utility;
- stable preferences; and
- equilibrium outcomes.

Rational choice is defined as maximizing individual utility. Utility is derived from preference satisfaction and the preferences of individuals are typically seen as stable. At least, they are seen as strictly individual – not influenced by societal or cultural factors. If they change, it is entirely due to individual change – aging and so on. This is the essence of the individualist perspective underlying rational choice models. Finally, when rational actors act, they are involved in exchanges of goods and services with others. Rational actors will furthermore exchange goods until a point is reached where no more gain appears and an equilibrium state is produced. They act based on a means–end calculation. Actors cannot get all they want, as they have limited access to resources (e.g., income). Hence, they would have to prioritize and find the way (means) that increases their preference satisfaction (end) the most.

The above concept of *the core of a science* is borrowed from Lakatos (1974), according to whom each science is characterized by what he terms both a 'hard core' and a 'protective belt'. I will use the concept of 'application area' rather than the protective belt to describe the context into which the core assumptions are placed when analyzing real-world phenomena. Once more, following Eggertsson (1990), the *standard application area* of neoclassical economics can be defined as follows:

- no information costs;
- no transaction costs; and
- private property rights for all goods, which are exchanged in competitive markets.

Transaction costs is probably the least familiar of the above terms. Arrow (1969, p. 48) defines transaction costs as the 'costs of running the economic system'. Transaction costs have also been defined as the costs of information gathering, contracting and controlling contracts (Dahlman, 1979).[3] In the standard neoclassical model, these costs are discarded.

The only institutional elements appearing in the neoclassical model are those of property rights. It is noted that it is the task of the state to form and guard these rights. However, to analyze how this comes about is taken to be outside of the topic of economics. Given the kind of rationality involved, the only form of interaction implied by the model is the trading of goods. It will, moreover, appear 'by itself' as long as utility can be increased by such exchanging of owned goods. Thus, the market is 'the natural order of things' in a model based on individualism and zero transaction costs. Hence, the market is not seen as an institutionally created structure.

A couple of comments are necessary. First, a lot of research among economists includes studies of decision-making under risk and uncertainty. This implies dispensing with the assumption that information is cost free as no information costs actually implies that all information is certain. Hence, what we may call mainstream economists do not strictly follow the standard neoclassical model as defined by Eggertsson and others. We also observe that the issue of transaction costs is increasingly being included in economic textbooks.

Finally, the above description of the standard application area links rational choice to actions in markets. Rational choice in such a context is often called *instrumental*. The actor calculates what is best for his or her given goods and prices in the market. Rational choice theory has also been used a great deal in situations where human actions are interdependent – that is, where what it is best to do depends on what others do. Then we move into the area of game theory, and in such contexts, rational choice implies that action is *strategic*. The individual does what is best for him or her given that others act on a similar basis.

New institutional economics[4]

While institutional issues are largely ignored by neoclassical economics, some economists started to ask if transacting (or coordinating) is so costly, it might be that markets are not always the best way to allocate resources. Why is not all interaction happening in markets if markets are the most efficient? Why do we have firms (Coase, 1937; Williamson 1975, 1985)? Maybe state allocations or regulations could be more efficient if transaction costs were lower than in market exchanges (Coase, 1960; Williamson, 2000)?

Douglass North has taken the above perspectives further in some seminal publications forming the basis for the tradition of new institutional economics – see, for example, North (1990, 1991). He has defined institutions as "the *rules of the game* in a society or, more formally. . . the humanly devised constraints that shape human interaction" (North, 1990, p. 3; my emphasis). We note that institutions are seen as rules and operate as constraints. The society is, moreover, seen as a game. New institutional economics builds largely on the core of the neoclassical economics model. Humans act to maximize individual utility and preferences are unaffected by the institutional context. Given such an understanding of humans and human action, the only way institutions can operate is as constraints.

The most important 'rules of the game' are those defining the rights each individual holds – for example, the rules concerning access to resources. Given these rules and the existing distribution of endowments, individuals transact to get what in the end is considered best for them. Transacting is, however, costly and uncertain. Institutions are, according to this position, invented not least to reduce transaction costs and uncertainty. They are *instruments* that make production and exchange become more predictable, simple and efficient. The money institution, the contract and the various measurement scales are all understood as being invented to simplify transactions.

Note that while institutions are human constructs, the individual actors are not, according to this position. It should be observed that while the later North (2005) has moved away from utility maximization as a good description of human choice, he does not grant any role to institutions in forming preferences. In that sense, the individualist tenets of rational choice institutionalism are kept intact.

Rational choice institutionalism in other social sciences

Models of rational choice are also used in other social sciences – notably in political science and sociology. While economists study how individuals and firms operate in markets, political scientists study decision-making mainly in political fora and organizations. As sociology is the scientific study of society, sociologists have a wide area of focus, overlapping both those of economists and political scientists. A lot of their research centers, however, around civil society and civil society institutions, covering issues like family, gender, class and so on.

The main point here is that political scientists and sociologists using the rational choice model have imported it into areas of life beyond where it originated – in economics and the study of markets. While this has also resulted in some adaptions of the model, the main issue here is that a wider set of human actions is studied from the perspective of instrumental exchange or strategic behavior.

Thinking in terms of 'trade' and strategic behavior might make sense when studying political processes. Rational choice models have played a key role in the development of the discipline since the 1960s (Shepsle, 2006). Focus has been on collective action, with the 'games politicians play' as a core area of analyses. Hall and Taylor (1996) argue that there has been increased emphasis on the role of institutions when analyzing the outcome of such processes. The extensive set of rules in place for political decision-making could explain the rather high level of stability characterizing political processes. Institutions enhance efficiency through reducing the costs of political transactions. Rational choice institutionalists in political science use assumptions similar to neoclassical economic theory regarding human action. What politicians maximize is, however, different. They focus on votes, prestige and so on.

The work of Elinor Ostrom – see, for example, Ostrom (1990, 1998) – will be visited on several occasions later in this book. She is seen by many as a rational choice institutionalist. It is notable that while she uses utility maximization (or actually, satisficing)[5] as the decision rule, she accepts that preferences are socially influenced. This illustrates that the assumption of fixed preferences is not always 'abided by' among political scientists using rational choice models as their basis. Ostrom emphasizes explicitly that preferences are formed by societal processes.

Rational choice theories have also played a noteworthy role in sociology, but to a much less extent than in political science. Again, it started in the 1960s. Homans (1961) is often cited as a key reference for this development. In this case, maximization concerns social approval (ibid.). Following rational choice perspectives, social processes are described as exchanges – see, for example, Coleman (1973, 1990). Sociologists have used rational choice theories studying topics as diverse as family/demography, gender, religion and organizations (e.g., Hechter and Kanazawa, 1997). As with Ostrom, some of these authors accept that preferences may be influenced by society – for example, the internalization of norms. This reflects a core tenet of sociology and implies that some authors operate with assumptions that do not adhere to a strict definition of rational choice. While social structures are important contexts in sociological analyses – see, for example, Coleman (1990) – 'rational choice sociologists' adhere nevertheless to methodological individualism.

4.5.2 Constructivist theories

Naming the group of scholars we will now look at as 'constructivist' demands a cautionary note at the very beginning. Scholars included under this label may label themselves quite differently. Some might favor a reference to 'cultural perspectives' (e.g., Haviland, 1999), some to a 'critical institutional approach' (Cleaver, 2012) and some to 'social practice models' (e.g., Young, 2002). This issue relates not only to what people are used to calling theories or positions, but also to the fact that the concept of constructivism itself is used with different meanings. Certainly, most authors understand institutions as humanly constructed, for example, North. What distinguishes constructivism, as the concept is used in this book, is that actors' perceptions, interests and values held are themselves influenced by institutions and the wider culture of a society.

What does the above mean? It does not imply that all preferences people hold are created by society and internalized by its members. Certainly, physical needs are very important and tastes may be to some extent genuinely individual – some like it sweet, others hot. However, even at this level, culture may play an important role in forming what we prefer. Furthermore, the values that people hold are typically taken to be strongly influenced by the society where one is raised or lives.

While constructivist models deviate from rational choice models in their understanding of how society influences the development of individuals, this then has implications regarding how to explain collective action and how to understand norms. Constructivists see collective action as both possible and essential to handling many problems in a society. The existence of collective actors like communities, trade unions, political parties, environmental organizations and so on, is difficult to explain from a purely individualist position. Such actors are offering common goods and services for their members in the sense that they work for protection of their common interests, values and so forth. From a rational choice perspective, the logic of free-riding would, however, obstruct collective action: if the organization does not exist, it does not pay for any individual to set it up. If it does exist, there is no reason for individuals to become a member with the costs involved, as the public good will be produced anyway and can be 'consumed for free'.

Some rational choice scholars like Olson (1965) tried to explain the existence of organizations by arguing that they also offered individual, not just common services – various individual membership favors like cheaper insurance and so on. While not an irrelevant argument, this solution has been criticized not least by showing that many organizations offer no such services. Alternative explanations have emphasized the building of trust in cases where people interacted over time. While again not irrelevant, even such an explanation falls short. Finally and more fundamentally, it has been emphasized that rational choice cannot explain why people hold the preferences and values they do, and even more importantly, why they change. Explaining this would have to go beyond rational choice (Scott, 2000).

The above issues demand more thorough discussion, and I will return to that in Chapter 5. Here I will just give a brief overview of the main positions. While Hall and Taylor (1996) make a distinction between what they term historical and sociological institutionalism, I will also add the tradition of classical economic institutionalism. In the present book, I will draw on all three, while the main basis is to be found in the latter tradition.

Classical institutional economics[6]

Classical institutional economics goes back to the late nineteenth/early twentieth century (e.g., Veblen, 1898; Commons [1934] 1990). It developed as a response to the emergence of neoclassical economics in the 1870s. Veblen criticized the view that preferences are purely individual, emphasizing the influence of society and its institutions on human desire (Veblen, 1899). While this tradition had a strong position especially in the USA until World War II, it lost much influence and did not really revive until the 1980s (e.g., Hodgson, 1988; Bromley, 1989).

Contrasting classical institutional economics with its main 'rival' – the neoclassical position – it sees first of all the human as *multirational* (e.g., Hodgson, 1988, 2007; Sjöstrand, 1995). The idea of maximizing individual utility as the only form of rationality finds little support. Rather, there can be different types of rationality, and the institutional context defines which is expected. In some contexts like a market, the dominant rationality may be to ensure what is best for the individual – 'maximizing individual utility'. In the family context, care is the dominant norm. Hence, considering what is right and wrong is an alternative form of rationality compared to the calculus of individual gain. What is right or wrong depends, moreover, on the kind of situation one is in. The focus among representatives of this school is, furthermore, not on equilibrium, but on change – on the evolution of institutions, perceptions, preferences and values (Hodgson, 1996).

Concerning the application theorems, classical institutional economics is based on much of the same understanding as that of the new institutional economists. Hence, the tradition emphasizes the importance of information and transaction costs for understanding human action and the functioning of institutional systems like markets, firms and organizations. They differ, however, regarding why such structures exist and change. While reducing transaction costs may be important, this tradition emphasizes the role of power and interest protection as important when explaining the development of economic structures like markets and firms (e.g., Schmid, 1987; Hodgson, 1988; Bromley, 2006). Finally, classical institutional economics is interested in studying a wide variety of institutional structures – for example, property structures beyond that of private property – and these again are discussed not only in relation to efficiency, but also in relation to the issue of power and interest protection (e.g., Schmid, 1987; Pitelis, 1993; Bromley, 2006). Thus, classical institutional economics challenges all the fundamental assumptions of the neoclassical model. Each has important consequences for the evaluation not least of public policies/governance.

Historical institutionalism

There is a lot of common ground between this tradition and classical institutional economics. The main distinction is maybe that the historical institutionalists are political scientists and sociologists and hence focus less on economic issues. Both put strong emphasis on the normative role of institutions and the role of power. Regarding the normative, the focus among historical institutionalists is to a large extent on what is the appropriate or right thing to do. A core development regarding this was a book by March and Olsen (1989, p. 22): "It is a commonplace observation in empirical social science that behaviour is contained or dictated by cultural dicta and social norms. Action is often based more on identifying the normatively appropriate behaviour than on calculating the return expected from alternative choices".

In this respect the historical school represented a further development of ideas of early sociologists like Durkheim, through Parsons, to Selznick, that emphasized the normative dimension of institutions quite strongly (see Scott, 2014) and it links clearly to perspectives taken up by classical institutional economists.

Other issues that characterize this tradition are the emphasis on power relations and power asymmetries. Important here is how the institutional structures facilitate, and obstruct, the access that various interest groups have to decision-making arenas. Historical institutionalists also strongly emphasize the role of path dependence in understanding the development of institutions – meaning that existing institutions influence what kind of changes will/can happen. This is not so only because it is a costly operation to undertake substantial changes in institutions, but also because identities of actors are formed by the existing ones.

Sociological institutionalism

While scholars of historical institutionalism and classic institutional economics have put special emphasis on the normative dimension of institutions, the development in mainstream sociology has taken a somewhat different direction. Again we must treat any distinction and 'grouping' with care. Sociology is quite heterogeneous. Nevertheless, we observe in recent decades a turn away from emphasizing the normative importance and more towards the cognitive significance of institutions. Institutions are not only formal rules and norms, but also symbolic systems, cognitive scripts and categorizations that make action possible and offer meaning to the situation. Hall and Taylor (1996, p. 948) note:

> Institutions influence behaviour not simply by specifying what one should do
> but also by specifying what one can imagine oneself doing in a given context. . .
> It follows that institutions do not simply affect the strategic calculations of
> individuals, as rational choice institutionalists contend, but also their basic
> preferences and very identity. The self-images and identities of social actors are said
> to be constituted from the institutional forms and signs provided by social life.

Referring to our previous presentation, this implies an emphasis on what
we termed conventions, not just as practical rules by which one organizes
interaction, but also as symbolic systems influencing perception. 'Facts' do
not present themselves to us in a straightforward way as assumed by rational
choice. What we observe and how we understand what we observe depend
on the concepts we have learned to use. Berger and Luckmann ([1967]
1991) played a key role in facilitating this shift in sociology towards more
emphasis on cognition. I think classical institutional economics would
prosper from a broader inclusion of this perspective, as I try to do in this
book.

It should also be mentioned that a lot of influence on sociological institutionalism came from organization theory. A core observation made here was that
organizations did not seem to choose practices that were the most efficient.
Hall and Taylor (1996, pp. 946–7) explain:

> [T]he new institutionalists in sociology began to argue that many of the
> institutional forms and procedures used by modern organizations were not
> adopted simply because they were most efficient for the task at hand, in line with
> some transcendent 'rationality'. Instead, they argued that many of these forms and
> procedures should be seen as culturally-specific practices, akin to the myths and
> ceremonies devised by many societies, and assimilated into organizations, not
> necessarily to enhance their formal means–ends efficiency, but as the result of
> the kind of processes associated with the transmission of cultural practices more
> generally. Thus, they argued, even the most seemingly bureaucratic of practices
> have to be explained in cultural terms.

Procedures typically spread through networks or organizational fields where
common problem definitions and solutions are copied. This 'isomorphism'
simplifies interaction as well as strengthens the legitimacy of what organizations do as they conform to common practices. Key references regarding this
trend are DiMaggio and Powell (1981, 1983), Meyer and Scott (1983) and
Scott (2014).

4.6   Main messages

In this chapter, I have defined the concept of an institution – understood as rules, symbols and practices. More specifically, institutions are defined as the conventions, norms and formally sanctioned rules of a society. They provide expectations, stability and meaning essential to human existence and coordination. Institutions support certain values, and produce and protect specific interests. Institutions are not only human constructs, they are also 'constructing the human' – that is, they influence the perceptions, interests and values of individuals. As such, society imprints itself upon its individuals through socialization or enculturation processes.

The process of institutional creation and socialization can be described in three phases: (1) externalization, (2) objectivation and (3) internalization. The first phase regards the creation of a new rule or practice by some people. The second concerns the observation of this rule or practice by somebody else as 'how things are or should be done'. The latter phase concerns these rules/practices becoming the way these others do things. This understanding of institutions is built on a weak or moderate form of constructivism, emphasizing agency, but formed within structures. Institutions are created by actors who are themselves formed by the institutions and cultures of society.

Regarding the wider literature, there are two important provisions to make regarding the perspectives of this book. First, organizations are treated as actors not institutions. They are constituted by institutions – that is, the rules and practices defining the organization. They are, however, best viewed as actors while somewhat more complex and 'abstract' than individuals. Second, institutions are in some parts of the literature seen only as constraints. This relates to a divide in the social sciences between disciplines/authors that see the individual as self-contained – as not formed by social processes – and those that see institutions as constitutive even of individuals. While the former (must) see institutions as external constraints, the latter understands institutions as important for what actors are and become. While the former perspective dominates mainstream/neoclassical economics, its 'cousin' 'new institutional economics' and a large fraction of political science, the latter perspective is dominant in sociology, anthropology and classical institutional economics.

The distinction made between conventions, norms and legal rules follows an underlying distinction between coordination and conflict. While conventions are practical solutions to coordination problems – enduring rules and practices that make interaction possible – norms go further as they support certain values as opposed to others. Hence, they operate in a 'landscape' of potential conflict, but reduce this potential by emphasizing which values should be protected. In situations where conflicts cannot be safeguarded only through defining common values, legal regulations may be invoked, drawing on the sanctioning power of a third party. In relation to this, it should be noted that conventions may not be as 'innocent' as the above seems to indicate. By categorizing phenomena as 'natural', they may have the power to conceal conflictual issues, actually being very effective in that respect.

Hence, institutions must be understood as power structures. They may empower as well as 'discipline' or create structures of domination. Based on an institutional perspective, I have made a distinction between 'epistemic and ideological power', 'positional power' and 'coordination power'. All these forms are important for environmental governance. The first regards what perspectives dominate the discourses of knowledge and value. The second concerns the distribution of power to act. The third describes the capacity to interact.

NOTES

1 I have chosen to use the concept of epistemic and normative power instead of Bourdieu's 'symbolic power' concept. This is because I will sometimes need to make a distinction between the epistemic and the normative.

2 One may ask about the status of the neoclassical model in contemporary economics. It still dominates textbooks and university curricula. At the same time, there are several developments within mainstream economics that point towards a process of change – for example, Brock and Colander (2000). My aim here is not to cover various developments in, for example, economics, but to offer a description of principal positions.

3 Because of this, information costs could be subsumed under that category. It is kept as a separate point since information gathering is also necessary for activities other than transacting.

4 The reader may be confused by the reference to 'new' institutional economics, as there has yet been no mention of any 'old'. The 'old' or 'classical' institutional economics, as I prefer to call it, actually developed in parallel to the neoclassical tradition – as both a critique and alternative model. The tradition of new institutional economics developed from the 1960s onwards. A revival of classical institutional economics occurred about 20 years later – much as a reaction to the 'new'. This 'modern' version of classical institutional economics will be briefly covered under Section 4.5.2 on 'constructivist theories'.

5 I will explain the difference in Chapter 5.

6 A more complete presentation is offered in Vatn (2005).

5

Theories of motivation and human actions

To understand why environmental resources are under pressure, we need to understand what motivates human action. Such insights are equally important for communities, states and international bodies when formulating policies and institutions to create better outcomes. While ecosystems are complex, so also are human motivation, action and interaction. The aim of this chapter is to give an overview of the main positions in the literature on these issues. As part of that, I will develop a distinct position based on institutional theory that will inform much of the later analyses in the book. Again, simplifications will be made. For those interested in deepening their insights, references used should offer interesting opportunities for further reading.

Human action or behavior[1] can be both automatic and reflected. Kahneman (2011) differentiates between 'thinking fast and slow', between what he terms System 1 (the automatic) and System 2 (mental effort). While these distinctions may underestimate the interaction between the two – the unconscious also plays a big role in reasoned actions – it clarifies that there are different types of processes involved when acting.

What motivates action is comprehended differently across the literature. Understanding these distinctions is crucial to grasp why scholars from various disciplines advocate different policies. In disentangling this, I will focus on the concept of rationality. Some see *rationality* as purely *individual* – what has previously been termed 'rational choice theory' – while others also include the concept of *social rationality*. Some see what is rational as independent of *institutional contexts*, while others put strong emphasis on institutions when understanding what acting rationally means. Certainly, not all action is based on complete calculations or fully reasoned. Humans are not endowed with unlimited capacities. When understanding action we therefore have to take into account that we are at best 'boundedly rational'. Moreover, much action is, as already mentioned, routinized. Hence, I will introduce the notion of *habit* – linking reflected action to automatic behavior.

5.1 Theories of human action

5.1.1 Individual rationality

Trying to clarify the above issues, I start by focusing on the model of individual rationality. It is developed most rigorously within neoclassical economics. As already emphasized in Chapter 4, it understands rationality as maximizing individual utility. Hence, it emphasizes selfishness. Moreover, it looks at the individual as 'isolated' in the sense that preferences are not influenced by social contexts or processes.

To act rationally in the meaning of maximizing individual utility demands 1) that preferences are rational – that the individual is able to rank options so that they can choose what offers the highest utility for her or him – and 2) that they choose according to that ranking, whether it is about what to have for dinner, which shirts to buy and so on. The qualities of different options are evaluated and compared to the price. What gives the highest preference satisfaction – utility – is chosen.

The concept of rational preferences is perhaps the most unfamiliar to the reader. The main issue concerns whether the individual is able to rank all options from the most to the least preferred and that this ranking is consistent – that is, transitive. The latter implies that if an individual considers good A as better than good B and good B better than good C, then A must be ranked above C for the preferences to be rational. Ranking option A as better than C, but nevertheless choosing C is also irrational as the choice is not consistent with what is defined as best.

The model of individual rationality implies that if the quality of a good goes down or the price increases, demand falls. It also implies that preferences and hence choices are stable across contexts and uninfluenced by social processes. There are many issues to discuss concerning how well this model represents actual choice:

- Are people self-contained in the sense assumed – for example, are preferences independent of cultural background and the context in which choices are made?
- Do people only think about themselves when choosing?
- Do people have the necessary information to make rational choices as defined?
- Are they able to do the necessary ranking and calculations? Do they really maximize?

In the rest of Section 5.1, I will discuss the above issues. I start with a short analysis of the assumption of the 'isolated' individual in the meaning of preferences being purely individual. Thereafter, I discuss whether choice is only based on egoistic motivations. I then contrast the model of individual rationality with that of social rationality. Finally, I look at the issue of habits and bounded rationality as responses to the last two questions presented above.

5.1.2 Preferences as individual vs socially constructed

Let me start with a personal observation. In the early 1990s, I stayed at an American University. A colleague of mine – an economist – visited Japan. Coming back, she was perturbed. In the case of some commodities, relative prices in Japan were so different from those observed in the USA. While apples in a nearby grocery store in Madison could be bought in large bags for a dollar, the Japanese could pay as much as 15 dollars for one apple. It was almost like the higher price the better. She noted that in Japan 'perfect apples' were used as gifts and as a sign of friendship. What my colleague caught a glimpse of was the social construction of preferences, and it seemed to shake her beliefs about a fundamental assumption in economics.

Is this, however, worrying? When travelling we all observe the tremendous role culture plays in forming what we do or prefer. A child born in India but adopted to Sweden grows up and becomes 'Swedish'. Her preferences and behavior resemble that of the Swedish family and community she grows up in. Studies of the role of culture on the shaping of individuals abound in disciplines like social anthropology and sociology (e.g., Haviland, 1999; Grusec and Hastings, 2007). As opposed to the assumption of standard economics, people depend on culture for their development – see also Etzioni (1988). This not only concerns language and abilities to communicate, but also preferences, norms and values. Cultures are responses to the various issues we face in life. Their response may vary a lot. We use different clothes and eat different foods. We respect different values and interact differently.

This view is also gradually taking hold among some economists. An example is Fehr and Gintis (2007) and their emphasis on the role of institutions like norms for human behavior, underlining how socialization shapes the preferences of individuals. Such a shift in understanding has, however, great implications for the overall model of economics. In Part Five we will discuss the implications of this for what are good policies. Here we will take a first step considering the implications for the theory of human action.

5.1.3 Do people only think about themselves?

Resent research – also among economists – raises serious doubts about whether people only think about themselves when acting. Box 5.1 offers a number of examples from experiments illustrating that people act in ways that deviate from the model of individual rationality. It does, however, also offer examples showing that we may come pretty close to acting in an individually rational manner – especially in cases resembling choices between commodities in market contexts.

When going to the shop, people typically think about what is best to buy for them. They evaluate the prices and quality of the various commodities offered. In a food store, we may assess whether the products are healthy for us – for example, their nutritional value, if they may contain pesticides and so on. Some may, however, also put emphasis on the production methods used and buy food they believe is produced in an environmentally friendly way. They act based on motives beyond selfishness.

Acting non-selfishly actually seems quite common. People may help others without being rewarded – even some they do not know or expect to meet again. Hence, they take on costs without expecting any 'payback'. When travelling, I often have to ask locals about the way to, for example, the hotel. I note that people – almost without exception – try to help. Some even go some lengths to ensure that I find my way. Similarly there are many examples showing that people may cooperate and share when managing common resources – see, for example, Ostrom (1990); Ostrom et al. (1994). The examples from experiments like ultimatum games, dictator games and public goods games as presented in Box 5.1 illustrate the same. Does that imply that the standard model of individual rationality is false because we may also act altruistically? Scholars disagree regarding this matter.

Economists like Andreoni (1990) and Frey (1997) have argued that while there are no *external rewards* involved when helping others – for example, no payments – people may experience *internal rewards*. Andreoni (1990) refers to a 'warm glow', explaining seemingly altruistic behavior as still being about own utility. Doing good to others is rewarded through feeling good, and what seemed to be an altruistic action is fitted to the model of individual rationality by expanding what creates individual utility. Frey (1997) makes a similar expansion of the standard model of individual rationality by referring to intrinsic motivation. The concept is borrowed from Deci (1971) and implies – in Frey's understanding – that the individual gains utility from performing the act itself.

BOX 5.1

WHAT DO EXPERIMENTS SAY ABOUT MOTIVATION AND HUMAN ACTION?

Experiments have to an increasing degree been applied in the social sciences – first in psychology, later in economics. This research documents that humans may – under certain circumstances – act in ways similar to the model of maximizing individual utility. Certainly, work like that of Slovic and Lichtenstein (1983) and Tversky and Kahneman (1986) casts some serious doubts on the human capacity to act consistently, especially when risk is involved – see also Section 5.1.6. Nevertheless, there are also many studies appearing over the years showing that people are able to act in ways that closely resemble the standard model of individual rationality – see, for example, Holt et al. (1986); Davis and Holt (1993). The choices involved are typically rather simple though, and resemble those faced in commodity markets. Moreover, Shogren (2006) offers a series of examples showing that by making the cost of 'irrational' behavior great enough people tend to act in an individually rational way.

While the above literature focuses on the capacity to maximize in individual choice situations, other experiments look at choices where other people are involved – looking at the willingness to share and cooperate. The 'ultimatum game' is one example (Güth et al., 1982). In this game, a proposer gets a sum of money, which she must divide between herself and an anonymous respondent. If the respondent accepts the split, both players get the money as divided by the proposer. If the respondent rejects the deal, the two participants get nothing. Over the years a series of studies

have been published within this area – for example, Roth et al. (1991); Hoffman et al. (1994); Blount (1995); Camerer and Thaler (1995); Henrich et al. (2001). While the individually rational thing to do would be to offer the lowest sum possible – for example, a dollar – to the respondent, Gintis (2000) sums up by concluding that most proposers make a higher offer with a 50–50 split being dominant. Moreover, respondents often turn down offers less than 30 percent.

While refusals of positive offers are difficult to explain by the standard rationality model, the proposer might act in an individually rational manner and offer more than the minimum, fearing refusals of very uneven splits. (Note, however, that s/he then assumes the respondent to be (potentially) 'irrational'.) The 'dictator game' has been developed to study this. In this setting, the respondent does not have the power to turn offers down. Proposers now reduce offers compared to the ultimatum format. Nevertheless, a large fraction of the proposers still make positive offers. The first study of this kind was made by Forsythe et al. (1994). Eighty percent of the participants in their game wanted to share. In this case, the modal offer was a split 70–30. Compared with findings from the ultimatum game, this suggests that a fraction of what is given in ultimatum games follows from the fear of refusal. As many still offer money to respondents in dictator games, this can, however, only be part of the explanation.

'Public goods games' concern a situation where a common resource is involved.

➡

Participants are typically offered a sum of money that he or she can keep or put in a common pool. For each dollar a participant puts into the pool, every participant receives a sum of money – typically 50 cents. Given this payoff, putting money into the pool pays for the group as a whole as long as there are three or more participants. It is nevertheless not individually rational to do so as each dollar is only rewarded by 50 cents to the one depositing the dollar. Despite this, quite substantial levels of cooperation are observed (Ledyard, 1995; Gintis, 2000). Biel and Thøgersen (2007) conclude after reviewing the literature, that even in one-shot public goods games 40–60 percent of participants cooperate. Ostrom (2000) shows that 30–40 percent of the participants rank the cooperative result as better than the situation that offers the most to themselves – that is, they do not prefer a situation where they themselves defect and all others cooperate. Of the participants, 25–30 percent were indifferent between these two outcomes.

Ostrom (1998) takes this position a bit further by accepting the role of socialization – that norms of a society are internalized and influence what is preferred. She expands the individual utility function with a set of so-called 'delta parameters'. A parameter of shame implies a cost – negative utility – when breaking a norm. A parameter of pride offers a benefit in the form of feeling good when following the norm. These parameters are culture specific. This way, a social construct – the norm – is understood to influence action through influencing what creates utility.

While there are merits to this explanation, there are also some issues that warrant further consideration. First, utility maximization demands that all values are in principle commensurable. A single comparative term must exist by which these values can be compared and ranked (Vatn and Bromley, 1994; O'Neill et al., 2008). It demands that it is possible to compare ordinary commodities like milk and T-shirts with guilt and guilt with pride. This is a strong assumption that cannot just be taken for granted.

Second, while introducing norms increases the capacity to explain certain behaviors, it leaves open the question of whether norms always work through changing individual utility. Certainly, guilt and pride are well-documented mechanisms. Do we, however, calculate how much guilt or pride we may encounter when making our choice? Put differently, is this kind of internal punishment or reward the way internalized norms work? In classical institutional theory, norms are seen as something that constitutes the self as well as offering meaning to various situations. Norms are images of what it means to act in a socially right or responsible way. This differs from the view of norms as constraints working through influencing the individual's calculation of utility. The aim of the next section is to develop this idea further.

5.1.4 Social rationality

An alternative way to think regarding 'internal rewards and punishments', is to emphasize that the very logic of choice – the *type* of motivation – may be of more than one kind – see, for example, Searle (2005); Hodgson (2007). Searle (2005) emphasizes deontological aspects of choice – the obligation to act in certain ways. Sen (1977) argues specifically that reducing all other-regarding preferences to a concern only for own utility is problematic. He hence distinguishes between sympathy and commitment where the former concerns selfish motivations for acting 'nicely' and the latter points towards a different logic – that of doing what is 'right' (Box 5.2).

BOX 5.2

RATIONALITY, SELFISHNESS AND DOING THE RIGHT THING

As a student of economics in the 1970s, I realized that what I found most valuable to do – for example, helping people without seeking a personal gain – had to be categorized as an irrational act according to the theory I was learning. I found this confusing, if not provocative. Alan Holland (2002) discusses the basic issues faced here. He notes that 'self-sacrifice' or acting nobly has no place in the model of standard economics. The implications of this may be huge. It defends selfishness to be the natural attitude and devalues or denies acts of other kinds. Certainly, models that expand the utility function to include intrinsic motivations may circumvent this problem – in the sense that acting other-regardingly can be accounted for. It nevertheless devalues 'noble' acts to become simply about oneself and the concept of 'self-sacrifice' is turned around and becomes no sacrifice after all.

This is fundamentally about what it means to be human. A model not allowing for true sacrifices may be seen as dehumanizing.

In relation to that, we note that feelings of pride and shame are real phenomena. One may still ask what role these feelings play for action. This is not a novel question. David Hume has already discussed this, referring to scholars at the time who understood honorable acts and friendship in terms of utility or pleasure. He noted: '[T]hey found, that every act of virtue or friendship was attended by a secret pleasure; whence they concluded, that friendship and virtue could not be disinterested. But the fallacy is obvious. The virtuous sentiment or passion produces the pleasure, and does not arise from it. I feel a pleasure in doing good to my friend, because I love him; but do not love him for the sake of that pleasure'. (Hume [1742] 1985, pp. 85–6)

In line with the latter, March and Olsen (1989, 1995) emphasize the logic of 'appropriateness'. As already mentioned in Chapter 4, they note that action is often based more on identifying the normatively appropriate behavior than on evaluating the returns expected from alternative choices. Appropriateness points toward what it is right to do in contexts where the interests of others are involved – that is, it is about what the situation 'demands' of us. In Chapter 3, we emphasized 'we' and 'they' conflicts. These conflicts demand balancing own interests against the interests of others. This demands commonly agreed rules. It does not lend itself to individual rationalization and calculations. It concerns agreeing about what the right principles are to follow in social contexts – whether of the 'we' or 'they' kind. Based on this, we acknowledge that there is not only individual or 'I' rationality. There are also rationalities pertaining to 'we' and 'they' contexts.

'We' rationality

'We' rationality concerns what is the right or appropriate thing to do for the group. In cases where choices are interdependent – for example, the use of a common-pool resource – people face the daunting task of balancing the interests of all the actors involved. These choice situations may resemble that of the prisoner's dilemma (Box 3.1) or public goods games (Box 5.1). Here cooperation gives the better result for the group as a whole, but it is not individually rational to cooperate. As an example, a fish stock may be overexploited. Reduced fishing efforts by everybody (cooperate) will increase the total net output from this fishery. The structure of the problem is, nevertheless, such that it is better for the single fisher to continue with the high fishing effort (defect) – cf. Box 3.1.

This is the classic example of 'the tragedy of the commons' (Hardin, 1968). As observed by many – for example, Bromley (1989); Ostrom (1990) – it was not a tragedy of the commons (that is, common property), but of open access. It is a situation characterized by no rules. It is exactly through forming institutions – rules about what is an appropriate use of a resource – that communities all over the globe have been able to avoid the potentially detrimental outcomes of using shared resources. Certainly, communities are not always successful. Failures are often observed (e.g., Cleaver, 2012), but to a much lesser extent than what the *standard* model of individual rationality predicts.

Rules or norms about what is proper action typically develop through communication. This is observed a great deal when communities establish rules concerning what uses are accepted, what investments are expected and how defection will be treated (e.g., Ostrom, 1990, 2005). Offering the opportunity to communicate in public goods games results in increased cooperation through making agreements about which rules to follow (Ostrom et al., 1994; Cardenas et al., 2000).

As indicated in Chapter 3, one reason for failure to cooperate in the above type of situations is related to the fact that many 'we' conflicts are asymmetric. Inequalities, asymmetric power relations, imply that (potential) gains and losses are not equally shared among participants (e.g., Benjaminsen and Lund, 2002; Cleaver, 2012). In such situations, it is more demanding to create rules that are accepted by everybody and ensure that they are followed. Another reason is related to a variation in people's willingness or inclination to cooperate. As is shown in ultimatum games (see Box 5.1), there is variation in willingness to share across participants. In public goods games typically about half the money given to participants is put into the common pool – ranging from a few giving all the money they get, to a few giving nothing, and the majority of participants lying somewhere in between. If participants are offered the opportunity to punish others, this opportunity will be utilized, and cooperation levels increase substantially (Ostrom et al., 1994; Fehr and Gächter, 2002) – see also Figure 5.1.

The research in this field shows several things. It shows that many participants choose cooperation as their first strategy in a setting with a common-pool resource. This is so despite the fact that no rules regarding sharing are specified for the 'game'. People seem to act as 'conditional cooperators', implying that they (1) see the situation as one where they should cooperate, and (2) reduce their cooperative will if others do not cooperate. Moreover, especially those inclined to cooperate are also willing to punish those not cooperating if there is an opportunity to do so. As punishing is costly for them, they face a personal loss by doing so. They are still willing to do it.

Two issues warrant further comment. Why are some willing to punish even if that actually results in a loss for that individual? Second, what are the implications of the individual variation observed? The Fehr and Gächter (2002) study is helpful in relation to answering these questions. In their experiment, people punish even if groups are reorganized between periods so that nobody meets the same people again and hence can possibly gain from punishing in earlier periods (see note to Figure 5.1). Hence, Fehr and Gächter conclude that the punishments are an example of altruism. As only others will gain from their punishment, the act is good only for the group, not themselves. Believers of the expanded model of individual

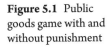**Figure 5.1** Public goods game with and without punishment

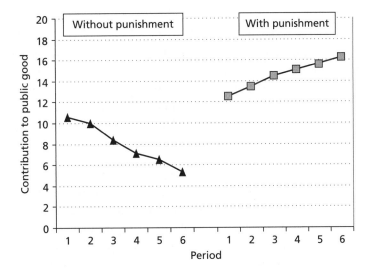

Note: A public goods game is played in groups. After each period, participants are informed about average contributions. In this case, two sets of games were organized – without punishment (WoP) and with punishment (WP). In WoP period 1, about ten units were on average contributed to the public good – this was half the money received as endowment per round. Over the six periods of WoP, contributions went down. Introducing the possibility to punish resulted in increased contributions. Typically, cooperators punished non-cooperators. Punishing was costly and could be bought by money from the endowment each got. The punishment implied reduced endowments of those not cooperating. Groups were reorganized between periods; hence, nobody met the same people again. Fehr and Gächter conclude therefore that the punishment was altruistic. Note that this may also explain why contributions go down in periods 1–6.

Source: Based on Fehr and Gächter (2002, Figure 2(b)).

rationality – that is, the model including intrinsic motivation – could argue, though, that people may punish because of intrinsic reward of punishing. One reason why I find this explanation weak is that it must imply that people feel good by hurting somebody – for example, of form of 'sadism'. It is hard to envision that this is what is going on here – see also the discussion about self-sacrifice in Box 5.2. I note, however, that we cannot (yet) disprove this explanation empirically.

Regarding implications of the individual variation observed, the experiment shows that punishment is not generally necessary to 'force' cooperation. Many will cooperate out of 'free will'. The cooperative will documented is, however, vulnerable to people acting selfishly. From the perspective of ensuring cooperation, it becomes important to form rules and have the opportunity to punish to protect cooperation against defection from people that are less inclined to cooperate.

'They' rationality

The Fehr and Gächter experiment not only illustrates aspects of 'we' rationality. It also offers indications of 'they' rationality. This form concerns what it is right to do for others – that is, acts are altruistic. It includes everyday observations of people helping somebody, even strangers. It includes individuals' reduced emissions of greenhouse gases to protect the climate for future generations and so on.

While most of us just accept such acts as altruistic, it has been notoriously difficult to prove that there is not selfishness involved. Batson and Shaw (1991) developed experiments to prove altruism defined as "a motivational state with the ultimate goal of increasing another's welfare" (p. 108). In contrast, selfishness is "a motivational state with the ultimate goal of increasing one's own welfare" (ibid.). In one of their experiments, respondents were offered different options to escape a potentially distressing situation – that is, observing somebody having to endure pain from 'electric shocks'.[2] For those becoming distressed to see this, an escape opportunity was offered, solving the problem if they were egoistically oriented. For altruistic individuals, escape would not help. The latter could avoid the problem by swapping with the person having to endure the 'shocks'. Some people chose to do so and the authors conclude that this proves existence of altruism. Sober and Wilson (1998) emphasize that economists have argued that the proof does not hold. These economists propose including internal rewards or punishments into the model – for example, shame – which redefines egoism in a way that is not refutable by the experiment.

Research on understanding altruism has not been able to produce any decisive empirical proofs regarding what is going on at the level of human motivation. Including internal rewards really renders the model untestable. It can neither be proved nor disproved through observation. It is always possible to come up with ideas about new internal rewards that may turn what is thought of as altruistic behavior into something that can be (potentially) explained through a model based on individual utility.

In this situation, some researchers have developed a conceptualization that takes into account these different understandings, distinguishing between three types of altruism – see, for example, Crowards (1997):

- selfish altruism;
- reciprocal altruism – solidarity;
- pure altruism.

The first covers 'I' rationality in the expanded form including internal rewards for 'acting nicely'. The second is parallel to the idea of 'we' rationality, while the third is another name for 'they' rationality. While all three are meaningful, differentiating between them through observation has so far proven futile – note the distinction made in Chapter 3 between the real and the empirical.

5.1.5 Habits

Habits are acquired patterns of action that typically occur automatically – see, for example, Verplanken and Aarts (1999).[3] While some behavior is reasoned, some is automated. At the same time, it is important to understand how social processes may result in automation – actually how 'collective reason' may become routine.

Not all habits have a social origin. They may be the result of individual processes. A person has at one point started to drink a glass of water first thing in the morning. Over time this type of behavior has become something he or she 'just does' without thinking about it. It has turned into a habit. At the same time, most habits are acquired in social contexts and hence he or she reflects that this is 'the way we used to do this'. The 'father' of institutional economics, Thorstein Veblen actually defined institutions as "*settled habits of thought* common to the generality of man" (Veblen, 1919, p. 239; my emphasis).

Conventions and norms of action tend to be habituated. We greet in a standard way, we greet in specific situations only; we sort waste and so on without asking if we should. However, these forms of action are the result of social construction – of reasoned action by those developing the convention and norms, but if successfully internalized appear later as habits.

One type of habit is 'rules of thumb'. According to Screpanti (1995), such rules evolve as a response to complexity. In such a situation, it is difficult to assess consequences of various acts. Hence, learning from each other may be a way to obtain better and more certain results. Screpanti therefore argues that rules of thumb are socially tested practices. They are common knowledge in practical form passed on between individuals. Farming is, as an example, a complex business. While it is impossible to assess and optimize all factors involved when producing a crop, experience is condensed into a set of rules or skills concerning 'what to do when'. This may involve issues like when to plough, how to plough, when to sow, how much to fertilize, and so on. The answer to these questions is tested ways of behavior – skills – and are passed on in the specific working environment, from generation to generation. Polanyi (1967) focuses on this issue when describing the dynamics and relevance of so-called 'tacit knowledge'.

There is a substantial debate in the literature about the relation between habituation and reasoned action – see, for example, Bourdieu (1990); Giddens (1991); Archer (2003). A core concept in this debate is that of reflexivity. If human action is habituated, is there any place for reflection – for reasoned action? If (sometimes) reasoned, when is it so and when not? No broadly accepted settlement of this question has yet been reached.[4] Rather, we have to accept that human action 'cycles' between being reasoned and automated. Understanding norms as a collective solution to a problem that individual reason cannot solve shows how difficult it is to demand individual reason as a necessary component of 'rational action'. The issue here is rather that of choosing to follow the norm or not. Sometimes we do so in an 'unreasoned' way. However, mostly we have to evaluate what norm it is now right to follow. Given the fact that there is complexity and uncertainty, it is, moreover, hard to define even habits as irrational.

5.1.6 Bounded rationality and satisficing

This brings us to the issue of bounded rationality. We previously asked: do people have the necessary information to make, for example, individually rational choices? Do they really maximize? Gathering information is often quite demanding. Figuring out what it is best to do is equally challenging. How do people go about these things? While some aspects – for example, calculating – are relevant only for situations where maximizing behavior is of interest, information gathering and evaluation of that information pertain to all theories of action presented so far.

The basic idea of bounded rationality is that the decision-maker transforms complex or intractable decision problems into tractable ones:

> One procedure. . . is to look for satisfactory choices instead of optimal ones. Another is to replace abstract global goals with tangible sub goals, whose achievement can be observed and measured. A third is to divide up the decision making task among many specialists, coordinating their work by means of a structure of communications and authority relations. (Simon, 1979, p. 501)

Of the three, satisficing is the one that has gained most attention. March (1994) concludes that satisficing implies setting a target. All solutions falling short of the target are exempted. The first solution passing it will be chosen.

It is exactly a type of 'shortcut' one would expect if information is costly to obtain and handle. Many economists interpret the writings of Simon and March as describing how actors economize on information costs. The target is a solution to the problem of optimal information search, which takes us back to the standard optimization calculus. This is not a true representation of Simon and March's position. They do not look at satisficing as a way to optimize on information handling. From their perspective, the problem humans face is caused by the costs of gathering and handling information, but satisficing is not disguised optimizing. It is something else. It is about pragmatic, tractable solutions to 'intractable' problems.

A challenge for the theory of satisficing is to define how people develop targets. While no agreed solution to that problem seems to exist, it may be a way to explain some habits or 'rules of thumb' as discussed above. However, they are not targets concerning acceptable levels of goal attainments. They are instead regularized procedures, capable of producing satisfactory results.

Hodgson (1988) makes several references to consumer behavior, documenting that only a small fraction of the purchases we make are based on deliberation over costs and qualities. Buying a car – high stakes – may be deliberate, while using it may turn into a habit. An important point here is that habits, first acquired as ways to handle complexities, later tend to become 'valuable in themselves'. Behavior, which is repeated, tends to be reinforced by its effect on how we perceive that the actual problem should be solved, transformed from one of many solutions to becoming a valuable act in itself (Box 5.3).

Habits are also important to human coordination as they make it easier to form expectations about the behavior of others. Indeed, in a complex world where information problems are pervasive and maximization unattainable, regularizing behavior is an important way to create a basis from which to form expectations. This suggests that rules of satisficing behavior, if settled in the form of habits, reduce the information and coordination problem in two ways. First, they reduce the need for information search for the decision-maker. They are given solutions to the problem. Second, by their very existence, they reduce the need for information search for other decision-makers too. Once such constructs are instituted, we know what to expect from each other.

BOX 5.3

INFORMATION, COGNITION AND INFORMATION OVERLOAD

Nørretranders (1991) offers a series of interesting observations on the understanding of consciousness. He concludes that consciousness is establishing order, or more precisely about removal of disorder in the form of information overload. While the amount of information reaching the human body is calculated to be about 11 million bits per second (!), the amount we can consciously handle is between 10 and 30 (!!), depending on skills. This implies that we need some way of sorting out what is important information – what should the conscious 'be bothered with'. As Nørretranders also contends, institutions – not least in the form of conventions – help us to handle this. Learned conventions help the unconscious to sort out what is the most important information among all those that we have been exposed to.

A personal experience illustrates the point. Many years ago, I stayed at an English university. The first day, I wanted to go from the department to the library. I was not used to left-side driving. I figured out that I should do the opposite of what I was used to in Norway – that is, walk on the right side of the road. Coming up the hill towards the library, I approached a turn. A car came towards me, and without thinking, I just jumped off the road. The car passed without anything happening. Standing there in the ditch, I felt embarrassed. Trying to reconstruct what had happened, I realized that I must have observed that the car seemed to move from the inside towards the outside when coming out of the turn. When my unconscious 'automatic screener' recognized that, it made me immediately look at the driver. Observing that she was looking down at her shoes, I jumped without thinking. Reconstructing, I realized that the car had been on the outside of the turn all the time – left-side driving. Moreover, I recognized that I had not looked at the driver, but at the passenger. . . My unconscious reactions were all predisposed to Norwegian traffic institutions. This example illustrates how the unconscious is very much 'primed' by the institutions we have learned. In England, my action seemed irrational. In Norway, it might have saved my life.

5.1.7 Summarizing theories of human action

In the above, we have described two main models of rational choice with subgroups:

1. *Individual rationality:*
   (a) maximizing individual utility – external rewards/material incentives, given preferences;
   (b) maximizing individual utility – both external and internal rewards, given preferences;

    (c)   maximizing individual utility – both external and internal rewards + socially constructed preferences and norms.
2. *Social rationality:*
    (a)   'we' rationality – solidarity; socially constructed preferences and norms;
    (b)   'they' rationality – true altruism; socially constructed preferences and norms.

Several issues have been emphasized. Do we maximize or is it about other choice rules – for example, norm following and/or satisficing? Do we think only about our own utility, or do we take the interest of others into account? If we also consider the interests of others when choosing, is it because we find that right or because even this offers individual utility? Finally, are the preferences and norms directing action a natural and given aspect of each individual or are they socially influenced?

Research clearly shows that people's preferences and norms are influenced by social processes/culture. We can conclude from this that models 1(a) and 1(b) are false. There are situations where choice is based mainly or exclusively on what is best for the individual – situations where negative implications of own actions for others are seen as non-existent or unimportant. While we are not be able to maximize – we are satisficers – there are many situations where the focus is on what is best for oneself. Regarding these situations, I find a transformed model 1(c), emphasizing satisficing instead of maximization, to be a reasonable model.

What then about situations where there are interdependencies – that is, 'we' or 'they' conflicts. It is clear that people have the capacity to take other people's interests into account. It is, however, not proven whether a model where we act on the basis of internal rewards (model 1(c)) or models emphasizing that we do what is appropriate (model 2), is best. The research community has – as of yet – not found a way to empirically distinguish indisputably between the two.

In relation to this, I note that I will use models of type 2 in the rest of the book when interpreting situations where some form of altruism is involved/where external rewards cannot explain what is observed. While model 1(c) is not empirically refuted,[5] I consider models of type 2 to be better in line with what we think is specific to being human – see also Box 5.2.

5.2 Institutions and human action

5.2.1 Institutions-as-rationality contexts

Given the above reasoning, how do people distinguish between 'I', 'we' and 'they' situations, and how do we know what to do in the different contexts? These problems cannot be solved on an individual basis simply because they demand a common understanding of what the rationality should be. We cannot individually define a common logic. It is here that institutions come in. They are developed to structure the decision environment by defining what kind of rationality should form the basis for our choices in various situations. Institutions can hence be seen as rationality contexts by signaling whether the choice situation is foremost about individual as opposed to common concerns (Vatn, 2005, 2009a). In some contexts, the institutional environment is oriented towards supporting individual rationality. In other settings, it is reinforcing social rationality. This is the basis for the institutions-as-rationality contexts theory.

We noticed earlier that in standard economics the individual is seen as 'isolated'. We have, however, already observed how the individual – his or her preferences and values – has a strong social component. Etzioni (1988) goes further and argues that to create the 'I' a 'we' is needed. He refers to research showing that people who are left alone lose their ability to act rationally also on an individual basis. Individual rationality may seem to depend on the social sphere, even at a basic level. From a more practical point of view, I note that institutions like accounting techniques, the bottom line, firms and markets, all support individual, calculative rationality.

While institutions play a key role in supporting individual rationality, they are constitutive of social rationality. Here norms play a core role defining expectations about when we should take the interest of others into account, and maybe defining in what way that should be done. In a community setting, people understand that acting selfishly is typically wrong. Hence, institutions may operate at two different levels. First, they may define which kind of rationality is expected – should I act cooperatively, should I reciprocate, may I think mainly about my own interests? Second, they may define more specific acts as expected – for example, to drive on the right side, to fish only on certain days and so on. Here the convention or norm guides the choice.

Markets tend to foster individual rationality also in the sense that social relations are largely transformed into instrumental ones. What the individual decides on is what to buy – which commodities to choose. Here issues like who has produced the commodity, under what conditions, with what environmental effects and so on, are suppressed. It does not imply that people may not be aware of such issues – consider, for example, consumer boycotts. Nevertheless, what the consumer sees in the shop is typically a commodity of a certain type with a given price. Its 'history' is typically not evident. There is nothing in the choice situation that demands that we take interests beyond our own into account. Rather, we are 'protected' against these.

Implicit in the above, few situations purely belong to one 'idealized' type of motivation. Certainly, throwing oneself into a cold river to try to rescue a stranger may be acting based on a strong 'they' norm only. Killing in self-defense may be based on pure self-interest. However, as illustrated above, even in the marketplace we may take issues beyond the 'I' into account. Acting on behalf of a community, self-interest may be involved. According to Etzioni (1988), there is always a tension between individuality and social belonging – between the individual utility on the one hand and norms and moral reasoning on the other.

In relation to this, one should also note that people are differently inclined. Some are more egoistic than others. This is well known from own life experiences, and has been scientifically documented – see also Section 5.1. The institutions-as-rationality contexts model does not hypothesize that individual action is uniform given a certain institutional context. What it says is that on average people act more selfishly in an institutional context emphasizing individual rationality than in one emphasizing social rationality. Being egoistically inclined does not imply that you are not sensitive to social demands. You just follow norms less strictly.[6]

It may be that the will to punish – recall the Fehr and Gächter (2002) experiment (Figure 5.1) – is a capacity that evolution has created to make it possible for groups to function well despite some 'hyper-individualists'. One may ask why has evolution not eliminated such traits and made all willing cooperators? One response might be that these capacities may be important for certain types of innovations, maybe also for the capacity to defend a group against external threats.

One may then ask where has the will to cooperate, share and help others come from? Ostrom (2000) reviews much of the literature on how our capacity to cooperate and learn norms may have evolved. She suggests (p. 143) that in the long period during which individuals operated in small groups as hunters and gatherers, survival was:

dependent not only on aggressively seeking individual returns but also on solving many day-to-day collective action problems. Those of our ancestors who solved these problems most effectively, and learned how to recognize who was deceitful and who was a trustworthy reciprocator, had a selective advantage over those who did not.

According to this thinking, our capacity to learn norms and follow them has been fostered by evolutionary mechanisms. The quote also indicates that individual variation could be a good thing as a population includes different capacities. Given that the future offers huge challenges concerning our capacity to cooperate – that is, environmental degradation as discussed in Chapter 2 – the question is whether our capacity to cooperate is strong enough.

5.2.2 Empirical evidence

The institutions-as-rationality contexts theory can explain how the logic of action can shift between contexts. Is it, however, empirically supported? Starting with everyday observations, most of us have probably encountered that what we could do in one context would maybe even be seen as provocative in other settings. We may shout and yell at a soccer match, but talk quietly at the dinner table. We may find it right to negotiate hard with the bank, but not with a friend. A CEO may feel obliged to act tough in negotiations with employees and sack people to fulfill the demands of the owners. Acting also as a parent, he or she may be the most caring person.

Experiments in economics and social psychology can offer further insights into this. Let me start with an experiment documented in Ross and Ward (1996). Here a public goods game was set up with two treatments including identical payoffs, meaning that the willingness to cooperate should be the same if payoffs were only what counted. Calling one treatment the 'Wall Street game' and the other the 'community game' resulted in significantly lowered willingness to cooperate – that is, payments to the common pool were lower in the 'Wall Street game'. This observation supports the institutions-as-rationality contexts hypothesis in that the cooperative will depend on the kind of institution alluded to.

An experiment by Gneezy and Rustichini (2000a) offers deeper insights into this. They performed a field experiment – an experiment in a real life situation. They utilized the fact that at many high school students collect money for charities. In the case documented, the researchers intervened in such an event at a high school in Israel. The authors write (p. 799):

Normally, the students are organized into groups according to the class in which they study, and each group is then divided into pairs of students who work together as a team. Each pair receives a certain number of coupons, which serve as receipts for the donors. The amount collected by each pair on the donation day depends mostly on the effort invested: the more houses they visit, the more money they collect.

The experiment differed from the traditional set-up in the sense that the students were divided into three clusters that were treated differently. Those under treatment 1 were informed "about the importance of the donation they were to collect, and that the society wished to motivate them to collect as much money as possible. They were told that the results of the collection would be published, so that the amount collected by each pair would become public knowledge" (ibid.). Those under treatment 2 and 3 got the same information. In the case of treatment 2 each pair was, however, told that they would themselves receive 1 percent of the money collected. The third group was told that they would get 10 percent.

The results from the experiment show that most money was collected in the standard situation – that of no economic incentive. Offering a payment of 1 percent resulted in a significant reduction. Increasing the payment resulted in a level of collected money lying between the two other treatments. The difference between 'no pay' and 10 percent pay was, however, not significant.

How to interpret this finding? The first issue to explain is why students collected any money at all when there was no payment. According to the standard model of individual rationality, they should not do so as they had to put effort into something offering nothing. A reasonable explanation is that they did this because it was an appropriate thing to do. There was a norm saying that students should act for a good cause by collecting money. Why then was there a substantial drop when a payment was offered? If the norm motivated people to collect money, shouldn't the offer of individual pay increase effort further? A reasonable understanding of this is that offering payments changed the logic from doing 'the right thing' to start thinking about 'what is best for me'. One percent pay could be seen as a lousy payment. While no payment is even more 'lousy', the lack of payment was not an issue in the 0 percent treatment. The experiment also shows a significant increase in effort from 1 percent to 10 percent payment. This supports the standard model of individual rationality. As soon as the logic is about individual gain, paying more results in increased effort. The experiment supports the institutions-as-rationality context theory, as moving to a context with payments seems to have changed the type of motivation.

Another study by Gneezy and Rustichini (2000b) regards late-coming in day-cares. Here a rather small fine to reduce tardy retrieval of children was instituted. 'Surprisingly', this actually exacerbated tardiness. The authors' prime explanation is that before the fine was installed, the parents were uncertain about which 'type' the owner was. By installing a rather low fine, it became evident that the owner was 'kind' and breaking the rule of late-coming was not so costly after all.

This explanation builds on the standard model of individual rationality, accepting that actors do not (always) have full information. Is it, however, plausible? The fact that there had been no fine on tardiness before should have proven 'kindness' beyond any doubt. An alternative explanation, also mentioned briefly by the authors, points toward the existence of a norm against late-coming. Introducing the fine shifted the logic by eroding that norm. The following steps offer a sensible interpretation: (1) a norm against late-coming allowed the day-care center to close at a fairly predictable time; (2) the norm was still not strong enough to make everybody appear before closing time (individual variation); (3) management introduced a fine for late retrievals with the expectation that the penalty would strengthen adherence to the norm; (4) the payment transformed the logic behind the interaction between parents and management into one of individual rationality.

Under the new institutional regime, parents seized the opportunity to pay to retrieve their children later than had originally been their rule. Paying may have solved problems parents faced in hectic afternoons. The fine was turned into a price for late-coming. It should finally be mentioned that when the fine was removed, late-coming was reduced, but not back to the original level. Introducing the logic of an individual incentive weakened the norm.

A study by Eek et al. (2001) shows another aspect, but of a similar kind. They asked respondents about their perception of private vs public day-cares. While private provisioning implied an expectation of treatment relative to the level of payment, public provisioning created expectations about equal treatment independent of pay (that is, payment differentiated by income). We see again that what is considered 'right' is a function of the institutional context.

There are several examples in the literature confirming that introducing payments changes 'the logic of the situation'. George Simmel (1978) made the observation that introduction of money into relationships induces people to think about each other in cost–benefit terms. In a more recent study, Vohs et al. (2006, p. 1154) conclude that results from a series of nine experiments:

suggest that money brings about a self-sufficient orientation in which people prefer to be free of dependency and dependents. Reminders of money, relative to nonmoney reminders, led to reduced requests for help and reduced helpfulness toward others. Relative to participants primed with neutral concepts, participants primed with money preferred to play alone, work alone, and put more physical distance between themselves and a new acquaintance.

5.2.3 Motivation in different institutional contexts

A way to summarize the ideas developed in this chapter would be to look more systematically at variations in types of motivations across key institutional contexts in a society. Table 5.1 exemplifies some characteristics of five such 'idealized'[7] contexts regarding the type of rationality and interaction formats involved and the way these are instituted through defining characteristic roles.

The market is an arena for trade facilitating enhancement of individual utility. While maximization is an unattainable goal, markets with their

Table 5.1 Rationality, interaction formats and roles in different institutional systems

Institutional system	Rationality and type of interaction	Roles
The market	Individual rationality Utility maximization or satisficing Trade	Consumer and producer
The firm	Individual rationality Profit maximization or satisficing Command	Employer and employees
The family	Social rationality Care taking Norms, reciprocity Communicative process	Parents and children
The political arena (the state)	Individual or social rationality Communicative process	Politicians and voters Citizens
The community (civil society)	Social rationality Norms, reciprocity Communicative process	Neighbors, friends, members of civil society organizations, working collectives

Source: Based on Vatn (2005).

various institutions make it easier to approximate the ideal. The institution of money is one example. In real markets, information problems are pervasive, resulting not least in rules to counteract cheating, false advertisement, insider trading and the like. Common norms of good business practices have therefore become important, showing that even in institutional contexts fostering individuality, norms/social control are important.

The firm in its type form is also constructed to facilitate maximization – in this case of profits. The firm is instituted around command, not trade. While many institutions are created to support decisions in firms, the goal of maximization is unattainable even in this case. Its environment is uncertain. In this context, growth/increase in market shares is a typical goal to increase external control and capacity to handle shocks/survive. Regarding internal control problems, individual incentives – 'carrots and sticks' – may be used. We may also observe normative 'measures' to build workers' identification with the goal of the firm. Therefore, even here a wider perspective on rationality than the instrumental logic of profit maximization may come into play.

Moving to the family, the 'type' logic is different. While some seem to view even this entity merely as an arena for trade – for example, Becker (1976) – the existence of concepts like love and care makes most people realize that there is more to this story. The role of parents is not least that of raising children and creating durable relationships. Certainly, gender issues remain high in debates about family structures, and in many cultures patriarchal domination is very visible. Perversions regarding child care are also observed – for example, heavy control, even abuse. It is, however, through the definition of what a perversion is that a society confirms what the specific rationality of an arena is or should be.

Turning to the political arena, it can resemble both categories of rationality. We observe political arenas governed dominantly by individual or interest competition (pure political games) to situations dominated by social rationality and communicative processes. Hence, which logic is fostered – instituted – varies across cultures. Politics is about taking sides – about defining which interests or values should thrive. At the same time, with no limits regarding what it is acceptable to do when fighting for certain interests, political processes could easily erode into 'war'. Therefore, the institutional structures specifying which acts are acceptable and which are not, are key to defining this arena. Many 'policy failures' observed around the globe follow from either weak insights into these issues, and/or lack of institutional capacity to do anything about it.

Civil society may be seen as the 'bed rock' of institutionalization. It is here that normative collectives are formed and thrive. While many value issues and conflicts are 'fought out' in the political arena, the legitimacy of the political process comes from its acceptance by civil society. Communities are networks of social relations. They are, however, more than this. They are the arenas where the cultural or common basis for any interaction – be it 'economic' or 'political' – are formed. Without this embeddedness – see, for example, Polanyi ([1944] 1957); Zukin and DiMaggio (1990); Dequech (2003) – there will no shared common understanding for interaction – in whatever form.

Certainly, civil society or community cultures vary. Hence, we observe variation across states regarding what is allowed to be treated as an economic problem and what rules exist for holding 'political office'. When civil society is weak, the political arena may degenerate into pure nepotism. Even in what are normally called well-functioning democracies there is great variation concerning what measures are allowed in, for example, election campaigns. It is especially interesting to see to what degree the 'market mechanism' is allowed to intrude into the political arena. In some societies, individual grants or grants from firms or organizations are accepted without limits to fund election campaigns. Other societies consider this a bribe. In some societies, political advertisements dominate elections, while in others the focus is more on debate and the testing of arguments.

It is in the political arena that decisions are made regarding which interests should be formally protected by the collective. Certainly, this creates a difficult balancing between the 'common' interest and the interests of specific groups. I will address this issue in Chapters 6 and 7. Here we shall just make the point that the way we manage to institute the political sphere will influence what is acceptable behavior and define what is allowed or legitimate regarding the priority of own interests, the interests of specific groups and the polity more at large. March and Olsen (1995) emphasize that governance takes place not least by the creation of what is appropriate through forming the role of an public official.

We have noted that people may act reciprocally or morally in markets and others selfishly in social arenas. If this is the case, there seems to be no clear relationship between behavior and the type of arena. First, the argument is not that institutions determine completely the rationality of action. The individual cannot be reduced just to structure. There is always an important element of individual choice and adaptation, and different individuals follow norms to a different extent. That is why I talk of 'types' of interactions.

Following the ideas underpinning critical realism, we may talk only of potentials as opposed to 'law-like' relations.

Second, we have already seen that markets are also dependent on a set of norms to function well. The various scandals in corporate businesses over the last years and the reactions to these serve as good examples. Third, norms are not just 'out there'. They become internalized. Through that process, they become part of the individual's character. This implies that they not only vary between arenas, but they also vary between individuals due to different upbringing and individual capacities. Some act more 'citizen like' in any arena, while others are more individualistic.

Societies must decide what institutional arena is best suited for treating which issue. Some goods are explicitly kept outside of the marketplace. Walzer (1983) talks about spheres of blocked exchange. In general this has to do with (how we perceive) the character of the goods. If only exchange value is perceived to be of relevance to us, trade will dominate. If other dimensions are of importance, it becomes rational to establish spheres based on a different logic.

Health care is a good example of the various issues involved here. Concerning this good or service, we observe very different solutions both across societies and across various dimensions of health. The basic question here is whether good health is a right for everybody or not – that is, whether the allocation of health care services should be governed by markets or by public rationing. Other areas where trade is restricted or not allowed concern personal integrity/the human being itself, education, retirement schemes, public offices, criminal justice, freedom of speech, friendship, human body parts and so on. Walzer (1983) lists altogether 14 spheres from which the logic of exchange is exempted either totally or to some degree.

As already indicated, the fundamental logic of an institutional system as described in Table 5.1 may be perverted. Walzer discusses the implication of this. He concludes that such occurrences do not violate the existence of various spheres. Rather, they are strong proof for the existence of different rationalities: "Dishonesty is always a useful guide to the existence of moral standards. When people sneak across the boundary of the sphere of money, they advertise the existence of the boundary. It's there, roughly at the point where they begin to hide and dissemble" (ibid., p. 98).

As already noted, some people are generally more caring than others. They also may be considerate in contexts where the expected logic is to compete. Others may be quite self-expressive even in situations where the fundamental logic is care. At the same time, we also build identity through our ability to move between rationalities. It is not that people that are sensitive to the distinction between 'I' and 'we' are seen as incoherent or psychologically unstable. Rather, it is those who are insensitive in these matters that are seen as 'abnormal'.

5.3 Main messages

The main message of this chapter is the existence of different forms of rationality. One fundamental observation is the need for protecting our own interests. At the same time, humans live in communities, requiring that we find ways to handle our relations to others. Regarding the topic of this book, we finally note that the physical environment 'forces' interdependencies upon us. Hence, a key issue regards how the interests of the individual, the group and the others are treated.

On the basis of this, I have defined two core types of rationality – that of individual and that of social rationality. The former concerns what is best for the individual. The latter may be divided into two sub-groups. First, there is 'we' rationality, regarding what is the better for the group one belongs to. Second, we have 'they' rationality regarding what it is right to do towards the other(s). Human capacities are limited. Hence, there is 'boundedness' to most actions. However, that is a different issue from observing that actions are oriented towards the interests of the individual, the group or the other(s).

While the individual has learned to observe these three levels – note this structure as fundamental to our language – it is not possible for an individual to sort out when to think in, for example, 'I' vs 'we' terms. Institutions as collectively defined rules and practices are helpful in specifying what kind of rationality is expected. They may, however, do more by defining in concrete terms what one is expected to do in specific contexts. Some norms are almost universal – defining what it means to be a 'good human' – while others are very context specific. The various roles we 'play' are examples of sets of norms defining relationships to members of the specific group(s) we are part of. As a species, we seem to have developed a distinct capacity to move between roles, in the same way as we are able to switch between languages.

The observations made in this chapter are of great importance to the issues we shall later raise regarding which type of institutions should be established for making choices about the environment. This concerns which type of rationality we find reasonable to institute for these kinds of issues. Some may argue that individual preferences and market transactions should govern both the formulation of goals and the choice of environmental actions. Others may favor institutional structures built around social rationality, norm building and common decision-making. The rest of the book will, to a large extent, be about evaluating the arguments behind these positions.

NOTES

1   In the literature we find a distinction between authors systematically referring to 'action' (e.g., in sociology) as opposed to those referring to 'behavior' (e.g., in economics and much of psychology). Here I will use the concepts synonymously.

2   Actually, the people did not face electric shocks. They were asked to act as if they received these. The respondents were not informed about the fake.

3   Their precise definition is: "learned sequences of acts that have become automatic responses to specific cues, and are functional in obtaining certain goals or end states" (Verplanken and Aarts, 1999, p. 104).

4   See Elder-Vass (2007) for a discussion of the problems faced here and an interesting sketch of a possible solution.

5   Note that Sober and Wilson (1998) argue that models of type 2 are better than models like 1(b) and 1(c) as they are simpler and would have a greater chance to survive evolutionary forces. In model 2, altruism works directly – as a force in and of itself. In models 1(b) and 1(c), it works via the utility function, the feeling of guilt and so on. Hence, in the latter case there are two steps and the chance of 'failures' might increase. I note the argument, but do not consider it a final proof.

6   Certainly, some people are not sensitive to norms. This kind of behavior is actually seen as abnormal. Similarly, people that are 'super social' – putting the interests of others before themselves – may also be seen as maladjusted.

7   I refer to the Weberian concept of 'ideal types'. This is a categorization meant to capture key characteristics of a phenomenon – that is, elements common to most cases of the defined category.

Part Three

The theory of environmental governance

In Part One we looked at what characterizes environmental resources and processes, including an assessment of the state of the world's environments. We looked at what these characteristics imply for humans that live in these environments, and analyzed how human action impacts on the quality of various ecosystems. We also emphasized the conflicts involved and how we could develop institutions to ensure future environments that are good to live in. In Part Two, we expanded on these aspects by deepening our understanding of institutions and human action, and the relation between the two. A key point was that institutions influence action not only through acting as constraints, but more importantly by influencing our perceptions, interests and types of motivation.

The next step involves looking at the theory of environmental governance as forming institutions and hence influencing action. In Chapter 6, I present a framework for analyzing environmental governance systems. In Chapter 7, I discuss criteria for evaluating governance structures and present perspectives on institutional change, drawing on insights from previous chapters. Part Three builds a platform for the preceding parts, where more focus is on what present governance structures look like in practice and how successful they have been in maintaining our physical environments.

6

A framework for analyzing environmental governance systems

The aim of this chapter is to develop a framework that can form the basis for analyzing environmental governance. In that respect it has been essential to form a framework that can foster interdisciplinary research. The chapter is divided into four main parts. First, I look at the concept of governance and its meaning. The following three sections build the framework step by step – that is, one section on resource regimes, one on governance structures and finally one presenting the full framework for the study of environmental governance systems.

6.1 Perspectives on governance

The concept of governance refers to 'steering'. Hence, there is an element of authority involved. Moreover, it encompasses both processes and structures. The process element refers to the shaping of priorities, how conflicts are acknowledged and possibly resolved, and how the coordination of people's actions regarding resource use is facilitated. The structural aspect refers to how these processes are organized and 'administered'. Governance demands some durability in both processes and structures.

Shaping priorities – formulating goals – pertains to all spheres of a society – social, political and economic. It refers, moreover, to all levels from the global to the local. Hence, we may talk of global governance when referring, for example, to the liberalization of trade and the development of global environmental agreements. Governance takes place at national levels through decision-making in parliaments, governments and ministries. Local government and a host of private and community-based organizations are also engaged in governing various resources. Governance encompasses steering of both public and private activities.

Coordination is a core aspect of governance. It concerns coordinating actions within and between different sectors of public administration as well as between such administrations and the private sector. Coordination can happen in various ways – in markets, by political bodies regulating private activities, and through cooperation such as partnerships between public agencies, firms and civil society actors.

Environmental governance refers to use, management and protection of environmental resources and processes. That is typically a conflictual issue. Hence, governance is also about taking sides or developing compromises. Who should get access to resources; whose interests should be protected? This may involve conflicts between a mining company and local herders; between hydropower companies and displaced local communities; that of using land for farming vs building activities or nature protection.

The processes mentioned above happen within structures. These refer both to actor constellations and to decision-making procedures. As already made clear, governance is more than government. It encompasses actors like firms and non-governmental organizations.[1] The processes undertaken within and between actors and actor networks will typically follow a certain set of procedures. The degree of formalization of these varies tremendously, with procedures within state administrations typically being the most rigorous and those in network structures being more variable.

From the above, we can conclude that governance is a complex concept – it covers a large variety of actors, objectives and forms of interaction. Attempting to simplify this complexity, I begin by explaining and exploring the concept of resource regimes.

6.2 Resource regimes

The concept of a resource regime is reserved here for institutions governing use and protection of environmental resources and processes. Two sets of institutions are key: (1) the rules concerning *access* to environmental resources; (2) the rules concerning the *interactions* within and between actors having access to such resources as well as being influenced by decisions regarding them.

The first set of rules covers property and use rights, including state and customary law, as well as relevant norms and conventions. The second element – the interaction rules – consists of rules regarding coordination with respect to the use of resources and the products produced thereof. Note that what is produced may be both goods/services and side-effects like pollution. Hence, the rules regulating the 'transfer' of side-effects of production are also included. Note that no productive or consumptive activity can avoid side-effects – see, for example, Baumgärtner (2000) – and it is therefore important to also consider this aspect when defining the concept of a resource regime.

6.2.1 Property and use rights

Property and use rights define 'access' to benefit streams from a resource. One may distinguish between different aspects of this. Schlager and Ostrom (1992, pp. 250–51) emphasize rights to access, to withdrawal, to management, to exclusion and to alienation:

- *access:* the right to enter a defined physical property;
- *withdrawal:* the right to obtain the 'products' of a resource (e.g., catch fish, appropriate water, etc.);
- *management:* the right to regulate internal use patterns and transform the resource by making improvements;
- *exclusion:* the right to determine who will have an access right, and how that right may be transferred;
- *alienation:* the right to sell or lease either or both of the above rights.[2]

The above definition of access is narrow, as it covers only the right to physically enter a place. Earlier in this chapter I used the concept with reference to its wider meaning. I would also like to add that an alienation right is thought by many to also include the right to consume or destroy the resource itself. This is termed a right to the capital – see, for example, Honoré (1961).

The combination of rights as defined specifies the position of various actors in relation to the resource. Hence, Schlager and Ostrom (1992) characterize an (authorized) user as one that has the right to access and withdrawal. I will also include right to manage as part of the definition of being a user. An owner holds all five rights.[3] Property respective use rights may, moreover, be individual, public or common.

Types of property

Delving deeper into the role of rights regarding resources, I will start by looking at the different types of property rights. Again, I find it helpful to think in terms of ideal types. It is standard to divide these rights into four groups – see also Bromley (1991, 2006):

- private property;
- common property;
- state (public) property;
- open access.

These are legal rules implying that a third party – a common authority – guarantees the right of the property owner to certain benefit streams. In this sense, a property right is a relation between the rights-holders and the rights-regarders as defined and supported by a specific authority structure. The third party may be a state. It may also be a 'traditional' authority. Hence, we divide between state law and customary law.

While the rights-holder in the case of *private property* is normally thought of as an individual, *common property* is likewise private property for a group of co-owners (Bromley, 1991). In the case of a *state property* regime, the ownership is in the hands of the state. Principally, ownership at lower public levels like the county or the municipality level is of the same form and by changing the label from state to public property, it is explicitly covered by this category. Finally, *open access* is a situation where there is no property.

If we look at a specific piece of land like a forest, it can be privately owned. This means that it is owned by a private person like a farmer or a private corporation as in the case of a forest company. This grants the individual or the firm certain rights and obligations regarding the use of the forest resources. It can also be owned by a specified group of inhabitants. It is common property. In this case, one will observe two kinds of rules: (1) those defining who are members of the commons, and (2) those defining the rights to use various resources involved – that is, which benefit streams can be utilized, by which members, to which degree and maybe also by which means.

The forest may also be owned by the state. This implies that while the resources are in principle owned by all persons having state membership, state-authorized representatives make decisions concerning resource use. Finally, open access implies that whoever wants to use a benefit stream from the forest may do so. A privilege exists for everybody. Certainly, open access is 'what was there in the beginning'. Transforming the relations into one of the three other property regimes could be motivated in two different ways of interest to us. First, it could be prompted by the wish of certain individuals or collectives to get exclusive access to a benefit stream. This is the distributional aspect. Second, it may be important to regulate the use of the resources – to avoid overuse or to regulate side-effects of different uses – to avoid the 'tragedy of open access'.

Property rights are complex

Private property may take several different forms. A piece of land may be owned by an individual, or it may be owned by several people. It is the form of that co-ownership that defines if it is individual or common property. In the case of individual property, individuals own shares – as in a joint-stock company. The owner can sell her or his share(s) without consulting other shareholders in the company. In the case of common property, individuals may use and manage the resource according to common rules, while the right to sell is with the group – not each individual owner or member.

State property looks like common property in the sense that no individual shares can be distinguished. There are, however, some clear distinctions. State or public property will normally be multi-objective – that is, concern a wide variety of benefit streams/capital. We observe that the public may run schools, hospitals, manage forests, infrastructure and so on. Common property is typically narrower in focus as it normally concerns only specific sets of benefit streams – for example, access to a common pasture or a specific forest.

An interesting case here is indigenous people's execution of common property rights to land and to specific resources like fish, game and pastures situated within a state dominated by another nationality. This ethnic group may have its own authority structures to grant, regulate and control the rights to the commons. In such cases we typically observe conflicts between the majority and minority nations regarding who owns the land itself – that is, whether the perceived property right by the indigenous people is only seen as a use right by the state (Hahn, 2000; Riseth and Vatn, 2009). Bolivia is a rather special case with formal acknowledgment of indigenous nations' rights, creating equality between indigenous and state jurisdictions. McNeish and Böhrt (2013, p. 202) conclude that "in this way transference has been made from a singular judicial system to a 'formal plural and equal judicial' system".[4]

Different types of third party

The above discussion about different types of property rights refers to a situation in which the (property) right is established under the authority of a state. Following Weber ([1922] 1958), it is, moreover, 'rationally legal'. This conceptualization points towards the fact that with modern state building follows a distinct definition of what legitimate authority is. It is territorial and built on certain principles regarding how power is granted to this third party. It does not necessarily demand democratic rule, while the claim that state power is only legitimate if based on democratic elections has been vastly expanded throughout the globe over the last 100 years.

There is, however, also customary law and customary rights. Here the authority – the third party – is 'traditional'. It is normally associated with tribal, but also monarchic authority. It refers to positions that are typically inherited. Hence, the basis for its legitimacy is different from that of a state where elections form the basis for granting third party power. The law may, moreover, not be written. Note that while the distinction between law and norms is sometimes based on whether the rule is written or not, I draw the distinction of whether there is a third party or not. It is notable that oral law is easier to 'change' than written law and may be continuously adapted. Third-level authority may also sometimes be unclear and customary law may sometimes look more like a norm or convention. Regarding the functioning of a third party role, there is clear difference between a parliament/modern court system and tribal leadership.

The above reflects the fact that institutions and authority have developed over time into new forms. The logic underlying modern democracies is different from other forms. This not only implies that authority can have many sources. It also means that different sources of authority may exist concurrently. To define what is legal or not in such a complex landscape is difficult and creates confusion regarding where to draw the line between what in this book are termed legal rules and norms; see, for example, Moore (2001); Tamanaha (2008).

In relation to the above, I want to emphasize three issues regarding the concepts used in the complex context of rights, formal and informal regulations:

- First, we have the distinction between the *de jure* and the *de facto* rights. The former stands for the legal – hence, the formal – definition of the right. The latter stands for the 'right in practice'. There may be a difference between the two, as the way 'things are done' may deviate from what the law defines. This may be the case even if the capacity to enforce the law is strong. We may talk about 'sleeping paragraphs'.
- Second, we have the concept of *legal pluralism*. Here different legal systems have competing solutions to the same problem. This may be because a law regulating, for example, landowners' rights to the capital may be in conflict with parts of environmental law. The property law grants such a right, while the environmental law defines certain resources as inalienable. This situation will typically result in conflicts over which

law has primacy. It may also result in struggles regarding whether compensation for lost property should be awarded. Another field of specific importance to us is the overlap and conflict between state and customary law, as found in many countries in the South. This may both reflect references to competing third parties as well as competing claims to resources. When countries in the South gained freedom in the period after World War II, the legal system established by colonial powers was often continued and conflicts between formal state ownership and customary rights still endure. Both kinds of legal pluralism are widespread (e.g., Merry, 1988; Tamanaha, 2008).

- Third, while the distinction between legal rules and norms may sometimes be difficult to draw – what is rightly defined as third vs second party control – the functioning of the law is difficult to envision if not supported by norms and conventions. One thing is that there is a general norm that the law should be accepted. Another is that a law cannot regulate all possible situations, and it will in practice have to be embedded in a wider set of norms and conventions to make it work. The difference lies in the kind of power that operates – the difference between 'power of the practical' (conventions), 'the power of appropriateness' (norms) and that of 'coercion' (legal rules).

All the above elements are crucial when studying property and use rights' systems. One has to understand the source of authority, the possible overlap between institutional systems – whether they are competing or reinforcing – and the underlying interest constellations that are key to comprehending the overall dynamics. In relation to that, it is important to observe how actors may move between competing rules – 'forum shopping' – and how rules may be 'bent and stretched'. To some extent it is 'functional' that rules are somewhat flexible – for example, rules regarding access to water that may have to cover situations of ample supply as well as periods of (severe) shortage. Cleaver (2012) shows how such flexibility is important, but may also be 'vulnerable' to the exercise of discretionary power and sometimes even outright manipulation for supporting certain individual interests.

6.2.2 Interaction rules

Our lives are formed through interaction. We engage with others directly through communication, cooperation and coordination, but also through competition. It is part of being social, of living in communities. It is also a consequence of the division of labor. We finally interact indirectly through side-effects of action – for example, pollution following from production and consumption.

There are several forms of interaction. Many are rule based. The following four types cover the most important given our purpose:

- trade;
- command;
- community rules;
- no rules.

When *trading*, goods and services are exchanged most typically against a payment. It is a voluntary form of exchange and in its 'ideal form' thought of as impersonal interaction.[5] What matters are the price, quantity and quality of the good or service. The power one can exert in this form of interaction depends primarily on one's wealth. Hence, while parties to a trade are formally equal, they may be unequal with respect to their actual purchasing power. We find trade mainly in markets and it is the dominant way to exchange commodities. It may, however, be used internally in organizations too. The so-called 'New Public Management' approach includes a variant of 'trade' in which services are sometimes sold between departments of the same public agency or between public agencies – see, for example, Sørensen and Torfing (2007). This stands in contrast to basing transfers to such agencies purely on budgetary – that is, command-based – procedures. We should finally note that the basis for trade is ownership of what is (to be) traded.

Command is founded on hierarchical power. This power can be used both within ('we') and between ('they') actors. Regarding command 'within', we observe that firms as well as public administrations are based on command (Williamson, 1975). Certainly, there is typically a contract – a trade – at the basis of being hired by a firm or a public body. Nevertheless, as employees of these organizations, the ultimate power to decide on the use of resources lies in the line of command. Note that the execution of such power may not be visible as direct force. It may be defined as appropriate behavior since creating a productive work environment may depend on offering autonomy to employers and a cooperative atmosphere. Hence, we may observe systems that resemble community rules. However, if somebody's activity is not in line with the goals of the firm or agency, the power of command will typically be used.

In the case of command 'between' actors – that is, one actor commanding another – we refer to third party authority – typically the state. This kind of power is used to form and protect property rights. It is also used to create structures for public funding and payments – taxes and subsidies – and is the type of interaction format relied upon when public standards are set concerning prescribed product quality and when rights and responsibilities for, for example, pollution are defined.

Moving next to *community-based interaction* rules, these are oriented at strengthening relations between individuals or groups. Cooperation is a key element. Relations are typically informal, and to a large extent based on norms, including rules of reciprocity. Community-based rules are characteristic responses to everyday challenges with respect to how people living together may treat each other as they go about organizing their activities.

Such interaction rules are observed within ('we') and between ('they') communities. Regarding rules 'within', we discern informal structures like neighborhoods and friendships, but also some formalized ones like families, villages, common properties and civil society organizations. Families include both command and norms/reciprocity – with rules varying considerably across cultures. The same goes for villages and common properties. Using the village as an example, we first perceive the village as an organized community with interaction rules based on command – for example, village assemblies, councils and chairs. Second, we perceive the village as a place where people cooperate, but also confront each other based on norms about what are acceptable actions.

Regarding community-based rules, which regulate relationships 'between' communities, norms of reciprocity are again a dominant form across cultures. Strengthening relations seems key. According to Bauman (1993), reciprocity can be seen as a non-immediate transaction, as in the form of gifts (Mauss [1925] 1965). The giving is done without calculating or discussing any immediate reward, as in the case of trade. Nevertheless, Bauman (1993, p. 57) writes:

> [I]n the long run, however, one expects gifts to be reciprocated, and in quantities judged to be needed to maintain parity. The readiness of gift-giving is not likely to survive indefinitely unless this expectation comes true. Unlike the case of the business transaction, profit is not the motive of the gift; more often than not it is benevolence that triggers the action. More importantly yet, gift-giving is not an episodic, not a self-contained act. On the contrary, it makes sense – as Claude Levi- Strauss has shown elaborating on Marcel Mauss's idea of *le don* – when seen as a tool of establishing stable and peaceful relationship between otherwise mutually isolated and/or hostile persons or groups.

It is notable that in the case of common property, we frequently observe rules that are more formalized than what pertains to standard reciprocity.

While these rules rest typically in decisions made by the members of the commons and the logic of reciprocity is often important, the format of the interaction will often take the form of command. This regards the definition of membership of the commons, as well as rules regarding withdrawal and management – see, for example, Ostrom (1990). The same also goes for the system of enforcement, which is often much more sensitive to social circumstances than typically found in state-based systems. Hence, there seems to be an element of care involved.

Finally, a fourth option is *no rules*. This implies that there are no commonly defined ways to interact. Hence, people are free to do whatever they wish, despite consequences for others. Side-effects like pollution are important given the focus of the present book, and we note that they typically begin as unregulated – as not in need of any specified interaction rules. This is partly so, since 'in the beginning' no harm was observed. Emissions were maybe small and were taken 'care of' by the self-cleaning capacity of the environment. The causal link between emissions and degradation may, moreover, be difficult to prove. Over time, problems become visible, and causes are defined. Then a fight over who has the right – that is, if the polluters may continue their practices or victims have the right to a clean environment – may appear. Nothing may be done, implying that 'no rules' pertain and rights are 'implicitly' given to polluters. No rule is also a rule.

6.2.3   Idealized resource regimes

Combining the four types of property rights and four main forms of interaction rules, we get 16 ideal-type *resource regimes* – Table 6.1. Note that here I only focus on interaction between and not within involved actors. Defined as types, the structure does not cover variations in detail or possible overlaps. Nevertheless, it offers a sufficiently rich structure to form a basis for analytical purposes.

All combinations in the table are observed in practice, while those represented by the cells on the diagonal tend to dominate.[6] Side-effects like pollution initially fall under the 'open access'/'no rules' category. Environmental governance can be seen as a way to change the resource regime to regulate this kind of 'unnoticed' cost shifting. There are interest conflicts related to whether and in which way property rights and interaction rules should be reformulated to handle side-effects.

The concept of a regime has different meanings throughout the literature. The definition of a resource regime as developed here differs from

Table 6.1 Idealized resource regimes

Type of interaction \ Type of property/use right	Private property/ use rights	State/ public property/ use rights	Common property/ use rights	Open access
Trade				
Command				
Community rules – cooperation, reciprocity				
No rules defined				

many other uses. Some conceptualizations of regimes include actors, resources, institutions and technologies – for example, the 'water regime' or the 'car regime' (Holtz et al., 2008; Marletto, 2010). In the literature on international agreements, the concept of an international regime is defined as a set of norms, formal rules and decision-making procedures created to regulate and coordinate action between states – that is, political bodies (e.g., Chasek et al., 2014). In the language of this book, actors like political bodies belong to the next level of concepts – that of the governance structure.

6.3 Governance structure

6.3.1 Actors and institutions

Moving to the concept of governance structure implies including actors. They can principally be divided into three groups: (a) those owning/ using productive resources – economic actors, (b) those having the power to define property/use rights and interaction rules – political actors, and (c) those ensuring democratic legitimacy of political action – civil society actors. Including actors at these levels implies that we also need to add a new set of institutions: the (formal and informal) rules and practices defining the policy process and interactions in the sphere of civil society. Based on this, a governance structure consists of the following:

1. *Actors – with their goals/motivations, capacities, rights and responsibilities:*
   (a) economic actors holding rights to productive resources;
   (b) political actors defining the resource regimes and the rules for the political process;
   (c) civil society actors that offer legitimacy to political actors and define the normative basis for the society.

2. *Institutions facilitating interaction:*
    (a) the resource regime: the rules governing the economic process: (i) rights to resources and (ii) rules of interaction;
    (b) the rules governing the political process (constitutional and collective-choice rules);
    (c) the institutions of civil society.

Note that the same person may be an economic and political actor, as well as participating in civil society. We talk here of roles. Economic actors may be private, state or community based. Regarding political actors, we may distinguish between local actors, actors at state and international level. Civil society organizations encompass non-governmental organizations (NGOs). We may define civil society as the arena for creating the normative basis of a society and civil society actors as the set of actors expressing the interests and will of citizens.

Looking at the institutions facilitating interaction – the interaction rules – we have already described key formats concerning the economic process. There are, however, also different forms of interactions in the political and civil society arenas. In the political arena, interaction rules form relationships between political bodies themselves and between these bodies and their constituencies – civil society. The rules governing the political processes are constitutional and collective-choice rules. Constitutional rules determine, for example, the bodies of political decision-making and who are eligible to participate in political decision-making. Collective-choice rules are rules that define the specific procedures of collective decision-making. Figure 6.1 summarizes.

Figure 6.1 The governance structure

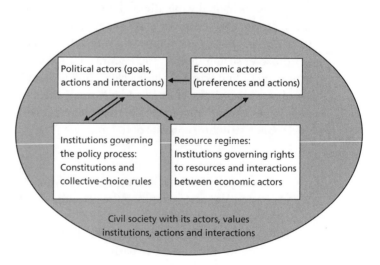

According to the figure, economic and political actors and institutions are *embedded* within civil society, implying that there are multiple channels and ways of influence.

In the following, I will expand the description of the main groups of actors and the institutions governing political and civil society processes. It is important to emphasize again that I focus on main *types*, while I also illustrate some key variations within each group of actors. The motivation is to characterize key features of each actor type to facilitate an analysis of actions and interaction regarding environmental governance.

6.3.2 Economic actors

Economic actors may be grouped as producers and consumers. In more subsistence-oriented economies, production and consumption units may be the same – for example, the household. Here, I will look mainly at what motivates the actions of these actors. I will put most emphasis on producers. Production based on private property is organized as firms or is household based. Firms may be grounded on sole proprietorship or various forms of joint ownership such as a stock-holding company – for example, the corporation. Regarding goals/motivations, firms are typically constructed to serve the interests of their owners in the form of maximizing profits and accumulating capital.

The situation may be different among smaller firms or units of household-based production. The family farm is typically envisioned as a unit maximizing the utility of the family rather than profits since it is a combined unit for both production and consumption – see, for example, Nakajima (1986). Issues regarding lifestyle and appropriateness of the production modes are also seen as important (e.g., Burton, 2004; Defrancesco et al., 2008; Kvakkestad et al., 2015). While household-based production outnumbers corporations vastly, the latter dominate globally with respect to the volume of commodity production.

Regarding production based on state or public property, some may be organized as firms, others as public management. If the state operates a hydroelectric power plant, manages a forest or runs the railways, it may be organized largely as a private firm. A difference from a private firm may, however, be observed in that the goal might encompass wider elements than profit-making. This is often the reason for keeping some resources that otherwise could be privatized under public governance. What might become a side-effect or 'negative externality' under the rule of private property, may be 'internalized' in the case of public ownership by defining a wider set of goals.

The state is also engaged in delivering public goods by establishing national parks, running public schools, public health care systems and so on, and facilitating individual resource use such as building and maintaining infrastructures. In these cases, the logic instituted is that of public management. All income may come from budget allocations and is hence based on taxes.

Production based on common property typically involves households sharing the responsibility for managing a pasture, a forest, or an irrigation system, among others. Common property organizations focus on balancing the common interest to the interests of the individuals/households involved. The products produced typically belong to the households. They normally also own the 'means' to utilize the common resource – for example, animals, tools and so on – and in that sense the goals may resemble that of household-based production more in general. The responsibility for the common resource may create social cohesion necessary for good results regarding managing this resource (Ostrom, 1990, 2005; Platteau, 2000). As pointed out by Baland and Platteau (1996), common property is, however, not 'inherently conservationist'. Population pressure may, as an example, force degradation. At the same time, these authors emphasize that it is not the regime per se that causes problems, rather its erosion. At the same time, common properties are not necessarily fair. Power asymmetries may exist and create substantial variations in access to resources internally in the commons – see, for example, Cleaver (2012).

Production based on common property is typically less expansive than production under pure private property – especially the corporate forms. Its aim is not to grow, as the focus is on the management of the productive capacity of a common resource. This is an effect of the aims instituted, of the way ownership is organized, but also the type of resources typically involved – for example, forests, pastures and fish. Common property organizations may be involved in increasing production – fish cultivation and irrigation facilities are typical examples. What it does not facilitate is turning capital into other uses – a dominant aspect of the corporate dynamics.

A special form of common property is the cooperative. Again, there is common ownership based on rules as defined above for common property organizations. Typically, the name 'cooperative' is used for co-ownership of human-made capital, while the term 'common property' is dominantly used for co-ownership in natural resources.[7] Hence, cooperatives exist as both consumer and producer cooperatives. A typical example of the latter is processing agricultural produce. It is, however, also a growing form used in decentralized production of energy.

Given the increasing importance of specialized production for sale implicit in the growth of the firm – not least corporate production – an implication is the 'creation' of the 'specialized' consumer. Economic theory assumes that production choices are directed by the consumers and their (given) preferences. As discussed in Chapter 5, their preferences may be molded by production interests. The creation of the consumer and the institutional dynamics of growth, welfare and consumption will be discussed further in Chapter 9.

6.3.3 Political actors

Regarding political actors, I find it reasonable to cover two 'types'. First, there are public authorities of which the state is the most prominent. Next are international organizations based on national governments – that is, international governmental organizations (IGOs).

Public authorities

A public authority has the power to decide in matters involving constitutional and collective-choice rules in a society, implying the power to formulate resource regimes and act as a third party regarding conflicts appearing between, for example, economic actors. The most developed public authority is the state. However, a village council, a municipal council, a clan leader may possess some of the same capacities. Here I will concentrate on the state, its role and powers as a public body and third-level authority.

According to Weber ([1921] 1946, p. 77; original emphasis) "a state is a human community that (successfully) claims the *monopoly of the legitimate use of physical force* within a given territory". He notes that this kind of force is not the only means of a state, but it is specific to it. Ideally, the modern or democratic state is seen as an organization to support the interests of its constituencies.

Democracy is one of many forms of political governance. Some countries are governed by different systems. Regarding democracy, the form and 'depth' varies substantially across countries. Hence, specifying what defines a democracy is difficult. March and Olsen (1995, p. 2) state:

> Democracy is a culture, a faith and an ethos that develop through interpretation, practice, wars and revolutions. It discovers new meanings and new possibilities in new experiences and ideologies. As a result, democratic traditions involve a richly evolving collection of diverse beliefs, processes and structures that are

neither easily characterized in concise terms nor summarized in a single systematic philosophy of governance.

They nevertheless note that there is something specific to democratic rule, and postulate four aspects of a democratic vision. First, there is a commitment to personal liberty and individual responsibility in its exercise. Second, there is the idea of popular sovereignty and political equality. Third, there is a faith in the role of individual and collective human reason in human affairs. Fourth, there is emphasis on procedural reliability and stability, on the rule of law and the regulation of arbitrary power.

March and Olsen (ibid.) present two contrasting ways to understand the state and political action more in general. The first is the 'exchange conception of political action'. The other is the 'institutional perspective'. The first is also called the 'pluralist' or 'liberal' perception of the state. It sees politics very much as a 'market', where different political actors compete for power and, based on the interests they represent, undertake bargains with other actors, and look for opportunities to make coalitions when necessary to advance their position. According to this perspective, political actors look very much like 'economic man'. They bargain to obtain what is best for them/ those they represent. March and Olsen note that some authors emphasize that the political bargains create results that are better for everybody – or at least are not worse for anyone. Others note that even if political action is 'voluntary exchange', some may systematically lose due to unequal initial access to resources and the fact that some then have an advantage when 'trading' – for example, neo-pluralist explanations (Turner, 1997).

March and Olsen (ibid.) support a perspective resembling that of classical institutional economics as presented in Part Two of this volume. They do not argue that the exchange model is entirely wrong; certainly, politics is full of strategic games. They emphasize, however, three aspects that I find important and that change the meaning of politics even as a bargain. First, the interests and positions of political actors are socially constructed. Second, the content of the positions politicians take may be changed through the political process by learning and deliberation. Finally, and most importantly, political action is based on a set of rules about what is appropriate and the creation of political actors is about the creation of a specific role and identity. This regards both the citizens and their representatives/the politicians as well as the administrators.

So creating a politician is about forming a role whose focus is on the common good. Certainly, the perception of what is the 'common good' differs.

There are different interests and people hold different values. However, the 'economic man' vision of the 'exchange perspective' cannot explain how politicians can represent anyone other than themselves. Hence, according to the exchange perspective, politics runs the danger of becoming an arena for personal interests only (O'Neill, 1998; Vatn, 2005). This is again used among many 'exchange theorists' as an argument for a minimal state.

The institutional understanding – on the other hand – emphasizes the opportunity and the importance of creating the role of the politician/administrator as acting on behalf of a community. March and Olsen (1995, pp. 35–6) write:

> Exchange traditions downplay the significance, or meaning, of the common good and doubt the relevance of social investment in citizenship. The assumption is that self-oriented interests cannot (and should not) be eliminated or influenced. . . Political norms are seen as negotiated constraints on fundamental processes of self-serving rationality rather than as constitutive.

March and Olsen, hence, stand in a tradition that emphasizes the constitutive process of creating citizens and their representatives. They note that (ibid., p. 37):

> proper citizens are assumed to act in ways consistent with common purposes that are not reducible to aggregation of their separate self-interests. . . Good citizens are pictured as willing to reason together. They deliberate on the basis of a sense of community that is itself reinforced by the process of deliberation. From this perspective, the real danger to a polity comes when no controlling standard of obligation is recognized and politics becomes the unchecked pursuit of interests.

The institutional position is therefore both normative and descriptive. It emphasizes what politics should look like in democracies. However, it also emphasizes the potential that lies in forming the political actors and the way politics is done to be able to create or at least move towards that ideal.

There is, however, a third position that should be mentioned – the Marxian understanding of the state. The argument comes in different forms, but advances the idea that the state is 'class dependent'. Marx himself pointed out in the Communist Manifesto that the state acts as an executive committee for the bourgeoisie class to protect their interests (Marx and Engels [1848] 1998). Miliband (1969) argues that the privileged class use the state to protect their interests through interpersonal ties between the economic elite and the state representatives. Yet another variant of Marxist critique comes from Poulantzas (1978). He defines the relationship and domination in much more structural terms. State officials may not consciously support the ruling class. Rather, it reflects a necessity. To advance policies that are in its interests is important for the state as it controls most of the productive resources of a society.

International governmental organizations (IGOs)

To increase international cooperation, a long list of IGOs was established after World War II. These were founded to address a series of issues like *development* (e.g., the Organisation for Economic Co-operation and Development and the World Bank); *trade* (e.g., the World Trade Organization); *environment* (e.g., the Global Environment Facility); and *production* (e.g, Organization of the Petroleum Exporting Countries). The United Nations and its system of sub-organizations is the dominating IGO. It includes a series of sub-organizations and programs of importance to environmental governance (e.g., UN Food and Agriculture Organization and the UN Environmental Program). It also hosts a series of environmental treaties with their secretariats.

Political actors need resources. The resource base is created in different ways depending on the type of actor. Broadly speaking, governments get their resources through taxation of income/economic activities and from public production. Governments are also the funders of IGOs.

6.3.4 Civil society actors

Civil society actors span a vast field from individuals/families to political parties. As emphasized, the normative basis for a society is found here. It develops both in organized and unorganized ways. Organized formats have gained increased importance in modern societies through the establishment of non-governmental organizations (NGOs). Traditionally, they are non-profit entities, spanning religious, environmental, cultural, humanitarian, human rights organizations and labor unions. Mass media are also important actors in civil society. The same regards research. I finally include political parties and organizations representing business among civil society actors. They somewhat transgress the categories of political and economic actors.

NGOs represent a variety of civil society voices and can be seen as a channel of participation in the democratic process of a society. Historically they have been organized as membership organizations only, typically at local and national levels, responding to special interests and needs. Some have, however, also become part of an international superstructure – international non-governmental organizations (INGOs). They may engage in global issues, but also in specific environment and development projects in, for example, developing countries. In such cases, they may operate 'from the outside in' as project managers. There is also an increasing trend towards establishing what one may call 'civil expert organizations' and 'think tanks'. These are not membership based, but funded through, for example, private donations and sometimes public support. While NGOs are important voices for civil society, they specialize in different ways and it is not a given that they always represent civil society voices.

Mass media are important channels regarding information from and across civil society actors. They vastly expand the opportunity for engagement in public discourses. Media are, however, not neutral intermediaries. They often set their own agendas. Due to their position, it also becomes interesting for other actors – not least economic actors – to influence mass media through ownership and control. This challenges the independency of media and represents an important topic with respect to the democratic capacity of civil society.

In modern societies, an important part of knowledge building is specialized in the form of institutionalized research in universities and research institutes. Research is not an actor in the same way as, for example, NGOs. It is specialized action in expanding various frontiers of knowledge and dependent on the creative force of human imagination. Its capacity to undertake independent thinking and be a 'critical and reflexive eye' regarding developments in society is important in nurturing a vibrant civil society.

Political parties are a kind of facilitative actor in their role in linking civil society and the formalized political arenas. They are, moreover, a kind of 'generalist organization' representing certain ideologies and interests concerning the development of societies. They produce and channel civil society voices into the political process. They also 'compete' for power at municipal and state levels – for example, for positions in parliaments and in the forming of governments.

Business representatives may play a very strong role in influencing policymaking, not as an extended channel of democracy, but because of their economic power. Certainly, here we not only encounter business or industry sector organizations – for example, various branch organizations – we also observe that single corporations like Exxon, BP, Shell and so on have the power to operate not only as economic actors, but also as influencing the political processes. Their role in policy formulations has become very strong in fields such as the environmental – see, for example, Chasek et al. (2014).

6.3.5 Rules governing political processes

In the section on political actors above, I discussed some issues related to the political process. At the basic level lie constitutional rules that typically govern both the relationship between the citizen and their political representatives and what powers these representatives have. Next, there is a set of collective-choice rules that structure the policy processes, be it at local, national or international level.

The relationship between the citizens and the politicians varies across political systems. In the case of democratic states, key rules concern voting rights, rights concerning ways the citizens can participate directly in political processes, including referendums. Regarding participation, the right to elect representatives to political bodies – foremost the parliament – is fundamental. Regarding further engagements of citizens, we observe some considerable variation. In a country like Switzerland many questions are put forward for referendums, while in most countries it is only in exceptional cases that the citizens decide directly on political issues, as such decision-making power is delegated to elected bodies. Over time, we see, however, a development towards opening up arenas for public participation. The literature talks of a 'deliberative turn' – see, for example, Dryzek (2002); Bäckstrand et al. (2010).

In democracies, there is a division of political power between the legislative (parliaments), the executive (governments) and the judicial (courts). The logic is to avoid concentration of political power – to build in some 'self-correcting' mechanisms. Regarding the relation between the legislative and the executive, two systems dominate – the parliamentary and the presidential. In the former case, the executive is based on majority support in the parliament, while in the latter case a president is elected and has the power to establish government.

Despite the tendency for increased citizen participation in politics, this has not resulted in changes in the rules for who decides – see, for example, Bäckstrand et al. (2010). Hence, decision-making in democracies is still delegated to the above units. This raises questions concerning accountability and transparency, which are key aspects of legitimate democratic rule. Elected politicians are accountable to the citizen first of all through elections, but also through institutionalized systems defining the rules of good conduct, what it means to break these – for example, corruption – and what the consequences of this are.

Regarding IGOs, I first note that they are constituted by sovereign states. The international arena is 'an anarchy' in the sense that there is no third party rule – no delegation of such power from nation states to international bodies. That means that there is no majority rule and countries may withdraw from negotiations, or not sign and ratify agreements. In the case of the World Trade Organization (WTO), a court procedure can make a judgment in cases where one member state accuses another of breaking the rules for international trade. WTO has, however, no power to enforce a solution except allowing member states to counter a state that has broken the WTO rules by setting up trade barriers – that is, 'trade wars'.

6.3.6 Civil society action and interaction

Action and interaction in civil society are much less formalized than in the political sphere. At the root, we have norms about what is seen as appropriate interaction between fellow citizens. While such norms exist for all arenas in society, they play a fundamental role for civil society. Many of these rules seem to permeate not least the political level as an extension of what is generally considered 'good behavior'. This does not imply that there are no formal rules regarding the civil society arena. Many constitutions have rules protecting the right to free speech, balanced against rules regarding offensive action or speech. Finally, the right to organize is a key issue that is often protected by law.

Systems facilitating deliberation are crucial for how vibrant and influential civil society is regarding not least supporting the policy processes. The rights to speech and organize are crucial elements. The issues, however, go further and involve the quality of community interaction and the capacity to access and engage in various arenas. Organized interests in the form of NGOs seem to dominate deliberative fora that are established throughout the years (Bäckstrand et al., 2010). Sometimes their access to such arenas is formalized. These organizations operate at local, national and international levels. Some specialize at one level, while others span them all. Hence, some NGOs have local and national bodies, while also being part of international confederations. These may next have access to, for example, forums for international environmental decision-making like UN processes. Logically, they only have the right to voice concerns and make proposals (Chasek et al., 2014).

Organized interests in civil society may facilitate open, public debate. They may, however, also influence the political level directly through participation in formalized networks and forums between state officials and civil society organizations. Finally, they may influence through lobbying. Certainly, the latter is a challenge for democratic rule, as both transparency and unequal access to such influence may be counter to fundamental democratic principles.

6.4 Environmental governance systems

To establish a full framework for the study of environmental governance systems (EGSs), we need to include a few more variables:

● environmental resources and processes;
● technologies and infrastructures;
● patterns of interaction; and
● outcomes – resource use and state of the resource.

The EGS framework as depicted in Figure 6.2 may seem quite complex. It includes, however, what I consider a minimum of aspects to be accounted for when studying environmental problems and their potential causes and solutions.

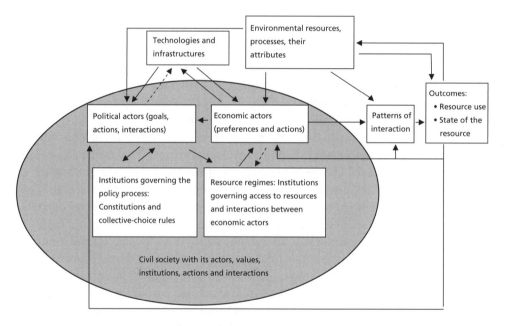

Figure 6.2 A framework for studying environmental governance systems – the EGS framework

While the reader acknowledges the elements in the lower part of the framework – the governance structure including resource regimes – I would like to emphasize four issues regarding the rest of the framework:

● The attributes of the environmental resources influence outcomes directly. As important, they are also assumed to influence (a) the choice of resource regime, (b) the actions of the economic actors, and (c) the pattern of interaction. Regarding (a) and (b) it is the way actors perceive resources and their attributes that is influential. Here the roles of research and other civil society actors are also important. Concerning (c) the reader may recall the difference between polluting a river and polluting a lake. Hence, different patterns of interaction appear due to interplay between choices made by single economic actors, the number of such actors involved and the characteristics of the resource.

- Similarly, the outcomes – the specific states of the resources – are assumed to influence both economic and political choices. Civil society as well as economic actors may, moreover, try to influence the policy process if environmental outcomes are not seen as acceptable. Again, it is the perception – in this case of outcomes – that counts.
- Technologies and infrastructures influence choices among the different categories of actors. If policy-makers want to shape technological development, they may change the resource regime, altering the conditions for technology production among economic actors.
- Political and economic actors are treated differently concerning interactions. Patterns of interactions between economic actors are emphasized as a separate variable. This is done to capture how this pattern is also influenced by the attributes and state of the resources.

The EGS framework is influenced by Ostrom's institutional analysis and development (IAD) framework (see Ostrom, 1990, 2005, and a framework by Oakersson, 1992).[8] It has, nevertheless, its own distinct characteristics established not least by the emphasis on the concept of governance structure with a differentiation between types of actors and forms of institutions and an explicit treatment of the interaction between the elements of the framework. The IAD framework operates with a separate action arena. In the EGS framework, these arenas are differentiated dependent on type of process. They are defined by the institutions framing economic as well as political and civil society processes.

The framework could support analyses on different scales – from the local to the global. For specific analyses, one would typically need to elaborate on the framework. If there is both a local, national and international component to the analysis, one will have to divide between local, national and international actors and institutions – developing a layered governance structure.

As emphasized in Chapter 2, the dynamics of environmental resources/processes vary a lot across types of resources/ecosystems. Ostrom and Cox (2010) emphasize a series of aspects regarding 'resource systems' and 'resource units' that may influence governance. They mention aspects such as 'boundary clarity', 'size', 'productivity', 'equilibrium property' (e.g., recharge dynamics, feedbacks), 'predictability', 'storage capacity', 'resource unit mobility', 'replacement rate', 'spatial and temporal heterogeneity' and 'economic value'. These concepts are ways to systematically map characteristics of resources and involved processes to be able to characterize challenges and opportunities regarding governance. In Chapter 12, I will look more in detail at issues concerning environmental governance, illustrating the importance of these factors.

Young (2002, 2008), among others, emphasizes the concept of 'fit' between the institutions and the characteristics of the environmental resources/processes. According to him: "The problem of fit is a matter of the match or congruence between biophysical and governance systems"[9] (Young, 2008, p. 26). If the resource regime does not fit the attributes of the resource system, problems may appear. This is certainly an important challenge for environmental governance. Fisheries regulation is a typical example where regimes have repeatedly failed to ensure the aims of the regulations due to both the specific biophysical complexities encountered and the difficulties faced as fish stocks migrate between and outside economic zones of different countries (e.g., Finlayson and McCay, 2000). Even in the case of more simple ecosystems, regimes have failed to achieve defined aims. Indeed, by increasing our understanding of the dynamics of the various ecosystems, one would expect that it would help to construct regimes that are a better 'fit'.

The fit concept is based on a 'hand–glove' metaphor. While appealing, it is, however, not straightforward to think in these terms (Vatn and Vedeld, 2012). As noted above, actions do not relate directly to the biophysical characteristics of resources, but to our perceptions of these. This concerns both our understanding of resource dynamics and which aspects of a resource or ecosystem the various interests want to emphasize. A forest can be turned into a pasture and vice versa. Both ecosystems can be well functioning given soils and climates. They just serve different purposes and interests.

Finally, how well a certain regime is able to produce wanted outcomes also depends on the status of the technology. A resource regime that works well given certain technologies may be a disaster given other regimes. There are many examples of collapses in environmental resources that appear after a change in technology that increases harvesting capacities – see the study by Finlayson and McCay referred to above, and Riseth and Vatn (2009; see also Box 6.1). Problems may not be acknowledged early enough, or the capacity

BOX 6.1

STUDYING SAMI REINDEER HERDING USING THE EGS FRAMEWORK

In the 1980s, overgrazing of the rich lichen pastures was observed in the Finnmark county of Norway. This was the direct result of strong growth in the number of reindeer. Until 1970, records show that the Sami held a relatively stable number of reindeer. In Vest-Finnmark, for example, the number varied around 40 000. In 1990, the number had increased to about 110 000. This led to severe problems for the whole business (Riseth and Vatn, 2009).

While the Sami communities – as a minority enclave within the Norwegian state – had been under political and cultural pressure from the Norwegian authorities for centuries, reindeer herding proved sustainable (Riseth, 2005). The main *resources* for herding are the reindeer and the pastures. It takes place on the undulating plains of the county and on the islands surrounding the main land. Herding is based on following the animals' natural migratory pattern and has been developed gradually from hunting to herding. Pastures are seasonal and the migration goes from the inner plains, with winter pastures dominated by lichen, through spring pastures with a mix of lichen, herbs and grasses, to the summer pastures in coastal areas dominated by grasses and herbs. This movement is reversed in the fall.

Regarding the *resource regime*, animals are private property while pastures are common property to groups of households – *siidas*. It is notable that the basis is customary and that the Norwegian state considers the land itself state property. The Sami society is acephalous – that is, lacking a third-level authority. Over time, there has

been a process of establishing such a level – that is, a system of reindeer herding districts – with much of the initiative coming from the Norwegian authorities. The experiences with this system are at best mixed (Riseth and Vatn, 2009).

The resource regime changed gradually throughout the 1950s with increased *market access* established for reindeer meat. Earlier, trade was mainly related to products from bone, skin and silver. From the mid-1960s, a process of *technological change* started with the introduction of snowmobiles and later all-terrain vehicles (ATVs). Together these changes set in motion a development that ended in the mentioned *outcome* of pasture degradation. While increased market access opened up an opportunity for increased production, the technological change made expansion easier. The lack of a common political power among the Sami, who could potentially have the power to restrict the expansion, is an important element in this story. A lack of a third party system made necessary institutional transformation from the 'inside' difficult. Instead, internal conflicts developed and some herders seized the opportunity to outcompete others. Important also is the fact the landscape in Finnmark is very open – difficult to demarcate pastures for the various *siidas*. It is, moreover, summer as opposed to winter pasture limited – implying that there is no strong natural limitation to herd expansion until overgrazing of the lichen pastures starts 'hitting back'.

The imposed reindeer herding districts were too weak to handle these challenges. The Norwegian government intervened

➡

with different support schemes. Reforms of the late 1970s and early 1980s aimed at co-management and optimization of production (Riseth, 2003). However, the form of these interventions and the fact that there was a lot of mistrust between the Sami and Norwegian officials made these initiatives ineffective. In fact, they seemed to increase rather than curb the problems (Riseth and Vatn, 2009). While there are many cases showing the	ability of local communities to adapt successfully to existing and new conditions – see, for example, Bromley (1992); Ostrom (1990, 2005); Ostrom et al. (2002) – this case illustrates the complexities involved. It illustrates the role of resource dynamics, market access and technological change. It illustrates the challenges when local authority is weak and when there is competition between systems of authority.

of the political system to undertake the necessary transformation of the resource regime may be too weak.

6.5   Main messages

Governance has both process and structural components. The processes concern shaping priorities – including acknowledging and possibly resolving conflicts – and facilitating coordination concerning people's use of resources. The structural dimension concerns the actors and institutions in place to facilitate priority-making and ensuring that goals are achieved. Certainly, these formulations and distinctions are purely analytical. In practice, governance processes are messy and structures are often quite incoherent.

Analyzing governance demands conceptualization. In this chapter, I have defined a series of concepts. I have, moreover, developed a framework where the main relationships between these concepts or variables are defined – the environmental governance system (EGS) framework. At the basis of the framework, we have the *resource regime*. It consists of (1) the rules governing *access* (wide meaning) to productive resources and (2) the rules concerning the *interactions* within and between actors having such access. While access is ensured by property and use rights – in the form of private, state, common property and open access – interaction may be governed by trade, command, community rules and, finally, no rules. The importance of informal as well as formal systems should be emphasized. The same regards the distinction between customary rights based on local third party rule and property rights defined by the state. These may in many instances be overlapping and competing – that is, legal pluralism.

The next level concerns the *governance structure*. It includes economic, political and civil society actors – that is, actors that hold rights to productive resources and actors that have the power to define the institutions that govern resource use – the institutions that define the rules and practices governing economic processes. Actors have different motivations. They also have different capacities, rights and responsibilities as defined by the institutions. Hence, institutional structures are key determinants of the power various actors have regarding protection of their interests.

Including next the *environmental resources/processes* and *technology/infrastructure* completes the framework of interacting variables producing *patterns of interaction* and *outcomes*. Analyses of concrete cases at, for example, local, national or global levels and possible interactions between these levels demand further specifications of the generic EGS framework as developed here. It represents a minimalized basis for the development of such expanded versions. In doing so, capturing the depth of both informal and formal structures is crucial. The latter is typically the easiest. Nevertheless, informal institutions may play key roles as well, as 'rules-in-use' may differ from 'rules-on-paper'. Hence, a concentration on formal rules will typically make the analysis incomplete – sometimes exceptionally so.

NOTES

1 Some argue that the concept of governance should not include government. Certainly, the concept of governance became 'popular' during the 1990s as an acknowledgement of the multitude of centers of power and of processes of 'steering' also outside the fields of governmental control. Nevertheless, I agree with Paavola (2007) that it is unreasonable not to include government as a core actor in governance.
2 Schlager and Ostrom (1992) actually refer to 'collective-choice rights'. This is because they focus on common-pool resources only – see Chapter 3, this volume.
3 Intermediate categories as defined by Ostrom and Schlager are 'claimant' (access, withdrawal and management rights) and 'proprietor' (all rights except alienation). As is seen from the text, I use 'claimant' and 'user' synonymously.
4 This system expands beyond the Weberian understanding of legality implying one source of ultimate power within the boundaries of a state.
5 In local markets, those trading would typically know each other.
6 Observe that in the case of resources under open access, only the 'no rules' apply for the transfer of the resources themselves.
7 The International Co-operative Alliance defines a cooperative as an association of people who voluntarily cooperate for their mutual benefit (ICA, 1995).
8 Another very influential framework at this level is the social-ecological systems framework – see, for example, Ostrom (2007).
9 By 'governance system' Young implies the same as 'resource regime'.

7

Evaluating and changing governance structures

As emphasized in Chapter 6, governance concerns shaping priorities, facilitating coordinated action and handling conflicts. Hence, governance has a clear normative dimension – and the issue that immediately surfaces is: what is 'good governance'? This demanding question is the topic of the present chapter. I start by presenting a set of criteria directed at evaluating governance and governance structures. Thereafter I move from the level of criteria to look at how governance structures influence (environmentally relevant) action. In the present chapter, I mainly accentuate theoretical aspects of this issue. I will have much more to say on the empirical side in Part Five. Dissatisfaction with outcomes – for example, with environmental conditions – may motivate changes in governance structures. I close this chapter with a brief presentation of theories of institutional change.

7.1 Criteria for evaluating governance and governance structures

Regarding criteria for the evaluation of governance and governance structures, we face two key issues. First, there is the issue of what it is considered best to do. What are good criteria for evaluating outputs? Second, there is the issue of process. How has one reached a decision on what it is best to do and how are policies implemented? The latter concerns how a society treats its members regarding decisions that are in some way common – how citizens are involved and respected in policy processes. Deciding upon such rules will often imply taking sides between interests. A core challenge then is how one treats the 'losers': How do we best evaluate governance structures and the policies they produce in a situation where there are typically both 'winners' and 'losers'?

Given the above, I find the criterion of *legitimacy* a meaningful basis for evaluating governance and governance structures. Legitimacy is fundamentally about justified authority. However, what 'justified' means varies across the literature. Traditionally, the literature on legitimacy has focused on 'due process', emphasizing legality. Over the years the perspective has broadened, also including emphasis on the form of participation (and fairness in distribution of power and outcomes – see, for example, Dryzek, 2002; Bäckstrand, 2006; Paavola and Adger, 2006; Okereke and Dooley, 2010). We may actually distinguish between three main definitions of 'justified authority':

- Decisions are made according to 'due process'. Decisions are made in accordance with the law, following predefined rules regarding how decisions should be made and implemented. This position is often termed the 'legal' definition of legitimacy. It refers neither to the quality of that process, nor to the content of the outcomes. It is a purely formal definition.
- Decisions are legitimate because the process is accepted. A decision is legitimate if it is accepted by those concerned. It is done in a way they consider right. Again, the focus is on procedure, but it expands beyond the purely formal element. It concerns people's beliefs about political authority – how common decisions should be made, not just how they are actually formalized. Understanding legitimacy as acceptability is often called the 'descriptive' understanding of legitimacy.
- What is legitimate has to abide by normative standards about what is a good process and outcome. While there can be no universal definition of such standards – they will typically have some historical and cultural specificity – the normative perspective goes beyond the descriptive, demanding justification for the standards as supported by reason and judged favorably by society (e.g., Habermas, 1979; Bernstein, 2005).

In relation to the second and third points above, one may also make a distinction between 'subjectivist/internal' and 'objectivist/external' standards for legitimacy. The first concerns the judgment made by the members of a community itself and links to the issue of acceptability. The second regards an evaluation against an external standard for what a legitimate decision should be like. While the 'internal' assessment may include both descriptive and normative elements, the 'external' evaluation would emphasize normative aspects only. In that respect, the evaluation may go beyond the normative issues as emphasized by the people involved and refer to general standards of appropriateness. Here we may link to Lukes's third face of power (see Lukes, 2005 and Chapter 4, this volume) describing how people may be 'moved' to take positions that are not in their own interest through, for example, manipulating their beliefs. If one limits the analysis only to 'internal' assessments, one risks losing important aspects of what should be included in the evaluation.

BOX 7.1

GOOD GOVERNANCE

Definitions of 'good governance' vary across the literature. Typically, the main interest in defining the concept is found among international organizations like the United Nations (UN), International Monetary Fund (IMF) and the World Bank. This seems related to the fact that these international governmental organizations (IGOs) are engaged in programs of various kinds across the world and need to evaluate the policy processes in the countries with which they are involved. In a communication 'What is Good Governance?' the UN Economic and Social Commission for Asia and the Pacific states: 'Good governance has 8 major characteristics. It is participatory, consensus oriented, accountable, transparent, responsive, effective and efficient, equitable and inclusive and follows the rule of law' (UN, 2009b, p. 1). Moreover, the UN states: 'It assures that corruption is minimized, the views of minorities are taken into account and that the voices of the most vulnerable in society are heard in decision-making. It is also responsive to the present and future needs of society' (ibid.).

The reader will recognize some commonality to the issues raised in the text. There are, however, important issues or differences. Setting up lists like this is fine, but they typically do not reflect on the theoretical basis regarding the underlying concept of legitimacy. Hence, lists may be inconsistent, drawing on competing theoretical foundations. As an example, being consensus oriented, efficient, equitable and following the rule of law, may not be easily reconciled as criteria. Also important is understanding how different governance structures may influence the preferences of actors and the goals they pursue. Hence, the meaning of, for example, participatory, accountable, effective and efficient depends on these structures. These fundamental questions are not raised in the 'official' statements on what is good governance.

There are important cleavages in the literature on legitimacy. The most important relates to the distinction between the 'republican' and the 'liberal' perspectives. Republican ideas go back to Aristotle and prioritize the polity (community) in the meaning of focusing on the common good. These ideas were influential in the case of both the American Revolution and the contemporary concept of communitarian democracy. The liberal tradition is younger, with a strong emphasis on individual freedom. It has motivated many modern institutions in Western countries. This split in positions links to the distinction between the positive and negative definitions of freedom – the perspective of freedom as being capable – as something that must be created by a community (positive) – vs freedom as absence from coercion (negative).

In the following, I will discuss these different aspects of legitimacy. I will start by presenting a conceptual framework for evaluating legitimacy. Next, I will go into some detail regarding each of the main elements of the framework.

7.1.1 Legitimacy – a conceptual framework

The literature distinguishes between the legitimacy of the decision-making process itself – 'input legitimacy' – and the legitimacy of results – 'output legitimacy' (e.g., Bäckstrand, 2006; see also Scharpf, 1999). Hence, this literature uses the concept of 'output' for what I have so far termed 'outcome'.

I will utilize the input–output distinction when developing a framework for studying legitimacy. I try, moreover, to include elements regarding both internal and external legitimacy. According to Bäckstrand, input legitimacy relates to the form of the policy process, and she emphasizes issues like responsibility, participation, accountability and transparency. She stresses the importance of how different interests are included in policy formulation and implementation processes, and how decision-makers are accountable to stakeholders and the wider society. According to her, output legitimacy concerns the effectiveness of policies in assuring wanted results.

I find her distinctions sound, while I would like to expand both the content of input and output legitimacy somewhat. I think a stronger focus on justice is warranted. This regards procedural justice (input) and distributive justice (output). I also find it important to include efficiency among the output criteria. I will refer here only to the concept of cost-efficiency – a choice that will be explained later.

Based on the above, I define the following set of criteria to evaluate legitimacy:

1. *Input (process) legitimacy:* the appropriateness and acceptability of decision-making processes on both principle grounds and with regard to the interests of various actors – for example, national authorities, civil society/local communities and business. The core concept is procedural justice, including issues like participation at different stages of the decision-making process, the transparency of the process and the accountability of decision-makers to wider constituencies.
2. *Output (result) legitimacy:*[1]
    (a) distributive justice: regards principles for allocation of benefits and burdens across activities in a society;
    (b) effectiveness: concerns the capacity to ensure that the defined goals are reached;
    (c) efficiency: concerns here the ability to reach goals set at lowest costs – cost-efficiency.

In the following, I will look in more detail at each of these concepts. As I try to clarify their meaning, the reader will notice that to offer a strictly limited set of definitions is neither desirable nor possible. The criteria must be formulated in a way that is open to including elements that are important for the specific contexts – to various local (internal) standards. Hence, the aim is to offer direction and not a complete set.

7.1.2 Input legitimacy

Input legitimacy is fundamentally about authority to decide – legitimacy justifies authority. It involves what conditions are set for decision-making, how power to decide is delegated, the form of and conditions for participation, how transparent the processes are and finally how the power to decide is made accountable. In the normatively oriented literature on 'input' legitimacy, authority is linked to fair process – to equal standing of all subjects. This is also called procedural justice – and is linked strongly to the institutions of democracy.

Rawls (1971) hence specifies the concept of (pure) procedural justice[2] with reference to 'fair procedure' in the meaning of equal opportunity. He emphasizes that this version of procedural justice focuses entirely on the procedures themselves and not on the expected outcomes that follow. They concern the quality of the process only.

Ensuring equal opportunity – in this case in the process of formulating goals and defining governance structures – is demanding. It is foremost defined as an equal right to participate. There are two dominant strands in the literature – the 'elitist' and 'egalitarian'. According to Webler and Renn (1995, p. 21): "the elitist or liberal view claims that political elites compete for votes similar to how entrepreneurs compete for customers. The populace has the right to determine which of the competing elites are allowed to govern, but the substance of the political decisions are made within these elite circles". The egalitarian view of democracy, on the other hand, is "inspired by the normative claim that the citizen be able to co-determine political decisions that affect his or her livelihood" (ibid.).

The two forms are based on different interpretations of what is fair or equal opportunity. In both cases, there is participation. The difference lies in what the participation is about – delegation of power to decide or direct involvement in concrete decisions. Both can be defended as legitimate based on the idea of equal opportunity. Certainly, there is disagreement in the literature about the quality of either argument.

In relation to this, I will note that the conceptualization of what democracy is has developed quite substantially over the centuries (e.g., Gutmann and Thompson, 2004). It reflects a move from a very narrow elitist view where large parts of the populace were not even given the right to vote – see Chapter 6. Similarly, the view that the capacity to deliberate over decisions was only a capability of elites is a persisting one, while there is substantial change in the thinking on these issues – note, for example, the work of Dewey (1927) and Habermas (1984).

According to Webler (1995, p. 38), egalitarian or "[p]articipatory democratic theorists emphasize that participation is consistent with political equality and popular sovereignty, because it provides every individual an equal and fair chance to defend his or her personal interests and values and to contribute to the definition of the collective will". Webler (ibid., p. 39) also emphasizes the issue of competence:

> When the purpose of public participation is to produce a collective decision,
> competent understandings about terms, concepts, definitions, and language use;
> the objectified world of outer nature (nature and society); the social-cultural world
> of norms and values; and the subjective world of all individuals are all essential.
> This is accomplished through the use of established procedures. How well the
> people in the discourse manage to apply these procedures is the measure of
> competence.

Hence, democracy – equal opportunity to participate – demands certain personal capacities and procedures that support competent dialogue as a basis for decision-making.

In practice, we observe that political decisions at national level are taken by parliaments, governments and various public bodies – that is, mainly representative bodies. Here, the basis for legitimacy is representative democracy, while various forms of hearings may be involved – implying inputs to the process from at least organized stakeholder/civil society groups. Participatory processes are mainly found in cases of local processes and projects. These may also take various forms. Inoue (1998) distinguishes between three levels: the top-down approach, a professional guided participatory approach and the endogenous bottom-up approach. In the top-down approach, local people are consulted about decisions *post factum* to the decision-making process. Within the professionally guided participatory approach, external professionals elaborate drafts and plans. People may be consulted, but only after outsiders have made core decisions. The bottom-up approach is locally initiated and characterized as a continuous learning process, where external professionals take actions according to local needs; they act as facilitators.

Arnstein (1969) and Pretty (1995) are examples of more detailed categorizations. Pretty specifies seven types: (1) manipulative participation, (2) passive participation, (3) participation by consultation, (4) participation for material incentives, (5) functional participation, (6) interactive participation and (7) self-mobilization. One may interpret the first six categories as specifications of Inoue's top-down and professionally guided approaches respectively. It is notable that unequal power relations may also characterize locally initiated and governed processes – see, for example, Cleaver (2012). Power asymmetries (may) exist both within and between levels of decision-making.

To the extent that power to decide is delegated, the issues of transparency and accountability are key. Transparency regards how open the process is, and how information about the decisions and the arguments behind them are made available to the public. It not only concerns availability in the sense that relevant documents are posted. The 'raw material' may be overwhelming. Therefore, it is also reasonable to demand that information is relevant, easily understood and delivered in a timely manner. Hence, Christiano (2003) emphasizes that transparency implies that people are able to see whether they are treated in a fair way given reasonable effort.

The issue of accountability is equally important. It concerns the basis on which decision-makers acquire their right to decide on behalf of others, including who has the right to take back their mandate. Bäckstrand (2006) notes that many new initiatives in environmental governance are network based with competing or overlapping authorities. In some situations, private actors and NGOs may be made responsible for activities that are usually seen as public obligations. Hence, standard assumptions about hierarchical accountability in representative democracy may not apply.

7.1.3 Output legitimacy

Regarding output legitimacy, I have emphasized three sub-criteria: distributive justice, effectiveness and efficiency.

Distributive justice regards principles for allocation of benefits and burdens across activities in a society. There are at least eight different principles regarding distributive justice developed in the literature: (1) strict egalitarianism; (2) the difference principle; (3) resource-based principles; (4) welfare-based prin-

BOX 7.2

DIFFERENT PRINCIPLES OF DISTRIBUTIVE JUSTICE

This box offers a very brief overview of key principles of distributive justice:

1 *Strict egalitarianism:* each individual should have the same level of material goods and services.
2 *The difference principle (Rawlsian principle):* each person has an equal claim to a fully adequate scheme of equal basic rights and liberties. Social and economic inequalities are acceptable under two conditions:
   (a) they are to be attached to positions and offices open to all under conditions of fair equality of opportunity; and
   (b) they are to be to the greatest benefit of the least advantaged members of society.
3 *Resource-based principles:* each individual should have access to the same amount of resources – equal opportunity.
4 *Welfare-based principles:* social welfare should be maximized. This implies some

way of summarizing individual welfare. Hence, a priori definitions of how welfare of each individual should count is necessary – that is, the definition of a social welfare function.
5 *Desert-based principles:* people should be rewarded according to their 'effort' – be it input of work, capital or loss of income (e.g., as an effect of protection of a biotope).
6 *Libertarian principles:* just outcomes appear as the result of free individual choice.
7 *Feminist principles:* equal status for all. 'The private is political' – referring to the observation that liberal theories of justice have been unable to treat injustice in the (protected) private sphere.
8 *Compensatory justice:* the poor have to carry a non-proportionate amount of environmental costs. This demands 'over-compensation' to correct for historical/ systemic injustice

ciples; (5) 'desert'-based principles; (6) libertarian principles; (7) feminist principles; and (8) compensatory justice. These are briefly explained in Box 7.2.

These principles are based to some extent on competing moral philosophies – see, for example, Rawls (1971); Nozick (1974); Anderson (1999); Sen (2009). Hence, as researchers – as well as citizens – we need to choose based on our own normative stand or on the position of our 'clients' if we do research in support of certain interest groups. What are relevant or good criteria depends also on the concrete topic – for example, which risks are involved (Sen, 2009; Forsyth, 2014). If the analysis is descriptive – that is, we want to map which principles of distributive justice have been discussed and used – there is really no reason to limit the list at the outset of a study. It is the case material that determines which is relevant. In the event of normative analyses – for example, critical assessments of principles used in concrete cases – the researcher has to define the principles used and offer motivations for the choice to make analyses transparent.

In a study of the process of instituting reduced emissions from deforestation and forest degradation (REDD+) at local level in Brazil and Tanzania, we chose to combine principles 1 and 5 (Vatn et al., 2013). The principle of desert, meaning being deserving of something, was used as REDD+ implies loss of (forest) livelihoods, and compensation is an issue. We also used the principle of egalitarianism as we found it to be a strong value among the local populations. In this case, the principles were competing – compensating for livelihoods paid according to individual loss of livelihoods (5) or paid equally independent of the costs for each person/family (1). In this research, we did not take a stand on what would be the best principle. Our aim was to understand what the distributive issues were and how people thought about the relevant principles (internalist perspective). At the same time we could raise questions regarding the dilemmas communities faced based on how they decided (externalist perspective).

Another example is criteria for sustainable development. Here we also observe competing positions. The famous Brundtland Commission (WCED, 1987) used a mix of egalitarianism (1) and the welfare-based principle (4) with emphasis on the needs of future generations not being compromised by the present. Others – like Pearce et al. (1989) – used a resource-based definition, emphasizing a non-negative development in human-made and natural capital over time.

Criteria may also be complementary. Feminist principles (7) may be combined with most of the others except principle 6. The same goes for compensatory justice (8). They may imply that women or people in developing countries are treated in a special way to break prior unjust actions. This can, however, happen within a framework of 'strict egalitarianism' (1), the 'difference principle' (2), resource-based principles (3) and so on. In the case of principles 1 and 2, principle 7 may even be viewed as implicit.

Turning to the criterion of *effectiveness*, this concerns how well the policy is at meeting its overall goals. This relates to a long list of issues. Let me illustrate by using a case. A government or parliament may have decided to protect 5 percent of the forests to safeguard biodiversity. It has decided to pay forest owners who freely set aside land for protection – that is, forest owners should be compensated for loss of livelihoods. Hence, the foundation is a desert based principle of justice where forest owners do not have an obligation to protect biodiversity.

Given this normative context, three issues regarding effectiveness seem of special interest. First, to reach the defined aim, necessary resources for compensation must be made available. Second, one must be able to target the 'right' forest owners – that is, those who own land that is interesting for biodiversity protection. Third, one must avoid so-called leakage. Increased protection of forests at one place may result in increased logging and so on at other places, reducing the net effect of wanted protection. Regarding both the second and third points, the motivations of forest owners are important. Do they accept the basis for the regulation as fair and hence follow the intention, or do they try to find ways 'around' it – in the worst case accepting payments, but still continue to log? The latter may happen if the government has low legitimacy and/or its agencies have little capacity to monitor.

Efficiency – as an economic term – concerns optimal resource allocation in a society. Regarding our case, the efficiency question is: how much forest should be protected? Reducing logging is costly since the value of timber is lost, and it may be that resource allocations other than (high levels of) protection are better for the overall welfare of society. Efficiency is obtained when – at the margin – the value of trees as timber equals their value in protection – see also Chapter 8, respectively Varian (2010). One challenge is that this criterion demands that all values are priced. This is problematic not least in the field of the environment. Moreover, prices are a function of how income is distributed. As the criterion is defined, it tries to circumvent the issue of distribution by taking the latter as given. Distribution is defined as a political, not an economic issue. As will be made clearer later – especially in Section 7.2 and Chapter 8 – this separation is not possible to defend either normatively or in a more technical sense. It implies that 'what becomes efficient' depends on the distribution of resources/income. Including both distributive justice and efficiency in a list of criteria for output legitimacy therefore becomes inconsistent.[3]

Due to this, we need to take a step back and resort to a concept of efficiency that a) does not demand that all values are monetized, and b) is less in conflict with the other criteria. The criterion of cost-efficiency serves our needs fairly well. It is defined as the ability to reach an externally set goal at lowest costs. In our example on forest protection, it implies reaching the target – e.g., the 5 percent target defined above – at minimum costs. This involves the direct cost of reduced deforestation – that is, the so-called opportunity costs (the loss of income). It also involves the costs related to decision-making, contracting, delivering payments, monitoring, reporting and so on – that is, the transaction costs.

Even these costs depend on the distribution of resources in a society. Hence, this criterion also cannot be treated independently of the criterion of distributive justice. On the other hand, to not include any criterion on cost would also be problematic – for example, may not capture strategies where little is gained, while costs are high. Due to the observed inconsistencies, it is important to localize where the chosen criterion or criteria for distributive justice influence the calculation of costs.

7.1.4 What if criteria are in conflict?

We have already mentioned one issue regarding conflicting criteria – that between principles of distributive justice and (cost-)efficiency. There may be conflict also at a higher level – between the criteria for input and output legitimacy. What is a good process may produce outputs considered bad and vice versa. Hence, there is a split between authors that prioritize input legitimacy and those emphasizing output legitimacy (Forsyth, 2014). Christiano (2003) terms the former 'proceduralists' and the latter 'instrumentalists'. Taken literally, it means that for the former any output is deemed legitimate if the process producing it is legitimate. For the latter any process is legitimate given that it produces legitimate outputs.

Several authors argue in favor of giving priority to input legitimacy if there is a conflict. Tyler (1990) and Sunshine and Tyler (2003) argue that outputs tend to be seen as legitimate among people if procedures are legitimate. Christiano (2003) reaches a similar conclusion based on a normative-philosophical reasoning, taking equal opportunity of interests as a basis. I would add that to the extent that chosen procedures influence outputs, a certain primacy to procedures or governance structures is unavoidable. This is so because if procedures are changed, a change in outputs may follow. The former determines the latter to some extent.

However, giving full primacy to procedures and no weight to outputs when in conflict seems unwarranted too. It is easy to offer examples of legitimate processes that could produce non-legitimate outputs. Christiano (2003) illustrates this by the case of a fully legitimate procedure producing the enslavement of a certain part of the population. Hence, giving priority to procedures demands defining some standards regarding outputs that are non-negotiable.

Rawls (1971) defines the concept of 'perfect procedural justice' as one that reliably produces the desired outputs. Personally, I think this is a productive way to think – that is, to try to develop governance structures that are able to produce just and sustainable outputs. This is very much the perspective of this book. At the same time, there are limits to this strategy – actually in two directions.

First, if a procedure ensures sustainability, but does so by compromising key principles regarding democratic decision-making, there is a conflict between the focus on ensuring a certain output and equal opportunity in the process of deciding. Second, if it compromises key distributive norms – for example, intra generational justice – it fails regarding output legitimacy. Hence, while I argue that the focus on process or governance structure is key, it is important to notice that not all problems can be solved by giving full primacy to procedural justice in the sense of the 'perfect'.

7.2 How governance structures influence environmental action

In Chapter 6, I defined the concept of governance structures including actors and institutions. Regarding actors, I distinguished between civil, political and economic. Regarding institutions, I differentiated between rules governing civil society interactions, policy processes (e.g., the processes of forming resource regimes) and rules governing the economic processes (the resource regimes themselves).

In Section 7.1, I discussed criteria for evaluating governance and governance structures – both processes and outputs. In the present section, I will look at how core aspects of governance structures may influence results or outputs in the form of the status of the environment. I say 'may', as we operate in a world of high complexity and can talk only about tendencies or potentials, not law-like phenomena.

Based on institutional theory as presented in Chapters 4 and 5, I have selected the following four dimensions or variables regarding what seems to be important aspects to emphasize when studying how governance structures influence environmental action:

- rights and responsibilities;
- transaction costs;
- perceptions;
- preferences and types of motivation.

In the following, I will clarify key relationships from a theoretical perspective. I will later – especially in Part Five – look more in depth at empirical studies that help inform on these issues.

7.2.1 The importance of rights and responsibilities

Rights and responsibilities are important for the political as well as economic process. The former refers to what it means to 'hold office', and act as a citizen. The latter regards rights concerning 'access' to productive resources (e.g., property and use rights) and rules regarding protection of economic/environmental resources. Having a protected right to income-generating resources is basic to sustaining one's life. Rights influence income distribution as well as one's economic power, which can next be turned into political power. These aspects were covered in Chapter 6. Here I will restrict the analysis to the issue of environmental degradation – to side-effects and the right to shift costs onto others, and to protect oneself against cost shifting.

I have already emphasized that production and consumption of goods and services imply a similar production of 'waste'. Economic activity also tends to change ecosystems through various forms of uses. While not all waste or landscape changes influence other people's opportunities, a vast amount of them do. Not all of these effects are negative. There are also impacts that are considered positive – the creation of a garden, a cultural landscape and so on. How should we think about these issues in terms of rights and responsibilities?

One way of terming the rights would be to protect 'victims' against all cost shifting from others. The idea can be illustrated by the 'polluter pays principle' (PPP). It emphasizes that those causing an environmental harm should have no right to do so. They should 'pay'. In the case of positive side-effects, the 'provider gets principle' (PGP) has been formulated. However, what is the basis for defining something as a cost or a benefit – a negative vs a positive effect? Figure 7.1 illustrates some of the challenges involved.

The line from 0 to 1 defines the interval between a 'destroyed' environmental resource/ecosystem (0) and an 'intact' or 'undisturbed' (1) environment. PS represents the present status indicating some deterioration in the original qualities due to some types of use. This reduced quality is evaluated as positive for the resource users that have moved the system from '1' to PS. They do, however, not consider the effect on others of such a change, as we assume

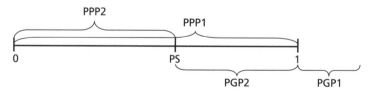

Figure 7.1 Rights, compensation principles and environmental status

that there are no incentives for them to do so – no legal regulations or norms restricting use.

So, what principles or rights could apply here? One solution is that the ones deteriorating the natural values should be responsible for all damages. This implies that no damage is allowed or that deterioration is accepted, but only against a payment set in relation to the damages caused. This rule is illustrated by PPP1. The 'polluter' is responsible for all damages happening in the interval 0–1. Similarly, she or he will be compensated if they manage to increase environmental qualities beyond what nature itself has produced (1) (that is, PGP1). The latter could be the creation of a cultural landscape or building a dam that reduces disastrous floods. An alternative rule is that the 'polluter' has the right to the PS (or in principle any other status between 0 and 1). If the environment is further deteriorated, she or he must pay (that is, PPP2). If they manage to increase the status, he or she will be compensated (PGP2).

The decision over these rights cannot be made independent of the cultural or political context in which these decisions appear. Distributional aspects and issues of *fairness/equity*, become typically very important when formulating rules of the above kind. A simple example from REDD+ may illustrate this. The idea behind the strategy is that the North pays the South to reduce deforestation. This is termed a cost-efficient way to reduce emissions of CO_2, hence, a low-cost strategy for the North to respond to its expected post-Kyoto obligations concerning emission cuts. If the PPP1 rule were instituted in this case, the South would have to pay itself for the avoided deforestation. Given that it is countries in the North that have advocated this solution not least to lower own costs for reducing greenhouse gas emissions – it is an offset solution (see Chapter 13) – compensation (PGP2) seems to be more legitimate. As important, the North has already cut its forests substantially as part of its development strategy without facing any responsibility for consequences on, for example, the climate. Finally, many poor communities in the South depend on forests for their livelihoods.

7.2.2 The role of transaction costs

In Chapter 4 we referred to Arrow's definition of transaction costs as 'the costs of running the economic system'. Before discussing the relationships between institutions, transaction costs and action, I find it necessary to widen the concept in two directions. First, according to the perspectives of this book, reference should be to all forms of governance structures be they political or economic, be they market, command or community based. Moreover, I find it wise to include also the costs of establishing new governance structures, not only those of using or 'running' them.

The focus on governance structures and transaction costs appeared first in the literature on industrial organization. Williamson (1975 and 1985) are seminal publications. He focused on explaining institutional arrangements in modern capitalism. He asked why we observe different forms of organization in different sectors – for example, the existence of vertical integration; the variation in contractual forms. Most basically, he asked why we have firms, if markets are more efficient at allocating resources.

His explanation was the variations found in transaction costs. These may differ substantially across the production of various types of goods and services as well as different resource regimes. He identifies three main factors, namely asset specificity, frequency and uncertainty. Asset specificity is considered the most important, and Williamson distinguishes between what he calls non-specific and idiosyncratic goods. The former concerns 'mass production' of, for example, nails and the latter concerns at the limit goods or services that are specific to each transaction – for example, a building or machine that is constructed only once to meet the demand of a specific actor. Transaction costs are assumed to increase the more idiosyncratic the good is.

Frequency is regarded the second most important factor. It concerns the relationship between sellers and buyers/contracting partners – that is, whether they are engaged in occasional or recurrent transactions. Concerning uncertainty, Williamson focuses foremost on 'behavioral uncertainty' where opportunism is a core factor. Frequency and behavioral uncertainty are linked in the sense that frequent transactions create trust and thus reduce uncertainty.

Hence, Williamson posits that the less specific the good is, the higher the frequency, and the lower the behavioral uncertainty, transactions in markets will dominate. The more idiosyncratic goods are, the lower the frequency and the higher the (behavioral) uncertainty, the greater is the chance that production will be brought under one authority – one management. These findings also have relevance for environmental governance.

While Williamson's explanations are challenged because there is no focus on power,[4] there are still several aspects of interest to us. Environmental goods or services tend towards being idiosyncratic as their qualities are largely site specific. Due to systems' complexity, large uncertainties prevail. Finally, observing action is often demanding – to clarify who and what causes the damage. Hence, there is large 'behavioral uncertainty' and danger for opportunistic behavior.

Common property and public property/state regulations are alternatives to private properties' trading in environmental services. These solutions may be favorable – even the only tenable options – in many cases due to the lower level of transaction costs. Why is it so? We talk here of public goods and mainte-nance of the quality of such goods is vulnerable to free-riding. The command power of states, but also common property organizations, guards against the opportunity to free-ride. Command power may also be important to be able to raise enough resources for environmental protection, to the extent that this is necessary. Finally, there are effects on 'behavioral uncertainty'. Levi (1998) argues that trust is important for a state's governance capacity. This increases the will to cooperate – and reduces the need for control. This observation seems of great importance for any governance context.

7.2.3   Institutions, interests and perceptions

Acting happens on the basis of beliefs – beliefs about what needs to be acted upon and beliefs about effects of action. These beliefs depend on our percep-tions about what the issues are and how the physical and social worlds 'work'. This is a key issue not least in the case of environmental governance. Because of high complexity and the subsequent high levels of unawareness and of uncertainty, 'fixing beliefs' (Bromley, 2006) is not in any way straightforward.

While perceptions are to a large extent based on sensing, what we sense is of different kinds. Being a farmer, one learns what are good and bad soils from the perspective of growing crops, what the patterns of weather are. When cooperating, we learn who is trustworthy and who is deceitful. We access information via written sources, the Internet and so forth. So, how is it that we make sense of all of this?

Certainly, some sense-making is quite direct. We learn that if it does not rain, plants die. We learn that some plants are poisonous and we may die if we eat them. However, the amount of information 'out there' is tremendous and comes in very different forms. Berger and Luckmann ([1967] 1991) are a key source regarding the 'sociology of knowledge'. They emphasize very strongly the collective element of perceiving and learning. The language is key. They write (pp. 35–6; original emphasis):

> The reality of everyday life appears already objectified, that is, constituted by an order of objects that have been designated *as* objects before my appearance on

the scene. The language used in everyday life continuously provides me with the necessary objectifications and posits the order within which these make sense and within which everyday life has meaning to me.

Therefore, the language offers words – predefined concepts – through which I learn to understand the world around me. It is based on experience – subjective experiences – that are objectified through the language, through 'models of mind'. Berger and Luckmann (ibid., p. 37; original emphasis) continue: "The reality of everyday life further presents itself to me as an intersubjective world, a world I share with others. . . I know that there is an ongoing correspondence between *my* meanings and *their* meanings in the world, that we share a common sense about its reality".

While there is a reality – see my emphasis on realist ontology in Chapter 3 – perceptions of it may differ. Moreover, not all reality can be observed. What we know of the world around us depends on how we conceptualize it. Hence, changes in conceptualizations may result in new insights and all the time we have to be 'critical' of our conceptualizations (see Section 3.4).

In Chapter 4, I illustrated the process of institutionalization – with the elements externalization, objectivation and internalization. This process is also illustrative of how we perceive and know. We learn through a social process of standardizing beliefs. In relation to this, we may talk of primary and secondary socialization – see, for example, Berger and Luckmann ([1967] 1991). Primary socialization includes learning about the norms of the culture we are raised in. We also learn about its conventions and its conventional ways of thinking – the knowledge of that society about what is and how we can influence what is. Secondary socialization is "the internalization of institutional or institution-based 'sub-worlds'" (ibid., p. 158). This refers not least to 'sub-worlds' of competence. Over the years, formalized education systems have been established in every country – including basic and higher education. The latter, especially, involves specialization. We learn to become a farmer, a plumber, a teacher, an engineer and so on. Specialized knowledge implies specialized vocabulary and special ways to perceive. This is a necessary element in modern societies. As some knowledges are 'particular', people develop different capacities to perceive. This makes it possible to develop skills and insights that would be impossible in a less specialized society, but it may also create conflicts, as we tend to see and value different things – see Trainor (2006). Box 7.3 offers an example of such a disagreement, covering different professional perceptions regarding the effect of a tax on nitrogen in fertilizers.

BOX 7.3

THE NITROGEN DISPUTE – THE SCIENTIFIC 'BATTLE'

In the late 1980s there was a debate across many Western European countries regarding how to reduce nitrogen losses from agricultural fields to various water bodies. Higher nitrogen losses per acre are generally associated with higher nitrogen fertilizer application rates. This resulted in a debate about introducing a tax on nitrogen (N) fertilizers. This was also the case in Norway. The proposal came from a group of researchers – economists – who were asked by Norway's Ministry of Agriculture to evaluate the effects of an N tax – see, for example, Simonsen (1989). The economists concluded that such a tax would reduce emissions of N, both through reducing what would become the optimal amount of N fertilizers bought and through ensuring that N in animal manure would also be better utilized. They concluded, however, that taxes needed to be high to be effective – for example, in the order of 100–300 percent. This proposal resulted in a tough debate between representatives of different professions. It even changed the cooperation on agri-environmental policies between the Ministry of Agriculture and the Ministry of Environment (Vatn et al., 2002) – see Box 10.1.

Regarding the disciplinary controversy, agronomists attacked the conclusions drawn by the economists. They referred to a Von Liebig model – standard in agronomy – arguing that N is typically a limiting factor of plant growth/yields. Given

this, yields would increase linearly as a function of adding N to the field up to a point where it would have no more effect. In such a situation, raising the price of N would not influence N use except when reaching a level where no use of N fertilizers is deemed optimal. In contrast, the economists built their analyses on 'smooth' yield functions. They argued that while the Von Liebig model might be right for the growth of each single plant, maybe each bit of land, the aggregate response over the whole field would not be characterized by such a breaking point. Given this conjecture, an increase in the N price would motivate profit-maximizing farmers to reduce use of N fertilizers gradually as the price grew.

It turned out to be almost impossible to reach any agreement based on observations. This is because yields in field experiments measuring responses to N are also influenced by a series of other factors like weather, micro-conditions regarding soils and so on. Hence, different yield functions could be 'fitted' to the observations, without any clear help from statistical methods to define the 'best fit'. The disciplinary conflict was never resolved. It is also notable that farmers may not have perceived the issue in ways similar to any of the disciplinary perspectives, while the agronomists argued that the extension service based its messages on the agronomic model (Vatn et al., 2002).

In the case of environmental governance, analyses frequently go beyond everyday language – that is, specialized knowledge is typically very important. Moreover, we cannot always build decisions on practical experience. We may resort to model-based analyses, scenarios and so on, normally with substantial uncertainty attached to conclusions. This raises tremendous challenges for democratic decision-making. Research on how citizens handle complexity and risk points towards the importance of 'social filters' in the process of 'fixing our beliefs' (Wildavsky, 1987). We often rely selectively on information from elites (political leaders, organizations, media outlets) that we trust (Krosnick et al., 2006). As an example, Kahan et al. (2012) studied attitudes towards climate change in the USA. Trusting the source of information was found to be key, and this trust seems related to peers whose arguments protect people's social position.

This indicates that interests influence perception, hence, our 'perceived truth'. We tend to 'see' what is helpful to us – both in the sense of practical needs and position and place in a society. Interest may be defined by social belonging, economic position, profession and so on. There is hence a tendency for people to relate themselves more strongly to information that confirms themselves in relation to other members in a group that have similar interests and values, and hence share common beliefs (Giddens, 1991; Schulz-Hardt et al., 2000).

This does not imply that knowledge and perceptions are purely interest based. It means, however, that for science to inform 'the public' and believe that this will change perceptions accordingly is a far too simple model. Rather, we need to engage in an open debate about positions and the different types of knowledge that are needed in that process. This places a lot of responsibility with the media. I see two great challenges here. One regards the role of 'special interest groups' that may use, for example, uncertainty and professional disagreements to create disinformation – see also Chapter 3. The other regards the 'fact' that the media seem to 'live off conflicts'. Hence, disagreements between researchers/disciplines receive much more emphasis than agreements. Again, the debate around climate change offers a very good example.

7.2.4 Institutions, preferences and motivations

While acting depends on beliefs, it also depends on preferences and motivation. The latter issue was developed in some considerable detail in Chapter 5. To complete Section 7.2, I will just summarize points made earlier:

- There is a distinct social component to the formation of preferences. Hence, different cultures are characterized by different conventions and norms regarding what are normal consumption patterns. Being socialized implies learning these conventions and norms.

- Our interests are strongly influenced by the rights we have and the type of role within which we operate. This shows up in our actions as different preferences. While roles are not straitjackets, they define what is seen as appropriate.

- Hence, people have the capacity to operate under different types of preferences and act in accordance with different types of rationalities. They may be motivated by what is best for themselves. They may also be motivated to act in ways that are best for the group they belong to or for others.

- So while people are characterized by multiple sets of preferences and a plurality of motivations, it is the institutional context that defines which type of motivation – and hence, what set of preferences – is expected.

These observations are crucial for environmental governance as it puts emphasis on two very important issues. First, human preferences can change through processes of socialization. Deliberation over what preferences are best to hold becomes both a possibility and a necessity in an interconnected world. Certainly, it is very demanding to keep such deliberations open and reflexive. Second, when establishing or changing resource regimes, when introducing policy instruments like laws and payments into a given resource regime, one needs to notice that it not only changes what seems 'optimal' or 'best to do', it may also change the very logic by which actors perceive the problems faced. We will return to these complex issues on many occasions in Part Five when looking at environmental governance in practice.

7.3   Changing governance structures

A key element of environmental governance is changing governance structures. This is an important part of any area of governance (Bromley, 2006). In the case of the environment, we find ourselves in the middle of a transformation process trying to develop institutional structures to ensure better use and protection of environmental resources and processes. Certainly, managing environmental resources has a long history. It is reasonable to argue that 'environmental governance' has been part of our history as long as humanity has existed. What is specific to our times is that our use of environmental resources has expanded vastly and that issues appear on all levels up to the global. To be able to study the processes of changing governance structures and to support the development of proposals for further changes, insights into concepts and theories of such changes are important. The aim of this section is to offer an introduction to key perspectives, also drawing on several theories and assessments made in earlier chapters.

While governance structures encompass both institutions and actors, my focus will mainly be on institutional change. I note that changes in institutions are also the basis for constructing new actors. At the same time, actors change institutions. While the process is constrained and difficult, it is dominantly a volitional activity (Giddens, 1984; Bromley, 2006).

Again, we enter a complex field of study. One issue relates to the fact that there are several theories of human action, and each points towards separate interpretations of institutional change. Another is that there are so many types of institutions, so many contexts in which institutional change happens, so many reasons for why change may be wanted, and so many causes for it still not happening. Therefore, it is very difficult to create 'the theory' of institutional change.

One element in this is the distinction between agency and structure. How can a structure be challenged that imprints itself upon actors who, moreover, see and evaluate the world around them based on these institutions? How can 'rule followers' suddenly become 'rule breakers'? How can habituated man (Veblen, 1919; Bourdieu, 1990) turn into reflexive or deliberative man (Giddens, 1991; Archer, 2003)? At the same time, there must also be reflexivity and creativity since institutions do change. The question is, nevertheless, how deliberate such changes are. Some oppose that idea. Hence, I will start by a brief overview of theories viewing institutional change as spontaneous versus designed. Next, I will offer an overview of various interpretations of the dynamics of institutional change. What can motivate such change and what 'does it take' to go from an idea about a need for change to make it happen?

7.3.1   Spontaneous vs designed

The idea of institutional change as spontaneous comes in different forms. The 'purest' version states that such change is not a result of any intention or 'plan'. It follows from individual actors developing a system of shared beliefs about how to act. Institutions are, moreover, sustained by self-enforcement – see, for example, Hayek (1988); Sened (1997); Aoki (2001). Hayek talks about spontaneous creation of various solutions and a selection of the best institutions happens as if it was 'a market for institutions'. The idea is similar to that of biological selection. It is 'governance without government' (Young, 2009).

Designing institutions implies that they are crafted or created through a reasoned process – see, for example, Shackle (1961); Bromley (2006). They are formed through deliberation among actors about what seems to be the better institutions to create given a defined challenge. This position refers mainly to political processes whether at local, national or international level. Some refer, however, also to processes of institutionalization within firms as the result of communication/negotiations between the involved parties – for example, owners and workers (Bromley, 2006) – or among participants of a common property (e.g., Ostrom, 2005).

There is a tendency to equate spontaneous institutional change with unintentional and bottom-up, and designed institutional change as intentional and top-down (Sened, 1997). I find this confusing, while not always wrong. The language comes closest to a spontaneously developed institution. It is self-enforcing since to make oneself understood one has to follow the rules of the specific language. Nevertheless, words are the result of a creation by somebody. Hence, there is the intention to say something not said before. Not all new words proposed 'survive', however. Hence, there seems to be a kind of 'spontaneous' selection process where a new word establishes itself if enough people use it. Certainly, words also 'die' when people stop using them.

Many conventions may actually be established this way. Nevertheless, one soon enters the area of intended and even top-down processes in the case of conventions; the length and time conventions are politically codified. There are also intentional/top-down elements involved regarding which side to drive on. Originally, driving was on the left side of the road or path. After the French Revolution, there was a top-down decision to change to right-side driving to create distance to the old political system. At the same time, left-side driving may have originated spontaneously. It has at least been argued that this was because people mainly defended themselves with the right hand (e.g., with a sword).

While this shows a mix of spontaneous and intended, as bottom-up and top-down, I note that in the area of norms, intention has definitely played a great role. This does not necessarily involve top-down – at least in the meaning of a third party. We can envision communities deliberating over what way one should treat each other. It is a process among fellow citizens. Norms are embedded in cultures and not based on or demanding third party legitimation. Hence, they are the result of 'bottom-up' processes, but not unintended. Rather, they are the result of human deliberation over what it should mean to live together in communities.

It is first when we get to formal rules with its third party that we can talk of both intended/designed and top-down institutional change. The solutions may be worked out in parliaments or by governments – local as well as national. Whether a village council or a national parliament makes the rule does not change the fundamental logic of the process and the type of authority involved. The process of creating the new solution may be concentrated around closed processes among political decision-makers. It may also involve citizens to various degrees. The political authority, however, typically draws the conclusion.

Frances Cleaver is among those who have challenged the idea of designed institutional change – for example, Cleaver (2012) – but from a different perspective than Hayek et al. She emphasizes two main limitations to the possibility to design. First, the existing set of institutions limits the opportunity to institutional change. They have to be worked out within or from what is existing. It is a form of rearrangement and implies strong path dependence. Second, studies of designed change tend to focus mostly on formal rules and may miss the informal power structures as well as people's capacity to 'work around' externally imposed rules if they are not serving their interests.

Institutions form us and our relations. Hence, it is most probably impossible to create a new set just by ignoring or demolishing all there is. Agency cannot simply free itself from all structure. Moreover, institutions are per definition durable. Hence, Cleaver is right when claiming that there are limits to change. At the same time, there is also an issue related to how great are the challenges we face. Perceived urgency may offer a basis for change that is more radical in the meaning less path dependent.

7.3.2 The dynamics of institutional change

The above indicates that institutional change happens in many different ways. While it is easier to study changes in formal than informal rules and practices – there are often written sources regarding both arguments and conclusions – the informal structures are at least as important to understand. However, why does change happen? I started by asking, how is it possible to change institutional structures if they represent the ways we see and think – consciously and unconsciously? I will start by making two observations. First, institutional change is pervasive – whether designed or not. Second, while institutions form or construct humans and we often or mostly act on the basis of learned conventions and norms – habituated behavior – humans are reflexive beings. I have emphasized earlier that even following a norm typically demands an evaluation of what kind of behavior is now expected and if one wants to follow what is expected.

So institutional change could follow from the simple fact that enough people decide *not to follow what is expected*. This may be because new values emerge – for example, environmental values – or new interests form. Human interactions take so many forms that no institutional structure is able to 'fix' it all. Alternatively, institutional change may follow from the fact that *what happens is unexpected*. Institutional structures may be built to facilitate economic growth, and then recessions appear. A system may be instituted to ensure management of a water resource, but suddenly depletion is observed. Trees start dying unexpectedly. The list is endless.

Bromley (2006) distinguishes between three steps in the process of institutional change. "The first step is recognition on the part of affected individuals that the status quo institutional setup induces particular behaviors, the aggregate of which gives rise to realized outcomes that are no longer regarded as acceptable or reasonable" (p. 73). The second step "concerns new created imaginings" (p. 74) – visions of alternative structures. The final one is policy formulation where alternative solutions are evaluated and the preferred change is effectuated. While Bromley emphasizes public policy-making, he also uses this structure to study other fields of society – for example, the business sector.

There are several things to comment on regarding these steps. Defining what is acceptable and reasonable is a demanding process. First, one needs to acknowledge that there is something 'wrong'. Oppressive regimes may continue not only because of power of physical control, but also mental 'control' – for example, Lukes's third dimension of power. Hence, what may be seen as illegitimate from 'outside' may continue unopposed. Second, defining something as not acceptable in the sense of being a basis for change demands that one understands what is happening and is able to define the most important causes. This includes asking if the problem is an institutional one. Regarding environmental problems, this is a key question. Finally, there is the issue of wrong for whom? One would expect that push for change is different if what is unacceptable concerns the 'powerful' as opposed to the 'powerless'.

These mechanisms are as important in the process of creating imaginings. Blyth (2003) emphasizes the role of ideas not least in this phase. He notes that in periods of (economic) crisis, ideas reduce uncertainty, making collective action and coalition building possible. In the struggle over existing institutions, these imaginings are weapons and act as blueprints for new structures. This process is a process of delegitimizing present structures and legitimizing alternatives.

Turning finally to the process of evaluating and choosing new structures, power relations are again a core aspect. This regards both what issues to prioritize for action, and if acting, whose interests to protect. In democratic societies, chosen solutions must follow what is understood as legitimate in the given context. This may not imply that solutions are neither 'fair' nor 'effective' seen from the outside. In practical formulations of new institutions, epistemic, normative and positional power are at play. One should therefore recognize the distinction between "victory and defeat in the political battle" versus the "victory and defeat in political argument . . . a question of truth and validity" (O'Neill, 1998, p. 1). As emphasized before, having the power to form other people's visions of *what is* – epistemic power – and *what should be* – normative power – influences the need for using one's positional power; the latter being more visible and exposing 'the battle'.

In relation to this, the issue of uncertainty is important. This regards both uncertainty regarding what causes a problem – that outcomes are not acceptable – and regarding what the effect of various institutional changes would be – for example, changes in resource regimes. This uncertainty 'demands' ways of 'fixing beliefs' about what the better understanding is (Blyth, 2003; Bromley, 2006). It may, however, also create inaction. Uncertainty may either create general 'paralysis' or be used to create such paralysis by those wanting nothing to happen. Again, it is reasonable to refer to the debate over climate change.

Following the EGS framework – see also Figure 7.2 – causes of 'bad' outcomes may be related to four factors:

- It may be 'natural' – that is, be the result of environmental dynamics.
- It may be a result of institutional structures that do not function as expected. This may be because they are not able to produce the desired actions or because they do not 'fit well' to the environmental dynamics. This may be because the rights structure is not well adapted to the characteristics of the problem. Transaction costs may be high and/or the kind of motivation structures/rationalities facilitated are counterproductive. Hence, changes may be necessary to facilitate shifts at all these levels. Changing the logic of economic action may possibly demand changes in actor structures too. Regarding environmental dynamics, I not only think of specific resources or processes, I also have in mind the overall

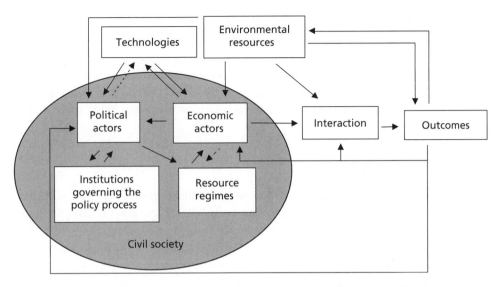

Figure 7.2 The EGS framework used for analyzing institutional change

pressures on the environment created by institutions fostering a growing economy.

- Problems may follow technological change. They could be 'unexpected' effects of new technologies – for example, the appearance of various types of pollution. They may, however, also originate because the new technology changes action and interaction patterns among economic actors – for example, more effective fishing gear results in increased catches. The existing resource regime may turn out to be ineffective in handling the new situation.
- The capacity of the civil society and/or the political system to adapt to new circumstances should finally be mentioned. Inaction may be caused by lacking ability to change. It should also be mentioned that to expand the capacity of the political system to act, new actors may have to be established – for example, new ministries, agencies and local political bodies.

Reflecting on these points brings us back to Cleaver (2012). She emphasizes three aspects that I think are important expansions of the above. First, she mentions that "institutions, established for one purpose, often evolve through bricolage to be multi-functional" (ibid., p. 87). She offers several examples of organizations that have evolved for one purpose – for example, water management – that expand their activities – to, for example, irrigation.[5] Second, she emphasizes complexity in institutional and organizational structures. Hence, action in one field of society – for example, managing water – will be influenced by institutions also developed for other areas. Finally, she emphasizes that change occurs through copying, bending and combining existing rules and logics. This is the idea of institutional bricolage. It is hard to be truly creative. It is easier to copy or mix existing solutions and tested solutions may seem 'safer' given all the uncertainties faced.

7.4 Main messages

Governance is to prioritize which values and interests to protect. This chapter has focused on three aspects of this issue. First, I looked at criteria for 'good governance' – what are legitimate governance and governance structures? Next, I discussed how governance structures influence outputs – in our case the quality of environmental resources and processes. Finally, I looked into the issue of changes in governance structures and what seem to be the main dynamics behind such changes.

Regarding criteria for 'good governance', I first recognized that to the extent governance implies favoring certain interests and values, this may mean that someone wins while others lose. Given this, some understand a decision as legitimate, if it follows 'due process'. A wider definition includes the premise that there is acceptance among those affected – internal legitimacy. Finally, there is also the position that legitimacy demands decisions to stand up well against a defined set of criteria or standards – external legitimacy. While analyses demand studies according to both internal and external criteria, I have proposed a set of external criteria using the distinction between input and output legitimacy: (1) *input (process) legitimacy,* which concerns the appropriateness and acceptability of decision-making processes both regarding fundamental principles concerning societal decisions and with regard to the interests of various actors involved; (2) *output (result) legitimacy* including (a) distributive justice; (b) effectiveness and (c) efficiency.

Studying governance structures and their legitimacy includes emphasis on outputs. In Section 7.2 of the chapter, I highlighted how institutions influence actions and hence output. I concentrated on four ways institutions affect action – that is, through their influence on (1) rights and responsibilities; (2) transaction costs; (3) perceptions; and (4) preferences and type of motivation. These are aspects that I will return to in later analyses when evaluating various existing and alternative governance structures.

Understanding institutional change is important for the study of environmental governance. While such change may be the result of unmanaged processes – being spontaneous – environmental governance depends dominantly on designed change. Environmental problems are, to a large extent, the result of institutional structures that motivate choices that are bad for our environments. Observing increased pressures on ecosystems stimulates searches for change in such structures. This kind of change is, however, demanding. It confronts interests protected by existing institutions. It is also easier to adapt existing institutions than to change the entire path of development. One might, however, ask if that suffices.

NOTES

1 In the literature, we encounter the so-called 3Es as the basis for evaluating policies – see, for example, Stern et al. (2006). The Es are effectiveness, efficiency and equity. The structure proposed in the text is inspired by the 3Es concept. However, including justice goes beyond equity as a criterion. Moreover, I think it is more fundamental than effectiveness and efficiency. Therefore, it is put first.

2 Actually, Rawls (1971) distinguishes between four types of procedural justice – including (a) 'pure procedural justice'; (b) 'perfect procedural justice'; (c) 'quasi-pure procedural justice'; and (d) 'imperfect procedural justice'. Perfect procedural justice concerns a procedure that reliably produces a wanted output. Hence, it combines the input and output side of legitimacy as defined in the main text. The types (c) and (d) are intermediate categories.

3 Not all principles in Box 7.2 are inconsistent with the efficiency criterion – for example, principle 6.

4 For those interested, Marglin (1991) offers a good exposition of an alternative (or supplementary) explanation focusing on power relations. He understands the firm as 'an instrument' to control labor and ensure that the surplus goes to owners. See also Chapter 9.

5 Note, however, that Cleaver here actually talks of organizations and not of institutions.

Part Four

Markets and governance

In this part of the book we shall look at markets as governance structures. There are two main reasons for giving particular space to this issue. First, markets are the dominant institutional structure regarding allocation of resources. Second, there is a strong trend towards increasing the use of markets when allocating environmental resources – to handle environmental conflicts. Hence, to understand the dynamics of environmental degradation and the potentials of this new trend, it is necessary to understand what markets are and do.

In Chapter 8, I will therefore introduce key concepts from the theory of markets as allocating goods and services. I will base the presentation on standard neoclassical (microeconomic) theory. I next widen the analysis by evaluating this theory, including a discussion about distributional issues, preference formation and transaction costs, drawing on previous insights from institutional theory.

In Chapter 9, I move from theory to practice – to a presentation of the process of creating markets. I will look at developments from when markets were mainly localized phenomena strongly embedded in social structures until they became more independent arrangements. I will next look at the vast expansion of markets after World War II and the institutional conditions for that to happen. I close with a discussion of the relationship between the concepts of efficiency and cost shifting.

8

The market

This chapter offers a short presentation of the theory of markets as found in standard textbooks in microeconomics – that is, the neoclassical exposition. I will first offer an overview of the neoclassical understanding of the economic process and contrast that to the perspective of ecological economics. Next follow three sections on the market and its actors – that is, on consumers and their demand, on producers and their supply, and, finally, on how supply and demand 'meet' in markets, creating equilibrium. I note that the presentation in these sections is simplified and reduced to the minimum necessary for discussions and expositions in later chapters. Then I describe markets as an institutional system and discuss how institutional conditions influence the results that markets produce – that is, what becomes a 'market equilibrium'. Finally, I will introduce the concept of 'market failure' and what it may mean that markets fail.

This chapter will include few references as it mainly offers a brief overview of standard textbook material. Those who would like to expand their insights into microeconomic theory could look at Asafu-Adjaye (2005), Schotter (2009) and Varian (2010).

8.1 The neoclassical view of the economic process

The neoclassical model was presented in Section 4.5. It included assumptions about the core – that is, rational choice as maximizing individual utility, stable preferences and equilibrium outcomes. The standard application area includes no information costs, no transaction costs and private property rights for all goods, which are exchanged in competitive markets. We noted that neoclassical or mainstream expositions may include changes in the application area. The presentations here will start out from the standard assumptions.

Figure 8.1 illustrates the mainstream economics description of the economic system. The actors are producers/firms and consumers/households. The main institutions are markets for goods and services (commodities) and

Figure 8.1 The economic system as envisioned in mainstream – neoclassical – economic thinking

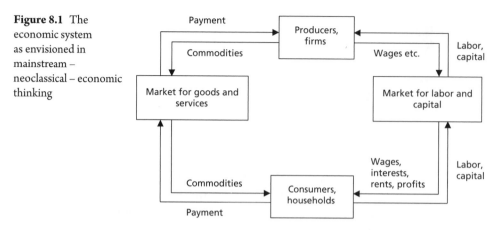

markets for input factors (labor and capital). So while commodities move from firms via markets to consumers against a payment, production factors move from households to the firms also against a payment dependent on the type of factor.

It is notable that the system is physically isolated – nothing enters or leaves. In the sub-branches of environmental and resource economics this delimitation is changed. Figure 8.2 illustrates this.

Figure 8.2 The economy–environment interactions as perceived in neoclassical environmental and resource economics

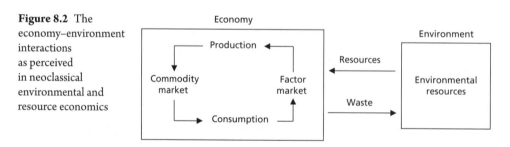

The expanded system includes links to environmental resources through two processes – the inclusion of natural resources in the economy and the production of waste that is emitted into the environment. These processes are typically treated in the sub-fields of resource and environmental economics. The latter also includes other fields beyond waste and pollution – for example, the production of positive side-effects/externalities.

This 'vision' of the economic system and its interaction with the environment has been challenged not least by ecological economists. The point is that the economy not only 'draws upon' but is also embedded in the physical environment – see, for example, Daly and Farley (2011). An alternative 'vision'

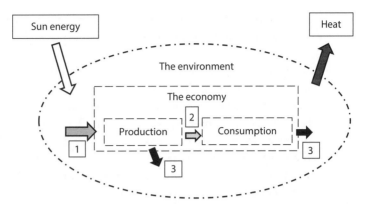

Note: The numbered arrows are flows of 1: inputs; 2: commodities: 3: waste.

Figure 8.3 The ecological economics understanding of the economy–environment interaction

would be to start from this premise and describe the economy as a subsystem of the physical environment as depicted in Figure 8.3 – see also Chapter 1.

Ecological economics emphasizes that the inputs of materials and energy to the economy – extraction here being part of production activities – by necessity results in a similar 'output' of waste. It understands the economic process in thermodynamic terms – see Chapter 2 – emphasizing that the size of the economy also has implications for the environment. The consequences of economic activity on the environment are understood as systemic and not as more or less accidental side-effects of economic activity as is standard in neoclassically inspired analyses.

8.2 Consumers, preferences and demand

According to the neoclassical model, consumers maximize individual utility – the utility that goods and services offer to them. Few economists think that the maximization assumption is literally true, but find it to be a good approximation that furthermore allows for mathematical treatments far beyond what models of, for example, satisficing, admit.

Consumer choice can be described as maximizing the value of a *utility function*:

$$U_j = f(q_1, q_2, \ldots, q_n)|M \tag{8.1}$$

where U_j is the total utility for individual j consuming n different goods and services (q) like food, clothes, housing, heating and so on given the income constraint M.

Consumers have different preferences[1] for the available goods and services. In maximizing their utility, consumers also take into account the price for each commodity and their income – their capacity to pay. Hence, maximization happens under a constraint of available income.

In standard expositions of preferences and utility, the focus is on so-called indifference curves. These show how much the amount of one good needs to be increased to compensate for the loss of one unit of another good while leaving the consumer equally well off. One piece of bread may be equally preferred to ten eggs. At the same time, the *marginal utility* of a commodity – the utility given by one more unit consumed – typically goes down as consumption of that good increases. Hence, simply adding five more eggs may not compensate a reduction in the amount of bread to half. More than that will be needed. At some point there is 'saturation' – for example, there is no increase in total utility by more consumption of the good. Marginal utility is zero.[2]

Given that the consumer is maximizing her or his utility, she or he is willing to pay a price for the good (e.g., eggs) that at maximum is equal to her or his marginal utility. The demand for a good depends on the marginal utility it offers – that is, in optimum the maximum willingness to pay equals the marginal utility. Hence, the willingness to pay goes down from the first to the second egg and so on. The higher the price, the less eggs will be bought. This is illustrated in so-called demand curves. Figure 8.4 shows the demand for eggs from consumer A.

Total demand is the sum of the demand from all consumers – that is, horizontal aggregation of individual demand curves in the figurative exposition. In Figure 8.5, this aggregation is illustrated in a case where there are only two consumers. We note that consumer B is not willing to pay as much for eggs as consumer A. Hence, at high prices only consumer A is willing to buy eggs.

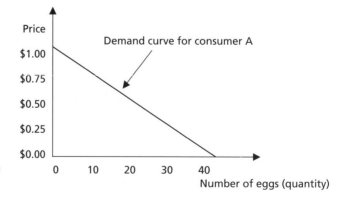

Figure 8.4 Consumer A's demand for eggs

Figure 8.5 Total demand as a function of individual demands

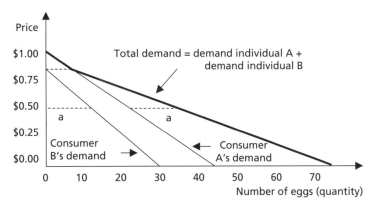

A key empirical observation is that demand for goods that are important for humans will be rather inelastic (e.g., food). This means that demand is not much changed if prices change (price insensitive). Demand curves are 'steep'. Demand for 'luxury' goods is rather elastic (e.g., diamonds) – that is, demand is very price sensitive. Demand curves are 'flat'.

8.3   Producers, costs and supply

Turning to production and supply of goods and services, the theory assumes that producers – that is, firms – maximize profits. They produce according to a production function:

$$q_i = g(x_1, x_2, \ldots, x_m) \qquad (8.2)$$

where q_i is the amount of good i produced on the basis of m inputs (x).

Example: Eggs = g(feed, water, labor, buildings, machinery, medical treatments). Using inputs is costly. They have alternative value – value in alternative uses – and the cost is understood as the loss of that value when used in the specific production such as eggs. *Fixed costs* are investments in, for example, buildings, machinery and so on. These will be costs that the producers face independent of the level of production. *Variable costs* are costs that are dependent on the size of production. In egg production, feed is a typical example. *Marginal costs* are the cost of the last unit of production (in mathematical terms the derivative of the total cost curve). In (egg) production inputs (feed) are assumed to offer diminishing returns. Adding 1 kg of feed to a group of egg-producing hens when the amount already given is low results in more extra eggs produced than if the amount of feed is already high. At the limit, hens cannot digest more. . . The marginal product is zero.

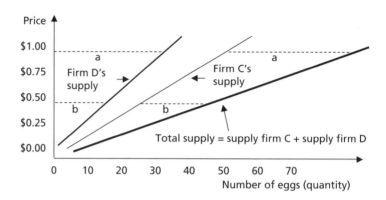

Figure 8.6 Total supply as a sum of supplies from individual firms

The assumption that the producer is maximizing his or her profits implies that he or she will demand a price that is equal to (or higher than) his or her marginal production costs. The reference to 'or higher than' relates to the fact that producers could certainly gain from selling at a price above the marginal costs. If there is competition among several producers and consumers are well informed, the neoclassical model of competitive markets – see Section 8.4 – implies that it is not possible to sell at higher prices.[3] From the above assumptions, it is possible to construct supply curves for various products – in our case eggs – see Figure 8.6. The total supply is the sum of the firms' marginal costs curves above the per unit average costs – the so-called 'break-even'.[4]

Here we observe that firm C is able to produce eggs at a lower price than firm D since marginal costs at all levels of production are below that of this firm.

8.4 The market, market equilibrium and efficiency

The market is a 'place' where goods and services are traded between producers and consumers against a payment. Combining Figures 8.5 and 8.6 we get the standard exposition of a market equilibrium where the number of eggs q is traded at price p – see Figure 8.7. In a situation where the market is competitive – that is, there are many producers and consumers – price and volume are assumed to settle at a level where marginal utility for consumers equals marginal costs for producers. That is, where demand and supply curves intersect. If price is below p, supply will go down and push the price upwards. If price is above p, demand will go down and push the price downwards.

Given the assumptions of the neoclassical model, the market equilibrium is understood as efficient. It is efficient in consumption as consumers get what

Figure 8.7 Market equilibrium

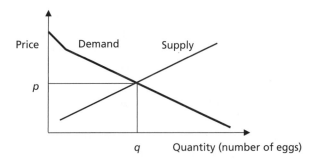

they want according to their individual preferences and to a price that equals marginal utility. It is efficient in production as competing firms are 'forced' to supply to the lowest costs possible. This leads – according to the theory – to economic efficiency in the sense that there is no alternative allocation of resources that makes some people strictly better off and leaves everyone else at least as well off as before. This outcome is called *Pareto optimal*. Any change from this situation will reduce welfare for some.

It is notable that this concept of efficiency avoids comparing the utility of one person against another. The early neoclassical economists like Jevons ([1871] 1957), Marshall ([1890] 1949) and Pigou (1920) built their analyses on the idea that interpersonal comparisons were possible. These authors concluded, for example, that redistribution from the rich to the poor could increase total utility or welfare in a society as the marginal utility of income (money) was understood as higher among the poor. In concrete terms, offering a dollar to a person earning 500 dollars a year would increase the utility of that person more than offering the same dollar to one earning 500 000 dollars.

This position came under heavy attack in the 1920s and 1930s as it was seen as unscientific. Individual utility could not be observed; hence, it could not be compared. Taking a stand on distribution was seen as normative. Economics should strive for value neutrality – become a positive science in the sense of physics. Hence, the Pareto principle was adopted as a normative 'minimum', assuming that if nobody were worse off, it would be acceptable to all.

8.5 The market as a governance system

Markets are institutional systems. They are based on the transformation of goods and services into commodities – that is, tradable units. To ensure this, a long series of institutions need to be in place. Let me offer a few examples:

- *Property rights to goods and resources:* private property is what is most typically emphasized, but public administrations, state-owned firms and common properties may also operate in markets.
- *The institution of money:* direct exchange of goods is possible and such trade is also market trade. Money makes trading much easier – reduces transaction costs – hence it makes it much easier to expand markets geographically.
- *Measurement scales:* weight, length, volume and so on.
- *Other constructs:* firms, banks, financial instruments like loans or stocks.

Before I continue the analysis, I need to emphasize that while the assumptions behind the neoclassical model leading to equilibriums as depicted in Figure 8.7 are unrealistic in many ways – note all kinds of information problems and the existence of transaction costs – I think the model captures something essential when emphasizing that markets facilitate satisfaction of individual preferences and the creation of profits. Moreover, I think the market itself strengthens the role of such motivations. What is problematic is the conclusion that markets are efficient governance structures. The aim of this section is to look more deeply at this issue.

The market equilibrium as described in Section 8.4 seems to be the result 'only' of individual preferences. Hence, it is neutral in the sense that people get what they want. This view is rather simplistic. Instead, the market equilibrium is influenced by several institutional, political and cultural factors. In Section 7.2, we looked at how different institutional aspects influence human choice. In the following, I will reformulate some of these observations to include them as far as possible in the conceptualizations of neoclassical theory and see how that influences the conclusions derived regarding efficiency. I will look at:

- the role of rights:
  - (a) distribution of rights to resources in a society influence income distribution;
  - (b) the rights regarding cost shifting;
- the social construction of preferences;
- transaction costs and various institutional structures – for example, markets vs firms vs state vs community systems.

This way I show how what appears as (Pareto) efficient is a function of the institutional structures created. This implies that institutional systems other than markets have their own optima. The 'best solutions' across these institutional structures demand normative judgments beyond those of markets

themselves. Therefore, to try to guard a theory on efficiency against normative claims turns out to be difficult. Rather, it conceals important value issues.

8.5.1 Economic efficiency – rights and income distribution

Starting with rights and the subsequent income distribution, their effect on
'what becomes efficient' is clearly acknowledged in mainstream economic
theory. By moving from the old perception of efficiency and welfare
enhancement through redistribution (the early neoclassical economists) to
the Pareto efficiency principle (the 'mature' neoclassical position), one tried
to draw a demarcation line between facts and values. It implied drawing a line
between economics and politics. Distribution was defined as a political question, while efficiency became something that a science – that is, economics –
could 'safely' handle.[5] Figure 8.8 illustrates the thinking.

The frontier UPF is the *utility possibility frontier* – that is, all possible situations that are Pareto optimal. At A, all efficiently produced goods and services are consumed by individual I. At B, all are consumed by individual II.
The UPF shows all efficient combinations between these two extremes. If
we are at the frontier – for example, UE – it is not possible to move in any
direction without reducing the utility of either individual I or II. While, individual I is much better off than individual II at UE, it would be a normative
claim to say that, for example, E is better from a societal point of view. If
we are at C, however, neoclassical economics has something to say. There
is an inefficiency, as it would be possible to increase production and move
to(wards) the UPF somewhere at or between D and UE. This will be a *Pareto
improvement* – at least one individual could be made better off without the
other being worse off. Maybe there are some restrictions on the trading in
markets and taking away these would increase efficiency – that is, moving
from C towards the UPF as described. Where to 'land' between D and UE
is not an economic issue, despite the fact that proposals (by economists)

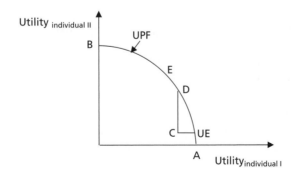

Figure 8.8 Pareto
optimality in utility
space

Figure 8.9 Market equilibria given equal and unequal income distribution

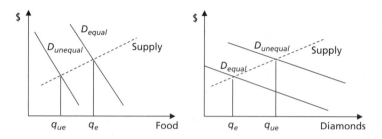

regarding how to move towards the frontier will rarely be neutral in distributional terms.

Figure 8.8 is very abstract. In Figure 8.9, I have transformed the states UE (unequal distribution) and E (equal distribution) in Figure 8.8 into their equivalent market equilibria for two commodities – food and diamonds. Given unequal distribution of income (UE), the total demand for food will be low and the demand for diamonds high, while given equal distribution (E) the opposite will be the case. To be blunt, unequal income distribution may imply that hunger is efficient.

The efficiency concept of neoclassical economics – the distinction between facts and value, between science and politics as implicit in this – is problematic. In Chapter 7, we developed the concept of legitimacy as a wider basis for evaluating governance structures and policies. While it is a demanding analysis, it brings the normative issues to the fore. While this is a 'challenge' to 'traditional ways' of demarcating science, it does what is necessary. It makes the normative issues regarding resource use in a society explicit. Avoiding them is impossible and results rather in hiding crucial aspects. Specifically one avoids the very strong favoring of *status quo* as is implicit in the Pareto principle. This is especially important in the case of environmental governance where distribution of rights – the explicit need to take a position on cost shifting – is a key issue.

8.5.2 Economic efficiency and cost shifting

Environmental problems evolve over time. At the start of a new economic activity, there is 'no problem' observed. As time passes, problems may appear and the question is raised: is this cost shifting really legitimate? In standard efficiency terms, the issue will have to be decided based on aggregate willingness to pay (WTP). In simple terms, this means who pays the most – those that want (more) commodities vs those that want (more) nature – decides the issue.

Let me illustrate with a case of water pollution following from the production of paper. This manufacturing results in the emission of sulfates that gradually reduces water quality. If people's willingness to pay for a clean environment is lower than the willingness to pay for paper, *status quo* emissions are optimal. If not, they should be reduced.

Is this, however, a legitimate basis on which to define the 'right' emission level? There are several issues involved here that should be emphasized:

- Even in cases where emissions are reduced, victims would typically have to endure some pollution caused by others. The argument is that no pollution would be inefficient as long as some are willing to pay for paper, or that cleaning discharges are costly. The 'optimum' is where marginal costs of reduced emissions equal the marginal gain in environmental quality.[6] However, victims may not consider this a legitimate basis for deciding on the level of pollution. They may claim that the environment should be unpolluted. It may be termed a rights issue, not one where other people's WTP can trump one's interest.
- Accepting the economic logic, one may next argue that the present income distribution influences what becomes an 'efficient emission level' as calculated based on WTP – simply because willingness depends on capacity to pay. One may raise the question whether the amount of clean environment should rather be seen as a rights issue than decided on the basis of the present income distribution.
- Responsibility for environmental damage is typically defined a long time after it has appeared. At the time when interference is proven and action is taken, there are many investments made in the specific production and many consumers have become accustomed to using the product produced. However, these investments and habits make it more costly to reduce emissions compared to a situation with responsibility for pollution defined from 'day one'. In the latter case, investments as well as consumption patterns would have been adapted to the required lower emissions from the beginning and more nature protection would have turned out to be cheaper, hence 'efficient' (Vatn, 2002).
- Last, even if one accepts the argument that choosing pollution levels should be based on efficiency evaluations, one is nevertheless faced with a right's/normative issue that cannot be dispensed from. It is observed that whether rights are with polluters or with victims – see Chapter 7 – influences 'the value of the environment' in economic terms. If the right is with polluters, it is victims' willingness to pay (WTP) that should be the basis for evaluating the value of a cleaner environment. If the right is with the victims, the measure should, however, be

the willingness to accept (WTA) compensation for pollution. There is strong evidence that WTA is much higher than WTP – typically in the order of two to four times (Kahneman and Knetsch, 1992; Horowitz and McConnell, 2002). Therefore, who has the right has tremendous influence on what 'becomes efficient'. Given a consistent treatment of the economic logic, the implication of this is that offering rights to victims (WTA) would make it efficient to protect much more nature than if rights are with polluters (WTP).

I will return to these topics in more detail in Part Five. At this stage, it is sufficient to have a grasp of the important links between the institutional basis of the economy and the concept of efficiency.

8.5.3 Economic efficiency and social formation of preferences

The argument regarding the influence of institutions and the socialization process on preferences has been clearly demonstrated in Chapter 5. Here I will illustrate how different preferences – as socially constructed – influence the market equilibrium ('what becomes efficient').

The example chosen (Figure 8.10) regards alcohol consumption in countries where there is a strong norm against such consumption – the 'Muslim' culture – vs countries without such a norm – here depicted 'non-Muslim'. What is efficient consumption is clearly defined by this norm. As depicted, there is no sale of alcohol under the 'Muslim' culture.

The core issue is the way institutions influence preferences and 'what becomes efficient'. A question following from that concerns whether markets themselves influence preferences. As is well established within marketing and business research, marketing increases sales and builds loyalty to brands – see, for example, Dekimpe and Hanssens (1995); Hooley et al.

Figure 8.10 Demand for alcohol in Muslim and non-Muslim countries

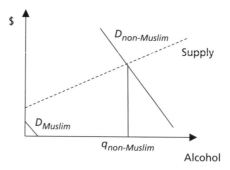

(2005). Hence, preferences are not a stable product even of cultures. They seem especially volatile in market economies.

There is a wider issue here that the above type of marketing research cannot enlighten. This regards how markets – by their capacity to deliver commodities of all kinds – push our perceptions and 'preferences' from non-market experiences towards goods and services that markets are able to deliver – that is, towards increased focus on commodities. Institutional theory would expect this kind of 'drift' to happen.

We observe that the stable individual preference – the bedrock of neoclassical economics – cannot be maintained. Rather, the basis for the evaluation of efficiency is an 'elastic' measure. If markets themselves influence the preferences of individuals, how can one argue that (even well-functioning) markets are efficient? Certainly, when preferences are dependent on the institutional structure itself, one cannot judge its favorability by using the measures made available by that structure itself. We are faced with a problem of circularity. In this situation, one is forced to ask what governance structures create the 'best preferences'? This is an 'outrageous' question to ask given neoclassical theory as based on Western ideas about 'individual autonomy or freedom'. However, we cannot escape the question. Rather, the issue is how to handle the question. How should societies settle their conventions and norms in an open dialogue where the issue is to define what 'we want to become'? What are legitimate processes for settling such questions? This concerns us both as individuals and as members of communities.

In relation to this, the distinction between needs and wants should also be mentioned. Preferences – while socially influenced – refer to subjectively observed wants. We buy what we want. What we want may or may not fulfill needs we have. In the literature, needs are understood in more 'objectivist' terms – see, for example, Max-Neef (1991); O'Neill et al. (2008). It is about what is good for us. To illustrate the difference: I may want a Coke, while the high content of sugar may not be healthy for me. Therefore, what we want may not be what we need. Also, this terrain is complex. Physical needs have an objective basis – for example, bodily needs for calories, proteins, minerals, clothing and so on. However, these needs may be satisfied in different ways. Some may get protein from eggs, others from beans. Moving to the social dimension of life, what is an objective need becomes even harder to define. The distinction between wants and needs also pertains here. Family, friendship and various other ways of belonging seem universal, while formats vary across cultures. Markets may satisfy wants, but not necessarily needs.

8.5.4 Economic efficiency and transaction costs

The final aspect I want to highlight is the consequence of assuming zero transaction costs when analyzing markets and market equilibria. In the market context, this implies that there are no costs related to acquiring information about the commodities available – their price and quality. There are no costs related to trading – for example, shopping, contracting. There are finally no costs related to ensuring that what is supposed to be delivered is actually delivered – for example, no enforcement costs.

Williamson (1985) notes that if transaction costs are zero – as in the standard neoclassical model – there is no way to distinguish between different governance structures on efficiency grounds. The argument is simple. People will have full information and will not accept anything but 'the best'. Moreover, they have all the power needed to enforce that, since the costs of such power are zero. Hence, outcomes will – according to Williamson – be the same independent of governance structures in the 'strange world' of zero transaction costs. While I acknowledge Williamson's argument as valid given his assumptions, I also note that he does not consider that different governance structures may create different individuals – that is, preferences and motivations – as discussed above.

Wallis and North (1986) estimated transaction costs to cover over half the gross national product in the US economy in 1970. This indicates that transaction cost economics is important.[7] The level of transaction costs, measured as the fraction of all costs, had approximately doubled since 1870. The increase does not imply that transacting has become less efficient over time. Rather, it is the opposite. Since these costs are reduced per unit of transaction, more transactions can be undertaken. The increase in aggregate transaction costs is rather an effect of the fact that economies grow and differentiate. As we specialize, we trade more and the costs of transacting become relatively more important than the costs of producing.

The point to raise then is, however, obvious: what governance structures are characterized by the lowest transaction costs – the lowest costs of interaction? Although this is not the only important criterion for evaluating governance structures for environmental governance (see Chapter 7), it is significant. As emphasized on several occasions, environmental problems are about human interaction. The more costly it is to be involved in necessary interactions that could mediate these problems, the fewer of them will be reconciled.

8.6   Markets and 'market failures'

Neoclassical theory acknowledges that markets may 'fail'. They also note that there are interactions between people that are not captured by markets. There are so-called 'external effects' – that is, services or disservices that go unnoticed by markets. This is a core issue in environmental economics.

This sub-discipline of neoclassical economics focuses on pollution. As this has no price – there is no cost of emitting – the amounts of emissions are too high. As emphasized above, this causes inefficiency. One way to solve the problem would be to try to include these disservices in the market by linking property rights to them. Another is to tax emissions at the level of their (marginal) damage to mimic the effect of a market price on emissions. This is the solution mostly emphasized in environmental economics analyses.[8]

While pollution is an example of a negative externality, there are also positive side-effects of production and consumption – that is, positive externalities. Examples would be cultural landscapes and well-maintained streets, homes and gardens. In this case, the lack of a price implies under-provisioning. Ever since Pigou (1920), the proposition has been to institute a subsidy on delivery of the positive side-effect to restore efficiency.

In environmental economics there is a general perception that externalities are accidental – see, for example, Baumol and Oates (1988). There are two main arguments against this view – one relates to the physical dimension, the other to the issue of motivation. Regarding the first, recall the ecological economics vision of the economic process as presented in Section 8.1. One conclusion we can draw from that perspective is that hardly any production or consumption process avoids external effects. On the one hand, ecosystems will be changed through the process of creating inputs to the economic process. On the other, all matter and energy that is included in the economic process will end up as waste at some point. Hence, externalities are pervasive phenomena. Therefore, there will be 'market failures' related to any transaction in the market. This is a disturbing observation regarding the focus on markets as ensuring efficiency. They will never do so. This does not imply that one should not use markets at all. Certainly, no system is able to guard against side-effects. Rather, the question will be what system will – in each concrete case – be best at handling side-effects? Formulated differently, what system will create the fewest side-effects? To analyze this, the issue – variations in transaction costs across governance structures – will be crucial. However, motivational issues will also be key.

Regarding these issues, we recall that according to the neoclassical model, actors maximize utility (consumers) or profits (firms). This implies that if costs can be shifted and done without violating any previously established and enforceable rights, then it will happen under the assumption of individual rationality – see, for example, Kapp (1971). One may ask why factories place themselves near water sources, and why chimney stacks are built high. Again, we observe that externalities cannot be viewed as accidental. Certainly, people or firms do not emit pollution to hurt others. Nevertheless, as they try to avoid costs falling upon themselves, they unavoidably shift them onto others. Examples and further discussions regarding environmental challenges as systemic features of market economies – whether physical or motivational – follow in Chapter 9 and in Part Five.

8.7　Main messages

Again, we have encountered how important concepts and models are to our understanding. This chapter began by contrasting the neoclassical and the ecological economics interpretation of the economic process. The former underlines the interaction of producers and consumers via markets. The latter emphasizes how the economy – market or non-market – is embedded in the environmental systems that support it. These two visions have very different implications for how we think about environmental governance.

To facilitate later discussions about economic instruments and markets in Part Five, we have looked at a set of core concepts from the neoclassical theory of the market – for example, the marginal utility and marginal cost concepts, demand functions, production functions and the market equilibrium. A basic conclusion in mainstream economics is that given certain assumptions – that is, those of the core and standard application theorems (see Chapter 4) – markets allocate resources in an efficient way. They create Pareto efficiency.

This conclusion is, however, contentious. I have shown that 'what becomes efficient' depends on institutional aspects, for example, the distribution of rights to resources, rights regarding cost shifting, the market-led construction of preferences and the level of transaction costs. So, important factors determining what is efficient are themselves influenced by the market institutions. To break out of this circularity, one needs to acknowledge that any governance structure influences rationality, distribution and costs. To evaluate which could serve us best, one needs to compare across such structures in an unbiased way. It demands developing criteria that are not internal to just one of the governance structures involved – for example, the market. In Chapter 7, I developed the concept of legitimacy to serve that purpose.

In closing the chapter, I brought together the ecological economics and institutional critique of mainstream economics in a discussion of the concept of 'market failure'. The former perspective shows us that market failures – for example, external effects – are not accidental, but rather pervasive. This points towards a need for thinking about environmental governance beyond 'correcting market failures'. The institutionalist critique emphasizes how markets facilitate self-regarding thinking. Given such thinking, cost shifting or creation of externalities is to be expected as a way for each firm or individual to 'protect' his or her interests. This way, the market facilitates a rationality that itself enhances environmental problems.

NOTES

1 Preferences are understood as a ranking of alternatives. The theory assumes preferences to be rational. This means that they are: *Complete:* Preferences are complete if the person is able to rank all goods or bundles of goods. This implies that for all x and $y \in X$: $x \geq y$ or $y \geq x$.
Transitive: Preferences are transitive if the ranking is such that x is better than y and y is better than z then x must be better than z. Formally: for all x, y and $z \in X$ where $x \geq y$ and $y \geq z$ then also $x \geq z$ must hold.
Continuous: Preferences are continuous if x is preferred over y and z is sufficiently close to y, then x is also preferred over z. This implies that the consumer is able to distinguish between goods even though the difference in the utility they offer is infinitesimal – see Varian (2010). Moreover, it is assumed that consumers choose what they prefer the most.

2 Historically, utility was seen as a quantitative measure of happiness – see, for example, Bentham ([1789] 1970); Marshall (1890). In modern economics it is dominantly seen only as a way to describe preferences (e.g., Varian 2010). It is not linked to happiness. Moreover, utility is understood as an ordinal concept – as a ranking of goods as revealed through choice.

3 Monopolists could, however, increase their profits by keeping prices above the marginal production costs by reducing production levels. They have the power to do so.

4 Actually, firms will – according to assumptions – start supplying as soon as average variable costs are covered. They will, however, then not be able to cover their fixed costs and will over time go bankrupt.

5 Neoclassical economists acknowledge that there are two value assertions behind even the Pareto principle – that one accepts the status quo distribution and that more is always better than less.

6 For readers that find this statement abstract or unintelligible, return to this passage after reading Chapter 12.

7 The transaction costs carried by individuals when searching for information, shopping and so on were not included. Transactions within firms were, however, incorporated.

8 This is curious. As long as the assumption of zero transaction costs is maintained – and that is typically the case in environmental economics – there is no reason for introducing taxes. It would be enough to define rights since actors can trade costlessly. Coase emphasized this already in 1960. Certainly, transaction costs are mentioned in newer texts on environmental economics. There is, however, yet no systematic treatment of the issue.

9

A brief history of markets and their actors

The aim of this chapter is to offer a few glimpses into the history of markets and its actors. I want to highlight two issues. First, markets and firms – even consumers – are socially constructed. Behind the process of forming and reforming especially markets and firms, we find social conflicts and political struggles influencing their form and importance. Understanding these struggles is important for comprehending the meaning of present arrangements and catching a glimpse of some alternative trajectories that were historically not pursued. Second, there are certain characteristics of the way we presently organize our economies – the dominating forms of markets and firms – that seem to have a strong impact on the way modern environmental governance is constructed. The chapter will highlight some of these.

9.1   The evolution of markets

The market I described in Chapter 8 is a theoretical or 'idealized' structure perceived as a 'natural order of things'. However, markets are not 'just there'. They do not simply evolve along a path of unfolding logic of individual rationality. They exist in many forms and the creation of, for example, the 'world market(s)' of today is a history of battles lost and battles won. Adam Smith saw markets as the result of a human propensity to truck, barter and exchange one thing for another (Smith [1776] 1976). The institutionalist understanding is different. We even have to be constructed as economic actors – see, for example, Veblen (1899); Polanyi ([1944] 1957); Callon (1998).

In this section, I will look at three issues. First, I will briefly describe a few important forms of markets, which all still exist. Second, I will discuss the development of so-called impersonal exchange – the one that comes closest to the textbook exposition of markets. Finally, I will look at the process of making land (nature) and labor tradable – that is, transform them into commodities. The last two topics are controversial in the sense that scholars in relevant fields tend to understand the issues and developments quite differently. I will offer a few indications regarding these disagreements, but again, the story I offer will have to be very limited in scope and depth.

Trade or exchanges have existed for a very long time. North (1991, p. 98) writes:

> The earliest economies are thought of as local exchange within a village (or even within simple hunter and gathering society). Gradually, trade expands beyond the village: first to the region, perhaps as a bazaar-like economy; then to longer distances, through particular caravan or shipping routes; and eventually to much of the world.

In the assessments of the expansion of markets and trade as presented by economic historians, a main focus is on division of labor and comparative advantage. Trade makes gains of specialization possible. People benefit from developing knowledge and skill in one craft and exchange their produce for all the other goods needed. Similarly, some products are more easily made in one place than another – for example, products from local ecosystems like spices, fur, fish, certain metals and so on.

North's description above hints at a certain succession in this process 'ending' in the 'impersonal' world market. In the case of trade within the local group – for example, village or tribe – North emphasizes the strong dependency on dense social networks. He cites Colson (1974, p. 59) who emphasizes that "[t]he communities in which all these people live were governed by a delicate balance of power, always endangered and never to be taken for granted: each person was constantly involved in securing his own position in situations where he had to show his good intentions".

A type of trade that goes beyond the local community is that of the bazaar. According to North, it has also existed for thousands of years. He sees it as a relatively impersonal form of exchange with rather high transaction costs. He writes:

> The basic characteristics are a multiplicity of small-scale enterprises with as much as 40 to 50 percent of the town's labor force engaged in this exchange process. . . a very finely drawn division of labor; an enormous number of small transactions, each more or less independent of the next; face to face contracts; and goods and services that are not homogeneous. . . There are no institutions devoted to assembling and distributing market information; that is, no price quotations. . . Systems of weights and measures are intricate and incompletely standardized. Exchange skills are very elaborately developed, and are the primary determinants of who prospers in the bazaar. (North, 1991, p. 103)

Hence, haggling over price and so on is a characteristic of this arena.

Caravan trade was an important way to establish trade between people living large distances from each other. Here exchanges were between strangers and it was an even greater problem to create necessary trust to make trade possible. How could one protect one's goods or 'property' and ensure acceptable terms of trade? North cites Clifford Geertz who gives a description of caravan trade in Morocco around 1900:

> Protection is personal, unqualified, explicit, and conceived of as the dressing of one man in the reputation of another. . . the essential transaction is that a man who counts 'stands up and says'. . . to those whom he counts: 'this man is mine; harm him and you insult me; insult me and you will answer for it'. (North, 1991, p. 104)

According to North (ibid.), tribal leaders found it rewarding to protect caravans, but they did not have the capacity to ensure protection through systems of formalized property rights.

We observe in all these cases a lack of or weak third party institutions creating a system depending on norms and threats to function. The anthropological literature throws a further and partly different light on so-called 'primitive forms of trade'. Here substantial effort has been on understanding the 'economy of the gift' – see, for example, Malinowski ([1922] 2002); Mauss ([1925] 1965); Gregory (1982); Graeber (2001). Malinowski emphasized 'exchange' of goods between individuals with the expectation of being returned at a later stage. It is characterized by reciprocity. Mauss emphasized that there was a kind of obligation involved, mainly as acts between representatives of groups. They were a way to build and maintain relations with others. Both authors saw 'the gift' as different from economic exchange. The basis was simply of a different kind, moving Gregory (1982) to emphasize a distinction between gifts and commodities. Gifts are embedded in political, religious and/or family institutions and do not represent a separate sphere like commodity markets.

Economic historians have emphasized the development of trade as local and personal, gradually becoming long distance and hence more and more impersonal. North (1981, 1991) sees this mainly as a development related to lowered transaction costs. He emphasizes not least how third party protection of property rights reduces transaction costs substantially (North, 1981). In North (1991) he also emphasizes three other institutional developments that facilitated this: (1) increased mobility of capital, due to shifts from usury law to interest; the evolution of the bill of exchange (implying a fixed date for repaying); more elaborate systems for accounting making it gradually possible to move from a family-based control system to more general or impersonal systems; (2) reduced information costs – especially the printing of manuals providing information on measurement scales, exchange rates between different monies and so on; (3) the transformation of uncertainty to risk – the techniques making it possible to calculate expected outcomes of investments, undertake portfolio diversification and hedge against risks.[1]

North indicates some of the institutional developments necessary to make markets 'work'. There are many engagements – both private and public – behind this development. North (1981, 1991) emphasizes not least the importance of protecting property rights through establishing third party enforcement – dominantly through state action.

This third party aspect has been subject to some considerable discussion among economists taking different positions regarding the institutional aspects of the economic process. Some like Sugden (1986), Hayek (1988) and Aoki (2001) emphasize the role of spontaneous order, and downplay the role of the state – see also Chapter 7. Others like Greif (2006, 2008) follow North and emphasize the important as well as the historic specificity of the creation of a 'modern state' as impartial and as ensuring impersonal exchanges through trade. Greif's argument is that not only is a third party necessary, he also argues that it was the capacity to constrain the power of this party – that is, the state – that made it possible to develop impersonal exchange.

The basis for the market economy in its impersonal form is the security of property rights and the enforceability of contract. Historically, a combination of norms and physical force was a basis for ensuring many forms of trade – see above. There are, however, limits to how far such a system is able to develop as there are strong limitations to private order contract enforcement institutions as Greif (2008) calls for example, reputation-based institutions.

Greif (2006, 2008) understands the development in a game-theoretical perspective. He thinks of institutional development in efficiency or cost–benefit terms. States or other 'sovereigns' may abuse rights. However, it is not the lack of power to abuse rights – that is, a weak state or sovereign – that creates the basis for secure property rights. Protection of rights demands a robust state. At the same time, a strong counterpower of private economic actors, standing up against the power of the state, is seen as necessary to avoid third party abuse. According to Greif (2008), this kind of situation existed in Western Europe – especially in England – from the late medieval period and into the industrial era. According to him, it created a historically quite genuine basis for building the necessary institutions for impersonal trade.

Referring to points made in Chapter 6 about the building of democracy as creating the role of citizens, politicians and administrators, one may note that Greif seems to overemphasize the role of economic interests as necessary for ensuring an 'impartial state'. Control of power abuse has shifted over time to be more about democratic culture and citizen control. Hence, while economic counterpower may have been important for the creation of a controllable state, other mechanisms may develop and over time become more decisive. The 'English' form of legal system backing property rights was historically unique. It had, however, the capacity to spread far beyond this specific context in parallel to the fact that the form of controlling the state itself changed.

The above development was a focus also of Karl Polanyi, and his book *The Great Transformation* (Polanyi [1944] 1957). He saw the development of the modern market as disembedding it from the wider social and political context and becoming a 'self-regulated' system. He pointed out that disembedding implied transforming all forces of production – also land and labor – into the commodity form. However, while commodities are produced for trade, land and labor are not. Polanyi (ibid., p. 71) writes: "A market economy must comprise all elements of industry, including land, labor and money. . . But labor and land are no other than the human beings themselves of which every society exists and the natural surroundings in which it exists". He continues (p. 73):

> Now, in regard to labor, land, and money such a postulate cannot be upheld. To allow the market mechanism to be sole director of the fate of human beings and their natural environment, indeed, even of the amount and use of purchasing power, would result in the demolition of society.

Polanyi built parts of his analysis on the process of 'commodifying' land and labor as happened in England throughout the seventeenth and nineteenth centuries. He noted the great despair that these developments created among the poor as they were driven from their land through the enclosure movement and forced to live unprotected off their labor only. It is notable that the enclosure – that is, the privatization of 'common land' – was driven by the English Parliament – at that time controlled by the landowning classes. He also emphasized the fact that the disembedded market economy was prone to crises – noting the number of recessions observed throughout the nineteenth century, culminating in the crisis of the 1930s. These developments demonstrate the limits of disembedding – of 'self-regulation'. The role of the state was therefore gradually expanded beyond protecting property to include some social security issues – through the creation of labor laws and economic safety nets for those who were out of a job, had reduced working capacity and so on.

9.2 The evolution of the firm and the modern consumer

9.2.1 The creation of the firm

Parallel to the history of markets is the creation of its actors – the producers and the consumers. Again, I can only cover a few key issues. A firm is a production unit. Historically, many forms have been created – for example, family farms, village-based co-production, cooperatives, factories, ancient river dynasties and modern globalized companies. In this landscape, it is difficult to draw a distinct line between what is a firm and what is not. It is clearly a business – a unit oriented to production – but can take many forms such as sole proprietorship, partnership or corporation.

From an institutional perspective, the firm is an institutional structure – a unit of command – see, for example, Coase (1937) and Williamson (1975, 1985). It is based on contracts with labor that subsume their capacities under the command of an owner or his or her agent. One perspective is to emphasize the firm as a way to reduce transaction costs – see the discussions in Chapter 7. Eggertsson (1990) clarifies by comparing a firm with using the market. The latter would imply that the consumer has to negotiate with several separate producers of inputs, putting together the final product themselves. Wanting a bicycle, he or she has to shop around for producers of wheels, frames, brakes and so on. First of all, this is time consuming and demands that the consumer has extensive knowledge of how to make the final product. It also demands that the different components are produced according to common standards so that they fit together.

Competing explanations for the creation of firms exist, however. Marglin (1991) argues, as an example, that the firm is not only a way to reduce transaction costs; it also secures greater surplus to owners. A short visit to the first English textile factories may illustrate the point. Originally, the weaving industry was organized as a 'putting out' system, where merchants/capital owners supplied home workers with weaving chairs and wool/yarn. This changed over time as workers were assembled in common buildings – factories. This, however, did not imply changes in production methods. The laborers ran weaving chairs practically as at home. No assembly line was established. The first woolen mills did not use water- or steam-based power, so even this could not be the reason for bringing workers together.

Marglin (1991) observes that the capital owners complained about the functioning of the labor market. If workers were paid more, they worked less. They had a certain need for consumption and instead, for increasing their effort, higher pay made them "stretch Saint Monday into Holy Tuesday" (p. 236). He also refers to "endless squabbles over product quality as well as embezzlement and fraud" (pp. 236–7). Thus, capitalists searched for ways to strengthen control to increase their revenues. The end result of this process was, according to Marglin, the factory.

Firms may also be seen as a way to pool capital. 'Modern' forms of organizing ownership of firms may illustrate the dynamics in this. At present, there is one dominant type of firm – the corporation. Again, the history is interesting. Bakan (2004) offers an analysis of its rise. Up until the end of the nineteenth century, the family firm and the partnership dominated as ways of organizing economic life. The dominance of the corporation was – according to Bakan – unexpected. He writes: "The corporation's dramatic rise to dominance is one of the remarkable events in modern history, not least because of the institution's inauspicious beginnings" (ibid., p. 5).

The first joint stock company was established in England in 1568 – the Company of the Mines Royal – based on the need to raise capital for activities of a size beyond what was possible even for partnerships. By 1688, 15 such firms with split management and ownership existed. There was much opposition to this institution, not least because of worries concerning the opportunities for fraud. Scandals followed, and in 1720 the right to establish corporate bodies was banned in England by the Bubble Act. This law was in power until 1825.

Meanwhile, the development of the corporation shifted to the United States. Corporations were established not least to raise enough capital to build railways, and they were looked upon as instruments of government. Moreover, several restrictions were put upon the corporate body. The stockholders had full liability. Corporations could only operate for narrowly defined purposes like railway building, for a limited amount of time and in certain locations. Hence, there were deliberate restrictions on how large a corporation could grow, defined to protect society against corporate dominance. They reflected the need for taking a multiplicity of interests and values into account.

The first restriction to fall was that of full liability. The idea of limited liability was instituted in England in 1851, substantially lowering the risks of investing in corporations and boosting their growth. Throughout the rest of the century, a process towards establishing the corporation as a legal person was, moreover, completed. According to Bakan, this happened "through a bizarre legal alchemy, [where] courts had fully transformed the corporation into a 'person'" (ibid., p. 16). The corporate person had taken the place of its owner. Gone was the 'grant theory' of corporations as instruments for government.

As important were the changes undertaken in the 1890s by the states of New Jersey and Delaware – emphasizing corporations as 'free individuals'. The rules requiring businesses to exist only for narrowly defined purposes, for limited time and to operate only within one state were repealed. The rules concerning control on mergers and acquisitions were also loosened. Finally, the rule against a company holding stocks in other companies was eliminated. Other states followed, and these changes resulted in a tremendous concentration of corporate power as the number of corporations in the USA fell quickly from 1800 in 1898 to 157 in 1904.

Veblen ([1904] 1958) offers an important addition to this story. He emphasizes that there was a shift from a 'money economy' to a 'credit economy' throughout the latter half of the nineteenth century, increasing the role of a secondary market for credit. This created a new form of uncertainty linked to the expectations of investors. Moreover, as markets expanded tremendously in the latter part of the nineteenth century, another kind of uncertainty appeared – unreliable demand. According to Veblen, the legal transformation and subsequent rise of the corporation in the 1890s in the USA was a response to these uncertainties. Cooperation between firms was a way to ensure a more secure environment for business investment and operation. Monopolization was a way to consolidate business in the face of uncertainties. Its development was, however, hindered by the Sherman Anti-Trust Act of 1890. The 'solution' among business people to this 'obstacle' was found in pushing for changes in the legal basis of the corporation, including among other elements the right for a corporation to own stocks in other corporations.

The concentration of corporate power provoked, however, a social and political reaction, reflected, for example, in the Trust Buster movement and the demand that corporations act in socially responsible ways. Some corporations were broken up. Some also changed their wage policies in response to this critique. In the 1930s, the concept of corporate social responsibility appeared in parallel to the New Deal policy. The latter reflected an ideology that remained dominant for several decades. This was superseded by neoliberalism that gained in strength from the late 1970s, changing the role of governments and reducing the power of labor unions as the process of economic globalization accelerated. I will soon return to this.

9.2.2 The development of consumers

Meanwhile, I will offer a few reflections on the development of the other market actor – the consumer. The consumer appears as a product of expanding markets as well as a prerequisite for it. In most of the 'life of humanity', the consumer role has had no meaning despite the fact that consuming was always a necessary part of living. It was – and still is for many – not separated from production.

So when could the 'consumer' be seen as a separate role? No definite answer can be given to this question; however, through the Industrial Revolution of the seventeenth and eighteenth centuries, mass production expanded and formed a basis for specialization in production. This resulted in increasing trade volumes and hence consumption, based on what others had produced, grew. In the second Industrial Revolution – from about 1860 – the accumulation of capital made it possible for some to increase consumption vastly beyond fulfillment of basic needs. Veblen (1899) describes a type of consumption where an important motivation was to show social power and prestige developing in the USA in the late nineteenth century – he termed it 'conspicuous consumption'.[2]

Through the twentieth-century development of mass consumerism, the level of consumption has expanded greatly among not only rich and middle class people, but also among workers in many parts of the world. Certainly, there is great variation, with about 1.2 billion people living on less than 1.25 US dollars a day (Olinto et al., 2013). We also observe trends in the West where the working class and parts of the middle class are losing out in many countries – see, for example, Piketty (2014).[3] At the same time, it is notable that average consumption measured as GDP per capita is estimated to be almost eight times higher in 1990 as compared to 1820 (Maddison, 2001).[4]

One issue is that the expansion of production and consumption has created challenges for maintaining the functioning of the world's ecosystems. Another is the question of whether it is actually offering a better life for people. Eradicating poverty is unquestionably a good and very important thing. However, does continued growth in consumption enhance life quality?

The literature is divided in this. Gabriel (2013) is among those emphasizing that consumerism has led to increased social mobility – consumers have been empowered. He states that "[i]t reinforces participation and equality by making liberty not an abstract right to public discourse but an expression of oneself through deliberate acquisition decisions and a realization of personal satisfaction in and through goods in daily experience" (p. 52).

At the same time, 'happiness research' documents that expanding income beyond 12 000–15 000 US dollars per person seems to add little to human well-being, measured as self-reported happiness – see, for example, Layard (2005). There are certainly limitations to this kind of measurement, but the findings across the literature are quite consistent. Subjective happiness appears not to increase with income, when income is above a certain threshold. Senik (2009) documents at the same time that distributional features matter for subjective well-being. Inequality is *ceteris paribus* associated with lower subjective well-being. This seems to be compatible with Veblen and the implicit point that one's rank in the social hierarchy is important for how well one feels.

Studies in consumption research – for example, Kasser and Kanner (2004); Solberg et al. (2004) – may throw further light on what is going on here. In line with Veblen, this research sees consumption as a form of social signifier. Consumption is important in building identity especially in post-modern societies with high consumption levels – see, for example, Ahuvia (2005); Ruvio and Belk (2013). This makes us easy 'prey' for advertisement. At the same time, Kasser et al. (2004, p. 22) argue that when people "concern themselves with materialistic goals, and when they espouse the values of the dominant consumer culture, the result is lower well-being". Max-Neef's work on the human needs matrix – including the dimensions of 'being', 'having', 'doing' and 'interacting' – may help explain this observation. He sees human needs as objective or universal. Our quality of life depends on how we are able to satisfy these. The *satisfiers* we choose – for example, material consumption – are instruments that may or may not fulfill needs (Max-Neef, 1991). High levels of consumption and low levels of satisfaction can easily co-exist if chosen satisfiers are not able to meet our needs.

The observation that material consumption may have limited capacity to ensure a good life may be good news for efforts to ensure sustainable development. One may argue that we will be as happy, maybe even happier, with less goods if less is distributed fairly equally. The latter may not be easy to achieve though as those 'at the top' will most probably defend their position. The research on 'loss aversion' – see, for example, Tversky and Kahneman

(1986) – offers added support to this challenge. People value losses more strongly than gains.

9.3   From Bretton Woods to the neoliberal era

The increase of corporate power throughout the late nineteenth century created, as we have seen, a countermovement. This resulted in various legal actions taken throughout the first part of the twentieth century including protecting the right for labor to organize. The economic crisis of the 1930s – the Great Depression – vastly reduced the legitimacy of the idea of self-regulated markets. The New Deal policy in the USA is maybe the most famous response of the time. It included public investments/relief programs, support to industries in economic despair, promotion of labor unions, unemployment compensation, maximum working hours and minimum wages – see, for example, Hamby (2004); Harrell et al. (2005).

The New Deal is a key example of a development from the 1930s and into the post-World War II period in most Western countries indicating an expanded role for the state in regulating markets and developing various systems of public support to the population. The idea of the welfare state was born,[5] although it took various forms. The so-called Nordic model was strongly influenced by social democratic perspectives including greater emphasis on redistributive taxation and expansion of state engagement in education, health services and so on. More liberal forms of welfare state policies – with larger emphasis on private sector engagement in, for example, education and health, reflecting a stronger belief in market provision – developed in, for example, England and the USA.

Throughout the nineteenth century, there was substantial growth in international trade that lasted into the twentieth century. Two World Wars and the crisis in the 1930s created disruptions that are very visible in the statistics on trade – Table 9.1. There was great uncertainty involved as countries that had their own currencies and stable trade conditions demanded coordination of exchange rates. Countries failed to do so, a fact that created new risks for business, which next gave birth to the rise of speculative financial transactions – themselves creating their own forms of risk. The 1929 stock market crash and the following bank crisis in 1931 were strong manifestations of a rather chaotic monetary system. To defend themselves, countries resorted to various protectionist measures throughout the 1930s.

Towards the end of World War II, the so-called Bretton Woods system was established. Developed countries tried to find a way to counteract the financial

Table 9.1 Value of world exports 1870–1998 (in million 1990 US dollars)

1870	1913	1950	1973	1998
50345	212425	295621	1690648	5817080

Source: Maddison (2001, p. 362).

instabilities experienced in the 1930s. While a complex story in itself – partly based on a fight between the UK and USA for world hegemony – it resulted in two new organizations: the International Monetary Fund (IMF) and the International Bank for Reconstruction and Development (IBRD), later part of the World Bank. The aim was to create a system of fixed exchange rates between the currencies. Due to the strengthened US economy – partly a consequence of the war – the US dollar became the basis for this system (Steil, 2013).

The Bretton Woods system focused on ensuring economic growth through liberalizing and expanding international trade. Given the experiences of the 1930s, it was concluded, however, that this demanded governmental control of markets. The Bretton Woods negotiations also included a proposal to establish an international trade organization. This failed and instead the General Agreement on Tariffs and Trade (GATT) was established in 1947. This was a multilateral agreement to ensure reduction of tariffs and other trade barriers.

The Bretton Woods system functioned quite well throughout the 1950s and into the 1960s. This period also coincides with the strongest period of economic growth observed. However, the system came under pressure during the 1960s. This was partly due to the fact that Europe and Japan were 'catching up' with the USA economically, and the dollar was not able to 'carry the burden' as reference currency as well as before.[6] This enabled 'speculative attacks' on the dollar and in 1971 the Nixon administration devalued the dollar – and by doing so "signaling, the end of the 'Bretton Woods System'" (Panic, 1995, p. 50).[7]

Through the 1970s and 1980s there was a gradual shift away from a belief in the need for political control towards thinking again that markets operate best if not 'interfered with'. These ideas were labeled 'neoliberalism'[8] and much of the intellectual basis is found in the work of Friedrich Hayek and Milton Friedman (Boas and Gans-Morse, 2009). These ideas gained significant political importance not least through the elections that brought Margaret Thatcher (1979) and Ronald Reagan (1981) into power in the

UK and the USA respectively. This brought forward a wave of 'deregulation' that spread far beyond these countries. It also materialized in what became the Washington Consensus – a list of demands imposed by the IMF and the World Bank for offering credit to developing countries that had become 'financially wrecked'[9] (Williamson, 1990). Finally, the idea of an international trade organization succeeded with the establishment of the World Trade Organization (WTO) in 1994.

The breakdown of the Bretton Woods system with the cessation of the mechanism that ensured fixed exchange rates for currencies implied increased risks for business. An almost immediate reaction to this was a tremendous growth in the volume of financial derivatives[10] – that is, methods to hedge against risk in markets (Pryke and Allen, 2000; Arnoldi, 2004). A rapid development in markets for derivatives happened. While the annual world GDP in 2000 was around 147 trillion US dollars, the derivatives market was in 1997 already close to five times this volume (Arnoldi, 2004).

While the basic logic behind derivatives and other financial instruments like securitization[11] seems to hedge against risk, the establishment of such products also lends itself to speculation. Through, for example, various forms of leverage,[12] it is possible for financial actors to create opportunities for arbitrage.[13] This may, however, create its own risks. It may increase volatility[14] – see, for example, McNally and Levi (2011). It may also result in systemic risks that under certain conditions may result in economic crises – see, for example, Tickell (2000); Hellwig (2009). Shin (2009) argues that the effect of various instruments to hedge against specific risks is actually to increase aggregate risk. The recent financial crisis of 2008 seems to be a notable illustration.

9.4 The limits of markets revisited

The above shows that there are substantial challenges related to the present organizing of the economy. Moreover, even if markets worked 'according to theory', there are limits to how well they can handle issues related to the physical environment. We remember Polanyi's ([1944] 1957) point that for markets to work well, land (or nature) also has to be turned into a commodity. This may change the meaning and role of nature. Another aspect concerns the technical limits to commodifying nature. I will close this chapter by looking at this.

According to the ecological economics perspective, there is a necessary relationship between production and waste creation – between economic value construction and environmental destruction. While private property and markets dominate commodity production, the creation of waste that necessarily follows, has to a large extent been unregulated – under open access. Historically, effects of waste creation were mainly local, and to the extent dealt with, this was done largely by defining various community norms. However, the tremendous growth in flows of waste over the last century has vastly transcended the community as a unit for coordination of such interdependencies.

In the section above, I have described the advancement of private property in resources. A key motivation has been to ascertain security for investments in time and capital through establishing a direct link between human activities/investments and individual returns from these. We have seen how the creation of the stock-holding company has increased the capacity for economies to grow. Furthermore, we have seen how various trade liberalization efforts have had a similar influence. This development is characterized by a separation of decisions over nature and hence separation of responsibilities. It would be a possible development if nature could be split in physically *inde*pendent parts and trade was costless. Then conditions for coordinating our economic activities via markets could work. However, if there is physical *inter*dependence, serious systemic problems may appear (Hagedorn, 2008; Vatn, 2008). To study this, we first need to look at the concepts of coordination and interdependency.

9.4.1 Coordination and interdependency

Markets coordinate action through matching supply and demand of commodities. We have seen that due to the costs of transacting, there may be issues involved even here. However, assuming that these are trivial[15] and that there are no external effects – that is, no physical interdependence – we may talk of a *simple coordination problem*. No physical interdependency implies that waste production does not create any harm. This is the standard assumption behind the analyses of trade as described in neoclassical economics. Markets are able to coordinate action and create Pareto-optimal outcomes.

These assumptions rarely hold. Hence, we face what I will term *complex coordination problems*. Here there is indirect interdependence. Actors' choices are interdependent because they take place in a common environment where choices have implications beyond each unit of decision-making. It is actually hard to imagine much production or consumption activity that does not involve some side-effects/harmful waste production spreading beyond those that engage directly with each other. Hence, what may be termed generalized interdependency is pervasive. If interferences are minor, building institutional structures that disregard them may be acceptable. If they are more significant, this seems not to be the case.

9.4.2 The firm–market–consumer regime and generalized interdependencies

In a system where natural resource use is divided into separate entities and all interaction happens through markets, the only way coordination of the utilization of natural resources and processes can happen is through the price mechanism. This demands that all resources are owned and that the price mechanism works properly. According to Hayek (1931, 1948) this mechanism is superior as it is able to solve the vast information problem that humans face when coordinating their activities. He emphasizes that knowledge is local and specific. If somebody wants to build a house, the terrain, weather conditions and the individual preferences are specific to creating that particular building. The strength of the market is that it does not depend on anyone possessing all this localized knowledge. The price mechanism distributes the information necessary "to coordinate the separate action of different people" (Hayek, 1948, p. 85).

The problem is that this price does not convey information regarding the effects on environmental resources and processes from producing building material and constructing the house. There are several issues involved. Here I will briefly discuss two. First, pricing environmental effects of production and consumption activities is problematic given the type of values involved. Second, if pricing was found acceptable, there is nevertheless no mechanism in markets themselves that ensure that environmental effects are captured by commodity prices. Pricing such effects would demand establishing property rights to all environmental resources. Moreover, it had to be possible to trade in all these properties.

Pricing the environment implies a 'condensation' of all information of its qualities into one metric – like the willingness to pay. This represents a tremendous reduction of information – see, for example, Vatn and Bromley (1994) and Martinez-Alier et al. (1998). Certainly, for coordination to be possible, some simplification is necessary. The question is whether pricing offers the relevant simplification for environmental governance to work well.[16] There are strong arguments against this being the case. One may ask if a utility-based measure is at all relevant in a domain like the common environment?[17] Even sidestepping the various ethical issues involved,[18] we observe challenges. Environments are different from place to place. Prices may work well for homogeneous goods. The opposite is the case if qualities vary. That will at minimum demand that prices are local.

So even if we assume that Hayek is right in his claim that the price of a commodity is the only message that is needed for actors to make their decisions on whether to buy a specific commodity or not in their local contexts, the argument must be turned on its head if side-effects are involved. For the market to work well then, everybody needs to possess all localized knowledge. However, prices carry no information about the changes in the environments from which the resources necessary to make that commodity were taken. If these consequences or costs are shifted beyond the firm making it, no information about them is captured. As important, prices on products carry no information about their costs as waste.

Turning to the second issue – that all environmental resources could and should be owned – I note that attaching private property to all environmental resources and processes is for practical purposes impossible. Here we face systems of interlinked processes, and dividing them into separate units would simply not work. Had it been possible, there is next the cost of establishing such rights and transacting over the various interdependencies involved via markets. By splitting up the resources into individual pieces, the number of transactions necessary to correct for side-effects – the generalized interdependencies – is vast. So, as Bromley (1990) has emphasized, what makes the internal system work well – the maximization of competing units in markets – also maximizes the transaction costs related to the bargaining over side-effects or cost shifting. In the case of global environmental problems – and assuming that every person in the world is somehow involved as in the case of climate change – the number of interdependencies is presently in the order of 7 billion × 7 billion – that is, every person is interdependent of everybody else. Handling such interdependencies through trade is certainly impossible.

The above shows that environmental problems are systemic. They follow from the creation of an economy treating systemic interdependencies as if there were only independence. In Part Five, I will discuss how we – through different adjustments of the economic system – have tried to handle the challenges faced. I will also discuss if what is being done moves us in the right direction, or if a more fundamental shift in our thinking may be needed.

9.5   Main messages

In this chapter, we have studied markets and their actors from an empirical perspective. We have seen how markets may take different forms. Historically, trade has been embedded in social structures and dominated by interpersonal relationships. In many instances, exchanges have taken more the form of reciprocal acts – for example, the 'gift economy' – than impersonal trade.

The creation of 'self-governed' or disembedded markets has taken a long time and has resulted in political counter-reactions, partly because of the power imbalances created and because of the crises that seem to follow from the operation of 'autonomous' markets.

The creation of markets has also resulted in a parallel creation of its actors – the separated producers and consumers. At the bottom lies an increased specialization that physically delinks production and consumption, to be reconnected, however, via markets. In modern societies, the firm is the dominant form of producer. Firms can be of many different types, and we saw how one form – the corporation – has come to dominate. We also recognized how there have been substantial political fights over what modes of firms to support. The corporation was delegitimized, partly banned for a long time. However, as markets expanded heavily in the late nineteenth century, these limitations fell. Parallel to this development, we observe a 'becoming' of the consumer and of mass consumption. The distribution of income within and across countries is, however, very skewed, implying that consumption levels vary substantially across the global population.

A market can be seen as a coordination instrument. It is an important institution, while having a tendency to fail – that is, economic crises are a recurring phenomenon. This has created political responses. Important in that respect is the Bretton Woods institutions that originated as a reaction to the economic crisis in the 1930s. Being quite successful in its own terms – not least in the sense of fostering a period of sustained economic growth not encountered before – the system in many ways collapsed in the early 1970s, paving the way for the so-called neoliberal era with renewed emphasis on 'self-regulation' of markets. An effect of this was a great expansion of the financial sector – partly as a reaction to the increased level of uncertainty and partly to try to make financial gains through speculation. A new crisis evolved in 2008, while it is yet unclear if that will cause a shift away from 'self-regulation' of markets.

In a book on environmental governance, the importance of studying markets is important for two reasons. First, it is the main institution in allocating resources for production and consumption – also environmental resources. Second, it may also be important in causing problems regarding the functioning of the natural environment. In relation to this, I argue that markets – despite the crises observed – may work quite well regarding coordination of production and consumption when there are no side-effects or externalities involved – that is, so-called simple coordination problems. The situation is, however, very different if there is physical interdependency. This is especially so if the interdependency goes beyond the close proximities of production and consumption. I call this situation a coordination problem with generalized interdependency. Many environmental problems have now reached a form and level characterized by such interdependency. This implies that our thinking around environmental governance may not only be about changing the frames within which markets and market actors operate. It may also demand changes in the market system itself.

NOTES

1. Later in Section 9.3 I will discuss the validity of this claim.
2. Certainly, there had also been groups before that who had excelled in consumption like the feudal lords and so on. 'Modern' or 'capitalistic' affluence is based on expansion of markets – including markets for labor. Block (2003, p. 283) notes, moreover, that "feudalism is characterized by the use of extra-economic coercion to extract surplus labor from agricultural producers. In contrast, in capitalism, surplus is extracted from the laboring classes through the purely economic mechanism of the wage contract".
3. According to estimates by Ortiz and Cummins (2011), the richest 20 percent of the world population receive 83 percent of global income while the poorest 20 percent receive just 1 percent of the total.
4. Total GDP in 1990 is – according to Maddison (2001) – 39 times that of total GDP in 1820. Population was five times as large.
5. The developments from the late nineteenth century can be seen as a kind of welfare state policy. One should also mention Bismarck and his social reforms from the 1870s. Esping-Andersen (1990) makes a distinction between a social democratic, conservative and liberal welfare state. Unique to the developments in the 1930s and onwards seems to be the social democratic influence.
6. The costs of the Vietnam War were also an influence.
7. Panic (ibid.) continues: "For the second time within a century, after initial success, a dominant country had failed to secure a viable, lasting international monetary system. The reason was the same in both cases: the inability of the country at the center of the system to maintain its economic supremacy. . .without sacrificing domestic welfare".
8. As Boas and Gans-Morse (2009) show, the concept of 'neoliberalism' refers to different ideologies and practical policies since the concept first came into use in the 1930s. Here I will only use it in the meaning defined in the text.
9. Williamson (1990) lists ten points including fiscal balance, cutting subsidies, tax reform, market-determined interest rates, trade liberalization, privatization, deregulation and legal security for property rights.
10. A derivative is a financial contract, a security that derives its value from one or more 'underlying' entity. The latter could be an asset like grain, timber and so on, but also an interest rate or an index. The value of the derivative is determined by fluctuations in the underlying asset, for example, stocks or bonds. Derivatives are used to hedge risk, but can also be used for speculation. Common derivatives include forwards, futures, swaps and options.
11. Securitization implies the creation of a financial instrument through combining different (financial) assets and subsequently offering repackaged instruments to investors. This process creates liquidity and allows small investors to buy shares into a larger pool of assets.
12. Leverage concerns ways to increase gains from investments – typically through using borrowed funds to invest in an asset. If the returns from the asset are above the interest paid on borrowed funds, the returns on equity can increase substantially. If this is not the case, the investor may face bankruptcy. Hence, leveraging increases risk and was an important element in the recent financial crisis.
13. Arbitrage means taking advantage of a price difference between two or more markets.
14. Volatility relates to risk and uncertainty about potential changes in the value of an asset. If volatility is high, there is a risk that prices can change quickly, and dramatically.
15. Trivial information problems imply that there is no uncertainty or risk. While interdependency due to information problems/asset specificity is the dominant issue discussed among economists – note Williamson (1985) – I will not analyze that issue here. My focus is on physical interdependence.

16 In his discussion of control hierarchies in natural systems, Pattee (1973) studies their structure–function duality – the interface between the detail of structure and the abstraction of function. Here he emphasizes that a function or control can only arise through some selective loss of detail. The question of importance in our case is what functions should be defined and supported and hence which loss of detail is preferable.

17 See also Chapter 11 for a more in-depth analysis.

18 As emphasized in the philosophical literature, ethical issues like those concerning the rights of species are different than issues concerning the utility of consumers – they belong to two incommensurable value dimensions (e.g., O'Neill, 1993; Holland, 2002). I will return to this issue in Chapter 11.

Part Five

Environmental governance in practice

I have so far characterized environmental challenges both conceptually and empirically, emphasizing the importance of human use, the issue of conflict and the need for cooperation and coordinated action (Part One). I next looked at what motivates human action and how institutions influence the level of selfishness, and the will to cooperate (Part Two). In Part Three, I developed a framework for analyzing environmental conflicts and coordination. I also looked at how to evaluate governance structures and outcomes, emphasizing the concept of legitimacy. In Part Four, I looked at the market – explaining its role as the dominant governance structure regarding present use of resources, and how its expansive logic is a challenge to our environments.

In this last and largest part of the book, I turn to studying how we have tried to handle the problems economic processes have created for the functioning of our physical environment, using the framework, concepts and perspectives developed so far. In Chapter 10, I focus on the policy process. I look at the process of establishing environmental policies, from priority setting/goal formulation to choosing and institutionalizing various policy instruments. Substantial emphasis is also put on the processes of goal formulation at the international level through the establishment of international environmental agreements.

In Chapter 11, I look in more depth at the process and methods of priority setting/goal formulation. The chapter is mainly devoted to studying different methods of decision support like cost–benefit analysis and deliberative methods. Chapter 12 is focused on an analysis of the ways environmental policies have been operationalized and various experiences with the use of different policy instruments – that is, changes in and adaptation of resource regimes. I distinguish between policies directed at use and protection of environmental resources on the one hand and policies directed at reducing pollution on the other.

The effectiveness of many environmental policies has been disappointing and this has stimulated an interest in developing alternatives. In Chapter 13, I analyze the dominant trend in that respect – that of making more use of markets in environmental policy. While 'the turn to the market' seems to be more dependent on state action than normally assumed, I also note problems with and limitations of this approach.

The main challenge regarding environmental policies is that it is an 'add on' to an economic system that is very expansive as well as seriously constraining what is politically possible in the domain of environmental governance. Chapter 14 is devoted to a discussion about what we have learnt from the previous 13 chapters regarding these limitations and how we could think about establishing alternative routes for developing a more sustainable future. I hope the reader finds my proposals engaging and supporting own thinking about alternative solutions. We live in times where too few are willing to think deeply about what far-sighted alternatives should look like. I do not possess the final answer, but the following five chapters may hopefully motivate many to think deeply about what changes are needed to make our societies and economies just and sustainable.

10
The policy process

The aim of this chapter is to give an overview of the policy process. This includes elements like agenda setting, definition of goals, formulation of actions and policy instruments, and implementation. While policy-making takes place at the level of different actors, I will here concentrate on public policy-making, treating business, non-governmental organizations (NGOs) and so on as participants in that process.

Public policy-making takes place both at local, national and international levels – that is, under different spatial jurisdictions. I also note that while public policy processes are typically quite formalized – they follow certain predefined rules and steps – their content is defined in an environment of competing perceptions, visions, values and interests. We may talk of opposing discourses or strategies backed by different interests. This regards both goals, definition of responsibilities and choice of policy instruments.

Aiming at covering these complexities, the present chapter is divided in five sections. First, I offer a brief overview of the stages of policy formulation in a somewhat idealized form. Thereafter I discuss a few prominent 'visions' regarding environmental governance strategies. In the third section, I present different ways these discourses may be operationalized in the sense of resource regimes and governance structures. Thereafter, I give an overview of the distinctiveness of decision-making from the local to the global level. In the last section, I look more in depth at the process of international policy formulation regarding key environmental issues spanning the field from climate change to the protection of the ozone layer. The emphasis here will be on problem formulation, goal and target setting. Issues regarding policy implementation will be analyzed in Chapter 12.

10.1 The stages of policy formulation

Policy-making can be described as a set of stages. Based on Turner (1997) we may define the following steps:

1. Recognizing that there is a problem that may demand action – agenda setting.
2. Defining the content of the problem.
3. Formulating and deciding on goals.
4. Defining alternative measures.
5. Evaluating options.
6. Deciding on actions and policy instruments.
7. Implementation.
8. Evaluation.
9. Possible reformulation of the problem, correction and supplementation.

While *measures* here refer to the actions that may solve or reduce a problem – for example, less car driving – *policy instruments* are the changes in conditions for human action that can motivate these measures to happen – for example, legal or economic instruments to facilitate less car driving. Certainly, the process may stop at any stage. One may go back to an earlier stage – for example, in the process of goal formulation, one may start redefining the problem; when choosing policy instruments, one may redefine goals.

Nevertheless, the above views the policy formulation process as very structured,[1] implying that the responsible political bodies systematically evaluate the issues of relevance to them. They prioritize which to look at by importance and gather necessary information to decide on what to do. The process is, moreover, believed to reflect the will of the people. From a social constructivist perspective, the 'rationalist' understanding implicit in the list of steps is hardly tenable. Looking first at the stages of problem recognition and definition, issues of cognition, perception and framing as discussed in Chapters 4 and 7 are important. To bring an issue to the attention of policy-makers may take a long time and be riddled with conflict.

In that process, the power to define issues is extremely important – including the power to avoid an issue being put on the agenda – see, for example, Bachrach and Baratz (1963). In relation to this, we need to remind ourselves about the complexity involved in environmental governance. The issues are often hard to define; there is uncertainty and ignorance. Demanding certainty as a basis for action hampers decisions; maybe obstructs an issue from being put on the agenda. Environmental governance faces great challenges here. Local, more easily defined issues with rather simple – often technical – solutions dominate agendas as opposed to fuzzy, long-term, global issues that may demand changes even at the level of the economic system.

The above understanding is important for analyzing the 'stages' of the process. The power to define which perceptions and perspectives should dominate, and the power to frame and allocate resources influence, for example, which issues are put on the agenda, what goals are chosen, which policy instruments are defined. In democracies, one would expect the citizens to decide. While there is some truth to the importance of 'casting one's vote' to influence politics, decision-making in modern democracies is influenced in ways outside this channel. It is also shaped by organized interest groups, what expertise dominates, and what perspectives govern various public bodies and agencies involved. Hence, Rokkan's statement (1966, p. 105), "Votes count, but resources decide", is still valid when studying policy formation.

Regarding *organized interests*, the capacity to raise awareness, influence or lobby policy processes seems important for outcomes at all stages – what is on the agenda, what goals and which policy instruments are chosen (e.g., Coen, 2007; Baumgartner et al., 2009). Some of this influence is on a case-by-case basis. More typically, it happens through organized *networks* between public bodies and private interests (e.g., Barley, 2010) and to some extent civil society. Typically, industry has a strong influence as environmental policy may demand changes in production processes and other investments to reduce emissions. It may fight such initiatives using uncertainty, loss of jobs and so on as arguments (e.g., Coen, 2004). Environmentalist pressure groups – for example, environmental non-governmental organizations (ENGOs) – also try to influence agenda setting, goals and chosen measures from their side. Their capacity to mobilize larger fractions of the citizens seems important for their success, while some ENGOs now seem to side rather with industry, trying to build an alliance for 'greening production' – that is, the 'civil expert organizations' mentioned in Chapter 6. This strategy seems to reflect the experience that mobilizing the citizens for moving political processes in a more environmentally benign direction goes too slowly (e.g., Dryzek et al., 2003), believing that changes may happen quicker if industry itself realizes the potentials in becoming 'green'.

Regarding the role of *science and expertise*, there is a series of important issues. Science has played a crucial role in establishing environmental policy as a new field of politics. Areas like climate change and ozone layer protection would hardly be imaginable without scientific work establishing the necessary insights into the 'invisible' problems faced and what causes them. At the same time, scientific 'advances' have themselves been part of the changes causing the problems – for example, synthetic chemicals. Moreover, and referring back to Chapters 2 and 3, the complexity of environmental problems represents a challenge to the dominant positivist and reductionist perspectives of modern science. Emergent properties and irreducible igno-rance pose fundamental challenges to the dominant vision of uniform scien-tific truth, next challenging the very notion of science as objective – see, for example, Funtowicz and Ravetz (1993); Norgaard (1994); Stirling (2006). In this landscape, it matters which sciences come to dominate a field – for example, whether the scientific basis behind biodiversity protection comes out of the tradition of conservation biology or non-equilibrium theory. Similarly, it matters if advice regarding choice of policy instruments comes from economists, psychologists or sociologists. It is also important what role science is given in the policy process. The 'rationalist' policy model is based on faith in scientific truth. This is no longer a tenable position. Political deci-sions will have to be made under uncertainty and in situations with compet-ing descriptions and value-based interpretations.

While politicians typically direct the policies in various fields, proposals for such decisions come dominantly from *administrative bodies* like ministries and public agencies. These bodies are also often delegated responsibility for the 'hammering out' of concrete policies. While external expertise as well as business and citizen representatives may play a role in formulating propos-als, the perspectives of administrative bodies themselves play a significant role regarding formulation of strategies, goals and policy instruments. These bodies are specialized regarding not only the issues they handle, but also the procedures and solutions. Hence, we may talk of administrative cultures or discourses based on standardized definitions and interpretations of prob-lems and solutions – see, for example, March and Olsen (1989); Vedeld and Krogh (2000); Vatn et al. (2002) – see also Box 10.1. These cultures reflect both internal competencies – for example, what disciplines dominate – and who the core 'clients' or 'user groups' are.

Therefore, what is 'appropriate' is not only about generic procedures and criteria at the level of government (March and Olsen, 1995). It regards topic- and agency-specific solutions as well. Hence, practices across fields like envi-ronment, transport, energy, agriculture and so on are typically quite different regarding the way policies are formulated and what kind of policy instru-ments dominate (e.g., Sabatier, 1999; Thornton, 2004). In relation to this, the above-mentioned networks between public agencies and external inter-ests are crucial. Such networks influence the internal processes of policy-making bodies. Hence, Meyer (1994, p. 32) notes that "[o]rganizations are interpenetrated with their environments, which may constitute (rather than affect) organizational identities, structures and activity routines". This resonates somewhat with the arguments by some Marxist traditions like that of Poulantzas (1978) – see Chapter 6 – emphasizing how political

BOX 10.1

THE NITROGEN DISPUTE – THE ROLE OF ADMINISTRATIVE CULTURES

In Box 7.3, I presented a dispute among scientists over the expected effect of taxes on nitrogen fertilizers. This debate became politicized, as it was transferred into a discussion among ministries involved in formulating environmental policies for Norwegian agriculture.

The problem of nutrient losses from agriculture to water bodies was acknowledged in the 1970s and a policy emerged with emphasis on information and fertilizer plans. Both the Ministry of Agriculture and the Ministry of Environment supported this policy. Until the late 1980s, there was substantial cooperation between the Ministry of Environment and the Department of Agronomy in the Ministry of Agriculture on this issue. The Agronomy Department had its basic competence in natural science/agronomy. At the same time, there was a strong 'culture' for cooperation with the farmers and their organizations in this department. The Ministry of Environment was 'agnostic' regarding the policy instruments used as long as reductions in emissions were ensured (Vatn et al., 2002).

The proposal of instituting a tax on nitrogen fertilizers 'disrupted' this cooperation because the Ministry of Environment shifted its position, thinking that strategies like a tax could be a better way to achieve the aims of reduced pollution. At the same time, the Policy Department of the Ministry of Agriculture – dominated by economists – saw pollution as an interesting issue as the tax proposal brought their competencies into play. Hence, there was a shift in alliances as the Ministry of Environment started to cooperate more with representatives from the Policy Department of the Ministry of Agriculture (ibid.).

For a while, it seemed that an agreement between the Ministry of Agriculture and Ministry of Environment on a fairly high tax level could be reached – that is, around 60 percent. However, an additional rule was invoked that put an end to it. The Ministry of Finance claimed that all tax revenues were general budget money – the responsibility of the Ministry of Finance. This was a problem for the Ministry of Agriculture–Ministry of Environment agreement as it also included considerations on the distributional effects, implying that farmers should be compensated for the costs of the tax through, for example, area payments. They needed the collected tax revenue for that purpose (ibid.). The Ministry of Finance did not accept this kind of earmarking.

administrations are structurally dependent on acceptance by key economic interests involved.

So if policies are routinized to a large extent and interest group domination is heavily institutionalized through administrative cultures and networks, how is it possible that, for example, a new area like environmental policy could establish itself? According to Chasek et al. (2014), there were a series of conditions that facilitated the establishment of environmental policy as an organized policy field in the late 1960s/early 1970s. The authors emphasize that economic growth based on economic considerations and technological change had created several problems for the functioning of the biosphere. Throughout the 1960s, this challenged the dominant development 'paradigm'. They write:

> In the early 1960s, the dominant paradigm came under steadily mounting attack. . . The 1962 publication of Rachel Carson's *Silent Spring* documenting the dangers to human health from synthetic pesticides marked the beginning of an explosion of popular literature about new scientific knowledge about new threats to the environment, including radiation, lead, toxic wastes, and air and water pollution. (Chasek et al., 2014. p. 30–31)

The 'wonders' of the second Industrial Revolution materialized in negative effects that even mobilized the streets. So by the early 1970s, a series of countries had established Ministries of the Environment and environmental protection agencies. One may say that a 'window of opportunity' (Kingdon, 1984; Farley et al., 2007) opened up throughout the 1960s and was seized by popular movements and radical politicians backed by the new growing body of scientific insights.

10.2 Three main discourses

Policy formulations cannot be made without reference to a 'system of perceptions' – an overarching vision or discourse. This is so for the single actor or agency to organize and give direction to its action. In a situation where there are multiple actors, paradigms or discourses are essential to creating a necessary common basis for thinking and acting. According to Hajer (1995, p. 44) discourses are "specific ensembles of ideas, concepts and categorizations that are produced and transformed in a particular set of practices and through which meaning is given to physical and social realities". They define the core variables to consider and the preferred solutions when policies are formulated.

Due to different interests and different types of knowledge, one would expect the field of environmental governance to be characterized by different and conflicting discourses. Bäckstrand and Lövbrand (2006) define three meta-discourses in present environmental governance:

1. *Ecological modernization.* The main feature is the idea that economic growth and environmental protection are compatible. The main strat-

egy is decoupling degradation from economic growth through markets, green technology, green regulation and trade. There is a 'weak version' that is "technocratic and neoliberal" and a 'reflexive version' that "adopts a critical approach to the limits of dominant policy paradigms and modern institutions" (p. 53). The authors note that the 'weak version' is the predominant discourse emphasizing market or 'market-based' solutions.

2. *Green governmentality.* Here the emphasis is on "stewardship of nature and an all-encompassing management of its resources". It is an expert-oriented management strategy based on the development in various new eco-knowledges. "Resting upon a notion of sound science, these well-trained environmental professionals provide credible definitions of environmental risks as well as legitimate methods to measure, predict and manage the same risks" (p. 54). Geoengineering is an example of a strategy to respond to climate change coming out of this discourse.

3. *Civic environmentalism.* Here the focus is on participation emphasizing the role of those that are faced with environmental problems and the power of deliberation. There is a reformist 'branch' emphasizing "a pluralistic global environmental order and affirms the rise of public–private partnerships between NGOs, business and governments" and a more radical discourse advocating a "fundamental transformation of consumption patterns and existing institutions" (p. 56).

Bäckstrand and Lövbrand (ibid.) note that the weak form of ecological modernization overlaps green governmentality. It is notable that while the civic environmentalist position played a significant role in the UN Conference on Environment and Development in 1992, the two other 'meta-discourses' have gained strong momentum in the years thereafter. The ideas presented under the notion of 'green economy' by the UN Environment Programme (UNEP, 2011a), the World Bank (2012a) and the OECD (2013) are ecologically modernist.

In relation to that, one should note that discourses 1 and 2 are both focusing largely on technological solutions. They are within the predominant vision of economic development with global trade, free enterprise and the promise of unbounded consumption. Hence, they are 'well adapted' to present economic power structures. Certainly, one may wonder how well adapted they are to the environmental challenges we face. While the ecological modernization discourse demands a nature that is very resilient, the green governmentality tradition is built on a vision that it can be controlled. Both perspectives are deeply rooted in Western attitudes and philosophies. So while environmental governance is much about institution building, it becomes quite clear that the knowledge and the core values on which this transformation is based, are very important.

10.3 Three main strategies regarding changes in governance structures

Environmental governance is about formulating new visions for the future. It is about establishing goals for our development, and it is about establishing the necessary institutions to help produce wanted outcomes. While we noted above three dominant meta-discourses as frames for thinking and acting, we may also identify three main perspectives or discourses regarding changes in governance structures. These can be organized with reference to the forms of interaction we defined in Chapter 6 – that is, expanded state command, more markets and trade, and more community and cooperative solutions.[2] While, for example, eco-modernization is more oriented to expanding markets and civic environmentalism to increased community, there is no strict 1:1 relationship between discourses as presented in Section 10.2 and the strategies presented below.

10.3.1 More government

The idea is that environmental problems can be reduced only through public action. The dominating perspective is that of seeing environmental problems as externalities or failing markets. Through legal regulations (e.g., prohibitions or prescriptions), economic incentives (e.g., taxes and subsidies) or changes in infrastructures, the conditions for choices by producers and consumers are changed to ensure more environmentally friendly action. Legal regulation has historically been the dominant strategy.

Governmental action is criticized for being slow and delivering weak results – see, for example, Carter (2007); Bäckstrand et al. (2010); Dryzek (2013). Dryzek (ibid.) emphasizes that this is the result of a series of problems with the rationality underlying governmental command – that is, administrative rationality as he denotes it. A key point here is that hierarchical organizations favor separation of complex problems and let them be handled by specialized competencies. Moreover, this form of public policy is too detached from the needs of people and is often not transparent. Its legitimacy has therefore been challenged. This has resulted in a search for alternative strategies. Among the proposed solutions is increased use of markets and business-led changes – that is, the eco-modernization paradigm or the neoliberal turn. Another is to focus more on the role of civil society, grassroots engagement and cooperation – the deliberative turn.

10.3.2 More market

The idea here is to create markets for environmental services: nature and its services represent huge values and by making them into commodities, their 'delivery' can be secured through trade. According to this view, the level of payments defines which resources to protect and what services to produce. Hence, the level of protection and service delivery is defined not by specifying common goals through political processes, but through the individual willingness to pay. The argument is that individual preferences should decide and that is guaranteed through establishing markets.

This strategy faces a great challenge regarding turning various aspects of the environment into tradable commodities. One issue regards the technical problems faced; how can natural processes be divided into distinct 'pieces' that can be traded? This was discussed in Chapter 9 – see also, for example, Vatn (2000); Gómez-Baggethun et al. (2010). Some recent developments towards establishing markets are observed – for example, in privatizing water services and creating markets for carbon emissions and biodiversity protection. Certification schemes are also a route that is being pursued. In the case of water, creating a commodity is technically rather simple, but privatization has nevertheless resulted in quite strong opposition (e.g., Shiva, 2002). When commodification through demarcation is difficult – like in the case of biodiversity protection – one may ask why people would be willing to pay at all, as the individual can only acquire a (small) part of the gain. At least this is hard to explain given the standard argument for markets as based on individual rationality. Finally, one may question why individual willingness to pay is a legitimate basis for prioritizing environmental values.

10.3.3 More civil society and community

The deliberative turn is another response to the weak performance of government action in the environmental field. The idea is based on (self-)mobilization of citizen and civil society organizations in cooperative action for environmental protection. Emphasis is on participation and deliberation – communication and cooperation – between multiple actors. According to Bäckstrand et al. (2010, p. 33): "The premise of deliberative rationality is that rational individuals and groups can deliberate around environmental problems and subsequently arrive at the most informed and also the most legitimate decisions". While deliberation may not ensure consensus, the model of "deliberative democracy rests on a general belief in reasoned argument as the best way of resolving moral conflict" (Lövbrand and Kahn, 2010, p. 50).

Deliberation has its strengths in developing common understanding and ideas regarding what should be done. Hence, it seems to be an important element in widening the basis for legitimate environmental policy and making it more effective in the sense that it is rooted in people's will and understanding. It can mobilize public opinion and help generate novel solutions (Lemos and Agrawal, 2009). However, there is no guarantee that deliberation produces environmentally friendly outcomes – that is, be 'environmentally effective' to paraphrase Bäckstrand et al. (2010). Moreover, deliberation itself may be weak at changing action, while it may form a basis for strengthening and developing new norms.

10.3.4 Hybrid solutions

The literature also discusses various combinations of the above strategies. The basic idea behind establishing hybrid forms is to compensate for weaknesses related to each main type. Hence, Lemos and Agrawal (2009, p. 79) state: "The emergence of these hybrid forms of environmental governance is based upon the recognition that no single agent possesses the capabilities to address the multiple facets, interdependencies and scales of environmental problems that may appear at first sight to be quite simple". They especially note the weakening of the state both as an effect of globalization and efforts to decentralize environmental management. Figure 10.1 captures key types of 'hybrid' governance structures.

Lemos and Agrawal describe several strengths of hybrids:

> [T]he involvement of market actors in environmental collaboration is typically aimed at addressing the inefficiencies of state action. . . by injecting competitive

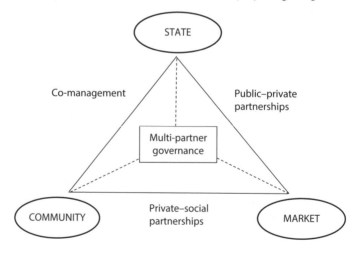

Source: Based on Lemos and Agrawal (2009).

Figure 10.1 Hybrid governance structures

pressure into the provision of environmental services. . . enabling greater profitability in the utilization of environmental resources. . . the addition of community and local voices to environmental governance is seen as providing the benefit of time- and place-specific information that may help solve complex environmental problems. . . at the same time allowing a more equitable allocation of benefits. . . Higher level of participation can help overcome the democratic deficit and lack of legitimacy that are often associated with market-focused instruments. (Lemos and Agrawal, 2009, pp. 79–80)

The authors also mention limitations. They note that public–private partnerships may themselves create democratic deficit and inequality. Greater efficiency in use of natural resources may imply higher rates of extraction, challenging intergenerational equity.[3] While partnerships may empower some groups, others may be disempowered. Especially in North–South contexts with large power asymmetries, hybrids may weaken the position of partners from the South. If partnerships do not offer real and equitable cooperation, they may just represent increased 'alleged' legitimacy, while skewed power relations continue. The authors note the view that:

new hybrid forms of environmental governance are allegedly part of a broader agenda to achieve corporate interests that economic globalization is all about (Paterson, Humphreys, and Pettiford 2003). In a world of weak states, deterritorialized action, and concentrated power, corporate interests and multilateral organizations can control and re-frame environmental action as a means to legitimize their preferences in terms of development models. (Lemos and Agrawal, 2009, p. 82)

Therefore, hybrid solutions may sometimes reduce participation from the wider public.

The argument behind, for example, increased use of markets and partnerships, was weak performance of state policies. This does not imply that other governance models are better. It may just reflect that problems are very difficult to handle. Failures may reveal the tremendous task to (re)direct economic activity towards sustainability in a system where (1) interactions in the production sphere are simplified through institutionally separated and self-regarding decision-making units (firms); (2) economic growth and capital accumulation are system's imperatives; (3) complex interactions in the environmental sphere are unavoidable. Strengthening the autonomy of the economic decision units through globalization has, moreover, weakened the capacity of states and municipalities as actors on the environmental arena. In relation to that, there are two important aspects. First, the power of states to direct activities of firms is weakened as the latter have the option to move production from one state jurisdiction to another. Moreover, the number of environmental problems that expand beyond local or national jurisdictions has increased extraordinarily.

This does not mean that new forms of governance are unimportant. Given the theoretical foundation of this book, one may posit that decentralization efforts including more community-based management may be important for ensuring sustainable management and use of certain resources. I hypothesize, however, that the expanded use of markets is to a large extent ineffective in the field of environmental governance. I also hypothesize that the role of states will be crucial for the foreseeable future. I will discuss these propositions further in Chapters 12 to 14.

10.4 Policy processes at different levels

As emphasized above, the effects of economic activity expand more and more beyond the domains of decision-making units – be they the firm, the community or the state. States are the most important decision units regarding political action. Some decision-making power is delegated to local levels, while the power to make laws and to a large extent institute taxes/fees rests with the state level. Firms are the dominant economic actors with the power to direct production – within the created legal and economic spaces.

Related to the above, we observe several challenges regarding environmental governance:

- First, while some impacts of production on environmental resources fall on resources operated by the firm itself, most affect other firms, municipalities, states and areas under no jurisdiction like air and international waters. This way a lot of economic action affects municipalities and states that have no influence over those 'producing' the harm.
- Intergovernmental organizations (IGOs) are formed to handle issues that go beyond the jurisdictions of states. However, these have limited power. States are considered sovereign entities, implying that they – in principle – decide themselves what international issues they engage in. Moreover, while they may be morally bound by agreements they ratify, IGOs typically have no formal power to ensure that treaties are followed by their parties. Hence, in the case of environmental problems, a country whose industry pollutes areas in other countries may not agree to do anything, or if agreeing, it may not comply.
- Multinational corporations, however, have the power to command their

production units wherever they can operate. Certainly, state-specific regulations may influence their activities. On the other hand, corporations may move the production to other countries, if they find the institutional conditions better.

Taken together, these points demonstrate some important asymmetries that may explain quite well why environmental problems are so hard to solve.

Impacts of consumption may be analyzed in similar ways. While certainly each consumption unit pollutes much less than a production unit normally does, the effects may be spread to the global scale even in this case. Consumption units – that is, households – are, however, less mobile compared to many firms. This makes it easier to regulate consumption than production. Moreover, regulating consumption is also a way to control production. As we will see later, regulation on consumption is rather rare, which may reflect a strong emphasis on individual freedom of choice.

While a main challenge is how to handle environmental impacts beyond the jurisdiction of individual states, the issue of delegation of power to the local level is also important. Certainly, in cases where knowledge and resource dependency are localized, there are strong arguments for such delegation. However, even in these cases, there may be side-effects going beyond the local jurisdiction that demand action at higher levels.

The situation described above has made visible the need for multilevel environmental governance (e.g., Eckerberg and Joas, 2004; Berkes, 2008). The idea is to specify responsibility at international, national and local levels and link these levels in a consistent way, making decisions interactive and mutually supportive. While it is important to make some progress in this sense, it is a demanding task given the existing distribution of power and the kinds of problems faced.

10.5 International environmental governance

As already noted, many environmental issues not only expand beyond the local to the national, they have also become regional, even global. In this section, I will look at the distinct challenges for international environmental governance as a specific type of 'two-level' governance. Thereafter I will illustrate these challenges by visiting a set of policy areas – climate change, biodiversity protection, fisheries management, toxic chemicals/transboundary air pollution and stratospheric air pollution. As international bodies and agreements have limited power to institute policy instruments – which mainly has to be done at state and local level – the main issue regarding international agreements is to define goals and distribute responsibility between states. Hence, this section is also an illustration of the first three stages of the policy formulation process – see Section 10.1 – at its most complex level.

10.5.1 International environmental governance – a complex two-level 'game'

As there is no political authority above nation states, the international relations literature – see, for example, Dunne et al. (2010); Devetak et al. (2011) – describes the international political arena as an anarchy. States are free to decide whether they will ratify any international agreement. What can be agreed is, moreover, a kind of 'least common denominator'. Three processes are involved. First, we have the process of each single country deciding on its position. Second, we have the process of agreeing on a common text at the international level. Finally, there is the procedure of ratification. If an international treaty is accepted by a government – is signed – it must take it to its parliament, which may or may not accept what is signed. It is after the agreement is accepted by the parliament that the final signature – the binding ratification – is made.

The field of international relations is oriented at international politics and studies negotiations and agreements at this level. It is a very complex literature with a series of (partly overlapping) positions regarding how to analyze and understand developments. Historically, the so-called realist or hegemonic power model dominated the scientific understanding. According to this model, it is the relative strengths of states that determine international regimes and agreements. Effectiveness depends on a hegemonic state that can take a lead and exercise power over weaker ones. Hence, agreements come about 'by force' of the strongest party. Chasek et al. (2014) note that this understanding may explain much of the development of the post-war international economic system, but not so much international environmental agreements since these are negotiated in a period with no clear hegemony. Moreover, the USA as the main 'hegemon' has not been especially interested in pushing for international environmental agreements.

Another approach within international relations is based on the 'exchange concept of political action' – see Chapter 6 – typically formulated in a game-theoretic bargaining format. Based on the standard assumptions of individual rationality, states seek solutions that are favorable to them. In the international arena, that is typically not possible without looking for coalitions.

The standard bargaining model is a so-called unitary actor model – that is, the states that are parties to the negotiations have a coherent set of interests. This model seems unable to explain some agreements. Putnam (1988) presents a model that takes into account the fact that conflicts are as much internal to states as they characterize the international level. Hence, he describes international negotiations as a simultaneous 'two-level game':[4] the "two-level approach recognizes that central decision-makers strive to reconcile domestic and international imperatives simultaneously" (p. 460). The international process may influence the national positions, as international processes may allow space for changes in national priorities since national minority positions may be able to create a basis for the 'better' international compromise. By accepting that states are not unitary, it is possible to understand international cooperation even where interests are in conflict.

A third line of thought acknowledges that while there is lack of a common authority at the international level, there may still not be lack of community. First of all, ties exist between countries and become established between leaders (for example, Haas et al., 1993; Finnemore and Sikkink, 1998). There is also the fact that certain norms about appropriate behavior are gradually forming at the international level (for example, Chayes et al., 1998). Hence, countries may experience pressure to accept agreements if they see it as important for their international standing, if they are afraid of being blamed for causing a breakdown in negotiations and so on. Certainly, this seems to be contingent on how dependent a country is on international support. The fact that the USA has not ratified most of the prominent international environmental agreements illustrates this point.

The epistemic community model is a special version of the international community thesis (Chasek et al., 2014). Here the focus is on the transnational networks of experts and bureaucrats that seem to play important roles in the forming of some agreement, and, in certain phases, of establishing treaties.

More fundamentally, the realist and liberal exchange understanding of international agreements is criticized for taking actors as given and is not understood as historically constructed – see, for example, Rupert (2010). This means also that these research traditions become very conservative in the sense that they do not question the basis on which 'hegemony is exercised' or 'games are played'. Two directions of analysis stand out. First, we observe a 'school' focusing on deliberation, emphasizing especially the opportunity for open dialogue among civil society groups at the international level that may challenge hegemonic worldviews – see, for example, Linklater (1996).

The anti-globalization movement illustrates that there is force in voicing different views regarding the model of development, but that it also has very limited influence on decisions. Second, we have critical theory emphasizing the role the globalized economic system and economic actors play in shaping international agreements. Here it is pointed out that in forming these agreements, states have to take into account the effect on the functioning of the (present) economic system – for example, the structural demands for growth and capital accumulation. Similarly, there is the role representatives of the business sector play in the process of negotiating environmental treaties.

Chasek et al. (2014) document a series of examples of how industry has pressured both national governments and been present at international forums, trying to oppose or weaken environmental agreements. They also show cases where industry has been divided, and some business representatives have supported environmental regulations. Such regulations may not only represent costs for business, they may also create opportunities for new investments. However, there is substantial risk related to investment in new technologies – for example, renewable energy. Hence, industry typically demands security for these investments in the form of long-term stability regarding conditions for investment. In that sense, international agreements may be a good thing.

Last, the role of ENGOs needs to be mentioned. They participate in processes at both the national and international level, voicing views from the environmentally engaged civil society. At the international level, they mainly operate through international environmental NGOs (IENGOs) like Friends of the Earth International – a federation of 77 national ENGOs (Chasek et al., 2014). Another example is WWF – the World Wide Fund for Nature. Some national ENGOs also operate at the international level – for example, some of the big US NGOs. Chasek et al. (ibid.) note that (I)ENGOs may have some influence through the agenda-setting process, but that they have much less to say when decisions are made.

(I)ENGOs play a role in building an international community of environmental values and norms. It is hard to estimate the importance of this, but the potential importance of such a process is substantial. It should be mentioned that the focus of Northern and Southern ENGOs is a bit different. While the ENGOs of the North have focused a lot on the effects of industrialization and hence pollution and climate change, ENGOs in the South have emphasized land use issues, rights to resources and issues regarding human rights, and distributive justice including the position of marginalized/indigenous peoples. While there are many examples of good cooperation between

ENGOs from North and South, this has resulted in conflict regarding some topics – for example, climate change (ibid.).

10.5.2 Climate change

In the following sections, I will look briefly at the development of a set of international environmental agreements. The aim is to describe their content and the process behind their development. This way I illustrate how knowledge about the stakes/the type of environmental issues involved, the state of technology and the interests among involved political and economic actors has influenced the agreed solutions. I focus mainly on environmental issues already covered in Chapter 2.

Regarding climate change, it took a long time from the observation that human activity influenced the climate – see, for example, Arrhenius (1896) – until the issue was put on the political agenda. As shown in Chapter 2, the use of fossil fuels increased considerably from about 1950. It was, however, in the 1980s that the consequences for the climate were first politically addressed. The first World Climate Conference was held in 1979, but attracted mainly scientists and NGOs. The Intergovernmental Panel on Climate Change (IPCC) was established in 1988 under the World Meteorological Organization (WMO) and the United Nations Environment Programme (UNEP). It laid the basis for a procedure to create a common knowledge base for negotiations and actions. Its first reports were delivered in 1991, documenting the importance of human emissions and reaffirming global warming as a serious threat (Chasek et al., 2014). At the Rio Conference in 1992, the UN Framework Convention on Climate Change (UNFCCC) was signed. It emphasized that the industrialized countries had a particular obligation to reduce emissions. It was suggested that these should be stabilized at the 1990 level by the year 2000 (UNFCCC, 2014).

A so-called Conference of the Parties (COP) was also instituted at the Rio Summit. Its role was to develop the general principles of the UNFCCC into more practical policies. The first COP was held in Berlin in 1995. Conflicts were tense. Reducing CO_2 emissions was seen by some as a threat to the present model of development. The science was questioned and there were issues related to political and economic hegemony. The EU was pushing for a binding commitment, while the so-called JUSCANZ group (Japan, USA, Canada, Australia and New Zealand) opposed negotiations for reduced emissions (Chasek et al., 2014). At COP3 – in Kyoto in 1997 – the Kyoto Protocol was nevertheless agreed, establishing a plan for reducing the emissions of greenhouse gases to a level on average about 5 per cent lower than that of 1990 by 2008–12. To be operative, the Protocol had to be ratified by at least 55 countries, covering at least 55 per cent of the total emissions of the so-called 'Annex I' countries – that is, industrial countries including Eastern Europe. The reduction levels were heavily debated at the Kyoto meeting and cuts were distributed unequally among Annex I states (UN, 1997). Those with perceived lower costs had to cut more.

The process continued to be difficult. At COP4 (Buenos Aires) the USA demanded 'meaningful participation' also by core developing countries for it to ratify the Protocol. In 2001, the USA finally withdrew after the Bush administration came into office. Then, at COP7 in Marrakesh the same year, the attending states agreed on a detailed set of rules for implementing the Kyoto Protocol. This agreement implied, however, a weakening of the original text since the USA did not join and the rules themselves were made less stringent to ensure that countries such as Japan, Russia and Canada would ratify (UNFCCC, 2014). In late 2004, Russia finally ratified, and the threshold of 55 per cent of emissions was reached. The Protocol became operative from February 2005.

The functioning period for the Kyoto Protocol ended in 2012. At the COP13 in Bali (2007) discussions about a post-Kyoto agreement began. Due to strong disagreements on levels and distribution of cuts, no agreement was reached in time. Hence, at the COP17 in Durban (2011), the parties agreed to postpone an agreement until 2015. At COP18 in Doha (2012) the functioning period for the Kyoto Protocol was extended to 2020. Developments during the COP19 in Warsaw (2013) and COP20 in Lima (2014) indicate that having a new agreement signed in 2015 may not be doable. It seems clear that no post-Kyoto agreement will materialize if obligations are not defined for developing countries as well. The discussion on overall levels of cuts, distribution of obligations to cut and the distribution of the costs thereof influences economic development.

This situation does not imply that countries do nothing. There is, however, a move from obligations to voluntary commitments or 'pledges' – that is, countries have stated levels of cuts they aim for by, for example, 2020 and 2050. The bilateral agreement between China and the USA on cuts just before the Lima COP in the fall of 2014 (Peel and Osofsky, 2014) is also seen as progress. The IPCC (2014a) states, in a rather diplomatic way that "Estimated global emissions levels in 2020 based on the Cancún Pledges are not consistent with cost-effective mitigation trajectories that are at least about as likely as not to limit warming to below 2°C relative to pre-industrial levels, but they do not preclude the option to meet this goal" (p. 24).

The topic of climate change is linked to some serious political and economic issues. Fossil fuels are literally the 'blood' of the economy. Cheap and highly concentrated energy has made it possible to grow economies in an unprecedented way. Many rich countries seem to go for solutions that maintain their hegemony, while developing countries are afraid of becoming 'cut off' from a development similar to that experienced by the North.

10.5.3 Biodiversity

While the climate change regime started from the global level and defined responsibilities for nation states, protection of biodiversity started at national level and moved later to the international – see, for example, Rosendal and Schei (2012). The first strategy was the establishment of national parks and nature reserves dating back to the nineteenth century. The development of multilateral agreements focusing on the protection of biodiversity began after World War II – that is, the International Convention for the Regulation of Whaling from 1946. From the 1970s and onwards there have been more comprehensive developments, not least under the lead of the UN. The Ramsar Convention on Wetlands of International Importance was established in 1971. In 1973, after the UN Conference on the Human Environment in Stockholm in 1972, the UN Convention on International Trade in Endangered Species (CITES) was established, and the Bonn Convention on the Conservation of Migratory Species was agreed upon in 1979 (Chasek et al., 2014). A series of bi- and multilateral agreements in fisheries around the globe – while mainly being directed at maintaining productive stocks for the world's fisheries – also has implications for species and habitat protection.

Under the Rio Summit in 1992, the more overarching UN Convention on Biological Diversity (CBD) was established (UN, 1992). The CBD is based on the precautionary principle. The underlying aim is to balance the opposing interests of economic utilization of biodiversity/genes and the need for protection. In accordance with this, the CBD focuses on (1) conserving biodiversity; (2) sustainable use of its components; and (3) sharing the benefits from, for example, commercial use of genetic resources. Again, a North–South conflict has been clearly visible. Furthermore, it is a typical framework convention, implying that more specific treaties have to be developed under the CBD to create a basis for concrete action. The International Tropical Timber Agreement (UN, 1994) and the Cartagena Protocol on Biosafety (UN, 2000) are examples of such treaties. It should also be noted that at the COP10 in Nagoya (2010), the parties to the CBD agreed on the so-called Aichi Biodiversity Targets stating that "By 2020, the rate of loss of all natural habitats, including forests, is at least halved and where feasible brought close to zero, and degradation and fragmentation is significantly reduced" (UN, 2010).

The CBD lacks a common procedure for producing 'certified knowledge' like that of the climate regime. The science is, however, less disputed, while we also here face issues challenging the present model of economic development with its implied habitat fragmentation and loss. Growing levels of pollution are also important, as well as the issue of rights to genetic resources. Chasek et al. (2014) emphasize that it has therefore not been easy to find ways to operationalize the CBD. They state that this reflects "the more diffuse nature of the regime's rules and norms, the absence of a strong lead-state coalition, the absence of an enforcement mechanism, and a general lack of political will" (p. 180). They note that the COPs under the CBD have been able to ensure some progress regarding the identification of global conservation priority areas and developing protocols on conservation and sustainable use. The developments regarding the issue of access to genetic resources and benefit sharing is much more conflict-ridden.

In relation to the latter, we note a rather deep rift between the ideas of the CBD and those governing international trade – that is, the WTO agreement. This became evident not least in the process behind the advancement of, on the one hand, the WTO Agreement on Trade-Related Aspects of Intellectual Property Rights (TRIPS), and the CBD on the other. Three issues have been addressed: (1) the right to patent biological material; (2) the right to trade genetically modified organisms (GMOs); and (3) the distribution of the income from the use of local species/genes by the GMO industry. These issues are interlinked. The TRIPS agreement emphasizes the importance of securing free trade and the right to use patents in the case of intellectual property – including modified genes and organisms. Certain compromises have already been made in the TRIPS agreement, implying that while microorganisms are generally patentable, states can exempt plants and animals of a higher order through national legislation (WTO, 1994). In 1999, a process of revising the agreement started. The USA claimed that the exceptions from patentability in the current agreement should be removed, while many developing countries – such as India and several African countries – favored a more restrictive policy (WTO, 1999). Because of these conflicts, the TRIPS revision is still not completed.

In the development of the Cartagena Protocol on Biosafety under the CBD, some of the above disagreements resurfaced. Although the USA had not ratified the CBD, it was still allowed to participate in the process. The main conflicts appeared between the so-called 'Miami countries' (Argentina, Australia, Canada, Chile, Uruguay and the United States) and 'The Like-minded Group' consisting of many developing countries. The EU took a middle position. The Miami countries wanted a solution that gave preference to the WTO rules. Developing countries wanted to give the Cartagena Protocol precedence over the WTO agreement. In WTO 'law' the rules for sanitary and phytosanitary measures – the SPS measures – are key. These rules demand that risk assessments have to be based on 'appropriate scientific evidence' – that is, that potential harm is proven. The argument behind the development of the Cartagena Protocol was that in many cases such evidence cannot be delivered. Since both harm and safety are difficult to prove, a precautionary practice should be allowed. The result was a protocol that granted more rights to regulate imports than implied by the WTO rules (Melchior, 2001), and the precautionary principle was granted a basic status in the Protocol (UN, 2000). However, the Protocol cannot be interpreted as changing a party's rights and duties in other areas of international law.

So, regarding biological material, the situation is characterized by competing international rules. To illustrate the implications of the situation, the EU *de facto* ban on imports of GMOs from 1999 is interesting. It was based on the Cartagena Protocol – specifically the acceptance of precautionary action. The ban followed a process within the EU, where not least civil society organizations reacted to the development of the GMO sector. A panel ruling by the WTO[5] in 2006 stated that bans of GM products by individual EU member states were illegal with respect to the SPS agreement. Since the USA was not a signatory either to the CBD or the Cartagena Protocol, it had argued that the Protocol had no power regarding trade between the USA and EU countries. In relation to this, it is notable that the ruling of the WTO panel nevertheless "sidestepped the issue whether EU legislation on biotechnology was illegal and did not express any opinion on whether GM foods were safe for consumption. It simply concluded that the EU had breached prior commitments under the SPS agreement by disallowing market access for some 21 products" (European Union Center of North Carolina, 2007, p. 5). While the WTO system is clearly the stronger of the two, the status of the precautionary principle is still not clarified internationally.

10.5.4 Fisheries

Until World War II, the main issues regarding fisheries concerned access to fishing grounds in coastal areas. Fish was an important resource that countries tried to protect for their own fishing industry. Some treaties were signed to regulate these conflicts – for example, the North Sea Fisheries Convention from 1882 (Stokke, 2012).[6] However, fisheries were dominantly open access. Fish resources were considered abundant. This perception changed after 1945. In part, it was seen that fishing influenced stocks, as reduced fishing during the war resulted in extraordinary catches in the post-war years. In addition, catch capacity was gradually increased through new fishing equipment, larger boats and so on.

Regulating fisheries is demanding. The resource is very valuable, as well as shifting between 'national waters' and between national waters and the open sea. Stokke (ibid., p. 98) writes: "The problem facing international fisheries regimes is how to balance utilization and conservation of a scarce resource while distributing the benefits among the states involved. Overcapacity results in fierce competition among and within states, rendering this problem malign, or politically difficult".

After 1945, a series of fisheries commissions were set up targeting specific fish stocks or regions. However, the regimes that were developed were weak. It was difficult to agree on measures that could constrain catches. Lack of capacity to follow up on what was agreed has also been an issue. By the adoption of the United Nations Convention on the Law of the Sea (UNCLOS) in 1982, the policy landscape changed. The convention covers access to all kinds of resources in the sea, on and under the sea floor. Pollution issues are also included. Regarding fisheries, the expansion of the jurisdiction of nation states through codifying 200-mile exclusive economic zones (EEZs) was a very important step (Jensen, 2012). While hurting non-coastal state interests, it simplified the basis for negotiating regional agreements and the possibility to control them (Stokke, 2012).

While UNCLOS simplified the development of more firm fish stock–related agreements, challenges were still tremendous. A new step was taken by the development of the Agreement on the Conservation and Management of Straddling Fish Stocks and Highly Migratory Fish Stocks (the UN Fish Stock Agreement for short), from 1995. It grew, to some extent, out of a conflict between Canada and the EU on the fisheries along the Canadian coast. From the 1960s, European vessels started fishing in 'Canadian waters'. Canada reacted by unilaterally establishing a 200-mile EEZ in 1977. The collapse in the Canadian East Coast cod fisheries around 1990 resulted in a moratorium on cod fishing from 1992 (Finlayson and McCay, 2000). This was a typical conflict between 'coastal states' and 'distant-water states'. Chasek et al. (2014) emphasize that a diplomatic deadlock was created due to the conflicting interests. The USA held a split position as it was also in many cases operating as a 'distant-water state'. However, in 1994, the country sided with Canada, and the UN Fish Stock Agreement would be agreed the year after.

It represented a framework for establishing regional fisheries management organizations and agreements. Important means to ensure the stated aim of sustainable use were strengthening the rights and responsibilities of flag states,[7] but also port states[8] and of other states that have signed a regional agreement. As late as the year 2000, only one of the six states with highest catches – the Russian Federation – had ratified the Agreement. China, Japan, Poland, the Republic of Korea and Spain had not (Juda, 2001). According to data from the UN (2013), all have now ratified.

The basis for most agreements is the specification of a total allowable catch (TAC) and distributing it between the parties to the agreement. Due to the conflicts involved, it has been difficult to agree on sufficiently low TACs. Historical catch levels tend to dominate as a basis for the distribution of TACs (Stokke, 2012).

As a result, the situation in the world's fisheries is not good. According to Chasek et al. (2014), about 30 percent of the marine fish stocks are overexploited. Stokke (2012) notes that the number of overfished stocks is now about twice the level before the establishment of the EEZs. Catches reached 86 million tons in 1996. This is five times the catches in 1950. Since 1996, catches have fluctuated between 77 and 86 million tons (Chasek et al., 2014). Stokke (2012) notes three reasons for the problems still faced. First, many coastal states have not taken the obligation to conserve resources seriously. Second, many fish stocks straddle from national zones into high seas and remain available to distant-water fishing vessels. Third, technology developments tend to outpace regime development.

10.5.5 Toxic chemicals and transboundary air pollution

According to Chasek et al. (2014), systematic production of chemicals for commercial purposes developed after World War II. The number of compounds is vast and around 100 000 chemicals are registered for commercial use in the EU alone. On top of this, follow emissions of pollutants from use of various inputs – for example, sulfur dioxide (SO_2) and nitrogen oxides (NO_x) from combustion of fossil fuels. Hence, we enter a very complex landscape. I will cover two regimes – the global regime on persistent organic pollutants (POPs) and a regional regime on transboundary air pollutants. These are important regimes in an area where most compounds are actually used without any environmental regulations at all.

The center stone in the global regime on POPs is the Stockholm Convention on Persistent Organic Pollutants from 2001. It covers 13 compounds – including the 'the dirty dozen' – counting several pesticides and insecticides like aldrin, chlordane, dichlorodiphenyltrichloroethane (DDT) and polychlorinated biphenyl (PCB). While regulation had been pushed by countries like Canada and Sweden back in the 1980s, it was first in 1995 – when the UNEP's Governing Council asked for an assessment of the 'the dirty dozen' – that a process towards establishing an international agreement took off. In 1997, the Council endorsed the assessment and negotiations of a text began. Quite a complex 'table of positions' evolved as countries had different needs regarding the use of the various compounds. The EU and Canada took on a lead role in the negotiations, while the USA, Japan and many developing countries used their veto power. NGOs mainly supported strict regulations while companies supported the 'vetoers'. African countries as well as health-oriented NGOs opposed the banning of DDT. To reduce the conflicts – to avoid vetoing by important parties – concepts like 'acceptable purpose' and 'specific exemptions' were created in the negotiation process (Chasek et al., 2014).

The result was a division of the pollutants into three categories (Stockholm Convention, 2001). The first group regards pollutants that should be eliminated. It is notable that there are several exemptions made, though, even from this list. This is the largest group of compounds. DDT was placed in a category of its own, defined as a pollutant where use should be restrictive. According to Van den Bergh (2008), it has still been in use in many developing countries. Finally, there was a category for POPs that were by-products of certain productions, which should be minimized or eliminated, but where it was seen as difficult to ensure zero emissions. The convention included a financial mechanism to support developing countries and countries 'in transition' to meet their obligations. A clear limitation of the Convention is a rather weak non-compliance procedure, and discussions at later COPs have resulted in little progress. It is also notable that while 180 countries have ratified the Convention, some important 'producer countries' like Israel, Italy, Malaysia and the USA have not ratified (Chasek et al., 2014). Since 2001, ten new substances have been included, while the process has been characterized by quite some disagreements among the parties and lists of 'acceptable purposes' and 'exemptions' have expanded.

The Long-range Transboundary Air Pollution Convention adopted in 1979 is an example of a regional agreement regulating polluting substances crossing national borders. It laid the groundwork for a 20-year process resulting in eight protocols regulating emissions of altogether six pollutants or groups of pollutants – SO_2, NO_x, VOCs (volatile organic compounds), POPs, heavy metals and ammonia. It started with engagement from the Nordic countries observing acidification of ecosystems, mainly caused – it was argued – by SO_2 emissions from the continent/UK and carried north by the wind. In the beginning, the 'source countries' were very skeptical that there was a problem. While the Nordic countries "scored an important intermediate success" by the establishment of the Convention, it was "little more than an empty shell" (Wettestad, 2012, p. 27). It laid the basis, however, for a gradual process of 'filling the shell'. Through a long list of protocols – for example, the Helsinki Protocol on SO_2 (1985), the Sofia Protocol on NO_x (1988), the Geneva Protocol on VOCs (1991), the Århus Protocol on heavy metals and POPs (1998).[9] In 1999, the various protocols were integrated into the overarching Gothenburg Protocol.

Wettestad (2012) emphasizes that there were several reasons for the ability to 'fill the shell'. In the late 1970s, a debate started in Germany about the effect of acid rain on its own forests. The breakdown of the Soviet Union resulted in a strong reduction from Eastern Europe simply due to reduced industrial production. Finally, the UK – which was the strongest opponent to regulations in this area – also changed its position as their coal-fired plants were shut down. This was not an effect of environmental concerns, but economic liberalization. The combined effects of regulations and economic developments have resulted in some considerable success regarding SO_2 emission reductions. On average, cuts are slightly above the aim of a 63 percent reduction. Wettestad (ibid.) notes, however, that critical loads are still exceeded in vulnerable areas. For most of the other compounds, results are behind the aims. Regarding ammonia, only about half of the 40 percent cut has been achieved (ibid.).

10.5.6 The agreements for stratospheric ozone depletion

Based on a growing scientific understanding that emissions of chlorofluorocarbons (CFCs) were a threat to the stratospheric ozone layer, a process towards establishing an international regulation started in the late 1970s. The ozone layer is important in protecting the earth against ultraviolet radiation – which at high doses causes skin cancer and damage to plants. In this case, the USA was the most engaged party seeking an international agreement. This was so despite the fact that it accounted for about 40 percent of the CFC production in the world. Together with Canada and the Nordic countries, they took a lead role. The EU opposed controls while being an even more important producer of CFCs than the USA. Chasek et al. (2014) note that developing countries like Brazil, China,

India and Indonesia were also skeptical due to the future opportunities in CFC production.

The first agreement on the protection of the ozone layer – the Vienna Convention from 1985 – affirmed the importance of protecting it, but did not mention the CFCs at all. Shortly after the signing of the Convention, new and strong evidence on the development of the 'ozone hole' was published, and in response to this, the USA pushed for further negotiations, resulting in the Montreal Protocol of 1987. It mandated that industrial countries reduce CFC emissions by 50 percent (UN, 1987). Chasek et al. (2014) emphasize that the change in the EU position implicit in this agreement was a result of several factors: some EU countries were pro-regulation in the first place; the significant role played by the executive director of UNEP; pressure by the USA and European NGOs; and reluctance by the EU to cause a failure in negotiations.

In the years following the signing, there has been a substantial strengthening of the Protocol through amendments. The EU actually shifted its position to take on a lead role. DuPont, a US chemical company, announced in 1988 that it would be able to produce a substitute to CFCs. Hence, an agreement of phasing out CFCs by 2000 – the so-called London Amendment – was agreed in 1990. A fund was also created to support developing countries to implement the Protocol. According to a report from the UNEP (2008), there was a steep reduction in the production of CFCs from 1989 and close to a phase-out by 2004. By 2009, the Protocol was ratified by all UN member states.

10.5.7 How to explain the different outcomes?

The five cases show some considerable variation in success or effectiveness. While the climate and biodiversity regimes are weak and results seem grossly inadequate compared to the challenges, the ozone layer policy seems to be a great success. The other fields studied seem to be characterized by results that are more variable.

The above hints at several reasons for why developing strong international agreements in the environmental realm is difficult. As emphasized by Underdal (2002), many of the problems are of a malign type. There are huge uncertainties involved. Hence, indisputable scientific proofs are hard to deliver. Easy technological fixes are typically not available. As emphasized – especially in Part Four of this book – the structure of the economic system in itself creates serious impediments as interests are so strongly formed around competition and growth. The way economic decision units are formed, the institutionalizing of the profit motive and pooling of capital through the institution of stocks have created a structure that has a tremendous force in changing the surface of the globe. It has created strong positive feedbacks between investments, technological development and mass consumption. Politically, the problem surfaces at two levels. States are afraid of losing out in the fight over attracting investments by making regulations too strict. Equally important is the 'compromise' of mass consumption. The legitimacy of the existing political system seems heavily based on the economy's ability to grow.

Comparing the climate and ozone agreements may offer some further insights into what is at stake here. The climate negotiations have not produced much despite the fact that they have been going on for 25 years. The science has been under ongoing attacks and this seems to have weakened civic engagement. The problems are expected to mostly surface rather far into the future and when it is necessary to act becomes an issue. As already emphasized, climate change and biodiversity loss challenge the existing development model at its basics. The conflict between rich and poor regarding the issue of justice is very strong and the intragenerational question creates problems for a solution to the intergenerational ones. It is also notable that the South is expected to be hit more than the North. The costs of decarbonizing the economy are substantial and the 'carbon industry' is politically very strong.

In the case of stratospheric ozone depletion, we observed a rather quick resolution. Here the science – while disputed at the start – was soon agreed upon by all parties. The depletion of the ozone layer was very quick and countries in the North were the potentially most exposed. A technological fix was soon found, while it is worrying to observe that a single industry – a few companies really – seems to have had such a big influence on the position of the EU early on. At the same time, I note the importance of the internal disagreements in the EU. Putnam's 'two-level game' also seems to help in understanding the EU positioning as developing over time.

Certainly, observing the series of 'benign' conditions that seem to have to be in place to create an effective international environmental agreement in the case of CFCs may seem disappointing regarding future opportunities. At the same time, I note that there are also a few positive signs. First, the process of international agreements seems to be taken as a 'serious business' among (most) countries engaged. If action was purely strategic, one may wonder why states engage so seriously in negotiating texts that are not formally binding. Countries seem to view their signatures as demanding commitment and follow up at least to some extent. This indicates that they acknowledge some norms of 'good conduct', while the qualification 'to some extent' may indicate that they 'look to each other'. An unofficial norm is established that deviates from the agreement, but is still effective. The hypothesis is that countries try to do the same as others. Being a 'lead state' may induce an interest in being at the front. Being among those that had to be persuaded, may result in lower than average compliance.

Second, there are examples where countries have been willing to take on costs of environmental regulations unilaterally – for example, the position of the EU at the Kyoto negotiations and its ratification of the agreement while knowing that the USA would not bind itself to any cuts. Hence, lead positions seem not just strategically based. Finally, the opening up of the 'negotiation' process by including various actors beyond the official representatives – mainly NGOs – creates grounds for communication with the wider public that may turn out to be very important. It broadens the societal 'conscious-ness' and it forms a basis for political action at the level of civil society. However, the power of mental models like the growth paradigm, the risks of becoming a 'loser' in international competition and the power of industry are certainly strong obstacles to ensuring more substantial breakthroughs.

10.6 Main messages

The process of formulating policies – defining aims and specifying actions – is complex. It can be portrayed as a set of steps that has to be made by the decision-maker to fulfill the demands of a legitimate process. At the same time, uncertainties and conflicts of interest rarely make the process straight-forward. We also note that the relationships between the formally designated policy-makers and interest groups from civil society and industry are impor-tant and take many forms, from formalized consultation procedures and net-works to lobbying.

Formulating policies demands a set of overarching principles or visions. These are fundamental beliefs about what type of actions are effective and necessary. Based on Bäckstrand and Lövbrand, I observed three meta-discourses – 'ecological modernization', 'green governmentality' and 'civic environmentalism'. The former two – especially the ecological moderniza-tion paradigm – dominate policy-making. Civic environmentalism is a form of countervision to that of continued economic growth with a 'greener face' and the belief in the controllability of environmental processes.

Principles and visions need to be transformed into action. Here we observed three main strategies – more governmental regulations, more markets and finally more civil society/community action. The latter two seem to be a reaction to observed 'government failure'. While noting this, I also argued that 'failures' may rather be the result of demanding issues than state action necessarily being the least effective. Following this, we looked at the fact that states are in a somewhat weakened position to formulate policies. Environmental issues have expanded beyond national borders and action often demands international agreements as well as local action to be effective. Regarding the former, states are sovereign, so agreements at the international level tend to become 'a least common denominator'. Economic interests are important regarding what can be agreed. While economic actors may dislike being regulated, economic globalization also weakens the position of states. It is, however, an error to believe that turning then to the market would necessarily do better.

I closed the chapter by going through the processes behind and content of a set of international environmental treaties. The 'least common denominator' hypothesis was largely supported, while the picture of an anarchy seems exaggerated. There is no third party at the international level. However, some elements of a community development are observed and some norms of good conduct are in effect. According to Chasek et al. (2014), more than 900 international environmental agreements – global or regional – have been established since 1970. Therefore, there is progress.

Nevertheless, we also observe many failures. In very urgent areas like climate change and biodiversity loss, we witness results that seem very weak compared to the challenges. In cases like fisheries, toxic chemicals and transboundary air pollution, the results are mixed. Some successes are observed across these fields, but generally outcomes are rather weak and problems are increasing in many areas. The policy regarding the ozone layer is one of very few 'pure success stories'.

The above picture can to large degree be explained by the existing interest constellations and how easy it is to find technological fixes. The ecological modernization paradigm dominates policy-making, and the traditional paradigm of development through economic growth is center stage. At the same time, we observe that rich countries are afraid of losing their position. Poor countries want – reasonably – to catch up. On top of this, globalization has reduced the capacity for political action. A combination of 'trickling down' and 'technological fix' strategies therefore dominate, while international negotiations systematically get stuck on how to define and distribute 'fair burdens'. The natural environment is, however, not resilient enough to stand such a development strategy and such political impasses. A cynical view would be to just conclude that the weakest will lose – whether they live today or tomorrow.

NOTES

1   For a review of the debate on the 'stages approach' within political science, see DeLeon (1999).
2   There are different ways that this is expressed in the literature. Bäckstrand et al. (2010) distinguish, for example, between hierarchies, markets and networks.
3   In relation to that, I will note that the authors seem to equate efficiency with technical efficiency or productivity.
4   My emphasis. While the international policy arena is maybe the closest one can get to strategic games as described in game theory, I find this understanding to be too narrow. There are also elements of a normative community evolving – see also the text.
5   In the WTO system there is a panel procedure set up to handle disagreements between members.
6   Stokke (2012) notes that the first known treaty regulating access to fishing grounds is from 1351 – between England and Castile (now part of Spain).
7   The state in which the vessel is registered.
8   The state where the catch is landed.
9   The Århus Protocol was actually an important basis for the Stockholm Convention from 2001.

11

Evaluating what it is better to do

In Chapter 10, we looked at the whole process of policy formulation from problem definition to implementation. Defining goals is the most important element in this process – involving an evaluation of what it is better to do given involved perceptions, values and interests. While the political process may take the form of a negotiated compromise between various positions, there is evaluation. In that vein, decision-makers may see a need to prepare decisions through a formalized process of evaluation. There may be a wish to consult the wider population. Issues may be complex, which in itself demands structured evaluation. Finally, there is the need to ensure process legitimacy, including increased transparency. Hence, developing material that prepares for the final political decision – so-called decision-support – is a typical element of policy processes in democracies.

The aim of this chapter is to present and evaluate different methods that can be used in developing such decision-support. I start by offering a brief overview of the process of evaluation, including a focus on the concepts of value, interests and value commensurability. Thereafter, I introduce the concept of value-articulating institutions. Methods used to assess people's values are institutionalized – that is, rule-based – systems for articulation. In the third section, I turn finally to three main types of value-articulating institutions – cost–benefit analysis, multicriteria analysis and deliberative methods – presenting their underlying assumptions and how they generate advice about what it is better to do.

11.1 The processes of evaluation

Some choices are routinized. We choose without evaluation. This chapter is about conscious choice – about choice that is in some way structured to reach a conclusion about what to prefer. Some choices are individual; some are collective. In this book we are looking at choices regarding the common good – the common environment – which implies decisions at different societal levels – at the level of a local municipality, a state or at the international level. This is a process of choosing between or balancing competing interests and values. While individual choice is complex, collective choice is even more so.

11.1.1 Values, interests, commensurability and incommensurability

What is *value* and what offers value are difficult to define. Values are about what gives direction in life, while being differently understood across the literature. Graeber (2001, pp. 1–2), for example, emphasizes three main streams of thought regarding the issue of value:

1. 'values' in the sociological sense: conception of what is ultimately good, proper, or desirable in human life;
2. 'value' in the economic sense: the degree to which an object is desired, particularly, as measured by how much others are willing to give up to get them;
3. 'value' in the linguistic sense, which goes back to the structural linguistics of Ferdinand de Saussere (1966), and might be most simply glossed as 'meaningful difference'.

The latter conceptualization shows that value can be defined in quite abstract terms. In this chapter I will refer only to the first two streams of thought.

The sociological perspective is focused on values as guiding principles in life. They are held by individuals, but are typically culture specific. Hence, they are socially constructed and often relate to what are considered common goods. While there is an acknowledgement of cultural specificities regarding values, there is also the argument that there is something specific to being a human – see, for example, Max-Neef (1991); Ryan and Deci (2000); O'Neill et al. (2008). Hence, universal ('objective') values like good health, personal relations, autonomy, competence/knowledge of the world, relations to the non-human world, aesthetic experiences and so on, are often-mentioned examples.

The economic perspective emphasizes pleasure or well-being, typically measured as exchange value – that is, how much one is 'willing to give up to get something' – for example, how much one is willing to pay for one good as opposed to another. Value is seen as subjective and related to individual welfare and measured as intensity of preferences.

Regarding the economic perspective, there is a distinction between exchange and use value. Some resources – like fresh air or water in a stream – may be very valuable to us in use, but have no exchange value. Hence, economic value, as defined above, depends on scarcity – physical or institutionally created (e.g., property rights). It is notable that exchange and use values are both consequentialist values. They gain their value from usefulness. The sociological perspective – as specified here – also includes other kinds of values. Hence, it is standard to distinguish between consequentialist, deontological and virtues ethics – see, for example, O'Neill et al. (2008).

While consequentialism is instrumental – things are valuable as a means to the end of pleasure or welfare – deontology emphasizes that things may be an end in themselves. This concerns not least the moral standing of individuals. This thinking originated with Kant, who argued:

> Beings whose existence depends, not on our will, but on nature, have none the less, if they are non-rational beings, only a relative value as means and are consequently called *things*. Rational beings, on the other hand, are called *persons* because their nature already marks them as ends in themselves. (Kant [1785] 1956, p. 91; original emphasis)

Some authors have expanded Kant's argument to include all sentient beings as having 'intrinsic value' (Regan, 1988) – a perspective that is important not least for the issue of animal rights.

Finally, virtues ethics concerns questions with regard to what kind of person one should or want to be – see, for example, MacIntyre (1986). It concerns issues like honesty, personal integrity and other aspects regarding our relations to others – including potentially other species.

There is also the concept of *interest*. In relation to the above, an interest is understood as reflecting the position of a person or group in a societal structure. An interest is hence defined by the fact that something is favorable or unfavorable to those holding this specific position. The interest of a producer may be different from the interest of a consumer – for example, high vs low price – while they may both hold similar values – that one should not hide information of importance for the trade, for example about the quality of the product or the fact that the buyer is unable to pay and so on. We may also move between positions – for example, from being a producer to becoming a consumer – without changing our values in the sociological sense.

Even values may be somewhat context dependent. Nevertheless, the difference between interests and values makes practical sense. This is observable in the distinction between interest and value conflicts – see, for example,

Aubert (1979). The former relates to issues where the actors are in agreement about the issues and values involved. They are 'just' in disagreement about the solution sought – typically the distribution of gains and losses. Such conflicts are typically treated through negotiations. A value conflict cuts deeper. The issue is fundamentally about the perception of a question and what normative implications various solutions have. Some may understand a forest mainly as a place for trees to grow to become timber for use, while others see it as a place for various species to live. While a conflict of interest may be decided through negotiations or 'trade', a values conflict may not be solvable or demand changes in value positions to create agreement. Fisher and Ury (1991) argue similarly.

The economic view of values implies that they are commensurable. There is one common measure of value that can be used to compare options. Typically, this measure is money. The sociological view may imply that such comparison is impossible or not meaningful. Values are plural. O'Neill et al. (2008, p. 74) write "that there are a number of distinct values, such as autonomy, knowledge, justice, equality, beauty etc., which are not reducible to each other nor to some other ultimate value such as pleasure". Sacrifice is an example of unwillingness to trade off. A person may refuse to trade, for example, his or her right to vote or a piece of land for development against any price. Such an act is "not a trade-off, but rather a refusal to engage in trade-offs" (ibid., p. 81).

11.1.2 Individual evaluations and choice

To make some of the above more concrete, let us start by looking at an individual choice – that of what shirt to buy. Although this is rather simple, it nevertheless involves a series of issues like deciding on the best 'mix' of attributes like cloth, cut, color, brand, price, what to choose if child labor is involved and so on. Added to the above issues of values and commensurability, we also need to include aspects related to the complexity of evaluation and the time it takes.

One way to describe the choice would be to envision it as a ranking of attributes according to a hierarchical or lexicographic order.[1] Such an order is actually an example of a form of incommensurability. As illustrated above, a good like a shirt is characterized by several attributes. We can order them as a vector $a = (a_1 . . . . a_n)$; where a_1 may be the brand, a_2 the cut, a_3 the color, a_4 the price, and so on. A ranking based on a lexicographical order implies evaluating according to the most important attribute first – for example, a_1. Hence, only shirts of a certain brand are evaluated. The rest are discarded.

Next, the evaluation is focused on the second most important attribute – for example, a_3. Maybe only dark-colored shirts will do, and so it goes until either one shirt is left, or two or more are ranked equally good and the choice can be made randomly among these.

Another procedure would be to produce a single value metric – a monetary measure – for each alternative and compare these to the price set for each. To produce such a metric – v^m – the individuals must weigh each attribute less the price. So the value v^m is the (scalar) product of two vectors – the vector describing the attributes $a = (a_1....a_n)$ of the commodity – and one describing the weights – $w = (w_1....w_n)$ of each attribute reflecting the individual's preferences. If the price is lower than the monetary equivalent of v^m, buying the shirt will produce a gain. Other shirts may still be chosen if the gain is larger. The single metric computation implies trading off the attributes against each other – for example, a shirt with a very good cut can be chosen even if it is not the preferred brand.

Despite the formal simplicity of these alternatives, the process is difficult for most goods. Hence, long experience may be required for them to work well. The ranking or calculation processes may be demanding in themselves. Hence, cognitive restrictions may create challenges for both methods. It may be difficult or time-consuming to define the set of attributes to evaluate. It may be difficult to construct the lexicographic structure necessary for ordering them, and defining the weights and transforming them into a monetary equivalent.

11.1.3 Social evaluations and choice

Moving to social or collective choice, there are further complications. People may disagree over choices regarding the common good. According to the above, they may have different interests regarding the alternatives to be considered or they may also hold different values. Hence, they may emphasize different attributes – for example, timber vs species richness in the case of a forest. Their weighting may be different or some may refuse trade-offs altogether – see, for example, Spash (2000).

Regarding the physical environment, some may think that the most important environmental challenge is about preserving certain landscapes. Others are more interested in the functionality of nature. Some may think it is important to expand renewable energy production, while others think the issue is more about effective energy use. Some think it is important to protect large predators, while others would rather see them become extinct. Hence, there are two problems involved: what issues should be prioritized for decision-making? What values should next form the basis for the evaluations involved? We see that those controlling the definition of the problems have great power. The assessments are defined by the alternatives put forward and how one perceives values.

Added to the fact that the values involved may themselves be incommensurable, collective decision-making includes a specific type of incommensurability that does not stem from value incommensurability itself. This concerns how to deal with the fact that people may hold various values. How can one decide whose values – person A's or person B's – should be prioritized? Even if we assume that values themselves are commensurable, how can one trade off a situation where person A wants to protect large predators while person B prioritizes domestic animals?

A specific aspect of this more general problem concerns the fact that the physical world is common to us. Therefore, what I do or prioritize influences what others can do and experience. Physical interdependencies create normative interlinkages. The economic perspective on values and preferences considers these as individual and therefore they need no defense. Rather, demanding justification is seen as paternalistic. However, if the preferences of one person – through the actions that they motivate – influences the opportunities for others, those others may reasonably ask whether these preferences are legitimate – that is, ask for a discussion about which preferences are acceptable (Vatn, 2000).

Various methods of evaluation produce different answers to the above issues and questions. To assess their characteristics – to evaluate their capacities and qualities – we need a basis for doing so. I find the concept of *value-articulating institutions* very helpful in this regard.

11.2 Value-articulating institutions

A main role of institutions is to signal how things are or should be done. This is important when people interact. Hence, they form and give meaning to various choice contexts. They are rationality contexts. A productive way of assessing specialized evaluation methods like cost–benefit analysis, multicriteria analysis and deliberative methods is to see them as rule structures facilitating the articulation of values and interests (Jacobs, 1997). They shape contexts for such articulation based on different rationalities. They are based on distinct principles concerning how to perceive the involved issues, values and interests and how they should be articulated and aggregated/traded off. They form perceptions and they define how perceptions can be expressed. In that respect, they all define explicit or implicit responses to the following three issues:

- *Participants:* who should participate, on which premises and according to which role and competence? How are they supposed to participate – in writing, orally, individually, via group meetings and so on?
- *Data:* what count as data and which form should value-based information take – for example, prices, weights, arguments? Are preferences or arguments taken as given, or is a process instituted to facilitate the development of these? Can incommensurable values be included? How is information conveyed to participants and how are data produced?
- *Recommending:* how are conclusions reached? Are they based on an aggregation of individual appraisals or evaluation of arguments?

Cost–benefit analysis, multicriteria analysis and deliberative methods have distinct 'answers' to these questions. They are based on different theoretical underpinnings, different understandings of what characterizes environments, values, human action and the role of process. If we see values as individual, we would search for a value-articulating structure that makes us elicit these preferences in the most precise and neutral way. If, however, we think that preferences or values are context dependent – that they develop and depend on the format of the involved processes – rather, we should ask which evaluation contexts are most relevant to employ for the problem or issue at hand. Furthermore, if we believe values are commensurable, we would choose a different method from when we believe they might be incommensurable.

11.3 Main types of value-articulating institutions

This section is devoted to clarifying the differences between key value-articulating institutions: cost–benefit analysis (CBA), multicriteria analysis (MCA) and deliberative methods like citizen juries and consensus conferences.[2] The aim is to focus on the principal differences. For those intending to use some of the methods in practical assessments, they need to look at sources that are more comprehensive. Some references are offered in the text.

We shall use the above list of the main aspects of value-articulating institutions to organize the analysis of similarities and differences. While CBA, MCA and the set of deliberative methods to be presented here do not cover all types of value-articulating institutions in existence, the ones selected should give good coverage of the main issues involved. While I find some value-articulating institutions more relevant for environmental decision-making than others, no value-articulating institution can be said to be ideal, following the complexities involved.

Some of the challenges encountered for these methods ensue from the character of societal or public choices, and are thus common to all appraisals. Dominantly the value-articulating institutions discussed here are used to assess 'projects' regarding transport, building of dams, regulation of a polluting substance, protection of species, technology assessments and so on. In each case, one has to define the alternatives, whose interests should count, which consequences are relevant, and how they should be accounted for. While these challenges are common to all the value-articulating institutions, they are solved differently. My aim is to clarify how the basic assumptions underlying the various value-articulating institutions influence the chosen solutions and how well they are able to handle the characteristics of environmental problems.

11.3.1 Cost–benefit analysis

Cost–benefit analysis is based on neoclassical welfare theory. The fundamental idea is quite straightforward. A project or action is prioritized according to how much benefit it gives less its cost. This way it supports the maximization of the total benefits for society. In principle, CBA can be used for both public and private decisions. Nevertheless, CBA is mainly developed for public decision-making – that is, when markets (as perceived) fail – implying that environmental decision-making is one of its core areas.

CBA typically evaluates a set of alternatives – for example, various ways of changing a transport system or which species to protect. Doing nothing is always an option to consider. According to Boardman et al. (2014, p. 6), a CBA includes the following steps:

1. Specifying the set of alternative projects.
2. Deciding whose benefits and costs count (standing).
3. Identifying the impact categories, cataloguing them, and selecting measurement indicators.
4. Predicting the impacts quantitatively over the life of the project.
5. Monetizing (attach money values to) all impacts.
6. Discounting benefits and costs to obtain present values.
7. Computing the net present value of each alternative.
8. Performing sensitivity analysis.
9. Making a recommendation.

For those who want to access a more complete description of the method, I refer to Hanley and Spash (1993); Hanley and Barbier (2009); Boardman et al. (2014).

Participants

CBA includes three main types of participants. There is a decision-maker, a group of experts and a selected number of laypeople. The decision-maker – be it a political body like a ministry, a county or local council, but sometimes also a firm or community – defines the issue and the alternatives to be considered. This may be done in cooperation with experts. Experts organize the whole process of evaluation and write up a report including advice to the decision-maker about the best choice. To do so, they have to describe and evaluate the effects of different alternatives. It is here that laypeople come in. They participate to the extent that there is a need to elicit project-specific willingness to pay estimates for the goods and services involved.

In that respect people participate as consumers of the various values involved – seen as goods and services. They are assumed to have preferences for the various alternatives and the cognitive capacity to handle the information conveyed. Geographical delimitation is a challenge. The rule is to include those impacted. Who that is depends on the definition of the goods and services. If a new road implies, for example, loss of habitat and endangers some species, one may argue that 'everybody' may actually be involved, despite the fact that the road is situated in a specific area. This is a difficult issue, while not specific to CBA.

Data

Data concern descriptions of the alternatives involved and measurement of relevant impacts. These issues involve the vector of attributes, and the problem is not least to define which systems boundaries are relevant – what aspects should and should not be included; what their geographical delimitation is and so on. This is especially crucial in the case of environmental issues.

In the CBA framework, definitions of what the impacts are, are seen as technical and taken care of by experts. These are regarded as purely factual issues. Hence, in a case of a transport problem, experts estimate resource use in building the system, how much land is lost, whether specific habitats will change, transport time, emissions of various types and so on. However, values enter the stage when assessing the relative importance of the different impacts. In CBA, valuation is done in monetary terms based on individuals' willingness to pay (WTP) as revealed in real markets or by methods like hedonic pricing and contingent valuation – see Box 11.1. Construction costs including buying land may be revealed from markets. Loss of habitat, reduced travelling time, changes in emissions are examples of changes where

BOX 11.1

VARIOUS METHODS TO ELICIT PEOPLE'S WILLINGNESS TO PAY FOR ENVIRONMENTAL VALUES

Environmental values typically do not have a price. In the case of CBA, prices are needed to make the assessment. If market prices do not exist, people's willingness to pay can be elicited through indirect methods. There are two kinds: revealed and stated preferences.

Revealed preferences: hedonic pricing and travel cost methods

Revealed preferences means that monetary values are obtained based on choices in markets. In the case of *hedonic pricing* environmental values are elicited from prices of goods whose value varies with some environmental characteristic. Typically, the market for housing is utilized. The value of environmental attributes like pollution and noise is assessed by using data on house prices in areas with, for example, clean as opposed to polluted air. This way the capitalized value of clean air as assessed by the buyer can be revealed. It is seen as a strength that it is actual WTP that is measured. The method has meaning only where the environmental values can be captured by the price of a complementary marketable good like a house.

Regarding the *travel cost method* the basis is the 'willingness to travel' to consume environmental goods or services. It is typically used for assessing the value of recreational goods like visiting national parks, forests, going fishing and so on. The resources spent to be able to consume a good or service – for example, travel costs, entry fees, value of the time spent – are taken as a proxy for the value of the good. Based on these costs, a demand curve for each site can be estimated. As with hedonic

pricing, it can only be used for a rather restricted set of environmental goods.

Stated preferences – contingent valuation and choice experiments

The limited area of applications regarding the above methods motivated the development of techniques that could elicit prices of environmental goods that are not in any way linked to marketed ones. *Contingent valuation* implies asking respondents for their willingness to pay for a good that is described to the respondent. The strengths and weaknesses of the contingent valuation method are in many ways opposite to those of hedonic pricing and the travel cost method. Contingent valuation can in principle be used to elicit values for whatever good (given that it can be converted into a price). It can be used to estimate the monetary value of a species, the existence of a protected area that one will never visit (or 'consume') and so on. Regarding weaknesses, the literature questions how realistic such an assessment is – for example, do people take the bidding seriously since it is not about actual payments; do they understand what the issue is about, as they may not actually experience them?

Choice experiments have become increasingly popular as they are seen as a more realistic way to elicit WTP than using contingent valuation. In this case, respondents are offered a number of discrete alternatives to choose from. Including at least one commodity among the alternatives makes it possible not only to get a ranking of options, but also to elicit WTP.

no market exists, and indirect methods may be used. Such analyses are costly, and so-called benefit transfer (Navrud, 2004; Navrud and Ready, 2007) is used to an increasing extent. This implies that benefit estimates for one situation – for example, estimating the value of a certain wetland – are used for a project where another wetland area is at stake. Normally the 'transfer' implies some correction due to changes in socioeconomic conditions.[3]

Monetization is a core feature of CBA and has several implications. First, social choices are based on the intensity of individual preferences as measured by the willingness to pay. Second, all values involved are considered commensurable. Values are also seen as compensable, implying that a loss observed in one attribute or good can be compensated by a gain in another. Finally, it is assumed that the individual – *as* an individual – is the ultimate judge regarding resource allocation and has well-informed preferences concerning the goods and services involved.

Recommending

CBA is a way to search for an optimal solution. It is defined as the alternative with the highest net present value (NPV) – measuring the difference between benefits and costs[4] as observed over time. As already emphasized, this demands that all impacts be measured in monetary terms. The net present value is defined as:

$$NPV = \sum_{t=0}^{T} \frac{B_t}{(1 + r)^t} - \sum_{t=0}^{T} \frac{C_t}{(1 + r)^t} \tag{11.1}$$

where B_t are benefits and C_t are costs in time period t, r is the discount rate and T is the time horizon of the project. Discounting (r is positive) implies that benefits and costs at a later point in time are valued less than present ones.

There are two important value issues involved here that go beyond the pricing itself. While some may experience the benefits, costs may fall on others. More precisely, net benefits may be positive for some and negative for others. It is rather unusual that all people involved gain from a project. Therefore, the NPV calculation of CBA does not ensure Pareto optimality as defined in Chapter 8. Instead, CBA is based on the rule of potential Pareto improvement. It implies that if the winners of a project gain more than losers lose – that is, following from the NPV being positive – the project is beneficial. It is notable that the rule does not demand that winners compensate the losers.[5]

The second value issue concerns discounting future effects. A social discount rate should be used. The choice of this rate is an ethical question (Hanley and Spash, 1993). There are some unresolved issues in economic theory about the choice of this rate – specifically the relationship between private (market) and social discount rates (see Portney and Weyant, 1999). Individuals, as members of a society (citizens), may have time preferences other than as consumers – that is, care more for the future. This may particularly apply to environmental benefits and costs. Individuals may have a time horizon related to their life expectancy, while society must also think of the coming generations. The issue has particularly come to the fore in the discussion about how to evaluate benefits and costs of climate change mitigation activities – see, for example, Spash (2002); Stern et al. (2006); Tol and Yohe (2006); Weitzman (2007).

Debates around CBA

The assumptions underlying CBA are much debated. Partly, they are problematic given the neoclassical model itself, as it abandons interpersonal comparison. By aggregating willingness to pay estimates, CBA implies such comparison.[6] Hence, the criterion of potential Pareto improvement is also a source of conflict among mainstream economists themselves. Beyond this, I note the following debated issues: (1) should social choice be made on the basis of individual preferences; (2) is willingness to pay a good measure of individual preferences and their intensity; (3) can all values be seen as commensurable; (4) should discounting be undertaken at all and should it be based on private discount rates; (5) what should one do in CBA if impacts are uncertain?

With regard to basing social choice on individual preferences, this is a consistent choice given mainstream economic theory. There is only one value measure – that of individual preferences. There are nevertheless at least two problems with this. First, what about the preferences of non-humans and future generations? They have no say, except through present individuals and their concern for them – see also O'Neill et al. (2008). Second, as implicit in the distinction between individual and social rationality (Chapter 5), there are individual and social preferences – that is, the distinction between consumers and citizens. One may argue that since CBA is typically used to assess common goods, it is the role of the citizen that should be catered for as it is our preferences as citizens that answer questions regarding what is a good society and what are good relationships with our environments – see also Vatn (2009b); Soma and Vatn (2010).

In addition, willingness to pay depends not only on preferences, but also on ability to pay. Consequently, results depend on the distribution of income. One way for CBA to deal with this latter problem is to assign different weights to rich and poor. Dasgupta and Pearce (1972) discuss some of the philosophical questions involved and practical ways of dealing with this. Such weighting is rarely done. Analysts may find it difficult to establish a basis for weights. It introduces yet another normative aspect into an analysis based on a theory seeking to be value neutral.[7]

One may also ask if WTP is the right monetary measure. It assumes that the consumer has no right to the environmental good or service; they have to pay for it. A measure that assumes the opposite situation is that of willingness to accept (WTA). Then the consumer is asked about required compensation to accept a loss of a good/service. Empirical research shows that WTA is typically two to four times the value measured as WTP – see Chapter 8. It is difficult to explain this fact with reference to neoclassical economic theory. We nevertheless note that the monetary value of, for example, protecting nature will be very different depending on the measure chosen – WTP or WTA – since what is an 'optimal amount of nature' will vary substantially. The advice for practitioners in the field is always to use WTP – see, for example, Arrow et al. (1993).[8]

The assumption of commensurability and compensability implies that values can be traded off. The issues involved here are discussed above. Added to this, CBA demands that the individual is informed and has preferences about the goods involved. It also demands that there are no (serious) problems for the individuals to undertake the necessary calculations and that they fully comprehend the issues involved.

Regarding discounting, O'Neill et al. (2008, p. 57) argue that it provides "a rationale for displacing environmental damage into the future, since the value placed upon damage felt in the future will be smaller than the same value of current consumption". This is a serious issue as environmental problems like climate change and biodiversity loss span many generations, and using discount rates even as 'low' as, for example, 3 percent, means effects beyond 50 years have little weight in calculating the NPV.[9]

CBA is able to handle uncertainties in the form of risk – that is, outcomes and probabilities are known – by moving to calculating *expected* NPV. These values can further be evaluated via sensitivity analysis. If there is uncertainty or ignorance involved, no probabilities exist. While some have tried to 'reformulate' uncertainty or ignorance into risk to stay within the framework, I find this to be a problematic practice. Alternatively, one may formulate constraints for impacts where effects are uncertain and remove alternatives not conforming to these constraints. As an example, if important habitats are involved, an option is to define how much habitat loss can be allowed, if any. Alternatives not passing this extra test should not be accepted despite high net present values – see, for example, Toman (1994). This brings a lexicographic ordering into the CBA analysis.

Sometimes, the CBA analysis is 'incomplete' in the sense that not all impacts are monetized. We observe that the analysis quite often involves some effects that are only orally described, leaving the 'weighting' of these to the decision-makers. This adaptation makes CBA resemble some versions of multicriteria analysis.

11.3.2 Multicriteria analysis

Advocates of MCA emphasize that environmental issues may foremost be viewed as conflicts between various interests or values. Decision-making is then about conflict resolution – about identifying the best compromise between conflicting ends. Conflicts may imply that interests and values are not easily traded against each other. MCA is formulated to handle values or criteria that are not straightforwardly transformed into one dimension like a monetary measure (Martinez-Alier et al., 1998). It can also handle the fact that weights may only be considered coefficients of importance, not signaling trade-offs/compensability (Munda, 1996). For those who want to access more complete descriptions of MCA, I refer to Munda (1995); Figueira et al. (2005); Munda (2007).

The steps of MCA very much resemble those of CBA. Issues regarding who participates, the data involved and how to conclude are nevertheless different. This also applies to the form of the process. Before I take a look at these issues, I present a matrix that is a typical example of the core of MCA in Table 11.1.

We observe that impacts or scores related to the various criteria (effect variables) are defined according to various scales of measurements, also including qualitative or ordinal scales. The table includes a weighting of the various criteria. As some types of MCA do not include such weights, they are put in parentheses.

Table 11.1 An example of a (simplified) MCA matrix regarding a transport problem

Criteria	Units/scales	Scores regarding the alternatives			(Weights)
		Highway (a)	Bus (b)	Train (c)	
Investments	Million US dollars	200	150	300	(0.25)
Maintenance	Million US dollars/ year	35	20	25	(0.15)
Time reduction (per person)	Minutes per day	25	10	15	(0.15)
Emissions of CO_2	Tons/year	1.250	320	120	(0.2)
Emissions of NO_x	Tons/year	480	150	10	(0.15)
Landscape effects	+++/– – –	– – –	– –	–	(0.1)

Participants

MCA originated in engineering and typically only involved a decision-maker and an analyst. As in CBA, the decision-maker may be a political body, a firm or a community. The roles and interaction of the involved parties are, however, somewhat differently interpreted. Consistent use of MCA in this format implies that the decision-maker is strongly involved in the problem formulation, and defines both the alternatives and the criteria. Traditionally, the scores have been assessed by the analyst who may seek assistance from specialist expertise. If weights are used, the decision-maker again sets these.

Over time, the use of MCA has expanded to societal decision-making, typically including stakeholders and/or citizens. They are involved in evaluating the various alternative solutions and rank them – either by ranking the criteria (weights) or the alternatives directly. They may also play a role in defining alternatives and criteria.

Concerning a stakeholder-based MCA, the idea is that the issues involve a set of specific interests. Banville et al. (1998) define stakeholders as those having a vested interest in an issue. They may be causing the problem and/or they may be affected by it. Defining who they are is not a simple issue. As clarified in the section on CBA, who has interests in an issue depends not least on how it is understood and framed. It is thus at the level of problem formulation that the structure is set, which then defines who should be involved.

The focus of a 'stakeholder MCA' is on generating the 'best' compromise often between conflicting interests involved. This part of the process may take different forms. One solution is to let each group of stakeholder representatives assess the various alternatives and conclude concerning their priorities. On the basis of this information, the analyst may develop a new set of alternative solutions that can be candidates for better compromises. Then the stakeholder groups assess these alternatives in a second round. In principle, several rounds can be included. The point is that the development of the final solution – the compromise – lies very much in the formulation and reformulation of the problem and then the alternatives. Stewart and Scott (1995) describe an example of this procedure for a hydroelectric dam project in South Africa where some people had to move depending on where the dam was placed.

Instead of involving stakeholders, a representative set of citizens can be invited to participate in the MCA assessments. In this case, the focus is more on defining the 'general interest' as perceived by these representatives than generating a compromise between the special interests as defined by stakeholders. Renn et al. (1993) suggest that a combination of stakeholders and citizens' participation may be preferable in that stakeholders may more clearly define what the issues are, while the citizens may be the most legitimate actor regarding the issue of values – evaluating which stakes or interests should be prioritized.

Data

MCA includes two sets of data: (1) estimation of impacts – that is, the scores – and (2) ranking of the various criteria – that is, weights. As already emphasized, MCA may be undertaken without using weights. Regarding scores, MCA analysts emphasize that problems are often ill defined. Data production is seen as a process of collective learning. MCA is a structured search process where the analyst supports the decision-maker and/or the actual interest group(s)/citizens in defining the problem, looking for alternatives, assessing their consequences, ranking the alternatives, maybe going back and formulating new alternatives and so on.

MCA hence assumes bounded rationality. The argument is that restricted cognitive capacity becomes especially important in situations characterized by complexity, maybe unfamiliarity. Over the years, we see a tendency to further problematize the setting of scores. Increasing disputes over the assessment and understanding of the effects of various solutions to a problem has reduced confidence in pure expert assessments. This is typical not least for environmental issues. A good example is the controversies around the use or release of genetically modified organisms, where the main conflict actually has been more about assessing the consequences of their use than over weighting these consequences (Stirling and Mayer, 2001). This has resulted in increased involvement of stakeholders or citizens in the process of assessing the scores.

Weighting of criteria is also a contested step of data production. As already emphasized, it should be undertaken either by the decision-makers themselves, by stakeholders or citizens. The choice here varies across types of MCA. MCA methods exist where weights are ordinal – representing only a ranking of the criteria – that is, so-called weak commensurability (O'Neill, 1993). Cardinal weights may also be used to indicate strong commensurability. They may signal trade-offs similar to CBA. They may also be treated as coefficients of importance, measuring how much more important a criterion is compared to another without implying that increased amounts of the less valued criterion can compensate for the loss related to the higher valued one. One may argue that it is three times as important to protect wolves as bears. Still, tripling the number of bears may not compensate for not protecting any wolves.

Recommending

As is implicit in the above, MCA is not one but many methods. There are differences depending on who participates and what various participants do. As important is the fact that there are various ways to compare alternatives. First, there are some MCA methods that are 'utility based' – for example, multi-attribute utility theory (MAUT). Here the focus is on utility functions/cardinal weights. MAUT-based methods are therefore quite similar to CBA concerning the assumptions about commensurable value dimensions and the potential for making trade-offs (compensability). These methods use aggregation procedures where a single value for the different alternatives involved is computed and thus a ranking of them can be made according to a one-dimensional criterion (Nijkamp et al., 1990). The main difference to CBA thus concerns the process of data production, including the form of participation and the way utility information is produced.

Another type of MCA emphasizes the aspect of incommensurable value dimensions, restricting possibilities for trade-offs. These methods are focused either on avoiding aggregation altogether, or on structuring it differently from MAUT. Hence, the distinction made above between CBA as focusing on commensurability and trade-offs, and MCA as focusing on weak commensurability/incommensurability and non-compensability is actually relevant for this second group of MCA procedures only. Some restrict

MCA to creating the matrix of scores, as basis for ranking of alternatives without using weights for the criteria. MCA becomes a choice experiment as described under CBA (Box 11.1), while adding the process of scoring. Other methods use calculative aggregation procedures – while different from MAUT. These vary according to assumptions about weights. They may be cardinal, but not involving compensability – for example, methods like ELECTRE, NAJADE – or weights may be ordinal – for example, REGIME. It is quite logical that MCA is not one, but a set of methods, as there are many ways of ranking projects when one moves away from commensurability and one-dimensional aggregation procedures. Different logics may then apply – see Vatn (2005) for a further discussion of this.

While MCA is seen as an iterative process, the assessment is at some point closed and the material presented to the decision-maker who – as in CBA – makes the final choice. Stakeholders or citizens may have agreed on a proposal, giving it considerable weight in the final evaluation. Alternatively, if no compromise is reached, in the end much more is left with the decision-maker.

Debates around MCA

There are several issues raised also regarding MCA. The issue of who should participate is core. At least among practitioners, there seems to be a lack of recognition of the effects of choosing various kinds of participants. However, it matters a great deal whether stakeholder representatives or citizens are involved regarding both the form of the process and what role interests and values play, and what kind of values are emphasized. The choice of representation influences outcomes of the process. At the same time, there are no objective criteria to turn to. This situation demands high levels of sensitivity to the issues involved by those organizing the evaluation.

The issue of weighting is another debated issue. Including cardinal weights makes MCA vulnerable to the same critique as CBA regarding incommensurability. One may even take that critique one step further as weights in MCA assume fixed trade-offs at least over the distribution of scores involved. Given the observation of plural values and restricted trade-offs, alternatives with thresholds, ordinal weights and no weighting at all may seem to better capture important aspects of the kind of values and interests involved. It is notable that MCA does not use discounting. Some view that as a weakness, others as a strength.

Some MCA methods like NAJADE and REGIME use some fairly complicated mathematics when producing a ranked order of alternatives. One thing is the quality of the assumptions that underpins the procedures. As important is the fact that there might be some alienation in the process of calculating ranked orders. The stakeholders or citizens involved may have problems understanding how the ranking is produced and hence prefer direct choice among described alternatives – see, for example, Refsgaard (2006).

11.3.3 Deliberative methods

While both CBA and most variants of MCA are based on a calculative logic, a third position in the literature is to accentuate the role of the argument and of potential preference changes following from communication about what should be done. Wilson and Howarth (2002, p. 441), moreover, note that "The paradox between the public nature of ecosystem services and the measurement of their economic value through individual expression has led to calls for more deliberative forms of environmental valuation to provide an alternative to standard valuation methods".

While the focus of this section is to characterize deliberative methods as an alternative for evaluating options regarding use and protection of environmental resources, one should be aware that the thinking about deliberation goes beyond that of project appraisals. It is also about the wider issue of democracy – of turning democracy by representation into a system more based on direct participation – see discussions in Chapter 10. For those interested in overviews regarding deliberative democracy, I refer to Dryzek (2002, 2013); Smith (2003); Bäckstrand et al. (2010).

Deliberation implies communication that induces "reflection upon preferences in non-coercive fashion" (Dryzek, 2002, p. 2). The idea goes to the heart of the issue of collective or social choice: the question of whether preferences can change, and whether consensus can be found concerning which values should have priority. The emphasis on deliberation has roots as far back as ancient Greece and its *polis*. In modern, twentieth-century developments, names like Dewey (1927), Arendt (1958), Habermas (1984, 1996), but also Rawls (1993), are central. A core idea is that of communicative rationality (Habermas, 1984) with its focus on the creation of understanding through dialogue and the force of the better argument. It is a form of common reasoning where consensus may be obtained via mutual learning, understanding and changes in what is preferred.[10] In the Habermasian (ideal) form, communication is thought to be free of coercion, strategic action and manipulation.

Participation

Again, there are three groups of participants – decision-makers, experts and laypeople. The latter are most consistently involved as citizens, while stakeholders may be called as 'experts' on the issue. One observes, however, cases where stakeholders are also included in the normative assessments. At least from a Habermasian perspective, this is problematic.

The definition of roles involved vary between formats of deliberative methods – see Box 11.2. In the case of focus groups, the only expertise normally included is the moderator. People meet to express views on a topic. There is no other expertise on factual issues. In the case of citizen juries, the jurors (citizens) hear 'witnesses' – that is, experts on various aspects of the topic, including stakeholders.

Data

Factual data may be presented in written form – often material produced by those organizing the deliberation and distributed before the meetings. Even more important is the opportunity to hear experts and to hold discussions with them to clarify issues. Deliberative methods provide opportunities for considerable in-depth evaluation of the knowledge and uncertainties involved. Given the complexities faced, engaging experts from different backgrounds and views increases the capacity of the deliberative process to capture what may be at stake.

Like MCA, deliberative evaluation can therefore be seen as a response to the bounded rationality of individuals. The process of deliberation not only makes the people involved aware of the needs and perspectives of others, which is the core of the communicative aspect. The citizens may also help each other to clarify what the issue is about and which way they themselves (should) think about the problem.

Also distinctive is the format of valuation. It is formulated through judgments and articulation of arguments. Moreover, this process is interactive with the evaluation of factual matters and issues related to the uncertainties and lack of knowledge involved. Hence, Joss (1998, p. 5) emphasizes that "The active involvement, in a dialogical way, of lay people, experts and interest-group representative allows for the subjects under consideration to be evaluated, beyond a purely scientific context, to include economic, legal, ethical and other social considerations".

BOX 11.2

KEY DELIBERATIVE VALUE-ARTICULATING INSTITUTIONS

Several forms of deliberative methods or institutions exist. I will restrict this brief presentation to three – that is, focus groups, citizen juries and consensus conferences.

Focus groups

A focus group is a small, randomly selected citizens' discussion group – typically up to ten people – led by a moderator. The aim is to explore the views of the people involved in a context that is supportive of bringing forward views and arguments. There are three distinct characteristics of a focus group. First, it is normally based on the knowledge of those participating – that is, no experts are called. Second, it does not propose a conclusion on what to do. The material is brought from the focus group to the decision-maker in the form of a summary of arguments. Finally, the subject area to discuss is defined by the organizers – see also Barbour (2007).

While focus groups seem to have originated in marketing research, it is being used in the environmental area (e.g., Burgess et al., 1988; Kerr et al., 1998; Butler, 2010; Van Assche et al., 2012). The so-called 'deliberative focus group' (Wakeford, 2001) is an example of a more comprehensive form, also involving external expertise.

Citizen juries

A citizen jury is also a small group of citizens (10–20 people) acting as jurors. It is led by a moderator, but deviates from a focus group in several ways. First, a citizen jury is expected to draw a conclusion on the actual matter in the form of a proposal to the commissioning body. Second, its discussions are supported by 'witnesses', dominantly experts, but also stakeholders, who present material for the jurors to support them in their deliberations. The jury is given the power to define which witnesses it wants to hear. The process will normally take three to five days. The method is presented more completely in Stewart et al. (1994) and Smith and Wales (1999).

Citizen juries have been used since the 1970s. Several applications relate to environmental problems (Kenyon et al., 2001) like the release of genetically modified organisms (Marris et al., 2001; Aasen and Vatn, 2013), wetlands and water management (Aldred and Jacobs, 2000; Huitema et al., 2010), and nanotechnology (Burri and Bellucci, 2008). The idea is to develop a consensus proposal. Nevertheless, consensus may not be possible and a voting procedure is applied.

Consensus conferences

A consensus conference has many of the same features as the citizen jury. We talk again about a small group of laypeople, which deliberate over an issue under the lead of a moderator. The method was developed in Denmark in the 1980s by the Danish Board of Technology as a means of incorporating the perspectives of the lay public within the assessment of new and/or controversial scientific and technological developments raising serious social and ethical concerns (Joss and Durant, 1995; Joss, 1998; Smith, 2003). Consensus conferences are used for issues similar to those mentioned for citizen jury above – see, for example, Einsiedel et al. (2001); Burri and Bellucci (2008); Dryzek et al. (2008). The main difference to a citizen jury is mainly that consensus conferences are focusing even more strongly on consensus. Thus, disagreement or the recommendation of a diversity of options is not encouraged (Wakeford, 2001).

Recommending

The format of the conclusion varies between the various deliberative methods. In the case of focus groups – see Box 11.2 – there is typically no aim to conclude by stating what should or should not be done. Rather, it is a form of recording and evaluating viewpoints and arguments. This is different in the case of citizen juries where a recommendation is made either through reaching a consensus or via voting. The basis for this conclusion is a common judgment of the factual information and the various arguments made.

Deliberative methods open up communication about what is of value and who it is of value to. O'Neill emphasizes that "dialogue involves not just recording given views and attitudes, but ideally the transformation of . . . actors' self-understandings . . . through conversation" (O'Neill, 2001, p. 488). Hence, while negotiations seek compromises between given interests, deliberation fosters critical examination of preferences and values and processes towards mutual understanding.

Dialogue tends to discourage strategic or instrumental behavior. It accentuates a focus on the common good since the dialogue logically is about 'we', not 'I'. It facilitates thinking in public interest terms – as citizens (Goodin, 1996). While, there might still be an interest in bringing forward arguments in favor of pure individual gains, one is forced to couch these in terms that can support the common good. This claim is then open for tests and counterarguments and if not found valid, the argument can be discredited as the disguised strategic action it really is. This way the advocate is also discredited. Elster (1998) handles a special aspect of this in his focus on the 'civilizing force of hypocrisy'. When one states that something is good for society, it binds the individual to what is said and obstructs the realization of the potential selfish motive behind the argument. Dialogue and public statements civilize behavior (Dryzek, 2002; Smith, 2003).

Debates around deliberative methods

There are also issues or problems in the case of deliberative methods and one concerns participation. We typically talk of small groups creating issues of representativeness. There are several responses to this challenge. First, there is the argument that the quality and relevance of the material brought forward is much better than, for example, methods with wider participation as the issues can be more intensively handled in smaller groups. Second, one may repeat the exercise with more groups, which is costly. Third, representation may not be about statistical representativity. O'Neill (2001) argues that since we are dealing with normative and political questions, statistical representation is not the issue. It is rather about establishing procedures by which representatives are acknowledged to act legitimately on behalf of others – of the society. While involving people as citizens actually reduces the problem, it is still a challenge for deliberative valuation to formulate rules and practices about who to call upon in each case and how interactions in meetings should be structured.

What about groups or individuals that have restricted capacity to present their views and participate in deliberation? Power-free communication may not be a possibility for powerless people. The institutional challenge in this case is whether one should create specific rules that help secure the defined rights of these groups in the deliberative process, or let them choose to be represented by 'advocates'. So while CBA has issues related to 'ability to pay', we here encounter issues related to 'ability to say'.

Another problem concerns the representation of future generations (Goodin, 1996; O'Neill, 2001). This is a problem common to all value-articulating institutions. Should we involve each other in guessing about what kind of lives the coming generations want to live? I think this is a wrong formulation of the problem as the future is always created by the present generation. According to the classic institutional perspective, we form those to come. Regarding this issue, there is hence no choice. It is our responsibility to create a world and a future that accord with what we believe creates the best opportunity for the coming generations to live good lives (Sunstein, 1993; Page, 1997). The issue of representing the future generations is not about speaking on behalf of them as much as it is about creating them and their opportunities.

Regarding the data, it has been observed that not only the quality of the knowledge represented by experts, but also the quality of their performance as witnesses, influence the understanding and appreciation of the information – see, for example, Aasen and Vatn (2013). This may be a serious issue warranting specific emphasis and reflexiveness regarding the potential biases.

Due to all the complexities involved, some have argued for combining deliberative methods and MCA – see, for example, Stagl (2003, 2006); Munda (2004, 2007); Wittmer et al. (2006). This solution can help to structure the assessment of a complex problem through the MCA system of scores. There is, however, a challenge related to ensuring that including MCA facilitates rather than constrains dialogue.

Finally, in developing arguments and concluding, there is the issue of maintaining the process and avoiding turning it into pure negotiation. Emphasizing the citizen role and focusing on the common good at the start of a deliberative process is a response to this challenge. Certainly, the vision of what the common good is may vary across individuals and (sub-)cultures. Hence, there may not be agreement. That is not counter to the very idea of deliberation and voting is a way to 'settle' disagreement.

In relation to this, one should note the difference between the standard electorate voting procedure of representative democratic systems – that is, isolated individuals voting in elections – and voting in a jury after a process of deliberation. Dryzek (2002) argues that the capability of deliberation to create a stronger sense of community – that is, of developing and emphasizing common values – narrows down the possibility of conflict.[11]

11.4 Main messages

The focus of this book is on collective choice – about common decisions regarding our shared environments. Evaluations of what it is best to do are founded on values and interests. How we understand these concepts has strong implications for what we think is a good or legitimate way of organizing collective choices and the evaluations that underpin them. The main distinction in this field is between a position that perceives values as individual preferences – how much we are willing to pay to obtain something – and the opinion that values are socially defined principles about what is the right way of acting. Seeing values as individual preferences points towards choosing the solution that maximizes the sum of preference satisfaction. Seeing them as socially constructed, points in a different direction – towards a dialogue over what are important values to support. It emphasizes the better argument. Another key issue regards whether values are considered commensurable or not. Finally, environmental issues may be difficult to comprehend. The way we think about complexity and the cognitive challenges faced is also of importance for the way collective evaluations and choices should be made.

Assumptions made about the character of values, complexity and cognitive capacity points towards different forms of evaluation – different value-articulating institutions. We have looked at three types – cost–benefit analysis, multicriteria analysis and deliberative methods. They diverge regarding (1) who should participate and according to what role and competence, (2) what are considered relevant data, and (3) how common recommendations should be reached.

While all value-articulating institutions involve both decision-makers and experts, they differ regarding who undertakes the value articulation and how it is done. In the case of CBA, we do this as consumers. Values are measured as individual preferences in the form of willingness to pay for various (environmental) qualities. Information about these qualities is normally presented in written or oral form to each individual. The aim of CBA is to find an optimal solution defined as the highest net present value through aggregating willingness to pay estimates. It is assumed that individuals have given preferences for the goods involved and the necessary capacity to evaluate the ability of different alternatives to satisfy their preference.

MCA covers several tools. The basis for all of them is that goods are multidimensional and that decisions are complex. The methods therefore concentrate on supporting participants with constrained capacities in a demanding evaluation process. MCA is furthermore focused on establishing the best compromise between conflicting values or interests. The various types of MCA tools differ with regard to assumptions made concerning whether values can be compared and traded off against each other – whether they are commensurable and compensable.

Regarding deliberative methods, people are mainly invited to participate as citizens, while stakeholders may be involved. Again, there are different formats, defined partly by the role of experts and the format of recommendations. While dialogue among the involved citizens is a key characteristic, some deliberative methods also place strong emphasis on expert–citizen interaction to clarify both factual and value-related issues. Also in the case of deliberative methods, cognitive capacity is considered restricted. The main rationale for communication is that through learning about various arguments, people may be able to reach agreements on what alternatives to prioritize. While the ideal solution is a created consensus, voting is an alternative when such consensus cannot be reached.

Choosing who should represent laypeople is a challenge for CBA, MCA and deliberative methods. The problem may seem smaller the larger the selected group. Therefore, it can be seen as less of a problem in CBA where WTP estimates are typically derived from rather large samples. However, it is clearly a trade-off between the width and depth of the analysis, between bringing many people in, and ensuring good understanding. Involving more people can furthermore not compensate for a wrong or illegitimate type of assessment. Given that environments are shared, there are strong arguments for favoring decisions based on communication and social preferences – on citizens' dialogue. Moreover, given the specific characteristics of environmental problems, I find it problematic to use methods that assume value commensurability and that assume that the factual issues involved are simple. Hence, I find that deliberative methods and some of the multicriteria value-articulating institutions conform best to the issues and values involved. This is so, despite the observation that no method is ideal.

This chapter has focused on decisions as 'single moments in time' – what it is best to do regarding a specific issue like developing a transport system for an area, protection of a specific habitat and so on. In relation to this, it is important to emphasize that decisions are rather continuous, where one decision forms the basis for the next. They are taken in context (O'Neill et al., 2008), where not only history, but also traditions regarding how decisions should be made are important. In that sense, it is essential to think about value-articulating institutions presented here as part of a wider system of value articulation and decision-making. That perspective is easily lost when looking at single methods and single choices.

NOTES

1 Formally, a lexicographic ordering is defined as $(a_1, a_2) \leq (a_1', a_2')$ if and only if $a_1 < a_1'$ or $(a_1 = a_1'$ and $a_2 \leq a_2')$.

2 Strictly speaking, in CBA it is the system used for pricing – for example, hedonic pricing, contingent valuation – that is, the value-articulating institution. Hence, Jacobs (1997) classifies CBA as a 'decision-recommending institution'. In the case of MCA and deliberative methods, the value articulation is an integrated part of the whole assessment. I think distinguishing between value-articulating institutions and decision-recommending institutions complicates the presentation and I therefore also refer to CBA as a value-articulating institution.

3 There are challenges related to using benefit transfers and the potential inconsistencies in basing monetary assessments on a theory assuming that preferences are purely individual and next including social variables when making corrections as part of the transfer. These issues are discussed in Spash and Vatn (2006).

4 Here the concept of opportunity cost of a choice is key. It is the value of the best forgone alternative. Therefore, if a road were to be built, forgone alternatives would be alternative uses of the resources used for building it. To the extent market prices exist, they are seen as a measure of the value of such forgone alternatives. Indirect methods may be used, as discussed in the text.

5 To take a stand on compensation is seen as normative – a political question. It is also notable that such compensation would be very costly to organize – transaction costs. In relation to that, it is argued that there will typically be no systematic winners or losers; hence, compensation can be disregarded. This assumption is not well founded. As the poor have less capacity to pay, they will mainly become losers given the rule of potential Pareto improvement.

6 One might ask if this is also not the case in market allocations. A cardinal willingness to pay measure – the price – is decisive here too. In this case it is, however, not necessary to assume that a kilogram of strawberries for £1.50 gives the same utility to person A as to person B even if they both buy it at that price. It only says that a kilogram of strawberries gives equal or more utility than alternative uses of this sum for each individual. If this transaction enters a CBA, the price of £1.50 is used as a measure of the benefit it gives to both A and B. Their benefits or 'utilities' are compared.

7 Munda (1996) argues that there is an inconsistency involved in assigning different weights to different individuals. Distributional weights must be seen as coefficients of importance. They define the relative importance of each individual. Munda argues that it is a problem when including these in a framework

otherwise based on trade-offs. He concludes: "Unfortunately, since CBA is based on a complete compensatory mathematical model . . . [distributional] weights can only have the meaning of a trade-off ratio, as a consequence a *theoretical inconsistency exists*" (p. 163; original emphasis).

8 Arrow et al.'s argument (1993) is that WTP is more 'realistic' as it is bound by the income of the respondent. WTA could in that sense be 'any figure'. I find it highly problematic that a potential measurement problem overrules a consistent treatment of rights – an issue that is clearly the more fundamental.

9 Given a discount rate of 3 percent, a benefit of 100 US dollars in year 50 has a NPV of 22.8. If the benefit accrues a 100 years from now, the NPV is 5.2 US dollars. Certainly, how future losses and gains are discounted has great implications for which long-term policies become most favorable or 'efficient' given CBA techniques.

10 The term *deliberative democracy* has different meanings in different literatures. Some equate it with the standard representative democracy of the liberal state, where the basic idea is that of individuals with given and stable preferences that do not change as a function of the context of interaction. It is the single individual, who through his or her personal reasoning, draws the conclusion about what he or she finds to be the right solution. Rawls is the most prominent representative of this position. Dryzek (2002, p. 15) suggests that "Rawls downplays the *social* or interactive aspect of deliberation, meaning that public reason can be undertaken by the solitary thinker. This is deliberation of a sort – but only in terms of the weighting of arguments in the mind, not testing them in real political interaction" (original emphasis). There is thus great variation between different deliberative schools concerning the implication of deliberation, the role of the group and the role offered for changed preferences. Interested readers can look at Bohman and Rehg (1997) and Dryzek (2002) for an exposition of various stances. The way the concept of deliberation is developed here implies the possibility for a discussion with others about which values to emphasize and what to prefer.

11 Boulding (1970) has argued similarly in that "a public requires some sort of organization, an organization implies community, a community implies some kind of clustering of the benevolence function . . . which denies the assumption of independent utilities" (cited in Schmid, 1987, p. 30). So, community is 'domain restriction' – that is, a clustering or 'homogenization' of values and preferences.

12

Policy instruments – institutions for environmental governance

In Chapter 10 I focused on the overall policy process – that is, the definition of goals and ways to operationalize these through instituting various policy instruments. In Chapter 11, I took this one step further by looking more specifically at how the formulation of goals could be supported by specifically designed evaluation processes. In the present chapter, I expand by analyzing experiences with various policy instruments. I define policy instruments in a wide sense – as (re)formulations of the resource regime. This may happen on two levels. First, it concerns establishment of and changes in the basic structures of property rights and types of interaction rules. Second, it concerns various regulations, given these structures, like the introduction of prohibitions, taxes and so on.

The analyses in this chapter are organized within the environmental governance system (EGS) framework developed in Chapter 6. I start by further explaining the concept of a policy instrument as indicated above. Thereafter come two sections where I offer insights regarding the form and effect of existing resource regimes and adaptations of these for (1) a set of environmental resources and (2) some types of pollution. This is the largest part of the chapter, which aims at illustrating how the dynamics between resource characteristics, technology and resource regimes influence the use and state of the chosen resources. Finally, I move from the empirical level to look at policy instruments from a more theoretical perspective where I summarize present understanding of how various regulations like legal instruments, economic incentives and information work.

12.1 Policy instruments understood as (re)formulations of the resource regime

I have emphasized that environmental problems typically arise because decisions that are physically interlinked are institutionally separated. From this perspective, environmental governance can be viewed as ways to try to institutionally (re-)connect what is already physically interconnected.

Related to this, changes in the basic structure of the resource regime as well as regulations put in place within an existing regime seem important to consider. Therefore I define policy instruments in a wide sense – as (re)formulations of the resource regime. This includes (1) establishment of/changes in property rights (private, state, common, open access) and types of interaction rules (trade, command, cooperation, no rules), and (2) various specific environmental regulations given these structures. The latter may involve introduction of legal regulations (e.g., prohibitions, prescriptions/emission standards, emission quotas) and economic incentives (e.g., taxes, subsidies, tradable emission quotas) linked to environmentally harmful activities. In most of the literature it is only (2) that are termed (environmental) policy instruments. I find including both levels above conceptually the most consistent. I also think that changes in the basic structures of resource regimes are as important for the status of our environments as the specific environmental regulations.

Disentangling this, let me start by looking at three directions environmental policy could take – see also Chapter 10:

- *The expansion of common property with community regulations.* This implies a system of common governance of resources where use by individual households or firms produces (negative) side-effects for other households/firms. By establishing common property – various community rules/norms regarding the use of the resource at stake like a fish stock, a forest, a water body – side-effects/interactions can be regulated through a common definition of who is allowed to do what concerning the common resource.
- *The expansion of private property operating in markets.* While individual property and markets may be seen as the cause of many environmental problems, there is also the argument that this is so because there is too little individual ownership. Hence, by expanding property rights to all ecosystem dimensions or side-effects of economic activity, these may then be traded in markets, ensuring that they are priced and this way looked after.
- *The expansion of state property or state regulation of private activities.* One may establish state property over the involved resource or emitting activities and regulate their use through direct command. The state may also change the conditions of economic activity for private actors – be they firms, common property entities or households/individuals. In this case,

the state establishes regulations like legal prohibitions, taxes, emission quotas and so on, signaling the costs of side-effects to those creating them. Also, the latter strategy implies changes in the rights structure either explicitly as in legal regulations, or implicitly through the introduction of, for example, environmental taxes.

Actually, the latter type of policy operates at two different levels. Expanding state property implies direct regulation of resource use as it is governed by the state/state agency. Regulating private decisions implies use of the third party power of the state. This power is also the basis for establishing private and common property in environmental resources.

The above three main options have different characteristics concerning the form of and capacity to handle environmental problems. In Chapter 7, I defined four main dimensions when studying the capacities of governance structures – that is, the distribution of rights and responsibilities, transaction costs, perceptions, and type of motivation. I will briefly summarize here what has been emphasized in earlier chapters in this regard.

Starting with *rights and responsibilities*, the main issue in all the above resource regimes concerns who is allowed to shift costs upon whom and to what extent this may happen. They differ, however, depending on how this is institutionalized. If we start off from a situation characterized by open access, establishing common property implies that cost shifting becomes an issue for common regulation among the co-owners. Creating state ownership has a similar capacity, while management is now delegated to elected representatives/the administration of state agencies and not undertaken by co-owners themselves. In the case of private property and markets, conditions for trading over side-effects/cost shifting must be established by defining rights regarding cost shifting. If resource owners are free to shift costs onto others through, for example, pollution, those others must pay the polluter to reduce emissions/cost shifting. If rights are with the victims, resource users may pay these to accept (some) emissions following from production. So while internal rules govern in the case of common and state property, trade defines the level of interference in the case of private properties operating in markets.

How effective and efficient these solutions are depends not least on the involved *transaction costs*. Economic theory emphasizes that firms operating in competitive markets – that is, a situation with many producers and consumers – results in efficient production. This is under the assumption of no or low transaction costs. It may, however, be very costly to assign private property rights to environmental resources as many are common-pool – that is, costly to demarcate. Moreover, even if demarcation is possible, it may be very costly to establish trade over side-effects of use as these are typically widespread and therefore impact upon many people/firms. Air and water pollution are good examples. Bringing resources under one authority – for example, as common or state property – may reduce transaction costs substantially. This depends, however, greatly on the types of resources and side-effects involved. Common property of a pasture or fish in a lake may have relatively low coordination costs (transaction costs) and can create well-coordinated use. In the case of air and water pollution, common property may not be a relevant solution. Here specific state regulation like standards and taxes may be the solution with the lowest transaction costs and have the best capacity to produce good results.

Regarding *perceptions*, I will now also include *articulation of values*. In the case of common property, focus is on balancing the common interest with the interests of the involved individuals/households. Hence, issues will typically be framed as questions regarding what should be permitted use. Value articulation is an integrated part of the process of making the internal rules – defining accepted practices. In the case of private property and trade, parties look for what can offer individual gains. Knowledge is private. Values are articulated through the process of defining prices – resting on the willingness to pay and accept compensation. Under the last option – state ownership or direct state regulation – the type of government is crucial. Assuming a democratic and well-functioning state, action should in principle reflect the values of its citizens, while we saw in Chapter 10 how both special interests and administrative cultures influence framing and perception. As in the case of common property, valuation is again part of rule-making. The state may want to bring the views of its citizens into that process using cost–benefit analysis or deliberative methods. Hence, states/state agencies may base their decisions actually on a perception that comes close to that of market and trade, while it may also favor deliberation.

Turning finally to *motivations*, these are also expected to vary across resource regimes. As emphasized in Chapters 5 and 7, motivation may be individually vs socially oriented, strategic vs cooperative. While firm managers are expected to maximize profits of the firm, communities are expected to be more oriented at fostering cooperation within their bounds. Public bodies are – at least in well-functioning democracies – built to be responsive to the demands from their citizens. The state is the only actor that can directly balance the interests of all living in its territory, while it depends on agreements with other states to handle cross-border issues. While it may act on the basis of social rationality within its bounds, it may act strategically in the international realm.

From the above, we see that regimes are not neutral regarding the costs of handling side-effects. They are not neutral regarding how highly a side-effect is valued, which interests and values become protected or whether people are willing to cooperate/think beyond their own interests when trying to sort problems out. In the following, I will discuss these issues both empirically and theoretically.

12.2 Use and protection of environmental resources

I distinguish in this chapter between use and protection of environmental resources on the one hand (the present section) and the question of pollution due to emissions from production and consumption on the other (Section 12.3). Regarding use of environmental resources, I will focus on the capacity of various resource regimes to ensure sustainable use. In that vein, the analyses will also include emphasis on distributive aspects.

I start this section with a short overview of general issues regarding choice and functionality of resource regimes for environmental resources. The presentation follows the EGS framework. This section forms the basis for subsequent analyses of resource regimes for a selected set of environmental resources – that is, land (forests and pastures), irrigation and fish. These are chosen to show how the dynamics between resource characteristics, technology and resource regimes influence resource use and the state of the resources. I will do so by trying to embed these analyses in studies of the political processes forming these regimes. The section closes with a similar focus on policies directed specifically at protection – limited to the issue of biodiversity.

12.2.1 General aspects

Developing resource regimes that work well for environmental – common-pool – resources is demanding and has become increasingly so (e.g., Dietz et al., 2003). According to the EGS framework, the characteristics of the resource, the technologies involved, the interests of various actors, and the political system influence the choice of resource regime as well as how they function. I will highlight here some issues of importance for the later analyses of specific resources.

The characteristics of the resource and the natural processes involved

Environmental resources and processes are typically characterized by high complexity and diverse types of processes. Based on the literature – see, for example, Ostrom (1990, 2005); Ostrom et al. (1994); Agrawal (2001); Young (2002); Young et al. (2008); Turner (2011) – the following aspects seem important regarding choice of resource regime and how effective they may be – how well they 'fit':

- the size of the resource and interactions between different resources;
- the mobility and variability of the resource;
- the storage capacities involved;
- the possibility to demarcate – create boundaries – around involved resources and processes.

The *size of the resource* influences to some extent what resource regime is relevant or feasible. Defining the size of a resource is, however, difficult. One may talk of a stand of trees and a fish stock. One may also talk of ecosystems, including interlinkages between such systems in space and time. Hence, fishing of one species typically influences the dynamics of the whole ecosystem. Due to the involved interactions, boundaries around a resource must therefore be somewhat pragmatically defined, knowing that each border established by defining use or property rights leaves some human interactions unregulated. The more borders, the larger the challenge.

The *mobility* of the resource seems to have rather profound implications on what regimes are feasible. While land and trees do not move, some resources related to land and trees – for example, microorganisms, soil, animals, birds – move. The same goes for resources like water and air. The challenges this creates for governance has been amply illustrated in Chapter 10.

There is also *variability*. The productivity of, for example, land, may change – between seasons, but also between the same season in different years due to variation not least in rainfall. *Storage capacities* also influence the way a resource may be used and the functionality of various resource regimes. Forests, herds, lakes and groundwater basins and so on have large storage capacities. Rivers, pastures and agricultural land have less.

It is a general assumption in most of the literature that sustainable use of common-pool resources demands that resources are *demarcated* – that access is somehow limited. That implies including some people and excluding others. Being common-pool resources, we face per definition high costs

Source: An adjusted version of
Bromley (1991).

Figure 12.1
Productivity of land
and possible types of
property regime

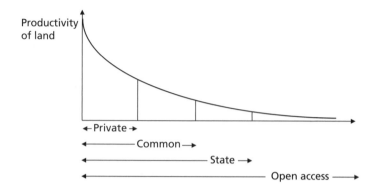

of exclusion – see Figure 3.1 in Chapter 3. So, limiting access may not be easy. In that respect, it is notable that exclusion costs vary. Using land for illustrative purposes, one may hypothesize a relationship as described in Figure 12.1.

Private property is the most costly to establish as it implies the highest number of properties – that is, borders – to define and protect. Hence, one will expect it to exist only on land that is or can be made fairly productive. Common property can also exist for land that is less productive as the involved people/households operate the land as a common unit. There are simply fewer borders to establish and protect, while there is increased demand for internal coordination. State property may be able to cover land of even lower quality due to the capacities of the state. At some point, the costs of establishing property rights are too high, and the land is left as open access. One may also choose open access for political and social reasons. All should have access. If the resource is common-pool – that is, there is rivalry – that implies the danger of exhaustion.

We observe that all property regimes are feasible for some land. Then a key question concerns what regime offers the best expected outcomes; what is considered the most legitimate solution?

The cost of exclusion depends on the characteristics of the resource. While drawing 'lines' may be necessary to establish governance, these may create their own problems. Land fragmentation is a good example of one type of issue involved (e.g., Fahrig, 2003). Decisions made on each owned unit of land may be effective in guarding productivity of that piece for defined uses. It may, however, also transform the landscape and this way vastly change the opportunities for species and processes that operate on larger scales than each owned plot. Hence, defining property rights may also create problems.

There are also important distributional issues involved. Private property might exclude some from the land and private land rights may become concentrated through trade. Common property may include all, but there may be elite capture – that is, informal privileges. The way income from state property is distributed depends on political priorities.

Technology and technological change

Regarding technology, two issues seem key. First, technological change may influence what resources become rival. Second, such change may also influence excludability/the costs of demarcation. So, it is not only the characteristics of the resource that influence if it is common-pool or not; technology is also important.

The capacity to extract resources influences when a resource becomes rival in use. This capacity is affected by the kind of technology involved. Without axes, cutting trees is difficult. Hence, rivalry is low. Chainsaws expand the extraction capacity further. The types of fishing gear and boats available affect the capacity to fish. An environmental resource that is vast compared to the capacity to extract can be under open access without creating problems regarding future use. With increased extraction capacity, the resource turns common-pool. Costs of demarcating properties and managing resources may also be altered as a result of technological change. Here the developments in various information technologies are key – for example, mapping systems. Remote sensing is an example of new opportunities regarding control/monitoring.

Economic actors

Access to resources is important for economic actors. One would therefore expect distribution of property/use rights to be a key issue. Power relations will be important. Also prominent is the need for coordination among users as environmental resources are typically common-pool. These issues have been amply discussed in previous chapters, emphasizing not least how various property rights regimes influence both motivations and the capacity to coordinate. Here I will add a reflection regarding the need for coordination related to the severity of rivalry in use. Rivalry is not only an effect of the characteristics of the resource. The number of people involved as well as the form and level of use – that is, the extraction pressure – also impact the level of rivalry. The literature identifies, moreover, that the size of the group involved is important, especially for the success of a common property regime – see, for example, Wade (1988); Baland and Platteau (1996);

Agrawal (2001); Ostrom (2005) – due to its influence on demarcation and coordination costs.

Regarding the latter, heterogeneity in income and ethnicity may be important. Agrawal (2001) notes that heterogeneity does not prohibit coordination, but makes it more difficult as it typically demands more use of force. To the extent that solving problems regarding use of environmental issues demands cooperation, the cultural basis for creating and maintaining cooperative will is important.

The political regime

The political regime concerns the actors involved, the interests they represent and the institutions governing the policy processes. Choice and functionality of the various resource regimes depend on these interests and capacities at all levels. They influence the will and capacity to establish various property regimes and institutionalize various regulations regarding the actions of economic actors.

At the basis lies the overall legitimacy of the political system. Here one may envision positive and negative cumulative circles. Good capacity increases the chance to deliver well, which next increases the capacity by enhancing the legitimacy of the system. Many developing countries experience the opposite. Lack of political capacity results in weak output, which next challenges the legitimacy of the system further.

Low capacity may restrict what options are available to the state. The state may not be able to ensure the necessary basis to manage the resources that it owns. This seems especially to be the case when there are conflicts over the rights to such resources. Problems are rampant when central governments undermine local authority (e.g., Bromley, 1992; Agrawal, 2001). It may be constrained regarding its capacity to institute environmental regulations for legal, economic or informational reasons. Corruption may be extensive (e.g., Robbins, 2000). All this will influence what regimes are observed, their legitimacy as well as ideas about reform.

As emphasized in Chapter 10, policies reflect interest constellations and ideologies, including overall perspectives regarding which resource regimes are seen to deliver well regarding the interests involved. These aspects are part of the political regime and crucial in understanding what solutions have been developed for specific resources.

12.2.2 Land

Turning to specific resources, I start by focusing on land. According to the Food and Agriculture Organization (FAO, 2012a) – see Chapter 2 – about 9 percent of the global land mass is arable. Half of it is grassland and forests – fairly evenly split. Three percent is inland water. The rest is deserts, glaciers and other non-productive land. Drawing the line between categories is not easy. These figures offer, nevertheless, a reasonable macro-perspective.

Land offers a number of potential income streams for human appropriation. A forest may deliver timber, fuelwood, animal feed, game, medicinal plants, various forms of leisure experiences and so on. Rights to such benefit streams may vary. Trees may be owned by some; others may have access to pastures; yet others to game. Next, rights may vary from 'full ownership' to 'use rights' in various combinations and formats – see also Chapter 6.

Structures regarding ownership and use rights for land vary across the globe. Even the meaning of property varies and we observe often-complex mixtures of legal and customary rights that may be in conflict/create uncertainty. Many developing countries apply the public trust doctrine for land. As an example, the President of Tanzania holds all land as a trustee for the people. In practice, land is managed by the Ministry of Lands (URT, 1999a). Private rights exist for agricultural land – partly based on statutory (that is, legal) and partly on customary rights. Communities may also own land – for example, forests.

While the law typically recognizes customary rights of occupancy, there may often be situations with competing claims, as well as huge power asymmetries. As pressures on land increase due to various processes, conflicts seem to increase in many developing countries. Merlet et al. (2014, p. 2) write:

> One kind of conflict over land rights arises when rural populations are marginalized and excluded from land that has been appropriated by a minority of agricultural producers that rely on salaried employees. Another kind of land related conflict arises in contexts where feudalism (a system in which large land owners take advantage of sharecroppers or tenant farmers) persists. Still other conflicts involve indigenous populations who are attempting to re-appropriate land (sometimes very large amounts of land) that they have been using for generations. These populations often practice forest agriculture and leave land fallow for long periods of time as it regenerates. This makes them particularly vulnerable to land grabbing by foreign parties. In semi desert areas and steppes, conflict between herd people and farmers has increased.

Foreign parties may be national and international. International investors are invited by governments and land is leased without involving local
communities. Land is appropriated by national residents who utilize the
fact that governments are weak. The scale of rights transfers is substantial
(e.g., Shanmugaratnam, 2014; Demissie, 2015).

Forests

Forests are dominantly owned by states. Agrawal (2007) concludes that,
globally, close to 84 percent of forests are under state/public ownership.
About 4 percent of this category is defined as 'community administered';
4.5 percent is common property/indigenous lands. Private property covers
almost 12 percent. There is a difference between developed and developing
countries. In the latter, state property is slightly more important (86 percent)
and private property clearly less so (5.6 percent). Common property/indig-
enous lands are more important – 8.3 percent. The figures are uncertain.

There are, as already emphasized, conflicts over tenure. Especially in developing countries communities claim customary rights to resources in state-
owned forests, as a large number of people live on land that is defined as state
owned. It is notable that colonial rule and the establishment of independent
nation states in the South implied establishment of state property to forests
under customary rule. A rather recent process of decentralization – transferring state forests to community tenure regimes – has been ongoing since the
late 1980s. Most probably, the number of legally defined community forests
is now larger than the data from Agrawal (2007) indicate.

There has been substantial debate regarding which property rights regime is
most effective at ensuring sustainable forestry. There are many examples of
successes and failures regarding all forms – see, for example, Ostrom (1990,
2005); Agrawal (2001, 2007); Ostrom and Nagendra (2006). In analyzing
this, it is important to note that forests may not necessarily be common-
pool. Many are sufficiently productive to cover the costs of establishing
private property, noting that the value of tradable resources also depends
on access to markets. At the same time, states may want to keep control
over forests, ensuring income from, for example, logging to cover their costs.
Communities may want to keep forests as common property not because of
prohibitive costs of establishing private rights, but because it facilitates their
present uses and ensures maintaining the community. Hence, the difference
between developed and developing countries may be explained by political
and cultural differences as well as differences regarding transaction costs and
access to markets for timber.

While there is a series of common challenges, each property regime faces specific issues regarding sustainable use. In the case of private property, a key topic concerns regeneration. To the extent that private ownership is motivated entirely by profitability, there is a question of whether replanting pays. Rather, income from timber harvests could be invested in other activities if that offers more income. What is economically the best thing to do depends on the speed of regrowth. In the North, forests tend to grow slowly and owners may not be motivated to replant. Hence, legal regulations are created, making owners responsible for regeneration (e.g., Bauer et al., 2004). Another case concerns time-limited private concessions in state forests – typically for 10–30 year periods. Here, problems of regeneration have been rampant, as loggers do not have much incentive to reforest. Legal regulations and forced payments to regeneration funds have created such incentives, but it has also been vulnerable to corruption – see, for example, Barr et al. (2010) and their study of Indonesia's Reforestation Fund. Public access to privately owned forests for hiking and some non-timber products like berries and mushrooms is a separate issue, regulated differently across countries – see, for example, Bauer et al. (2004). These rights are quite extensive in, for example, Scandinavia, while very restricted in countries like the USA.

Regarding state property, similar issues as those for private property may pertain. The state may be in need of financial means to develop the country, and forests represent a form of capital that can be easily transformed into cash. Hence, there is pressure towards deforesting. Similarly, states may support agricultural development, and allow people to encroach on state forests as long as they convert it to agricultural uses (e.g., Movik et al., 2012). Establishing state ownership may also interrupt well-functioning customary institutions. If the state does not have the capacity to enforce its own rules, there is a danger that state property deteriorates into *de facto* open access, since the customary systems involved may also erode – see, for example, Baland and Platteau (1996); Ostrom (2005); Chhatre and Agrawal (2009). There may also be a problem related to lack of presence, implying weak capacity to adapt to ecological dynamics – see, for example, Folke et al. (1998).

Common property also has its strengths and weaknesses. Similar to state property, it may reduce transaction costs of establishing and managing the regime. It is also seen as a flexible system where the larger size of the involved land offers wider opportunities to the people involved regarding resource use. It increases flexibility and hence reduces risk as compared to private property. If a disease or drought hits one part of a forest, use can be reallocated to other parts through collective decisions.

There is a rather substantial literature on common property and under what conditions it may be successful. Ostrom (1990, 2005) is well known for her so-called design principles. These are based on observations regarding factors that seem important to ensuring successful common property management – for forests, but also other common-pool resources – see Box 12.1. In his review of the overall literature in this field, Agrawal (2001) presents an even longer list of facilitative factors including also external factors and factors related to the type of resource. The number of households involved is important. Nested systems may, however, mitigate problems related to large commons. He mentions 'well defined boundaries', 'shared norms',

---

BOX 12.1

OSTROM'S DESIGN PRINCIPLES FOR ENDURING GOVERNANCE OF COMMON-POOL RESOURCES

Ostrom (1990, 2005) has defined the following principles for enduring institutions for governing common-pool resources:

1 *Clearly defined boundaries:* resources and included individuals/households.
2 *Proportional equivalence between benefits and costs:* the amount of resources a user is allocated is proportional to her or his costs (labor, materials etc.).
3 *Collective-choice arrangements:* – those affected by the rules have the power to make them.
4 *Monitoring:* accountable also to users/ are the users themselves.
5 *Graduated sanctions:* violations are graduated depending on seriousness and context of offence.
6 *Conflict resolution mechanism:* users and their officials have access to low-cost local arenas for conflict resolution.
7 *Minimal recognition of rights to organize:* government recognizes the right to local self-organization.
8 *Nested enterprises:* – governance organized in layers – important for large-scale resources.

Frances Cleaver (2012) discusses both the universality of the principles and their basis in rational choice thinking. She questions the tendency to equate 'institutional robustness with clearly delineated formal structures and with the role "crafting" plays in regularizing repeated interactions' (p. 14). She notes that studies from the South 'illustrate the dynamic evolution of institutions (involving both conflict and reconciliation) that occurs when modernizing states try to impose standard policies, laws, organizational structures in localities where there may be very different ideas about equitable distribution and decision-making and pre-existing norms and arrangements for managing resources' (pp. 14–15). Cleaver emphasizes the importance of understanding local power structures as crucial for interpreting 'what is' and 'what can be'. At the same time she acknowledges that Ostrom (2007) also recognizes that the principles are potential indicators rather than a panacea for sustainable governance.

'appropriate leadership', 'fairness in allocation of benefits', 'rules that are easy to understand', 'locally devised rules', 'ease of enforcement', 'graduated sanctions', 'accountability of monitors', 'low exclusion cost technologies', 'low level of market integration' and 'time to adapt to technology change and market integration'. Padgee et al. (2006) reach similar conclusions from their meta-study. They also emphasize 'congruence between biophysical and socioeconomic boundaries'.

Community, fairness and locally devised sanctioning tend to strengthen the legitimacy and effectiveness of common property – see also McKean (1992); Blaikie et al. (1992); Chhatre and Agrawal (2008). A specific aspect of this is the fact that resources under common property are often crucial for the survival of the poorer segments of rural populations – see, for example, Vedeld et al. (2007). Common property may, however, be vulnerable to elite capture.

Many common property regimes have been under pressure and there are several examples of failures. This ownership category has also been misinterpreted as open access – note Hardin (1968) and the confusion he created by terming open access as common property. Hence, there was a period through the 1970s and 1980s where privatization or shift to state ownership was heavily advocated. Agrawal (2001) notes that this was a misguided process. Referring to Baland and Platteau (1996) he notes that:

> the privatization of common-pool resources or their appropriation and regulation by central authorities tends to eliminate the implicit entitlements and personalized relationships that are characteristic of communal property arrangements. These steps, therefore, are likely to impair efficiency, and even more likely to disadvantage traditional users whose rights of use seldom get recognized under privatization or expropriation by the state. (Agrawal, 2001, p. 1653)

From the late 1980s, we observe a countermove – a process of decentralization. This is a response to demands from local communities/indigenous peoples and from international donors (Agrawal, 2007). It is based on the general idea that forest management can be made better when users are involved in rule-making and being responsible for forest management. Decentralization has, however, also been shown to be demanding. It takes two main forms. First, there is establishment of so-called community-based forest management (CBFM). That is in reality re-institutionalization of common property. Second, there is joint forest management (JFM). In the latter case the property right is still with the state or a local public body, and the regime is one of co-management – that is, a hybrid form. Box 12.2 offers a brief overview of the process and formats in Tanzania.

BOX 12.2

COMMUNITY-BASED AND JOINT FOREST MANAGEMENT IN TANZANIA

The development in Tanzania regarding forest ownership and management serves as an example of the situation in many developing countries. In the pre-colonial era, ownership of land was vested with the clan. The overall authority of allocation was a responsibility of the chief. Tanzania came under German colonial rule in the 1890s. After World War I, the British took over based on a League of Nations mandate. Both regimes saw forests as a source of income for the colonial rulers. Timber was very important, while the colonialists viewed the traditional slash and burn agriculture as unsound. Forest reserves were estab-lished and, by the end of British rule in 1961, about 11 percent of mainland forests of Tanzania was under such governance (Kilihama, 2014). Moreover, game reserves and national parks were also created on vast areas of land. People lost access to resources (Hofstad, 1990), often through eviction. Some forests were declared native forest reserves, while the rest was general land – *de facto* open access.

Independence did not change the situation much. The same categories of ownership continued, while the estab-lishment of local government authorities implied a transfer of native forest reserves into local government reserves. Various programs combating deforestation and erosion were instituted, with rather weak results (Kilihama, 2014). From the 1990s a process of decentralization – the establish-ment of participatory forest management (PFM) – started. It was formally supported by the National Forest Policy (URT, 1998), the Village Land Act (URT, 1999b) and the

Forest Act (URT, 2002). It takes two forms: community-based forest management (CBFM) and joint forest management (JFM). The former implies establishment of village forests and transfer of property rights to the village level. The latter regards co-management in local or central government forest reserves.

According to Kilihama (2014), almost 7.8 million ha were under PFM by 2012. This is about 23 percent of the forest area in mainland Tanzania. The amount under CBFM was about 2.3 million ha, while the figure for JFM was 5.4. It is notable, however, that the formalization process is lagging heavily behind. In the case of CBFM, forest borders and management rules are defined locally, while the formalization by the authorities is not finalized in a large number of cases. Looking at JFM, agree-ments on joint management are signed in only about 25 percent of the cases where agreements have been negotiated. Kilihama (ibid.) emphasizes that the main reason for this is the lack of a defined benefit-sharing mechanism.

There is yet limited experience with the effect of PFM in Tanzania. Blomley et al. (2008) undertake a comparative study of forest status in traditional forest reserves and in forests under CBFM and JFM. In their case studies, PFM seems to do better than both standard state ownership/man-agement and open access. Moreover, JFM seems to do better than CBFM. They note also that PFM systems that have lasted for a while do better than newly established ones. They do emphasize though problems with elite capture.

Agrawal (2007) indicates that from the mid-1980s until about 2005 as much as 200 million hectares have been transferred to community tenure – that is, about 5 percent of all forests. The assessment of the success varies substantially across the literature, indicating that it is demanding and that the way decentralization is done is important. Phelps et al. (2010) emphasize that decentralization has mainly targeted low-value forests. States have kept control over forests of high commercial value, but also areas set aside for biodiversity conservation. The authors conclude that:

> [o]utcomes vary, but effective decentralization reforms have increased local actors' benefits and rights to forests, reduced costs of protection, and provided opportunities for biodiversity conservation. A recent analysis of 80 forest commons across 10 countries shows that rulemaking autonomy at the local level is associated with greater forest carbon storage and higher livelihood benefits. (Phelps et al., 2010, p. 312)

Somanathan et al. (2009) are careful in their conclusion regarding cases of decentralization in the Indian Himalayan region when stating that village-managed forests do at least as well as state-owned forests regarding resource conservation. They note, however, that village management costs – transactions costs – are an order of magnitude lower than for state-managed forests. Based on data from Nepal, Agrawal and Gupta (2005) remark that decentralization may not help the poor. At least, participation in established user groups is dominated by the already better off. Hence, to reach the poorer segments, specific institutional mechanisms need to be built – see also Grieg-Gran et al. (2005).

Ribot et al. (2006) note that decentralization may fail because it is not done in a proper way. In a study covering data from decentralization processes in Bolivia, Indonesia, Nepal, Nicaragua, Senegal and Uganda, they conclude that the state tends to still keep control. Decentralization is mainly nominal. They note four points as important for obtaining more successful decentralization – (see pp. 1881–82). First, 'to be honest' – to realize that arguments used to compromise democratic decentralization are often not the ones stated; second, to 'strengthen accountability from top to bottom' beyond the electoral process; third, 'ensure autonomous decision power at local level'; and fourth, 'build a broad coalition' of interest to counteract centralizing forces – that is, increase influence beyond state administrative bodies that build their power basis on central management. All points emphasize that decentralization is a much more profound process than just 'shifting rights'.

Pastures

According to Asner et al. (2004) and Reid et al. (2008) about 25–45 percent of the earth's land surface can be defined as pastureland – rangelands.[1] Most rangelands are of low productivity as the more productive parts have been turned into agriculture. About 1 billion people depend on such resources as part of their livelihoods (Reid et al., 2014).

Some pastures are relatively stable regarding productivity – for example, European mountain pastures. Most pastures are, however, found in dry environments characterized by high variability in precipitation. In such contexts herding is mainly undertaken by pastoralists that traditionally move across vast areas, adapting grazing patterns according to ecological conditions (e.g., Fernández-Giménez, 2002; Turner, 2011; Moritz et al., 2013; Reid et al., 2014). This creates a dilemma for herders. Turner (2011) notes that on the one hand, herders depend on a resource regime where transaction costs of moving are low – that is, where ideally herders can move freely and gain access to new resources when demanded. That is open access. On the other hand, side-effects of such free movement need to be handled to avoid overgrazing.

How is this dilemma resolved institutionally? First, the situation varies substantially across the globe, illustrating the importance of technical, cultural as well as political issues. In the west of the USA and parts of South America, individual ownership – typically over large tracts of land – dominates. In Africa and Asia some kind of common property arrangements dominate while being on land that is formally owned by the state (Lane, 2000; Turner, 2011; Reid et al., 2014). According to these authors, customary rights extend from camps and water sources. They are somewhat 'fuzzy' – that is, more clearly defined and respected close to camps and water sources. The system depends on an intricate balance between mobility, flexibility and reciprocity. It depends on continuous renegotiations of access to land.

Moritz et al. (2013) argue that in West Africa pastures are under open access – meaning in this case that every herder has an explicitly defined right to roam freely. Their understanding deviates from, for example, Turner (2011), and there seems to be some disagreement regarding how to best characterize the governance structures for pastures in the Sahel. The fact that there does not seem to be a wide 'tragedy of open access' in the area may be used as proof of the existence of effective community regulations. At the same time, it is notable that resources are quite resilient and the herder dilemma may not always be that demanding to handle. Grasslands are actually much less vulnerable to overgrazing under dry than wet conditions as pastures can recover due to an abundance of seeds (Reid et al., 2014). There are also 'bottleneck seasons' keeping the number of animals down. Robinson and Whitton (2010) make a similar argument for Central Asian conditions. The dominant focus on subsistence is another element to an explanation – see, for example, Fernández-Giménez (2002); Robinson and Whitton (2010). This situation may shift, with greater focus on production for a market as expansion, then acquires new economic meaning, increasing the potential for overgrazing (e.g., Riseth and Vatn, 2009).

The literature on pastoralism is actually more concerned with the 'tragedy of enclosure'. Trying to attach formalized property rights to rangelands – especially privatization (Reid et al., 2014) – may cause its own problems as it demands changed resource use – for example, farming. This may result in unsustainable use of water resources and overgrazing in nearby areas.

The greater issue is, however, the marginalization of herder communities and all the obstacles that arise regarding this way of life. States often prioritize agriculture before herding. Land that herders regard as theirs may be offered to farmers or leased to, for example, private agricultural companies. This may have negative effects on herding activities in the areas left due to fragmentation (Hobbs et al., 2008). Governments also push for sedentarization; herding becomes concentrated around villages and overgrazing may occur.

The geographical level at which pastoralism appears in many parts of the world demands a kind of nested system, and the role of higher-level political bodies is important – see, for example, Moritz et al. (2013); Reid et al. (2014). States may be good facilitators. This seems to be the case in, for example, the Chad region (Moritz et al., 2013). The dominant picture is, however, the opposite, as state ownership is currently used to limit the role of pastoralists in management and investment. Often users end up in a situation where they do not have the right to reallocate land to respond to changes in local conditions. Hence, active state ownership has often fostered land use conflicts and the breakdown of collective action within and across pastoral groups (McCarthy et al., 1999; Lane, 2000; Benjaminsen et al., 2009a).

12.2.3 Irrigation

Irrigation is predominantly a common-pool management issue. Water extraction – whether individual or collective – typically influences water availability both for other users and for ecosystems. Sources for irrigation vary – for example, rivers, lakes, groundwater, water tanks and so on. According to the FAO (2015), almost 25 percent of all arable land is 'equipped for irrigation', a doubling since 1961. Irrigation systems depend on access to water, land and infrastructure. It is standard to divide between state, community, and privately owned. The former two types dominate. Many systems are nested – a community-level organization is part of a system where the state is involved at higher geographical scales – for example, river basins. It is again important to note that (formalized) property rights are only one element of a resource regime. Norms and conventions also play a very important role in their functioning – see, for example, Meinzen-Dick (2014).

State-owned irrigation systems are often technically rather advanced. Nevertheless, there are many examples showing that they do not function well – see, for example, Tang (1994); Gulati et al. (2004); Araral (2005); Meinzen-Dick (2014). There can be problems with organizing and financing maintenance and operation. Issues regarding information transfer are significant and users/farmers do not seem engaged enough in these systems, even if they depend on them. Payments of fees are often lacking and local people typically expect the state to do the maintenance.

Also, systems organized by local communities have their faults. Nevertheless, the literature seems to conclude that overall functioning is better for this type of system than the state-run system – see, for example, Tang (1994); Gulati et al. (2004); Meinzen-Dick (2007, 2014). These arrangements are typically smaller than state-owned structures, while medium-sized systems are also observed. Meinzen-Dick (2007, p. 15202) notes that:

> the majority of systems with effective farmer management had long histories
> and farmers with strong property rights over the systems and decision-making
> authority on constitutional, collective-choice, and operational rules. By contrast,
> the externally initiated programs seeking to develop farmer organizations in larger,
> state-run systems often involved the top-down imposition of a rigid structure of
> user groups and uniform rules that would allow state agencies to recognize and
> interact with WUAs [water user associations].

Tang (1994) notes that while farmer-owned systems dominantly employ local farmers on a part-time basis and typically against no payment, rule conformance is still better than when full-time government agents operate as guardians – see also Bardhan (2000).

Systems organized by local communities seem somewhat vulnerable to inequality – see, for example, Bardhan and Dayton-Johnson (2002). Relationships are complex, though. Heterogeneity in income, wealth and ethnicity tend to influence cooperation negatively. However, in cases where very rich people are involved, systems may work better again, possibly due to the interest and capacity these people have in maintaining the system. Formalizing water rights is demanding – especially in a developing country context. Customary rights dominate and water grabbing is a problem.

Turning to private systems, these may be single farm based. Private interests may also operate systems for larger areas, financing them through sale of water services. Such systems have existed for a long time in the USA, for example. In the 1980s and 1990s there was interest in expanding such large-scale systems using markets for water. This development concerned not only water for irrigation, but also domestic use, mining and so on. The idea was to ensure better use of a scarce resource. Chile and Australia are the main examples. Bauer (1997) argues that markets for irrigation water in Chile have resulted in a shift in water use towards more valuable crops. Trades are, however, limited due to high transaction costs. According to Solanes (2013) water rights were handed out for free and made tradable without restrictions. This has resulted in a monopolization of ownership, creating strong power asymmetries in markets. There are also negative effects on third parties and on the environment in general. Similar experiences are observed in Australia (Tisdell, 2001; Young, 2012). Tisdell (2001) emphasizes that environmental consequences of privatizing water are less in the USA as it is accompanied by state regulations regarding total use.

It is notable that community ownership could also result in similar negative outcomes if not constrained. While communities live in and depend on local environments, many systems around the world – also community based – seem on an unsustainable path due to salinization.

12.2.4 Fisheries

Fisheries are both marine and freshwater based. Catches of wild fish in 2011 totaled about 90.4 million tons. Of this, 78.9 million tons were from marine harvests and 11.5 from inland fisheries. Comparably, aquaculture produced almost 65 million tons. The total volume of captured wild fish was only about 20 million tons in 1950. Although for marine fisheries volumes peaked in the first half of the 1990s, inland fisheries seem to have had steady growth in the whole period (FAO, 2012b).

Increased catches have resulted in overexploitation – see also Chapter 10. One may think that this is because fisheries have generally been open access. With the development in fisheries technology – for example, improved boats and gear – this would be an expected development. The situation is, however, not that simple. It is certainly very difficult to control fisheries since the resource is mobile and difficult to observe. Nevertheless, some fisheries have long been regulated.

Welcomme (2001) and Allison and Ellis (2001) document the existence of both community and state regulations of inland fisheries. Gear limitations, closed areas and seasons, and access control are all observed, while quantity regulations are rare. According to Welcomme (2001), limitations on access – boundary rules – are one of the most widespread methods used: "In many societies tradition limits access to the fishery to certain ethnic groups or social groupings and even within these there are controls on who actually fishes" (p. 213). States may also regulate access to freshwater fisheries. Welcomme notes (ibid., p. 214):

> In state-regulated systems the state retains ownership of the fishing rights, but assigns them explicitly or tacitly to particular user groups. In most countries open waters such as large lakes and rivers belong to the state, although the right to fish such waters may be designated to a particular group.

Sipponen et al. (2010) document systems with private ownership to inland waters in Europe. In the Nordic countries, landowners along a lake may own both water and fish. Management may be undertaken through a cooperative organization among landowners – see, for example, Salmi and Muje (2001).

Regulations have also become important in marine fisheries, while the physical characteristics of the oceans make this more demanding at least compared to smaller lakes. State regulations have become increasingly important. We do, however, also observe traditional common property arrangements. These seem to exclusively concern coastal/inshore fisheries – see, for example, Acheson (1975); Berkes (1985); Jentoft and Kristoffersen (1989); Schlager (1994); Allison and Ellis (2001). Schlager (1994) documents a study of 30 coastal fisheries worldwide. She verifies extensive existence of fishers' organizations regulating use of technology and defining assignment rules. The former is directed at avoiding physical interference at sea. The latter concerns regulation of access to the best fishing grounds. She notes that there were no direct regulations of the volume of catches, but that the rules regarding use of technology may have such an effect. She notes that due to lack of information – high natural variability in fisheries and problems with observing catches – it is difficult to develop regimes to regulate what is captured. Rapid technological development has put a strain on traditional systems, and state regulations are growing in importance. Market integration also plays a role here. According to Berkes (1985, p. 201), "community control over the fishing effort appears to be very difficult to achieve in commercial fisheries in general. . . if a given stock is not overexploited, this is probably related to insufficient market demand rather than to community-level controls".

The greatest challenges are observed in open sea fisheries with fish stocks straddling from one country to another. In Chapter 10 we discussed the development of exclusive economic zones (EEZs). This gave nation states better control and in a sense, fish stocks became state property when they were in their waters. As we also saw, a system of inter-state agreements was developed to regulate fishing of straddling stocks. This has reduced, but far from eliminated, problems; the number of overfished stocks has continued to increase.

State regulations of inshore and open sea fisheries take a variety of forms. We observe restrictions on gear, spatial regulations (territorial use rights), actions to reduce the size of the fishing fleet and so on (Arnason, 2012; Emery et al., 2012). A fairly new concept is that of total allowable catch (TAC). Backed by a development in fisheries' science, estimations of fish stocks and their variations have formed the basis for embarking on quantitative regulations. In the case of international agreements, TACs have to be split between participating countries. Next, they are split between individual operators. These individual quotas (IQs) have sometimes been made tradable – individual tradable quotas (ITQs) (e.g., Grafton, 1996; Arnason, 2012). According to Arnason (2012), harvests under ITQs may presently cover up to 25 percent of global marine harvests.

The ITQ system has been heavily debated. Economists generally defend it (e.g., Grafton, 1996; Arnason and Gissurarson, 1999; Hannesson, 2004; Arnason, 2012). The main argument is that trade will ensure efficiency, as the right to fish will wind up in the hands of those that can fish at least cost. Given that there is a TAC, shifting to an I(T)Q is also helpful to avoid 'the race to fish'. In a system with a non-distributed TAC, everybody will try to fish as much as possible before the TAC limit is reached and the fishery closed. This may result in overcapacity. ITQs seem to have avoided this problem, while an IQ system would also do so.

In 2008, 18 countries used ITQs "to manage several hundred stocks of at least 249 species" (Chu, 2009, p. 217). According to Diekert et al. (2010) only two of these are in South America and Africa (Chile and Namibia); ITQs may fit best in simpler ecosystems – the 'single species environments' of the North (Degnbol et al., 2006; Ban et al., 2009). Chu (2009) has studied

20 marine fisheries under an ITQ system. She observes that biomass has increased on average. The picture varies, however, with improvements in 12 out of the 20. She notes that the decline in six stocks may follow from too high TACs, low harvest compliance, and natural causes, while it may also demonstrate the difficulty in managing a dynamic resource. She notes that ITQ programs may have little effect in the case of highly migratory species.

There are also a series of other critiques of ITQs that need to be mentioned. First, there has been a 'tradition' to hand out quotas for free. Hence, the resource rent is offered fully to those staying in business (Bromley, 2009; Pinkerton and Edwards, 2009). This has been criticized in the sense that fish is 'common property' and the rent should go to the society/the state and not to individuals (e.g., Weitzman, 2002; Bromley, 2009).

Second, there are other distributional issues going beyond 'privatization of common resources'. ITQs tend to be concentrated on a limited ownership including absentee ownership, with small investors being excluded from the field (Palsson and Helgason, 1997; Pinkerton and Edwards, 2009). Local fishing communities seem to lose out in this process. Early on, this raised the issue of granting quotas to fishing communities. To keep the permit to fish in local ownership, trading would then have to be abolished. Helgason and Palsson (1998) document strong sentiments among fishers against trading the right to fish – referring to fish as a 'common resource'.

Third, while ITQs may support conservation of targeted species, they do not solve pressing issues regarding the ecosystems involved – see, for example, Degnbol et al. (2006); Branch (2009); Gibbs (2010). It may increase problems of discarding small fish/bycatches to maximize the value of the quota. There are generally weak or no incentives in ITQs to take the wider ecosystem issue into account – for example, habitat destruction and so forth. Degnbol et al. (2006) and Hilborn (2007) emphasize that fishing is a multi-goal activity – economic, social and environmental – and policies need to adapt to that fact.

A response to this has been a push – especially by ENGOs – towards establishing marine protected areas. This may be a helpful strategy as it offers direct protection for habitats and reduces pressures on stocks. It may also be rather easy to monitor. The strategy, however, is best for relatively stationary species. Marine protected areas may also attract fishers in adjacent waters due to potentially increased stocks. Hence, supplementary measures may be needed. Degnbol et al. (2006) note that experiences with marine protected areas are mixed. In that respect they refer to insufficient stakeholder participation, inadequate institutional capacity and too strong a focus on natural science competence and/or too little on economics and social sciences.

The above observations have led to an increased focus on co-management among states and fisher communities – see, for example, Hanna (1995); McCay et al. (1995); Pomeroy and Berkes (1997); Jul-Larsen et al. (2003); Jentoft et al. (2009). As in previous cases visited in this chapter, co-management could be a way to combine the need for local knowledge and engagement with the need for higher-level coordination and power. It could also empower local communities. As noted before, co-management is not easy to organize. Allison and Badjeck (2004) document problems regarding participation and elite capture also in fisheries.

Jentoft et al. (2009) note that co-management nevertheless could be helpful as a way to resolve the complex property rights situation regarding aquatic resources. The combination of state ownership and local customary rights creates several challenges. Jentoft et al. see co-management as:

> a process that brings legal systems, and their constituent organizations and groups, together within a single framework. For fisher organizations, which frequently have distinct legal perspectives, co-management is an essential path to legitimacy. For the state, other legal systems are a resource that management can draw upon. (Jentoft et al., 2009, p. 27)

Co-management may avoid erosion of the institutional fabric in fishers' communities. It establishes an arena for deliberating and mitigating discrepancies. Based on an empirical study for India, the authors note that successful co-management depends on well-organized local communities with specific institutions for fisheries management that the state respects.

In the 1980s and 1990s, ITQs had a kind of panacea status especially among many economists (Davis, 1996). Over time there is clearly increased realization that a single instrument may not work. While there are still disagreements – see, for example, Pinkerton and Edwards (2009); Turris (2010) – few argue that one solution fits all anymore. Hence, Grafton et al. (2008) offer a somewhat different message to Grafton (1996). The same goes for Arnason (2012) and Arnason and Gissurarson (1999). A need to move towards interdisciplinarity is acknowledged. That would help build strategies that are better able to take the complex set of goals involved into account. The political battle regarding 'weighting' goals would, however, remain.

12.2.5 Biodiversity protection

Important drivers of biodiversity loss is land conversion (e.g., urbanization, forest clearings, landscape fragmentation), overharvesting, landscape fragmentation and pollution. Economic expansion – for example, agriculture, fishing, industrial developments, growth of cities and infrastructures, building of dams, mining – are all examples of practices that cause this. While the issue of pollution will be discussed in Section 12.3, I focus here on area management.

Protection of certain lands and waters constitutes a substantial part of environmental policy. Chape et al. (2005, p. 444) note that such protection is not new:

> Setting aside natural areas to maintain their intrinsic values. . . has been part of human endeavour for millennia, occurring in all regions of the planet where humans have settled. Historically, the motivation for protecting natural areas has ranged from the religious to resource or species management, including initiatives such as designating sacred groves and limiting or prohibiting the exploitation of particular species in certain areas. For example, those areas set aside by Pacific Islanders; European hunting reserves; and the forest, elephant, fish and wildlife reserves established by the Mauryan rulers of India in the second and third centuries BC.

A 'modern era' of protected areas started in 1872 with the establishment of the Yellowstone National Park. This form of legal regulation is still the dominating strategy to protect habitats and biodiversity. From a rather 'slow start' there has been a substantial increase in protected areas from about 1960. At that time, the total area globally was about 1.6 million km² (Naughton-Treves et al., 2005). According to Juffe-Bignoli et al. (2014) the area is now close to 23 million km² – that is, 15.4 percent of land and inland water areas; 3.4 percent of the world's oceans is under some form of protection.

This expansion is partly a result of scientific developments regarding conservation and principles for establishing and managing protected areas. International conservation organizations like the World Wide Fund for Nature (WWF), the International Union for Conservation of Nature (IUCN) and academic organizations have been key actors. Chape et al. (2005) emphasize the work of the IUCN and the World Commission on Protected Areas. UN processes – for example, the Convention on Biodiversity (CBD) – are also very important. IUCN has defined six categories of protected areas:

Ia: Strict nature reserve; Ib: Wilderness area; II: National Park; III: Natural monument or feature; IV: Habitat/species management area; V: Protected landscape/seascape; VI: Protected area with sustainable use of natural resources (IUCN, 1994).

There is substantial debate about the effect of area protection both regarding protection of biodiversity and its economic and social impacts. There is actually scant documentation of the effects of area protection on biodiversity. It is difficult to undertake such analyses. Agreeing on a common set of indicators is demanding. Next, establishing data series for such indicators is difficult as one normally lacks necessary historical data. Given this, one needs to be careful when interpreting findings. The available material is, however, quite consistent. According to a set of large-scale analyses – see, for example, Bruner et al. (2001); Chape et al. (2005); Naughton-Treves (2005); Hayes (2006); Barber et al. (2012); Porter-Bolland et al. (2012) – protected areas seem to result in recovered natural vegetation, increased vegetation cover and species abundance. The picture is complex, however, and in some cases protection has not succeeded in better conditions or reduced negative trends. We also observe that protected areas tend to become 'islands' in a heavily utilized landscape, which causes its own problems – see, for example, Naughton-Treves et al. (2005); DeFries et al. (2005). Finally, some areas are protected not only legally, but also by 'natural isolation' like some parks in the Amazon (e.g., Barber et al., 2012).

The fact that protected areas are effective, raises a counter-question. Is this the only alternative? Hayes (2006, p. 2064) compares 163 forests in 13 countries and concludes that there are "no statistically significant differences in forest conditions between legally protected forests and forests governed by users who establish and recognize forest rules". So, forests under well-regulated forms of common property may be as effective regarding protection of forests as protecting by law.

Understanding this, it is important to note that protection implies reduced use. This has created considerable conflict across the globe. People who lose livelihoods from establishment of national parks may not respect the 'border'. They need their livelihoods and locally devised rules may result in better forest status despite some use. Moreover, elites may often be the first not to respect protection. Brockington and Igoe (2006) show how corrupt officials continue to facilitate logging in protected areas, how mining, road building and so on may continue. McElwee (2006) documents similar as she also notes that eviction is a process of changed power relations strengthening the position of state agencies and private interests.

That protection creates conflict is the case in both developing and developed countries – see, for example, Schmidt-Soltau (2003); Brockington (2004); Roth (2004); Hutton et al. (2005); Brockington and Igoe (2006); Bergseng and Vatn (2009); Benjaminsen and Bryceson (2012). The situation is clearly most problematic in developing contexts where compensations for loss of rights/livelihoods and eviction are often small or even non-existent (e.g., Schmidt-Soltau, 2003; Brockington and Igoe, 2006; Vedeld et al., 2012). While property rights are mostly clarified and legal processes regarding compensation exist in developed countries, the situation is different in most developing countries where the state owns the land and local people have customary 'use rights' only. National authorities very often appropriate local rights, prohibit agriculture and impose human exclusion when establishing protected areas. This approach became a norm during the colonial period and seems inherited by the national governments after independence (Adams and Hulme, 2001).

Roth (2004) emphasizes that there is a long history of nature protection in the South going back to the legacy of protecting a (believed) pristine nature, as was the ideological basis for, for example, Yellowstone.[2] Eviction is maybe the most serious socioeconomic effect of protection – see, for example, Schmidt-Soltau (2003); Brockington (2004); Brockington and Igoe (2006); Rangarajan and Shahabuddin (2006); West et al. (2006); Agrawal and Redford (2009). Moving in itself is demanding for people. Moreover, there are few 'no-man's-lands' to move to. The literature documents problems related to the functioning of the law and the courts as local claims on land are often not respected (e.g., Brockington, 2004). Brockington and Igoe (2006) document that eviction from park areas in Africa is common for a majority of areas. They find much less in South America.

Schmidt-Soltau (2003) emphasizes that compensating for displacement is, moreover, a difficult solution as life will never be the same after one is forced to move. Some people he interviewed felt they were turned into beggars. Moreover, he notes:

> In discussions with park managers, it appeared that those conservation projects that refused to compensate indigenous forest dwellers in the region, did so because they thought that recognizing traditional land titles would jeopardize their resettlement programmes, since it would be impossible to refund the losses of the inhabitants 'equally' in cash or in kind. The logic of the projects was therefore to refuse legal recognition in order to avoid endless discussions on how to compensate the un-commensurable. (Schmidt-Soltau, 2003, p. 533)

As information about eviction became widely known, this delegitimized traditional 'fence and fine' as a strategy for protection. There have been several responses to this development. We observe less emphasis on eviction and a substantial number of people continue to live within protected areas – against the law – see, for example, West et al. (2006). The World Bank (2002)[3] has developed rules regarding resettlements when people are displaced, emphasizing consultation, feasible resettlement alternatives and "prompt and effective compensation" (p. 3). These rules are as much a response to resettlements regarding development projects. Agrawal and Redford (2009) document that these may be in the order of ten times that of eviction due to protection.

Another response has been to accept sustainable use in protected areas. Hence, from 1990, the relative share of category VI in the IUCN system has increased substantially (Juffe-Bignoli et al., 2014). The emphasis on co-management – as discussed in Section 12.2.2 – should also be mentioned as a way to create new income opportunities. Finally, there is the idea of payment for ecosystem services (PES), which has been developing from the 1990s (Wunder et al., 2008). This is seen as a way to expand the financial basis for protection through utilizing people's willingness to pay – the market – for nature's services, covering costs related to loss of livelihoods among local people. I will return to an analysis of PES in Chapter 13.

Regarding human use and human livelihoods, it is notable how different the situation is across the globe. While reports from Asia and Africa document conflicts between authorities and local people, the situation is somewhat different in parts of Latin America – especially the Amazon. Here there is much more focus on keeping people in the forest as a way to protect it. A main strategy has therefore been to define indigenous territories and establish conditions for sustaining traditional life forms – see, for example, Barber et al. (2012). The conflict here concerns expansion of cattle ranging, soybean production, dam construction and mining.

The difference from Africa seems related to different livelihood strategies, lower population pressure and the capacity of indigenous (local) people to mobilize support – nationally and internationally. There are also similar situations in Asia where indigenous people protect their lands through the way they live – for example, Indonesia. Here political force behind protection is however weak. Emphasis is on, for example, logging and palm oil production and indigenous people do not have the standing as potential 'partners' in protecting forest landscapes (Carlson et al., 2012).

Overall, the situation in developed countries is quite different. Here the distinctions between state, private and common property is much clearer – that is, fewer issues regarding competing claims/legal pluralism. A large fraction of protected areas is on publicly owned land and is largely uncontroversial. Conflicts relate mainly to protection of large predators (e.g., Hiedanpää and Bromley, 2012) and mandated protection on privately owned land (e.g., Bergseng and Vatn, 2009). This is so despite quite clear procedures regarding compensation for lost income. Processes from mandated protection to voluntary measures are observed – that is, that landowners offer land to be protected against a payment. Formats vary. In Norway voluntary protection is organized in the form of cooperation between the state and the forest owner's organization (Skjeggedal et al., 2010; Barton et al., 2013). The US Conservation Reserve Program and the Australian Bush Tender Program are examples of systems using auctions. Here landowners participate in a bidding procedure where the state pays winners for setting aside land for protective purposes (Zandersen et al., 2009).

Habitat protection has also become part of spatial planning. This is illustrated by the EU Birds and Habitats Directives. These directives form a basis for a system of protection sites – that is, the Natura 2000 ecological network. They are, however, also supposed to influence physical interventions like road building, city expansion, construction of industrial sites and so on. According to Beunen (2006), it has been difficult to ensure consistent legal practices in this field. The overall legitimacy is also questioned in the sense that the re are "many newspaper articles devoted to the little animals that stopped the construction of roads, business parks or housing developments" (p. 611). This reflects the fact that in situations with very high market values for land, biodiversity protection may be difficult to defend. An alternative strategy has evolved implying that developers may instead be allowed to destroy a habitat against paying for protection or restoration of a habitat elsewhere – on land that is cheaper. I will discuss the strategy of offsetting in Chapter 13.

12.3 Emissions and pollution

Pollution may influence human health directly as well as impacting the status of environmental resources and processes. There are issues concerning the quality of products consumed – for example, substances in food, clothing, building material and so on that directly influence us. There are also issues regarding emissions impacting the quality of land, water and air, which may cause damage to our health. Finally, emissions may reduce the productive capacity of various resources, influencing the vitality of ecosystems and the conditions for various life forms.

All civilizations have most probably had some 'emission regulations' – for example, rules regarding interference related to common environments like water use, feces disposal and so on – see, for example, Steinbeck (2005); George (2008) – but industrialization has brought a new dimension to human interference. Holder and Lee (2007) describe how eighteenth-century industrialization in England resulted in new regulations. Conflict resolution was based on traditional property and tort law.[4] It seems like the English law-makers tried to draw a line between 'natural use' of resources – legally protected – and use that went beyond 'natural use' – wrongful acts. Pollution from, for example, production activities executed in 'normal ways' was not 'wrongful'.

An important shift occurred as late as the 1960s, including a widening of the focus to incorporate emphasis on the functioning of ecosystems and the impact of modern industrial production methods and consumption growth on life-supporting systems. It resulted in the establishment of public administrations directed at environmental problems. Countries established Ministries of the Environment, Pollution Agencies and general laws regarding environmental protection as a basis for more specific regulations in various fields. These included legally based standards, informational measures, economic instruments and infrastructures (Holder and Lee, 2007).

It is notable that in the case of pollution, policies focus dominantly on regulations of side-effects of economic activities without making any fundamental changes in resource regimes like ownership structures and role of markets. In the beginning, legal regulations directed at firms dominated – for example, standards, emission licensing, prohibitions – often combined with informational instruments. From the 1980s, we observe a move towards increased use of economic instruments. There are, however, two issues involved that relate to property rights and interaction rules. First, legal and economic policy instruments redefine rights – either explicitly or implicitly – as they change the rights to emit. Second, there is an increased focus on more use of markets not least in distribution of responsibilities regarding emission cuts. The latter issue will only be briefly touched upon in the coming sections. Chapter 13 is devoted to a study of that trend.

Regulations of polluting activities/substances are more developed in rich as opposed to poor countries. Table 12.1 offers some indications regarding the development for three key types of emissions – carbon dioxide, sulfur dioxide and nitrogen oxides (CO_2, SO_2 and NO_x).

Table 12.1 Emissions of CO_2, SO_2 and NO_x for world total and selected countries and regions[a]

	CO_2 in billion tons[b]			SO_2 in million tons			NO_x in million tons		
	1990	2000	2010	1990	2000	2010	1990	2000	2010
World total	22.4	24.8	33.6	122.1	102.9	97.4	81.0	81.1	77.3
Australia, Japan, New Zealand	1.4	1.6	1.6	2.7	2.6	2.8	3.7	3.7	3.4
Canada and USA	5.2	6.2	5.9	24.4	18.5	16.4	23.4	19.9	18.3
Centrally planned Asia, and China	2.8	4.0	9.1	22.0	28.4	30.9	7.8	12.3	13.8
Central and Eastern Europe	1.0	0.7	0.7	11.1	5.9	4.1	3.5	2.8	2.0
Latin America and Caribbean	1.0	1.3	1.7	6.7	6.3	6.8	5.5	6.4	6.0
South Asia	0.8	1.3	2.3	4.8	7.6	11.0	3.1	5.4	7.6
Sub-Saharan Africa	0.5	0.5	0.7	4.8	5.4	4.9	2.6	3.7	3.7
Western Europe	3.5	3.5	3.4	17.9	7.9	3.1	14.1	10.8	7.5

Notes:
[a] Regions (selected) as defined by Nakicenovic and Swart (2000).
[b] From fossil fuels and cement.

Sources: Based on Cofala et al. (2006); CDIAC (2015).

Regarding the world total, we observe that emissions of SO_2 and NO_x have declined from 1990 to 2010. For CO_2 the picture is opposite. For Central and Eastern Europe, emissions have gone down for all compounds. In regions like Western Europe and North America, CO_2 emissions are fairly stable, while SO_2 and NO_x emissions are reduced. In developing countries, emissions increase for all compounds, while starting at low levels as measured per capita. The region defined as 'centrally planned Asia, and China' – also including Cambodia, Hong Kong, Republic of Korea, Laos, Mongolia and Vietnam – has quite steeply increasing figures for all compounds. CO_2 emissions are more than tripled. This is mainly explained by the development in China, where emissions have expanded almost 340 percent in 20 years. Nevertheless, average emissions per US citizen is almost three times that of an average Chinese citizen – 17.6 vs 6.2 tons CO_2 – by 2010.

According to Smith et al. (2011), SO_2 emissions peaked already in the 1970s in Canada/USA and Western Europe. The world total peaked around 1980, while data from (former) Soviet Union indicate a peak around 1990. Many regions like centrally planned Asia and China, and South Asia, most probably have not peaked yet. The data reflect aspects of economic development – for example, the collapse of the Soviet Union that resulted in a vast reduction in industrial production in the 1990s, and the tremendous growth in GDP in countries like China and India in the relevant period.

Another feature is the deindustrialization happening in the West, implying that a lot of manufacturing has moved to China, India and so on. Druckman and Jackson (2009) show that if including the CO_2 emissions behind imports corrected for exports, the emissions that the UK has been responsible for actually increased in the period 1990–2004. The official statistics show a reduction as they cover only what is emitted directly from the country. Peters et al. (2011) document that this is a general trend for developed countries taken together – offering data for the period 1990–2008. Emissions of SO_2 and NO_x are heavily linked to CO_2 emissions. Hence, much of the increase in emissions in countries like China and India is an effect of a global redistribution of manufacturing.

Section 12.3 will be divided into five subsections. First, I will describe a set of general aspects regarding the 'pollution problem' and its regulation, again using the EGS framework. Environmental instruments are instituted nationally while production is globalized. I discuss implications of this for choice of policy instruments in a second subsection. Thereafter three sections follow where I study more specifically the type of instruments used regarding air and water pollution, emissions of greenhouse gases and domestic solid waste. The focus is on how the choice of policy instruments varies across pollutants and countries. Where possible, I will link this to reflections on political culture, distributional issues, effectiveness and efficiency.

12.3.1 General aspects

The characteristics of the environmental resources and the technologies involved

In the case of pollution, I find it best to combine the discussion of the characteristics of the environmental resources involved and the technologies used. This facilitates an integrated focus on the combined natural and human-made production and consumption systems. As emphasized in Chapter 8, thermodynamics is important for understanding emission processes – be they from production (including extraction) or consumption. Figure 12.2 is a reproduction of Figure 8.3 in Chapter 8, illustrating the flow of resources – matter and energy – from the environment through the economy, all ending as emissions. Whether the emitted substances pollute depends on the form in which the matter is released, its volume and the characteristics of the environment. As evident from resilience theory, ecosystems have certain capacities when it comes to handling inputs of matter (and energy).[5] As an example, the acidic effect of SO_2 or NO_x depends on the amount of lime in soils and water.

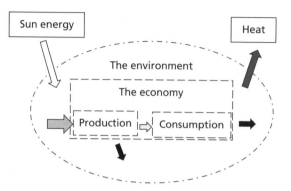

Figure 12.2 The economy–environment interaction – inputs, commodities and waste

Technology has similar importance. Some technologies may create environmental problems; others may help reduce them. Technological change may make more resources available for use. The combustion engine – as an example – was the impetus for vast expansion in the use of fossil fuels. We also observe that technological change has resulted in a vastly increased capacity to transform matter into 'new' forms – for example, the 100 000 synthetic chemicals produced industrially. The type of production processes involved also affects whether there will be problems. NO_x – as an example – is an emitted substance from combustion. Technologies have also been developed to reduce the amount of polluting substances leaving a production process – for example, renewable energies and scrubbers reducing SO_2 emissions from coal-fired energy plants. 'Closing' production processes reduces matter flows to air and water through recycling.

Changes in emission levels may be ensured by introducing legal standards, economic instruments and so on. I will later look at what characterizes these types of policy instruments. Here we shall concentrate on an issue linked to matter flows – where should one regulate in the process from input through production and consumption to emissions, whether by legal, economic or other means? Why is this an issue? Shouldn't one always regulate emissions as they cause the damage? It is an issue because it is costly to regulate – transaction costs – and these costs depend on where one regulates in the chain from input to emissions.

Let me illustrate with an example. Using fossil fuels results in emissions of CO_2. One could regulate on emissions – for example, by taxing them. However, one would then need to tax a tremendous number of activities – actually all firms and individuals. If instead we tax the input of the fuel, the number of actors to tax – fossil fuel producers – would be vastly reduced as well as transaction costs. Moreover, the effect would be the same.[6] The incentive to reduce emissions would be similar whether the tax is on the fuel or on the emissions through the impact on the cost of using fossil fuels. Moreover, it does not matter where on the globe CO_2 is emitted. It will be mixed in the atmosphere anyway. The emission is the same whether one regulates on inputs or emissions – it is homogeneous – while the costs of regulating would be very much lower if regulating on inputs.

Fossil fuels also include sulfur. Here the situation is different as the spatial aspect is important. SO_2 does not mix in the atmosphere like CO_2. Instead it deposits dependent on winds and precipitation. Effects would therefore vary geographically. Moreover, most of the SO_2 is emitted mainly from a relatively low number of coal-fired power plants. Finally, depending on the technology used, the amount of SO_2 will vary. Emissions are not homogeneous. Using input taxes will tax all coal, even though not all of the sulfur will be emitted, or emitted to sensitive ecosystems. In this case, it may both be possible – fairly low cost – and more precise to regulate emissions instead of inputs.

A third option would be to regulate on the production process. If it is too costly to regulate on emissions, and too imprecise to regulate on inputs, one could prescribe certain technologies that one knows pollute less. One could then operate with different demands on technologies dependent on where the emissions happen. In a place where recipients are vulnerable, strict demands regarding technology could be set. In other places, one could regulate more 'softly'. This form of regulation would be somewhat inflexible, but the reduction in control costs compared to measuring emissions could make it a favorable solution under some conditions. Figure 12.3 illustrates how one could balance transaction costs and 'loss of precision'.

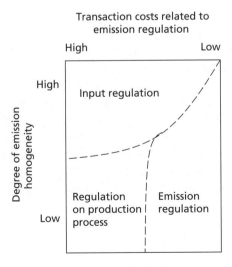

Figure 12.3 Best point of instrument application

Economic and civil society actors

As discussed in Chapter 8, firms have good economic reasons to emit, as reducing emissions following from any production process is costly. If firms are truly profit maximizers with full information, it can be shown that any (environmental) regulation will increase their costs. This will reduce profits even if parts of the costs can be passed through to consumers via higher prices. If producers do not have full information, regulations may in some cases result in reduced costs. There are examples where increased monitoring of emissions has resulted in better 'trimming' of the production process with economic gains for the factory – see, for example, Harrington et al. (2004a). In any case, one would expect firms to be negative to environmental policies as well as being weak on self-regulation.

This could change if consumers demanded products with less of an ecological footprint. Consumers may 'vote' with their money – see, for example, Shaw et al. (2006). There are examples of consumer boycotts – for example, some fast-food chains have been boycotted as a reaction to environmentally unfriendly meat production (Garrett, 1987); oil companies have been targeted for environmental damage and lobbying against climate policies (Skjærseth and Skodvin, 2001); non-certified tropical timber producers have met with protest against unsustainable harvest practices (Klooster, 2005). At the same time authors like Delacote (2009) emphasize that consumer boycotts are weak, being vulnerable to free-riding. I may add that there is also a large information problem involved. It is very demanding for each consumer to establish which product has the lowest environmental impact. This alone may prohibit any substantial effect of 'consumer regulation'.

Environmental NGOs may have more power, both to facilitate consumer boycotts and to make environmental effects of certain production methods, products and actions of specific firms visible. Young (2009) emphasizes their role as 'watchdogs' – informing on firms that do not abide by regulations. They also organize consumer or local community boycotts – see, for example, Child and Tsai (2005); Klooster (2005); Haufler (2009). Companies that have experienced effective boycotts seem clearly influenced by such reactions as it threatens their ability to earn money, even survive – see, for example, Child and Tsai (2005). Despite several examples of success, some – like Blackman (2010) – nevertheless question the overall effectiveness of such community pressure.

The political regime

So it seems reasonable that political action – changes in resource regime – will dominate the environmental field. Then the capacity of the political system in place is of utmost importance regarding the choice of regulations as well as their functioning. Any environmental policy is vulnerable to 'weak government' due not least to lack of capacity to develop, monitor and enforce regulations – see, for example, O'Connor (1995); Blackman and Harrington (2000); Blackman (2010). Issues regarding corruption also prohibit effective environmental policies to a substantial degree – see, for example, Pellegrini and Gerlagh (2006); Cole (2007).

Table 12.1 is an illustration of this. The picture is, however, not a simple one. Increasing pollution levels are not only about regulatory capacity. Governments in developing countries predominantly emphasize economic growth above environmental protection. The government of China cannot be termed weak. It is also reasonable to claim that the suppression of an active civil society is part of the story. In China, pressure from outside the Communist Party has been virtually non-existent as civil society is heavily repressed. This may be changing. Finally, we note the point mentioned above about a deindustrialization of the West.

12.3.2 National policies in a globalized economy

Firms operate under competition. Especially with increased globalization policy-makers would have to take into account whether regulations make the country less attractive for investors. This seems to have influenced pollution regulations – both regarding who carries the costs and how 'tight' the regulations have become – see, for example, Ulph and Ulph (1995); Harrington et al. (2004a); Fredriksson et al. (2004) – see also later presentations regarding specific policies. This situation emphasizes the need for well-functioning international agreements to make it possible to strengthen national regulations.

At the same time it is notable that while firms were heavily against regulations in the early phase of modern environmental regulations – see, for example, Harrington et al. (2004a) – they seem over time to have become more focused on ensuring 'a level playing field' (Young, 2009). It is a relative disadvantage that is the most difficult for them to handle.

The literature on 'pollution havens' is interesting in that respect – that is, the issue of whether 'dirty industries' leave countries with stricter environmental regulations and settle in countries with less restrictive policies. We have already noted the effect of the global restructuring of industrial activity in general, also implying a shift in the distribution of pollution. The pollution haven literature adds to this by focusing especially on dirty industries. The literature has been somewhat inconclusive regarding this latter issue. Kellenberg (2009) argues that this is largely the effect of researchers treating environmental policies as exogenously determined – that is, not seen as a way for governments to strategically attract companies (and avoiding companies leaving). This is certainly a great weakness of many earlier studies, and Kellenberg's study confirms that environmental policies are influenced by strategic considerations – see also the above references to Ulph and Ulph (1995); Harrington et al. (2004a); Fredriksson et al. (2004). A recent global study by Deng and Hu (2015) uses investment network theory and reaches a conclusion similar to Kellenberg's. They conclude:

> Our findings reveal that the factor endowment effect[7] coexists with the pollution haven effect. Both of them decide the pattern of international specialization and host countries' positions in the global network, making countries that have obvious capital advantage more likely specialize in pollution-intensive products, while others that have obvious environmental regulation advantage specialize in clean products. (Deng and Hu, 2015, p. 3954)

While the situation in many developing countries is bad, the 'export of pollution' is balanced by various factors. First, even in countries with stricter regulations, the issue of competitiveness is taken clearly into account in the way policies are formulated and costs distributed. In formulating policies, industrial interests are of great importance. Second, many industries are dependent on local resources – for example, mining (see also Kellenberg, 2009 on this). Hence, moving the activity is a non-option. Third, NGOs act as watchdogs, establishing a counteractive force to escape regulations. Finally, multinationals operating in countries with weak environmental regulations may not (always) take advantage of that. They may well use the same technology as in countries where they have originated stricter regulations (e.g., Child and Tsai, 2005). This may reflect that when established, more environmentally friendly technologies are not that costly to use. Environmental concerns may moreover be internalized among staff. These firms may, however, also use higher standards to increase their competitiveness in the developing countries they operate in to outcompete national businesses. This happens through pushing governments for stricter regulations (ibid.).

12.3.3 Air and water pollution

Turning to concrete policy areas. I note first that literature on various policies is voluminous, while focusing dominantly on 'cases' – for example, the situation in single countries for one pollutant. Moreover, the focus of the analyses varies, and it is not possible to offer a review that can systematically compare, for example, key variables like efficiency/transaction costs, distributional effects, motivational responses and so on.

I will therefore mainly focus on the choice of policy instruments. Regarding this subsection on air and water pollution, I have chosen to concentrate on wastewater, SO_2, NO_x, nitrates, heavy metals/lead and CFCs. To the extent possible – data and space – I will comment on issues related to political conflicts, effectiveness, efficiency and distribution. It is notable that the literature is dominated by analyses for developed/OECD countries. This reflects the stronger emphasis on pollution regulation in these countries – see discussions around Table 12.1.

In all focused areas, we find use of both legal regulations and economic instruments. Informational instruments and infrastructure developments are also observed. Instruments are very often combined. Harrington et al. (2004b) compared environmental policies in Europe and the USA. They conclude:

> The most important characteristic in U.S. and European environmental policies is that countries employ a mix of traditional regulatory approaches and economic incentives. This is true not only for a nation's total portfolio of environmental policies but also, more surprisingly, for each nation's approach to individual problems. (Harrington et al., 2004b, p. 240)

Wastewater

Wastewater is one of the early areas of environmental regulation. Regarding domestic wastewater, building of necessary infrastructures – starting in urban areas – has been key. Such systems exist across the globe, while certainly of differing quality. Originally, the focus was on 'getting rid of' the waste in the sense of discharging wastewater without any cleaning to chosen recipients. It is, however, notable that systems of local recycling have existed for a long time. Just disposing of wastewater to water bodies has proven unsustainable; nevertheless, recently, treatment facilities have been built to reduce emissions (George, 2008). The global situation is not good, however. It is estimated that 2.6 billion people do not have sanitation (ibid.). Fees are often charged for covering the costs of cleaning domestic waste.

Special programs may exist for wastewater from industries. In the USA a system of taxes on emissions was proposed in the early 1970s. According to Harrington (2004), this was criticized both by the industry and by environmentalists. The former opposed this solution as they were opposed to taxes in general and questioned the basis for a regulation at all. The latter saw it as a 'license to trash'. In practice, a system of standards was therefore used. Even this was questioned by the industry and many cases were taken to court, resulting in delays and weaker regulations. Over time, industrial wastewater was also increasingly treated through wastewater plants. This way an economic instrument – the fee charged for the cleaning service – was introduced and seemingly accepted by the industry.

Bressers and Lulofs (2004) present the system for industrial water pollution in the Netherlands. At its basis lies the Surface Water Pollution Act from 1970, including a licensing regime and a system of quality standards for surface water that takes into account natural background levels and varies between regions. A number of sewage treatment plants were built to ensure effectiveness, and a fee on discharges from industries was instituted early on. Hence, there are many parallels with the US system, while conflicts were less.

SO_2 and NO_x

As we saw in Chapter 10, SO_2 and NO_x have been a topic for international agreements developing in the 1970s. It is notable that only 23 countries have ratified the Helsinki Protocol on SO_2. Organisation for Economic Co-operation and Development (OECD) members dominate, while a few non-members from Eastern Europe have also ratified. This does not, however, mean that other countries do not have policies in this area – like the USA and China. Finland, Norway and Sweden are examples of countries focusing on input taxes – that is, taxing the sulfur content of the fuels. Germany has used a purely regulatory approach directed at emissions. The USA has established a cap-and-trade system on emissions. China has used a system of emission fees (Blackman and Harrington, 2000).

According to Wätsold (2004), the German system was directed at large power plants using emission limit standards "expressed in mg/m³ waste gases, which was depending on the fuel, size, and remaining operating time of the plant" (p. 33). Reductions obtained between 1983 and 1990 were almost 90 percent. Wätsold (ibid., p. 37) concludes that "our analysis suggests that the German command-and-control approach was most likely the best choice in terms of efficiency. The reason is that the policy aim was to reduce SO_2 emissions as much and as soon as possible". I note from the above that the regulatory system included some flexibility though, by varying limits per fuel type, age of the plant and so on. It should also be mentioned that by using legal means, there were no costs to the industry in the form of taxes or fees.

In the USA a total cap on emissions was set for the energy sector as a whole. This limited volume could also be seen as a 'right to emit' and was distributed for free to the various plants – so-called grandfathering. Similar to the German situation, this reduced costs for the industry compared to a tax. The system implied that firms could trade these rights between themselves to further reduce the costs of abatement – that is, those that could reduce emissions cheaply could be paid by those that had high costs to do more and the latter less than the initial obligations. Burtraw and Palmer (2004) argue that the US cap-and-trade was more efficient than a system like the German one, under US conditions with rather large differences in abatement costs between firms. It is, however, notable that cuts in the US case were much lower than in Germany – about 30 percent from 1980 to 1995. In such a situation trading makes more sense than a situation close to a phase-out.

China has used a system based on a combination of emission standards and fees. As we saw in Table 12.1, the policy has not been successful – that is, emissions increased in the order of 50 percent between 1990 and 2010. This is partly an effect of the tremendous increase in GDP and energy use in this period. It has, however, also been argued that it follows from weak monitoring and a system where costs for fees are compensated in a way such that it has actually made it profitable to increase emissions(!) (Blackman and Harrington, 2000). Zhang et al. (2007) argue that some of these incentive problems have been corrected.

Turning to NO_x, the focus of policies seems to be directed at two main sources: emissions from power plants/industrial boilers and motor vehicles. In the latter case, the dominant policy strategy has been prescribed installment of catalytic converters in cars. Regarding regulations of the energy sector/industrial boilers, there seems to be a tendency among OECD countries to combine legal regulations with a fee system. For example, France has a system based mainly on emissions standards complemented with a tax. The tax is 'paid back' through subsidies for cleaner technologies (Millock and Sterner, 2004) – reducing distributional effects. Sweden has a similar system, with a higher tax. In this case, it is the size of the tax that is the main incentive to reduce emissions. It is also refunded, in this case automatically – that is, without any link to technology investments (ibid.). In the case of the USA, NO_x-oriented regulations started out with a focus on standards and for new sources only. Some flexibility was added to the regulatory system before a cap-and-trade solution similar to that for SO_2 was instituted (Burtraw and Evans, 2004).

Nitrates

Nitrate emissions to water bodies became an issue in the 1970s and 1980s especially in Europe. There were two main sources identified: wastewater and fertilizers. Regarding the latter, we observe strong emphasis on information campaigns and fertilizer plans. Taxing nitrogen in industrial fertilizers was also adopted in some European countries – see, for example, Rougoor et al. (2001); Vatn et al. (2002). However, the tax needed to be very high to induce a considerable reduction in use of such fertilizers (Vatn et al., 1997). This created, as we have seen (see Box 7.3 and Box 10.1), quite strong political controversies not least related to the cost to farmers, but also disagreement over effectiveness.

In developing countries, the situation is partly opposite to Europe. Hence, several African countries subsidize fertilizers to increase yields – see, for example, Banful (2011). Problems with misuse of the money and so on have been manifest, and some programs have been stopped due to this, but they are now being reinstituted (ibid.). China has been subsidizing nitrogen fertilizers heavily. Berger (2014) documents that fertilizer levels are very high – even far beyond the economic optimum for farmers given the level of subsidies.

Heavy metals/lead

Regarding heavy metals, I have chosen lead in gasoline as example. It was added to boost octane levels and first introduced in the USA in the early 1920s. Alternatives existed – for example, ethanol – but these were more expensive for the industry. There were already controversies from the beginning about potential negative health effects. Despite some quite strong evidence, the industry managed to counter the claims and it took 50 years before health effects were accepted as proven and policies were introduced (Kovarik, 2005).[8] In the USA, this happened in 1974. According to Newell and Rogers (2004), it was a reaction not only to health problems, but also to protect catalytic converters in cars introduced to reduce NO_x and SO_2 emissions. All gasoline stations were instructed to offer unleaded alternatives. Standards regarding the amount of leaded compounds in gasoline were later defined and tightened. As small refineries had problems abiding by the regulations, a cap-and-trade system was instituted to offer them more flexibility. This was despite an aim of a complete phase-out (ibid.).

Europe was even slower to react than the USA. In 1981 the EU fixed an upper limit on lead content in gasoline at 0.4 grams per liter. At the same time, no member state was allowed to reduce content below 0.15 g/l due to free trade considerations within the EU. A reduced gasoline tax on non-leaded fuels was also instituted. Finally, the EU formulated a ban on leaded gasoline (Hammar and Löfgren, 2004). Lead phase-out has become the story across the globe too. According to UNEP (2014), only three countries still use leaded gasoline – all in Asia[9] – and three more combine leaded and unleaded.[10]

CFCs

Turning finally to CFCs, there is also a similar development with a situation close to a phase-out in 2004 (UNEP, 2008). As emphasized in Chapter 10, the Montreal Protocol set limits on CFC emissions, which were tightened over time. Developed and developing countries faced different claims on the speed of a phase-out. In the case of EU and the USA, a combination of legal regulations (emission/technology standards) and economic instruments is observed. In this case, the USA actually used input taxes, possibly reflecting the strong public reaction to the information offered about the development of the 'ozone hole' and the existence of a rather cheap substitute. The EU on the other hand turned to using a cap-and-trade system on CFCs with quite strict cuts in volumes (Hammitt, 2004). The difference may reflect the fact that the EU was lagging behind the USA at the time the Montreal Protocol was adopted due to opposition in some European countries against CFC regulations. To follow up on the demands of the Protocol, faster reductions were necessary.

12.3.4 Emissions of greenhouse gases

As we saw in Chapter 10, reaching a binding international agreement on emission reductions is very difficult. The Kyoto Protocol is weak. Regulating emissions of greenhouse gases is also demanding because there are many sources. While CO_2 dominates, two more gases are especially important – that is, methane (CH_4) and nitrous oxide (N_2O). Finally, there are the emissions of fluorinated gases. This implies that policies need to be directed at a long series of compounds and processes.

As we saw in Chapter 10, the Kyoto Protocol defines obligations to cut greenhouse gas emissions from the so-called Annex I countries. Moreover, it included three 'flexibility mechanisms' to reduce costs of cutting: (1) trading emission quotas between the Annex I (developed and some transition) countries; (2) joint implementation (JI) between the same countries – that is, Annex I countries could pay for measures in other Annex 1 countries; (3) the clean development mechanism (CDM), allowing Annex I countries to invest in measures in developing countries as part of their obligations. The latter have no greenhouse gas emission restrictions, but by developing projects for reduction of emissions, they can be granted certified emission reductions (CERs) that can be sold to Annex I countries/actors. The latter can then count this as part of their own reductions.

All these solutions are in use. The EU, Switzerland, Australia and New Zealand have established a cap-and-trade system. Recently South Korea, Kazakhstan and the US state of California have also done so. Hence, countries or states not bound by the Kyoto Protocol use the instrument. Regarding the cap-and-trade system and CDM, a more thorough investigation will follow in Chapter 13, where I focus on the trend towards more use of markets in environmental policy.

Other instruments are also in place. Gasoline taxes exist in many European and a few other countries (Sterner, 2007). In some countries such taxes have been motivated by the effect on climate change – for example, Scandinavia (Blackman and Harrington, 2000). It is notable that they typically originated before the Kyoto Protocol. The Sterner (2007) analysis points toward these taxes – if high – having had a clear effect on emissions. He concludes that "Had Europe not followed a policy of high fuel taxation but had low US taxes, then fuel demand would have been twice as large" (p. 3194). It is notable that taxes are on the input – on gasoline. Actually, emission quotas are not operationalized in the form of controlling emissions, but as regulations of inputs of coal, oil and gas. The much lower costs of input regulation as well as no loss in precision seems to explain this.

12.3.5 Domestic solid waste

I will close this section with brief coverage of the systems in place for handling domestic solid waste. It is an example of an area where infrastructure improvement is a key policy measure. This is especially the case for domestic waste where pick-up and sorting facilities close to home have been important. Hoornweg and Perinaz (2012) indicate quite substantial collection rates in what they term high-income countries – that is, 98 percent – while the average for low-income countries is in the order of 40 percent. 'Upper middle' and 'lower middle' fall in between. There is a lot of uncertainty regarding these data – especially concerning waste disposal. The authors nevertheless state that low- and lower-middle-income states dispose most of the waste in open dumps. They also state that several middle-income countries have poorly operated landfills – a form of controlled dumping. Most waste is generated in high-income countries – both per capita and in total. Landfill dominates, followed by recycled waste and 'waste-to-energy' systems. From the data, one can conclude that sorting of waste is not very common globally.

While the issue of littering is also greatly influenced by local norms, several states have introduced legal prohibition against it. This is more widespread and strict for toxic waste, but is also established for domestic waste, at least in many developed countries. Fees are often used to cover the cost of managing waste treatment systems. In the case of countries/municipalities that promote sorting, necessary infrastructures have been key. Some countries have also included economic incentives to try to increase the degree of sorting. Box 12.3

BOX 12.3

INCENTIVE SYSTEMS TO INCREASE SORTING OF DOMESTIC WASTE – THE CASE OF NORWAY

In a study with doctoral candidate Marit Heller, we document the effect on the degree of sorting for three different payment systems: (1) a flat fee, (2) a frequency-based fee, and (3) a weight-based fee. The latter two systems are so-called incentive based as households pay less to the community the lower the amount of unsorted waste. Also in the case of the frequency-based fee and weight-based fee, there is a fixed component.

Waste sorting facilities have been in place in Norway for quite some time – first established in towns, later including rural areas. The level of sorting became quite substantial in the traditional systems without any economic incentive to sort – that is, with flat fees. We note therefore that availability of sorting facilities plus normative persuasion was quite effective. In recent years some municipalities have introduced economic incentives – as the government has motivated such a solution. In our study we compare three municipalities with flat fees and three with frequency-based fees. Stated levels of sorting were actually significantly lower in the latter case, while effects are small (Heller, unpublished manuscript).

One group of municipalities shifted from flat fees to weight-based fees from 2009, but returned to flat fees again two years later. Our study (Heller and Vatn, under review) documents several motivational issues related to the weight-based fees. People started redefining categories – for example, paper diapers were increasingly defined as paper. This resulted in rising costs for the inter-municipal company handling the waste since the need to re-sort the waste after it was collected increased. Illegal disposal of waste such as burning or throwing waste into the countryside also increased. At the same time, we observe that the respondents were split almost 50–50 in their stated response to the weight-based fee. One half said the economic incentive motivated them to increase sorting. These scored relatively low on a scale measuring environmental concern. The other half – scoring significantly higher on the scale – did not see any meaning in the incentive. They were not demotivated either. While the dominant motivation for sorting waste among the groups was norm based – a sense of duty or responsibility – the incentive seems to have induced a partial shift to a more calculative attitude among the half that became motivated by the incentive. The system was ended due to the extra costs incurred (re-sorting), increased littering in the countryside and general resistance to the weight-based fee system. After the flat fee was reintroduced, sorting levels seem unchanged.

offers some key findings of an analysis of these systems for Norwegian municipalities. Some pronounced motivational effects are observed, possibly because an economic incentive has been introduced in a situation where substantial levels of sorting were already obtained through practical and normative means.

12.4 Policy instruments – some theoretical issues

I will close the chapter with a theoretical analysis of the main policy instruments as referred to in Sections 12.2 and 12.3. I will distinguish between legal, economic, informative policy instruments and environmentally friendly infrastructure development. I will also add a short note on making public activities themselves more environmentally friendly. Issues regarding rights/distribution, transactions costs and motivation will be emphasized.

12.4.1 Formal rules – legal instruments

The law is fundamental in defining rights to resources. Moreover, it may define what is the 'permitted' or 'right' thing to do given what one owns/is offered the right to use. The basis for the law is the state and its legitimated right to command its citizens. It is based on coercive, but also normative power (Etzioni, 1975). Sometimes its main role is to codify existing norms to strengthen their function. In 'modern' societies more relationships and conflicts have become regulated in the form of legal prohibitions and prescriptions. There is more formalization, while its content and efficacy still depends on its normative acceptance across society.

The legal system is typically a kind of hierarchy. Laws about how to regulate relationships between the state and its citizens and between different citizens form a fundamental basis for any regulation. It is impossible to understand the character and content of environmentally oriented laws without understanding how rights to land and its attached resources are defined more generally. Hence, understanding environmental law and regulations demands understanding the systems for property rights and the regulations of these. In the case of environmental policy more specifically, many countries have chosen to establish a general law that defines the conditions for more detailed environmental regulations.

Regarding motivation, the 'logic of the law' can be understood in two different ways. Based on the idea of individual rationality, the evaluation of the law will follow a cost–benefit assessment. The law is followed if expected costs of punishment are higher than the expected gains of breaking the law and vice versa. From the perspective of social rationality, the law is followed because it is right to do so. It is a principle to follow the law whatever gains that breaking it may offer. This is the normative content and effect of the law.

Tyler (1990) and Sunshine and Tyler (2003) emphasize the normative acceptance of the law and its policing as fundamental for its effectiveness. Tyler (1990) found that compliance with the law bore little relationship to the level of punishment. Instead he observed situations with high compliance when punishments were low and low compliance when they were high. He found that the 'willingness to follow the law' was strongly dependent on the legitimacy of that law in society. He concluded that normative issues are important for explaining behavior. This supports the understanding that the law is more than an external punishment structure.

Regarding transaction costs, using the law may be 'low cost' to the extent it is able to build or support an existing normative community regarding what it is right to do. It simply reduces control costs if the law is 'self-policing'. Looking more specifically at environmental policy instruments, there are reasons to argue that transaction costs are lower for emission standards/ individual quotas, than for tradable quotas, as there is the same need regarding control of compliance, while the trade adds the costs of trading. The potential for reduced abatement costs may still make a system with trade better regarding overall costs. The conclusion here, however, depends on the specific case, as was also illustrated in the above empirical analyses.

As we have seen, legal regulations were often preferred by the industry because it implied less cost for them compared to a tax on emissions. Similarly tradable emission quotas were favored over taxes. The income for the state/ public would be equally lower as compared to a tax. This is the other side of the coin. I will explain the difference regarding distributional effects after having looked at economic and informational instruments in more detail.

12.4.2 Economic instruments

Regarding economic instruments, I make a distinction between markets and taxes/subsidies. I will start by looking at the latter. Regarding the former, I will only look at tradable quotas. Chapter 13 is devoted to a more complete analysis of markets in environmental governance.

Taxes and subsidies

The logic of economic instruments is to introduce an incentive for individuals and firms to reduce actions that are environmentally damaging. They

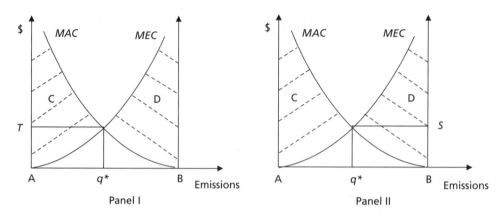

Figure 12.4 Taxing emissions (Panel I) and subsidizing emission reductions (Panel II)

are based on remunerative power (Etzioni, 1975). Environmental taxes imply putting a cost on damaging nature. Environmental subsidies are paid for delivering environmental services/reducing damages. Economic policy instruments are based on the theory of rational choice. It is notable that they may work even if actors are boundedly rational. Effects may then, however, be lower than what is expected from 'theoretical assumptions'.

Figure 12.4 illustrates the way environmental taxes are thought to work as presented in environmental economic textbooks – see, for example, Kolstad (2000); Perman et al. (2011).

The figure focuses on emissions of a pollutant. It depicts the marginal environmental costs (*MEC*; curved line rising to the right) as a function of the level of emissions. This cost is assumed to be based on people's willingness to pay (WTP) for a clean(er) environment. The higher the emissions, the lower the quality of the environment and the higher the WTP. Similarly, there is the cost of abatement, where the marginal abatement costs (*MAC*; curved line rising to the left) are key. These costs regard all kinds of changes that reduce emissions – for example, changes in production processes, cleaning emissions, reduced production levels. They are assumed to increase the more emissions are reduced. The logic is that reducing emissions by a small amount when they are high – for example, at B – is not that costly. The closer one comes to zero emissions, the higher the costs of reducing emissions with one more unit.

The underlying cost–benefit reasoning implies that there might be both too much and too little pollution. In B there is too much – $MEC > MAC$ – while in A there is too little – $MAC > MEC$. The optimal point of emissions – q^* – is where $MEC = MAC$. How can emitters be motivated to emit q^*? This is possible by introducing a tax T on the emissions – see Panel I of Figure 12.4. To the right of q^*, it is economically beneficial to abate – the costs are lower as the MAC is below the tax T. To the left, the firm or individual would rather emit and pay the tax as T is lower than MAC. The economic reasoning leads the agents to emit q^*. Marginal abatement curves will normally vary between firms. It can, however, be shown that if the rationality assumptions hold, this variation does not matter for the end result. The tax will ensure that the total emissions will be q^*, while firms with low abatement costs will reduce emissions relatively more than those with higher levels.

Introducing a tax (T) on emissions implies assuming that rights are with the victims of the pollution. Introducing a subsidy (S) implies assuming rights to be with the polluters. Otherwise, the reasoning behind a subsidy is similar to that of a tax. Paying polluters a subsidy at level S will motivate them to cut emissions from B to q^* – see Panel II in Figure 12.4. So, to the right of q^*, they will abate and receive the subsidy. To the left of q^* the cost of abatement is higher than S and emissions will prevail. One may argue that it is wrong to pay anyone for reducing a harm, as there should be no harm in the first place. It is also obvious that a tax and a subsidy will have different distributional effects. This is an important rights question that I will soon return to.

Areas C and D represent the net gain from introducing a tax respectively as subsidy. I note that the costs of setting up and running the tax/subsidy system – the transaction costs – must be less than areas C (when using a tax/rights with the victim) or D (when using a subsidy/rights with the polluter) in Figure 12.4 for there to be any gain from state regulations. Taxes or subsidies on emissions demands measuring the emissions, which may be quite difficult in many cases. Hence, taxing inputs of substances that later end up as pollutants may be an alternative to reduce transaction costs – see the discussion in Section 12.3.1.

The standard exposition also assumes that there is no relationship between the monetary value of environmental damage and the rights structure. In Chapter 11, we noted, however, that willingness to accept compensation (WTA) (rights are with the victim – WTA_{Rv}) are typically two to four times that of WTP (rights with the polluter – WTP_{Rp}). Following a consistent use of the concepts, a tax implies that one should use WTA estimates and a subsidy that one should use WTP.

Figure 12.5 illustrates the potentially large difference between the 'optimal emission levels' and the levels of the 'right' tax and subsidy. Rights with the victim implies a much lower 'optimal' emission level – q^{*WTA} – than rights with the polluter – q^{*WTP}. To the extent policies are based on monetary estimates, this error has vast practical implications as 'optimal levels' of emissions vary substantially.

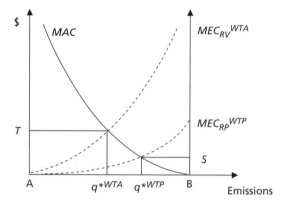

Figure 12.5 The efficient level of emissions – WTP vs WTA estimates of environmental damages

The solutions in Figures 12.4 and 12.5 demand that both abatement and environmental costs are measured in monetary terms. According to our discussions in Chapter 11, it may be problematic to measure environmental effects this way. As we have seen, international agreements are typically based on defining emission reductions as percentages of the level at a certain base year. The basis is not WTP, but a standard or 'acceptable level'. To reach such a level, one may use legal regulations. Taxes or subsidies can also be used – see Figure 12.6. Instituting a tax or subsidy equal to the level of marginal abatement costs (MAC) where the emissions equals the standard – q_{es} – offers the incentive to reduce emissions to that level.

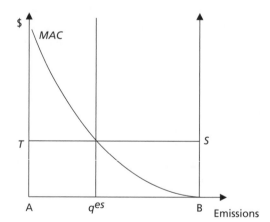

Figure 12.6 The case of a set standard for emissions, using taxes or subsidies

The so-called polluter pays principle (PPP) has become the standard way of formulating victims' rights in the case of environmental degradation. As normally instituted in most states, we again observe confusion as full polluter's responsibility is not instituted – consider Figure 12.7.

Figure 12.7 Polluters pays principle, environmental taxes and the efficient level of emissions

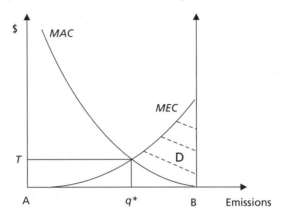

The figure shows the PPP solution where a tax $T = MEC = MAC$ is instituted. The MEC is, however, assumed to be based on WTP estimates. This is inconsistent since there are victims' rights. WTA should have been used. Moreover, the victims are not protected by an undisputable right to a clean environment. Instead regulation occurs first when some negative consequences are observed and their cause is proven. Then emissions are actually at B. This implies that one starts off from a situation of some emissions, maybe even at high levels. One then evaluates if a regulation is worthwhile – that is, if the MEC is higher than the MAC at B. If so, a tax should be instituted. It will, however, be relatively low given that it is based on WTP. In practice one also has to evaluate the level of transaction costs given state regulations. If we start from B and these costs are larger than area D, no regulation suddenly becomes optimal. This situation will be more frequent as the MEC curve is based on WTP and not WTA. High transaction costs actually 'protect' the polluters and not the victims as would have been the case with a consistent use of PPP.[11]

A basic question concerns who has the responsibility of proving that harm is inflicted. A consistent use of victims' rights would imply that before anyone is given the opportunity to engage in, for example, some productive undertaking, they must document the (likely) environmental effects of their planned activity. If damaging emissions will follow, they will be taxed from day one. As the PPP is normally practiced, the burden of proof is instead with the regulator. In this sense, we actually observe again a kind of a mix between victims' and polluters' rights. Note also that despite taxing, victims have to endure some pollution, whatever 'optimal level' is referred to.

Tradable quotas

Tradable quotas are an economic instrument based on a legal regulation in the form of a quota or cap – typically on emissions – that is made tradable. In Sections 12.2 and 12.3 we looked at several cap-and-trade systems. The environmental protection lies in the cap. The trading system is instituted to reduce the costs of reaching the cap. Figure 12.8 illustrates this in a situation of so-called grandfathered quotas.

The figure shows a stylized situation where the total emission quota Q is divided equally between two firms – that is, $q_1 = q_2$ and $Q = q_1 + q_2$. Being grandfathered means that the firms get emission quotas for free. Hence, rights are in that sense with polluters. Alternatively, emission quotas could be sold – for example, auctioned – in the first place. This would be a situation very much resembling that of an emissions tax, where the quota price – at least 'in theory' – would equal the tax.

Given quotas q_1 and q_2, we see that it will be much more costly for Firm 1 to reduce emissions to the allowed level than it is for Firm 2. The marginal abatement cost at q_1 is about three times the costs for Firm 2 at q_2. However, Firm 2 can sell some of its emission quota to Firm 1. If Firm 1 reduces emissions only to q_1^* and pays Firm 2 to reduce to q_2^*, the total emission is still Q (as $q_1^* - q_1 = q_2 - q_2^*$). As the marginal abatement costs for the two firms are equal, costs are minimized. The hatched areas represent the net gains from this trade.

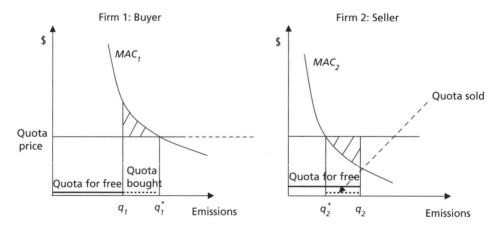

Figure 12.8 Tradable quotas – grandfathered

12.4.3 Information

Information programs are an important part of environmental policies. While it has typically been an element of legal regulations and economic incentive programs, information may also play a role on its own. Dietz and Stern (2002) emphasize that its role has been increasing and define it as a new tool for environmental protection. One reason for its expansion may be that as 'low hanging fruits' like large point sources have been regulated, policy-makers are faced with issues involving the actions of 'everybody'. This may demand a shift in focus.

Information as a policy instrument can be 'pure information' – providing information about 'the facts'. It may also have an educational element. According to Dietz and Stern (ibid., p. 5), "Education includes the provision of information in a systematic and structured way, but usually goes further, encouraging deeper understanding and, perhaps, values and norms regarding behaviors".

Seen from the perspective of standard rational choice theory, information has no role as there is full information. Expanding this model – as was done in Chapter 5 – and accepting that information is costly/actors are boundedly rational, information programs become important as a way to ensure that relevant information is easily available. Therefore, information packages may be an important part accompanying legal prescriptions or the introduction of economic incentives to inform about the changes and spread knowledge about ways to adapt to new circumstances. Labeling of products is another way of supporting and simplifying information. Product certification is an important element of this.

From a social constructivist perspective, the role of information goes further. It may both have the capacity to change the perception of an issue – for example, that climate change is happening and may cause several problems. Moreover, it may change our habits and preferences – change conventions and norms – and so influence motivations fundamentally.

From the perspective that behavior is habituated, change demands transformations in our modes of response. Change is both 'habit breaking' and 'habit taking' (Hiedanpää and Bromley, 2014). These are profound processes that may not be easy to establish, despite 'the push' from legal and economic incentives. Training/education may be necessary. As habits are social constructs – see the discussion in Chapter 5 – the process may also have to go beyond the action of individuals and engage the community – small and large scale – in a common process of defining what should now be the acceptable way of acting. Rules and habits around waste sorting are a key example. People's adaptation to information about climate change may be another. While we seem to be at the start of such changes, some people are already using alternative/renewable energy, changing their mode of transport and so on.

Schwartz's norm activation theory (Schwartz, 1977) offers a somewhat different understanding. He emphasizes that information through creating 'awareness of consequences' may result in an individual's 'ascription of responsibility' leading next to changed behavior. While I think this understanding offers important insights, I would add that this process is not only happening at the individual level, there is a social dimension to it. Ascription of responsibility depends on socially constructed norms. These may even change as a result of information and education. Moreover, the processes around 'awareness raising' and 'ascription of responsibility' are largely social in that an 'agreement about what is a problem' and 'what are acceptable responses to it' is something that is typically developed in communication with others.

Should the state try to motivate norm changes? Wilbanks and Stern (2002, p. 340) note that "in our society, we tend to believe that government roles in shaping human behavior should be quite limited". While I note that people's preferences can never be 'independent' and that economic forces may be more important than governments in forming us, the authors raise an important issue. As we have seen, environmental problems cannot be solved on the basis of individual and independent action. Collective engagement is key. State action seems to be crucial in that respect – whether it regulates through legal, economic, informational or other means. The issue of what is legitimate state action cannot be tackled by asking for a minimum state. Rather, it must emphasize openness and deliberation in an active dialogue with and across civil society. The key aspect of 'information as an instrument' seems to reside here. It concerns the creation of arenas for communication and deliberation over what are reasonable responses to the problems we face.

12.4.4 Distributional and motivational aspects of policy instruments

Before I turn to a discussion about infrastructure development as a policy instrument, I want to briefly discuss a few distributional and motivational issues with relevance to the three types of instruments studied so far.

Distributional aspects

As we have seen, especially in Section 12.3, distributional aspects were key regarding choice of policy instruments and their specifications. Figure 12.9 is helpful in disentangling this. It illustrates the costs for polluters facing an emission tax T. A limit q_{es} is set on emissions. For simplicity I treat all polluters as one.

In the case of a tax T, the polluter pays area A to the state as tax – the tax T times the emitted volume q_{es}. Added to that is the cost of abatement – area B as the sum of the marginal abatement costs.[12] The total costs for polluting agents are tax + abatement costs = A + B. In the case of a legal regulation – that is, in the form of an emission standard set that the polluters must comply with – the polluter only faces the abatements costs B. Using a subsidy is even better for the polluter. Dependent on its form, it could actually generate net income for the polluter despite investments in abatement – that is, the subsidy is larger than B. An informational measure implies no direct costs for the firm. If it is motivated by this to abate – for example, it realizes that its present practices are bad – it will have to carry abatement costs.

Given the above, it is not difficult to understand why industries tend to favor standards over taxes, while we have seen several examples of taxes being repaid. Then distributional effects resemble that of a legal regulation. The argument against standards from an economic point of view is that they rarely lead to the least-cost solution as all firms have to reduce emissions down to the same standard. A least-cost (cost-efficient) solution could be obtained if those with low abatement costs abate more than those with higher costs. This will follow from using a tax – that is, assuming that agents maximize and are well informed about the tax and their individual $MACs$.

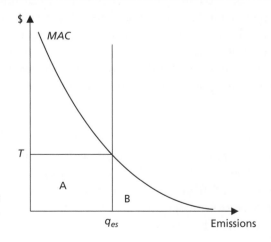

Figure 12.9 The costs for polluters of a tax on emissions

A tradable quota has in theory the same capacity to produce cost-efficient outcomes as a tax – see Figure 12.8. If quotas are auctioned, costs for the industry equal that of a tax.[13] If quotas are grandfathered, costs for the polluting sector are similar to a legal standard. There will, however, be some internal distributional effects due to the trade involved. Those selling quotas (those with low abatement costs) will have a monetary gain and the buyers (those with high abatement costs) an outlay of similar size. While grandfathering reduces overall costs for an industry, the initial distribution of quotas may nevertheless become a politically tense issue as it influences who earn income – who become sellers and buyers. The conflict is often resolved by defining individual quotas as a percent-wise cut based on historical emissions.

As touched upon in Section 12.2, there have been negative reactions to establishing private rights (quotas) in environmental assets like air and fish. As common goods they should not be owned by individuals/firms. In several cases it is therefore emphasized that the quota is not a property right, but an 'allowance' (e.g., the American Clean Air Act) or a 'license' as is the wording in many fisheries regulations. This practice is criticized by some economists since it creates uncertainty for the firms holding such 'licenses'; see, for example, Arnason and Gissurarson (1999). The state keeps the right to the fish and may chose to reallocate licenses. Other economists like Weitzman (2002, p. 326) were "shocked" by the fact that licenses were given for free, implying that license holders were offered the rents of natural systems – that is, the value of the fish stock itself.

We also observe different reactions to tradable quota systems depending on which problem or sector we look at. Individually tradable quotas – ITQs – have created much more conflict in the fishing industry than in the field of air pollution – compare the quota system in Icelandic fisheries with the US trading scheme for sulfur emissions. This may be due to differences in distributional consequences, societal aspects and the dynamics of the environmental issue. Regarding societal aspects, the fishing industry in Iceland is much more integrated in the communities involved and has a very long history with strong traditions compared to the US energy industry.

Motivational issues

The above analysis of economic instruments assumed that actors are maximizing individual utility/profits. As discussed in Chapter 5, bounded rationality and satisficing are more relevant descriptions of actors than maximization. Moreover, people may act on the basis of social as opposed to individual rationality. These issues may influence the effect of policy instruments.

Bounded rationality implies some 'stickiness' to individual behavior like habits. Individuals (and firms) choose what they see as a satisfactory solution to a problem. According to this theory, they will stick to this solution if no 'major' changes in their environment occur. Hence, a tax on fossil fuels or electricity may not result in a change in use before it reaches a certain (high) level. An element in this is the cost of information gathering that may itself vary. In the case of electricity, you do normally not observe it from everyday use as you get a bill, for example, every third month. In the case of gasoline for your car, the information on price changes is available every time you fill the tank.

The policy implications of the observation of bounded rationality are partly that one may have to add other instruments to economic ones. Information campaigns are one option as discussed above. Policies regarding waste sorting is a prime example. Moreover, making sorting a habit has been supported in many countries through TV programs for children, activities in schools and so on. Finally, new norms may be established.

That action may be based on social as well as individual rationality creates challenges for environmental policy. In Chapter 5 we documented examples where people in some situations actually deliver less if paid for delivery. People may collect less money for charity if paid to do so – see Gneezy and Rustichini (2000a). Fining late-coming increased such behavior – Gneezy and Rustichini (2000b). The cases documented in Box 12.3 also showed motivational changes. Frey (1997) terms this 'crowding out'; Bowles (2008) talks of undermining 'moral sentiments'.

Similar observations are made even in the business sector. In a study of sanctioning systems, including fines for environmentally bad conduct, Tenbrunsel and Messick (1999) observe that control may actually reduce compliance up to a certain level of control. If control is strengthened further, compliance starts increasing again due to the fact that punishment/fines are increased to a level where they cannot just be disregarded. The public agency controlling emission reductions, hence, faces a dilemma. If it controls firms that anyway intend to follow the restriction, the 'internal' motivation of these firms may be reduced and a worse situation may appear. If it makes too few controls, however, those that have not internalized a norm of emissions reductions may go on as before and the credibility of the whole system may be at stake. The agency may solve this dilemma by using different strategies for different types of firms – that is, only heavy controls on what they see as potential rule violators. This demands that it is possible for the agency to classify firms as 'nice' and 'bad'.

A way of understanding this is to turn to the idea of plural rationalities and that institutions signal which rationality is expected. If an environmental issue is moralized – that is, there are norms defining what is right behavior – establishing payments, taxes, fines or controls on behavior may shift the rationality from one of, for example, doing what is right or best for the group ('we' rationality) to calculating what is best for the individual ('I' rationality). While the issue we now look at is very complex – it is difficult to offer simple explanations that make sense in all situations – I believe that Figure 12.10 captures some of what is going on.

The figure distinguishes between 'I-' and 'we'-motivated behavior – between individually oriented – also called strategic or instrumental – behavior, and norm-based behavior. In quadrants A and D the state and the agents (firms/households/individuals) perceive the rationality or logic of the situation similarly. In A they see the situation as governed by individual rationality. In D they see it as ruled by norms. In the first case (A) economic incentives will function well. In the latter, reciprocity or voluntary compliance should be the rule.

Quadrant B describes a situation covering many of the examples given above. They are all 'counterintuitive' from an economic perspective. The state uses policy instruments assuming the agent is acting individually rational, while the agents look at the situation as being one of norm following. In such a situation, the response is likely to be 'perverted'. Norms are eroded. People are offered money for something considered a duty. Money then makes them offer less

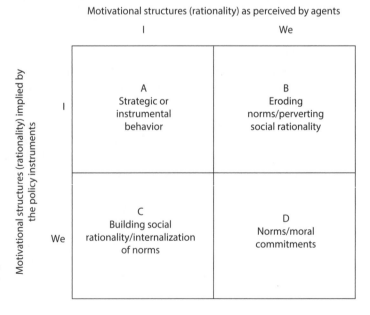

Figure 12.10
Motivational structures, policy instruments and behavior

or nothing at all. People are motivated to act environmentally friendly and become demotivated through being paid for it or being met with controls showing that those controlling them do not trust that they will comply.

Quadrant C describes a situation where the state may support a process of norm building where no norm previously existed. The case of smoke regulation may serve as a good example. Nyborg and Rege (2003) document a study of smoking behavior in Norway. In 1988 smoking was forbidden in certain public spaces (public transport, meeting rooms etc.). This then influenced smoking in other arenas like private homes, where more disapproval of smoking was observed or smokers started to ask if they could smoke, went outdoors without asking for permission to smoke indoors and so on. Nyborg and Rege propose an explanation building on the assumption that non-smokers experienced a more negative effect of smoking in homes because they had learned how pleasant it could be without smoking as this was now experienced less often in public spaces. This may be part of the explanation, but still a bit hard to believe as most spaces would also before 1988 be characterized by non-smoking experiences – for example, most outdoor areas.

An alternative explanation would suggest that a new norm structure was established in the wake of the law. Banning smoking in some places resulted in smoking becoming less acceptable in general. Those smoking may also feel obliged to acknowledge that smoking is negative for non-smokers more in general. The non-smokers may have similarly felt that it was now acceptable to simply say no to a smoker in their home. This response seems to have become socially acceptable quite quickly. A new norm was internalized favoring the interests of non-smokers.

12.4.5 Infrastructures facilitating environmentally friendly action

This is another large area that will be treated very briefly here. Our case above regarding waste sorting illustrated how physical infrastructures may be key to facilitating environmentally friendly action. This is just one of many examples. It may span the field from 'nudges' (Sunstein, 2013) – for example, small 'cues' that lead us to changed behavior like re-use of towels in hotels – to rebuilding the entire transport system of a region or town to facilitate lower emissions. The issue is simple. People cannot travel collectively if there is no such system operating. Increasing fuel taxes may – as an example – have little effect if alternatives do not exist.

Similarly, energy systems and the way cars are fueled will be influenced by availability of infrastructure. The latter example can be used to illustrate one of the challenges we face when transforming a system to become more environmentally friendly. Electric cars and cars run on for example, hydrogen, will depend on availability of stations along roads that deliver these forms of energy. However, until 'enough' car drivers use these types of energy sources, there is no incentive for private gasoline stations to offer these energy forms. On the other hand, that number will not materialize before the service is available. Such types of 'Catch 22' situations abound in the process of transforming the economy to solutions that are better in environmental terms and would need public action regarding infrastructure developments to 'break the cycle'.

12.4.6 Making public activities more environmentally friendly

Above we saw that states may protect habitats on land they own. This is an example of a type of policy that has much wider implications. State administrations and state-owned firms may change their use of resources and emission practices to protect the environment. This concerns internal budgetary processes in public bodies. It concerns investment practices and daily operations of publicly owned facilities. While one could think that this is a field where changes could be easily obtained through orders from the top, public officials also act in habituated ways. Public investments are made in a situation with competing aims, of which environmental implications are but one and often not a highly prioritized issue.

Climate change is an area with increasing focus regarding the action of public bodies and the governance of own activities – both concerning mitigation (e.g., Wheeler, 2008) and adaptation (Amundsen et al., 2010). The former involves issues like insulation of buildings, energy use, transportation and so on. It is obvious that there is large potential for change here that is yet not utilized. Wheeler (2008, p. 488) emphasizes that many states and municipalities in the USA have developed mitigation plans. He concludes that: "most of these plans lack the strong actions and political and institutional commitment needed to mitigate emissions or adapt to climate change".

A few countries – for example, Brazil, Germany and Portugal – have been experimenting with so-called fiscal transfers (e.g., Ring, 2008a and 2008b; Santos et al., 2012). The idea here is that transfers of resources from the central/federal government to lower levels depend in part on the environmental status of these areas and actions taken. This money is generally payments to cover education, social security and so on. While potentially effective, such a system needs to balance between the need to ensure equal opportunity across the country regarding such services and the effects on environmental quality.

12.5 Main messages

This chapter has focused on an analysis of policy instruments in environmental governance. I have defined such instruments as (re)formulations of the resource regime. It includes therefore changes in property rights and interaction rules as well as the introduction of more specific environmental regulations of legal, economic and informational form.

The analysis has been organized on the basis of the EGS framework, emphasizing how characteristics of the environmental resource, technology, interest constellations and existing political regimes have influenced (1) choice of policy instruments and (2) the outcomes regarding resource use and status of the resource. Rights/distributional aspects, transaction costs and motivational issues have been highlighted both when trying to understand choice of instruments and outcomes. The area is vast and the literature varies in its emphasis. Given that, my analysis had to take the form of illustrations rather than a complete enquiry where all aspects of an institutional analysis were systematically dealt with for each selected topic.

I divided the analysis between use and protection of environmental resources on the one hand and issues regarding pollution on the other. Both areas illustrate the importance of the overall political regime for the form of environmental governance. In the South, the issue of access to environmental resources and the conflict between different interests in that respect came to the fore as the main issue. In relation to that, the weak protection of local rights to environmental resources was especially noticeable. While pastoralists' interests are particularly vulnerable, the challenge is a general one. Some development towards strengthening local rights is, however, discernable.

Building institutions for economic growth has been a fundamental priority in both the North and the South. Trade liberalization has been a key element in this and has weakened the possibility for effective environmental governance. States are the main actors in formulating concrete environmental policies. They have the power to institute policy instruments like legal regulations and environmental taxes. This is very difficult to do in a globalized economy. Therefore industry has had a strong influence on the formulation of environmental policies – both regarding ambitions and form. It has been necessary for states to minimize costs for national businesses. International environmental agreements have to some extent helped to counter the structural asymmetry that characterizes the governance of international trade and of the environment. We have, however, seen that their effect has been rather weak. This is reasonable, given the strong focus on liberalizing trade and the fact that environmental problems 'know no borders'. Hence, environmental policy has developed into a global 'prisoner's dilemma'.

The 'fish regime' illustrates the international feature of environmental issues, while the characteristics of the resource play a specific role for the choice and potential success of regimes. Fish move in and out of national jurisdictions. Expanding these (EEZs) has made it easier to regulate fishing effort. International agreements regarding specific fish stocks have still been necessary. Defining which countries have a right to fish and how much to catch has been a very demanding task. There has been progress in this area – a fact that offers some hope for cooperative outcomes in the international realm. Nevertheless, the often too high TACs and the existence of large open access areas at sea make it clear that we have only come halfway. Distribution of national quotas and the right to trade these have been very controversial issues, illustrating that environmental governance is very much about whose interests get protection and which model for development is dominant. Here markets with their type of efficiency have been favored above protecting the interests of communities and facilitating a cooperative logic.

Also in the case of regulating pollution, the characteristics of the problem have had strong influence on chosen policies. One thing is the international aspect. Another is how these characteristics materialize into the costs of regulation – transaction costs. While climate policies are aimed at regulating, for example, CO_2 emissions, it is the input of fossil fuels that in practice is regulated. In the case of SO_2 from power plants, regulations are mainly on emissions. This is made possible through the low number of emitters. Emissions of NO_x from cars is – as an example – dominantly regulated through prescribed technologies. It is important to note that (perceived) resource characteristics and involved technologies do not determine policies. They do, however, limit the options.

Technological change is an important cause of environmental problems. We saw this in forestry management and in fisheries. It was also a dimension in all pollution problems analyzed. Increased production capacity/capacity to catch is one aspect here. Another is changed production and consumption processes that new technologies facilitate – for example, fossil fuel use. Finally, we observed the tremendous increased use of synthetic compounds in processes and products. All these changes are made to create economic opportunity while dominantly pushing developments towards ecological limits. Environmental regulations change the basis for creating such opportunities and have in some fields been successful in reducing problems – for example, ozone layer protection. Here we observe both banning of certain substances and limitations to the level of allowable use.

Environmental policy is directed at changing behavior of economic actors. Legal and economic instruments dominate. We have already noted the strong emphasis observed regarding avoiding policy instruments that reduce the profit of firms 'too much'. Hence, environmental taxes are often repaid, quotas are typically grandfathered and made tradable. Individual rationality has been basis for choice of instruments. This is logical as most policies have been directed at firms. There seems to be a trend towards the internalization of some norms regarding environmental standards among some segments of business. In this respect, it is hard to distinguish between what is genuine concern and what is reflecting a worry that one may lose market shares if one gets exposed as environmentally unfriendly. Only a small number of environmental policies are directed at consumers. Examples are fuel taxes and waste treatment. In the latter case, infrastructure development and creation of norms have been essential. It is notable that to the extent environmentally friendly action is normatively based, introducing economic incentives to strengthen such action may easily fail.

We observe rather few changes in the basic property rights and interaction rules of the economy. A key example of the opposite is some changes in rights to environmental resources in the South – including both a strengthening of rights of local communities and expansion of access to these resources by various international economic actors. The expansion of the jurisdiction of coastal states – the creation of EEZs – is another example of changes in rights to resources. Finally, any environmental regulation in the form of, for example, prohibitions, prescriptions or taxes and so on represents a (implicit) change in the rights structure. The right to shift costs is changed. Nevertheless, the most important observation is that private property to resources and interaction through trade dominate as before. Actually this resource regime has been strengthened throughout the era of environmental regulation since the 1970s. Some argue that this is not a problem. Rather, the role of markets should be expanded further – also in the field of environmental policy. Others argue that environmental policies will only be able to create marginal corrections to an overall negative trend as long as environmental issues do not penetrate the formulation of the basic structures of resource regimes. These issues will be discussed in the next two chapters.

NOTES

1   Above, I indicated that it was about 25 percent. The higher figures here seem to depend on where the borderline is drawn concerning forests and deserts, or other non-productive land.

2   Until recently it was unknown that this park was established through eviction (Nabokov and Loendorf, 2004).

3   As cited in Schmidt-Soltau (2003). The rules were revised in 2013.

4   Tort law is applied by courts to provide relief to people who have suffered harm from the wrongful acts of others.

5   I will mainly focus on matter. Energy lost may also influence surrounding environments – for example, heated water. Nevertheless, it is the matter flow that is by far the most important when talking about pollution.

6   See Vatn (1998) for the derivation of this result.

7   Factor endowment is commonly understood as the amount of land, labor, capital, and institutional conditions for industrial activity in a country.

8   Kovarik (2005, p. 384) writes: "Early warnings were ignored by industry, and as leaded gasoline became more profitable, scientists willing to support industry were financed as guardians of the scientific criteria for lead's health impacts. Controversy erupted in 1924 after refinery accidents left workers dying from violent insanity. In efforts to protect their profits, industry executives falsely claimed there was no alternative to leaded gasoline. Fifty years passed before scientific, court, and regulatory challenges had any influence. When independent research finally emerged, the results were damning enough to support an international phase-out of leaded gasoline".

9   Afghanistan, Myanmar and North Korea.

10 Algeria, Yemen and Iraq.

11 The reader may note that after having raised issues regarding how reasonable it is to use monetary measures of environmental costs, I nevertheless assume such measures here. I observe that while the principal arguments regarding the way PPP is operationalized do not change by turning to non-monetary measures, it is much easier to explain the issues raised in the text by using graphs – that is, assuming monetary measures.

12 Total abatement costs are the sum of the marginal abatement costs – that is, the area under the MAC curve. This is a simplification, though, as there are also fixed (abatement) costs.

13 There are, however, some added transaction costs following from the process of auctioning.

13

The turn to the market

Throughout the last 30 years, we observe an increased use of economic instruments like taxes in environmental policy – see Chapter 12. We also witness increased belief in using markets – interaction through trade – to solve environmental problems. This materialized in the idea of trading emission permits – as introduced already in the 1980s. Throughout the 1990s the idea of 'payments for ecosystem services' (PES) evolved. The development of certification and offset programs add to the development.

Given the theoretical basis for this book and the discussions – especially in Chapter 9 – one may wonder how markets can be a solution to environmental problems. The aim of this chapter is to look at the experiences obtained in various fields and evaluate the prospects of expanding markets to handle environmental challenges. I start with looking at the theory behind using markets to solve environmental problems. In the empirical part, I will focus on three issues. First, I ask to what extent what are called markets in environmental services really are markets. Next, I will undertake a brief evaluation of the legitimacy of some of the most important systems developed. Last, I will use the experiences obtained in a brief discussion of governance structures for reduced emissions from deforestation and forest degradation (REDD+) – a system presently evolving.

13.1 The theory of markets as a solution to environmental problems

Proponents of expanded use of markets argue that they are more efficient than traditional command-and-control policies – see, for example, Pagiola and Platais (2007). They are seen as a way to maintain freedom of choice and are expected to create more resources for protection. This is in line with the rather recent discourse on the 'green economy' – see, for example, UNEP (2011) and World Bank (2012a) – as well as the ideas of ecological modernization where focus has been on ensuring 'better' development and not fighting industry and consumption (Kull et al., 2015).

Markets demand property rights to the traded objects. Coase (1960) suggested that if rights are defined and transaction costs are low or zero, markets will handle environmental problems efficiently. Coase insisted that given low or zero transaction costs, the only thing the state needs to do is to ensure that rights are clarified. Figure 13.1 depicts the market for emissions of a polluting substance, and for emission reductions.

The reader will note the similarity to Figure 12.4 on environmental taxes and subsidies. The difference is that we now talk about a price – p – that is established through trade. The idea is that a market will establish as soon as there is a gain from trade settling at a price defined by the level of the (marginal) abatement costs (MAC) and the (marginal) environmental costs (MEC). The latter will appear as willingness to pay (WTP) if rights are with the polluter and as willingness to accept compensation (WTA) if rights are defined to be with the victim(s).

Given the standard assumption in economic theory of individually rational actors and no transaction costs, the trade will settle at an emissions q^* and price p^*. This will – according to the assumptions – be the case independent of who has the right. This is the so-called 'Coase theorem'. Rights must be defined, but who has the right is not important given that transaction costs are zero. The argument goes like this. If rights are with the polluters, they will not abate and emission levels are initially at B. If victims want to reduce the emissions, they need to approach the polluter(s) and pay for abatement. If they pay less than p^*, emissions will be higher than q^*. In this situation marginal environmental costs ($MEC = WTP$) are higher than the marginal abatement costs (MAC). Both parties will gain from increased payments and more

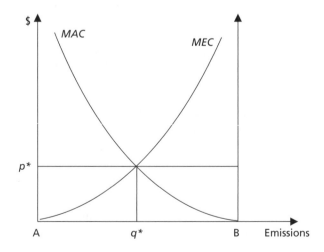

Figure 13.1 The efficient level of emissions with zero transaction costs

abatement. The optimal solution – maximizing gains for both parties – will be an agreement where the price $p = MEC = MAC = p^*$.

If rights are with the victim, the reasoning is similar. Now no emissions are allowed. However, the producer realizes that paying the (to become) victims to accept some pollution will be better for both. Again, the trading parties will settle at the price $p^*(= MAC = WTA)$. According to this reasoning, the optimal level of emissions is the same independent of who has the right in the first place.

It is important to note that Coase was explicit on seeing the rights issue as 'symmetrical'. Both the emitter and those 'consuming the emissions' would have to be around for there to be pollution. This perspective has political implications. It goes against the polluter pays principle. Moreover, as environmental problems are rarely observed before some time after the emissions have started, one will typically be at B in Figure 13.1 when the question of whose rights should govern is raised. Then 'maintaining a right' to the polluters may not be questioned, as the result regarding the quality of the environment would be the same as when 'shifting' it to victims.

There are several issues that make this Coasean conclusion unreasonable. Let me start with the assumption about zero or low transaction costs. In practice, these are rather high due to the characteristics of the goods and services involved.[1] We may discuss the implications of this with reference to Figure 13.2.[2]

Figure 13.2 shows the gains from trading in emissions – the hatched areas. If rights are with the victims – that is, no emissions (we are at A) – the net gain

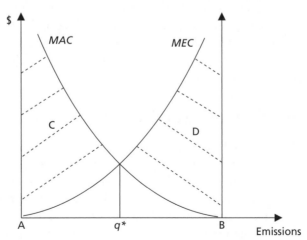

Figure 13.2 The efficient level of emissions under bargaining given positive transaction costs

involved by moving to a situation with q^* emissions is the hatched area C. Similarly, if rights are with the polluters – gains from trading are D. If transaction costs are less than C respectively D, the optimum will still be q^*. There are gains from trading. If transaction costs are greater than C respectively D, the gains from trade are lower than the costs and there is no reason to trade. So, if transaction costs are high, the definition of who has the right actually defines the level of 'optimal emissions'. In a market setting, there will then be no emissions if rights are with victims and unregulated pollution levels if rights are with polluters.

The level of transaction costs may vary substantially depending on how costly it is to demarcate the good/service – that is, defining property rights – how costly it is to measure emissions, and finally how many polluters and victims are involved in the trading. The case of climate change illustrates this clearly. Here millions of firms and billions of households/individuals are involved as both polluters and victims. If action is to be taken in the form of trade between the individual emitters and victims, at least 7000 000 000 × 7000 000 000 deals need to be made.[3] It is easy to see that within a market structure, all (potential) gains from trade vanish due to the high transaction costs. This is so despite the fact that gains from avoiding climate change may be extremely high.

The Coasean reasoning also omits the wealth effect of the rights' distribution itself – see Chapter 8. The party that gets the right acquires an implicit income transfer. If rights are with the victims, they will receive income in the form of the compensation paid. If rights are with the polluters, instead victims will have to pay. This will influence the capacity – hence, willingness to pay. Second, we saw in Chapter 11 that WTA is typically two to four times larger than WTP. The wealth effect explains only (a minor) part of that difference. There also seems to be an effect of the rights distribution itself. Losing a right is fundamentally different from gaining one – see, for example, Tversky and Kahneman (1986); Vatn and Bromley (1994). Coase did not consider this.

13.2 Are they markets?[4]

Much of the literature on markets in environmental governance perceives the environment as services – as ecosystem services.[5] They are the object of trade. One may ask if this is a reasonable way to perceive nature – see the discussion in Chapter 3. Here I raise a different question based on the above reasoning on transaction costs: how can markets in ecosystem services establish themselves? In an assessment of this, I will focus on the four most

---

BOX 13.1

THE GENERAL TREND OF PRIVATIZING PUBLIC PROPERTY

Following the neoliberal trend from the late 1970s, we observe a process towards privatizing public property – for example, infrastructure, schools, health and water services. This has been driven mainly by efficiency arguments – the belief that private business is more efficient. Establishing competition is part of this reasoning. This development has caused a lot of debate. My assessment of the literature is that this trend has resulted in more negative effects than positive. Privatization does not seem to offer more efficient solutions – see, for example, Levin (2001); Homedes and Ugalde (2005); Prasad (2006); Allen and Pryke (2013). Part of the reason is that

goods are public – for example, knowledge – or management demands coordination – for example, transport systems like trains. Moreover, the issue is as much about distributional effects and the quality of the activity as about efficiency per se. Hence, Romanow (2002) concludes that Canadians regard health care to be a moral and not a business issue. Similar arguments are found in McGregor (2001) and Homedes and Ugalde (2005). Privatization of the university sector influences open access to knowledge. It is therefore argued that knowledge loses its character as a public good (Ritzer, 2011; Blacker, 2013).

---

important types – that is, payments for ecosystem services, certification, carbon markets and biodiversity offsets. The development towards more use of markets in ecosystem services is parallel to the process towards privatizing public property. While it is not a topic I will delve into here Box 13.1 offers a very brief summary of some of the developments.

13.2.1 Payments for ecosystem services (PES)

PES is the archetype of a market in environmental governance. Wunder (2005, p. 3) defines PES as:

1. a *voluntary* transaction where
2. a *well-defined* ES (environmental service) (or land use likely to secure that service)
3. is being 'bought' by a (minimum one) ES *buyer*
4. from a (minimum one) ES *provider*
5. if and only if the ES provider secures ES provision (*conditionality*).

Looking at the experience, PES in the form of direct trade between a buyer and a provider/seller seems, however, rare. A well-known case is that of

Vittel – a water company operating in France. To ensure better quality of its products, it has formed contracts with nearby farmers to reduce nitrate inflow to water bodies (Perrot-Maître, 2006).

Despite the existence of direct trade, it is evident that most PES projects involve intermediaries. These may be firms/traders, NGOs, but also public bodies at various levels as well as intergovernmental organizations like the UN Global Environment Facility and the World Bank. We even observe double or triple sets of intermediaries – that is, states paying the intergovernmental organization, paying another state, paying providers/sellers of ecosystem services. Finally, some intermediaries are private–public partnerships like the so-called conservation trust funds (Spergel and Wells, 2009) – see Figure 13.3.

Concerning PES with intermediaries, Milder et al. (2010) have reviewed existing registers. According to their data, PES projects with intermediaries amounted to about 23.5 billion US dollars in 2009. Moreover, their data show that public funding based on taxes or fees dominates as the source of payments. While there is some uncertainty concerning the completeness of sources and the categorization of programs,[6] I consider the strong role of public actors to be a robust finding. According to the Milder et al. data, payments for watershed protection is the service with the largest total[7] – about 14 200 million US dollars globally. Public authorities raised 99.9 percent of the resources.[8] 'Landscape beauty and recreation' is the second largest – calculated to about 7300 million US dollars. In this case, I have calculated that publicly raised funding covered about 70 percent. Private payments were typically directed at private goods and services like hunting and fishing fees. Concerning biodiversity protection, 99 percent of a total of 1465 million US dollars was based on public funding.[9] Finally, regarding projects directed at carbon sequestration and storage, Milder et al. (2010) only include land use/forest sinks. The level of these was about 170 million US dollars. Taken together, the data indicate that about 90 percent of the finances for PES in 2009 – that is, transaction (a) in Figure 13.3 – was created on the basis of taxes and fees – by command not trade. If we remove payments for private goods – for example, fishing and hunting – the figure is 99 percent.

Figure 13.3 The structure of actors involved in PES

What then about the transactions between intermediaries and sellers or providers – the transaction **(b)**? Again, no easily accessible data are available. If transaction **(a)** is trade, then so is **(b)**. Regarding publicly raised money, transaction **(b)** may take the form of auctions or other forms of contract-based payments. The US Conservation Reserve Program and the Australian Bush Tender system are examples where auctioning/competitive bidding is used. These systems qualify as trades. They seem, however, to have a rather limited spread. Porras et al. (2008) note that auctions are not used in any of the PES projects they have studied – all in developing countries.

Concerning what I have termed above 'other forms of contract-based payments', many more examples exist. Agri-environmental schemes – for example, those of the EU – include some contract-based systems, which nevertheless hardly qualify as a trade. Rousseau and Moons (2008) therefore term most as subsidies.

While about 75 percent of PES resources are spent in the North (based on Milder et al., 2010), PES are often thought of as an invention of the South. Costa Rica is among the pioneers. The Environmental Services Payment Program (ESPP) has been operating since 1997 and is administered by FONAFIFO, the National Forestry Financing Fund. ESPP is a public program and the government appoints the board/administration of FONAFIFO, formulates statutes and secures the finances (FONAFIFO, 2013). For the period 1997–2009, altogether 99 percent of the funds were public. ESPP uses individual contracts. It differentiates payments according to the status of the ecosystem. Hence, we seem to encounter a hybrid solution – a combination of command and trade.

Programs with combined emphasis on environmental issues and poverty alleviation – for example, the Socio Bosque program in Ecuador – are even less trade oriented. All costs are covered by public funds. Contracts are used, but they are uniform and not based on negotiations. The combination of environmental and social goals seems to make trade less relevant.

While no complete overview exists regarding the form of public payments, one can safely conclude that a substantial part of PES is non-market. If we look at public services, 99 percent of the money used comes from public budgets. Only a rather small – while unknown – fraction of these resources is next used for trading.

Why is it so? Why do markets not work well for PES? I see two main reasons. First, ecosystem services are typically public goods. We then face the standard free-rider problem. The costs of paying for production of ecosystem services fall upon each single buyer, while typically large numbers of beneficiaries experience the gains. Hence, almost all private funding for PES was related to private goods like hunting.

Second, we have the issue of transaction costs. It is very costly for each beneficiary to trade with the sellers. Intermediaries may simplify trading. Public bodies are in a sense 'intermediaries'. States or local public bodies can often collect the resources needed with very low costs using their capacity to command – for example, through taxes or fees. In the case of water projects, it is normal for the public water agency to simply make an addition to the standard water bill to raise the necessary revenues. This way transaction costs are reduced considerably compared to using the market.

Concerning the second transaction more specifically – the payments to sellers (**b**) – I note that trading is more common than when raising resources (**a**). Nevertheless, trade is a rather marginal phenomenon. I see three potential explanations for this. Transaction costs again limit the amount of trade. Second, there is both a lack of familiarity and skepticism among actors involved especially with auctions over ecosystem services (e.g., Porras et al., 2008). A third point relates to the fact that programs often combine environmental and distributional considerations, reducing the room for trading. The Scottish Grampian Challenge Fund is a good illustration. It started as a competitive tendering system. Zandersen et al. (2009, p. 69) write:

> [L]andholders disliked the uncertainty in the tendering process, finding it 'unfair' either because neighbours received more cash, because it was hard to know what to bid or because bidders found out they had underbid. . . As a result the Forestry Commission introduced a new fixed-price scheme in 2003.

13.2.2 Certification systems

As opposed to PES, certification programs are based on trade. They utilize consumers' willingness to pay an extra premium for specific qualities. They exist for a wide variety of products. In our case, the important ones are mainly found in agriculture, forestry and fisheries. The logic behind certification is to set standards for products and/or production methods. These may foremost relate to product quality/health aspects – that is, the private good dimensions. They may, however, also be linked to environmental standards – for example, environmentally friendly production methods. The idea is that 'concerned' consumers are willing to pay an extra premium for these products and this way support more sustainable production systems.

Several certification schemes exist – for example, the Rainforest Alliance's ECO-O.K. program; the Smithsonian Migratory Bird Center's 'Bird Friendly' label; the UTZ certification scheme; the East African Organic Products Standard (EAOPS); the certification standards by the Forestry Stewardship Council and the Sustainable Forest Initiative; and the Marine Stewardship Council's fishery certification program (see Bishop et al., 2008; Forest Trends & Ecosystem Marketplace, 2008; Marine Stewardship Council, 2013). Many actors are involved – private, NGOs, and public authorities. While private actors seem to dominate, some of these initiatives are best characterized as public–private partnerships.

Forest Trends & Ecosystem Marketplace (2008) estimates the market for certified agricultural products to represent about 2.5 percent of the global food market. Nathaniel and Jenkins (2012) indicate the total value of these products to be about 64 000 million US dollars. This figure also includes 'fair trade' products. Hence, we cannot specify the amount of 'eco-certified' products. In the case of forestry, the same source indicates a traded volume of about 54 000 million US dollars. While these figures are high compared to those for biodiversity-related PES programs, one should note that only a (small) fraction of the price relates to payments for, for example, ecosystem services – (part of) the price premium. This fraction is unknown. It should be noted that at least in the case of certified organic food, the extra willingness to pay may largely be linked to the private services – the perceived higher consumption qualities.

13.2.3 Carbon markets

Also in this case, transactions are dominantly taking the form of trades. We have already noticed that most carbon-related PES systems are trade based. However, the large volumes of transactions are found in cap-and-trade systems. The market was established through the emission reduction liabilities that Annex 1 countries were assigned by the Kyoto Protocol. The same protocol included – as we saw in Chapter 12 – a set of flexibility mechanisms establishing the basis for carbon markets – for example, emissions trading and the clean development mechanism (CDM).

There are actually several carbon markets, of which the EU Emissions Trading System (EU ETS) is by far the largest. According to the World Bank (2012b), the total value of the existing carbon markets in 2011 was 176 020 million US dollars. Of this, the EU scheme accounted for almost 85 percent – 147 848 million US dollars. The next largest volume was the CDM market – 25 323 million US dollars. It should be mentioned that the total value also includes 569 million US dollars from what is termed the voluntary market – that is, a fraction that, while small, is outside the cap-and-trade system. So, while there is trade, state action – the formulation of a cap with liabilities that are made tradable – has been necessary for the market to establish. Carbon markets are founded on command.

Regarding the EU ETS, firms can trade allowances bilaterally or through brokers, on one of six exchanges (Hintermann, 2010). In the case of CDM, states operate as buyers – see, for example, the German Development Bank (KfW, 2015); the Norwegian State (Norwegian Ministry of Finance 2011). The main role of the state is, however, that of regulator – formulating caps, distributing individual permits, defining rules for trading, and controlling compliance.

It is important to remember that it is the size of the cap that defines the environmental impact of cap-and-trade systems. I also note that the regulation in this case is largely on an already existing commodity – fossil fuels – which makes market operations much simpler than in the case of, for example, biodiversity. I also reiterate that the choice of cap-and-trade as opposed to taxes on fossil fuels may be explained by the practice of grandfathering quotas, implying that costs are reduced for industry. This may be especially important in cases where not all countries have reduction responsibilities, as is the situation with the Kyoto Protocol.

13.2.4 Biodiversity offsets with habitat banking

The Business and Biodiversity Offsets Program (BBOP, 2009, p. 6)[10] defines biodiversity offsets as:

> measurable conservation outcomes resulting from actions designed to compensate for significant residual adverse biodiversity impacts arising from project development and persisting after appropriate prevention and mitigation measures have been implemented. The goal of biodiversity offsets is to achieve no net loss, or preferably a net gain, of biodiversity on the ground.

The concept of 'residual adverse biodiversity impacts' refers to losses that cannot be avoided on-site. Offsetting implies compensating for these residuals off-site.

Biodiversity offset is a rather new strategy – sometimes including so-called habitat banking.[11] The USA and Australia have been pioneers – for example, the US Compensatory Mitigation (also known as wetlands mitigation) and

BioBanking in New South Wales, Australia (Madsen et al., 2010). We also find such programs in Canada, Brazil and in Europe (EFTEC et al., 2010; Santos et al., 2011). Finally, there are a few examples in developing countries.

Biodiversity offsets are of various types. Some systems are clearly non-market, like the German system with compensation pools. These are integrated into municipal planning of land use and decisions are in our terminology based on command. The compensation scheme linked to the EU Natura 2000 is similarly a purely regulative measure (Conway et al., 2013). Regarding systems where trade is involved, there are examples of 'voluntary' systems (UNEP, 2012),[12] implying that firms or individuals are willing to pay independent of a cap or regulation.

Nevertheless, in the case of trades, liability-based systems are dominant. A defined conservation objective forms the basis – for example, a limit/cap on how much land can be 'developed' in an area. The offset implies that trading is allowed to compensate for loss at the 'development site' (on-site) against increases at the 'rehabilitation site' (off-site). The role of intermediaries is again very important. Such brokers may be so-called 'habitat banks' – for example, the Environment Bank. Intermediaries may make it possible to pool activities and this way avoid the piecemeal characteristics of single offsets. It is notable that the concept of a habitat bank is also used for a 'bank of land' off-site – land that is developed to be traded in offset programs.[13]

Madsen et al. (2010) estimate the annual market size to be at minimum 1.8–2.9 billion US dollars.[14] About 85 percent of the traded volumes are found in North America. Trade-based biodiversity offsets dominantly take the form of markets with intermediaries, where payments both to and from the intermediary take the form of a trade. Public bodies are involved as regulators – defining goals, controlling trades, performances and so on.

13.3 Analyzing the legitimacy of markets in environmental services

As emphasized in Chapter 7, there is both input (process) legitimacy and output legitimacy. Using this structure, in the following I will offer a brief evaluation of the various markets for environment services as presented above. While I try to comment on what I find to be the most important issues, it is not possible to more than touch the surface regarding empirical findings. There is tremendous variation regarding issues, actors and contexts. As an example, payments to forest owners mediated by an NGO are quite different from carbon deals between specialized traders.

13.3.1 Input (process) legitimacy

Input legitimacy concerns here the appropriateness and acceptability of using the market for ensuring protection of environmental resources and processes. It has been a highly contested turn in policy. This implies that there is no 'reasonable agreement' on whether using markets is an appropriate perspective and strategy. The main argument in favor of markets is that they will increase effectiveness and efficiency compared to public regulations. This is an important argument, but as we have seen, a contested one. Arguments against using the market go beyond the above. One issue regards the commodification of nature. This critique challenges the specific way of perceiving and treating nature when transformed into something tradable – see, for example, Gómez-Baggethun et al. (2010); Kosoy and Corbera (2010); Sullivan (2013a) for discussions. Linked to this is questioning the view that nature is a service for humans – understanding nature in purely instrumental terms. Defining individual property rights to a common environment is another aspect that is questioned. Connected to the market perspective is also the idea that environmental protection can be combined with economic growth. This is a contested position, too (e.g., Spash, 2012).

I find all these arguments compelling, implying that humanity needs to define limits to how far markets should be allowed to expand. At the same time, the limit cannot be set at zero. Nobody takes that position. We have traded environmental resources in the form of timber, milk and so on for a long time. The challenge for us is to define in practice where the limits for markets should be set. We debate whether genes should be tradable. Trade in species is regulated. We debate whether fishers should be allowed to own and trade fishing rights. Should one be allowed to destroy a habitat if it pays? Is it acceptable to do so if one ensures protection somewhere else? The list of contestations over where the limit should be drawn could be made very long. My main point is to emphasize that these issues – while often termed 'efficient resource use' – influenced by the language of the market – are not about efficiency, but about our view of our physical environment and our common relations to nature.

While these are fundamental ethical and political issues that have no scientific answer, it is nevertheless possible to analyze certain aspects of procedural legitimacy of markets in environmental services. As we saw in Chapter 7, a key concept is 'equal opportunity to participate'. In markets, the willingness and capacity to pay are key. Therefore, equal opportunity depends on equal income distribution. The fact that this distribution is highly skewed across the globe questions the basis for increased use of markets as ensuring 'equal opportunity'.

Trading is also costly, and participating in, for example, PES, is not an opportunity for all because of transaction costs. Intermediaries may be helpful in that they reduce such costs. At the same time, important power asymmetries are observed not least due to the position intermediaries have, being advantaged especially regarding information about markets. The strong position of these actors is observed both regarding PES (Corbera et al., 2007b; Vatn, 2010) and biodiversity offsets (Sullivan and Hannis, 2015). Munden (2011) argues more generally that intermediaries are in a position to capture much of the rents created. Spash (2011) notes that the financial sector is quite active in promoting markets in ecosystem services, seeing this as an important area for their growth. It is problematic if their private interests become a driver behind market expansion in the field of environmental protection.

The basic question is whether we should participate in such protection mainly as consumers or citizens. The principal arguments in that regard have been discussed before – especially in Chapter 11 – concluding that this is a citizen's issue. While a different matter, one may nevertheless question whether the political system in practice offers more 'equal opportunity' than the market. There is no simple answer to this question. Regarding political processes, experts and politicians play key roles defining what should be protected. Participation from the wider public is low. Their influence is mainly exercised through elections, membership in environmental organizations and debates in media. Despite these channels, the arguments for more use of deliberative processes are strong. At the same time, turning to the market is not an adequate response to faulty political processes. The distinction between citizens with value articulation via arguments and consumers with articulation via payments is a principal one.

In relation to this, it is important to emphasize that markets to a large extent are politically framed, even created. As we saw in Section 13.2, the dominant markets in ecosystem services are established through politically set caps. The value articulation is therefore political, while trading is established to ensure cost-efficiency. In that sense, it is the establishment of market actors and their role in the political process that is the issue. Simply stated: who controls the political process, traders or citizens?

The issues of transparency and accountability link to this. To the extent that states are democratically governed, political actors are accountable to the public. In markets, accountability is an issue between buyers and sellers. Due to the combined effect of public goods characteristics and high transaction costs, many people who have an interest in the outcomes of these deals are not part of the transaction. Moreover, if deals are private, the parties to the trade control the flow of information. Intermediaries will have a lot of power in these cases, and there may be limits to how transparent their actions can be due to information disclosure rules. Certainly, governments may be corrupt and information concealed. The principal difference between private and public 'deals' concerning the duty to inform is nevertheless important.

13.3.2 Output legitimacy

Effectiveness

Effectiveness concerns the capacity to ensure that defined goals are reached. Generating the required resources is one aspect; another concerns targeting; a third the capacity to change behavior. As we saw in Section 13.2, to the extent that markets are based on voluntarily created payments – for example, PES and certification – they seem unable to generate large sums of money for environmental protection. The main reasons seem to be transaction costs and free-rider issues. Certainly, building higher levels of environmental consciousness may strengthen this capacity of markets, while one may ask why that engagement should not instead be turned into political action.

In cap-and-trade-based systems, there is a lot of money involved. However, these are not resources used for protection. They concern payments for shifting obligations between involved actors. The protection lies in the cap, while trading reduces the cost of keeping within the limit. One may argue that lowering costs makes a stricter cap possible. At the same time, as most emission permits are grandfathered, states forgo the opportunity to raise resources through selling permits in the first place.

Regarding the effect on environmental qualities, I will offer a few observations regarding each of the four systems covered in Section 13.2. Starting with PES, I have chosen to illustrate by looking at agri-environmental programs in the EU and USA on the one hand and PES programs in Costa Rica on the other. I remind that PES programs dominantly take the form of state subsidies. Markets exist, but they are in a clear minority.

Both the EU and the USA have a set of agri-environmental policies. Baylis et al. (2008) note that while the EU focuses more on landscape amenities, the USA emphasizes soil loss/pollution more strongly. There are historical reasons for this and reflect a different priority among citizens (ibid.).

EU programs are typically broad and use mainly subsidies. US programs like the Conservation Reserve Program use auctioning. It has been documented that both policies have had an effect related to stated goals, but research in the field shows challenges. Regarding the EU programs, they have resulted in increased biodiversity – especially in grassland areas and 'simple' landscapes – that is, landscapes with a low proportion of semi-natural habitats (e.g., Kleijn and Sutherland, 2003; Kleijn et al., 2006; Batary et al., 2010). They have also reduced land abandonment in more marginal agricultural areas and ensured maintenance of certain farming processes (Baylis et al., 2008). The Conservation Reserve Program is targeted towards more narrowly defined goals – soil erosion/land retirement – which makes trading easier. It has ensured the required retirements (Claassen et al., 2008), while Sullivan et al. (2004) note that about half the area would be taken out of production anyway.

Regarding the effect of PES in developing countries, there is rather scant documentation – see, for example, Alix-Garcia et al. (2012). There is particularly a problem with a lack of good baselines. Costa Rica is probably the country with the most well-documented studies of conservation instrument effectiveness.[15] Studies at national level report seemingly low effectiveness of PES (e.g., Daniels et al., 2010; Pattanayak et al., 2010). Such national-level studies do not, however, reflect the large within-country variations due to differences in the quality of implementation and/or in the response of subgroups of the population – see, for example, Daniels et al. (2010); Arriagada et al. (2012). Studies of protected area effectiveness for the three decades preceding the introduction of PES indicate somewhat higher effectiveness on avoided deforestation (Andam et al., 2008; Pfaff et al., 2009). Porras et al. (2013) have reviewed impact evaluation studies of PES in Costa Rica comparing it with national parks. They conclude that PES at best is as effective as the average effectiveness of national parks in avoiding deforestation in the decades before PES.

Regarding certification, I note that it may be driven by care for the environment. It utilizes the profit motive of firms and the willingness of consumers to pay voluntarily for common goods like biodiversity. While offering opportunities, a limitation regarding effectiveness is found in this mix of motivations. First, for certification to work there must be a marketable product involved. Hence, if protection of an ecosystem demands reduced production, certification is of limited effect. Another limitation relates to what level of extra payments consumers are willing to offer for the commodity sold. Being individual payments for public goods, the willingness depends not least on the strengths of local norms regarding what responsibility consumers should take. While the certified section concerning agricultural products is fairly low, it is increasing (Forest Trends & Ecosystem Marketplace, 2008), indicating that such norms are gradually strengthening.

Carbon trading represents by far the largest market in this field. There are two observations of importance concerning the functioning of markets based on caps. First, the 'strictness' of the cap is important for the effectiveness of the system. It has been a continuous problem with the EU ETS that the caps set have been too large. Especially in the present situation with economic recession, the demand for energy has fallen and many firms do not need all the permits they have been granted. The market has hence been flooded with allowances resulting in prices falling to levels far below what was expected (Chaffin, 2012). This has given increased impetus to those proposing instituting carbon taxes instead of cap-and-trade.

While the idea of a cap is to ensure strict reductions, there are ways they can be circumvented. Both in the case of the EU emission trading scheme and the CDM there have been reports of fraud – see, for example, Schneider (2007); Sovacool and Brown (2009); World Bank (2010). There is a motivational reason for that. Those who are parties to the trade have no direct interest in the quality of what is traded. The buyer is after as cheap allowances/certified emission reductions as possible, and is not necessarily concerned with whether reductions are real. Similarly, the seller wants as high net revenues as possible from the trade, implying that lowered real delivery compared to what is contracted on paper is tempting. This illustrates how cap-based markets differ from traditional commodity markets in that none of the parties to the trade has any specific interest in whether what is traded is delivered. That interest is with the regulator – the state – as representing its citizens.

Turning finally to biodiversity offsets, I note that also here a substantial part is non-market. In the case of markets, Santos et al. (2011) emphasize the key role of the regulator for effectiveness. Its tasks are even more demanding here than in the case of carbon markets as the 'service' is typically much more complex. This may explain the rather limited use of biodiversity offsets, even though it is spreading. I especially note that defining baselines and specifying what is an equal offset in terms of the qualities involved is very demanding. The regulator also needs to follow developments over time both on- and off-site. The costs of control might be quite high and if not reclaimed from the parties to the trade, projects that are not efficient may be carried through if they offer separate gains for these actors. Another aspect concerns the capacity of public authorities to facilitate and control. This may explain why we see few biodiversity offsets in developing countries.

A positive aspect of biodiversity offsets is that they may make higher levels of biodiversity protection acceptable to the extent that costs for protection are reduced. At the same time, there are vast challenges, and the strategy has become highly controversial – see, for example, Sullivan (2013b). It is notable that not all offset programs follow the standard as defined by BBOP (2009). Madsen et al. (2010) mention as examples the Brazilian Forest Code offsets and 'developer's offsets', where monitoring problems and lack of clear guidelines as to what determines an 'ecological equivalence' are observed.

I have already mentioned the difficulty of defining what is 'equal'. Draining, for example, a wetland close to the sea for building purposes, can be mitigated by establishing a new one or expanding an existing one upstream. How then to evaluate 'equivalence' or 'likeness'? Which aspects are to be included – biodiversity, water management and purification, landscape values, opportunities for people to experience wildlife and so forth? How can one ensure that one system delivers the 'same' as another in a case with such compounded complexities? The closer in space the rehabilitation site lies, the larger the chance of minimizing 'net losses'. On the other hand, the gains of trading will typically be lower, too. Hence, the stricter these restrictions are, the lower will be the potential gains of trade.

A specific aspect of this is the problems following from the incentive structures. These are parallel to those of carbon markets. The interest of the parties to the trade is to get the credits. The interest in the services lies mainly with the public as represented by the regulator. Hence, the literature documents a rather low fraction of projects as successfully fulfilling the criteria set – see, for example, Gibbons and Lindenmayer (2007); Benayas et al. (2009); Briggs et al. (2009); Suding (2011). A specific problem relates to the observation that fewer measures than expected are taken on-site. Offsetting is typically cheaper, and we observe an 'erosion' of the BBOP rules.

Efficiency

Turning to efficiency, I have limited the focus to cost-efficiency, including transaction costs – see Chapter 7. Trading may reduce costs of reaching targets. Referring to the analysis in Section 12.3, I note that the empirical evidence is a bit mixed – for example, the German 'command-and-control' and US trading systems for reducing SO_2 emissions were both presented as efficient solutions. While I think there are certainly situations where trading may reduce the costs, the conclusion is not universal. The context is important. Moreover, trading seems to demand a certain type of aim. Trading demands demarcation and high level of specificity. Hence, it is easier to use for more easily defined 'services'. We saw this in the above comparison between EU and US agri-environmental programs. The US Conservation Reserve Program is rather narrowly focused, and trading is facilitated. The aims of the EU programs were wider and flat rate payments in the form of per area subsidies dominate. Certainly, higher levels of precision could be obtained by more differentiated systems – see, for example, Batary (2010); Gonthier (2014). That would, however, demand more data and control – that is, higher transaction costs.

Regarding cost-effectiveness, the issue of unequal income is important. In the case of carbon trading through CDM and REDD+, firms and governments from the North pay for actions in the South. A key motivation in many cases is the lower costs of action there. However, people in the South are poor and 'the poor sell cheap' (Martinez-Alier, 2002). To the extent that poverty is the reason for actions being 'low cost', there are certainly tremendous problems involved with using cost-efficiency as a criterion.

Moving to transaction costs, Wunder et al. (2008) conclude that for PES projects they have studies – all in developing countries – the level of these costs tend to lie in the order of 30–100 percent compared to the payment – that is, 15–50 percent of total costs. The authors find that set-up costs are typically higher than running costs. This reflects that many of these payments are 'single trades' covering rather idiosyncratic services. In the case of CDM, Michaelowa and Jotzo (2005) indicate transaction costs in the order of 0.3–1 euros per tCO_2 for large projects (20 000–200 000 tCO_2 per year) to 10 euros per tCO_2 smaller ones (2000–20 000 tCO_2 per year). This compares to a price per tCO_2 in the EU market at about 5 euros in 2013 (World Bank, 2014b).

In case of agri-environmental programs, transaction costs vary tremendously depending on type of good, form and point of instrument application. Rørstad et al. (2007) document transaction costs ranging from 1–2 percent of total costs (payments plus transaction costs) for flat rate acreage and livestock payments with simplified control. In the case of payments for more specific amenities with substantial controls involved, transaction costs were up to 35 percent of total costs. The difference is mainly explained by the complexity of what is paid for. Certainly, here we encounter an important trade-off. Transaction costs can be reduced substantially by measuring simple proxies like land under defined management. Using proxies comes, however, often against a large loss in precision.

The volume transacted – for example, hectares involved per trade – seems very important for the level of transaction costs as a large fraction of these costs is fixed – see the data for CDM offered above. Furthermore, where a methodology for estimating emission reductions is not in place at the outset, this increases transaction costs substantially (Michaelowa and Jotzo, 2005). Coggan et al. (2013) document similar findings for offsets, while noting that asset specificity (biodiversity) plays a very important role for the level of transaction costs.

The high per unit transaction costs following from small quantities is a great obstacle against involving smallholders in environmentally oriented projects – for example, forest conservation. As already emphasized, various forms of collective agreements – like basing agreements on communities instead of individual households – have been documented to have substantial effects on the level of transaction costs (Corbera et al., 2007a; McAffe and Shapiro, 2010; Mahanty et al., 2013).

Distribution

This takes us to the last dimension of output legitimacy – that of distribution. Here I will concentrate on PES and CDM for forest projects – that is, afforestation and reforestation projects (CDM_{AR}). This limitation reflects partly the lack of publications regarding distributional aspects of, for example, the EU ETS and biodiversity offsets. In the case of PES/CDM_{AR}, I concentrate on the developing country experience, as I find distributional aspects most important in this context. Before starting my analysis, I will remind the reader about the distributional effect of the initial allocation of rights. As discussed above and in Chapter 12, rights have wealth effects. Grandfathering tradable quotas in, for example, carbon offers substantial income to those granted these quotas.

This issue is also relevant in the case of PES/CDM_{AR} in developing countries. Rights are (implicitly) with providers. There may be many very strong arguments for this. Increased delivery of ecosystem services comes at the expense of important livelihoods for poor people with few alternatives. In the case of CDM, we also encounter a situation where the North pays to 'save its own skin' – that is, to reduce costs of its own obligations following from the Kyoto agreement.

Based on this, payments should (at least) cover costs faced by those having to change their use of, for example, forest resources. The technical term is 'opportunity costs' – the costs of opportunities lost. Some authors state that actual payments are lower, in some cases much lower than opportunity costs – see, for example, Porras et al. (2008); Kosoy et al. (2008); Gross-Camp et al.

(2012); Mahanty et al. (2013). Wunder and Alban (2008) argue against this conclusion. They emphasize that trades are voluntary and sellers would not sell if they lose. They also point to the fact there may be other potential gains to sellers than the payment, for example, increased tenure security, local gains from conservation, strengthened relationships between buyers and sellers – for example, between upstream and downstream dwellers in the case of water protection – see also Corbera et al. (2007a); Porras et al. (2008); Muradian et al. (2008). These issues are important. We need, however, to mention that while increased tenure security is a good thing for those acquiring it, formalization may reinforce existing inequalities, even result in exclusion as observed in several African cases (Ensminger, 1996; Sjaastad and Cousins, 2009; Benjaminsen et al., 2009b).

The argument that voluntary trades will result in a better (or at least as good) situation for both parties, is questionable. There are rather strong arguments against assuming that people involved actually maximize profits – know their opportunity costs (e.g., Frank, 1987; Pattanayak et al., 2010). In a recent study by Janet Fisher of a PES program in Uganda, she interviewed participants about their basis for participating. While receiving payments was a key motivation for participation:

> [o]nly 11 percent of participants reported calculating the profitability of the carbon strategy compared to other land uses. A much higher percentage (43 percent) reported that although they hadn't calculated anything, they were motivated by the future benefits of the project, often citing timber. The remainder (46 percent) said they had made no calculation, just planted. (Fisher, 2012, p. 50)

Who participates then in these programs – who is paid? First of all, receivers of payments are owners or users of land including concessionaries (in the case of plantations) – see Porras et al. (2008); Wunder et al. (2008); McAffe and Shapiro (2010); Krause and Loft (2013). Most receivers of payments have a formalized property right and having this right seems to be a great advantage for being eligible to participate in PES and CDM_{AR} projects. Since community 'ownership' is dominantly informal – that is, customary rights – private ownership dominates in PES and CDM_{AR}. Communally owned land is not well represented in PES schemes – see for example, Porras et al. (2008). This is often due to lack of formalization/lack of accepted borders. Cases where communities are paid are, however, observed – see Corbera et al. (2007a); Alix-Garcia et al. (2012); Ingram et al. (2014). There is a trend towards increased inclusion of land under common property. Prioritizing smallholders, making landholders who can document possession, although not full legal tenure, is also a feature of some PES programs (Porras et al.,

2013). Therefore, use rights may suffice, but overall it is an advantage for participation to have formalized property rights.

The poorer segment of rural populations is underrepresented in PES/ CDM$_{AR}$. This seems explained by the fact that they (1) need all land for their survival; (2) large fractions are landless or hold customary rights only (see also Unruh, 2008); (3) the costs of contracting varies in a way that systematically disfavors the poor – see, for example, Grieg-Gran and Bishop (2004); Corbera et al. (2007a); Wunder et al. (2008); (4) participation in PES/ CDM$_{AR}$ demands a level of knowledge that the poor often do not have – see, for example, Bosselmann and Lund (2013); Mahanty et al. (2013).

Women are generally underrepresented in PES programs as they often lack property rights. Commonly owned land is, moreover, frequently under a patriarchal system of decision-making (e.g., Corbera et al., 2007b). A notable counter-example is the Bolsa Floresta program in Brazil where payments go exclusively to the female head of the household (Viana, 2008). The PES program in Costa Rica has also taken measures to increase the number of women included (Porras et al., 2013).

To the extent that payments are low, it may not be problematic that few small-holders are involved in PES/CDM$_{AR}$. The situation is probably more difficult for the landless surviving on renting marginal land. As PES may increase the value of such land, the landless may be unable to pay what is demanded and are put in an even more difficult situation – see, for example, Sullivan (2010); Nakakaawa et al. (2011); Mahanty et al. (2013). It is also significant that where money is paid to communities, there is the risk of 'elite capture', emphasizing the need for ensuring transparency. Jindal et al. (2008) note that this is especially a problem where property rights are unclear.

13.4 Reduced emissions from deforestation and forest degradation (REDD+) – the new market?

In the present climate negotiations, reduced deforestation and forest degradation (REDD+) is a key issue. Deforestation counts presently for about 10–12 percent of all losses of carbon dioxide to the atmosphere. REDD+ is proposed as a cost-effective way of halting deforestation especially in the tropics. The idea was first presented at COP11 in 2005 in Montreal. Important decisions about a process for including REDD in a post-Kyoto agreement was made at COP13 in 2007 in Bali. In 2005 the focus was on deforestation. In Bali it expanded to forest degradation and discussions about including enhancement of forest carbon stocks – hence the + (Angelsen, 2008).

REDD+ is thought of by many as a PES program linked to a global carbon market. The idea has been to offer industrial countries the opportunity to fulfill some of their obligations according to a post-Kyoto agreement by paying for REDD+ in developing countries and obtaining carbon credits/ (CERs). An alternative international model for REDD+ has been the so-called 'fund model' where mainly public authorities in the North donate resources that are next paid to national funds/governments in the South to finance REDD+. An international fund could also be offered the power to issue CERs and hence be based on private funding.

Vatn and Vedeld (2013) discuss different models for national REDD+ governance structures – that is, (1) market, (2) independent national funds, (3) funds in the state administration and (4) budgetary support. They evaluate both process and output legitimacy, referring to experiences with PES and CDM and so on. What stand out are the many challenges that organizing REDD+ will face. The choice of solution must depend on the local contexts in each case – especially the political culture, which present institutions are in place, and the potential of REDD+ in the actual country. They conclude, however, that the market system seems to be the weakest alternative for a national REDD+ architecture. Its main appeal lies in its capacity to attract private funding. The authors note, however, that a global REDD+ fund given the power to offer CERs would make the other three solutions equally strong in this respect. The potential to find cost-effective REDD+ options is also an argument for the market solution. It does, however, not compensate for the weaknesses of markets regarding lack of political accountability/democratic control, low capacity to avoid leakage,[16] permanence, coordination across sectors, high transaction costs, and expected distributional consequences.

Regarding the other three options, Vatn and Vedeld (2013) found that the arguments for funds in the state administration and budgetary support are quite strong compared to that of separate national funds like conservation trust funds. This particularly concerns accountability/democratic processes, coordination across sectors, capacity to avoid leakage, co-benefits and maybe transaction costs. They noted that if REDD+ becomes large – that is, much land is involved – it seems problematic to establish a system for combating deforestation and forest degradation that is separated from state decision-making and administrative bodies. Using state budgets may, however, not ensure the necessary transparency. Corruption has been a substantial problem in public administrations in many developing countries. Therefore a separate fund – still positioned so that coordination with relevant ministries and state agencies is argued to offer the best compromise in many contexts. Utilizing and strengthening the capacity of existing regional and local administrations is part of this argument – that is, avoiding the costly operation of establishing a separate REDD+ administration 'all the way down' to the locality where the forest is.

The issue of democratic deficit and the negative experiences with state protection strategies discussed in Chapter 12 demand caution. The fact that REDD+ is assumed to bring resources to compensate for lost livelihoods offers the opportunity to build REDD+ on community-based solutions. It also offers many temptations for people who are 'well positioned' in systems where transparency is weak. Grabbing money is much easier than grabbing land/trees. . . Transparency regarding use of resources and strong emphasis from the international community on the importance of local compensation is therefore very important. National funds are considered better than both markets and budgetary support in this sense.

REDD+ was initiated partly because it was believed to be cheap (e.g., Stern et al., 2006) and partly because it was believed to offer quick solutions. In a study of the introduction of REDD+ at the local level in Brazil (RDS Rio Negro) and Tanzania (Kilosa district), Vatn et al. (2013) observe again that creating a 'commodity' to sell is very demanding. It is institutionally profound in the sense of establishing both land rights and rules regarding use. It changes human relationships. Only in the Tanzanian case, did one come close to trying to 'sell a service'. However, the communities did not accept a 'trade' that would disrupt local distributive norms. Hence, payments were made equal per individual – independent of how important community forests were for their livelihoods.

The North's emphasis on cost-efficiency implicit in REDD+ is, moreover, in conflict with the South's emphasis on the need for compensatory justice in climate change policies (Ikeme, 2003). I reiterate again that cost-efficiency is not a neutral measure of costs as it is heavily influenced by the initial distribution. As already emphasized, making payments according to such costs is not at all innocent in equity terms. While REDD+ also includes an aspect of poverty reduction, the focus on cost-efficiency could result in maintaining global inequalities. Hence, the equity dimension warrants separate attention when building governance structures for REDD+. While protecting forests in the South is important, I note that the process of finding legitimate ways of doing so has only just begun.

13.5 Main messages

The turn to the market is foremost motivated by gains in efficiency. The theoretical basis for that claim depends on clearly defined rights to what is to be traded and low costs of trading – transaction costs. Environmental resources are complex and defining rights at a level where trade becomes possible is in many cases difficult. If possible, it may demand simplifications that are problematic.

The analysis of key markets in environmental services – PES, certifications, carbon markets and biodiversity offsets – shows first of all that what may seem to be a market is really not a system based on trade. PES is seen as the archetype of a Coasean solution. Here 'consumers' of environmental services are thought to trade with providers of such services to increase delivery. It turns out that almost all PES money comes from public purses. They are raised through command – taxes and fees – and payments dominantly take the form of subsidies. Certification and the systems for carbon are examples of markets, while certification is a rather marginal phenomenon. Biodiversity offsets are partly instituted as a pure regulatory measure, and partly as markets.

When disentangling the reasons for this, we note that markets in ecosystem services must be politically created to grow large. Carbon markets and biodiversity offsets are based on politically created caps. While the protection of the environment lies in the cap, trading is allowed to reduce the costs for business of such caps. In the case of PES, trades are based on voluntary commitment. The free-rider problem and the fact that transaction costs are rather high, limit the materialization of such commitments. These factors also seem to explain the rather weak importance of certification.

Regarding the legitimacy of markets, the analysis shows challenges related to the implied simplification of complex values and processes. Trade is built upon instrumental human–nature relationships. Participation in markets depends on capacity to pay and one may reasonably ask if it is the consumer and not the citizen that should have a say. While these arguments are very important, I observe that no system avoids simplification. The question is what system is least problematic in that sense. I also observe that we cannot avoid instrumental relations to nature. The issue is in what form and to what extent.

The analysis of the effectiveness, efficiency and distributional effects undertaken was mainly illustrative of a series of issues and challenges. Discussing effectiveness, the above question of motivation for paying resurfaces as markets seem ineffective in raising funds for environmental protection/provision of ecosystem services. Those involved in carbon trading/biodiversity offsets seem, moreover, interested mainly in getting the credits – not the ecosystem service itself. This is a challenge since traders have substantial power to influence the content of trades. The simplifications necessary to foster trade are important. There is also a motive to simplify to reduce costs for the involved parties. While targeting is important to facilitate trade, it influences what aims can be formulated. The more complex issues are, the less suitable it is to transact via markets.

This takes us to the efficiency issue. The main challenge here seems again to be how markets frame what kind of goals can be pursued. Markets demand commodification – i.e., the good/service must be measurable in monetary terms and demarcated. This implies typically great simplification of complex values. Given that commodities can be defined, trading may reduce costs of delivery. This is, however, not given because of high transaction costs. Carbon is easier to trade than biodiversity. So, where markets may work well is a highly contextual issue. Finally, fraud is also a challenge.

Regarding distribution, the main issue concerns the initial definition of rights and the implied wealth effects. This is especially important in the case of cap-and-trade systems. My analyses of PES and CDM_{AR} raise some doubt regarding the assumption that those trading will all be winners. One thing is that 'the poor sell cheap'. Another is that 'providers' of ecosystem services may not know their costs or do not think about the issue in such terms. Third person effects of trades – for example, the effect on the landless – are important to acknowledge.

I do not claim that there is no room for trade. Public policy instruments are not always the best. They also face issues regarding simplification, transaction costs, even fraud. The public has, however, to always 'be there'. Markets are politically created. Sometimes these structures may help us, but often they do not, or there is a need for tight regulations to scrutinize their capacities. To reiterate the obvious: no governance structure is ideal. Contextual analyses are always necessary. One issue seems, however, not context dependent. This is the importance of the policy process and of citizens' engagement.

NOTES

1   Coase (1960) also discussed situations where transaction costs were positive. He then emphasized that the state may have to be involved more widely than by 'just' defining the rights. Nevertheless, his emphasis was purely on the effects on transaction costs, emphasizing that private trades could be more efficient than state regulations even if transaction costs related to markets are quite large.

2 In a complete discussion, one needs to distinguish between fixed and variable transaction costs. In Vatn (2005, Section 13.2) I undertake such an analysis.

3 Seven billion refers to the number of people presently living on our planet.

4 A substantial part of this section is based on a newly published paper of mine – Vatn (2015).

5 Some authors use the concept 'environmental services' instead. I have found no fundamental difference in the meaning of the two concepts.

6 While it is hard to evaluate to what extent all relevant programs are captured, I also note the issue of what is relevant to include as PES. One such issue is discussed in note 8.

7 As some of their sources refer to 2008, even 2007, it is unclear if all data really are for 2009. The authors say nothing about adjustments and so on of older data. Nevertheless, figures are presented as of 2009.

8 Milder et al. (2010) also include here a category 'Private, regulated'. It covers offset-based systems. Hence, while being termed PES by these authors, they are based on a liability and hence not 'voluntary' as I assume PES programs to be. It should be mentioned that the volume of this category is estimated at 1100 million US dollars and is excluded in the figure presented in the text.

9 Also here Milder et al. (2010) refer to a category 'Private, regulated'. Again, it is about offset/banking systems. The volume is estimated to 380 million US dollars.

10 BBOP is a collaboration of more than 75 organizations and individuals including companies, financial institutions, government agencies and civil society organizations.

11 The Habitat Bank Ltd writes at their homepage: "the term habitat bank refers to a) privately or publicly owned land managed for its natural resource value and b) the delivering body, such as The Environment Bank Ltd., that brokers arrangements between developers and land owners/managers to provide a "no-net-loss" policy of ecosystem services including biodiversity".

12 One example is the Brisas copper and gold project in Venezuela.

13 See note 11.

14 Madsen et al. (2010, p. vii) emphasize quite strongly that this is a low estimate "as about 80 percent of existing programs are not transparent enough to estimate their market size".

15 I am heavily indebted to David Barton regarding the evaluation of the Costa Rican experiences. The paragraph builds on an unpublished text of his.

16 That deforestation is just moved to another place.

14

Environmental governance – the need for new institutions

In Chapter 1, I described the following aim:

This book is about how people and societies handle the issues of coordination and conflict regarding use and protection of their physical environments. It is about clarifying what characterizes the challenges and how people have gone about solving them. It concerns how we should study these issues to facilitate a better understanding of how and why we have created present challenges. It is, however, also about facilitating thinking about better solutions to growing problems.

While we have hinted at aspects of the last part of the aim, I devote the final chapter of the book to a more systematic treatment of this demanding issue.

The previous chapters show that problems are far from solved. While there are areas of progress – for example, some local pollution is reduced in some parts of the world – in general, trends are negative – especially regarding issues like biodiversity loss and climate change, but also a series of pollution issues. The problems we face are very serious. I also contend that present strategies seem to have limited possibilities for success. At the same time, I note that it is difficult to prescribe what it is best to do. First, issues are very complex, and history has persuasively shown that there are no 'easy fixes'. Second, changes do not flow from the study desk. They are concretized in civil society deliberations and fought over in political negotiations. At the same time, ideas about change – how to think about change and possible directions to take – often flow from desks. My ambition is to deliver some inputs to a debate regarding how to think about future options and to some extent also indicate directions.

I start with framing the problem based on the analysis in previous chapters. Thereafter I will summarize some prevailing responses to future policies for reducing environmental problems. I ask if more of today's medicine will do. Concluding that these strategies are characterized by some serious limitations, I continue by presenting ideas regarding how one could think about alternative solutions. I close the chapter with a brief discussion about the realism of these strategies.

14.1 Framing the problems

The problem can be formulated in simple, while somewhat blunt terms. To reduce pressures on our environments to a tolerable level – to ensure sustainable futures – we simply need to prioritize this goal. Environmental management and protection must be taken much more seriously in policy formulations. Next we need to change human action in ways that conform well to this new priority. This implies strengthening the capacity for collective action – to coordinate our use of environmental resources from local to global levels. This is easy to state, but maybe impossible to do. It is difficult first because it is so hard to change priorities. It is also very difficult to create governance structures that effectively change actions and produce results that are in line with potentially shifted priorities.

First of all, while urgency may be a good basis for shifting priorities – note how nations are able to mobilize during war and immediate threats to health – environmental problems are unfolding in ways that typically do not confront us as urgencies. In Chapter 2, we looked at the issue of resilience. We noted that natural environments are able to withstand external pressures quite well. This may seem good as it offers time to adapt. This capacity masks the fact, however, that we may be heading for something bad. Resilience is a limited capacity, and when thresholds are passed, the system will change its dynamics – that is, the conditions for the life forms that produce and are produced by it change. So, from a policy perspective, resilient environments are not just a good thing, as they obscure signals regarding what is going on and may offer the illusion that we are safe. Before the system 'flips', we may see no or few indications that indisputably show that we are moving towards serious problems. In such a structure, it is hard to mobilize the necessary political support for policy changes.

There are also good reasons to continue prioritizing economic growth since a very large fraction of humanity lives in poverty. It is an ethical necessity to support better conditions for the present poor. There are two questions to ask in relation to this. First, the fruits of economic growth are very unevenly distributed. Is the present model for development able to eradicate poverty even if there were no serious environmental limits? Second, why is this goal still so high on the agenda in rich countries? We have seen that people do not seem to be happier beyond a certain, rather modest, level of consumption. In a world of environmental risks, one would expect that 'rational' societies would reduce or stop consumption growth simply because there would be little to gain while much to lose.

There seems to be a quite simple answer to this. The economic system depends on growth to function well. At the same time it offers an enlarged tax base that makes reconciling competing interests easier in the political sphere. There is more to divide and politicians do not need to confront the fundamental issues regarding unequal access to resources and primary income. At the same time, ensuring stability is an important task for states. In our economy low or no growth implies unemployment. It threatens the legitimacy of political systems and may create insurmountable political and social problems.

Hence, I agree with Jackson (2009) that we are caught in an institutional impasse. If the economy continues to grow, we face increasing environmental problems. If it stops growing, social problems will surmount. Given present institutions, growth as well as no growth/de-growth are unsustainable, while for different reasons. These issues have been touched upon earlier. At the basis of the system lies the motive of profit-making and the implied capital accumulation. The increased level of corporate power building up over the last decades has resulted in high levels of profits and accumulated capital searching for new investment opportunities. This drives expansion. The deregulated financial sector has added to the pressure by its vastly increased creation of debt. If that was not enough, the weakened position of labor in many countries has resulted in increased debt-based consumption (Foster and Magdoff, 2009; Tienhaara, 2010).

All of this has put an increased demand on the future to 'pay back'. This would not in itself represent a problem if these expansive economic decision units had not at the same time operated in common environments. Production and consumption is coordinated via markets in ways that create strong positive feedbacks: more production generates income that offers the opportunity to invest and consume even more. There are, however, no signals in the system of firms and consumers operating in markets for commodities that capture effects on the environment – what I have termed *side-effects*. There is no systemic set of negative feedbacks controlling form and scale of economic activity.

While this explains environmental degradation, stopping growing would also create substantial challenges, illustrated by the effect of economic recessions.

Investing becomes more risky. Growth creates the best environment for investment as it lowers the risk of losses, while recessions are characterized by spirals of increased risk, reduced investments, reduced demand and further increased risk. So we must continue to grow our economies, not because it offers better lives, but because not growing – under current institutional conditions – would create huge social costs and political instability.

Being caught between this Scylla and Charybdis, facilitating growth has been prioritized as an aim in itself. There is both a national and international dimension to this. It is reasonable that leaders in poor countries want their economies to grow, while the path should be different from that pursued by the rich. The greatest challenge is with the rich countries. We need to find a path of development that does not depend on growth. This kind of global compromise seems far away. We are actually going in the opposite direction. In the 1992 Rio Summit the compromise was that of 'sustainable development'. In the Rio+20 Summit in 2012 the phrase was changed to 'sustained growth' while it should also be 'inclusive' (UN, 2012b).

While environmental challenges are acknowledged, they are not considered serious enough. Resilient ecosystems up to the 'earth system' mask impending problems. Being caught in a conflict over economic expansion and environmental protection, we may simply downplay the role of somewhat disturbing signals, terming messengers of worrying trends as unserious 'alarmist' or 'doomsday prophets'. There may also be a systems dimension to that reaction. We have become used to 'progress' understood as ever-expanding commodity creation. The present economy is good at that. It is, moreover, what we have learned to expect. Jackson (2009, pp. 163–4) reflects this well when he notes that our society is:

> designed to favour a particularly materialistic individualism and to encourage the relentless pursuit of consumer novelty because this is exactly what keeps the economy going. The erosion of commitment is a structural requirement for growth as well as structural consequence of affluence. Growth calls on us to be myopic, individualistic novelty seekers, because that's exactly what's needed to perpetuate the economic systems.

So while some gain more than others, we are all in some sense 'caught'. The losers are the future generations, while we cannot – given our 'myopic visions' – imagine that this will be the outcome.

In this situation we need to be better at handling early warnings and to create institutions that are able to deal with the form that environmental risks take. A key strategy would be to develop governance structures less dependent on economic growth to function well. Less growth will reduce the risk of pushing ourselves beyond limits. It will make it easier to act on 'early warnings' and use our ingenuity to create even greater distance to potential disasters. This way we get more time to respond to such warnings.

Creating distance to thresholds or tipping points demands developing strategies that minimize environmental disturbances of whatever use of environmental resources there will be. Reduced dependency on growth creates a macro-environment that makes it less challenging for us to devise the necessary actions regarding problems that will show up in various contexts from the local to the global. Developing such strategies is very demanding, while I think it is almost impossible to handle emerging challenges if the growth spiral and the underlying power relations continue.

14.2 More of today's medicine?

14.2.1 Greening growth

Given the perspective of this book, it is as expected that the solution proposed by strong actors is not less growth, but 'green growth' and more markets. The proposals respond to the challenges in a way that does not confront the present developmental model or the institutional structures it is built upon. They are system compatible. Given the daunting task to change ideologies and institutions, greening growth may be the best to hope for.

The pressure towards more markets in environmental policy has been visible for quite some time and reflects neoliberal ideology as well as strong economic interests pushing for the expansion of markets. There is both a structural and actor-oriented explanation for this development. The logic of the economic system is expansion and there will be a continuous push for expanding the 'limits of markets' – to find new areas for investment and profits. At the same time, investors are powerful actors that influence 'mainstream' thinking towards the belief that this is a good development and should be further facilitated. Economic structures facilitate certain types of interests and actions as they similarly obstruct other visions, interests and behaviors.

The idea of the 'Green New Deal' (UNEP, 2011) and 'green growth' (e.g., World Bank, 2012a) were launched as a response to the 2008 financial crisis. It is notable that the ideas were a reaction to the crisis itself, as well as seeing the crisis as a 'window of opportunity' for redirecting growth. Making growth green would imply 'killing two birds with one stone'. The positive connotation regarding Roosevelt's 'New Deal' policy as a response to the economic crisis of the 1930s was used to legitimate 'going green' 75 years later. So 'going green' was seen as (more) realistic if it could be the answer to an economic crisis.

While illustrating the weakness of environmental crises as a 'self-standing' argument for change, the 'Green New Deal' also points towards the need for changes in technologies – not least the necessity to transform energy systems to more use of renewables. This is in itself a very important and demanding task and would be a necessary element in any strategy towards sustainable futures. In the present situation, it must be understood as part of 'ecological modernization' and 'green governmentality' strategies. It is formulated as a way to change our relationships with nature without having to change the relationships between each other as human actors. This seems politically less demanding.[1]

The idea is that of decoupling – of ensuring growth without negative environmental consequences. From a perspective of environmental preservation and protection, the problem is not increased GDP itself, but what growth demands of physical resources and waste creation. If growth and less resource use could become twins – if the form of physical interactions between nature and humans could change that way – the basic institutions could prevail and tough political decisions could simply be circumvented. This is, however, also the limitation of the idea of a 'Green New Deal'. It will at best postpone problems. The danger lies in making us even more 'addicted' to the growth paradigm and camouflaging the fundamental challenges.

The immediate effect of the Green New Deal was rather limited (HSBC, 2009) and it lost momentum over time (Røpke, 2015). It did not evoke serious enough engagement by states. Investment in green technologies would require public economic support as most of these technologies would not compete well with dirtier ones – for example, renewable energies are more costly than fossil fuels. It would also demand facilitative infrastructure developments. Support for such public facilitation has been weakened over almost 30 years with neoliberal policies relying more on markets.

There are also limits to decoupling. Present trends show only 'relative decoupling' at best – see, for example, Haberl et al. (2006, 2011); Jackson (2009). Material flows grow at a speed pretty much at the level of GDP growth. This implies that the unit of material inputs per unit of GDP is fairly constant over time. There is a positive development regarding energy as there is a reduction in energy inputs per unit of production. Total energy use is nevertheless growing.

The fact that technological developments in energy systems and substitution towards less energy-intensive products only results in relative and not absolute decoupling is partly explained by the 'Jevons paradox'. As energy use becomes more efficient – less costly – there is simply more income left to consume more energy. So while the amount of energy used per unit of GDP goes down, total energy use continues to rise.

Also important is the fact that the shift to renewables is slow. As noted above, it demands public support. Some are also afraid that de-carbonizing the economy will result in reduced economic growth. Stern et al. (2006) argued, however, that stabilization of CO_2 in the atmosphere would only come at a cost of 1 percent of global GDP. The CO_2 target in their analyses was, however, high – 550 ppm. Lower levels would imply higher costs and PricewaterhouseCoopers estimated that a reduction in emissions by 50 percent would reduce global GDP by 3 percent (Jackson, 2009). While reductions most probably have to be higher, the costs do not seem to be that daunting even in growth terms. With 'normal' GDP growth rates at 2–3 percent it would not be much to talk about.

While climate change is only one of several environmental challenges, the debate about the reasonableness of the present de-carbonizing analyses is illuminating regarding the issues we are confronted with. First, there are issues regarding the assumptions made in such analyses. Future opportunities and costs of alternative technologies – that is, the rate of 'technological progress' – have to be assumed. Macroeconomic models typically include standardized expectations about such progress, defined as a certain percentage per year. While generally quite problematic, the difficulties with such assumptions are more pronounced given that we talk of a complete rearrangement of our energy systems, not just marginal adaptations.

Cheap energy was an important factor behind the unprecedented growth rates of the economy observed after 1950. Moreover, four out of five economic recessions since 1970 seem related to increased energy costs – oil price 'shocks' (Jones et al., 2004; Hamilton, 2009). Increasing energy prices curb growth, while recessions tend to push prices down, facilitating growth again. Hall and Klitgaard (2012) argue that when energy costs measured as percentage of total GDP lie around 5 percent, economic growth is strong. When reaching a level of about 10 percent, recessions tend to occur under present resource regimes.

The energy cost of energy production is an element in this equation. This is expressed by the concept of energy return on investment (EROI). It measures how much energy is produced by each unit of energy input. While there are challenges related to what to include in such analyses, resulting in variations in calculations, it is generally accepted that the EROI of fossil fuels is high; it has been in the order of 30:1 or above (Hall et al., 2014). The high rate of output compared to the input is certainly very important for the capacity of fossil fuels to ensure economic expansion. The EROI is, however, going down and Gagnon et al. (2009) document a reduction for oil and gas from about 30:1 in 1995 to about 18:1 in 2006. Also important are EROIs for renewables. According to Hall et al. (2014) there is substantial disagreement about the EROI for these energy sources, but they are much lower than those of fossil fuels. Renewable energy sources will be more costly also because they are less 'energy dense'; 'tend to be intermittent'; 'lack transportability'; 'demand new infrastructures' (ibid.).

While high energy costs may reduce growth potentials, I note that this observation also depends on present economic structures. 'Greening the economy' in the sense of moving to an energy system based on renewables may not necessarily curb growth. It will, however, reduce prospects for profits and growth in consumption. It seems clear that investments in renewables offer less opportunity for high profits as EROI is lower and more investments are needed in the energy sector. More investments may imply higher GDP growth, while this is not easy to ensure through markets as profits fall. It will most probably demand much higher levels of public investment also because of the infrastructures needed. Even if growth rates may go down as an effect of costlier energy, a transition to renewable energy will require many new jobs to be created. Due to the lower EROI compared to fossil fuels, more labor input would be necessary per unit of energy. So, the main effect will be on profits and consumption. The reduced level of profits points towards a need for more engagement in production by communities and states. Consumption will be relatively lower due to higher needs for investment and higher maintenance costs of energy systems.

The environmental crisis will demand a lot of new jobs not least in nature restoration and maintenance. Hertsgaard (1999, p. 19) even emphasized: "A growing minority of experts within corporate and government circles believes that restoration of the environment could become a source of virtually limitless profit for consumers and companies alike in the coming century". While we observe the stupidity in this as a basis for limitless profits, it is not an unreasonable scenario that environmental recreation and maintenance will become increasingly important given the fact that we 'need to grow' to curb effects of growth. It may be a 'self-perpetuating' system, albeit producing less and less welfare.

At the same time, one must not underestimate the cost of economic expansion to ensure economic stability. Simple arithmetic shows this. A growth rate of 3 percent per year implies that the economy doubles about every 25 years. While maybe not seeming that much, it implies that the economy will be 16 times larger in 100 years. If we contend that a growth rate below 2 percent implies a danger of recession, we are on a path where we demand the economy to grow six to eight times per 100 years to 'stay stable'.

It is easy to understand that ensuring environmental protection is much more demanding – maybe illusory – if the economy has to grow at such a speed just to 'stay stable'. Rather, it seems reasonable to keep what may be left as space for increased consumption – if any – to those who are poor, and use all technological progress to reduce/minimize environmental impacts of total consumption. Before I turn to that issue, I will, however, make a summary comment to the type of policies presently used to protect the environment.

14.2.2 The problem of 'ex post' state regulations

We may understand current environmental policy as being part of a two-stage process – see Chapters 12 and 13. First, economic growth and capital accumulation are facilitated through establishing a resource regime that is very expansive. Property rights are defined as if no harm would appear from resource use/production. Second, when problems (necessarily) appear, specific regulations may be put in place to try to reduce these side-effects. This may happen a long time after the problems originated. This is because it takes time before problems become visible (the resilience effect); before it is clear what causes the problem (the complexity effect); and political support is created to make a change (the conflict of interest effect). In that process, the state is faced with some quite daunting issues – a kind of structural path dependency that heavily restricts *ex post* action:

- At the time of regulation, large investments have been made in the relevant production. This will increase the cost of regulation – that is, the abatement costs – compared to a policy where regulations were set up to influence these investments at the outset. The difference between the costs of *ex post* and *ex ante* regulations – that is reactive as opposed to proactive policies – may be substantial as investments made under the assumption of no harm have to be changed/reversed. Alternatively, one could build policies on the presumption that all production will result in harm – the ecological economics perspective – evaluate their potential seriousness and regulate before production is allowed. Note that the time between starting a certain production/using a particular technology for the first time until problems are visible and harm proven may be very long and at the time of 'possible action', the number of wrong investments will be tremendous. This problem is more pertinent the higher the growth rates – see also Chapter 8 on this.

- At the point when the issue of a possible regulation is on the political agenda, strong interests are created that will oppose such regulation. This concerns the producers involved who will protect the above-mentioned investments and jobs. However, consumers may also be negative to changes as the product causing the damage might have to be withdrawn or it will be more costly to buy. Serious distributional effects may appear too – note the effect of higher energy costs.

- The governments find themselves in a situation characterized by international competition and regulations are constrained by the fact that companies may move and jobs may be lost – see Chapter 12.

So, there are a lot of reasons why this kind of regulation will be weak. Given 'normal' levels of economic growth, governments not only chase moving targets, they may become more and more behind.

Industries may also fight policies in court. This was briefly mentioned in Chapter 12. As emphasized above, investing is risky. The possibility of an environmental regulation adds to the uncertainties embedded in markets. Hence, industry wants to reduce the opportunity for governments to regulate, arguing that if production was initially legitimate, industry should not face losses at a later stage despite the fact that harm may appear.

One recent example is the Swedish company Vattenfall suing Germany for 6 billion dollars at the Washington-based International Centre for Settlement of Investment Disputes[2] over losses following the closure of nuclear power plants where Vattenfall has made investments. Another example is the Philip Morris tobacco company suing Australia for lost profits because the government took action to reduce teenage smoking.

The right of states to form national policies has become an issue in trade liberalization agreements over the years, challenging the autonomy of states' legal jurisdictions. One thing is that a company may move if a state develops policies that that are not as favorable as those of other states. In addition, states can be sued for policy changes that endanger profits. This has become a tense issue in the negotiations between the EU and the USA on the so-called TTIP – The Transatlantic Trade and Investment Partnership. While negotiations are kept secret, information has been revealed regarding a system for an investor–state dispute settlement. If made part of the final agreement, it would allow corporations to sue governments for actions limiting a corporation's future profits.

This challenges democracy at its very basis. It restricts the opportunities to formulate forceful environmental policies. Moreover, it shows a development where *ex post* regulations may become not only very costly in societal terms, but will also shift all costs onto the state. Step by step, the basis for this kind of regulation is weakened, reducing its legitimacy further.

14.3 Thinking about alternatives

Given the above, we need to think in new ways. In the following, I will present a series of ideas that I find worth evaluating and developing further. I do not think of them as *the* solution. I think of them as a way to think based on the perspectives advanced in this book. I want to challenge the reader and hopefully provoke a debate about future directions of economic development.

Fundamentally, the issue is about *responsibility* for future living conditions and how such responsibility is instituted. It is also about how acts of responsible actors are coordinated. Problems do not typically appear as a result of single decisions, but are the result of many acts. This increases the challenges considerably. Two strategies need to be combined. First, and as an overall risk-reducing strategy, we need to curb the growth of the economy. Second, environmental consequences of production and consumption within this limit need to be reduced. To facilitate this, we should develop integrative institutions (Hagedorn, 2008; Vatn, 2008).

Regarding growth, a key issue is finding strategies for economic development for the South that do not repeat the errors of the North. It may also imply building consumer responsibility in the form of an anti-consumerist culture. This is especially important in the North, but also needs to be part of a far-sighted Southern strategy. Noting that the problem is not economic growth per se, but the amount of ecosystem transformation and the form and amount of waste generated, an important strategy may be to develop a regulatory system focused on minimizing the inputs of materials to the economy – the so-called material throughput. Finally, creating economic institutions less dependent on 'growth to ensure stability' seems crucial.

There is certainly overlap between the above strategies to curb growth and strategies more specifically oriented at reducing environmental impacts of a given level of production and consumption. Present institution building has focused on individualizing and separating decision-making. Separation simplifies choice, but must inevitably create decisions that are incompatible with the dynamics of the natural systems and must systematically end up with shifting or displacing costs of actions upon other actors. First, it seems we need to develop a new kind of firm based on different principles of ownership and operation as compared to the corporation. Let me for now indicate the direction by calling it 'the cooperation'. Second, it seems necessary to build a governance structure above that level that is able to communicate between these reorganized economic actors in ways that (1) facilitate and support their pursuit of sustainability, and (2) link decisions at different levels of impact. Some issues can be decided upon locally – when consequences are only local and no higher-level structures are needed. Other decisions affect processes at higher levels due to various interlinkages in scale and time, as in the case of fishing regimes, regional or global pollution, regional or global biodiversity concerns, and climate change.

In the following I will offer some short descriptions of each strategy as mentioned above. I will highlight both opportunities and challenges. I will principally emphasize ideas to facilitate a discussion about directions to take. I will also offer some concrete illustrations. It is my view that ensuring sustainable development demands developing institutions – resource regimes – that have not been envisioned yet. At the same time, before the creation of money, of states, of corporations, these things were inconceivable. What is essential is willingness to think about alternatives as well as observe developments that may already be underway and could grow if offered support.

14.3.1 A new strategy for development

It all starts with defining where we want to go – the overall vision of what a good society looks like. Economic growth may be a strategy to eradicate poverty, and is legitimated by this expectation. The negative effect of high present consumption levels for future generations is, however, an issue that delegitimizes such a strategy. One response to the latter has been to demand development to be sustainable. As noted in Chapter 4, the World Commission on Environment and Development (WCED, 1987, p. 43) defined sustainable development as "development that meets the needs of the present without compromising the ability of future generations to meet their own needs". The Commission emphasized needs and this way it went beyond the idea of preference satisfaction as is standard in economic welfare analysis. It continued by stating that sustainable development:

> contains within it two key concepts: the concept of 'needs', in particular the essential needs of the world's poor, to which overriding priority should be given; and the idea of limitations imposed by the state of technology and social organization on the environment's ability to meet present and future needs. (Ibid.)

It hence also explains that there is not only an intergenerational, but also an intragenerational aspect to sustainable development. At the same time, limits are seen as related to technology and social organization – that is, institutions – only. The belief expressed by the Commission was that economic growth is both possible and important. Technological and institutional change will make that possible without challenging environmental limits.

The conclusion of the Commission was strongly embraced in the 'Rio process'. This could be because it did not demand a fundamental break with existing policies – just 'do growth better'. At the same time, major institutional reforms like the establishment of World Trade Organization (WTO) and further trade liberalizations have materialized without any links to the Rio process or to the concept of sustainable development. It is highly questionable if this has ensured 'doing growth better'. Whether the Commission and the following Rio process were sidelined or co-opted is maybe not that important. What is significant is that sustainable development – even as defined by the Commission – seemed to demand a break with present development goals and strategies – while still being placed within the 'growth paradigm'.

The literature on alternative goals for development makes a distinction between a subjective notion of welfare and a more objectivist account of needs. This literature breaks with consumerism and GDP growth as a way to ensure good quality of life – see, for example, Max-Neef (1991); Jackson (2009); Latouche (2009); Rauschmayer et al. (2011). Important inspirations are found in Sen (1999, 2009) and Nussbaum (2003, 2011). Let me start with Sen to illustrate the issues involved. He is critical of the present strategy of development focusing on GDP as a good measure of well-being. His position is based on a criticism of the utilitarian concept of welfare – that is, preference satisfaction – both because he sees what is valuable to be multidimensional and that preferences are adaptive (Sen, 1995, 1999). Here he is much in line with arguments presented earlier in this book. It follows from this that measuring progress in monetary terms (one-dimensional/GDP) and based only on people's preference satisfaction is weak and does not confront the most important issues regarding what a good life is. Rather, he focuses on the issue of creating human capabilities. These are 'achievable functionings' – what makes us able to do and be. In practical terms, it relates to issues like being healthy, having a job, having social networks, ensured political liberties and economic and social rights.

Sen avoids establishing a 'finite list' of capabilities that should be ensured. His point is not that a good life has to have a specific set of achievable functionings. The point is that it is functioning in all its plurality as understood by reasoned people themselves that is important. We note that Sen is, moreover, supporting a positive understanding of freedom. It is something that should be created, demanding active engagement by society. Nussbaum (2003, 2011) goes further in that she develops a defined set of capabilities that a parliament should guarantee to its citizens through its constitution.

While breaking with the consumerist logic, there is nothing explicit in Sen that ensures sustainable development. In that respect, Sen's concept of capabilities as freedom is silent (Nussbaum, 2003).[3] However, the freedom of one may limit the freedom of others. In this sense Max-Neef (1991) and his emphasis on the distinction between needs and satisfiers moves us forward. Needs can be met in different ways – by different satisfiers. We may, for example, get the calories and nutrients we need by eating vegetarian food as well as non-vegetarian. We may experience nature locally or far away. High levels of needs satisfaction can be created through very different levels of material consumption. This is also an argument strongly advocated by the so-called de-growth movement (see, for example, Schneider et al., 2010; Kallis et al., 2012).

A good life need not to be consumerist. Nevertheless, to embrace a future where consumption should be in some way limited raises a series of tough issues. It may demand that we have to take a stand as a community on the content of consumption, on what is good vs bad consumption, on what is sufficient or enough. Focusing on capabilities and needs will help. It offers a positive direction. There is, however, a large difference between thinking about capabilities and needs as a way to ensure freedom and eradicate poverty and seeing them also as a basis for curbing growth. In the latter sense it goes blatantly against the kind of consumerist liberties that have become so strong a value at least in some parts of the world.

So we must ask: are we able to develop a necessary common vision about responsibility and care? While I am not sure, I am sure that for it to be successful, it must be a bottom-up process. It must come out of a deliberative process including an evaluation of what it means to be human in a world of physical limits. It is no less than a tremendous cultural change, challenging some very strong values regarding modern ways of living. Nevertheless, it does not seem hopeless. Responsibility for offspring is also a fundamental value. Under the belief that there is no conflict between growing consumption and sustainability, we have been made to believe that the future is safe – that growth actually produces more for those coming. However, if that is not true, if we realize rather that present growth reduces opportunities for the future, there are some fundamental values in all cultures that may be vitalized.

Now it is possible to see that the dogma that technological change will always come to our rescue is actually problematic. It has become 'ideology'. It distracts our focus away from a discussion about common responsibilities regarding the future of our civilization. For sure, we need technological change – considerable change too – directed at changing production processes to reduce environmental impacts, including a de-carbonizing of the economy. However, the opportunities for technological change do not eliminate our responsibility to search for a new development path. It is the other way around. We need to ensure technological development that fits such a path.

14.3.2 Consumer responsibility

Let us assume that a set of values directed at responsibility and care have gained momentum in a democratic process regarding the direction development should take. How could it come about in practice? How could it be institutionalized? I will now discuss this in a series of steps starting with consumer responsibility.

From the above, a new development path has to imply changes in consumption – beginning with the situation in rich countries. Indeed, a lot of environmental damage follows from production activities. However, without consumption, there is no production. Whether we conclude that what is necessary is reduced material consumption (de-growth), stabilizing it (steady state) or reducing the pace (slow growth) is not the issue here. That question has to be answered through deliberation and political processes. I will limit myself to discuss what it might take to find a path where consumption growth is lower than what the present nexus of markets and firms need to function well.

To act in an environmentally friendly way, we need to know what our actions imply and we need to have a sense of responsibility. According to Schwartz

(1977) there is both 'awareness of consequences' and 'ascription of responsibility'. Regarding knowledge, there are two key dimensions with regard to the effectiveness of consumer action. First, we must want to know and next we must be able to know. The literature on this – see, for example, Heiskanen (2005); Feinberg and Willer (2010); Kahan et al. (2011); Pidgeon (2012) – offers some interesting, albeit disturbing observations.

Heiskanen (2005) reports a Finnish study on consumer awareness of a series of environmental problems by concluding that "What we ended up with then, was a picture of a highly well-intentioned, but extremely ignorant consumer" (p. 185). She notes 'the obvious', that if people do not know what acts cause which problems, it is hard to envision any effective changes in behavior. Pidgeon (2012) has made a broad review of public understanding of climate change. He notes an increased awareness up until about 2007, followed by a trend of reduced focus and sense of importance. The situation varies across countries, while he also notes that the issue of knowing is not just about facts. He states that "There is substantial evidence that the variation of attitudes towards climate change is influenced both by people's broader ideological beliefs and by their beliefs about threats to their fundamental values" (p. S90). This also has a knowledge dimension as climate denialism seems to follow a political right–left divide. Feinberg and Willer (2010), Kahan et al. (2011) and McCright and Dunlap (2011) support the interpretation that values influence what we believe – that is, there is a "tendency of individuals to form risk perceptions that are congenial to their values" (Kahan et al., 2011, p. 147).

The issue of information demand and information overload may also seem important. To know the effect of one's own actions, one needs to know both the effect of the act itself – for example, driving the car, using a certain detergent – and how the car, the fuel and the detergent were produced. This is demanding and time pressures may make it difficult even for the most engaged to ensure that he or she are well informed – see, for example, Carrigan and Attalla (2001); Heiskanen (2005); Wells et al. (2011). Labeling has been seen as a way to communicate better between consumers and producers. Understanding labels is, however, also time consuming and often demands quite a lot of technical competence. Eco-labeling may simplify matters, but there is still the issue of trust in the source and criteria used.

This takes us to the motivational side. In Chapter 13 we saw that there is some consumer engagement in buying eco-labeled products. The trend is, however, rather weak. Added to the informational challenges is the issue of motivation or 'ascription of responsibility'. Much of the literature emphasizes consumption as important in building identity – see, for example, Ahuvia (2005); Ruvio and Belk (2013). Carrigan and Attalla (2001) emphasize that the "importance of brand image for products such as clothing takes precedence over ethical criteria" (pp. 570–71). Caruana and Crane (2008) note how consumer responsibility is constructed in a 'dialogue' between consumers and corporations. They note an important mechanism related to the role of corporations in defining what consumer responsibility means. Their study of Responsibletravel.com, illustrates how:

> the construction of the responsible consumer shifts the locus of choice – from whether to consume tourism or not (the concerned citizen's position), to which type of tourism to consume (responsible or mainstream). . . By shifting from the former to the latter, the text assures us that most, if not all, of the relevant social, ethical and environmental issues have been attended to. (Caruana and Crane, 2008, p. 1513)

So, the market implies a necessary twist in the focus of environmental engagement – to what can be traded. More fundamentally, consumer responsibility confronts us with some difficult motivational conflicts. One thing is that we face the challenge of being different from the 'normal' consumer. Another is the fact that effects follow from the sum of individual actions. Single acts typically have no consequences; it is the pattern of interaction that counts. We are confronted with the standard free-rider problem of collective action. In such a situation people have to act on the basis of principles, not consequences – see also Moisander (2007). While some engaged individuals may develop personal principles like 'I never go by plane', 'I consume less' we are now rather in the field of expanding to common rules – of socially constructed images of what is the right thing to do. We talk of citizen – cooperative – rather than consumer – individualized –action.

I do not want to underestimate individual and small group action – not least in 'testing out' new consumption patterns and ways to live in a more environmentally friendly way. Development of subcultures of less consumerist forms of living is important. They can, however, hardly be more than informative experiments. On a larger scale, we observe disconnected consumers facing high information/transaction costs when trying to act in an environmentally friendly way in markets. We observe a consumer facing motivational conflicts, where actions for most of us – that is, the ones not highly motivated – do not become meaningful before being part of a cultural shift. Finally, we note that if successful in creating reduced consumption, economic collapse lies round the corner.

This does not imply that I think each of us does not have an ethical responsibility towards future generations, as well as those living now. This is, however, a citizen's responsibility, implying political action to support shifts towards resource regimes that function well with lower production levels and that ensure production processes that are environmentally acceptable. Some of that political activism may take the form of political consumerism (Micheletti et al., 2004). To be effective, it seems necessary to expand beyond the market sphere though and into the political.

14.3.3 Political responsibility[4]

Sustainable futures are basically about political responsibility – about formulating a common direction and creating necessary changes in resource regimes. This demands, however, also strengthening the power of the political sphere – of the state – and of its underpinning – civil society. The belief in individualism and a self-governed economy has led development astray – resulting in 'development betrayed' as Norgaard (1994) has termed it. Individualized choice cannot solve common challenges. It is as simple as that.

What is not simple is how to regain political power over the economy, and how to do so in a democratic way. While good ideas have been developed regarding expanding and deepening political participation – see, for example, Dryzek (2002, 2013); Bäckstrand et al. (2010) – making it happen is challenging. There are several issues that need to be observed. Politics must be oriented more at directing the economy and less on crisis management of a globalized market. Next, the political must be much more far-sighted. We need to find ways that, for example, take policy beyond electorate cycles of three to four years. Finally, there must be public engagement, which next requires access, influence and time. This is necessary to ensure legitimacy and citizen backing and force.

I talk here about redirecting, about changing direction and facilitating a process against which it becomes easier to discuss the large challenges we face. The issues involved would – given the framing of this book – be of the following kind:

- *Redirection.* I have already emphasized the need for a different direction of development. Here I just reiterate that, with an all-encompassing 'liberal state', the issue of what a good life is, is something for the single individual to decide upon. The crucial question here is where to draw the line between individual and collective choice. Some individual liberties need to be strengthened – for example, those of political participation – while at the same time we need to find ways where we can deliberate over and negotiate conclusions regarding what physical space or 'footprint' each of us should be free to operate.

- *Redistribution.* Democratization and thinking about such 'limited spaces' demand a strong focus on redistribution. It is necessary on its own terms. Given a project directed at curbing growth makes it even more important to ensure equal opportunity regarding access to resources and development of capabilities. The literature on consumption as referred to at various points in this book also shows that a strong reason for increased material consumption is to 'keep one's position' in the race for ever-increased consumption. Redistribution reduces the impetus to grow.
- *Regulation.* Understanding the key role of the political as forming the economic system is very important in general, but crucial when we talk of sustainable development. Ideally it implies putting reason – collective reasoning – above satisfying wants. Özler and Obach (2009) document the significant impact of state regulations on per capita ecological footprint. Schnoor (2008, p. 8615) notes that an important positive effect of the financial crisis is that "'regulate' is no longer a dirty word".[5] I see three key areas that demand stricter regulation in the future: (1) the use of environmental resources, (2) the direction of technological development, and (3) the development of infrastructures. Fundamentally, it is a shift from dominance of competition towards more cooperation and coordination.
- *Reforming the firm.* Regulating is demanding and may become impossible given certain resource regimes. One issue regards the vast information demands and transaction costs. Another regards the motivational structures instituted in economic actors – especially the firms. If production units were (1) less dependent on growing, (2) more willing and able to engage in environmental consequences of their actions, and (3) observing political action as something necessary for their own mission and survival, that could greatly increase the capacity of the overall governance structure to produce required outcomes.
- *Reformulating the international order.* As important for political action is changing the international order to strengthening political power and will over economic logic and corporate power. Important here is a change in the globalized economic order.

Each of the above represent tremendous challenges. While all seem important, I certainly acknowledge that 'getting there' is very demanding. To the extent strategies of the above kind can be sufficiently agreed upon, thinking about steps in the right direction – specifically steps that can reinforce each other – becomes important. I will return to that in a closing section. Here

I will say a few words on 'regulation', while a discussion regarding 'reforming the firm' and 'reformulating the international order' follows in separate sections.

Strengthening public capacity to regulate is an important part of a strategy for sustainable development. One option that should be further developed regards regulation on the input of material and energy into the economy – that is, a shift from *ex post* to *ex ante* regulation. It will avoid some of the problems discussed above regarding various path dependencies and has the potential to reduce the transaction costs through simplifying management and control of the regime. A strict input regime would imply demanding proof of 'no harm' or 'reasonable harm' before accepting an economic activity to start. Regulation could take the form of input quotas or taxes on the use of (some) environmental resources.

We have already seen some use of this strategy in fisheries (total allowable catches – TACs) and regulations of nitrogen inputs. Actually taxes and emission quotas in CO_2 are also in practice restrictions on inputs of fossil fuels. These systems have, however, been instituted *ex post* and not been part of a general strategy of input or 'throughput' regulation as already proposed by Daly (1977). The experiences gained point not least towards the importance of care when distributing such input quotas. There is also the question of whether quotas should be tradable. Using fishing as an example, quotas could be offered to individual fishers/firms and traded in markets. They could also be given to communities and managed through community rules. The choice here would influence decision processes and the role of society as opposed to the market. It would also influence effectiveness of the regulation and the long-run distribution of income and settlements. Narrow efficiency calculations – heavily emphasized in present discussions – would miss most of these issues including maintaining long-run coherence of societies. The latter seems crucial to fostering the acceptance of the overall goal of sustainability with its focus on sufficiency.

Regulating inputs is important in reducing the scale of material throughput. It does, however, not influence the form of resource use and the material transformations happening through production and consumption. It will therefore not be possible to avoid regulations on production processes and so on to ensure reasonable pressures on the environment, while input regulations will reduce the challenges.

An element in this is directing technological change. One thing is that markets cannot drive the kind of change now needed – at least not alone.

They are too myopic, too focused on individual gain and too 'path depend-ent'. What is now needed is a deliberate shift in paths – especially regarding energy systems. Private firms and markets may play an important role in this. They need, however, direction through coordinated research and infrastruc-ture developments.

14.3.4 The responsible firm

Expanding public responsibility for the environment is important, but very difficult to ensure given present resource regimes. To repeat from the above: if production units were (1) less dependent on growing; (2) more willing and able to engage in environmental consequences of their actions, and (3) observing political action as something necessary for their own mission and survival, this could greatly increase the capacity of the overall govern-ance structure to produce needed outcomes.

The concept of corporate social responsibility is well known. The research on the system – while documenting some positive developments – reveals that rather few businesses are involved and that the instruments used are weak – see, for example, Utting (2008); Sjåfjell (2011); Sneirson (2011). These observations are not least due to the fact that shareholder interests are the dominant interest in corporate governance.

One reason corporate social responsibility is not effective therefore is that it is an 'add on' to a system that is directed at goals other than environmental sustainability. There are some people who have tried to go further, creat-ing new forms of business – for example, so-called social enterprises – that combine to various degrees the logic of social welfare with that of com-merce (e.g., Ridley-Duff and Bull, 2011; Esposito, 2013; Lee and Battilana, 2013). They combine individual and social rationality in different ways. These enterprises take many different forms and some are also directed at environmental concerns. The idea that companies should have responsibili-ties to society – responsibilities beyond making profits – has been around for centuries. The development of the cooperative is a core example here. What are now observed are new legal forms facilitating institutional types like the community interest company in the UK and the benefit corporation in the USA (Esposito, 2013). Laws underpinning these types are in place to ensure that companies can operate without facing lawsuits if they do not give primary emphasis to profit maximization.

These are interesting experiments, and need further encouragement as learning about their potential and limitations is very important. Ensuring a business form that functions well if there is low or no overall economic growth is demanding. The reduced emphasis on profits is obviously taking the development of the firm in the right direction. Further, a development from 'community interest' to community ownership may even strengthen the basis for institutionalizing wider aims. Cooperatives and public organizations have shown that profit is not a necessary basis for production units to function well.

So, a shift in ownership structures with the implied shift in goals seems a very important strategy for a transformation to a sustainable development path. Several issues warrant specific attention when discussing the possibilities and obstacles involved. First, to move this from an experimental phase operating in small niches to become a basis for the entire economy demands a tremendous shift in rights to capital. It seems hard to envision this happening through donations. It cannot happen through vastly expanding the capital base either and gradually shifting capital accumulation to these new forms. Such relative redistribution is limited by the fact that we need to curb growth. Hence, absolute redistribution through taxation would be necessary, while the shift could get some support from the market if consumers were willing to 'massively' turn their demand towards products from the new types of firms. There is a potential for synergies here. Nevertheless, scaling up new business forms becomes a demanding project.

Second, while the above implies a shift in motivation for production instituting social and environmental responsibility at its basis, coordination between firms is still a problem regarding environmental consequences. We face some of the same challenges regarding green consumption. It is – as an example – much easier to ensure socially rather than environmentally responsible production. The former concerns action related to staff and local community and is 'direct' and measurable in local terms. In the case of the environment, the relation is typically 'indirect' – there is generalized interdependency – see Chapter 9. It is the sum of actions of all firms with respect to the specific environments that is the issue. In some cases those environmental effects go all the way up to the global level.

I see no way of instituting such responsibility at the level of single firms in a meaningful and operational way. Defining the aim to be – among other things – environmentally responsible production is certainly changing the way the unit will operate. It is, however, almost impossible to envision how this unit can take the environmental interaction with other firms directly into account. There is also the challenge of how to institute 'modesty' in production volumes and sale. In a sense, this goes against the iron law of markets: 'expand or die'.

Therefore, a crucial element in creating the 'new business' – *the cooperation* – is to ensure that a cooperative will also engage with the political will. A new form of 'social contract' between firms and society should be established where the firm is looked at as an 'instrument' for society, not a way for owners to enrich themselves. This implies an expansion of the power of the state and demands strengthening democratic control – transparency and accountability – much beyond today's situation even in the most developed democracies.

14.3.5 Responsible interaction

The above indicates a need to accept more state command and cooperative forms of governance and less competition. Nevertheless, it is hard to envision a development without substantial interaction via trade. I take as a given that commodity markets will also be important, while differently framed, in the future. Given the above ideas regarding the role of the state, changed foundations for firms and expanded role of communities, there is one key area of analysis left. That concerns international trade and the power of the state.

As we saw in Chapter 9, the volume of international trade has vastly increased not least since 1950, being facilitated by reducing both import and export regulations. This has shifted the power relations between states and multinational corporations – between politics and economics. None of the above ideas seem able to materialize to any meaningful size without changing the international regime.

This is again a very demanding issue. It is, however, possible to indicate principal directions to take. One could be to establish a 'fourth level of power' – an international governance structure where states restrict their sovereignty and accept a form of international government that can balance the interests of environmental protection against the interests of trade and a global division of labor. The second strategy would be to continue with states mainly as sovereign, but limit trade of commodities and free movement of capital to regain political power that way.

Both solutions challenge the existing governance structures to an extent far beyond any of the changes discussed in previous sections. It seems, however, impossible to avoid thinking about reforms in these directions. Personally, I favor a system that is based on limiting the role of 'free' international trade.

While for sure there is the issue of whether any of the above are 'realistic' ideas, I find regulating trade both more doable and also more democratic. A world government is extremely unrealistic. Moreover, democratic control of a global government – if ever feasible – is very difficult to foresee. Certainly, establishing a world environmental organization (e.g., Biermann, 2000) or upgrading the UN Environment Programme to become a UN specialized agency like the World Health Organization (e.g., Biermann et al., 2012) may be helpful in increasing the power of international environmental agreements and tilt the balance somewhat from the much stronger trade regime to become more in favor of environmental care.

Regarding the option of trade regulations, one could envision developments where countries are allowed to regulate imports – for example, through tariffs – dependent on the exporting country's environmental action. This could take a series of different forms. A fairly 'standard way' concerns cases where the environmental impact comes with the traded good – for example, bio-invasion from products or ballast water. This regulation could be based on normal polluter pays principles – see, for example, Perrings et al. (2005). It is the imported good that degrades the environment. More wide-ranging forms could be illustrated by the US ban on imports of tuna from Mexico to protect dolphins, and on shrimp to protect turtles (Copeland and Taylor, 2004). Yet more radical forms would be allowing trade restrictions when relevant international environmental agreements are broken. As this may motivate countries not to ratify such treaties in the future, a move even including acceptance of import restrictions in cases where countries are unwilling to sign and ratify international environmental agreements that a 'large majority' of states support, is also an option that would strengthen the power of such agreements. These ideas are principally along the lines of how the WTO tries to ensure that international trade rules are followed. From that perspective, they cannot be considered radical – rather conventional. What is radical is to accept such systems to favor environmental as opposed to goals regarding free trade.

The above would imply restrictions on the sovereignty of individual states to regain state power, making it possible to prioritize the environment more strongly. A policy focused on trade restrictions also depends on certain restrictions on the sovereignty of individual countries. Note that today there is a discussion about such restrictions, but with the opposite aim – see the above discussion about offering companies the right to sue states for regulations that threaten the value of their investments. It is interesting to note that this kind of reduction in the power of states is acceptable. The fact that trade distortion is a trumping argument, while environmental distortion is seen as a non-legitimate argument in international discourses, illustrates very obviously the existing power relations.

Piketty (2014) proposes a global capital tax to reduce inequality across the world. Such a tax will in itself make environmental policies easier, as higher levels of equality also reduce the pressures towards 'excessive' consumption growth. There will simply be less need to catch up with those who 'have more'. Moreover, this type of tax offers another opportunity – that of moving capital invested in standard corporate production towards new business forms. Taxes are publicly owned and states may use such revenues to offer investment support in the form of transfers or loans with low interest rates to social enterprises – whether under private, community or state ownership.

14.4 Utopia and realism

Are the above ideas purely utopian? Given the existing systems and current pressures for further strengthening of corporate and financial power, proposing to 'turn this tide' in the above direction may seem so unrealistic that it only causes shaking heads. I will close with two responses to such a reaction.

First, Piketty (2014) notes that his idea of a global tax on capital is utopian, but still useful. He notes first that "even if nothing resembles this ideal put into practice in the foreseeable future, it can serve as a worthwhile reference point, a standard against which alternative proposals can be measured" (p. 515). Moreover, it is possible to move step by step, while keeping in the right direction. If we are not willing to think 'outside the box', we only support the prolongation of a system that is not built to handle the problems we are facing.

Second, if the above is utopian, what is the alternative? Why is status quo incrementalism protected because it is realistic? Where is 'realism' taking us? What is really radical in the present situation? I would argue that continuing along the present development path will result in very radical changes in our living conditions though not of the utopian form. My aim has first of all been to trigger debate and in that respect try to support a free dialogue around alternative ways of thinking. My point is that the issues we are facing means questioning the way we organize ourselves and look for alternative governance structures with less bleak futures. Other people may have other and perhaps better ideas – that would be wonderful.

It is my conviction that we are at the start of a large transformation of the institutions of our economy. We are faced with tremendous challenges and it will take a long time to shift priorities and make them materialize in new governance structures. We will make a lot of errors, we will need to learn what does not work, retreat and find new ways. It will be a process that demands some considerable patience and hence needs to be begun before problems overwhelm us.

Discussing alternative governance structures necessary for establishing a sustainable economy does not imply an argument in favor of 'getting the institutions right' and then rescuing the environment. It is first of all about values and where we want to go. Resource regimes and the wider governance structures are just means in that process. Moreover, we cannot wait to act more seriously on, for example, climate change and biodiversity loss until we have developed all the ideas regarding necessary structural changes. What we need to do, however, is to bear the long run in mind when we act to realize short-run or intermediate goals. This is a very important point. I do not believe in revolutions, although the long-run aim must be quite revolutionary. Rather, we talk of larger and smaller synergistic steps in a certain direction.

In writing this book, I have often thought about the members of the British parliament who created the 18th century Bubble Act. They were thinking about how institutions change power relations. They were afraid of corporate power – not because they were engaged in protecting natural environments, but because they judged the opportunities for fraud unacceptable. I have sometimes wondered what these members of parliament would have said if they had been asked to judge today's challenges. Maybe they would have considered the environmental challenges we are facing to be the ultimate form of fraud? It is not possible to know. I am, however, quite sure what future generations will think.

NOTES

1 This argument rests on a simplification. Turning to renewals may also cause conflict between people as illustrated in the case of wind farms.
2 ICSID is an international arbitration organization mediating between international investors. ICSID is a member of the World Bank Group.
3 Sen has also been criticized for underestimating power relations and lack of emphasis on the political context of economic development – see, for example, Navarro (2000). This is, however, not a key issue here.
4 Added to institutional issues emphasized in this text, the focus on macroeconomic policies is also important for the development of a sustainable economy. While in this chapter I briefly discuss tax reforms and distributional issues, analyses directed at macroeconomic principles for a sustainable economy are warranted. Røpke (2015) offers an interesting input to that discussion. Her important work is complementary to my analysis.
5 I am grateful to Tienhaara (2010) for these references.

References

Aasen, M. and A. Vatn, 2013. Deliberation on GMOs: a study on how a citizens' jury affects the citizens' attitudes. *Environmental Values*, **22**(4): 461–81.

Acheson, J.M., 1975. The lobster fiefs: economic and ecological effects of territoriality in the Maine lobster fishery. *Human Ecology*, **3**(3): 183–207.

Adams, W.M. and D. Hulme, 2001. Changing narratives, policies and practices in African conservation. In D. Hulme and M. Murphree (eds): *African Wildlife and Livelihoods: The Promise and Performance of Community Conservation*. London: James Currey, pp. 9–23.

Agrawal, A., 2001. Common property institutions and sustainable governance of resources. *World Development*, **29**(10): 1649–72.

Agrawal, A., 2007. Forests, governance, and sustainability: common property theory and its contributions. *International Journal of the Commons*, **1**(1): 111–36.

Agrawal, A. and K. Gupta, 2005. Decentralization and participation: the governance of common pool resources in Nepal's Terai. *World Development*, **33**(7): 1101–14.

Agrawal, A. and K. Redford, 2009. Conservation and displacement: an overview. *Conservation and Society*, **7**(1): 1–10.

Ahuvia, A.C., 2005. Beyond the extended self: loved objects and consumers' identity narratives. *Journal of Consumer Research*, **32**(1): 171–84.

Aldred, J. and M. Jacobs, 2000. Citizens and wetlands: evaluating the Ely citizens' jury. *Ecological Economics*, **34**(2): 217–32.

Alix-Garcia, J.M., E.N. Shapiro and K.R.E. Sims, 2012. Forest conservation and slippage: evidence from Mexico's National Payments for Ecosystem Services Program. *Land Economics*, **88**(4): 613–38.

Allen, J. and M. Pryke, 2013. Financialising household water: Thames Water, MEIF, and 'ring-fenced' politics. *Cambridge Journal of Regions, Economy and Society*, **6**(3): 419–39.

Allison, E.H. and M.C. Badjeck, 2004. *Fisheries Co-management in Inland Waters. A Review of International Experience. Sustainable Fisheries Livelihood Programme (SFLP)*. Rome: FAO and DFID.

Allison, E.H. and F. Ellis, 2001. The livelihoods approach and management of small-scale fisheries. *Marine Policy*, **25**(5): 377–88.

Amundsen, H., F. Berglund and H. Westskog, 2010. Overcoming barriers to climate change adaptation – a question of multilevel governance? *Environment and Planning C: Government and Policy*, **28**(2): 276–89.

Andam, K.S., P.J. Ferraro, A. Pfaff, G.A. Sanchez-Azofeifa and J. Robalino, 2008. Measuring the effectiveness of protected area networks in reducing deforestation. *Proceedings of the National Academy of Sciences of the United States of America*, **105**(42): 16089–94.

Anderson, E.S., 1999. What is the point of equality? *Ethics*, **109**(2): 287–337.

Andreoni, J., 1990. Impure altruism and the donations to public goods: a theory of warm glow giving. *The Economic Journal*, **100**(401): 467–77.

Angelsen, A. (ed.), 2008. *Moving Ahead with REDD: Issues, Options and Implications*. Bogor, Indonesia: CIFOR.

Aoki, M., 2001. *Toward a Comparative Institutional Analysis*. Cambridge, MA: The MIT Press.

Araral, E. Jr., 2005. Bureaucratic incentives, path dependence, and foreign aid: an empirical institutional analysis of irrigation in the Philippines. *Policy Sciences*, **38**(2–3): 131–57.

Archer, M., 2003. *Structure, Agency, and the Internal Conversation*. Cambridge, UK: Cambridge University Press.

Arendt, H., 1958. *The Human Condition*. Chicago, IL: University of Chicago Press.

Arnason, R., 2012. Property rights in fisheries: how much can individual transferable quotas accomplish? *Review of Environmental Economics and Policy*, **6**(2): 217–36.

Arnason, R. and H. Gissurarson, 1999. *Individual Transferable Quotas in Theory and Practice*. Reykjavik: University of Iceland Press.

Arnoldi, J., 2004. Derivatives. Virtual values and real risks. *Theory, Culture & Society*, **21**(6): 23–42.

Arnstein, S., 1969. A ladder of citizen participation. *Journal of the American Institute of Planners*, **35**(4): 216–24.

Arrhenius, S., 1896. On the influence of carbonic acid in the air upon the temperature of the ground. *Philosophical Magazine and Journal of Science, Series 5*, **41**(251): 237–76.

Arriagada, R.A., P.J. Ferraro, E.O. Sills and S.K. Pattanayak, 2012. Do payments for environmental services affect forest cover? A farm-level evaluation from Costa Rica. *Land Economics*, **88**(2): 382–99.

Arrow, K., 1969. The organization of economic activity. Issues pertinent to the choice of market versus nonmarket allocation. In *The Analysis and Evaluation of Public Expenditure: The PPB System. Vol. 1*. Washington, DC: US Government Printing Office, pp. 59–73.

Arrow, K., R. Solow, P.R. Portney, E.E. Leamer, R. Radner and H. Schuman, 1993. Report of the NOAA Panel on Contingent Valuation. *Federal Register*, **58**(10): 4601–14.

Asafu-Adjaye, J., 2005. *Environmental Economics for Non-Economists. Techniques and Policies for Sustainable Development*. Singapore: World Scientific.

Asner, G.P., A.J. Elmore, L.P. Olander, R.E. Martin and A.T. Harris, 2004. Grazing systems, ecosystem responses, and global change. *Annual Review of Environmental Resources*, **29**: 261–99.

Aubert, V., 1979. *Sosiologi. 1. Sosialt samspill*. [Sociology. 1. Social Interaction]. Oslo: Universitetsforlaget.

Bachrach, P. and M.S. Baratz, 1963. Decisions and nondecisions: an analytical framework. *The American Political Science Review*, **57**(3): 632–42.

Baert, P., 2005. *Philosophy of the Social Sciences. Towards Pragmatism*. Cambridge, UK: Polity Press.

Bai, Z.G., D.L. Dent, L. Olsson and M.E. Schaepman, 2008. Proxy global assessment of land degradation. *Soil Use and Management*, **24**(3): 223–34.

Bakan, J., 2004. *The Corporation – the Pathological Pursuit of Profit and Power*. New York: Free Press.

Baland, J.M. and J.P. Platteau, 1996. *Halting Degradation of Natural Resources: Is there a Role for Rural Communities?* Oxford: Clarendon Press.

Ban, N., I.R. Caldwell, T.L. Green, S.K. Morgan, K. O'Donnell and J.C. Selgrath, 2009. Diverse fisheries require diverse solutions. *Science*, **323**(5912): 338–9.

Banful, A.B., 2011. Old problems in the new solutions? Politically motivated allocation of program benefits and the "new" fertilizer subsidies. *World Development*, **39**(7): 1166–76.

Banville, C., M. Laundry, J.-M. Martel and C. Baulaire, 1998. A stakeholder approach to MCDA. *Systems Research*, **15**(1): 15–32.

Barber, C.P., M.A. Cochrane, C. Souza Jr. and A. Veríssimo, 2012. Dynamic performance assessment of protected areas. *Biological Conservation*, **149**(1): 6–14.

Barbour, R., 2007. *Doing Focus Groups*. London: Sage Publications.

Bardhan, P., 2000. Irrigation and cooperation: an empirical analysis of 48 irrigation communities in South India. *Economic Development and Cultural Change*, **48**(4): 847–65.

Bardhan, P. and J. Dayton-Johnson, 2002. Unequal irrigators: heterogeneity and commons management in large-scale multi-variate research. In E. Ostrom, T. Dietz, N. Dolsak, P.C. Stern, S. Stonich and E.U. Weber (eds): *The Drama of the Commons*. Washington, DC: National Academy Press, pp. 87–112.

Barkow, J.H., L. Cosmides and J. Tooby, 1992 (eds). *The Adapted Mind: Evolutionary Psychology and the Generation of Culture*. Oxford: Oxford University Press.

Barley, S.R., 2010. Building an institutional field to corral a government: a case to set an agenda for organization studies. *Organization Studies*, **31**(6): 777–805.

Barr, C., A. Dermawan, H. Purnomo and H. Komarudin, 2010. Financial governance and Indonesia's Reforestation Fund during the Soeharto and post-Soeharto periods, 1989–2009. A political economic analysis of lessons for REDD+. *Occasional Paper No. 52*. Bogor, Indonesia: CIFOR.

Barton, D.N., S. Blumentrath and G. Rusch, 2013. Policyscape – a spatially explicit evaluation of voluntary conservation in a policy mix for biodiversity conservation in Norway. *Society & Natural Resources: An International Journal*, **26**(10): 1185–201.

Batary, P., A. Baldi, D. Kleijn and T. Tscharntke, 2010. Landscape-moderated biodiversity effects of agri-environmental management: a meta-analysis. *Proceedings of the Royal Society B, Biological Sciences*, **278**(1713): 1894–902.

Batson, C.D. and L.L. Shaw, 1991. Evidence for altruism: toward a pluralism of prosocial motives. *Psychological Inquiry*, **2**(2): 107–22.

Bauer, C.J., 1997. Bringing water markets down to earth: the political economy of water rights in Chile, 1976–95. *World Development*, **25**(5): 639–56.

Bauer, J., M. Kniivilä and F. Schmithüsen, 2004. Forest legislation in Europe. How 23 countries approach the obligation to reforest, public access and use of non-wood forest products. A study implemented in the framework of the European Forest Sector Outlook Study (EFSOS). *Geneva Timber and Forest Discussion Paper No. 37*. Zurich: United Nations.

Bauman, Z., 1993. *Postmodern Ethics*. Oxford: Blackwell.

Baumgartner, F.R., J.M. Berry, M. Hojnacki, D.C. Kimball and B.L. Leech, 2009. *Lobbying and Policy Change. Who Wins, Who Loses, and Why*. Chicago, IL: Chicago University Press.

Baumgärtner, S., 2000. *Ambivalent Joint Production and the Environment. An Economic and Thermodynamic Analysis*. Heidelberg: Physica Verlag.

Baumol, W.J. and W.E. Oates, 1988. *The Theory of Environmental Policy*. 2nd edition. Cambridge, UK: Cambridge University Press.

Baylis, K., S. Peplow, G. Rausser and L. Simon, 2008. Agri-environmental policies in the EU and United States: a comparison. *Ecological Economics*, **65**(4): 753–64.

BBOP (Business and Biodiversity Offsets Programme), 2009. *Biodiversity Offset Design Handbook*. Washington, DC: Forest Trends. Accessed 8 July 2015 at http://bbop.forest-trends.org/guidelines/odh.pdf.

Becker, G., 1976. *The Economic Approach to Human Behavior*. Chicago, IL: University of Chicago Press.

Benayas, R.J.M., A.C. Newton, A. Diaz and J.M. Bullock, 2009. Enhancement of biodiversity and ecosystem services by ecological restoration: a meta-analysis. *Science*, **325**(5944): 1121–4.

Benjaminsen, T.A. and I. Bryceson, 2012. Conservation, green/blue grabbing and accumulation by dispossession in Tanzania. *The Journal of Peasant Studies*, **39**(2): 335–55.

Benjaminsen, T.A. and C.E. Lund, 2002. Formalisation and informalisation of land and water rights in Africa: an introduction. *European Journal of Development Research*, **14**(2): 1–10.

Benjaminsen, T.A., F.P. Maganga and J.M. Abdallah, 2009a. The Kilosa killings: political ecology of a farmer–herder conflict in Tanzania. *Development and Change*, **40**(3): 423–45.

Benjaminsen, T.A., S. Holden, C. Lund and E. Sjaastad, 2009b. Formalisation of land rights: some empirical evidence from Mali, Niger and South Africa. *Land Use Policy*, **26**(1): 28–35.

Bentham, J. [1789] 1970. *Introduction to the Principles of Morals and Legislation*. London: Methuen.

Berger, A. and M.F. Loutre, 2002. An exceptionally long interglacial ahead? *Science*, **297**(5585), 1287–8.

Berger, L., 2014. Understanding the social construction of unsustainable human behaviour. The example of agricultural non-point-source pollution in Lake Tai, China. PhD dissertation, Berlin: Humboldt-Universität.

Berger, P. and T. Luckmann [1967] 1991. *The Social Construction of Reality. A Treatise in the Sociology of Knowledge*. London: Penguin Books.

Bergseng, E. and A. Vatn, 2009. Why protection of biodiversity creates conflict – some evidence from the Nordic countries. *Journal of Forest Economics*, **15**(3): 147–65.

Berkes, F., 1985. Fishermen and 'the tragedy of the commons'. *Environmental Conservation*, **12**(3): 199–206.

Berkes, F., 2008. Commons in a multi-level world. *International Journal of the Commons*, **2**(1): 1–6.

Bernstein, S., 2005. Legitimacy in global environmental governance. *International Law & International Relations*, **1**(1–2): 139–66.

Beunen, R., 2006. European nature conservation legislation and spatial planning: for better or for worse? *Journal of Environmental Planning and Management*, **49**(4): 605–19.

Bhaskar, R. [1975] 2008. *A Realist Theory of Science*. London: Verso.

Bhaskar, R., 1989. *Reclaiming Reality: A Critical Introduction to Modern Philosophy*. London: Verso.

Bhaskar, R., 1991. *Philosophy and the Idea of Freedom*. Oxford: Blackwell.

Biel, A. and J. Thøgersen, 2007. Activation of social norms in social dilemmas: a review of the evidence and reflections on the implications for environmental behavior. *Journal of Economic Psychology*, **28**(1): 93–112.

Biermann, F., 2000. The case for a world environment organization. *Environment: Science and Policy for Sustainable Development*, **42**(9): 22–31.

Biermann, F., K. Abbott, S. Andresen, K. Bäckstrand, S. Bernstein and M.M. Betsill et al., 2012. Navigating the anthropocene. Improving earth system governance. *Science*, **335**(6074): 1306–7.

Bishop, J., S. Kapila, F. Hicks, P. Mitchell and F. Vorhies, 2008. Building biodiversity business. London and Gland: Shell International Limited and the International Union for Conservation of Nature. Accessed 8 July 2015 at http://www.iucn.org/dbtw-wpd/edocs/2008-002.pdf.

Blacker, D., 2013. *The Falling Rate of Learning and the Neoliberal Endgame*. Alresford, UK: Zero Books.

Blackman, A., 2010. Alternative pollution control policies in developing countries. *Review of Environmental Economics and Policy*, **4**(2): 234–53.

Blackman, A. and W. Harrington, 2000. The use of economic incentives in developing countries: lessons from international experience with industrial air pollution. *Journal of Environment and Development*, **9**(1): 5–44.

Blaikie, P., J. Harriss and A. Pain, 1992. The management and use of common-property resources in Tamil Nadu, India. In D. Bromley (ed.): *Making the Commons Work. Theory, Practice and Policy*. San Francisco, CA: ICS Press, pp. 247–64.

Block, F., 2003. Karl Polanyi and the writing of *The Great Transformation. Theory and Society*, **32**(3): 275–306.

Blomley, T., K. Pfliegner, J. Isango, E. Zahabu, A. Ahrends and N. Burgess, 2008. Seeing the wood for the trees: an assessment of the impact of participatory forest management on forest condition in Tanzania. *Oryx*, **42**(3): 380–91.

Blount, S., 1995. When social outcomes aren't fair: the effect of causal attributions on preferences. *Organizational Behavior and Human Decision Process*, **63**(2): 131–44.

Blyth, M., 2003. *Great Transformations. Economic Ideas and Institutional Change in the Twentieth Century*. Cambridge, UK: Cambridge University Press.

Boardman, A., D. Greenberg, A. Vining and D. Weimer, 2014. *Cost–Benefit Analysis: Concepts and Practice*. 4th edition. Harlow, UK: Pearson.

Boas, T.C. and J. Gans-Morse, 2009. Neoliberalism: from new liberal philosophy to anti-liberal slogan. *Studies in Comparative International Development*, **44**(2): 137–61.

Bohman, J. and W. Rehg, 1997. *Deliberative Democracy: Essays on Reason and Politics*. Cambridge, MA: The MIT Press.

Bosselmann, A.S. and J.F. Lund, 2013. Do intermediary institutions promote inclusiveness in PES programs? The case of Costa Rica. *Geoforum*, **49**: 50–60.

Boulding, K., 1970. The network of interdependence. Paper presented at the Public Choice Society Meeting, 19 February.

Bourdieu, P., 1989. Social space and symbolic power. *Sociological Theory*, **7**(1): 14–25.

Bourdieu, P., 1990. *The Logic of Practice*. Stanford, CA: Stanford University Press.

Bowles, S., 2008. Policies designed for self-interested citizens may undermine 'the moral sentiments': evidence from economic experiments. *Science*, **320**(5883): 1605–9.

Branch, T.A., 2009. How do individual transferable quotas affect marine ecosystems? *Fish and Fisheries*, **10**(1): 39–57.

Bressers, H.T.A. and K.R.D. Lulofs, 2004. Industrial water pollution in the Netherlands. In W. Harrington, R.D. Morgenstern and T. Sterner (eds): *Choosing Environmental Policies. Comparing Instruments and Outcomes in the United States and Europe*. Washington, DC: Resources for the Future, pp. 91–116.

Briggs, B.D.J., D.A. Hill and R. Gillespie, 2009. Habitat banking – how it could work in the UK. *Journal for Nature Conservation*, **17**(2): 112–22.

Brock, W. and D. Colander, 2000. Complexity and policy. In: D. Colander (ed.): *The Complexity Vision and the Teaching of Economics*. Cheltenham, UK and Northampton, MA, USA: Edward Elgar Publishing, pp. 73–96.

Brockington, D., 2004. Community conservation, inequality and injustice: myths of power in protected area management. *Conservation and Society*, **2**(2): 411–32.

Brockington, D. and J. Igoe, 2006. Eviction for conservation: a global overview. *Conservation and Society*, **4**(3): 424–70.

Bromley, D.W., 1989. *Economic Interests and Institutions. The Conceptual Foundations of Public Policy*. Oxford: Basil Blackwell.

Bromley, D.W., 1990. The ideology of efficiency: searching for a theory of policy analysis. *Journal of Environmental Economics and Management*, **19**(1): 86–107.

Bromley, D.W., 1991. *Environment and Economy: Property Rights and Public Policy*. Oxford: Basil Blackwell.

Bromley, D.W. (ed.), 1992. *Making the Commons Work. Theory, Practice and Policy*. San Francisco, CA: ICS Press.

Bromley, D.W., 2006. *Sufficient Reason: Volitional Pragmatism and the Meaning of Economic Institutions*. Princeton, NJ: Princeton University Press.

Bromley, D.W., 2009. Abdicating responsibility: the deceit of fisheries policy. *Fisheries*, **34**(6): 280–90.

Bruner, A.G., R.E. Gullison, R.E. Rice and G.A.B. da Fonseca, 2001. Effectiveness of parks in protecting tropical biodiversity. *Science*, **291**(5501): 125–8.

Burgess, J., M. Limb and C.M. Harrison, 1988. Exploring environmental values through the medium of small groups: 1. Theory and practice. *Environment and Planning A*, **20**(3): 309–26.

Burri, R.V. and S. Bellucci, 2008. Public perception of nanotechnology. *Journal of Nanoparticle Research*, **10**(3): 387–91.

Burton, R.J.F., 2004. Reconceptualising the 'behavioural approach' in agricultural studies: a socio-psychological perspective. *Journal of Rural Studies*, **20**(3): 359–71.

Burtraw, D. and D.A. Evans, 2004. NO_x emissions in the United States: a potpourri of policies. In W. Harrington, R.D. Morgenstern and T. Sterner (eds): *Choosing Environmental Policies. Comparing Instruments and Outcomes in the United States and Europe.* Washington, DC: Resources for the Future, pp. 133–57.

Burtraw, D. and K. Palmer, 2004. SO_2 cap-and-trade program in the United States. A 'living legend' of market effectiveness. In W. Harrington, R.D. Morgenstern and T. Sterner (eds): *Choosing Environmental Policies. Comparing Instruments and Outcomes in the United States and Europe.* Washington, DC: Resources for the Future, pp. 41–66.

Butler, C., 2010. Morality and climate change: is leaving your TV on standby a risky behaviour? *Environmental Values*, **19**(2): 169–92.

Bäckstrand, K., 2006. Multi-stakeholder partnerships for sustainable development: rethinking legitimacy, accountability and effectiveness. *European Environment*, **16**(5): 290–306.

Bäckstrand, K. and E. Lövbrand, 2006. Planting trees to mitigate climate change: contested discourses of ecological modernization, green governmentality and civic environmentalism. *Global Environmental Politics*, **6**(1): 50–75.

Bäckstrand, K., J. Kahn, A. Kronsell and E. Lövbrand (eds), 2010. *Environmental Politics and Deliberative Democracy. Examining the Promise of New Modes of Governance.* Cheltenham, UK and Northampton, MA, USA: Edward Elgar Publishing.

Callon, M. (ed.), 1998. *The Laws of Markets.* Oxford: Blackwell.

Camerer, C. and R.H. Thaler, 1995. Anomalies. Ultimatums, dictators and manners. *Journal of Economic Perspectives*, **9**(2): 209–19.

Cardenas, J.C., J. Strandlund and C. Willis, 2000. Local environmental control and institutional crowding-out. *World Development*, **28**(10): 1719–33.

Carlson, K.M., L.M. Curran, G.P. Asner, A. McDonald Pittman, S.N. Triggand and J.M. Adeney, 2012. Carbon emissions from forest conversion by Kalimantan oil palm plantations. *Nature Climate Change*, **3**, 283–7.

Carpenter, S.R., 2005. Eutrophication of aquatic ecosystems: bistability and soil phosphorus. *Proceedings of the National Academy of Sciences*, **102**(29): 10002–5.

Carrigan, M. and A. Attalla, 2001. The myth of the ethical consumer – do ethics matter in purchase behavior? *Journal of Consumer Marketing*, **18**(7): 560–77.

Carson, R. [1962] 2002. *Silent Spring.* Boston, MA: Houghton Mifflin.

Carter, N., 2007. *The Politics of the Environment: Ideas-Activism-Policy.* 2nd edition. Cambridge, UK: Cambridge University Press.

Caruana, R. and A. Crane, 2008. Constructing consumer responsibility: exploring the role of corporate communication. *Organization Studies*, **29**(12): 1495–519.

CDIAC (Carbon Dioxide Information Analysis Center), 2015. Database. Accessed 13 February 2015 at http://cdiac.ornl.gov/.

Chaffin, J., 2012. Emissions trading: cheap and dirty. *Financial Times*, 2 February 2012.

Chape, S., J. Harrison, M. Spalding and I. Lysenko, 2005. Measuring the extent and effectiveness of protected areas as an indicator for meeting global biodiversity targets. *Philosophical Transactions of the Royal Society B*, **360**(1454): 443–55.

Chapin, F.S. III, G.P. Kofinas and C. Folke (eds), 2009. *Principles of Ecosystem Stewardship. Resilience-Based Natural Resource Management in a Changing World.* New York: Springer.

Chasek, P.S., D.L. Downie and J.W. Brown, 2014. *Global Environmental Politics.* 6th edition. Boulder, CO: Westview Press.

Chayes, A., A.H. Chayes and R.B. Mitchell, 1998. Managing compliance: a comparative perspective. In E.B. Weiss and H. Jacobson (eds): *Engaging Countries: Strengthening Compliance with International Environmental Accords*. Cambridge, MA: The MIT Press, pp. 39–62.

Chhatre, A. and A. Agrawal, 2008. Forest commons and local enforcement. *PNAS*, **105**(36): 13286–91.

Chhatre, A. and A. Agrawal, 2009. Trade-offs and synergies between carbon storage and livelihood benefits from forest commons. *PNAS*, **106**(42): 17667–70.

Child, J. and T. Tsai, 2005. The dynamic between firms' environmental strategies and institutional constraints in emerging economies: evidence from China and Taiwan. *Journal of Management Studies*, **42**(1): 95–125.

Christiano, T., 2003. The authority of democracy. *The Journal of Political Philosophy*, **12**(3): 266–90.

Chu, C., 2009. Thirty years later: the global growth of ITQs and their influence on stock status in marine fisheries. *Fish and Fisheries*, **10**(2): 217–30.

Claassen, R., A. Cattaneo and R. Johansson, 2008. Cost-effective design of agri-environmental payment programs: U.S. experience in theory and practice. *Ecological Economics*, **65**(4): 737–52.

Claussen, M., C. Kubatzki, V. Brovkin, A. Ganopolski, P. Hoelzmann and H.-J. Pachur, 1999. Simulation of an abrupt change in Saharan vegetation at the end of the mid-Holocene. *Geophysical Research Letters*, **26**(14): 2037–40.

Cleaver, F., 2012. *Development through Bricolage. Rethinking Institutions for Natural Resource Management*. London: Routledge.

Cline, W.R., 2007. *Global Warming and Agriculture – Impact Estimates Per Country*. Washington, DC: Center for Global Development, Peterson Institute for International Economics.

Coase, R.H., 1937. The nature of the firm. *Economica*, **IV**(16): 386–405.

Coase, R.H., 1960. The problem of social cost. *The Journal of Law and Economics*, **3**: 1–44.

Coen, D., 2004. Environmental and business lobbying alliances in Europe: learning from Washington? In D. Levy and P. Newell (eds): *Business in International Environmental Governance: A Political Economy Approach*, Cambridge, MA: The MIT Press, pp. 197–220.

Coen, D., 2007. Empirical and theoretical studies in EU lobbying. *Journal of European Public Policy*, **14**(3): 333–45.

Cofala, J., M. Amann and R. Mechler, 2006. *Scenarios of World Anthropogenic Emissions of Air Pollutants and Methane up to 2030*. Laxenburg, Austria: International Institute for Applied Systems Analysis (IIASA).

Coggan, A., E. Buitelaar, S. Whitten and J. Bennett, 2013. Factors that influence transaction costs in development offsets: who bears what and why? *Ecological Economics*, **88**: 222–31.

Cohen, J.E., 1995. Population growth and earth's human carrying capacity. *Science*, **269**(5222): 341–6.

Cole, M.A., 2007. Corruption, income and the environment: an empirical analysis. *Ecological Economics*, **62**(2–3): 637–47.

Coleman, J.S., 1973. *The Mathematics of Collective Action*. London: Heinemann.

Coleman, J.S., 1990. *Foundations of Social Theory*. Cambridge, UK: Belknap.

Colson, E., 1974. *Tradition and Contract: The Problem of Order*. Chicago, IL: Adeline Publishing.

Commons, J.R. [1934] 1990. *Institutional Economics. Its Place in Political Economics*. New Brunswick, NJ: Transaction Publishers.

Conway, M., M. Rayment, A. White and S. Berman, 2013. *Exploring Potential Demand for and Supply of Habitat Banking in the EU and Appropriate Design Elements for a Habitat Banking Scheme. Final Report Submitted to DG Environment*. London: ICF GHK Consulting Ltd in association with BIO Intelligence Service.

Copeland, B. and M.S. Taylor, 2004. Trade, growth, and the environment. *Journal of Economic Literature*, **42**(1): 7–71.

Corbera, E., K. Brown and W.N. Adger, 2007a. The equity and legitimacy of markets for ecosystem services. *Development and Change*, **38**(4): 587–613.

Corbera, E., N. Kosoy and M. Martinez-Tuna, 2007b. Equity implications of marketing ecosystem services in protected areas and rural communities: case studies from Meso-America. *Global Environmental Change*, **17**(3–4): 365–80.

Cordell, D., J.-O. Drangert and S. White, 2009. The story of phosphorus: global food security and food for thought. *Global Environmental Change*, **19**(2): 292–305.

Costanza, R., R. d'Arge, R. de Groot, S. Farber, M. Grasso, B. Hannon et al., 1997. The value of the world's ecosystem and natural capital. *Nature*, **387**(6630): 253–60.

Crowards, T., 1997. Nonuse values and the environment: economic and ethical motivations. *Environmental Values*, **6**(2): 143–67.

Crutzen, P.J., A.R. Mosier, K.A. Smith and W. Winiwarter, 2007. N_2O release from agro-biofuel production negates global warming reduction by replacing fossil fuels. *Atmospheric Chemistry and Physics Discussion*, **7**: 11191–205.

Dahl, R.A., 1957. The concept of power. *Behavioral Science*, **2**(3): 201–15.

Dahlman, C.J., 1979. The problem of externality. *The Journal of Law and Economics*, **22**(1): 141–62.

Daily, G. (ed.), 1997. *Nature's Services. Social Dependence on Natural Ecosystems*. Washington, DC, Island Press.

Daly, H., 1977. *Steady-State Economics*. San Francisco, CA: W.H. Freeman and Company.

Daly, H. and J. Farley, 2011. *Ecological Economics. Principles and Applications*. 2nd edition. Washington, DC: Island Press.

Daniels, A.E., K. Bagstad, V. Esposito, A. Moulaert and C.M. Rodriguez, 2010. Understanding the impacts of Costa Rica's PES: are we asking the right questions? *Ecological Economics*, **69**(11): 2116–26.

Dasgupta, P.S. and D.W. Pearce, 1972. *Cost–Benefit Analysis: Theory and Practice*. London: Macmillan.

Davis, A., 1996. Barbed wire and bandwagons: a comment on ITQ fisheries management. *Reviews in Fish Biology and Fisheries*, **6**(1): 97–107.

Davis, D.D. and C.A. Holt, 1993. *Experimental Economics*. Princeton, NJ: Princeton University Press.

Deci, E.L., 1971. Effects of externally mediated rewards on intrinsic motivation. *Journal of Personality and Social Psychology*, **18**(1): 105–15.

Defrancesco, E., P. Gatto, F. Runge and S. Trestini, 2008. Factors affecting farmers' participation in agri-environmental measures: a Northern Italian perspective. *Journal of Agricultural Economics*, **59**(1): 114–31.

DeFries, R., A. Hansen, A.C. Newton and M.C. Hansen, 2005. Increasing isolation of protected areas in tropical forests over the past twenty years. *Ecological Applications*, **15**(1): 19–26.

Degnbol, P., H. Gislason, S. Hanna, S. Jentoft, J.R. Nielsen and S. Sverdrup-Jensen et al., 2006. Painting the floor with a hammer: technical fixes in fisheries management. *Marine Policy*, **30**(5): 534–43.

Dekimpe, M.G. and D.M. Hanssens, 1995. The persistence of marketing effects on sales. *Marketing Science*, **14**(1): 1–21.

Delacote, P., 2009. On the sources of consumer boycotts ineffectiveness. *The Journal of Environment & Development*, **18**(3): 306–22.

DeLeon, P., 1999. The stages approach to the policy process. What has it done? Where is it going? In P.A. Sabatier (ed.): *Theories of the Policy Process*. Boulder, CO: Westview Press, pp. 19–32.

Demissie, F., 2015. *Land Grabbing in Africa: The Race for Africa's Rich Farmland*. London: Routledge.

Deng, Y. and H. Xu, 2015. International direct investment and transboundary pollution: an empirical analysis of complex networks. *Sustainability*, **7**(4): 3933–57.

Dequech, D., 2003. Cognitive and cultural embeddedness: combining institutional economics and economic sociology. *Journal of Economic Issues*, **37**(2): 461–70.

Devetak, R., A. Burke and J. George, 2011. *An Introduction to International Relations*. 2nd edition, Cambridge, UK: Cambridge University Press.

Dewey, J., 1927. *The Public and its Problems*. New York: Holt.

Diekert, F.K., A.M. Eikeset and N.C. Stenseth, 2010. Where could catch shares prevent stock collapse? *Marine Policy*, **34**(3): 710–12.

Dietz, T. and P.C. Stern, 2002. Exploring new tools for environmental protection. In T. Dietz and P.C. Stern (eds): *New Tools for Environmental Protection. Education, Information and Voluntary Measures*. Washington, DC: National Academy Press, pp. 3–15.

Dietz, T., E. Ostrom and P.C. Stern, 2003. The struggle to govern the commons. *Science*, **302**(5652): 1907–12.

DiMaggio, P. and W.W. Powell, 1981. *The New Institutionalism in Organizational Analysis*. Chicago, IL: University of Chicago Press.

DiMaggio, P. and W.W. Powell, 1983. The iron cage revisited: institutional isomorphism and collective rationality in organizational fields. *American Sociological Review*, **48**(2): 147–60.

Dolman, P., 2000. Biodiversity and ethics. In T. O'Riordan (ed.): *Environmental Science for Environmental Management*. Harlow, UK: Pearson Education Limited, pp. 119–48.

Druckman, A. and T. Jackson, 2009. The carbon footprint of UK households 1990–2004: a socio-economically disaggregated, quasi-multi-regional input–output model. *Ecological Economics*, **68**(7): 2066–77.

Dryzek, J.S., 2002. *Deliberative Democracy and Beyond. Liberals, Critics, Contestations*. Oxford: Oxford University Press.

Dryzek, J.S., 2013. *The Politics of the Earth. Environmental Discourses*. 3rd edition. Oxford: Oxford University Press.

Dryzek, J.S., R.E. Goodin, A. Tucker and B. Reber, 2008. Promethean elites encounter precautionary publics. The case of GM foods. *Science, Technology and Human Values*, **34**(3): 263–88.

Dryzek, J.S., D. Downes, C. Hunold, D. Schlosberg with H.-K. Hernes, 2003. *Green States and Social Movements: Environmentalism in the United States, United Kingdom, Germany, and Norway*. Oxford: Oxford University Press.

Dunne, T., M. Kurki and S. Smith (eds), 2010. *International Relations Theories. Discipline and Diversity*. 2nd edition. New York: Oxford University Press.

Eckerberg, K. and M. Joas, 2004, Multi-level environmental governance: a concept under stress? *Local Environment*, **9**(5): 405–12.

Eek, D., A. Biel and T. Gärling, 2001. Cooperation in asymmetric social dilemmas when equality is perceived as unfair. *Journal of Applied Social Psychology*, **31**(3): 649–66.

EFTEC (Economics for the Environment Consultancy), IEEP (Institute for European Environmental Policy) and IUCN (International Organization for Conservation of Nature), 2010. *The Use of Market-Based Instruments for Biodiversity Protection – The Case of Habitat Banking – Technical Report for EC DG Environment*. London: EFTEC.

Eggertsson, T., 1990. *Economic Behavior and Institutions*. Cambridge, UK: Cambridge University Press.

Ehrlich, P.R. and A.H. Ehrlich, 1992. The value of biodiversity. *Ambio*, **21**(3): 219–26.

Ehrlich, P.R. and J. Holdren, 1971. Impact of population growth. *Science*, **171**(3977): 1212–17.

Einsiedel, E.F., E. Jelsoe and T. Breck, 2001. Publics at the technology table: the consensus confer- ence in Denmark, Canada, and Australia. *Public Understanding of Science*, **10**(1): 83–98.

Elder-Vass, D., 2007. Reconciling Archer and Bourdieu in an emergentist theory of action. *Sociological Theory*, **25**(4): 325–46.

Elster, J. (ed.), 1998. *Deliberative Democracy*. Cambridge, UK: Cambridge University Press.

Emery, T.J., B.S. Green, C. Gardner and J. Tisdell, 2012. Are input controls required in individ- ual transferable quota fisheries to address ecosystem based fisheries management objectives? *Marine Policy*, **36**(1): 122–31.

Ensminger, J., 1996. Culture and property rights. In S. Hanna, C. Folke and K.G. Mäler (eds): *Rights to Nature: Ecological, Economic, Cultural, and Political Principles of Institutions for the Environment*. Washington, DC: Island Press, pp. 179–204.

Esping-Andersen, G., 1990. *The Three Worlds of Welfare Capitalism*. Princeton, NJ: Princeton University Press.

Esposito, R.T., 2013. The social enterprise revolution in corporate law: a primer on emerging corporate entities in Europe and the United States and the case for the benefit corporation. *William & Mary Business Law Review*, **4**: 639–767.

Etzioni, A., 1975. *A Comparative Analysis of Complex Organizations*. New York: Free Press.

Etzioni, A., 1988. *The Moral Dimension: Toward a New Economics*, New York: Free Press.

European Union Center of North Carolina, 2007. The EU US dispute over GMOs. Risk perceptions and the quest for regulatory dominance. *EU Briefings*. Accessed 21 June 2015 at http://europe.unc.edu/wp-content/uploads/2013/08/Brief0705-GMOs.pdf.

Evans, L.T., 1980. The natural history of crop yield: a combination of improved varieties of crop plants and technological innovations continues to increase productivity, but the highest yields are approaching limits set by biological constraints. *American Scientist*, **68**(4): 388–97.

Faber, M., R. Mansetten and J. Proops, 1996. *Ecological Economics. Concepts and Methods*. Cheltenham, UK and Brookfield, VT, USA: Edward Elgar Publishing.

Fahrig, L., 2003. Effects of habitat fragmentation on biodiversity. *Annual Review of Ecology, Evolution, and Systematics*, **34**(1): 487–515.

FAO (Food and Agriculture Organization), 2009. Global agriculture towards 2050. *How to Feed the World. High-level Expert Forum*. Accessed 11 June 2015 at http://www.fao.org/fileadmin/ templates/wsfs/docs/Issues_papers/HLEF2050_Global_Agriculture.pdf.

FAO (Food and Agriculture Organization), 2010. *Global Forest Resources Assessment 2010. Main Report*. Rome: FAO.

FAO (Food and Agriculture Organization), 2012a. FAOSTAT. Accessed 31 January 2012 at http://faostat3.fao.org/home/E.

FAO (Food and Agriculture Organization), 2012b. *The State of World Fisheries and Aquaculture 2012*. Rome: FAO. Accessed 28 June 2015 at http://www.fao.org/docrep/016/i2727e/ i2727e.pdf.

FAO (Food and Agriculture Organization), 2015. FAOSTAT. Accessed 6 February 2015 at http:// faostat3.fao.org/home/E.

Farley, J., D. Baker, D. Batker, C. Koliba, R. Matteson and R. Mills et al., 2007. Opening the policy window for ecological economics: Katrina as a focusing event. *Ecological Economics*, **63**(2–3): 344–54.

Fehr, E. and S. Gächter, 2002. Altruistic punishment in humans. *Nature*, **415**(6868): 137–40.

Fehr, E. and H. Gintis, 2007. Human motivation and social cooperation: experimental and analytical foundations. *Annual Review of Sociology*, **33**(3): 1–22.

Feinberg, M. and R. Willer, 2010. Apocalypse soon? Dire messages reduce belief in global warming by contradicting just-world beliefs. *Psychological Science*, **22**(1): 34–8.

Fernández-Giménez, M.E., 2002. Spatial and social boundaries and the paradox of pastoral land tenure: a case study from postsocialist Mongolia. *Human Ecology*, **30**(1): 49–78.

Figueira, J., S. Greco and M. Ehrgott, 2005. *Multiple Criteria Decision Analysis. State of the Art Surveys*. Berlin: Springer.

Finlayson, A.C. and B.J. McCay, 2000. Crossing the threshold of ecosystem resilience: the commercial extinction of northern cod. In F. Berkes and C. Folke (eds): *Linking Social and Ecological Systems. Management Practices and Social Mechanisms for Building Resilience*. Cambridge, UK: Cambridge University Press, pp. 311–38.

Finnemore, M. and K. Sikkink, 1998. International norm dynamics and political change. *International Organization*, **52**(4): 887–917.

Fisher, G., M. Shah, H. van Velthuizen and F. Nachtergaele (eds), 2001. *Global Agro-ecological Assessment for Agriculture in the 21st Century. Summary Report of the IIASA Land Use Project*. Laxenburg, Austria: International Institute for Applied Systems Analysis (IIASA).

Fisher, J., 2012. No pay, no care? A case study exploring motivations for participation in payments for ecosystem services in Uganda. *Oryx*, **46**(1): 45–54.

Fisher, R. and W. Ury, 1991. *Getting to Yes. Negotiating an Agreement Without Giving In*. London: The Random House Group.

Folke, C., F. Berkes and J. Colding, 1998. Ecological practices and social mechanisms for building resilience and sustainability. In F. Berkes and C. Folke (eds): *Linking Social and Ecological Systems: Management Practices and Social Mechanisms for Building Resilience*. Cambridge, UK: Cambridge University Press, pp. 414–36.

FONAFIFO (Fondo Nacional de Financiamento Forestal), 2013. Website. Accessed 20 December 2013 at http://www.fonafifo.go.cr/home/index.html.

Forest Trends & the Ecosystem Marketplace, 2008. *Payments for Ecosystem Services: Market Profiles*. Washington, DC: Forest Trends. Accessed 8 July 2015 at http://ecosystemmarketplace.com/documents/acrobat/PES_Matrix_Profiles_PROFOR.pdf.

Forsyth, T., 2014. Climate justice is not just ice. *Geoforum*, **54**: 230–32.

Forsythe, R., J.L. Horowitz, N.E. Savin and M. Sefton, 1994. Fairness in simple bargaining experiments. *Games and Economic Behavior*, **6**(3): 347–69.

Foster, J.B. and F. Magdoff, 2009. *The Great Financial Crisis: Causes and Consequences*. New York: Monthly Review Press.

Frank, R.H., 1987. If Homo Economicus could choose his own utility function, would he want one with a conscience? *The American Economic Review*, **77**(4): 593–604.

Fredriksson, P.G., J.A. List and D.L. Millime, 2004. Chasing the smokestack: strategic policymaking with multiple instruments. *Regional Science and Urban Economics*, **34**(4): 387–410.

Frey, B.S., 1997. *Not Just For the Money. An Economic Theory of Personal Motivation*. Cheltenham, UK and Lyme, NH, USA: Edward Elgar Publishing.

Funtowicz, S. and J.R. Ravetz, 1993. Science for the post-normal age. *Futures*, **25**(7): 735–55.

Gabriel, R. 2013. *Why I Buy: Self, Taste, and Consumer Society in America*. Chicago, IL: University of Chicago Press.

Gagnon, N., C. Hall and L. Brinker, 2009. A preliminary investigation of the energy return on energy investment for global oil and gas production. *Energies*, **2**(3): 490–503.

Galloway, J., 2005. The global nitrogen cycle: past, present and future. In W. Steffen, A. Sanderson, P.D. Tyson, J. Jäger, P.A. Matson and B. Moore III et al.: *Global Change and the Earth System. A Planet Under Pressure*. 2nd edition. Berlin: Springer Verlag, pp. 122–3.

Garrett, D.E., 1987. The effectiveness of marketing policy boycotts: environmental opposition to marketing. *Journal of Marketing*, **51**(2): 46–57.

Gaventa, J., 1980. *Power and Powerlessness. Quiescence and Rebellion in an Appalachian Valley*. Oxford: Clarendon Press.

George, R., 2008. *The Big Necessity. Adventures in the World of Human Waste*. London: Portobello Books.

Giampietro, M., 2003. *Multi-Scale Integrated Analysis of Agroecosystems*. London: CRC Press.

Gibbons, P. and D.B. Lindenmayer, 2007. Offsets for land clearing: no net loss or the tail wagging the dog? *Ecological Management and Restoration*, **8**(1): 26–31.

Gibbs, M.T., 2010. Why ITQs on target species are inefficient at achieving ecosystem based fisheries management outcomes. *Marine Policy*, **34**(3): 708–9.

Giddens, A., 1984. *The Constitution of Society*. Cambridge, UK: Polity Press.

Giddens, A., 1991. *Modernity and Self-identity: Self and Society in the Late Modern Age*. Stanford, CA: Stanford University Press.

Gintis, H., 2000. Beyond homo economicus: evidence from experimental economics. *Ecological Economics*, **35**(3): 311–22.

Gneezy, U. and A. Rustichini, 2000a. Pay enough or don't pay at all. *Quarterly Journal of Economics*, **115**(3): 791–810.

Gneezy, U. and A. Rustichini, 2000b. A fine is a price. *The Journal of Legal Studies*, **29**(1): 1–17.

Goldewijk, K.K., 2005. Three centuries of global population growth: a spatial reference population (density) database for 1700–2000. *Population and Environment*, **26**(4): 343–67.

Gómez-Baggethun, E., R. de Groot, P.L. Lomas and C. Montes, 2010. The history of ecosystem services in economic theory and practice: from early notions to markets and payment schemes. *Ecological Economics*, **69**(6): 1209–18.

Gonthier, D.J., K.K. Ennis, S. Farinas, H.-Y. Hsieh, A.L. Iverson, P. Batary et al., 2014. Biodiversity conservation in agriculture requires a multi-scale approach. *Proceedings of the Royal Society B*, **281**(1791).

Goodin, R., 1996. Enfranchising the earth, and its alternatives. *Political Studies*, **44**(5): 835–49.

Graeber, D., 2001. *Toward an Anthropological Theory of Value. The False Coin of Our Own Dreams*. New York: Palgrave Macmillan.

Grafton, R.Q., 1996. Individual transferable quotas: theory and practice. *Reviews in Fish Biology and Fisheries*, **6**(1): 5–20.

Grafton, R.Q., R. Hilborn, L. Ridgeway, D. Squires, M. Williams and S. Garcia et al., 2008. Positioning fisheries in a changing world. *Marine Policy*, **32**(4): 630–34.

Graves, J. and D. Reavy, 1996. *Global Environmental Change*. London: Longman.

Gregory, C., 1982. *Gifts and Commodities*. London: Academic Press.

Greif, A., 2006. History lessons. The birth of impersonal change: the community responsibility system and impartial justice. *Journal of Economic Perspectives*, **20**(2): 221–36.

Greif, A., 2008. Coercion and exchange: how did markets evolve? Stanford, CA: Stanford University – Department of Economics; Canadian Institute for Advanced Research (CIFAR). Accessed 19 June 2015 at http://papers.ssrn.com/sol3/papers.cfm?abstract_id=1304204.

Grieg-Gran, M. and J. Bishop, 2004. How can markets for ecosystem services benefit the poor? In D. Roe (ed.): *The Millennium Development Goals and Conservation: Managing Nature's Wealth for Society's Health*. London: IIED; Russell Press, pp. 55–72.

Grieg-Gran, M., I. Porras and S. Wunder, 2005. How can market mechanisms for forest environmental services help the poor? Preliminary lessons from Latin America. *World Development*, **33**(9): 1511–27.

Gross-Camp, N.D., A. Martin, S. McGuire, B. Kebede and J. Munyarukaza, 2012. Payments for ecosystem services in an African protected area: exploring issues of legitimacy, fairness, equity and effectiveness. *Oryx*, **46**(1): 24–33.

Grusec, J.E. and P.D. Hastings (eds), 2007. *Handbook of Socialization: Theory and Research*. New York: Guilford Press.

Gulati, A., R.S. Meinzen-Dick and K.V. Raju, 2004. *Institutional Reforms in Indian Irrigation*. New Delhi: Sage.

Gunderson, L.H., C.R. Allen and C.S. Holling (eds), 2010. *Foundations of Ecological Resilience*. Washington, DC: Island Press.

Güth, W., R. Schmittberger and B. Schwarze, 1982. An experimental analysis of ultimatum bargaining. *Journal of Economic Behavior and Organization*, **3**(4): 367–88.

Gutmann, A. and D. Thompson, 2004. *Why Deliberative Democracy?* Princeton, NJ: Princeton University Press.

Haas, P.M., R.O. Keohane and M.A. Levy (eds), 1993. *Institutions for the Earth: Sources of Effective International Environmental Protection*. Cambridge, MA: The MIT Press.

Haberl, H., F. Krausmann and S. Gingrich, 2006. Ecological embeddedness of the economy. A socioecological perspective on humanity's economic activities 1700–2000. *Economic and Political Weekly*, **XLI**(47): 4896–904.

Haberl, H., M. Fischer-Kowalski, F. Krausmann, J. Martinez-Alier and V. Winiwarter, 2011. A socio-metabolic transition towards sustainability? Challenges for another great transformation. *Sustainable Development*, **19**(1): 1–14.

Habermas, J., 1979. *Communication and the Evolution of Society*. Boston, MA: Beacon Press.

Habermas, J., 1984. *The Theory of Communicative Action. Vol. One: Reason and the Rationalization of Society*. Boston, MA: Beacon Press.

Habermas, J., 1996. *Between Facts and Norms, Contributions to a Discourse Theory of Law and Democracy*. Cambridge, MA: The MIT Press.

Hagedorn, K., 2008. Particular requirements for institutional analysis in nature-related sectors. *European Review of Agricultural Economics*, **35**(3): 357–84.

Hahn, T., 2000. Property rights, ethics and conflict resolution. Foundations of the Sami economy in Sweden. Dissertation. *Agraria No. 258*. Uppsala: Dept of Economics, Swedish University of Agricultural Sciences.

Hajer, M.A., 1995. *The Politics of Environmental Discourse: Ecological Modernization and the Policy Process*. Oxford: Clarendon Press.

Hall, C.A.S. and K. Klitgaard, 2012. *Energy and the Wealth of Nations: Understanding the Biophysical Economy*. New York: Springer.

Hall, C.A.S., J.G. Lambert and S.B. Balogh, 2014. EROI of different fuels and implications for society. *Energy Policy*, **64**: 141–52.

Hall, P.A. and R.C.R. Taylor, 1996. Political science and the three new institutionalisms. *Political Studies*, **44**(5): 936–57.

Hamby, A.L., 2004. *For the Survival of Democracy: Franklin Roosevelt and the World Crisis of the 1930s*. New York: Free Press.

Hamilton, J., 2009. Causes and consequences of the oil shock of 2007–2008. *Brooking Papers on Economic Activity*. Accessed 9 July 2015 at http://www.brookings.edu/~/media/Projects/BPEA/Spring%202009/2009a_bpea_hamilton.PDF.

Hammar, H. and Å. Löfgren, 2004. Leaded gasoline in Europe. Differences in timing and taxes. In W. Harrington, R.D. Morgenstern and T. Sterner (eds): *Choosing Environmental Policies. Comparing Instruments and Outcomes in the United States and Europe*. Washington, DC: Resources for the Future, pp. 192–205.

Hammitt, J.K., 2004. CFCs: a look across two continents. In W. Harrington, R.D. Morgenstern and T. Sterner (eds): *Choosing Environmental Policies. Comparing Instruments and Outcomes in the United States and Europe*. Washington, DC: Resources for the Future, pp. 158–74.

Hanley, N. and E.B. Barbier, 2009. *Pricing Nature. Cost–Benefit Analysis and Environmental Policy*. Cheltenham, UK and Northampton, MA, USA: Edward Elgar Publishing.

Hanley, N. and C. Spash, 1993. *Cost–Benefit Analysis and the Environment*. Aldershot, UK and Brookfield, VT, USA: Edward Elgar Publishing.

Hanna, S., 1995. User participation and fishery management performance within the Pacific Fisheries Management Council. *Ocean Coastal Management*, **28**(1–3): 23–44.

Hannesson, R., 2004. *The Privatization of the Oceans*. Cambridge, MA: The MIT Press.

Hansen, J., M. Sato, P. Kharecha, D. Beerling, R. Berner and V. Masson-Delmotte et al., 2008. Target atmospheric CO_2: where should humanity aim? *Open Atmospheric Science Journal*, **2**(1): 217–31.

Hardin, G., 1968. The tragedy of the commons. *Science*, **162**(3859): 1243–8.

Harrell, D.E., E.S. Gaustad, J.B. Boles, S.F. Griffith, R.M. Miller and R.B. Woods, 2005. *Unto a Good Land: A History of The American People. Vol. 2: From 1865*. Grand Rapids, MI: Wm. B. Eerdmans.

Harrington, W., 2004. Industrial water pollution in the United States. In W. Harrington, R.D. Morgenstern and T. Sterner (eds): *Choosing Environmental Policies. Comparing Instruments and Outcomes in the United States and Europe*. Washington, DC: Resources for the Future, pp. 67–90.

Harrington, W., R.D. Morgenstern and T. Sterner, 2004a. Overview: comparing instrument choices. In W. Harrington, R.D. Morgenstern and T. Sterner (eds): *Choosing Environmental Policies. Comparing Instruments and Outcomes in the United States and Europe*. Washington, DC: Resources for the Future, pp. 1–22.

Harrington, W., R.D. Morgenstern and T. Sterner (eds), 2004b. *Choosing Environmental Policies. Comparing Instruments and Outcomes in the United States and Europe*. Washington, DC: Resources for the Future.

Haufler, V., 2009. Transnational actors and global environmental governance. In M.A. Delmas and O.R. Young (eds): *Governance for the Environment. New Perspectives*. Cambridge, UK: Cambridge University Press, pp. 119–43.

Haviland, W.A., 1999. *Cultural Anthropology*. Orlando, FL: Harcourt Brace & Company.

Hayek, F.A., 1931. *Prices and Production*. London: Routledge and Son.

Hayek, F.A., 1948. *Individualism and Economic Order*. London: University of Chicago Press.

Hayek, F.A., 1988. *The Fatal Conceit: The Errors of Socialism, Vol. 1 of Collected Works of F.A. Hayek*. London: Routledge.

Hayes, T.H., 2006. Parks, people, and forest protection: an institutional assessment of the effectiveness of protected areas. *World Development*, **34**(12): 2064–75.

Hechter, M. and S. Kanazawa, 1997. Sociological rational choice theory. *Annual Review of Sociology*, **23**(1): 191–214.

Heiskanen, E., 2005. The performative nature of consumer research: consumers' environmental awareness as an example. *Journal of Consumer Policy*, **28**(2): 179–201.

Helgason, A. and G. Palsson, 1998. Cash for quotas: disputes over the legitimacy of an economic model of fishing in Iceland. In J.G. Carrier and D. Miller (eds): *Virtualism. A New Political Economy*. Oxford: Berg, pp. 117–34.

Heller, M., unpublished manuscript. The effect of waste fee schemes on the degree of waste sorting in households. Department of International Environment and Development Studies, Norwegian University of Life Sciences.

Heller, M. and A. Vatn, under review. The divisive and disruptive effect of a weight based waste fee. Ecological Economics.

Hellwig, M.F., 2009. Systemic risk in the financial sector: an analysis of the subprime-mortgage financial crisis. *De Economist*, **157**(2): 129–207.

Henrich, J.R., R. Boyd, B.S. Bowles, C. Camerer, E. Fehr and H. Gintis et al., 2001. In search of homo economicus: behavioral experiments in 15 small-scale societies. *American Economic Review, Papers and Proceedings*, **91**(2): 73–8.

Hertsgaard, M., 1999. A global green deal. *The Nation*, **1**: 18–23.

Hicks, B. and C. Nelder, 2008. *Profit from the Peak: The End of Oil and the Greatest Investment Event of the Century*. Hoboken, NJ: John Wiley & Sons.

Hiedanpää, J. and D.W. Bromley, 2012. Contestations over biodiversity protection: considering Peircean semiosis. *Environmental Values*, **21**(3): 357–78.

Hiedanpää, J. and D.W. Bromley, 2014. Payments for ecosystem services: durable habits, dubious nudges, and doubtful efficacy. *Journal of Institutional Economics*, **10**(2): 175–95.

Hilborn, R., 2007. Defining success in fisheries and conflicts in objectives. *Marine Policy*, **31**(2): 153–8.

Hintermann, B., 2010. Allowance price drivers in the first phase of the EU ETS. *Journal of Environmental Economics and Management*, **59**(1): 43–56.

Hobbs, N.T., K.A. Galvin, C.J. Stokes, J.M. Lackett, A.J. Ash and R.B. Boone et al., 2008. Fragmentation of rangelands: implications for humans, animals, and landscapes. *Global Environmental Change*, **18**(4): 776–85.

Hodgson, G.M., 1988. *Economics and Institutions: A Manifesto for a Modern Institutional Economics*. Cambridge, UK: Polity Press.

Hodgson, G.M., 1996. *Economics and Evolution. Bringing Life Back into Economics*. Ann Arbor, MI: The University of Michigan Press.

Hodgson, G.M., 2007. The revival of Veblenian institutional economics. *Journal of Economic Issues*, **XLI**(2): 325–40.

Hoffman, E., K. McCabe, K. Shachat and V. Smith, 1994. Preferences, property rights, and anonymity in bargaining games. *Games and Economic Behavior*, **7**(3): 346–80.

Hofstad, O., 1990. A simple model of wood supply and clearing of African woodlands with special reference to Tanzania. *Journal of World Forest Resource Management*, **5**(1): 47–57.

Hoggan, J. and R. Littlemoore, 2009. *Climate Cover Up. The Crusade to Deny Global Warming*. Vancouver: Greystone Books.

Hohfeld, W.N., 1913. Some fundamental legal conceptions as applied in judicial reasoning. *Yale Law Journal*, **23**(1): 16–59.

Hohfeld, W.N., 1917. Fundamental legal conceptions as applied in judicial reasoning. *Yale Law Journal*, **26**(8): 710–70.

Holder, J. and M. Lee, 2007. *Environmental Protection. Law and Policy*. Cambridge, UK: Cambridge University Press.

Holland, A., 2002. Are choices tradeoffs? In D.W. Bromley and J. Paavola (eds): *Economics, Ethics and Environmental Policy. Contested Choices*. Oxford: Blackwell, pp. 17–34.

Holling, C.S., 1973. Resilience and stability of ecological systems. *Annual Review of Ecological Systems*, **4**: 1–24.

Holt, C.A., L. Langan and A.P. Villamil, 1986. Market power in oral double auctions. *Economic Inquiry*, **24**(1): 107–23.

Holtz, G., M. Brugnach and C. Pahl-Wostl, 2008. Specifying 'regime' – a framework for defining and describing regimes in transition research. *Technological Forecasting & Social Change*, **75**(5): 623–43.

Homans, G., 1961. *Social Behaviour: Its Elementary Forms*. London: Routledge and Kegan Paul.

Homedes, N. and A. Ugalde, 2005. Why neoliberal health reforms have failed in Latin America. *Health Policy*, **71**(1): 83–96.

Honoré, A.M., 1961. Ownership. In A.G. Guest (ed.): *Oxford Essays in Jurisprudence*. Oxford: Clarendon Press, pp. 107–47.

Hooley, G.J., G.E. Greenley, J.W. Cadogan and J. Fahy, 2005. The performance impact of marketing resources. *Journal of Business Research*, **58**(1): 18–27.

Hoornweg, D. and B.-T. Perinaz, 2012. *What a Waste: A Global Review of Solid Waste Management*.

Washington, DC: World Bank. Accessed 7 July 2015 at http://siteresources.worldbank.org/INTURBANDEVELOPMENT/Resources/336387-1334852610766/What_a_Waste2012_Final.pdf.

Horowitz, J.K. and K.E. McConnell, 2002. A review of WTP/WTA studies. *Journal of Environmental Economics and Management*, **44**(3): 426–47.

HSBC (Hong Kong and Shanghai Banking Corporation), 2009. *A Climate for Recovery. The Colour of Stimulus Goes Green*. London: HSCB Global Research.

Huitema, D., C. Cornelisse and B. Ottow, 2010. Is the jury still out? Toward greater insight in policy learning in participatory decision processes – the case of Dutch citizens' juries on water management in the Rhine Basin. *Ecology and Society*, **15**(1): Art. 16.

Hume, D. [1742] 1985. Of the dignity or meanness of human nature. In *Essays Moral, Political, and Literary, Vol. I*. Indianapolis, IL: Liberty Press.

Hutton, J.M., W.M. Adams and J.C. Murombedzi, 2005. Back to the barriers? Changing narratives in biodiversity conservation. *Forum for Development Studies*, **32**(2): 341–70.

ICA (International Co-operative Alliance), 1995. Co-operative identity, values and principles. Accessed 23 March 2015 at http://ica.coop/en/whats-co-op/co-operative-identity-values-principles.

Ikeme, J. 2003. Equity, environmental justice and sustainability: incomplete approaches in climate change politics. *Global Environmental Change*, **13**(3): 195–206.

IMF (International Monetary Fund), 2012. IMF data. Accessed 4 February 2012 at http://www.imf.org/external/data.htm.

Ingram, J.C., D. Wilkie, T. Clements, R.B. McNab, F. Nelson and E.H. Baur et al. 2014. Evidence of Payments for Ecosystem Services as a mechanism for supporting biodiversity conservation and rural livelihood. *Ecosystem Services*, **7**: 10–21.

Inoue, M., 1998. Evaluation of local resource management systems as the premise for introducing participatory forest management. *Journal of Forest Economics*, **44**(3): 15–22.

IPCC (Intergovernmental Panel on Climate Change), 2007a. *Climate Change 2007: Impacts, Adaptation and Vulnerability*. Accessed 11 June 2015 at https://www.ipcc.ch/publications_and_data/publications_ipcc_fourth_assessment_report_wg2_report_impacts_adaptation_and_vulnerability.htm.

IPCC (Intergovernmental Panel on Climate Change), 2007b. *Climate Change 2007: Synthesis Report*. Accessed 11 June 2015 at https://www.ipcc.ch/publications_and_data/publications_ipcc_fourth_assessment_report_synthesis_report.htm.

IPCC (Intergovernmental Panel on Climate Change), 2014a. *Climate Change 2014: Synthesis Report*. Accessed 11 June 2015 at http://www.ipcc.ch/report/ar5/syr/.

IPCC (Intergovernmental Panel on Climate Change), 2014b. *Climate Change 2014: Impacts, Adaptation and Vulnerability*. Accessed 11 June 2015 at http://www.ipcc.ch/report/ar5/wg2/.

IUCN (International Union for Conservation of Nature), 1994. *Guidelines for Protected Area Management Categories*. Gland, Switzerland: IUCN.

Jackson, T., 2009. *Prosperity Without Growth. Economics for a Finite Planet*. London: Earthscan.

Jacobs, M., 1997. Environmental valuation, deliberative democracy and public decision-making. In J. Foster (ed.): *Valuing Nature? Economics, Ethics and Environment*. London: Routledge, pp. 211–31.

Jahnke, R.A., 2000. The phosphorus cycle. In M.C. Jacobson, R.J. Charlson, H. Rhode and G.H. Orians (eds): *Earth System Science: From Biogeochemical Cycles to Global Change*. Amsterdam: Academic Press, pp. 360–76.

Jensen, Ø., 2012. Law of the sea: protection and preservation of the marine environment. In S. Andresen, E.L. Boasson and G. Hønneland (eds): *International Environmental Agreements. An Introduction*. Abingdon, UK: Routledge, pp. 67–82.

Jentoft, S. and T. Kristoffersen, 1989. Fishermen's co-management: the case of the Lofoten Fishery. *Human Organization*, **48**(4): 355–65.

Jentoft, S., M. Bavinck, D.S. Johnson and K.T. Thom, 2009. Fisheries co-management and legal pluralism: how an analytical problem becomes an institutional one. *Human Organization*, **68**(1): 27–38.

Jevons, W.S. [1871] 1957. *Theory of Political Economy*. 5th edition. New York: Augustus M. Kelly.

Jindal, R., B. Swallow and J. Kerr, 2008. Forestry-based carbon sequestration projects in Africa: potential benefits and challenges. *Natural Resources Forum*, **32**(2): 116–30.

Jones, D., P. Leiby and I. Paik, 2004. Oil price shocks and the macroeconomy: what has been learned since 1996? *The Energy Journal*, **25**(2): 1–32.

Joss, S., 1998. Danish consensus conferences as a model for participatory technology assessment. *Science and Public Policy*, **25**(1): 2–22.

Joss, S. and J. Durant, 1995. The UK national consensus conference on plant biotechnology. *Public Understanding of Science*, **4**(2): 195–204.

Juda, L., 2001. The United Nations Fish Stocks Agreement. In O.S. Stokke and Ø.B. Thommessen (eds): *Yearbook of International Co-operation on Environment and Development 2001/2002*. London: Earthscan Publications, pp. 53–8.

Juffe-Bignoli, D., N.D. Burgess, H. Bingham, E.M.S. Belle, M.G. de Lima and M. Deguignet et al., 2014. *Protected Planet Report 2014*. Cambridge, UK: UNEP-WCMC.

Jul-Larsen, E., J. Kolding, R. Övera, J.R. Nielsen and P.A.M. van Zwieten, 2003. Management, co-management or no management? Major dilemmas in southern African freshwater fisheries. 1. Synthesis report. *FAO Fisheries Technical Paper. No. 426/1*. Rome: FAO.

Kahan, D.M., H. Jenkins-Smith and D. Braman, 2011. Cultural cognition of scientific consensus. *Journal of Risk Research*, **14**(2): 147–174.

Kahan, D.M., E. Peters, M. Wittlin, P. Slovic, L. Larrimore Quellette and D. Braman et al., 2012. The polarizing impact of science literacy and numeracy on perceived climate change risk. *Nature Climate Change*, **2**: 732–5.

Kahneman, D., 2011. *Thinking, Fast and Slow*. London: Allen Lane.

Kahneman, D. and J.L. Knetsch, 1992. Valuing public goods: the purchase of moral satisfaction. *Journal of Environmental Economics and Management*, **22**(1): 57–70.

Kallis, G., C. Kerschner and J. Martinez-Alier, 2012. The economics of degrowth. *Ecological Economics*, **84**: 72–180.

Kant, I. [1785] 1956. *Groundwork of the Metaphysics of Morals*. London: Hutchinson.

Kapp, K.W., 1971. *The Social Costs of Private Enterprise*. New York: Schoken Books.

Kasser, T. and A.D. Kanner (eds), 2004. *Psychology and Consumer Culture: The Struggle for a Good Life in a Materialistic World*. Washington, DC: American Psychology Association.

Kasser, T., R.M. Ryan, C.E. Couchman and K.M. Sheldon, 2004. Materialistic values: their causes and consequences. In T. Kasser and A.D. Kanner (eds): *Psychology and Consumer Culture: The Struggle for a Good Life in a Materialistic World*. Washington, DC: American Psychology Association, pp. 11–28.

Katz, D., 2006. Going with the flow: preserving and restoring instream water allocation. In P.H. Gleick (ed.): *The World's Water 2006–2007. Biennial Report on Freshwater Resources*. Washington, DC: Island Press, pp. 29–39.

Kellenberg, D.K., 2009. An empirical investigation of the pollution haven effect with strategic environment and trade policy. *Journal of International Economics*, **78**(2): 242–55.

Keller, E.A. and D.B. Botkin, 2008. *Essential Environmental Science*. Hoboken, NJ: Wiley.

Kenyon, W., N. Hanley and C. Nevin, 2001. Citizens' juries: an aid to environmental valuation? *Environment and Planning C: Government and Policy*, **19**(4): 557–66.

Kerr, A., S. Cunningham-Burley and A. Amos, 1998. The new genetics and health: mobilising lay expertise. *Public Understanding of Science*, **7**(1): 41–60.

Kerschner, C., C. Prell, K. Feng and K. Hubacek, 2013. Economic vulnerability to peak oil. *Global Environmental Change*, **23**(6): 1424–33.

KfW, 2015. Website. Accessed 8 July 2015 at https://www.kfw-entwicklungsbank.de/International-financing/KfW-Entwicklungsbank/.

Kilihama, F.B., 2014. Evolution and status of participatory forest management in Tanzania and future direction. *Tanzania Journal of Forestry and Nature Conservation*, **83**(1): 5–26.

Kingdon, J., 1984. *Agenda, Alternatives, and Public Policies*. Boston, MA: Little, Brown & Co.

Kleijn, D. and W.J. Sutherland, 2003. How effective are European agri-environment schemes in conserving and promoting biodiversity? *Journal of Applied Ecology*, **40**(6): 947–69.

Kleijn, D., R.A. Baquero, Y. Clough, M. Diaz, J. de Esteban and F. Fernandez et al., 2006. Mixed biodiversity benefits of agrienvironment schemes in five European countries. *Ecology Letters*, **9**(3): 243–54.

Klooster, D., 2005. Environmental certification of forests: the evolution of environmental governance in a commodity network. *Journal of Rural Studies*, **21**(4): 403–17.

Kluser, S. and P. Peduzzi, 2007. *Global Pollinator Decline: A Literature Review*. Geneva: UNEP/GRID-Europe.

Kolstad, C., 2000. *Environmental Economics*. Oxford: Oxford University Press.

Konikow, L.F. and E. Kendy, 2005. Groundwater depletion: a global problem. *Hydrogeology Journal*, **13**(1): 317–20.

Kosoy, N. and E. Corbera, 2010. Payments for ecosystem services as commodity feticism. *Ecological Economics*, **69**(6): 1228–36.

Kosoy, N., E. Corbera and K. Brown, 2008. Participation in payments for ecosystem services: case studies from the Lacandon rainforest, Mexico. *Geoforum*, **39**(6): 2073–83.

Kovarik, W., 2005. Ethyl-leaded gasoline: how a classic occupational disease became an international public health disaster. *International Journal of Occupational and Environmental Health*, **11**(4): 384–97.

Krause, T. and L. Loft, 2013. Benefit distribution and equity in Equador's Socio Bosque Program. *Society and Natural Resources*, **26**(10): 1170–84.

Krosnick, J.A., A.L. Holbrook, L. Lowe and P.S. Visser, 2006. The origins and consequences of democratic citizens' policy agendas: a study of popular concern about global warming. *Climate Change*, **77**(1–2): 7–43.

Kull, C.A., X.A. de Sartre and M. Castro-Larrañaga, 2015. The political economy of ecosystem services. *Geoforum*, **61**: 122–34.

Kvakkestad, V., P.K. Rørstad and A. Vatn, 2015. Norwegian farmers' perspectives on agriculture and agricultural payments: between productivism and cultural landscapes. *Land Use Policy*, **42**: 83–92.

Laherrere, J., 2006. Oil and gas: what future? Groningen Annual Energy Convention, 21 November 2006. Accessed 11 June 2015 at http://oilcrisis.com/laherrere/groningen.pdf.

Laherrere, J., 2012. Personal communications – additional material to Laherrere (2006) – e-mails 4 February 2012 and 7 February 2012.

Lakatos, I., 1974. Falsification and the methodology of scientific research programmes. In I. Lakatos and A. Musgrave (eds): *Criticism and the Growth of Knowledge*. Cambridge, UK: Cambridge University Press, pp. 91–196.

Lamoreux, J.F., J.C. Morrison, T.H. Ricketts, D.M. Olson, E. Dinerstein and M.W. McKnight et al., 2006. Global tests of biodiversity concordance and the importance of endemism. *Nature*, **440**(7081): 212–14.

Lane, C., 2000. *Custodian of the Commons: Pastoral Land Tenure in East and West Africa*. London: Earthscan Publications.

Latouche, S., 2009. *Farewell to Growth*. Cambridge, UK: Polity Press.

Lau, K.M. and K.M. Kim, 2006. Observational relationships between aerosol and Asian monsoon rainfall, and circulation. *Geophysical Research Letters*, **33**(21): L21810.

Layard, P.R.G., 2005. *Happiness: Lessons from a New Science*. New York: Penguin Press.

Ledyard, J.O., 1995. Public goods: a survey of experimental research. In J.H. Kagel and A.E. Roth (eds): *The Handbook of Experimental Economics*. Princeton, NJ: Princeton University Press, pp. 111–94.

Lee, M. and J. Battilana, 2013. How the zebra got its stripes: imprinting of individuals and hybrid social ventures. *Harvard Business School Organizational Behavior Unit Working Paper No. 14-005*.

Lemos. M.C. and A. Agrawal, 2009. Environmental governance and political science. In M.A. Delmas and O. Young (eds): *Governance for the Environment. New Perspectives*. Cambridge, UK: Cambridge University Press, pp. 69–97.

Levi, M., 1998. A state of trust. In V. Braithwaite and M. Levi (eds): *Trust and Governance*. New York: Russell Sage Foundation.

Levin, H.M. (ed.), 2001. *Privatizing Education: Can the Marketplace Deliver Choice, Efficiency, Equity, and Social Cohesion?* Boulder, CO: Westview Press.

Levin, S.A. (ed.), 2009. *The Princeton Guide to Ecology*. Princeton, NJ: Princeton University Press.

Linklater, A., 1996. The achievements of critical theory. In S. Smith, K. Booth and M. Zalewski (eds): *International Theory: Positivism and Beyond*. Cambridge, UK: Cambridge University Press, pp. 279–98.

Lövbrand, E. and J. Kahn, 2010. The deliberative turn in green political theory. In K. Bäckstrand, J. Kahn, A. Kronsell and E. Lövbrand (eds): *Environmental Politics and Deliberative Democracy. Examining the Promise of New Modes of Governance*. Cheltenham, UK and Northampton, MA, USA: Edward Elgar Publishing, pp. 47–64.

Lukes, S., 2005. *Power. A Radical View*. 2nd edition. New York: Palgrave Macmillan.

Mace, G., H. Masundire and J. Baillie, 2005. Biodiversity. In H. Hassan, R. Scholes and N.J. Ash (eds): *Ecosystems and Human Wellbeing: Current State and Trends*. Washington, DC: Island Press, pp. 77–122.

MacIntyre, A., 1986. *After Virtue*. London: Duckworth.

Maddison, A., 2001. *The World Economy: A Millennial Perspective*. Paris: OECD.

Madsen, B., N. Carroll and K.M. Brands, 2010. *State of Biodiversity Markets: Offset and Compensation Programs Worldwide*. Washington, DC: Ecoystem Marketplace. Accessed 8 July 2015 at http://www.ecosystemmarketplace.com/documents/acrobat/sbdmr.pdf.

Mahanty, S., H. Suich and L. Tacconi, 2013. Access and benefits in payments for environmental services and implications for REDD+: lessons from seven PES schemes. *Land Use Policy*, **31**: 38–47.

Malinowski, B., 1922 [2002]. *Argonauts of the Western Pacific. An Account of Native Enterprise and Adventure in the Archipelagoes of Melanesian New Guinea*. Abingdon, UK: Routledge.

March, J.G., 1994. *A Primer on Decision Making. How Decisions Happen*. New York: Free Press.

March, J.G. and J.P. Olsen, 1989. *Rediscovering Institutions. The Organizational Basis of Politics*. New York: Free Press.

March, J.G. and J.P. Olsen, 1995. *Democratic Governance*. New York: Free Press.

Marglin, S.A., 1991. Understanding capitalism: control versus efficiency. In B. Gustafsson (ed.): *Power and Economic Institutions. Reinterpretations in Economic History*. Aldershot, UK and Brookfield, VT, USA: Edward Elgar Publishing, pp. 225–52.

Marine Stewardship Council, 2013. Get certified! Fisheries. Accessed 9 February 2013 at http://www.msc.org/get-certified/fisheries.

Marletto, G., 2010. Structure, agency and change in the car regime. A review of the literature. *CREI Working Paper No. 6/2010.* Accessed 16 June 2015 at http://host.uniroma3.it/centri/crei/pubblicazioni/workingpapers2010/CREI_06_2010.pdf.

Marris, C., B. Wynne, P. Simmons and S. Weldon, 2001. *Public Perceptions of Agricultural Biotechnologies in Europe, Final Report of the PABE Research Project.* Accessed 20 June 2010 at http://www.keinegentechnik.de/bibliothek/basis/studien/eu_studie_akzeptanz_biotech_011201.pdf.

Marshall, A. [1890] 1949. *The Principles of Economics.* 8th edition. London: Macmillan.

Martinez-Alier, J., 2002. *The Environmentalism of the Poor.* Cheltenham, UK and Northampton, MA, USA: Edward Elgar Publishing.

Martinez-Alier, J., G. Munda and J. O'Neill, 1998. Weak comparability of values as a foundation of ecological economics. *Ecological Economics,* **26**(3): 277–86.

Marx, K. and F. Engels [1848] 1998. *Manifest der Kommunistischen Partei.* London: J.C. Burgbach. Translated and reprinted as K. Marx and F. Engels: *The Communist Manifesto,* introduction by M. Malia, New York: Penguin.

Mauss, M. [1925] 1965. *The Gift: Forms and Functions of Exchange in Archaic Societies.* Translation by I. Cunnison. New York: Northon.

Max-Neef, M. (with A. Elizalde and M. Hopenhayn) 1991. *Human-Scale Development – Conception, Application and Further Reflection.* New York: Apex Press.

Maxwell, J.A., 2012. *A Realist Approach for Qualitative Research.* Los Angeles, CA: Sage.

Mayumi, K. and M. Giampietro, 2006. The epistemological challenge of self-modifying systems: governance and sustainability in the post-normal science era. *Ecological Economics,* **57**(3): 382–99.

McAffe, K. and E.N. Shapiro, 2010. Payments for ecosystem services in Mexico: nature, neoliberalism, social movements, and the state. *Annals of the Association of American Geographers,* **100**(3): 579–99.

McCarthy, N., B. Swallow, M. Kirk and P. Hazell, 1999. *Property Rights, Risk and Livestock Development in Africa.* Washington, DC: ILRI and IFPRI.

McCay, B.J., C.F. Creed, A.C. Finlayson, R. Apostle and K. Mikalsen, 1995. Individual transferable quotas (ITQs) in Canadian and US fisheries. *Ocean Coastal Management,* **28**(1–3): 85–155.

McCright, A.M. and R.E. Dunlap, 2011. The politization of climate change and polarization in the American public's views of global warming, 2001–2010. *The Sociological Quarterly,* **52**(2): 155–94.

McElwee, P.D., 2006. Displacement and relocation redux: stories from Southeast Asia. *Conservation and Society,* **4**(3): 396–403.

McGregor. S., 2001. Neoliberalism and health care. *Journal of Consumer Studies,* **25**(2): 82–9.

McKean, M.A., 1992. Management of traditional common lands (*itiaichi*) in Japan. In D. Bromley (ed.): *Making the Commons Work. Theory, Practice and Policy.* San Francisco, CA: ICS Press, pp. 63–98.

McNally, R. and M. Levi, 2011. A crude predicament. The era of volatile oil prices. *Foreign Affairs,* **90**(4): 100–101. Accessed 19 June 2015 at http://www.relooney.com/NS3040/0_New_10333.pdf.

McNeish, J.-A. and A.C.A. Böhrt, 2013. An accumulative rage: legal pluralism and gender. In A. Sieder and J.-A. McNeish (eds): *Gender Justice and Legal Pluralities. Latin American and African Perspectives.* Abingdon, UK: Routledge, pp. 200–223.

MEA (Millennium Ecosystem Assessment), 2005. *Ecosystems and Human Well-being: General Synthesis.* Washington, DC: Island Press.

Meadows, D.H., D.L. Meadows and J. Randers, 1992. *Beyond the Limits. Global Collapse or a Sustainable Future.* London: Earthscan Publications.

Meinzen-Dick, R.S., 2007. Beyond panaceas in water institutions. *Proceedings of the National Academy of Sciences of the United States of America,* **104**(39): 15200–205.

Meinzen-Dick, R.S., 2014. Property rights and sustainable irrigation: a developing country perspective. *Agricultural Water Management*, **145**: 23–31.

Melchior, A., 2001. *Nasjonalstater, globale markeder og ulikhet: Politiske spørsmål og institusjonelle utfordringer* [Sovereigns, Global Markets and Inequality: Political Issues and Institutional Challenges]. Oslo: Norsk utenrikspolitisk institutt.

Merlet, M., C. Jamart and S. L'Orpelin, 2014. Land and water rights hotspots. *Land and Water Division Working Paper No. 8.* Rome: FAO.

Merry, S.E., (1988). Legal pluralism. *Law & Society Review*, **22**(5): 869–96.

Meyer, J.W., 1994. Rationalized environments. In W.R. Scott and J.W. Meyer (eds): *Institutional Environments and Organizations. Structural Complexity and Individualism*. Thousand Oaks, CA: Sage Publications, pp. 28–54.

Meyer, J.W. and W.R. Scott, 1983. *Organizational Environments: Ritual and Rationality*. Beverly Hills, CA: Sage Publications.

Meyer, W.B. and B.L. Turner II, 1992. Human population growth and global land-use/cover change. *Annual Review of Ecology and Systematics*, **23**(1): 39–61.

Michaelowa, A. and F. Jotzo, 2005. Transaction costs, institutional rigidities and the size of the clean development mechanism. *Energy Policy*, **33**(4): 511–23.

Micheletti, M., A. Follesdal and D. Stolle (eds), 2004. *Politics, Products and Markets. Exploring Political Consumerism Past and Present*. London: Transaction Publishers.

Milder, J.C., S.J. Scherr and C. Bracer, 2010. Trends and future potential of payment for ecosystem services to alleviate rural poverty in developing countries. *Ecology and Society*, **15**(2): Art. 4.

Miles, E., A. Underdal, S. Andresen, J. Wettestad, J.B. Skjærseth and E. Calin, 2002. *Environmental Regime Effectiveness. Confronting Theory with Evidence*. Cambridge, MA: The MIT Press.

Miliband, R., 1969. *The State in Capitalist Society*. London: Weidenfeld and Nicolson.

Millock, K. and T. Sterner, 2004. NO$_x$ emissions in France and Sweden. In W. Harrington, R.D. Morgenstern and T. Sterner (eds): *Choosing Environmental Policies. Comparing Instruments and Outcomes in the United States and Europe*. Washington, DC: Resources for the Future, pp. 117–32.

Mirowski, P., 1989. *More Heat than Light. Economics as Social Physics, Physics as Nature's Economics*. Cambridge, UK: Cambridge University Press.

Moisander, J., 2007. Motivational complexity of green consumerism. *International Journal of Consumer Studies*, **31**(4): 404–9.

Water for Food, Water for Life. A Comprehensive Assessment of Water Management in Agriculture. London: Earthscan Publications.

Moore, S.F., 2001. Certainties undone: fifty turbulent years of legal anthropology, 1949–1999. *Journal of the Royal Anthropological Institute*, **7**(1): 95–116.

Moritz, M., P. Scholte, I.M. Hamilton and S. Kari, 2013. Open access, open systems: pastoral management of common-pool resources in the Chad Basin. *Human Ecology*, **41**(3): 351–65.

Movik, S., G. Birikorang, A. Enright, G. Kajembe, L. Lima and S. Marostica et al., 2012. *Socioeconomic Conditions in REDD+ Pilot Areas: A Synthesis of Five Baseline Surveys*. London: International Institute for Environment and Development.

Munda, G., 1995. *Multicriteria Evaluation and a Fuzzy Environment. Theory and Applications in Ecological Economics*. Heidelberg: Physica-Verlag.

Munda, G., 1996. Cost–benefit analysis in integrated environmental assessment: some methodological issues. *Ecological Economics*, **19**(2): 157–68.

Munda, G. 2004. Social multi-criteria evaluation (SMCE): methodological foundations and operational consequences. *European Journal of Operational Research*, **158**(3): 662–77.

Munda, G., 2007. *Social Multi-Criteria Evaluation for a Sustainable Economy*. Berlin: Springer.

Munden, L., 2011. *The Munden Project. REDD and Forest Carbon: Market-Based Critique and*

Recommendations. Accessed 15 July 2015 at http://www.rightsandresources.org/documents/files/doc_2215.pdf.

Muradian, R., M. Martinez-Tuna, N. Kosoy, M. Perez and J. Martinez-Alier, 2008. Institutions and the performance of payments for water-related environmental services. Lessons from Latin America. Working Paper. The Netherlands: Development Research Institute, Tilburg University.

Myers, N., R.A. Mittermeier, C.G. Mittermeier, G.A.B. da Fonseca and J. Kent, 2000. Biodiversity hotspots for conservation priorities. *Nature*, **403**(6772): 853–8.

Myhre, G., 2009. Consistency between satellite-derived and modeled estimates of the direct aerosol effect. *Science*, **325**(5937): 187–90.

Nabokow, P. and L. Loendorf, 2009. *Restoring a Presence. American Indians and Yellowstone National Park*. Norman, OK: University of Oklahoma Press.

Nakajima, C., 1986. *Subjective Equilibrium Theory of the Farm Household*. New York: Elsevier.

Nakakaawa, C.A., P.O. Vedeld and J.B. Aune, 2011. Spatial and temporal land use and carbon stock changes in Uganda: implications for a future REDD strategy. *Mitigation and Adaptation Strategy and Global Change*, **16**(1): 25–62.

Nakicenovic, N. and R. Swart (eds), 2000. *Special Report on Emissions Scenarios. Contribution to the Intergovernmental Panel on Climate Change*. Cambridge, UK: Cambridge University Press. Accessed 29 June 2015 at http://www.ipcc.ch/ipccreports/sres/emission/index.php?idp=0.

Nash, R.F., 1989. *The Rights of Nature. The History of Environmental Ethics*. Madison, WI: The University of Wisconsin Press.

Nathaniel, C. and M. Jenkins, 2012. The matrix: mapping ecosystem service markets. Accessed 8 July 2015 at http://www.ecosystemmarketplace.com/pages/dynamic/article.page.php?page_id=5917.

Naughton-Treves, L., M.B. Holland and K. Brandon, 2005. The role of protected areas in conserving biodiversity and sustaining local livelihoods. *Annual Review of Environmental Resources*, **17**(30): 219–52.

Navarro, V., 2000. Development and quality of life: a critique of Amartya Sen's development as freedom. *International Journal of Health Services*, **30**(4): 661–74.

Navrud, S. 2004. Value transfer and environmental policy. In T. Tietenberg and H. Folmer (eds): *The International Yearbook of Environmental and Resource Economics 2004/2005. A Survey of Current Issues*. Cheltenham, UK and Northampton, MA, USA: Edward Elgar Publishing, pp. 189–217.

Navrud, S. and R. Ready (eds), 2007. *Environmental Value Transfer: Issues and Methods*. Dordrecht: Kluwer Academic Publishers.

Nelson, G.C., M.W. Rosegrant, J. Koo, R. Robertson, T. Sulser and T. Zhu et al., 2009. *Climate Change. Impact on Agriculture and Cost of Adaptation*. Washington, DC: International Food Policy Research Insitute (IFPRI).

Newell, R.G. and K. Rogers, 2004. Leaded gasoline in the United States. The breakthrough of permit trading. In W. Harrington, R.D. Morgenstern and T. Sterner (eds): *Choosing Environmental Policies. Comparing Instruments and Outcomes in the United States and Europe*. Washington, DC: Resources for the Future, pp. 175–91.

Nicolis, G. and I. Prigogine, 1989. *Exploring Complexity. An Introduction*. New York: W.H. Freeman and Company.

Nijkamp, P., P. Rietveld and H. Voogd, 1990. *Multicriteria Evaluation in Physical Planning*. Amsterdam: North-Holland.

Nöel. J.F. and M. O'Connor, 1998. Strong sustainability and critical natural capital. In S. Faucheux and M. O'Connor (eds): *Valuation for Sustainable Development*. Cheltenham, UK and Lyme, NH, USA: Edward Elgar Publishing, pp. 75–98.

Norgaard, R.B., 1994. *Development Betrayed. The End of Progress and a Co-evolutionary Revisioning of the Future*. New York: Routledge.

Nørretranders, T., 1991. *Mærk Verden. En beretning om bevisthed* [Feel the World. A Report on Consciousness]. Copenhagen: Gyldendal.

North, D.C., 1981. *Structure and Change in Economic History*. New York: W.W. Norton.

North, D.C., 1990. *Institutions, Institutional Change and Economic Performance*. Cambridge, UK: Cambridge University Press.

North, D.C., 1991. Institutions. *Journal of Economic Perspectives*, **5**(1): 97–112.

North, D.C., 2005. *Understanding the Process of Economic Change*. Princeton, NJ: Princeton University Press.

Norwegian Ministry of Finance, 2011. *Statens kvotekjøp* [The State's Quota Acquisition]. Accessed 8 July 2015 at http://omega.regjeringen.no/nn/dep/fin/Tema/berekraftig-utvikling/statens-kvotekjop-2.html?regj_oss=1&id=485754.

Novacek, M.J. and E.E. Cleland, 2001. The current biodiversity extinction event: scenarios for mitigation and recovery. *Proceedings of the National Academy of Science*, **98**(10): 5466–70.

Nozick, R., 1974. *Anarchy, State and Utopia*. New York: Basic Books Inc.

Nussbaum, M.C., 2003. Capabilities as fundamental entitlements: Sen and social justice. *Feminist Economics*, **9**(2–3): 33–59.

Nussbaum, M.C., 2011. Capabilities, entitlements, rights: supplementation and critique. *Journal of Human Development and Capabilities*, **12**(1): 23–37.

Nyborg, K. and M. Rege, 2003. On social norms: the evolution of considerate smoking behavior. *Journal of Economic Behavior & Organization*, **52**(3): 323–40.

Oakersson, R.J., 1992. Analyzing the commons: a framework. In D. Bromley (ed.): *Making the Commons Work. Theory, Practice and Policy*. San Francisco, CA: ICS Press, pp. 41–59.

O'Connor, D., 1995. *Managing the Environment with Rapid Industrialization: Lessons from the East Asian Experience*. Paris: OECD.

Odum, E.P. and G.W. Barrett, 2005. *Fundamentals of Ecology*. 5th edition. Belmont, CA: Thomson Brooks/Cole.

OECD (Organisation for Economic Co-operation and Development), 2003. *The World Economy: Vol. 1: A Millennial Perspective and Vol. 2: Historical Statistics. The World Economy, 1950–2001*. Paris: OECD.

OECD (Organisation for Economic Co-operation and Development), 2013. *Putting Green Growth at the Heart of Development*. Paris: OECD. Accessed 21 June 2015 at http://dx.doi.org/10.1787/9789264181144-en.

Ohlson, M., K.J. Brown, H.J.B. Birks, J.-A. Grytnes, G. Hörnberg and M. Niklasson et al., 2011. Invasion of Norway spruce diversifies the fire regime in boreal European forests. *Journal of Ecology*, **99**(2): 395–403.

Okereke, C. and K. Dooley, 2010. Principles of justice in proposals and policy approaches to avoided deforestation: towards a post-Kyoto climate agreement. *Global Environmental Change*, **20**(3): 82–95.

Olinto, P., K. Beegle, C. Sobrado and H. Uematsu, 2013. The state of the poor: where are the poor, where is extreme poverty harder to end, and what is the current profile of the world's poor? *Economic Premise No. 125*. Washington, DC: World Bank. Accessed 19 June 2015 at http://siteresources.worldbank.org/EXTPREMNET/Resources/EP125.pdf.

Olson, M., 1965. *The Logic of Collective Action: Public Goods and the Theory of Groups*. Cambridge, MA: Harvard University Press.

O'Neill, J., 1993. *Ecology, Policy and Politics. Human Well-Being and the Natural World*. London: Routledge.

O'Neill, J., 1998. *The Market. Ethics, Knowledge and Politics*. London: Routledge.

O'Neill, J., 2001. Representing people, representing nature, representing the world. *Environment and Planning C: Government and Policy*, **19**(4): 483–500.

O'Neill, J., A. Holland and A. Light, 2008. *Environmental Values*. London: Routledge.

Oreskes, N. and E.M. Conway, 2010. *Merchants of Doubt*. New York: Bloomsbury Press.

Ortiz, I. and M. Cummins, 2011. Global inequality: beyond the bottom billion. A rapid review of income distribution in 141 countries. *UNICEF Social and Economic Working Paper*. New York: UNICEF.

Ostrom, E., 1990. *Governing the Commons: The Evolution for Collective Action*. Cambridge, UK: Cambridge University Press.

Ostrom, E., 1998. A behavioral approach to the rational choice theory of collective action. Presidential address, American Political Science Association, 1997. *American Political Science Review*, **92**(1): 1–22.

Ostrom, E., 2000. Collective action and the evolution of social norms. *Journal of Economic Perspectives*, **14**(3): 137–58.

Ostrom, E., 2005. *Understanding Institutional Diversity*. Princeton, NJ: Princeton University Press.

Ostrom, E., 2007. A diagnostic approach for going beyond panaceas. *Proceedings of the National Academy of Sciences*, **104**(39): 15181–7.

Ostrom, E. and M. Cox, 2010. Moving beyond panaceas: a multi-tiered diagnostic approach for social-ecological analysis. *Environmental Conservation*, **37**(1): 451–63.

Ostrom, E. and H. Nagendra, 2006. Insights on linking forests, trees, and people from the air, on the ground, and in the laboratory. *PNAS*, **103**(51): 19224–31.

Ostrom, E., R. Gardner and J. Walker, 1994. *Rules, Games, & Common-Pool Resources*. Ann Arbor, MI: The University of Michigan Press.

Ostrom, E., T. Dietz, N. Dolsak, P.C. Stern, S. Stonich and E.U. Weber (eds), 2002. *The Drama of the Commons*. Washington, DC: National Academy Press.

Özler, S.I. and B.K. Obach, 2009. Capitalism, state economic policy and ecological footprint: an international comparative analysis. *Global Environmental Politics*, **9**(1): 79–108.

Paavola, J., 2007. Institutions and environmental governance: a reconceptualization. *Ecological Economics*, **63**(1): 93–103.

Paavola, J. and W.N. Adger, 2006. Fair adaptation to climate change. *Ecological Economics*, **56**(4): 594–609.

Padgee A., Y. Kim and P.J. Daugherty, 2006. What makes community forestry management successful: a meta-study from community forests throughout the world. *Society and Natural Resources*, **19**(1): 33–52.

Page, T., 1997. On the problem of achieving efficiency and equity, intergenerationally. *Land Economics*, **73**(4): 580–96.

Pagiola, S. and G. Platais, 2007. *Payments for Environmental Services: From Theory to Practice*. Washington, DC: World Bank.

Palaniappan, M. and P.H. Gleick, 2011. Peak water. In P.H. Gleick (ed.): *The World's Water. Vol. 7. The Biennial Report on Freshwater Resources*. Washington, DC: Island Press, pp. 1–16.

Palsson, G. and A. Helgason, 1997. Figuring fish and measuring men: the ITQ system in the Icelandic cod fishery. In G. Pálsson and G. Pétursdóttir (eds): *Social Implications of Quota Systems in Fisheries*. TemaNord Fisheries Report No. 593. Copenhagen: Scantryk, pp. 189–218.

Panic, M., 1995. The Bretton Woods system: concepts and practice. In J. Michie and L.G. Smith (eds): *Managing the Global Economy*. Oxford: Oxford University Press, pp. 37–54.

Paterson, M., D. Humphreys and L. Pettiford, 2003. Conceptualizing global environmental governance: from interstate regimes to counter-hegemonic struggles. *Global Environmental Politics*, **3**(2): 1–10.

Pattanayak, S.K., S. Wunder and P.J. Ferraro, 2010. Show me the money: do payments supply environmental services in developing countries? *Review of Environmental Economics and Policy*, **4**(2): 254–74.

Pattee, H.H., 1973. The physical basis and origin of hierarchical control. In H.H. Patte (ed.): *Hierarchy Theory. The Challenge of Complex Systems*. New York: George Braziller, pp. 71–108.

Pearce, D.W., A. Markandya and E. Barbier, 1989. *Blueprint for a Green Economy*. London: Earthscan Publications.

Peel, J. and H.M. Osofsky, 2014. *Climate Change Litigation. Regulatory Pathways to Cleaner Energy*. Oxford: Oxford University Press.

Pellegrini, L. and R. Gerlagh, 2006. Corruption, democracy, and environmental policy. An empirical contribution to the debate. *The Journal of Environment & Development*, **15**(3), 332–54.

Perman, R., Y. Ma, M. Common, D. Maddison and J. McGilvray 2011. *Natural Resource & Environmental Economics*. 4th edition. Harlow, UK: Pearson Education Limited.

Perrings, C., 1997. Ecological resilience in the sustainability of economic development. In C. Perrings: *Economics of Ecological Resources. Selected Essays*. Cheltenham, UK and Lyme, NH, USA: Edward Elgar Publishing, pp. 45–63.

Perrings, C., K. Dehnen-Schmutz, J. Touza and M. Williamson, 2005. How to manage biological invasions under globalization. *Trends in Ecology and Evolution*, **20**(5): 212–15.

Perrot-Maître, D., 2006. *The Vittel Payments for Ecosystem Services: A 'Perfect' PES Case?* London: International Institute for Environment and Development.

Peters, G.P., J.C. Minx, C.L. Weber and O. Edenhofer, 2011. Growth in emission transfers via international trade from 1990 to 2008. *PNAS*, **108**(21): 8903–8.

Petit, J.R., J. Jouzel, D. Raynaud, N.I. Barkov, J.-M. Barnola and I. Basile et al., 1999. Climate and atmospheric history of the past 420,000 years from the Vostok ice core, Antarctica. *Nature*, **399**(6735): 429–36.

Pfaff, A., J. Robalino, G.A. Sanchez-Azofeifa, K.S. Andam and P.J. Ferraro, 2009. Park location affects forest protection: land characteristics cause differences in park impacts across Costa Rica. *The B.E. Journal of Economic Analysis & Policy (Contributions)*, **9**(2): Art. 5.

Phelps, J., E.L. Webb and A. Agrawal, 2010. Does REDD+ threaten to recentralize forest governance? *Science*, **328**(5976): 312–13.

Pidgeon, N., 2012. Public understanding of, and attitudes to, climate change: UK and international perspectives and policy. *Climate Policy*, **12**(S1): S85–S106.

Pigou, A.C., 1920. *The Economics of Welfare*. London: Macmillan.

Piketty, T., 2014. *Capital in the Twenty-First Century*. Cambridge, MA: The Belknap Press of Harvard University Press.

Piketty, T. and E. Saez, 2003. Income inequality in the United States, 1913–1998. *Quarterly Journal of Economics*, **118**(1): 1–39.

Pimm, S., G. Russell, J. Gittleman and T. Brooks, 1995. The future of biodiversity. *Science*, **269**(5222): 247–350.

Pinker, S., 1994. *The Language Instinct*. London: Penguin Books.

Pinkerton, E. and D.N. Edwards, 2009. The elephant in the room: the hidden costs of leasing individual transferable fishing quotas. *Marine Policy*, **33**(4): 707–13.

Pitelis, C., 1993 (ed.). *Transaction Costs, Markets and Hierarchies*. Oxford: Blackwell.

Platteau, J.-P., 2000. *Institutions, Social Norms, and Economic Development*. Amsterdam: Harwood Academic Publishers.

Polanyi, K., [1944] 1957. *The Great Transformation. The Political and Economic Origins of Our Time*. Boston, MA: Beacon Press.

Polanyi, M., 1967. *The Tacit Dimension*. London: Routledge.

Pomeroy, R.S. and F. Berkes, 1997. Two to tango: the role of government in fisheries co-management. *Marine Policy*, **21**(5): 465–80.

Porras, I.T., M. Grieg-Gran and N. Neves, 2008. All that glitters: a review of payments for watershed services in developing countries. *Natural Resource Issues No. 11*. London: International Institute for Environment and Development.

Porras, I.T., D.N. Barton, A. Chacón-Cascante and M. Miranda, 2013. *Learning From 20 Years of Payments for Ecosystem Services in Costa Rica*. London: International Institute for Environment and Development.

Porter-Bolland, L., E.A. Ellis, M.R. Guariguata, I. Ruiz-Mallén, S. Negrete-Yankelevich and V. Reyes-García, 2012. Community managed forests and forest protected areas: an assessment of their conservation effectiveness across the tropics. *Forest Ecology and Management*, **268**(15): 6–17.

Portney, P.R. and J.P. Weyant (eds), 1999. *Discounting and Intergenerational Equity*. Washington, DC: Resources for the Future.

Postel, S.L., G.C. Daily and P.R. Ehrlich, 1996. Human appropriation of renewable fresh water. *Science*, **271**(5250): 785–8.

Poulantzas, N., 1978. *State, Power, Socialism*. Thetford, UK: Lowe & Brydone Printers Ltd.

Prasad, N., 2006. Privatisation results: private sector participation in water services after 15 years. *Development Policy Review*, **24**(6): 669–92.

Pretty, J. 1995. Participatory learning for sustainable agriculture. *World Development*, **23**(8): 1247–63.

Pryke, M. and J. Allen, 2000. Monetized time-space: derivatives – money's 'new imaginary'? *Economy and Society*, **29**(2): 264–84.

Putnam, R.D., 1988. Diplomacy and domestic politics: the logic of two-level games. *International Organization*, **42**(3): 427–60.

Ramankutty, N. and J. Foley, 1999. Estimating historical changes in global land cover: croplands from 1700–1992. *Global Biogeochemical Cycles*, **13**(4): 997–1027.

Ramankutty, N., J.A. Foley and N.J. Olejniczak, 2002. People and the land: changes in global population and croplands during the 20th century. *Ambio*, **31**(3): 251–7.

Randall, A., 1987. The problem of market failure. *Natural Resources Journal*, **23**(1): 131–48.

Rangarajan, M. and G. Shahabuddin, 2006. Displacement and relocation from protected areas: towards a biological and historical synthesis. *Conservation and Society*, **4**(3): 359–78.

Rauschmayer, F., I. Omann and J. Frühmann, 2011. *Sustainable Development. Capabilities, Needs, and Well-being*. London: Routledge.

Rawls, J.A., 1971. *A Theory of Justice*. Cambridge, MA: The Belknap Press of Harvard University Press.

Rawls, J., 1993. *Political Liberalism*. New York: Columbia University Press.

Reeburgh, W.S., 1997. Figures summarizing the global cycles of biogeochemically important elements. *Bulletin of Ecological Society of America*, **78**(4): 260–67.

Refsgaard, K., 2006. Process-guided multicriteria analysis in wastewater planning. *Environment and Planning C: Government and Policy*, **24**(2): 191–213.

Regan, T., 1988. *The Case for Animal Rights*. London: Routledge.

Reid, R.S., M.E. Fernández-Giménez and K.A. Galvin, 2014. Dynamics and resilience of rangelands and pastoral peoples around the globe. *Annual Review of Environmental Resources*, **39**: 217–42.

Reid, R.S., K.A. Galvin and R.L. Kruska, 2008. Global significance of extensive grazing lands and pastoral societies: an introduction. In K.A. Galvin, R.S. Reid, R.H. Behnke and N.T. Hobbs (eds): *Fragmentation in Semi-Arid and Arid Landscapes: Consequences for Human and Natural Systems*. Dordrecht: Springer, pp. 1–24.

Renn, O., T. Webler, H. Rakel, P. Dienel and B. Johnson, 1993. Public participation in decision-making: a three-step procedure. *Policy Science*, **26**(3): 189–214.

Ribot, J.C., A. Agrawal and A.M. Larson, 2006. Recentralizing while decentralizing: how national governments reappropriate forest resources. *World Development*, **34**(11): 1864–86.

Ridley-Duff, R. and M. Bull, 2011. *Understanding Social Enterprise. Theory & Practice*. London: SAGE Publications Ltd.

Ring, I., 2008a. Integrating local ecological services into intergovernmental fiscal transfers: the case of the ecological ICMS in Brazil. *Land Use Policy*, **25**(4): 485–97.

Ring, I., 2008b. Compensating municipalities for protected areas: fiscal transfers for biodiversity conservation in Saxony, Germany. *GAIA – Ecological Perspectives for Science and Society*, **17**(S1): 143–51.

Riseth, J.Å., 2003. Sami reindeer management in Norway: modernization challenges and conflicting strategies – reflections upon the co-management alternative. In S. Jentoft, H. Minde and R. Nielsen (eds): *Indigenous Peoples: Resource Management and Global Rights*. Delft, The Netherlands: Eburon, pp. 229–47.

Riseth, J.Å., 2005. So the last shall be first, and the first last? Sami reindeer management vs. other land users in mid-Scandinavia. In G. Cant, A. Goodall and J. Inns (eds): *Discourses and Silences: Indigenous Peoples, Risks and Resistance*. Christchurch, New Zealand: Department Geography, University of Canterbury, pp. 35–55.

Riseth, J.Å. and A. Vatn, 2009. Modernization and pasture degradation. A comparative study of two Sámi reindeer pasture regions in Norway. *Land Economics*, **84**(1): 87–106.

Ritzer, G., 2011. *The McDonaldization of Society*. 6th edition. London: Sage Publications Ltd.

Robbins, P., 2000. The rotten institution: corruption in natural resource management. *Political Geography*, **19**(4): 423–43.

Robbins, P., 2012. *Political Ecology*. 2nd edition. Chichester, UK: Wiley-Blackwell.

Robinson, S. and M. Whitton, 2010. Pasture in Gorno-Badakhshan, Tajikistan: common resource or private property? *Pastoralism*, **1**(2): 198–217.

Rockström, J., W. Steffen, K. Noone, Å. Persson, F.S. Chapin III and E. Lambin et al., 2009. Planetary boundaries: exploring the safe operating space for humanity. *Ecology and Society*, **14**(2): Art. 32.

Rodell, M., I. Velicogna and J.S. Famiglietti, 2009. Satellite-based estimates of groundwater depletion in India. *Nature*, **460**(7258): 999–1002.

Rokkan, S., 1966. Norway: numerical democracy and corporate pluralism. In R.A. Dahl (ed.): *Political Opposition in Western Democracies*. New Haven, CT: Yale University Press, pp. 70–115.

Romanow, R.J., 2002. *Building on Values. The Future of Health Care in Canada. Final Report*. Ottowa: Commission on the Future of Health Care in Canada. Accessed 8 July 2015 at http://www.cbc.ca/healthcare/final_report.pdf.

Røpke, I., 2015. Complementary system perspectives in ecological macroeconomics. The example of transition investments during the crisis. *Ecological Economics* [online]. Accessed 16 July 2015 at http://www.sciencedirect.com/science/article/pii/S0921800915001032.

Rørstad, P.K., A. Vatn and V. Kvakkestad, 2007. Why do transaction costs of agricultural policies vary? *Agricultural Economics*, **36**(1): 1–11.

Rosendal, K. and P.J. Schei, 2012. Convention on biological diversity: from national conservation to global responsibiliy. In S. Andresen, E.L. Boasson and G. Hønneland (eds): *International Environmental Agreements. An Introduction*. Abingdon, UK: Routledge, pp. 119–33.

Ross, L. and A. Ward, 1996. Naive realism: implications for social conflict and misunderstanding. In E.S. Reed, E. Turiel and T. Brown (eds): *Values and Knowledge*. Mahwah, NJ: Lawrence Erlbaum Associates, pp. 103–35.

Roth, A.E., V. Prasnikar, M. Okuna-Fujiwara and S. Zamir, 1991. Bargaining and market behavior in Jerusalem, Ljubljana, Pittsburg and Tokyo: an experimental study. *American Economic Review*, **81**(5): 1068–95.

Roth, R., 2004. On the colonial margins and in the global hotspot: park–people conflicts in highland Thailand. *Asia Pacific Viewpoint*, **45**(1): 13–32.

Rougoor, C.W., H. van Zeijts, M.F. Hofreither and S. Bäckman, 2001. Experiences with fertilizer taxes in Europe. *Journal of Environmental Planning and Management*, **44**(6): 877–87.

Rousseau, S. and E. Moons, 2008. The potential of auctioning contracts for conservation policy. *European Journal of Forest Research*, **127**(3): 183–94.

Rupert, M., 2010. Marxism and critical theory. In T. Dunne, M. Kurki and S. Smith (eds): *International Relations Theories. Discipline and Diversity*. 2nd edition. New York: Oxford University Press, pp. 157–76.

Ruvio, A.A. and R.W. Belk, 2013. Conflicting selves and the role of possessions: a process view of transgenders' self-identity conflict. In A.A. Ruvio and R.W. Belk (eds): *The Routledge Companion to Identity and Consumption*. Abingdon, UK: Routledge, pp. 141–7.

Ryan, R.M. and E.L. Deci, 2000. Self-determination theory and the facilitation of intrinsic motivation, social development, and well-being. *American Psychologist*, **55**(1): 68–78.

Sabatier, P.A. (ed.), 1999. *Theories of the Policy Process*. Boulder, CO: Westview Press.

Sachs, N.M., 2011. Rescuing the strong precautionary principle from its critics. *University of Illinois Law Review*, **2011**(4): 1285–338.

Salmi, P. and K. Muje, 2001. Local owner-based management of Finnish lake fisheries: social dimension and power relations. *Fisheries Management and Ecology*, **8**(4–5): 435–42.

Santos, R., I. Ring, P. Antunes and P. Clemente, 2012. Fiscal transfers for biodiversity conservation: the Portuguese local finances law. *Land Use Policy*, **29**(2): 261–73.

Santos, R., P. Clemente, P. Antunes, P. Schröter-Schlaack and I. Ring, 2011. Offsets, habitat banking and tradable permits for biodiversity conservation. In I. Ring and C. Schröter-Schlaack (eds): *Instrument Mixes for Biodiversity Policies. POLICYMIX Report 2/2011*, Leipzig: Helmholtz Centre for Environmental Research – UFZ, pp. 59–88.

Sayer, A., 1992. *Method in Social Science. A Realist Approach*. 2nd edition. London: Routledge.

Scharpf, F., 1999. *Governing in Europe. Effective and Democratic?* Oxford: Oxford University Press.

Schellnhuber, H.J., 1999. 'Earth system' analysis and the second Copernican revolution. *Nature*, **402**(Supplement): C19–C23.

Schlager, E., 1994. Fishers' institutional response to common-pool resource dilemmas. In E. Ostrom, R. Gardner and J. Walker (eds): *Rules, Games, & Common-Pool Resources*. Ann Arbor, MI: The University of Michigan Press, pp. 247–65.

Schlager, E. and E. Ostrom, 1992. Property-rights regimes and natural resources: a conceptual analysis. *Land Economics*, **68**(3): 249–62.

Schlesinger, W.H., 1991. *Biogeochemistry. An Analysis of Global Change*. 1st edition. London: Academic Press.

Schmid, A.A., 1987. *Property, Power, and Public Choice. An Inquiry into Law and Economics*. New York: Praeger.

Schmidt-Soltau, K., 2003. Conservation-related resettlement in Central Africa: environmental and social risks. *Development and Change*, **34**(3): 525–51.

Schneider, F., G. Kallis and J. Martinez-Alier, 2010. Crisis or opportunity? Economic degrowth for social equity and ecological sustainability. Introduction to this special issue. *Journal of Cleaner Production*, **18**(6) 511–18.

Schneider, L., 2007. *Is the CDM Fulfilling its Environmental and Sustainable Development Objectives? An Evaluation of the CDM and Options for Improvement. Report Prepared for WWF*, Berlin: Institute for Applied Ecology. Accessed 8 July 2015 at http://cleanairinitiative.org/portal/node/2253.

Schnoor, J., 2008. Global financial and environmental crises. *Environmental Science and Technology*, **42**(23): 8615.

Schotter, 2009. *Microeconomics. A Modern Approach*. Mason, MI: South-Western Cengage Learning.

Schulz-Hardt, S., D. Frey, C. Luthgens and S. Moscovici, 2000. Biased information search in group decision making. *Journal of Personality and Social Psychology*, **78**(4): 655–69.

Schwartz, S., 1977. Normative influences on altruism. In L. Berkowizt (ed.): *Advances in Experimental Social Psychology, Vol. 10*, New York: Academic Press, pp. 222–9.

Scott, J., 2000. Rational choice theory. In G. Browning, A. Halcli and F. Webster (eds): *Understanding Contemporary Society: Theories of the Present*. London: Sage Publications, pp. 126–38.

Scott, W.R., 2014. *Institutions and Organizations: Ideas, Interests and Identities*. 4th edition. Los Angeles, CA: Sage Publications.

Screpanti, E., 1995. Relative rationality, institutions and precautionary behaviour. In J. Groenewegen, C. Pitelis and S.E. Sjöstrand (eds): *On Economic Institutions – Theory and Applications*. Aldershot, UK and Brookfield, VT, USA: Edward Elgar Publishing, pp. 63–84.

Searle, J.R., 2005. What is an institution? *Journal of Institutional Economics*, **1**(1): 1–22.

Sen, A., 1977. Rational fools: a critique of the behavioral foundations of economic theory. *Philosophy and Public Affairs*, **6**(4): 317–44.

Sen, A., 1995. Gender, inequality and theories of justice. In M.C. Nussbaum and J. Glover (eds): *Women, Culture and Development*. Oxford: Clarendon Press, pp. 259–73.

Sen, A., 1999. *Development and Freedom*. Oxford: Oxford University Press.

Sen, A., 2009. *The Idea of Justice*. London: Allen Lane/Penguin Group.

Sened, I., 1997. *The Political Institution of Private Property*. Cambridge, UK: Cambridge University Press.

Senik, C., 2009. Income distribution and subjective happiness: a survey. OECD Social, Employment and Migration Working Papers, No. 96. Paris: OECD. Accessed 19 June 2015 at http://www.oecd.org/officialdocuments/publicdisplaydocumentpdf/?cote=DELSA/ELSA/WD/SEM%282009%2924&docLanguage=En.

Shackle, G.L.S., 1961. *Decision, Order and Time in Human Affairs*. Cambridge, UK: Cambridge University Press.

Shanmugaratnam, S., 2014. The land question, internal conflicts and international statebuilding in South Sudan. In S. Takeuchi (ed.): *Confronting Land and Property Problems for Peace*. Abingdon, UK: Routledge.

Shaw, D., T. Newholm and R. Dickinson, 2006. Consumption as voting: an exploration of consumer empowerment. *European Journal of Marketing*, **40**(9/10): 1049–67.

Shepsle, K.A., 2006. Rational choice institutionalism. In R.A.W. Rhodes, S.A. Binder and B.A. Rockman (eds): *Oxford Handbook of Political Institutions*. Oxford: Oxford University Press, pp. 23–38.

Shiklomanov, I.A., 1993. World fresh water resources. In P.H. Gleick (ed.): *Water in Crisis*. New York: Oxford University Press, pp. 13–24.

Shin, H.S., 2009. Securitization and financial stability. *The Economic Journal*, **119**(536): 309–32.

Shiva, V., 2002. *Water Wars. Privatization, Pollution and Profit*. London: Pluto Press.

Shogren, J., 2006. A rule of one. *American Journal of Agricultural Economics*, **88**(4): 1147–59.

Simmel, G., 1978. *The Philosophy of Money*. London: Routledge and Kegan Paul Ltd.

Simon, H.A., 1979. Rational decision making in business organizations. *The American Economic Review*, **69**(4): 493–513.

Simonsen, J.W., 1989. *Miljøavgifter på kunstgjødsel-N og -P* [Environmental Taxes on N and

P Fertilizers]. Report to the Ministry of Agriculture, Akershus: Department of Agricultural Economics, Agricultural University of Norway.

Sipponen, M., M. Mitchell and J. Vanberg, 2010. Does a property rights regime affect the outcome of European inland commercial fisheries? *Knowledge and Management of Aquatic Ecosystem*, **399**(6): 06p1–6p12.

Sjaastad, E. and B. Cousins, 2009. Formalisation of land rights in the South: an overview. *Land Use Policy*, **26**(1): 1–9.

Sjåfjell, B., 2011. Why law matters: corporate social irresponsibility and the futility of voluntary climate change mitigation. *European Company Law*, **8**(2–3): 56–64.

Sjöstrand, S.-E., 1995. Towards a theory of institutional change. In J. Groenewegen, C. Pitelis and S.-E. Sjöstrand (eds): *On Economic Institutions. Theory and Application*. Aldershot, UK and Brookfield, VT, USA: Edward Elgar Publishing.

Skjærseth, J.B. and T. Skodvin, 2001. Climate change and the oil industry: common problems, different strategies. *Global Environmental Politics*, **1**(4): 43–64.

Skjeggedal, T., V. Gundersen, K.A. Harvold and O.I. Vistad, 2010. *Frivillig vern av skog – evaluering av arbeidsform. Samarbeidsrapport NIBR/NINA* [Voluntary Protection of Forests – an Evaluation of the Practice. Joint NIBR/NINA Report]. Oslo: NIBR.

Slovic, P. and S. Lichtenstein, 1983. Preference reversals: a broader perspective. *American Economic Review*, **73**(4), 596–605.

Smith, A. [1776] 1976. *An Inquiry into the Nature and Causes of the Wealth of Nations*. Chicago, IL: University of Chicago Press.

Smith, G., 2003. *Deliberative Democracy and the Environment*. London: Routledge.

Smith, G. and C. Wales, 1999. The theory and practice of citizens' juries. *Policy and Politics*, **27**(3): 295–308.

Smith, S.J., J. van Ardenne, Z. Klimont, R.J. Andres, A. Volke and S. Delgado Arias, 2011. Anthropogenic sulfur dioxide emissions: 1850–2005. *Atmospheric Chemistry and Physics*, **11**: 1101–16.

Sneirson, J.F., 2011. The sustainable corporation and shareholder profits. *Wake Forest Law Review*, **46**: 541–59.

Sober, E. and D.S. Wilson, 1998. *Unto Others. The Evolution and Psychology of Unselfish Behavior*. Cambridge, MA: Harvard University Press.

Solanes, M., 2013. Viewpoint – the Washington Consensus, Chilean water monopolization and the Peruvian draft Water Law of the 1990s. *Water Alternatives*, **6**(2): 207–17.

Solberg, E.G., E. Diener and M.D. Robinson, 2004. Why are materialists less satisfied? In T. Kasser and A.D. Kanner (eds): *Psychology and Consumer Culture: The Struggle for a Good Life in a Materialistic World* [Kindle edition]. Washington, DC: APA, pp. 558–971.

Solow, R.M., 1974. Intergenerational equity and exhaustible resources. In *Review of Economic Studies. Symposium on the Economics of Exhaustible Resources*. Edinburgh: Longman, pp. 29–45.

Solow, R.M., 1993. Sustainability: an economist's perspective. In R. Dorfman and N. Dorfman (eds): *Economics of the Environment*. New York: Norton.

Soma, K. and A. Vatn, 2010. Is there anything like a citizen? A descriptive analysis of instituting a citizen's role to represent social values at the municipal level. *Environmental Policy and Governance*, **20**(1): 30–43.

Somanathan, E., R. Prabhakar and B.S. Mehta, 2009. Decentralization for cost-effective conservation. *PNAS*, **106**(11): 4143–7.

Sørensen, E. and J. Torfing (eds), 2007. *Theories of Democratic Network Governance*. Basingstoke, UK: Palgrave Macmillan.

Sovacool, B.K. and M.A. Brown, 2009. Scaling the policy response to climate change. *Policy and Society*, **27**(4): 317–28.

Spash, C.L., 2000. Multiple value expression in contingent valuation: economics and ethics. *Environmental Science Technology*, **34**(8): 1433–38.

Spash, C.L., 2002. *Greenhouse Economics. Values and Ethics*. New York: Routledge.

Spash, C.L., 2011. Terrible economics, ecosystems and banking. *Environmental Values*, **20**(2): 141–5.

Spash, C.L., 2012. Green economy, red herring. *Environmental Values*, **21**(2): 95–9.

Spash, C.L. and A. Vatn, 2006. Transferring environmental value estimates: issues and alternatives. *Ecological Economics*, **60**(2): 379–88.

Spergel, B. and M. Wells, 2009. Conservation trust funds as a model for REDD+ national financing. In A. Angelsen (ed.): *Realising REDD+: National Strategy and Policy Options*. Bogor, Indonesia: CIFOR, pp. 75–84.

Stagl, S., 2003. Multicriteria evaluation and participation: in search of theoretical foundations. Paper presented at Frontiers 2 – European Applications in Ecological Economics conference, 11–15 February, Tenerife, Spain.

Stagl, S., 2006. Multicriteria evaluation and public participation: the case of UK energy policy. *Land Use Policy*, **23**(1): 53–62.

Steffen, W., A. Sanderson, P.D. Tyson, J. Jäger, P.A. Matson and B. Moore III et al., 2005. *Global Change and the Earth System. A Planet Under Pressure*. 2nd edition. Berlin: Springer Verlag.

Steil, B., 2013. *The Battle of Bretton Woods: John Maynard Keynes, Harry Dexter White, and the Making of a New World Order*. Princeton, NJ: Princeton University Press.

Steinbeck, S.J., 2005. *An Abridged History of Onsite Wastewater Early Years to Present*. Revised by B.H. Grimes, PhD and N. Deal, MS, REHS, Onsite Water Protection Branch, Environmental Health Section, Division of Public Health, North Carolina Department of Health and Human Services.

Stern, N., S. Peters, V. Bakhshi, A. Bowen, C. Cameron and S. Catovsky et al., 2006. *Stern Review: The Economics of Climate Change*. London: HM Treasury.

Sterner, T., 2007. Fuel taxes: an important instrument for climate policy. *Energy Policy*, **35**(6): 3194–202.

Stewart, T.J. and L. Scott, 1995. A scenario-based framework for multicriteria decision analysis in water resource planning. *Water Resources Research*, **31**(11): 2835–43.

Stewart, T.J., E. Kendall and A. Coote, 1994. *Citizens' Juries*. London: Institute of Public Policy Research.

Stirling, A., 1998. Risk at a turning point? *Journal of Risk Research*, **1**(2): 97–109.

Stirling, A., 2006. Uncertainty, precaution and sustainability: towards more reflective governance of technology. In J.P. Voss, D. Bauknecht and R. Kemp (eds): *Reflexive Governance for Sustainable Development*. Cheltenham, UK and Northampton, MA, USA: Edward Elgar Publishing, pp. 225–72.

Stirling, A. and S. Mayer, 2001. A novel approach to appraisal of technological risk: a multicriteria mapping study of genetically modified crop. *Environment and Planning C: Government and Policy*, **19**: 529–55.

Stockholm Convention, 2001. *Stockholm Convention on Persistent Organic Pollutants*. Geneva: UNEP. Accessed 21 June 2015 at http://chm.pops.int/default.aspx.

Stokke, O.S., 2012. International fisheries politics, from sustainability to precaution. In S. Andresen, E.L. Boasson and G. Hønneland (eds): *International Environmental Agreements. An Introduction*. Abingdon, UK: Routledge, pp. 97–116.

Stork, N.E., 1997. Measuring global biodiversity and its decline. In M.L. Reaka-Kudla, D.E. Wilson and E.O. Wilson (eds): *Biodiversity II. Understanding and Protecting our Biological Resources*. Washington, DC: Joseph Henry Press, pp. 41–68.

Suding, K.N., 2011. Toward an era of restoration in ecology: successes, failures and opportunities ahead. *Annual Review of Ecology, Evolution, and Systematics*, **42**: 465–87.

Sugden, R., 1986. *The Economics of Rights, Co-operation and Welfare*. Oxford: Basil Blackwell.

Sullivan, P., D. Hellerstein, L. Hansen, R. Johansson, S. Koenig and R. Lubowski et al., 2004. *The Conservation Reserve Program: Economic Implications for Rural America. Agricultural Economic Report, No. 834.* Washington, DC: US Department of Agriculture, Economic Research Service.

Sullivan, S., 2010. The environmentality of 'Earth Incorporated': on contemporary primitive accumulation and the financialisation of environmental conservation. Paper presented at the An Environmental History of Neoliberalism conference, Lund University, 6–8 May.

Sullivan, S., 2013a. After the green rush? Biodiversity offsets, uranium power and the 'calculus of casualties' in greening growth. *Human Geography*, **6**(1): 80–101.

Sullivan, S., 2013b. Banking nature? The spectacular financialisation of environmental conservation. *Antipode*, **45**(1): 198–217.

Sullivan, S. and M. Hannis, 2015. Nets and frames, losses and gains: value struggles in engagements with biodiversity offsetting policy in England. *Ecosystem Services*. Accessed 8 July 2015 at http://dx.doi.org/10.1016/j.ecoser.2015.01.009.

Sunshine, J. and T.R. Tyler, 2003. The role of procedural justice and legitimacy in shaping public support for policing. *Law and Society Review*, **37**(3): 513–47.

Sunstein, C.R., 1993. Endogenous preferences, environmental law. *Journal of Legal Studies*, **22**(2): 217–54.

Sunstein, C.R., 2013. *Simpler: The Future of Government*. New York: Simon and Schuster.

Tamanaha, B.Z., 2008. Understanding legal pluralism: past to present, local to global. *Sydney Law Review*, **30**(3): 375–411.

Tang, S.Y., 1994. Institutions and performance in irrigation systems. In E. Ostrom, R. Gardner and J. Walker (eds): *Rules, Games, & Common-Pool Resources*. Ann Arbor, MI: The University of Michigan Press, pp. 225–45.

TEEB (The Economics of Ecosystems and Biodiversity), 2010. *Mainstreaming the Economics of Nature. A Synthesis of the Approach, Conclusions and Recommendations of TEEB*. Accessed 14 June 2015 at http://www.unep.org/pdf/LinkClick.pdf.

TEEB (The Economics of Ecosystems and Biodiversity), 2012. Bank of natural capital. *TEEB4me. com*, accessed 14 June 2015 at http://www.teeb4me.com/.

Tenbrunsel, A.E. and D.M. Messick, 1999. Sanctioning systems, decision frames and cooperation. *Administrative Science Quarterly*, **44**(4): 684–707.

Thornton, P.K., 2004. *Markets from Culture: Institutional Logics and Organizational Decisions in Higher Education Publishing*. Stanford, CA: Stanford University Press.

Thornton, P.K., P.G. Jones, P.J. Erickson and A.J. Challinor, 2011. Agriculture and food systems in Sub-Saharan Africa in a 4°C+ world. *Philosophical Transactions of the Royal Society*, **369**(1934): 117–36.

Tickell, A., 2000. Dangerous derivatives: controlling and creating risk in international money. *Geoforum*, **31**(1): 87–99.

Tienhaara, K., 2010. The tale of two crises: what the global financial crisis means for the global environmental crisis. *Environmental Policy and Governance*, **20**(3): 197–208.

Tisdell, J.G., 2001. The environmental impact of water markets: an Australian case-study. *Journal of Environmental Management*, **62**(1): 113–20.

Tol, R.S.J. and G.W. Yohe, 2006. A review of the Stern Review. *World Economics*, **7**(4): 233–50.

Toman, M.A., 1994. Economics and 'sustainability': balancing trade-offs and imperatives. *Land Economics*, **70**(4): 399–413.

Toman, M.A., J. Pezzey and J. Krautkraemer, 1995. Neoclassical economic growth theory and 'sustainability'. In D.W. Bromley (ed.): *The Handbook of Environmental Economics*. Oxford: Basil Blackwell, pp. 139–65.

Trainor, S.F., 2006. Realms of value: conflicting natural resource values and incommensurability. *Environmental Values*, **15**(1): 3–29.

Tsigaridis, K., M. Krol, F.J. Dentener, Y. Balkanski, J. Lathière and S. Metzger et al., 2006. Change in global aerosol composition since preindustrial times. *Atmospheric Chemistry and Physics*, **6**: 5143–62.

Turner, J., 1997. The policy process. In B. Axford, G.K. Browning, R. Huggins, B. Rosamund and J. Turner (eds): *Politics. An Introduction*. London: Routledge, pp. 409–39.

Turner, M.D., 2011. The new pastoral development paradigm: engaging the realities of property institutions and livestock mobility in dryland Africa. *Society and Natural Resources*, **24**(5): 469–84.

Turris, B.R., 2010. A rejoinder to E. Pinkerton et al., the elephant in the room: the hidden costs of leasing individual transferable fishing quotas. *Marine Policy*, **34**(3): 431–6.

Tversky, A. and D. Kahneman, 1986. Rational choice and the framing of decisions. In R.M. Hogarth and M.W. Reder (eds): *Rational Choice: The Contrast Between Economics and Psychology*. Chicago, IL: University of Chicago Press.

Tyler, T.R., 1990. *Why People Obey the Law*. New Haven, CT: Yale University Press.

Ulph, A. and D. Ulph, 1995. Trade, strategic innovation and strategic environmental policy. A general analysis. Discussion Paper, *Economics, Energy and Environment*, **4**:181–208.

UN (United Nations) General Assembly, 1982. *World Charter for Nature*. Accessed 16 June 2015 at http://www.un.org/documents/ga/res/37/a37r007.htm.

UN (United Nations), 1987. *The Montreal Protocol on Substances that Deplete the Ozone Layer*. Accessed 22 June 2015 at http://ozone.unep.org/new_site/en/Treaties/treaties_decisions-hb.php?sec_id=5.

UN (United Nations), 1992. *The Convention on Biological Diversity*. Accessed 21 June 2105 at http://www.biodiv.org/doc/legal/cbd-en.pdf.

UN (United Nations), 1994. *International Tropical Timber Agreement*. Accessed 21 June 2015 at http://www.itto.int/itta/.

UN (United Nations), 1997. *The Kyoto Protocol to the United Nations Framework Convention on Climate Change*. Accessed 21 June 2015 at http://unfccc.int/resource/docs/convkp/kpeng.pdf.

UN (United Nations), 2000. *The Cartagena Protocol on Biosafety to the Convention on Biological Diversity. Text and Annexes*. Accessed 21 June 2015 at http://www.biodiv.org/doc/legal/cartagena-protocol-en.pdf.

UN (United Nations), 2009a. *Water in a Changing World. The United Nations World Water Development Report 3*. Paris: UNESCO. Accessed 11 June 2015 at http://webworld.unesco.org/water/wwap/wwdr/wwdr3/pdf/WWDR3_Water_in_a_Changing_World.pdf.

UN (United Nations), 2009b. *What is Good Governance?* Bangkok: United Nations Economic and Social Commission for Asia and the Pacific. Accessed 18 June 2015 at http://www.unescap.org/sites/default/files/good-governance.pdf.

UN (United Nations), 2009c. *World Population Ageing 2009*. New York: United Nations. Accessed 11 June 2015 at http://www.un.org/esa/population/publications/WPA2009/WPA2009-report.pdf.

UN (United Nations), 2012a. UN data. Accessed 4 February 2012 at http://data.un.org/.

UN (United Nations), 2012b. *The Future We Want*. Accessed 18 April 2015 at http://www.uncsd2012.org/content/documents/727The%20Future%20We%20Want%2019%20June%201230pm.pdf.

UN (United Nations), 2013. *The United Nations Agreement for the Implementation of the Provisions* of the United Nations Convention on the Law of the Sea of 10 December 1982 relating to the Conservation and Management of Straddling Fish Stocks and Highly Migratory Fish Stocks (in force as from 11 December 2001). Overview. Last updated 31 July 2013. Accessed 21 June 2015 at http://www.un.org/depts/los/convention_agreements/convention_overview_fish_stocks. htm.

Underdal, A., 2002. One question, two answers. In E. Miles, A. Underdal, S. Andresen, J. Wettestad, J.B. Skjærseth and E. Calin: *Environmental Regime Effectiveness. Confronting Theory with Evidence.* Cambridge, MA: The MIT Press, pp. 3–45.

UNEP (United Nations Environmental Programme), 1992. *Rio Declaration on Environment and Development.* Accessed 14 June at http://www.jus.uio.no/lm/environmental.development.rio. declaration.1992/portrait.a4.pdf.

UNEP (United Nations Environmental Programme), 2008. *Backgrounder. Basic Facts and Data on the Science and Politics of Ozone Protection.* Accessed 15 July 2015 at http://ozone.unep.org/ Events/ozone_day_2009/press_backgrounder.pdf.

UNEP (United Nations Environmental Programme), 2011. *Towards a Green Economy: Pathways to Sustainable Development and Poverty Eradication.* Accessed 21 June 2015 at http://www.unep. org/greeneconomy/GreenEconomyReport/tabid/29846/language/enUS/Default.aspx.

UNEP (United Nations Environmental Programme), 2012. *Biodiversity Offsets: Voluntary and Compliance Regimes. A Review of Existing Schemes, Initiatives and Guidance for Financial Institutions.* Accessed 8 July 2015 at http://www.unepfi.org/fileadmin/documents/ Biodiversity_Offsets-Voluntary_and_Compliance_Regimes.pdf.

UNEP (United Nations Environmental Programme), 2014. Leaded petrol phase-out: global status April 2014 [map]. Accessed 6 July 2015 at http://www.unep.org/Transport/PCFV/ pdf/Maps_Matrices/world/lead/MapWorldLead_April2014.pdf

UNFCC (United Nations Framework Convention on Climate Change), 2014. First steps to a safer future: introducing The United Nations Framework Convention on Climate Change. Accessed 10 July 2015 at http://unfccc.int/essential_background/convention/items/6036.php.

Union of Concerned Scientists. 2007. *Smoke, Mirrors, and Hot Air.* Accessed 12 February 2012 at http://www.ucsusa.org/sites/default/files/legacy/assets/documents/global_warming/ exxon_report.pdf.

Unruh, J.D., 2008. Carbon sequestration in Africa: the land tenure problem. *Global Environmental Change,* **18**(4): 700–707.

URT (United Republic of Tanzania), 1998. *National Forest Policy.* Dar es Salaam: Ministry of Natural Resources and Tourism, Forestry and Beekeeping Division.

URT (United Republic of Tanzania), 1999a. *The Land Act No. 4.* Dar es Salaam: Ministry of Lands, Housing and Human Settlements Development.

URT (United Republic of Tanzania), 1999b. *Village Land Act (and Regulations) No. 5 of 1999.* Dar es Salaam: Ministry of Lands, Housing and Human Settlements Development.

URT (United Republic of Tanzania), 2002. *The Forest Act, No. 7 of 7th June 2002.* Dar es Salaam: Ministry of Lands, Housing and Human Settlements Development.

Utting, P., 2008. The struggle for corporate accountability. *Development and Change,* **39**(6): 959–75.

Van Assche, K., S. Bell and P. Teampau, 2012. Traumatic natures of the swamp: concepts of nature in the Romanian Danube Delta. *Environmental Values,* **21**(2): 163–83.

Van den Bergh, H., 2008. Global status of DDT and its alternatives for use in vector control to prevent disease. Background document for the preparation of the business plan for a global partnership to develop alternatives to DDT. Geneva: UNEP. Accessed 21 June 2015 at http:// www.pops.int/documents/ddt/Global%20status%20of%20DDT%20SSC%2020Oct08.pdf.

Van Kauwenbergh, S.J., 2010. *World Phosphate Rock Reserves and Resources.* Muscle Shoals, AL:

International Fertilizer Development Center (IFDC). Accessed 11 June 2015 at http://pdf. usaid.gov/pdf_docs/PNADW835.pdf.

Varian, H.R., 2010. *Intermediate Microeconomics: A Modern Approach*. 8th edition. New York: W.W. Norton Company.

Vatn, A., 1998. Input vs. emission taxes. Environmental taxes in a mass balance and transactions cost perspective. *Land Economics*, **74**(4): 514–25.

Vatn, A., 2000. The environment as a commodity. *Environmental Values*, **9**(4): 493–509.

Vatn, A., 2002. Efficient or fair: ethical paradoxes in environmental policy. In D. Bromley and J. Paavola (eds): *Economics, Ethics and Environmental Policy: Contested Choices*. Oxford: Blackwell, pp. 148–63.

Vatn, A., 2005. *Institutions and the Environment*. Cheltenham, UK and Northampton, MA, USA: Edward Elgar Publishing.

Vatn, A., 2008. Sustainability: the need for institutional change. In P. Utting and J. Clapp (eds): *Corporate Accountability and Sustainable Development*. New Delhi: Oxford University Press, pp. 61–91.

Vatn, A., 2009a. Cooperative behavior and institutions. *Journal of Socio-Economics*, **38**(1): 188–96.

Vatn, A., 2009b. An institutional analysis of methods for environmental appraisal. *Ecological Economics*, **68**(8): 2207–15.

Vatn, A., 2010. An institutional analysis of payments for environmental services. *Ecological Economics*, **69**(6): 1245–52.

Vatn, A., 2015. Markets in environmental governance. From theory to practice. *Ecological Economics* **117**: 225–33.

Vatn, A. and D. Bromley, 1994. Choices without prices without apologies. *Journal of Environmental Economics and Management*, **26**(2): 129–48.

Vatn, A. and P.O. Vedeld, 2012. Fit, interplay and scale – a diagnosis. *Ecology and Society*, **17**(4): Art. 12.

Vatn, A. and P.O. Vedeld, 2013. National governance structures for REDD+. *Global Environmental Change*, **23**(2): 422–32.

Vatn, A., E. Krogh, F. Gundersen and P.O. Vedeld, 2002. Environmental taxes and politics – the dispute over nitrogen taxes in agriculture. *European Environment*, **12**(4): 224–40.

Vatn, A., L.R. Bakken, P. Botterweg, H. Lundeby, E. Romstad and P.K. Rørstad et al., 1997. Regulating nonpoint-source pollution from agriculture – an integrated modelling analysis. *European Review of Agricultural Economics*, **26**(2): 207–29.

Vatn, A., G. Kajembe, R. Leiva-Montoya, E. Mosi, M. Nantongo and D.A. Santos Silayo, 2013. *Instituting REDD+. An Analysis of the Processes and Outcomes of Instituting REDD+ in Two Pilot Areas – RDS Rio Negro (Brazil) and Kilosa (Tanzania)*. London: International Institute for Environment and Development (IIED).

Veblen, T., 1898. Why is economics not an evolutionary science. *Quarterly Journal of Economics*, **12**(4): 373–97.

Veblen, T., 1899. *The Theory of the Leisure Class: An Economic Study of Institutions*. New York: Macmillan.

Veblen, T., [1904] 1958. *The Theory of Business Enterprise*, New York: The New American Library.

Veblen, T., 1919. *The Place of Science in Modern Civilisation and Other Essays*. New York: Huebsch.

Vedeld, P. and E. Krogh, 2000. Rationality in the eye of the actor. Economists and natural scientists in a discourse over environmental taxes. In T.L. Napier, S.M. Napier and J. Tvrdon (eds): *Soil and Water Conservation Policies: Successes and Failures*. Boca Raton, FL: CRC Press, pp. 285–318.

Vedeld, P., A. Jumane, G. Wapalila and A. Songorwa, 2012. Protected areas, poverty traps and conflicts – livelihood case study from Mikumi National Park, Tanzania. *Forest Policy and Economics*, **21**: 20–31.

Vedeld, P.O., A. Angelsen, J. Bojö, E. Sjaastad and G. Kobugabe Berg, 2007. Forest environmental incomes and the rural poor. *Forest Policy and Economics*, **9**(7): 869–79.

Verplanken, B. and H. Aarts, 1999. Habit, attitude, and planned behaviour: is habit an empty construct or an interesting case of goal-directed automaticity? *European Review of Social Psychology*, **10**(1): 101–34.

Viana, V.M., 2008. Bolsa Floresta (Forest Conservation Allowance): an innovative mechanism to promote health in traditional communities in the Amazon. *Estudos Avancados*, **22**(64): 143–53.

Viner, R.M., C. Coffey, C. Mathers, P. Bloem, A. Costello and J. Santelli et al., 2011. 50-year mortality trends in children and young people: a study of 50 low-income, middle-income, and high-income countries. *The Lancet*, **377**(9772): 1162–74.

Vitousek, P.M., P.R. Ehrlich, A.H. Ehrlich and P.A. Matson, 1986. Human appropriation of the products of photosynthesis. *Bioscience*, **36**(6): 368–73.

Vohs, K.D., N.L. Mead and M.R. Goode, 2006. The psychological consequences of money. *Science*, **314**(5802): 1154–6.

Vörösmarty, C.J., P. Green, J. Salisbury and R.B. Lammers, 2000. Global water resources: vulnerability from climate change and population growth. *Science*, **289**(5477): 284–8.

Wade, R., 1988. *Village Republics: Economic Conditions for Collective Action in South India*. Oakland, CA: ICS Press.

Wakeford, T., 2001. A selection of methods used in deliberative and inclusionary processes. *PLA Notes*, **40**(February), 29–31. Accessed 25 June 2015 at http://pubs.iied.org/pdfs/G01306.pdf.

Wallis, J.J. and D.C. North, 1986. Measuring the transaction sector in the American economy, 1970–70. In S.L. Engerman and R.E. Gallman (eds): *Long-Term Factors in American Economic Growth, Vol. 51 of The Income and Wealth Series*. Chicago, IL: University of Chicago Press, pp. 95–148.

Walzer, M., 1983. *Spheres of Justice. A Defence of Pluralism and Equality*. New York: Basic Books.

Wätsold, F., 2004. SO_2 emissions in Germany: regulations to fight Waldsterben. In W. Harrington, R.D. Morgenstern and T. Sterner (eds): *Choosing Environmental Policies. Comparing Instruments and Outcomes in the United States and Europe*. Washington, DC: Resources for the Future, pp. 23–40.

WCED (World Commission on Environment and Development), 1987. *Report from the UN World Commission on Environment and Development: Our Common Future* [Brundtland Report]. Accessed 14 June 2015 at http://www.un-documents.net/wced-ocf.htm.

Weber, M., [1921] 1946. Politics as vocation. In H.H. Gerth and C. Wright Mills (translators and eds): *From Max Weber: Essays in Sociology*. New York: Oxford University Press, pp. 77–128.

Weber, M., [1922] 1958. The three types of legitimate rule. English translation by H. Gerth, *Berkeley Publications in Society and Institutions*, **4**(1): 1–11.

Webler, T., 1995. 'Right discourse in citizen participation: an evaluative yardstick. In O. Renn, T. Webler and P. Weidemann (eds): *Fairness and Competence in Citizen Participation. Evaluating Models for Environmental Discourse*. Dordrecht: Kluwer Academic Publishers, pp. 35–87.

Webler, T. and O. Renn, 1995. 'A brief primer on participation: philosophy and practice. In O. Renn, T. Webler and P. Weidemann (eds): *Fairness and Competence in Citizen Participation. Evaluating Models for Environmental Discourse*. Dordrecht: Kluwer Academic Publishers, pp. 17–34.

Weitzman, M.L., 2002. Landing fees and harvest quotas with uncertain fish stocks. *Journal of Environmental Economics and Management*, **43**(2): 325–38.

Weitzman, M.L., 2007. A review of 'The Stern Review on the Economics of Climate Change'. *Journal of Economic Literature*, **45**(3): 703–24.

Welcomme, R.L., 2001. *Inland Fisheries. Ecology and Management*. London: Blackwell Science Ltd.

Wells, V.K., C.A. Ponting and K. Peattie, 2011. Behavior and climate change: consumer perceptions and responsibility. *Journal of Marketing Management*, **27**(7–8): 808–33.

West, P., J. Igoe and D. Brockington, 2006. Parks and peoples: the social impact of protected areas. *Annual Review of Anthropology*, **35**(1): 251–77.

Wettestad, J., 2012. Reducing long-range transport of air pollutants in Europe. In S. Andresen, E.L. Boasson and G. Hønneland (eds): *International Environmental Agreements. An Introduction*. Abingdon, UK: Routledge, pp. 23–7.

Wheeler, S.M., 2008. State and municipal climate change plans. The first generation. *Journal of the American Planning Association*, **74**(4): 481–96.

WHO (World Health Organization), 2008. *The Global Burden of Disease: 2004 Update*. Geneva: WHO. Accessed 11 June 2015 at http://www.who.int/healthinfo/global_burden_disease/GBD_report_2004update_full.pdf?ua=1.

Wilbanks, T.J. and P.C. Stern, 2002. New tools for environmental protection: what we know and need to know. In T. Dietz and P.C. Stern (eds): *New Tools for Environmental Protection. Education, Information and Voluntary Measures*. Washington, DC: National Academy Press, pp. 337–48.

Wildavsky, A., 1987. Choosing preferences by constructing institutions: a cultural theory of preference formation. *The American Political Science Review*, **81**(1): 3–22.

Williamson, J., 1990. What Washington means by policy reform. In J. Williamson (ed.): *Latin American Readjustment: How Much Has Happened?* Washington, DC: Institute for International Economics, pp. 5–20.

Williamson, O.E., 1975. *Market and Hierarchies. Analysis and Antitrust Implications*. New York: Free Press.

Williamson, O.E., 1985. *The Economic Institutions of Capitalism*. New York: Free Press.

Williamson, O.E., 2000. The new institutional economics: taking stock/looking ahead. *Journal of Economic Literature*, **XXXVIII**(3): 595–613.

Wilson, O.E., 2001. *The Diversity of Life*. London: Penguin Books.

Wilson, M.A. and R.B. Howarth, 2002. Discourse-based valuation of ecosystem services: establishing fair outcomes through group deliberation. *Ecological Economics*, **41**(3): 431–43.

Wittgenstein, L.J.J., [1922] 1974. *Tractatus Logico-Philosophicus*. London: Routledge.

Wittmer, H., F. Rauschmayer and B. Klauer, 2006. How to select instruments for the resolution of environmental conflicts? *Land Use Policy*, **23**(1): 1–9.

World Bank, 2002. *Operational Policy 4.12: Involuntary Resettlement*. Washington, DC: The World Bank.

World Bank, 2010. *State and Trends of the Carbon Market 2010*. Washington, DC: The World Bank.

World Bank, 2012a. *Inclusive Green Growth: The Pathway to Sustainable Development*. Washington, DC: The World Bank.

World Bank, 2012b. *State and Trends of the Carbon Market 2012*. Washington, DC: The World Bank.

World Bank, 2014a. Poverty overview. Accessed 23 March 2015 at http://www.worldbank.org/en/topic/poverty/overview. Last updated 8 October 2014.

World Bank, 2014b. *State and Trends of Carbon Pricing*. Washington, DC: The World Bank.

World Bank, 2015. CO_2 emissions (metric tons per capita). Accessed 21 February 2015 at http://data.worldbank.org/indicator/EN.ATM.CO2E.PC/countries.

World Resources Institute, 2012. Total GHG emissions in 2007. Accessed 11 June 2015 at http://cait2.wri.org/wri/Country%20GHG%20Emissions?indicator[]=Total%20GHG%20Emissions%20Excluding%20Land-Use%20Change%20and%20Forestry&indicator[]=Total%20GHG

%20Emissions%20Including%20Land-Use%20Change%20and%20Forestry&year[]=2007& chartType=geo.

WTO (World Trade Organization), 1994. *Agreement on Trade-Related Aspects of Intellectual Property Rights*. Accessed 21 June 2015 at https://www.wto.org/english/tratop_e/trips_e/t_agm0_e.htm.

WTO (World Trade Organization), 1999. *Review of the Provisions of Article 27.3(b), IP/C/W/163 (99-4812). Communication from Kenya on Behalf of the African Group*. Geneva: World Trade Organization.

Wunder, S., 2005. Payments for environmental services: some nuts and bolts. *CIFOR Occasional Paper No. 42*. Bogor, Indonesia: CIFOR.

Wunder, S. and M. Alban, 2008. Decentralized payments for environmental services: the cases of Pimampiro and PROFAFOR in Ecuador. *Ecological Economics*, **65**(4): 685–98.

Wunder, S., S. Engel and S. Pagiola, 2008. Taking stock: a comparative analysis of payments for environmental services programs in developed and developing countries. *Ecological Economics*, **65**(4): 834–52.

Young, M., 2012. Australia's rivers traded into trouble. *Australian Geographic*, 9 May. Accessed 23 March 2015 at http://www.australiangeographic.com.au/topics/science-environment/2012/05/opinion-australias-rivers-traded-into-trouble/.

Young, O.R., 2002. *The Institutional Dimension of Environmental Change. Fit, Interplay, and Scale*. Cambridge, MA: The MIT Press.

Young, O.R., 2008. Institutions and environmental change: the scientific legacy of a decade of IDGEC research. In O.R. Young, L.A. King and H. Schroeder (eds): *Institutions and Environmental Change. Principal Findings, Applications and Research Frontiers*. Cambridge, MA: The MIT Press, pp. 3–45.

Young, O.R., 2009. Governance for sustainable development in a world of rising interdependencies. In M.A. Delmas and O.R. Young (eds): *Governance for the Environment. New Perspectives*. Cambridge, UK: Cambridge University Press, pp. 12–40.

Young, O.R., L.A. King and H. Schroeder (eds), 2008. *Institutions and Environmental Change. Principal Findings, Applications and Research Frontiers*. Cambridge, MA: The MIT Press.

Zandersen, M., K.G. Bråten and H. Lindhjem, 2009. *Payment for and Management of Ecosystem Services: Issues and Options in the Nordic Context. TemaNord Report No. 571*. Copenhagen: Kailow ExpressApS.

Zhang, K., W. Zongguo and L. Peng, 2007. Environmental policies in China: evolvement, features and evaluation. *China Population, Resources and Environment*, **17**(4): 1–7.

Zillén, L., D.J. Conley, T. Andrén, E. Andrén and S. Björck, 2008. Past occurrences of hypoxia in the Baltic Sea and the role of climate variability, environmental change and human impact. *Earth-Science Reviews*, **91**(1–4): 77–92.

Zukin, S. and P. DiMaggio, 1990. Introduction. In S. Zukin and P. DiMaggio (eds): *Structures of Capital. The Social Organization of the Economy*. Cambridge, UK: Cambridge University Press, pp. 1–36.

Index